THE LAW OF SUCCESSION

AUSTRALIA AND NEW ZEALAND
The Law Book Company Ltd.
Sydney : Melbourne : Perth

CANADA AND U.S.A.
The Carswell Company Ltd.
Agincourt, Ontario

INDIA
N.M. Tripathi Private Ltd.
Bombay
and
Eastern Law House Private Ltd.
Calcutta and Delhi
M.P.P. House
Bangalore

ISRAEL
Steimatzky's Agency Ltd.
Jerusalem : Tel Aviv : Haifa

PARRY AND CLARK THE LAW OF SUCCESSION

Ninth Edition

by

J. B. CLARK, M.A., LL.B. (Cantab.)
of Lincoln's Inn and the North Eastern Circuit, Barrister,
Professor of Law in the University of Newcastle upon Tyne

LONDON
SWEET & MAXWELL
1988

First Edition	1937
Second Edition	1947
Third Edition	1953
Fourth Edition	1961
Second Impression	1963
Third Impression	1965
Fifth Edition	1966
Sixth Edition	1972
Second Impression	1976
Seventh Edition	1977
Eighth Edition	1983
Ninth Edition	1988

Published in 1988 by
Sweet & Maxwell Limited of
11 New Fetter Lane, London
Computerset by Promenade Graphics Limited,
Cheltenham, Gloucestershire
Printed by Hazell Watson and Viney Limited,
member of the BPCC plc, Aylesbury, Bucks.

British Library Cataloguing in Publication Data

Parry, *Sir* David Hughes
Parry & Clark on the law of succession.—
9th ed.
1. England. Succession. Law
I. Title   II. Clark, J.B. (John Bryan), *1926*–
344.2065′2

ISBN 0–421–35980–3
ISBN 0–421–35990–0 Pbk

©
Sweet & Maxwell
1988

PREFACE

The main developments in the law of succession since the last edition five years ago originate from statute. The Inheritance Tax Act 1984 has much improved the rules as to the incidence of tax on gifts by will. The Insolvency Act 1986, as modified by the Administration of Insolvent Estates of Deceased Persons Order 1986, now governs the administration of the insolvent estate of a deceased person. Again this has made a welcome improvement to the old rules, though the manner in which this was done is to be deplored. The 1986 Order should have carried a health warning that applying the Order to the Act may damage your health. The Order makes the relevant provisions of the Insolvency Act apply to the administration of a deceased's insolvent estate subject to five pages of "modifications" specified in the Order and subject to "any further such modifications as may be necessary to render them applicable to the estate of a deceased person." The Order tinkers in detail with the wording of many sections of the Act and (in case the five pages of modifications prove inadequate) leaves it to the weary succession lawyer to tinker for himself as may be necessary.

The Non-Contentious Probate Rules 1987 make a number of detailed changes and replace the 1954 Rules. Finally the Family Law Reform Act 1987 completes the reform of the rules governing illegitimacy.

There has of course been the usual crop of case law developments over the last five years—particularly those relating to the Inheritance (Provision for Family Dependants) Act 1975 and the judgment in *Re Williams* on the admission of extrinsic evidence of a testator's intention under section 21 of the Administration of Justice Act 1982.

I have tried to state the law on the basis of the material available to me on April 5, 1988.

University of Newcastle upon Tyne   J. B. Clark
April 5, 1988.

CONTENTS

TABLE OF CASES

lxxii TABLE OF STATUTES

TABLE OF RULES AND ORDERS

TABLE OF RULES OF THE SUPREME COURT

CHAPTER 1

THE NATURE OF A WILL AND OTHER DISPOSITIONS TAKING EFFECT AT DEATH

1. A WILL

A. A WILL IS INTENDED TO TAKE EFFECT ONLY AT DEATH

A will is the expression by a person of wishes which he intends to take effect only at his death. In order to make a valid will a testator must have a testamentary intention, *i.e.* he must intend the wishes to which he gives deliberate expression *to take effect only at his death*. It is not, however, necessary that the testator should intend to make, or be aware that he is making, a will.[1]

A will is ambulatory. A will has no effect until the testator dies.[2] This is the basic characteristic of a will and it is usually expressed by saying that a will, by its very nature, is ambulatory until the testator's death. Thus a will cannot confer benefits whilst the testator is still alive. If a testator makes a will giving his house Blackacre to James, James takes no interest in Blackacre so long as the testator is still alive. A will does not limit the testator's rights of ownership and accordingly he remains free to sell or make an *inter vivos* gift of Blackacre during the rest of his lifetime.

Document intended to take effect only at death is a will. A document intended by a person to be his will is usually worded so as to describe itself as his "Will." If the document is intended to be supplementary to a will it is usually worded so as to describe itself as a "Codicil." Indeed a professional draftsman invariably inserts words describing the document as a will or a codicil at the beginning of the document, so as to make the nature of the document clear immediately.[3] However, it is certainly not necessary for a document which is intended to operate as a will or codicil to describe itself as such. Whatever form it takes, any

---

[1] *Milnes* v. *Foden* (1890) 15 P.D. 105; *Re Stable* [1919] P. 7 (soldier's privileged will): see *post* pp. 41–42 and 44–45.

[2] But revocation of a previous will by another will or codicil takes effect when the latter is executed if the testator's intention to revoke is absolute, see *post*, pp. 67 and 70.

[3] Two alternative forms of commencement of a will in common use are: "This is the last Will of me James Smith . . . ," or "I James Smith of (address and description) hereby revoke all wills codicils and other testamentary dispositions heretofore made by me and declare this to be my last Will. . . . "

document can be proved[4] as a will or codicil if (i) the person executing it intended it to take effect only at his death and (ii) it was duly executed. To be duly executed, normally a document must have been signed and witnessed in accordance with the formalities required by the Wills Act 1837.[5] As Lord Penzance put it in *Cock* v. *Cooke*,[6] "It is undoubted law that whatever may be the form of a duly executed instrument, if the person executing it intends that it shall not take effect until after his death, and it is dependent upon his death for its vigour and effect, it is testamentary." Thus a document duly executed by a person who intended it to take effect only at his death can be admitted to probate as a will or codicil even though in form it appears to be instructions for a will,[7] a cheque,[8] a letter,[9] a deed,[10] or a statutory nomination.[11]

Ascertaining intention. In deciding whether a document can be proved as a will or codicil, the court ascertains the intention of the person who executed it both from the language of the document and from extrinsic evidence.

If the document appears to be testamentary on the face of it, a rebuttable presumption arises that the deceased intended it to take effect only at his death. Clearly this presumption arises if a document describes itself as a will or codicil. It has been suggested that the presumption arises if the document, whatever its form, has been signed and witnessed in accordance with the formalities required by the Wills Act 1837.[12] The presumption may be rebutted by cogent extrinsic evidence proving that the document was not intended to take effect at death. Thus the court refused probate of a will on proof that the deceased made it in jest as a specimen of a will made in as few words as possible.[13]

Conversely, if a document does not appear to be testamentary on the face of it, the burden of proving that the maker of the document intended it to take effect only at his death lies on those seeking probate

---

[4] *Post*, pp. 160 *et seq.*

[5] *Post*, p. 29: exceptionally a privileged testator may make an informal will without any formalities, see *post*, p. 39.

[6] (1866) L.R. 1 P. & D. 241, 243: see *Robertson* v. *Smith* (1870) L.R. 2 P. & D. 43; *In the Goods of Coles* (1871) L.R. 2 P. & D. 362.

[7] *Torre* v. *Castle* (1836) 1 Curt. 303; *Godman* v. *Godman* [1920] P. 261, 281 *et seq.*, (reviewing the authorities); *Re Meynell* [1949] W.N. 273 (where the testator's instructions to his solicitor for his will were duly executed with the required formalities because the testator's physical condition made him liable to die suddenly).

[8] *Bartholomew* v. *Henley* (1820) 3 Phill. 317.

[9] *In the Goods of Mundy* (1860) 2 Sw. & Tr. 119.

[10] *In the Goods of Morgan* (1866) L.R. 1 P. & D. 214.

[11] *In the Goods of Baxter* [1903] P. 12: see *post*, p. 15. A nomination under a pension scheme, although ambulatory, has been held to operate under the pension scheme trust deed and rules, and not as a testamentary disposition, and need not obey the formalities applicable to a will, *Re Danish Bacon Co. Staff Pension Fund Trusts* [1971] 1 W.L.R. 248: for criticism see Chappenden, [1972] J.B.L. 20.

[12] *Per* Barnard J. in *Re Meynell* [1949] W.N. 273 (the document contained an attestation clause): perhaps this suggestion ought to be limited to documents containing an attestation clause (*post*, p. 37) or some other indication of the document's testamentary nature.

[13] *Nichols* v. *Nichols* (1814) 2 Phill. 180 ("I leave my property between my children; I hope they will be virtuous and independent; that they will worship God, and not black coats"); see *Lister* v. *Smith* (1865) 3 Sw. & Tr. 282 (sham codicil).

of it.[14] This burden can be discharged by extrinsic evidence. Thus in *Jones* v. *Nicolay*,[15] where an order on a banker to pay £4,000 at 12 days' sight to X was signed by its maker T and attested by two witnesses, extrinsic evidence was admissible to prove that this was done when T knew he was dangerously ill and that T intended the order to be a codicil to his will.

Comparison with inter vivos disposition by deed. Unlike a will, an *inter vivos* disposition of property by deed takes effect forthwith or, if the deed is executed by the grantor conditionally on the occurrence of some event other than his own death, it takes effect on the occurrence of that event. However, if the condition is that the deed shall take effect only at the death of the grantor, it cannot take effect as a disposition *inter vivos*[16] but operates as a will or codicil if it was duly executed. In *In the Goods of Morgan*[17] the deceased during his lifetime executed three deeds of gift conveying property to trustees for the benefit of his children: each deed of gift contained a clause directing that it was not to take effect until after his death. The court held that the three deeds of gift together contained the will of the deceased and granted probate of them as they had been signed and witnessed in accordance with the appropriate formalities. In the absence of such a clause in each deed of gift showing the deceased's intention, the result would have been the same if extrinsic evidence had proved that the deceased intended these deeds to take effect only at his death.[18] On the other hand, if these deeds had not been signed and witnessed in accordance with the formalities required by the Wills Act 1837, they would not have constituted a valid will unless the deceased was privileged and so entitled to make a will without any formalities.[19]

A settlement of property does not become a will merely because it postpones the possession of property by, or even the vesting of property in, a beneficiary until the death of the settlor. For instance, a settlor may execute a settlement by deed of Whiteacre on the settlor for life, with remainder to X in fee simple if X survives the settlor. Under this settlement X's interest only vests in him if he survives the settlor. Nevertheless, provided the settlor intended the settlement to take effect forthwith or on the occurrence of some event other than his own death, the settlement constitutes an *inter vivos* disposition.

B. A WILL IS REVOCABLE UNTIL DEATH

Another important characteristic is that a will, by its very nature, is revocable by the testator until his death. A testator cannot make his will irrevocable during his lifetime. Thus a declaration by a testator in his

[14] *King's Proctor* v. *Daines* (1830) 2 Hagg.Ecc. 218.
[15] (1850) 2 Rob. 288.
[16] *Governors and Guardians of the Foundling Hospital* v. *Crane* [1911] 2 K.B. 367.
[17] (1866) L.R. 1 P. & D. 214.
[18] *In the Goods of Slinn* (1890) 15 P.D. 156.
[19] *Post*, p. 39.

will that it is irrevocable does not prevent him from subsequently revoking it.[20]

Joint will. If two or more persons duly execute the same document as the will of both of them, it constitutes a joint will and is treated as the separate will of each of them.[21] Each is therefore free to revoke or vary the joint will so far as it applies to him at any time, whether or not the other person is still alive.[22] If one dies leaving the joint will unrevoked, probate will be granted of the joint will as the will of the deceased testator.[23] If the other dies leaving the joint will unrevoked, probate will be granted of the joint will as the will of the other deceased testator. Joint wills are rarely made: their sole merit is that a joint will can effectively exercise a power given to two persons jointly to appoint by will.[24]

C. A Testator Can only Leave One Will

A testator may leave more than one expression of his testamentary intentions: he may, for instance, leave several documents worded so as to describe themselves as his will or as codicils to his will. But as the Privy Council pointed out in *Douglas-Menzies* v. *Umphelby*,[25] however many testamentary documents a testator may leave,

"it is the aggregate or the net result that constitutes his will, or, in other words, the expression of his testamentary wishes. The law, on a man's death, finds out what are the instruments which express his last will. If some extant writing be revoked, or is inconsistent with a later testamentary writing, it is discarded. But all that survive this scrutiny form part of the ultimate will or effective expression of his wishes about his estate. In this sense it is inaccurate to speak of a man leaving two wills; he does leave, and can leave, but one will."

This case concerned two testamentary documents, one disposing of the testator's estate in Great Britain and the other disposing of his estate in Australia, and accordingly in its judgment the Privy Council did not advert to the possibility of an oral expression of his testamentary intentions by a privileged testator. To take account of this possibility it may be better to say that a testator can only leave one will which is the net result of every valid expression of his testamentary intentions during his lifetime. This is the strict meaning of the word "will."

Frequently the word "will" is used in a different sense to denote a particular expression by a testator of his testamentary intentions—*e.g.* "the deceased made a formal will in England and later made an informal privileged will whilst serving as a soldier in Northern Ireland."

---

[20] *Vynior's Case* (1609) 8 Co.Rep. 81b; *In the Estate of Heys* [1914] P. 192, 197.

[21] *Re Duddell* [1932] 1 Ch. 585.

[22] *Hobson* v. *Blackburn and Blackburn* (1822) 1 Add. 274.

[23] The practice, adopted in *In the Goods of Piazzi-Smyth* [1898] P. 7 of proving only that part of the joint will which becomes operative upon the death of the first to die, is not now followed. The Principal Registry maintains an index of joint wills which have been proved in respect of one of the testators.

[24] *Re Duddell, supra.*

[25] [1908] A.C. 224, 233.

D. CONDITIONAL WILL

A testator may state in his will that he intends it to take effect only if some specified condition is satisfied—*e.g.* "If I survive my wife and inherit under her will . . . ,"[26] or " . . . in case anything should happen to me during the remainder of the voyage."[27] If the specified condition is not satisfied, the will does not take effect.

On the other hand, a testator may refer in his will to a possible future event merely in order to show his reason for making his will. An instance is *In the Goods of Dobson*[28] where the will began with the words, "In case of any fatal accident happening to me, being about to travel by railway, I hereby leave. . . . " The testator survived his railway journey and on his death Lord Penzance held that the will was not conditional, saying "the testator's meaning seems to me to have been this: 'My mind is drawn to the consideration that all railway travelling is attended with danger, and therefore I think that I had better make my will'."

It is a question of construction whether words used in a will (i) show that the testator intended it to take effect only if a specified condition is satisfied (a conditional will), or (ii) refer to a possible future event in order to show his reason for making his will (an unconditional will). When deciding this question the court considers the provisions of the will, read as a whole in the light of the surrounding circumstances in which it was made.[29] In *In the Goods of Cawthorn*[30] a testator wrote out but did not execute his will, which began with the words, "In the prospect of a long journey, should God not permit me to return to my home, I . . . make this my last will." Some months after returning home from his journey he executed his will in the presence of two witnesses and extrinsic evidence proved that he was not then contemplating any journey. The court held that the will was unconditional and was therefore admissible to probate.

If a conditional will contains a clause revoking a previous will but the specified condition is not satisfied, the conditional will is entirely inoperative and the previous will remains unrevoked.[31] However a conditional codicil which referred to a previous will was admitted to probate, though the specified condition was not satisfied, on the ground that it would have the effect of republishing the will, or of making the will valid if it had not been duly executed.[32]

A conditional will must be distinguished from a conditional gift in a will. For instance, a gift by will of "£200 to X if he swims the English

---

[26] *In the Estate of Thomas* [1939] 2 All E.R. 567.

[27] *In the Goods of Robinson* (1870) L.R. 2 P. & D. 171.

[28] (1866) L.R. 1 P. & M. 88: see *Burton* v. *Collingwood* (1832) 4 Hagg. 176 ("lest I should die before the next sun").

[29] *In the Goods of Spratt* [1897] P. 28 (where many of the cases are considered); *Re Govier* [1950] P. 237 (joint will; "in the event of our two deaths"). For admissible extrinsic evidence see *post*, pp. 418 *et seq.*

[30] (1863) 3 Sw. & Tr. 417 (the journey was from Bideford to Shrewsbury).

[31] *In the Goods of Hugo* (1877) 2 P.D. 73; *In the Estate of O'Connor* [1942] 1 All E.R. 546.

[32] *In the Goods of Mendes da Silva* (1861) 2 Sw. & Tr. 315; *In the Goods of Colley* (1879) 3 L.R.Ir. 243: but see *Parsons* v. *Lanoe* (1748) 1 Ves.Sen. 189, 190. For republication see *post*, p. 80.

Channel" is a conditional gift: if X does not satisfy the specified condition, the gift to him fails but the will as a whole still takes effect.

E. CONTENTS OF A WILL

The main function of most wills is to dispose of the testator's property after his death. By his will the testator may make gifts, either directly to a person beneficially or to trustees upon trust. Another important function of most wills is to appoint one or more executors to administer the testator's estate after his death.[33] Sometimes wills deal with various other matters in addition to (or instead of) disposing of the testator's property or appointing executors.

The corpse of the testator. The law recognises no property in the dead body of a human being. It follows that a testator cannot by will dispose of his dead body: a direction in a will to executors to deliver the testator's dead body to another person is therefore void.[34] The executors are entitled to the custody and possession of the testator's dead body until it is buried and the duty of disposing of the body falls primarily on them, at any rate if the testator leaves assets sufficient for this purpose.[35]

If a deceased has expressed wishes during his lifetime as to the disposal of his body, either in his will or otherwise, these wishes are generally not legally enforceable against his personal representatives, though they may well have effective moral force. For instance, wishes expressed in favour of, or against, cremation have no legal but only moral force.[36] However certain wishes have some legal effect. Thus, under the Human Tissue Act 1961, if a person, either in writing at any time or orally in the presence of two witnesses during his last illness, requests that his body or some specified part be used after his death for therapeutic purposes or for purposes of medical education or research, the person lawfully in possession of his body after his death *may* authorise this.[37] In the absence of such a request he *may* authorise this if, having made such reasonable inquiry as may be practicable, he has no reason to believe that the deceased had expressed an objection to his body being so dealt with after his death.[38]

A testator needs to ensure that his wishes as to the disposal of his body are quickly brought to the notice of the person in possession of it

---

[33] *Post*, pp. 140 *et seq.*

[34] *Williams* v. *Williams* (1882) 20 Ch.D. 659.

[35] *Rees* v. *Hughes* [1946] K.B. 517, 524 and 528: the duty can also fall on other persons, see *Halsbury's Laws* (4th ed., 1975), Vol. 10, para. 1017. For the payment of funeral expenses see *post*, pp. 255–256.

[36] Until 1965 reg. 4 of the Cremation Regulations 1930 (S.R. & O. 1930 No. 1016) made it unlawful to cremate the remains of any person who was known to have left a written direction to the contrary: this was revoked by the Cremation Regulations 1965 (S.I. 1965 No. 1146), reg. 7(*a*)).

[37] Human Tissue Act 1961, s.1(1).

[38] *Ibid.* s.1(2): he must also have no reason to believe that the surviving spouse or any surviving relative of the deceased objects. As to a request by a person for anatomical examination of his body, see Anatomy Act 1984, s.4(1) and (2).

after his death: indeed minutes count if his body is to be used for purposes of a transplant. If he merely expresses his wishes in his will, there is a danger that no one will read it and learn of his wishes until after his funeral, particularly if the will is deposited for safe custody with a solicitor or bank. If the testator is unwilling to make his wishes known openly in his lifetime, he needs to inform his executors and any persons who are likely to be with him at his death that his will contains these wishes. Alternatively he can express these wishes in a letter left with his executors and to be opened immediately after his death.[39]

Appointment of testamentary guardians. Each of the parents of a legitimate child may by will appoint one or more guardians of the child.[40] The mother of an illegitimate child may do so[41] but an appointment by the father is ineffective unless he was entitled to the legal custody of the child under an order in force immediately before his death.[42] The adopter of a child under an adoption order may also do so.[43]

The appointment may be made in respect of every child born, or (in the case of an appointment by a father) *en ventre sa mère*, at the appointor's death. In most cases a will appoints one or more guardians "of my infant children" so as to include children born after the date of the will.

A guardian acts jointly with the surviving parent unless the latter objects, in which case the guardian may apply to the court. But a guardian does not act jointly in this way if the testator's appointment of guardians is worded so as only to take effect "in the event of my wife (or husband) predeceasing me." If each of the parents appoints guardians, they act jointly after the death of both parents.[44]

Exercise of testamentary powers of appointment. By his will the testator may exercise any power of appointment conferred on him and exercisable by will.[45] For instance, he may under a settlement have a life interest and a power to appoint the settled property by will among his children or remoter issue.

The testator may exercise a testamentary power of appointment either (i) by a will made in writing and duly executed in accordance with the formalities required by the Wills Act 1837[46] or (ii) by an informal will if the testator is privileged.[47] Occasionally the instrument creating a power of appointment by will purports to require special formalities to

---

[39] H.M.S.O. issue a Kidney Transplant Donor Card which is intended to be kept with the donor at all times in a place where it will be found quickly.

[40] Guardianship of Minors Act 1971, s.4; s.3 assumes that more than one person may be so appointed. The appointment may be made by a privileged will: Wills (Soldiers and Sailors) Act 1918, s.4.

[41] *Re A., S. v. A.* (1940) 164 L.T. 230.

[42] Guardianship of Minors Act 1971, s.14(3), as amended by Domestic Proceedings and Magistrates' Courts Act 1978, s.36(1): see Family Law Reform Act 1987, s.6 for amendment to 1971 Act to come into force on appointed day (not yet in force on April 4, 1988).

[43] Adoption Act 1976, s.39.

[44] Guardianship of Minors Act 1971, s.4.

[45] For the rules of construction governing the exercise of powers of appointment see *post,* pp. 428 *et seq.*

[46] Wills Act 1837, s.10: see also *Re Barnett* [1908] 1 Ch. 402.

[47] *Re Wernher* [1918] 2 Ch. 82 (general power); *Re Earl of Chichester's W.T.* [1946] Ch. 289 (special power over personalty: *obiter* as to special power over realty).

be observed when the power is exercised—for example, three witnesses to the will instead of two witnesses as required by the Wills Act 1837. To deal with this, section 10 of the Act provides that, despite this special requirement, an appointment made by a will which is in writing and duly executed in accordance with the formalities required by the Act shall be valid "so far as respects the execution and attestation thereof." Section 10 thus makes it unnecessary to observe special formalities concerning execution and attestation but any other requirements must be observed, otherwise an appointment is void.[48] However, even special formalities concerning execution and attestation must be observed in an informal will, to which section 10 is not applicable.

F. Solicitor's Duty of Care in Preparation of Will

Duty to client. If T employs a solicitor S to prepare a will for T containing a gift to B, and owing to S's negligence the gift to B is void, S is liable in damages to T both in contract and in tort.[49] If T discovers during his lifetime that the gift to B is void, the damages recoverable by T are the costs of making a new and valid will or otherwise putting matters right[50]: if the discovery is made after T's death, it seems that T's estate would only recover nominal damages.[51]

Duty to beneficiary under will. But in this situation S also owes a duty in tort to B to use proper care in carrying out T's instructions. In *Ross* v. *Caunters*[52] the gifts by T's will to B failed because B's husband was an attesting witness of the will. S was negligent because, when S sent the will to T for execution, S failed to warn T that the will should not be witnessed by the spouse of a beneficiary, and, when T returned the will to S after execution, S failed to observe that it had been witnessed in this way. Megarry V.-C. held that B was entitled to recover from S by way of damages the value of the gifts to which B would otherwise have been entitled under T's will. Thus a solicitor who prepares a will for a client owes a duty, not only to his client but also to a beneficiary under the will, to use proper care in carrying out the client's instructions.

---

[48] *Cooper* v. *Martin* (1867) 3 Ch.App. 47 (requirement as to time of appointment). A requirement that the consent of a specified person be obtained to the appointment must, for instance, be observed.

[49] *Ross* v. *Caunters* [1980] Ch. 297, 306–308: see also *Midland Bank Trust Co. Ltd.* v. *Hett, Stubbs and Kemp* [1979] Ch. 384; Supply of Goods and Services Act 1982, ss.12–14. Whether a solicitor has a duty to draw his client's attention to the effect of marriage on a will (*post*, p. 59) depends on the circumstances, *Hall* v. *Meyrick* [1957] 2 Q.B. 455, 475–476 and 482.

[50] *Ross* v. *Caunters* [1980] Ch. 297, 303.

[51] *Ibid.* at p. 302.

[52] [1980] Ch. 297: see R. E. Megarry (1965) 81 L.Q.R. 478. For Wills Act 1837, s.15 (which deprives an attesting witness and his spouse of any benefit under the will which he attests) see *post*, pp. 334 *et seq.* See also *Gartside* v. *Sheffield Young & Ellis* [1983] N.Z.L.R. 37 (solicitor owes duty to B to prepare will for execution by T within reasonable time from T's instructions); *Clarke* v. *Bruce Lance* [1988] 1 All E.R. 364, Bates 59 A.L.J. 327.

G. Contract to Make, or Not to Make, a Will

Validity of contract.[53] A contract by which T promises P to leave to P by will specific property[54] (such as T's house), a pecuniary legacy,[55] or the whole or a specified share of his residuary estate, is valid. Of course, under general principles of contract law, such a promise must either be made under seal or be supported by valuable consideration; there must be an intention to create legal relations,[56] and the terms of the contract must not be uncertain.[57] Moreover, if the contract relates to land, it is not enforceable unless there is a signed memorandum satisfying section 40 of the Law of Property Act 1925,[58] though it is enforceable in equity if the equitable doctrine of part performance applies.[59]

Similarly, a contract by which T promises P not to revoke or alter T's existing will, or a particular gift in it, is valid.[60] Such a contract is construed as prohibiting intentional revocation by T[61] but not automatic revocation of his will if T marries[62]: thus if T marries, thereby automatically revoking his will, T does not commit any breach of contract.[63] A contract not to revoke may be drafted in such wide terms as to purport to prohibit automatic revocation by marriage as well as intentional revocation. However, in so far as it operates in restraint of marriage, such a prohibition is void on grounds of public policy.[64]

Remedies for breach. If T commits a breach of his contract with P to leave specific property, a pecuniary legacy, or the whole or part of his residuary estate to P, after T's death P is entitled to recover damages from T's estate for loss of the promised benefit.[65] In appropriate circumstances in an action for specific performance, the court may order T's

---

[53] For a remedy under the doctrine of proprietary estoppel see Snell's *Principles of Equity* (28th ed., 1982), pp. 558 *et seq.; Griffiths* v. *Williams* (1977) 248 E.G. 947; *Jones (A.E.)* v. *Jones (F.W.)* [1977] 1 W.L.R. 438; *Greasley* v. *Cooke* [1980] 1 W.L.R. 1306; *Re Basham* [1986] 1 W.L.R. 1498 (P acted to detriment, relying on belief, encouraged by D, that P would receive D's property on D's death: held P entitled to whole of D's estate). As to future reform consider the New Zealand Law Reform (Testamentary Promises) Act 1949, for which see Hardingham, *The Law of Wills* (1977), pp. 252 *et seq.*

[54] *Synge* v. *Synge* [1894] 1 Q.B. 466 (to leave P life interest in house); *Parker* v. *Clark* (1960) 1 W.L.R. 286 (to leave house and contents to P, Q and R jointly).

[55] *Hammersley* v. *De Biel* (1845) 12 Cl. & F. 45; *Graham* v. *Wickham* (1863) 1 De G. J. & Sm. 474.

[56] *Parker* v. *Clark* [1960] 1 W.L.R. 286, 292–294 (not a mere family arrangement).

[57] *MacPhail* v. *Torrance* (1909) 25 T.L.R. 810 (to make ample provision: too vague).

[58] *Maddison* v. *Alderson* (1883) 8 App.Cas. 467; *Re Gonin* [1979] Ch. 16. But T's estate may be liable on a *quantum meruit* to P for services rendered to T, *Deglman* v. *Guaranty Trust Co. of Canada* [1954] 3 D.L.R. 785.

[59] *Wakeham* v. *MacKenzie* [1968] 1 W.L.R. 1175 (T promised to leave house and contents to P if P gave up her flat and moved in and looked after him for life; P did so: held part performance): see *Re Gonin* [1979] Ch. 16, 30–31; Pettit (1968) 32 Conv.(N.S.) 384.

[60] *Robinson* v. *Ommanney* (1882) 21 Ch.D. 780; (1883) 23 Ch.D. 285.

[61] Intentional revocation occurs where the revocation is effected by destruction, another will or codicil, or duly executed writing; see *post*, pp. 63 *et seq.*

[62] *Post*, p. 59.

[63] *Re Marsland* [1939] Ch. 820.

[64] *Robinson* v. *Ommanney, supra*, where the contract not to revoke was held to be divisible, and valid in so far as it prohibited intentional revocation.

[65] *Hammersley* v. *De Biel* (1845) 12 Cl. & F. 45 (legacy); *Schaefer* v. *Schuhmann* [1972] A.C. 572, 585 *et seq.*

personal representatives to transfer the property bound by the contract (e.g. T's house) to P.[66]

T commits a breach of his contract with P not to revoke T's existing will if T intentionally revokes it.[67] P cannot stop T from revoking this will by an action for specific performance or an injunction, but P is entitled to recover damages from T, or after his death from T's estate, for loss of the promised benefit under this will.[68]

Testator's duty during his lifetime. If T contracts with P to leave *specific* property to P, and later T during his lifetime alienates the property to Q, T thereby repudiates the contract. P may at once sue T for damages which are assessed subject to a reduction for the acceleration of the benefit and also, if the benefit of the contract is personal to P, subject to a reduction for the contingency of his failing to survive T.[69] If P can intervene before a purchaser for value obtains an interest in the property, P can obtain a declaration of his right to have it left to him by will and an injunction to restrain T from disposing of it in breach of contract.[70]

But a contract by T to leave by will *all* his assets (or a share of them) at his death to P does not impose on T a duty not to dispose of any of his assets during his lifetime, unless the contract contains a term to this effect. However the contract does impose on T a more limited duty not to make *inter vivos* dispositions which in substance have a testamentary effect—such as a voluntary settlement whereby T settles property on himself for life, remainder to Q.[71]

Effect of lapse. Normally a gift by T's will to P fails by lapse if P predeceases T.[72] It is a question of construction of the contract between T and P whether (i) the benefit of the contract is personal to P who takes the risk of lapse, so that T is discharged from liability if P predeceases T,[73] or (ii) the benefit of the contract is not personal to P but accrues for the benefit of P's estate, so that T ought to make provision in his will against lapse.[74]

---

[66] *Re Edwards* [1958] Ch. 168, 175–176 (contract to devise house to P): see *Coverdale* v. *Eastwood* (1872) L.R. 15 Eq. 121 (contract to settle all T's property on P in strict settlement): the court may order any person holding the asset as T's successor in title to transfer it (*Synge* v. *Synge* [1894] 1 Q.B. 466, 471) unless he is a purchaser without notice or protected by the registration provisions applicable to interests in land, see Snell's *Principles of Equity* (28th ed., 1982), pp. 46 *et seq.*

[67] *Robinson* v. *Ommanney* (1882) 21 Ch.D. 780; (1883) 23 Ch.D. 285.

[68] *Ibid.*: probably in appropriate circumstances the court may order T's personal representatives to transfer the promised asset to P.

[69] *Synge* v. *Synge* [1894] 1 Q.B. 466; *Schaefer* v. *Schuhmann* [1972] A.C. 572, 586: see *Parker* v. *Clark* [1960] 1 W.L.R. 286.

[70] *Synge* v. *Synge, supra,* at p. 471; *Schaefer* v. *Schuhmann, supra.*

[71] *Jones* v. *Martin* (1798) 5 Ves.Jun. 266; *Fortescue* v. *Hannah* (1812) 19 Ves.Jun. 67; *Logan* v. *Wienholt* (1833) 1 Cl. & F. 611; *Re Bennett* [1934] W.N. 177 (Q the ostensible owner but T retained the income): cf. *Palmer* v. *Bank of New South Wales* (1975) 133 C.L.R. 150 (opening joint bank account with Q not testamentary).

[72] *Post,* p. 336.

[73] *Re Brookman's Trust* (1869) L.R. 5 Ch.App. 182; *Schaefer* v. *Schuhmann* [1972] A.C. 572, 586: see *Jones* v. *How* (1848) 7 Hare 267; *Needham* v. *Smith* (1828) 4 Russ. 318.

[74] See *Re Brookman's Trust, supra,* 191. See W. A. Lee (1971) 87 L.Q.R. 358, 361–362.

Effect of insolvency. A contract to leave by will specific property or a pecuniary legacy to P may merely impose an obligation on T to make a will containing such a gift; in that case P, like any other beneficiary under a will, takes the risk that T's estate may turn out to be insolvent, or insufficient to satisfy the gift, and if it does P takes nothing, or a reduced benefit.[75] However such a contract is more likely to impose an obligation on T to make the gift effective; in that case T commits a breach of contract if T's estate is insolvent, or insufficient to satisfy the gift, and P is entitled to be treated as a creditor for the value of the property[76] or the amount of the legacy,[77] and to rank for payment with T's other creditors of the same degree.[78] Thus the effect of insolvency depends on the extent of the obligation imposed on T by the contract.

A contract by T to leave by will the whole or a specified share of his residuary estate to P is different because T's residuary estate available for distribution is only ascertained after T's debts and funeral and testamentary expenses have been paid. P takes the risk that T's estate may turn out to be insolvent, and if it does P takes nothing and has no claim as a creditor for breach of contract.[79]

H. Mutual Wills

The Court of Chancery created the doctrine of mutual wills[80] in order to remedy the unconscionable revocation of a will in certain circumstances.

Three requirements must be satisfied:

(1) *Mutual wills made pursuant to an arrangement.* The first requirement of the doctrine is that two or more persons make an arrangement as to the disposal of some or all of their property on death and execute mutual wills pursuant to the arrangement.[81] Usually the persons are husband and wife. The mutual wills may take the form of a joint will or separate wills.[82] Each of the mutual wills makes provision for the other person in some way. Sometimes each will gives the other person a life interest, with remainder to the same beneficiary[83]; probably remainders to different beneficiaries in the two wills would suffice if this was

---

[75] See *Graham* v. *Wickham* (1863) 1 D.J. & S. 474, 484–485; *Eyre* v. *Monro* (1857) 3 K. & J. 305, 308.

[76] *Schaefer* v. *Schuhmann* [1972] A.C. 572, 586.

[77] *Graham* v. *Wickham* (1863) 1 D.J. & S. 474; *Eyre* v. *Monro* (1857) 3 K. & J. 305.

[78] For the order of priority of T's debts see *post*, pp. 288 *et seq.*

[79] *Jervis* v. *Wolferstan* (1874) L.R. 18 Eq. 18, 24; *Schaefer* v. *Schuhmann* [1972] A.C. 572, 586.

[80] See generally R. Burgess (1970) 34 Conv.(n.s.) 230; J. D. B. Mitchell (1951) 14 M.L.R. 136; T. G. Youdan (1979) U. of Toronto L.J. 390.

[81] Probably it would suffice if the first to die executes a mutual will and dies believing that the survivor has done so.

[82] *Re Hagger* [1930] 2 Ch. 190 (joint will); *Re Green* [1951] Ch. 148 (separate); *Re Cleaver* [1981] 1 W.L.R. 939 (separate).

[83] *Re Hagger, supra.*

the arrangement.[84] Sometimes each will gives the other person an absolute interest, with an alternative gift in case the other dies first.[85]

(2) *Agreement for survivor to be bound.* The second requirement is that the parties agree that the survivor shall be bound by this arrangement. This requirement normally takes the form of an agreement by the parties not to revoke their mutual wills. For instance, in *Re Hagger*[86] a husband and wife made a joint mutual will which contained a declaration by them that it should not be altered or revoked save by their mutual agreement: it was implicit in this declaration that the parties agreed that the survivor should be bound by this arrangement. This requirement can also be satisfied by an agreement to leave property by will. Thus in *Re Green*[87] a husband and wife made mutual wills which recited an agreement between them that, if the survivor had the use of the other's property for life without any liability to account, the survivor would provide by will for the carrying out of the wishes expressed in the other's will.

The agreement by the parties that the survivor shall be bound by this arrangement can be proved by declarations to this effect in the mutual wills or by clear and satisfactory extrinsic evidence.[88] A "mere honorable engagement" between the parties does not suffice.[89] In order to bring this agreement to the knowledge of any interested beneficiary and to facilitate proof of it in the future, it is advisable for the mutual wills to contain such declarations or for the parties to hand to any interested beneficiary a written declaration of their agreement signed by them.

The fact that the parties agreed to make, and did make, mutual wills in almost identical terms at the same time is not sufficient to establish that they agreed that the survivor should be bound. In *Re Oldham*[90] a husband and wife made mutual wills at the same time, giving the other an absolute interest with the same alternative gift in case the other died first. The husband died first and the wife took her husband's property under his mutual will. She later remarried and died, having made a new will which provided for her second husband and which departed entirely from her earlier mutual will. Astbury J. held that the doctrine of mutual wills was not applicable and upheld the wife's new will, saying that "the fact that the two wills were made in identical terms does not necessarily connote any agreement beyond that of so making them."[91]

(3) *Binding event occurs.* The arrangement becomes binding in equity on the survivor either (i) when the first of them dies, leaving his mutual will unrevoked and believing the agreement that the survivor shall be

[84] Snell's *Principles of Equity* (28th ed., 1982), p. 190, n. 33.
[85] *Re Green, supra; Re Cleaver, supra: cf. Re Oldham* [1925] Ch. 75, 84 and 87–88.
[86] [1930] 2 Ch. 190.
[87] [1951] Ch. 148.
[88] *In the Estate of Heys* [1914] P. 192. *Re Cleaver* [1981] 1 W.L.R. 939 (proof on balance of probabilities).
[89] *Re Cleaver, supra*, at pp. 945, 947–948.
[90] [1925] Ch. 75: see also *Gray v. Perpetual Trustee Co. Ltd.* [1928] A.C. 391; *Re Cleaver, supra.*
[91] [1925] Ch. 75. 88–89.

bound still stands, or (ii) when this occurs and the survivor accepts the benefit under the other's will. There are dicta in favour of both these alternatives but as yet no decision between them. In favour of the first alternative Clauson J. said *obiter* in *Re Hagger*[92] that the arrangement became binding in equity on the survivor when the first of them dies "even though the survivor did not signify his election to give effect to the will by taking benefits under it." The adoption of this first alternative would stop the survivor being free to escape from the arrangement by disclaiming the benefit under the other's will and thereby to take under any consequent intestacy of the other person.[93] On the other hand, there are several dicta which appear to favour the second alternative[94] and it has been argued that it is the survivor's acceptance of the benefit under the other's will which constitutes fraud justifying equity's intervention.[95] Perhaps the choice between the two alternatives ought to depend on the agreement of the parties—under their agreement was the survivor to be bound by the arrangement on the death of the first to die *or* on the acceptance by the survivor of the benefit under the other's will?

Whichever alternative applies, this third requirement is not satisfied if the first of them dies having revoked his mutual will before his death in breach of the arrangement.[96] Again, it is not satisfied if the first of them dies knowing the agreement to be bound no longer stands because the other has already repudiated it. To quote Lord Camden's eloquent words in *Dufour* v. *Pereira*,[97]

"A mutual will is a revocable act. It may be revoked by joint consent clearly. By one only, if he gives notice, I can admit. But to affirm that the survivor (who has deluded his partner into this will upon the faith and persuasion that he would perform his part) may legally recall his contract, either secretly during the joint lives, or after at his pleasure, I cannot allow."

Each is under an obligation not to revoke his will without notice to the other during the other's lifetime.[98]

Remedy of constructive trust. If these three requirements are satisfied equity enforces the arrangement against the survivor by treating him as holding the property concerned on a constructive trust to apply it in accordance with his mutual will.[99] To quote Lord Camden again in *Dufour* v. *Pereira*,[1]

"he, that dies first, does by his death carry the agreement on his part

[92] [1930] 2 Ch. 190, 195.
[93] See J. D. B. Mitchell (1951) 14 M.L.R. 136, 138.
[94] *Per* Sir Robert Collier in *Denyssen* v. *Mostert* (1872) L.R. 4 P.C. 236, 253: *per* Gorell Barnes P. in *Stone* v. *Hoskins* [1905] P. 194, 197; *per* Astbury J. in *Re Oldham* [1925] Ch. 75, 86. In the leading case of *Dufour* v. *Pereira* (1769) Dick. 419, 2 Hargr.Jurid.Arg. 304, Lord Camden used different phrases which have been cited in support of each alternative.
[95] See Hanbury and Maudsley's *Modern Equity* (12th ed., 1985), p. 320.
[96] *Stone* v. *Hoskins* [1905] P. 194.
[97] (1769) 1 Dick. 419; the quotation is from 2 Hargr.Jurid.Arg. 304, 308.
[98] *Birmingham* v. *Renfrew* (1937) 57 C.L.R. 666, 682.
[99] *Birmingham* v. *Renfrew* (1937) 57 C.L.R. 666; *Re Cleaver* [1981] 1 W.L.R. 939.
[1] 2 Hargr.Jurid.Arg. 304, 310.

into execution. If the other then refuses, he is guilty of a fraud, can never unbind himself, and becomes a trustee of course. For no man shall deceive another to his prejudice. By engaging to do something that is in his power, he is made a trustee for the performance, and transmits that trust to those that claim under him."

This constructive trust takes effect when the binding event occurs. Hence a beneficiary under the mutual wills, who survives the first but predeceases the second testator, does not lose his benefit by lapse. In *Re Hagger*[2] a husband H and wife W made a joint mutual will by which they gave their properties at Wandsworth (held by them jointly) to trustees upon trust for the survivor for life, and after the survivor's death to divide the proceeds of sale of the properties among certain named beneficiaries including P. The will included a declaration that it should not be altered or revoked save by their mutual agreement. The arrangement between them was incompatible with the right of survivorship applicable to their joint tenancy; accordingly the arrangement severed their joint tenancy and henceforth they held the Wandsworth properties as tenants in common.[3] W died in 1904 and H accepted his life interest under the will in her share of the properties. P died in 1923 and H died in 1928, having made a different will in 1921. Clauson J. decided that from W's death H held his share of the Wandsworth properties "on trust to apply it so as to carry out the effect of the joint will"[4]; thus from W's death P was entitled to a vested interest in remainder in H's share (as well as W's share) of these properties and there was no lapse by reason of P's death in H's lifetime.

This constructive trust does not stop the survivor from revoking his mutual will which, like any other will, is by its very nature revocable until his death. If the mutual will of the survivor is revoked and he makes a new will, any appointment of executors in his new will is effective (though they differ from the executors named in his mutual will), and on his death the new will must be admitted to probate.[5] But the survivor's personal representatives take the property concerned subject to the constructive trust, and to that extent the new will is ineffective.[6] In short equity frustrates but does not prevent the unconscionable revocation of a mutual will.

Where it applies, the equitable doctrine of mutual wills has the considerable merit of making the arrangement enforceable by any beneficiary under the constructive trust: on the other hand, a contract not to revoke is only enforceable by the contracting parties.

Property bound. What property is bound by the constructive trust depends on the construction of the arrangement embodied in the mutual wills. The arrangement may only apply to certain identified

---

[2] [1930] 2 Ch. 190.
[3] *Re Wilford's Estate* (1879) 11 Ch.D. 267; *In the Estate of Heys* [1914] P. 192; *Szabo v. Boros* (1967) 64 D.L.R. (2d) 48.
[4] [1930] 2 Ch. 190, 195.
[5] *In the Estate of Heys, supra.*
[6] *Re Cleaver* [1981] 1 W.L.R. 939. The doctrine of mutual wills applies where the survivor's mutual will is revoked by his marriage, *Re Green* [1951] Ch. 148: but see Law Reform Committee, *The making and revocation of wills*, Cmnd. 7902 (1980), p. 26.

property. On the other hand it may apply to a part,[7] or the whole,[8] of each person's residuary estate.

If the constructive trust applies for example to a part, or the whole, of each person's residuary estate, the question arises to what extent the survivor is free to dispose during his lifetime of (i) such of the other's property and (ii) such of the survivor's own property (including his after-acquired property) as are bound by the arrangement. As regards the other's property, this question only arises if the survivor took an absolute interest, and not a mere life interest, under the other's will. In the Australian case of *Birmingham* v. *Renfrew*[9] Dixon J. suggested that often the purpose of such an arrangement is to allow the survivor full enjoyment of both the capital and income of the property for his own benefit during his lifetime, though subject to him not making *inter vivos* gifts calculated to defeat the intention of the arrangement. "I do not see any difficulty in modern equity in attaching to the assets a constructive trust which allowed the survivor to enjoy the property subject to a fiduciary duty which, so to speak, crystallized on his death and [during his lifetime] disabled him only from voluntary dispositions *inter vivos*"[10] which were calculated to defeat the intention of the arrangement.[11] This floating constructive trust finally attaches to such property as the survivor leaves at his death.

It is rarely sensible for persons to make mutual wills.[12] If they insist on doing so, they ought carefully to consider what provision should be made in their arrangement for possible future events, such as the remarriage of the survivor or the birth of children to the survivor. Again, mutual wills ought clearly to define what property of each person is intended to be bound by the arrangement and what powers are intended to be conferred on the survivor to dispose of such property during his lifetime.

2. A STATUTORY NOMINATION

Several statutes permit a person entitled to certain funds or investments to dispose of them by a written nomination operating at his death. Instances include a sum payable by a Friendly Society,[13] Industrial and Provident Society,[14] and Trade Union[15]: in each case the sum nomi-

---

[7] *Re Green, supra* : see [1950] 2 All E.R. 913, 919: see also *Re Gillespie* (1968) 69 D.L.R. (2d) 368 (assets of H and W at death of first to die held bound).

[8] *Re Cleaver, supra.*

[9] (1937) 57 C.L.R. 666. See J. D. B. Mitchell (1951) 14 M.L.R. 136 and R. Burgess (1970) 34 Conv.(N.S.) 230, 240 *et seq.*

[10] *Birmingham* v. *Renfrew, supra*, at pp. 689–690: approved in *Re Cleaver* [1981] 1 W.L.R. 939, 945–947.

[11] *Re Cleaver, supra*, at p. 947 ("No objection could normally be taken to ordinary gifts of small value").

[12] See Law Reform Committee, *The making and revocation of wills*, Cmnd. 7902 (1980), p. 26; D. W. Fox (1975) 119 S.J. 380.

[13] Friendly Societies Act 1974, ss.66 and 67.

[14] Industrial and Provident Societies Act 1965, ss.23 and 24.

[15] Trade Union and Labour Relations Act 1974, Sched. I, para. 31 (as amended by Employment Protection Act 1975, Sched. 16, Pt. III, paras. 31 and 32); Trade Union (Nominations) Regulations 1977 (S.I. 1977 No. 789) and 1984 (S.I. 1984 No. 1290).

nated cannot exceed £5,000.[16] National Savings Certificates[17] and savings in the National Savings Bank[18] also pass under a nomination if it was made before May 1, 1981: in each case no monetary limit applies.

Comparison with a gift by will. A statutory nomination, like a will, has no effect until the nominator dies and is therefore ambulatory during the nominator's lifetime.[19] It follows that the nominee takes no interest in the nominated funds or investments so long as the nominator is still alive; during his lifetime the nominator remains free to deal with the nominated funds or investments as he pleases. Again, if the nominee predeceases the nominator, the nomination fails.[20] Similarly a gift by will normally fails by lapse if the beneficiary predeceases the testator.[21]

However, in several other respects a statutory nomination differs from a will:

(i) A person who has attained 16 years of age can make a statutory nomination but normally a person must attain 18 years before he can make a valid will.[22]

(ii) The formal requirements are different. In the case of money payable by a Friendly Society, for instance, a statutory nomination must be by writing under the nominator's hand, delivered at or sent to the registered office of the society or branch, or made in a book kept at that office.[23] In some cases signature by the nominator in the presence of an attesting witness was also required.[24] The formal requirements as to signature and attesting witnesses are different for a will and a testator is not required to deposit his will anywhere but may retain possession of it during his lifetime.[25]

(iii) Although the marriage of the nominator or testator automatically

---

[16] Administration of Estates (Small Payments) Act 1965, ss.2 and 6; Administration of Estates (Small Payments) (Increase of Limit) Order 1984 (S.I. 1984 No. 539), para. 2.

[17] National Debt Act 1972, s.11; Savings Certificates Regulations 1972 (S.I. 1972 No. 641), regs. 13–18 (as amended by S.I. 1981 No. 486).

[18] National Savings Bank Act 1971, ss.2 and 8(2); National Savings Bank Regulations 1972 (S.I. 1972 No. 764), regs. 33–38 (as amended by S.I. 1981 No. 484).

[19] *Ante*, p. 1.

[20] *Re Barnes* [1940] Ch. 267: see also Savings Certificates Regulations 1972, reg. 16(1); National Savings Bank Regulations 1972, reg. 35(1); Trade Union (Nominations) Regulations 1977, reg. 3(1).

[21] For lapse, and the exceptions to lapse, see *post*, pp. 336 *et seq.*

[22] Exceptionally an infant who is a privileged testator can make a valid will: see *post*, p. 42.

[23] Friendly Societies Act 1974, s.66(1).

[24] Savings Certificates Regulations 1972, reg. 14; National Savings Bank Regulations 1972, reg. 33(2).

[25] s.126 of the Supreme Court Act 1981 makes provision for the voluntary deposit of a will in the Court's custody by a testator during his lifetime: very few wills are so deposited: for the deposit procedure see the Wills (Deposit for Safe Custody) Regulations 1978 (S.I. 1978 No. 1724). ss.23–25 of the Administration of Justice Act 1982 (when brought into operation, s.76(5) and (6)) make provision for voluntary deposit in the custody of the Principal Registry of the Family Division, which is to register any will so deposited and function as the national body for the purposes of the Council of Europe Convention on the Establishment of a Scheme of Registration of Wills, Cmnd. 5073 (1972).

revokes both a nomination and a will,[26] the other rules governing revocation are rather different. A statutory nomination may be revoked by a notice complying with the same formal requirements as a statutory nomination but (unlike a will) cannot be revoked by a will or codicil.[27]

A person can, and often does, dispose of such funds or investments by will instead of employing a statutory nomination. Indeed, if a person contemplates making a will, it is usually better for him to dispose of all his assets by will and not to employ a statutory nomination. He can then, if he wishes, revoke or vary any of its provisions by a subsequent will or codicil. A statutory nomination once made tends to be forgotten. The risk of this occurring is a major disadvantage because the nomination will not be revoked or varied by any subsequent will or codicil. On the whole the recent changes which stop savings in the National Savings Bank and National Savings Certificates from being disposed of by new nominations in the future are to be welcomed. A nomination of such assets made before the relevant closing date is not of course affected.

3. A DONATIO MORTIS CAUSA

A *donatio mortis causa* is "a singular form of gift"[28] derived in part from civil law. It is not a gift *inter vivos* nor is it a gift by will. It has its own distinct requirements which are:

1. It must be intended by the donor to be conditional on his own death.
2. It must be made by the donor in contemplation of death.
3. Before his death the donor must part with dominion over the subject matter of the *donatio*.
4. Finally this subject matter must be capable of passing by *donatio mortis causa*.

The burden of proof of these requirements lies on the donee. A *donatio mortis causa* may be established by the sole evidence of the donee if the court after sifting it carefully consider his evidence trustworthy.[29]

A. Requirements of a Donatio Mortis Causa

1. Intended to be conditional on death. The donor must intend the gift to become absolute only at his own death. Meanwhile the gift is

---

[26] For the two exceptions to the general rule that a will is revoked by the marriage of the testator see *post*, pp. 59 *et seq.*

[27] See *ante*, nn. 13–18; *Bennett* v. *Slater* [1899] 1 Q.B. 45. For the effect of divorce on a gift by will to the former spouse see *post*, p. 344.

[28] *Per* Buckley J. in *Re Beaumont* [1902] 1 Ch. 889, 892. He continued, "It may be said to be of an amphibious nature, being a gift which is neither entirely *inter vivos* nor testamentary."

[29] *Re Dillon* (1890) 44 Ch.D. 76, 80; *Re Farman* (1887) 57 L.J.Ch. 637.

revocable. There must be "a clear intention to give, but to give only if the donor dies, whereas if the donor does not die then the gift is not to take effect and the donor is to have back the subject matter of the gift."[30]

Proof of intention. The donor need not express this intention in words. It may be inferred from the circumstances in which the gift was made. In *Gardner* v. *Parker*[31] X, who was seriously ill and confined to his bed, gave to Y a bond for £1,800, saying, "There, take that and keep it." X died two days later. Leach V.-C. held that this was a valid *donatio mortis causa*, inferring from the circumstances that X intended the gift to be conditional on his own death. Even if the donor knows that he is certain to die within a short time, there seems no reason why he should not show the necessary intention that the gift should become absolute only at his own death.[32]

Other forms of intention. There can be no *donatio mortis causa* if the donor intends to make an immediate gift *inter vivos*. In that case the gift stands or falls as an ordinary gift *inter vivos*[33]: if it is invalid as a gift *inter vivos*, it may become effective after the donor's death under the rule in *Strong* v. *Bird* which is considered later.[34]

Again, there can be no *donatio mortis causa* if the donor intends to make a gift by will, *i.e.* intends the wishes he expresses to take effect at his death but does not intend to part with dominion over the asset during his life.[35] In order to make a *donatio mortis causa*, the donor must part with dominion over the asset in his lifetime and this involves a mental intention on his part to do so.

2. Contemplation of death. This peculiar requirement is home-grown English law and is not derived from civil law. Of course the donor cannot form the necessary intention that the gift should become absolute only at his own death without contemplating death. But it is not sufficient for the donor to contemplate the possibility of death at some time or other in the future. This second requirement is only satisfied if he contemplates death "within the near future, what may be called death for some reason believed to be impending."[36] However he need not contemplate immediate death or be on his death bed when he makes the *donatio mortis causa*. In *Wilkes* v. *Allington*[37] this requirement was satisfied because, at the time of the *donatio*, the donor knew that he had cancer and believed himself to be a doomed man: he did not know how long he had to live but he was satisfied that he had not long to live. A month later he caught a chill on a bus journey on his way home from market and died from pneumonia. The court held that the *donatio mortis*

---

[30] *Re Craven's Estate* [1937] Ch. 423, 426.
[31] (1818) 3 Madd. 184; see also *Re Lillingston* [1952] 2 All E.R. 184 and *Re Mustapha* (1891) 8 T.L.R. 160.
[32] See *Wilkes* v. *Allington* [1931] 2 Ch. 104, 111.
[33] *Edwards* v. *Jones* (1836) 1 My. & Cr. 226; *Tate* v. *Hilbert* (1793) 2 Ves.Jun. 111.
[34] *Post*, p. 25.
[35] *Solicitor to the Treasury* v. *Lewis* [1900] 2 Ch. 812; *cf. Re Ward* [1946] 2 All E.R. 206.
[36] *Re Craven's Estate (No. 1)* [1937] Ch. 423, 426.
[37] [1931] 2 Ch. 104; see also *Re Richards* [1921] 1 Ch. 513 (contemplation of death from critical operation but died without operation: *d.m.c.* held valid).

causa was valid because it was not conditional on his death from the particular cause contemplated by him.

Would it suffice if the donor *mistakenly* believed that he had cancer and was a doomed man? Probably it would because the second requirement appears to be concerned with the donor's subjective assessment of his situation.[38] Again it would probably suffice if the donor contemplated death from some dangerous mission which he was about to undertake.[39] Contemplation of death by suicide may also suffice as suicide is no longer a crime.[40]

3. Parting with dominion.[41] Before his death the donor must part with dominion over the subject matter of the *donatio*. Two elements are required—(a) the donor's intention to part with dominion and (b) a sufficient delivery or transfer of the subject matter of the gift, or of something representing it, to the donee.

(1) *The donor's intention.* The donor must intend to part with dominion over the asset to the donee.[42] In *Reddel* v. *Dobree*[43] X when in declining health delivered a locked cash box to Y, telling her that the box contained money for her, that he wanted the box from her every three months whilst he lived, and that at his death Y was to go to his son for the key. The court held that there was no *donatio mortis causa*. X intended to retain dominion over the contents of the box during his lifetime: he had kept control of the key and had reserved to himself in advance the right to deal with the contents. Again, there is no *donatio mortis causa* if X merely intends Y to have custody of a locked box and its key in her capacity of X's housekeeper.[44]

However, the donor may have the requisite intention to part with dominion even though he imposes on the donee a trust—for instance, a trust to make a certain payment to another person, or to pay the donor's funeral expenses.[45]

(2) *Delivery.* There must be a sufficient delivery in the donor's lifetime.[46] If the donor does not part with dominion in his lifetime the

---

[38] *Cf. Thompson* v. *Mechan* [1958] O.R. 357 (donor regarded air travel as perilous) where the Ontario Court of Appeal adopted an objective assessment: see (1965) 81 L.Q.R. 21.

[39] *Agnew* v. *Belfast Banking Co.* [1896] 2 I.R. 204, 221.

[40] Suicide Act 1961, s.1. Before this Act contemplation of death by suicide did not suffice, *Re Dudman* [1925] Ch. 553; *Agnew* v. *Belfast Banking Co., supra.* See also *Mills* v. *Shields* [1948] I.R. 367.

[41] See W. H. D. Winder (1940) 4 Conv.(N.S.) 382.

[42] *Birch* v. *Treasury Solicitor* [1951] Ch. 298, esp. at pp. 304–306; *Hawkins* v. *Blewitt* (1798) 2 Esp. 662.

[43] (1834) 10 Sim. 244.

[44] *Trimmer* v. *Danby* (1856) 25 L.J.Ch. 424 (box contained X's securities, including bonds indorsed by X as belonging to Y: no *d.m.c.* as no delivery of bonds to Y); *Wildish* v. *Fowler* (1892) 8 T.L.R. 457 ("Take care of this" by sick lodger to landlady: no *d.m.c.*).

[45] *Hills* v. *Hills* (1841) 8 M. & W. 401; *Hudson* v. *Spencer* [1910] 2 Ch. 285; *Birch* v. *Treasury Solicitor* [1951] Ch. 298, 304.

[46] *Ward* v. *Turner* (1752) 2 Ves.Sen. 431; *Cant* v. *Gregory* (1894) 10 T.L.R. 584 (no delivery of mortgage deed as donee refused to accept it).

donatio mortis causa fails. In *Bunn* v. *Markham*[47] C, believing himself near death, directed the words, "For Mrs. and Miss C" to be written on sealed parcels containing money and securities, and declared that the parcels were to be delivered to Mrs. and Miss C after his death. C then directed the parcels to be replaced in his iron chest of which he kept the keys. Following C's death the court held that there was no *donatio mortis causa* because there had been no act of delivery and the donor had never parted with dominion over the parcels in his lifetime.

Delivery in the donor's lifetime is essential but it is immaterial that the delivery is made before, or after, the donor expresses his intention to make the *donatio*. For instance, in *Cain* v. *Moon*[48] a daughter delivered a deposit note to her mother for safe custody. Two years later when the daughter was seriously ill she told her mother, "the bank-note is for you if I die." The court held this to be a valid *donatio mortis causa*—the antecedent delivery sufficed and it was not necessary for the mother to hand back the note and for the daughter to re-deliver it when she expressed her intention to make the *donatio*.

(a) PARTIES TO THE DELIVERY. The delivery may be made by the donor or by his duly authorised agent,[49] and it may be made to the donee or to an agent for the donee.[50] But delivery by the donor to his own agent does not suffice.[51] If the donor intends to make a *donatio* to two donees H and W jointly, delivery may be made to W both for herself and as agent for H.[52]

(b) DELIVERY OF A CHATTEL. There must be either actual delivery of a chattel (*e.g.* the donor hands his watch to the donee) or delivery of the means of obtaining the chattel (*e.g.* the donor hands to the donee the key of the box which contains the watch)[53]: the latter suffices because the donor thereby parts with dominion over the chattel. A merely symbolic delivery, such as the delivery of a watchstrap as a symbol for the watch, does not suffice.[54] Handing over the key to the box which contains the watch is sufficient even though the donor does not hand over the box itself.[55] On the other hand, it probably does not suffice if the donor delivers to the donee one of two keys to the box but keeps the

---

[47] (1816) 7 Taunt. 224: see also *Hardy* v. *Baker* (1738) West t. Hard. 519 (donor told his servant to deliver property to donee after donor's death: no *d.m.c.*); *Bryson* v. *Brownrigg* (1803) 9 Ves. 1 (donor told his wife to move securities intended for his daughter to another drawer in his bureau: no *d.m.c.*); *Miller* v. *Miller* (1735) 3 P.Wms. 356 (oral gift of coach and horses to wife but no delivery: no *d.m.c.*); *Re Miller* (1961) 105 S.J. 207.

[48] [1896] 2 Q.B. 283: see also *Re Weston* [1902] 1 Ch. 680.

[49] *Re Craven's Estate (No. 1)* [1937] Ch. 423.

[50] *Moore* v. *Darton* (1851) 4 De G. & Sm. 517, 520 (*sed quaere* whether on the facts the donor's lady's maid was the donee's agent).

[51] *Farquharson* v. *Cave* (1846) 2 Coll.C.C. 356, 367; *Powell* v. *Hellicar* (1858) 26 Beav. 261; *Re Kirkley* (1909) 25 T.L.R. 522.

[52] *Birch* v. *Treasury Solicitor* [1951] Ch. 298, esp. at pp. 303–304.

[53] See generally A. C. H. Barlow (1956) 19 M.L.R. 394, where the *d.m.c.* cases are discussed.

[54] *Ward* v. *Turner* (1752) 2 Ves.Sen. 431.

[55] *Re Craven's Estate (No. 1)* [1937] Ch. 423, 428. The delivery of the means of obtaining the chattel suffices even though the chattel is not bulky and is capable of manual delivery, *Jones* v. *Selby* (1710) Prec.Ch. 300 (key delivered to trunk containing government tally); *Re Mustapha* (1891) 8 T.L.R. 160.

other key,[56] or delivers the box but keeps the only key to it,[57] because such conduct generally indicates that the donor does not intend to part with dominion.

In *Re Lillingston*[58] L in contemplation of death handed to P a packet of jewellery and the keys to her trunk, telling her that the trunk contained the key to her Harrods safe deposit, which in turn contained the key to her city safe deposit. L said that she wished P to have all her jewellery and that after her death P could go and get the jewellery in these safe deposits. L and P agreed that the packet of jewellery should be kept in the trunk, which was in L's room, and P placed the packet in the trunk. L then said, "Keep the key: it is now yours." The court held that there had been a valid *donatio mortis causa* of the packet of jewellery and of the jewellery in the two safe deposits. As Wynn-Parry J. put it, it did not matter "in how many boxes the subject of a gift may be contained or that each, except the last, contains a key which opens the next, so long as the scope of the gift is made clear."[59] Again, it did not matter that under the terms of the contract between L and Harrods P also needed L's signed authority to withdraw the jewellery from the Harrods safe deposit—L had transferred partial dominion to P and this sufficed.[60]

(c) DELIVERY OR TRANSFER OF A CHOSE IN ACTION. Similar rules apply if the subject matter of a *donatio* is a chose in action which is transferable by delivery. Thus, in the case of bearer bonds, there must be either actual delivery of the bonds to the donee or delivery of the means of obtaining them, such as the key of the box which contains the bonds.[61]

If the chose in action is not transferable by delivery there must be either a valid transfer[62] or the delivery of a document which amounts to a transfer.[63] In *Birch* v. *Treasury Solicitor*[64] B in contemplation of death handed to H and W her Post Office Savings Bank book, London Trustee Savings Bank book, Barclays Bank deposit pass book, and Westminster Bank deposit account book, intending that the money in these banks should belong to H and W in the event of her death. The Court of Appeal held that this was sufficient delivery to establish a *donatio mortis causa* of each of these bank accounts. The test to apply was to ask whether the particular document delivered " 'amounts to a transfer' as being the essential indicia or evidence of title, possession or production of which entitles the possessor to the money or property purported to

---

[56] *Re Craven's Estate (No. 1), supra,* at p. 428.

[57] *Re Johnson* (1905) 92 L.T. 357.

[58] [1952] 2 All E.R. 184.

[59] *Ibid.* p. 191: see also *Re Mustapha* (1891) 8 T.L.R. 160 (key delivered to wardrobe which contained key to safe which contained bonds).

[60] See also *Re Wasserberg* [1915] 1 Ch. 195.

[61] *Re Wasserberg, supra* (key to bank box containing bearer bonds); *Re Harrison* [1934] W.N. 25 (delivery of key but no intent to part with dominion).

[62] *Staniland* v. *Willott* (1850) 3 Mac. & G. 664 (*d.m.c.* by valid legal transfer of shares in public company). For the requirements for a valid transfer *inter vivos* see *Re Rose* [1952] Ch. 78.

[63] The phrase used by Lord Hardwicke L.C. in the leading case of *Ward* v. *Turner* (1752) 2 Ves.Sen. 431, 444.

[64] [1951] Ch. 298: see also *Re Dillon* (1890) 44 Ch.D. 76 (delivery of banker's deposit note) and *Moore* v. *Darton* (1851) 4 De G. & Sm. 517.

be given."[65] This test was satisfied because in the case of each bank the production of the bank book was necessary upon any withdrawal from the account. However it was held to be unnecessary for the document to express the terms of the contract out of which the chose in action arose, *i.e.* in this case the terms of the contract between B and each bank.

4. Property capable of passing by donatio mortis causa. In general most, if not all, pure personalty is capable of being the subject matter of a *donatio*. Thus bonds,[66] an insurance policy,[67] a banker's deposit note,[68] and savings certificates[69] have all been held capable of passing by *donatio mortis causa*. The following categories of property need separate consideration:

(1) *Land.* Lord Eldon in *Duffield* v. *Elwes*[70] took the view *obiter* that land cannot be the subject of a *donatio* and probably neither realty nor leaseholds is capable of passing by *donatio*.[71] However in *Duffield* v. *Elwes* the House of Lords held that a mortgage can be the subject of a *donatio* by delivery of the mortgage deed—the mortgage debt passes under the *donatio* and it carries the mortgage security along with it.[72]

(2) *Cheques and promissory notes.* A cheque or promissory note drawn by a third party passes by *donatio*: this is so even though it is not transferable at law by delivery, having been made payable to the donor and not having been indorsed by him.[73] But a cheque drawn by the donor upon his own bank cannot be the subject of a *donatio* because it does not constitute property, but is merely an order to his bank which is revoked by the donor's death.[74] Similarly there cannot be a *donatio* of a promissory note drawn by the donor himself—again it does not constitute property but is merely a promise to pay money.[75] However there may be a valid *donatio* if the donee receives payment on the cheque

---

[65] [1951] Ch. 298, 311: *cf. Delgoffe* v. *Fader* [1939] Ch. 922 (production of bank book unnecessary for withdrawal: no *d.m.c.* by delivery of book).

[66] *Snellgrove* v. *Baily* (1744) 3 Atk. 214 (donor delivered bond to donee saying, "in case I die it is yours": held *d.m.c.*); *Gardner* v. *Parker* (1818) 3 Madd. 184 (bond for £1,800); *Re Wasserberg* [1915] 1 Ch. 195 (bearer bonds).

[67] *Witt* v. *Amis* (1861) 1 Best & Sm. 109 (insurance policy on donor's life); *Amis* v. *Witt* (1863) 33 Beav. 619.

[68] *Re Dillon* (1890) 44 Ch.D. 76: *cf. Re Mead* (1880) 15 Ch.D. 651.

[69] *Darlow* v. *Sparks* [1938] 2 All E.R. 235 (war and national savings certificates); *Beatrice Finch* (1958) in Lawton's *Guide to the Law of Trustee Savings Banks* (3rd ed., 1962), p. 1026 (*d.m.c.* of premium savings bond). See also *Re Lee* [1918] 2 Ch. 320 (registered Exchequer bond: *d.m.c.* by delivery of Exchequer bond deposit book) and *Re Richards* [1921] 1 Ch. 513 (*d.m.c.* of registered Victory Bonds), and distinguish *Re Andrews* [1902] 2 Ch. 394.

[70] (1827) 1 Bli.N.S. 497, 530, 539 and 542–543.

[71] But *cf.* Pettit, *Equity and the Law of Trusts* (5th ed., 1984), p. 104, n. 19, citing *Cooper* v. *Seversen* (1956) 1 D.L.R. (2d) 161, 166 (land conveyed).

[72] (1827) 1 Bli.N.S. 497, 541, quoting Lord Mansfield in *Martin* v. *Mowlin* (1760) 2 Burr. 969, 979: see also *Wilkes* v. *Allington* [1931] 2 Ch. 104.

[73] *Veal* v. *Veal* (1867) 27 Beav. 303 (*d.m.c.* of unindorsed promissory notes payable to donor or order); *Re Mead* (1880) 15 Ch.D. 651 (*d.m.c.* of unindorsed bills of exchange payable to donor or order); *Clement* v. *Cheesman* (1884) 27 Ch.D. 631 (*d.m.c.* of unindorsed cheques payable to donor or order).

[74] *Re Beaumont* [1902] 1 Ch. 889: see also *Re Swinburne* [1926] Ch. 38, 47.

[75] *Re Leaper* [1916] 1 Ch. 579.

from the bank in the donor's lifetime[76] (or even afterwards before the bank is apprised of the donor's death[77]), or if the donee negotiates the cheque for value in the donor's lifetime.[78]

(3) *Company shares.* In *Ward* v. *Turner*[79] Lord Hardwicke held that the delivery of receipts for the purchase price of South Sea annuities was not a sufficient delivery of the annuities to the donee by way of *donatio*. He said that a *donatio mortis causa* of company stock could not be made "without a transfer, or something amounting to that," and the receipts were "nothing but waste paper."[80] However he certainly never suggested that company stock was not capable of passing by *donatio*. In *Staniland* v. *Willott*[81] the donor in contemplation of death made a valid legal transfer of company shares to the donee and the Lord Chancellor held that this constituted a *donatio mortis causa*, which had been revoked by the donor's recovery from his illness.

Unfortunately in *Moore* v. *Moore*[82] the court misunderstood the effect of *Ward* v. *Turner* and held that railway stock could never be the subject of a *donatio*. This decision was followed in *Re Weston*[83] where the court held that building society investment shares could not be the subject of a *donatio*. The decision in *Staniland* v. *Willott* was not cited in either *Moore* v. *Moore* or *Re Weston*, and both these first instance decisions must be regarded as of doubtful authority. Probably company and building society investment shares are capable of passing by *donatio mortis causa* if the donor makes a valid transfer of them to the donee or, perhaps, delivers a document which amounts to a transfer.

B. EFFECT OF A DONATIO MORTIS CAUSA

Revocable until death. A *donatio mortis causa* is revocable until the death of the donor. Revocation is automatic if the donor recovers from his illness from which he contemplated death.[84] Alternatively the donor may expressly revoke the *donatio* by resuming dominion over the property[85] or, perhaps, by merely informing the donee of the revocation.[86] There is, however, no revocation if the donor resumes possession of the property in order to hold it in safe custody for the donee but does not

---

[76] *Bouts* v. *Ellis* (1853) 17 Beav. 121, affirmed 4 De G.M. & G. 249; it suffices if the bank accepts the cheque during the donor's lifetime. *Re While* [1928] W.N. 182; *Re Beaumont* [1902] 1 Ch. 889, 895 (may be sufficient if bank gives undertaking to donee to hold amount of cheque for donee).

[77] *Tate* v. *Hilbert* (1793) 2 Ves.Jun. 111, 118.

[78] *Rolls* v. *Pearce* (1877) 5 Ch.D. 730.

[79] (1752) 2 Ves.Sen. 431.

[80] *Ibid.* at pp. 443–444.

[81] (1850) 3 Mac. & G. 664: see also *Re Craven's Estate (No. 1)* [1937] Ch. 423 (*d.m.c.* of shares transferred to donee).

[82] (1874) L.R. 18 Eq. 474.

[83] [1902] 1 Ch. 680: see also *Griffiths* v. *The Abbey National B.S. (1947)* [1938–1949] Reg.Rep. 14 (delivery of building society shares pass book; held *d.m.c.* by Registrar of Friendly Societies).

[84] *Staniland* v. *Willott* (1850) 3 Mac. & G. 664.

[85] *Bunn* v. *Markham* (1816) 7 Taunt. 224: see also *In the Estate of Mulroy* [1924] 1 I.R. 98.

[86] *Jones* v. *Selby* (1710) Prec.Ch. 300, 303.

resume dominion over it.[87] Again, the donor cannot revoke a *donatio* by his will.[88]

If the *donatio* transferred the donor's title to the property to the donee, then on revocation the donee holds the property on trust for the donor and must re-transfer it to the donor.[89]

Death of donor. Assuming there has been no revocation, on the death of the donor the *donatio* become absolute.

Often a *donatio* vests the donor's title to the property in the donee. This occurs where the donor makes a "complete" delivery or transfer, such as would suffice in the case of a gift *inter vivos*. In this case the donee's title becomes unconditional at the donor's death and no action on the part of the donor's personal representatives is needed to perfect the donee's title. But there may be a valid *donatio* even though the delivery or transfer does not vest the donor's title in the donee. In the case of a chattel or a chose in action transferable by delivery, the donor may make a delivery which suffices for a *donatio mortis causa* but would not suffice in the case of an *inter vivos* gift.[90] Again, a *donatio* of a chose in action not transferable by delivery may be made by the delivery of a document which amounts to a transfer, though it does not effectively transfer the donor's title to the donee. For instance, a valid *donatio* may be made by the delivery to the donee of a mortgage deed, though the legal title to the mortgage debt and the mortgage security remains vested in the donor.[91] Where the donor makes a *donatio* by an "incomplete" delivery or transfer, the donor's personal representatives hold the legal title on a trust imposed by law for the donee. If need be, the donee is entitled to require the personal representatives to lend their names to any necessary action, on receiving an appropriate indemnity from the donee.[92] In short, if the requisites for a valid *donatio* are satisfied, after the donor's death equity perfects an incomplete delivery or transfer to the donee. "The [equitable] principle of not assisting a volunteer to perfect an incomplete gift does not apply to a *donatio mortis causa.*"[93]

Comparison with a legacy. The basic differences between a *donatio mortis causa* and a legacy given by will are that a *donatio* must be made by the donor in contemplation of death (not so a will, which can be made at any time), and that a *donatio* requires the donor to part with dominion over its subject matter before his death (not so a will). There are also some subsidiary differences—for instance, the methods of revocation are different, and if the *donatio* vested the donor's title to the property in the donee no action on the part of the donor's personal

---

[87] *Re Hawkins* [1924] 2 Ch. 47 (*d.m.c.* by delivery of envelope containing money to donee; envelope then placed in donor's deed box for safe custody).

[88] *Jones* v. *Selby, supra.*

[89] *Staniland* v. *Willott* (1852) 3 Mac. & G. 664.

[90] *Re Wasserberg* [1915] 1 Ch. 195.

[91] *Duffield* v. *Elwes* (1827) 1 Bli.N.S. 497.

[92] *Duffield* v. *Elwes, supra; Re Wasserberg, supra; Re Lillingston* [1952] 2 All E.R. 184.

[93] *Per* Lindley L.J. in *Re Dillon* (1890) 44 Ch.D. 76, 83.

representatives is needed to perfect the donee's title.[94] However, in some respects a *donatio mortis causa* resembles a legacy:

(i) A *donatio* fails if the donee predeceases the donor[95]: similarly a legacy normally fails by lapse if the legatee predeceases the testator.[96]

(ii) Property given by *donatio* is liable for the debts of the donor, but only on a deficiency of the assets of his estate.[97]

(iii) In general a *donatio mortis causa* is subject to the rules of satisfaction. A *donatio* may therefore be satisfied by a legacy given to the donee by the donor's later will if the donor intended the legacy to be in satisfaction of the *donatio*.[98] It has been held that the mere fact that the legacy is of equal amount to the *donatio* does not raise a presumption that the donor intended it to be in satisfaction of the *donatio*.[99]

4. THE RULE IN STRONG v. BIRD

A. THE ORIGIN OF THE RULE

Forgiveness of a debt. *Strong* v. *Bird*[1] was decided in 1874 and concerned the forgiveness of a debt. B borrowed £1,100 from his stepmother, who was living in his house and paying him £212 10s. each quarter for her board. They agreed that B should repay the loan by a deduction of £100 from the stepmother's next 11 quarterly payments. The stepmother deducted £100 from her next two quarterly payments but she then refused to make any further deductions and expressly forgave B the debt. She continued to make quarterly payments of £212 10s. to B until her death. By her will she appointed B her sole executor and B proved the will. When she forgave B the debt there was no release of the debt at law because her forgiveness of the debt was not made under seal or supported by valuable consideration.[2] But B as executor could not sue himself for the debt and therefore as from her death B was no longer liable for the debt at common law.[3] Normally equity compels a debtor

[94] As to the rules of private international law governing the validity of a *d.m.c.* see *Re Korvine's Trust* [1921] 1 Ch. 343 (*cf. Re Craven's Estate (No. 1)* [1937] Ch. 423) and Dicey and Morris, *The Conflict of Laws* (11th ed., 1987), pp. 942–946.
[95] *Tate* v. *Hilbert* (1793) 2 Ves.Jun. 111, 120; *Walter* v. *Hodge* (1818) 2 Swans. 92, 99.
[96] *Post*, p. 336.
[97] *Smith* v. *Casen* (1718) 1 P.Wms. 406; *Ward* v. *Turner* (1752) 2 Ves.Sen. 431, 434; *Tate* v. *Leithead* (1854) Kay 658, 659; *Re Korvine's Trust* [1921] 1 Ch. 343, 348; *cf.* Warnock-Smith [1978] Conv. 130: see *post*, p. 273. As to the liability for debts of general and specific legacies see *post*, pp. 265 *et seq.* and 298–300.
[98] *Jones* v. *Selby* (1710) Prec.Ch. 300; *Hudson* v. *Spencer* [1910] 2 Ch. 285: for satisfaction see *post*, pp. 446 *et seq.*
[99] *Hudson* v. *Spencer, supra* (delivery of £2,000 deposit notes to housekeeper; two days later donor made will giving £2,000 legacy to her: held she took both *d.m.c.* and legacy).
[1] (1874) L.R. 18 Eq. 315.
[2] *Pinnel's Case* (1602) 5 Co.Rep. 117a; *Foakes* v. *Beer* (1884) 9 App.Cas. 605: in some circumstances the debtor may have a defence under the doctrine of promissory or quasi-estoppel.
[3] *Jenkins* v. *Jenkins* [1928] 2 K.B. 501.

executor to account for the amount of his debt at the instance of the deceased's creditors or the beneficiaries under the deceased's will or intestacy. However, Jessel M.R. held that B was not liable to account because his stepmother had a continuing intention to forgive him the balance of the loan. The debt was released at law and there was "no equity against him" to make him pay the debt. In short, the step-mother's continuing intention to forgive the debt rebutted the equity of the deceased's creditors or beneficiaries to make him pay the debt.[4]

Imperfect gift of property. The rule in *Strong* v. *Bird* has been extended from the forgiveness of a debt to an imperfect gift of property made by the deceased during his lifetime. In *Re Stewart*[5] the deceased bought and paid for three bearer bonds through his brokers a few days before his death. He handed to his wife an envelope which contained the brokers' letter announcing the purchase and the bought note, and said to her, "I have bought these bonds for you." However, the bonds were not delivered to the wife and immediately before his death she had no legal or equitable interest in the bonds. The wife was one of his executors and she and the other executors proved his will. Neville J. held that the wife was beneficially entitled to the bonds under the principle of *Strong* v. *Bird*, which he stated in this way[6]:

"where a testator has expressed the intention of making a gift of per-sonal estate belonging to him to one who upon his death becomes his executor, the intention continuing unchanged, the executor is entitled to hold the property for his own benefit. The reasoning by which the conclusion is reached is of a double character—first, that the vesting of the property in the executor at the testator's death com-pletes the imperfect gift made in the lifetime, and, secondly, that the intention of the testator to give the beneficial interest to the executor is sufficient to countervail the equity of beneficiaries under the will, the testator having vested the legal estate in the executor."

This reasoning appears unconvincing. The legal title to the bonds vested in the wife in her *fiduciary* capacity as one of the executors appointed by the deceased, and not as intended donee. Why should this complete the imperfect gift made in the deceased's lifetime? How-ever, *Re Stewart* has been followed at first instance[7] and has been con-sidered by the Court of Appeal[8] and has never been judicially doubted. In the present state of the case law authorities the rule in *Strong* v. *Bird* is applicable to an imperfect gift of any property, whether real or personal, made by the deceased during his lifetime.

---

[4] *Re Applebee* [1891] 3 Ch. 422, 429–430; *Re Pink* [1912] 2 Ch. 529: see also *Re Gonin* [1979] Ch. 16, 34.

[5] [1908] 2 Ch. 251: see also *Re Griffin* [1899] 1 Ch. 408, 412.

[6] [1908] 2 Ch. 251, 254.

[7] *Re James* [1935] Ch. 449 (imperfect gift of a house); *Re Comberbach* (1929) 73 S.J. 403; *Re Nelson* (1947) 91 S.J. 533. See also *Carter* v. *Hungerford* [1917] 1 Ch. 260: *Re Ralli's W.T.* [1964] Ch. 288; *Re Gonin* [1979] Ch. 16, 35 ("a simple rule of equity").

[8] *Re Freeland* [1952] Ch. 110: see also *Cope* v. *Keene* (1968) 42 A.L.J.R. 169 (High Court of Australia).

B. Requirements of the Rule

1. Deceased's intention. For the rule in *Strong* v. *Bird* to apply the deceased must show during his lifetime a present intention of forgiving the debt or of making a gift of particular property (as the case may be), and this intention must continue unchanged until his death. It is not enough if the deceased merely intends, or promises, to make a gift on a future occasion.[9]

(1) *Not a testamentary intention.* If the deceased's intention is to forgive the debt, or to make the gift, at his death or by his will, the rule in *Strong* v. *Bird* is not applicable. Such an intention is testamentary and has no effect unless the deceased shows such an intention in his duly executed will. In *Re Hyslop*[10] the deceased by his will appointed X, who owed him £100, to be one of his executors. After his death a letter written by the deceased to X was found; the letter showed that the deceased intended to cancel the debt due from X. The will, but not the letter, was admitted to probate. The court held that X was liable in equity to pay the debt to the deceased's estate. The rule in *Strong* v. *Bird* was not applicable because the deceased's intention to cancel the debt was testamentary. The letter was not duly executed as a will and was therefore not admissible in evidence and had to be disregarded.

(2) *No change of intention.* The deceased's intention of forgiving the debt, or of making the gift, must continue unchanged until his death. This requirement is not satisfied if the deceased later takes security from X for the debt which she has previously forgiven,[11] or later lends to Y the car which she previously intended to give to X.[12]

2. Property vests in donee. The other requirement of the rule in *Strong* v. *Bird* is that the debt, or the subject matter of the gift, must become vested in the intended donee. It suffices if it becomes vested in him as sole executor (as in *Strong* v. *Bird*) or as one of several proving executors (as in *Re Stewart*[13]).

Does it suffice if it becomes vested in him as administrator? In *Re James*[14] it was held to be sufficient that it had vested in the intended donee as one of two administratrices appointed by the court. In that case S became entitled to his father's house on the latter's death

---

[9] *Re Innes* [1910] 1 Ch. 188; *Re Freeland, supra,* (promise to give car when put in running order: rule not applicable); *Cope* v. *Keene, supra.*

[10] [1894] 3 Ch. 522: see also *Re Pink* [1912] 2 Ch. 529, 536 and 538–539; *Re Greene* [1949] Ch. 333 and *Brown* v. *Selwin* (1735) Cas.t.Talb. 240 (also reported in 3 Bro.P.C. 607 *sub nom. Selwin* v. *Brown*).

[11] *Re Eiser's W.T.* [1937] 1 All E.R. 244.

[12] *Re Freeland, supra,* at p. 121; *Re Wale* [1956] 1 W.L.R. 1346. See Kodilinye [1982] Conv. 14, 26–28.

[13] [1908] 2 Ch. 251. In *Re Stewart* the other executors took probate and the wife later took a grant of double probate (*post,* p. 176). *Quaere* whether the rule applies if the executor does not prove, see Kodilinye [1982] Conv. 14, 18–19.

[14] [1935] Ch. 449: see also *Re Ralli's W.T.* [1964] Ch. 288 (H made imperfect gift of her interest under T's will to her marriage settlement trustees of whom X was one; later X was appointed trustee of T's will; H died; X held H's interest on the trusts of the marriage settlement).

intestate. S "gave" the house to his father's housekeeper, handing her the title deeds, but he did not convey the house to her. She occupied the house as donee and S had a continuing intention to give the house to her until his own death intestate nine years later. The housekeeper was appointed to be one of two administratrices of S's estate. The legal estate in the house therefore vested in the housekeeper jointly with the other administratrix. Farwell J. held that under the rule in *Strong* v. *Bird* this perfected the imperfect gift of the house made by S in his lifetime. However, in *Re Gonin*[15] Walton J. doubted whether the rule ought to apply to an administrator who (unlike an executor) is appointed by the court and not by the deceased: it would seem "an astonishing doctrine of equity" that the gift is perfected if the intended donee manages to obtain a grant of letters of administration, but is not perfected if another person equally entitled to a grant does so.[16]

Some other problems still await solution.[17] For instance, does the rule apply to an executor by representation?[18] And is the rule binding on the deceased's creditors, as well as on the beneficiaries entitled under his will or intestacy? Probably the answer to each question is no.

C. AN IMPERFECT RULE

There may be something to be said for not perfecting any imperfect gift made by the deceased in his lifetime—then at his death all his assets pass under his will or intestacy. There is perhaps more to be said for perfecting all the imperfect gifts made by the deceased in his lifetime provided his intention to give continues unchanged until his death—this gives effect to the deceased's intention when he is no longer able to perfect the gifts himself. But what can be said for the rule in *Strong* v. *Bird* under which an imperfect gift (or the forgiveness of a debt) is only perfected if the property (or debt) vests in the donee in a *different capacity*, and in a *fiduciary capacity* at that?

---

[15] [1979] Ch. 16, 34–35.
[16] *Ibid.* at p. 35; but see (1977) 93 L.Q.R. 486; Kodilinye [1982] Conv. 14, 16–17. As to persons entitled in the same degree to a grant see *post*, p. 153.
[17] For the effect of the Inheritance (Provision for Family and Dependants) Act 1975, see *post*, p. 126, n. 18.
[18] *Post*, p. 144.

CHAPTER 2

THE MAKING OF WILLS

1. FORMALITIES

A. Formal Wills

Section 9 of the Wills Act 1837 provides that:

"No will[1] shall be valid unless—
 (a) it is in writing, and signed by the testator, or by some other person in his presence and by his direction; and
 (b) it appears that the testator intended by his signature to give effect to the will, and
 (c) the signature is made or acknowledged by the testator in the presence of two or more witnesses present at the same time; and
 (d) each witness either—
  (i) attests and signs the will; or
  (ii) acknowledges his signature,
  in the presence of the testator (but not necessarily in the presence of any other witness),
but no form of attestation shall be necessary."

This provision, which is quoted as amended by section 17 of the Administration of Justice Act 1982, applies if the testator dies after December 31, 1982.[2] Section 9 in its original form[3] (together with the Wills Act Amendment Act 1852) applies if the testator dies before January 1, 1983. The differences between the rules governing the execution of a will on a death after 1982, and on a death before 1983, are explained in this section.

Section 9 applies to all wills required to be executed in accordance

---

[1] "will" includes a testament, a codicil, an appointment by will or by writing in the nature of a will in exercise of a power, and any other testamentary disposition; Wills Act 1837, s.1. A nomination under a pension scheme is not a testamentary disposition, *Re Danish Bacon Co. Staff Pension Fund Trusts* [1971] 1 W.L.R. 248: for criticism see Chappenden [1972] J.B.L. 20.

[2] Administration of Justice Act 1982, ss.73(6) and 76(11).

[3] Section 9 in its original form reads "No will shall be valid unless it shall be in writing, and executed in manner hereinafter mentioned; (that is to say), it shall be signed at the foot or end thereof by the testator, or by some other person in his presence and by his direction; and such signature shall be made or acknowledged by the testator in the presence of two or more witnesses present at the same time, and such witnesses shall attest and shall subscribe the will in the presence of the testator, but no form of attestation shall be necessary."

29

with English internal law,[4] except wills of privileged testators and "statutory" wills of mentally disordered patients.[5] The court has no power to admit to probate an authentic will which is invalid under section 9.[6]

1. In writing. Under section 9 a will must be in writing but there are no restrictions as to the materials[7] on which, or by which, it may be written, or as to what language[8] may be used. It may be handwritten or typed and a printed or lithographed form[9] may be used; most "home-made" wills are made by filling up the spaces on printed will forms in the testator's handwriting. No particular form of words need be used: "all for mother" has been held to be a valid will.[10]

A will may be made in pencil or in ink or in a combination of the two, but there is a presumption that the pencil writing in such a combination was only deliberative and it will be excluded from probate unless the court decides that it represented the testator's definite intention.[11]

2. Signed by the testator.

(1) *Methods of signature by the testator.* Instead of signing his name[12] the testator may sign by marking the will in some way intended by him as his signature. Thus initials,[13] a stamped signature,[14] or a mark such as a cross, or an inked thumb mark,[15] or a mark of any shape,[16] are all sufficient if intended by him as his signature. A mark suffices though the testator's hand was guided by another person[17] and it is immaterial whether the testator could write or not. A mark is a useful method of signature for illiterates and those suffering from severe physical disability: it is desirable for the attestation clause to state that the testator signed with his mark.

In *In the Goods of Chalcraft*[18] the testatrix was dying and signed a codicil "E. Chal" but was unable to complete her signature: this was

---

[4] For the rules of private international law governing the formal validity of wills see Dicey and Morris, *The Conflict of Laws* (11th ed., 1987), pp. 1011 *et seq.*; Theobald on *Wills* (14th ed., 1982), Chap. 1. For the Convention on International Wills see ss.27, 28 and 76(5) and (6) of the Administration of Justice Act 1982.

[5] For privileged testators see *post*, p. 39 and for statutory wills see *post*, p. 47.

[6] See Law Reform Committee, 22nd Report, *The making and revocation of wills*, Cmnd. 7902 (1980), pp. 3–4: for reform see *post*, p. 38.

[7] *Hodson* v. *Barnes* (1926) 43 T.L.R. 71 (writing on empty egg shell).

[8] *Whiting* v. *Turner* (1903) 89 L.T. 71 (will written in French language); *Kell* v. *Charmer* (1856) 23 Beav. 195 (sums bequeathed represented in letters using jeweller's private code).

[9] Interpretation Act 1978, s.5 and Sched. 1.

[10] *Thorn* v. *Dickens* [1906] W.N. 54 ("probably the shortest will ever known").

[11] *In the Goods of Adams* (1872) L.R. 2 P. & D. 367.

[12] Signing in an assumed name suffices; *In the Goods of Redding* (1850) 2 Rob.Ecc. 339.

[13] *In the Goods of Savory* (1851) 15 Jur. 1042.

[14] *In the Goods of Jenkins* (1863) 3 Sw. & Tr. 93.

[15] *In the Estate of Finn* (1935) 105 L.J.P. 36 ("merely a blot" as his thumb slipped and the mark smudged).

[16] *In the Estate of Holtam* (1913) 108 L.T. 732 ("a sort of broken line"); *In the Goods of Kieran* [1933] I.R. 222. A seal intended as his signature probably suffices, *In the Estate of Bulloch* [1968] N.I. 96, 99.

[17] *Wilson* v. *Beddard* (1841) 12 Sim. 28.

[18] [1948] P. 222; *cf. Re Colling* [1972] 1 W.L.R. 1440.

held to be a sufficient signature on the ground that what she wrote was intended by her to be the best that she could do by way of writing her name. In another case[19] the will began "I, Emma Cook" and the testatrix wrote the words "Your loving mother" at the end: the court admitted the will to probate, being satisfied that the testatrix meant the words "Your loving mother" to represent her name.

(2) *Signature on the testator's behalf.* The will may be signed by some other person in the testator's presence and by his direction. The person signing may be one of the attesting witnesses[20] and he may sign his own name instead of that of the testator.[21]

(3) *Connection of signature with pages of will.* If a will is written on more than one page, of which only the last is duly executed, all the pages ought to be attached in some way at the time of execution so as to constitute a single testamentary document. In order to reduce the risk of fraud or accidental loss it is desirable that the pages should be securely attached—for instance, sewn together with lawyers' green tape. However, it suffices if at the time of execution the pages are held together by the testator's finger and thumb[22] or pressed together on a table by the testator with his hand.[23] Moreover it suffices if at the time of execution the pages, though not touching, are all in the same room and under the control of the testator.[24]

(4) *Position of signature—death before 1983.* The amended section 9 of the Wills Act 1837 (applicable on a death after 1982) does not require the signature to be at the end of the will. The original section 9 (applicable on a death before 1983) required the signature to be "at the foot or end" of the will. This led to several unsatisfactory decisions in which the court insisted upon strict compliance[25] and as a result the Wills Act Amendment Act 1852 was passed to give a wider meaning to this requisite.

(a) WILLS ACT AMENDMENT ACT 1852. The Act in rather verbose language provided *inter alia*:

(i) that the signature may be so placed "at or after, or following, or under, or beside, or opposite to the end of the will, that it shall be apparent on the face of the will" that the testator intended to give effect by his signature to the will;

(ii) that a blank space may intervene between the end of the will and the signature;

(iii) that the signature may be placed in or under the attestation clause,[26] or beside or under the signatures of the witnesses; and

---

[19] *In the Estate of Cook* [1960] 1 W.L.R. 353.

[20] *Smith* v. *Harris* (1845) 1 Rob.Ecc. 262.

[21] *In the Goods of Clark* (1839) 2 Curt. 329.

[22] *Lewis* v. *Lewis* [1908] P. 1.

[23] *In the Estate of Little* [1960] 1 W.L.R. 495.

[24] *In the Goods of Tiernan* [1942] I.R. 572; *Sterling* v. *Bruce* [1973] N.I. 225.

[25] *e.g. Smee* v. *Bryer* (1848) 1 Rob.Ecc. 616 (will held invalid because the signature of the testatrix was not placed in eight-tenths of an inch left blank at the bottom of a page but on the next page).

[26] *Post,* p. 37.

(iv) that the signature may be placed on a page on which no part of the will is written, even if there is room for it at the bottom of the previous page.

The 1852 Act ended with two prohibitions—a signature can never operate to give effect to any part of the will (i) which is underneath or which follows the signature in space or (ii) which was inserted later in time after the signature was made.

(b) THE END OF THE WILL. The provisions of the 1852 Act were applied by the court in a lenient manner in order to save wills from invalidity. In *Re Roberts*[27] the testator's holograph[28] will filled a sheet of paper, leaving a margin at the left of the page, but no space for his signature and the attestation clause at the foot of the page. The testator turned the page sideways and wrote them in the margin, so that the attestation clause began at the foot of the margin and his own signature was written at the top of the margin (*i.e.* physically opposite the beginning of the will). The court decided that the will was validly executed, treating the whole of the margin as opposite to the end of the will. The decision in *In the Goods of Hornby*[29] went much further. In that case the testator's holograph will filled most of a sheet of paper and in writing it out the testator left an oblong space ruled off on one side of the page about halfway down, with the intention of placing his signature in it. The court held that the testator's signature in this space was "in the intention of the testator, at the end of the will,"[30] and admitted the will to probate. Thus the whereabouts of the end of the will was made to depend on the intention of the testator.

On the other hand in *Re Stalman*,[31] where a testatrix signed her will at the top of the page because there was no room left at the bottom, the Court of Appeal held the will to be invalid as the signature was at the beginning, and not at the end, of the will and the first prohibition in the 1852 Act applied. Probably the result would have been different if the testatrix had written, "I declare this to be the end of my will" at the top of the page before she signed.[32]

(c) THE ORDER OF PAGES. Similar leniency was shown in applying the provisions of the 1852 Act to wills consisting of more than one page. In *In the Estate of Long*[33] the holograph will of the testatrix was written on both sides of a sheet of paper: on one side appeared the heading of a will, the appointment of an executor, and an attestation clause with the signatures of the testatrix and attesting witnesses, and on the other side appeared a list of bequests. The whole will was written before it was executed. The court admitted the whole will to probate, reading the will as beginning with the bequests and ending with the signatures. How-

---

[27] [1934] P. 102: see also *In the Goods of Coombs* (1866) 1 P. & D. 302.

[28] *i.e.* written by the testator in his own handwriting.

[29] [1946] P. 171: for criticism see Hardingham, *The Law of Wills* (1977), p. 30; Hodgekiss (1953) 26 A.L.J.R. 575.

[30] *Per* Wallington J., at p. 179.

[31] (1931) 145 L.T. 339: see also *Re Harris* [1952] P. 319; *In the Estate of Bercovitz* [1962] 1 W.L.R. 321.

[32] See *In the Goods of Kimpton* (1864) 3 Sw. & T. 427.

[33] [1936] P. 166: see also *In the Goods of Smith* [1931] P. 225.

ever this lenient approach was only possible if the will was a "circle"[34] and the court could break into the circle by taking the second page as the starting point. This approach was impossible if an incomplete sentence at the bottom of the duly executed first page ran on to the top of the second page,[35] or if the duly executed first page contained a bequest to "my sisters and friends" and the second and third pages expanded this bequest by listing the legatees[36]: in each of these cases the first page had to be read first and it alone was admissible to probate.

(d) INTERPOLATION. Words which followed the signature in space could be treated as preceding it by reason of the testator's use of signs of interpolation. For instance, in *In the Goods of Birt*[37] the testator used asterisks with the words "see over" in order to interpolate the rest of a sentence, which was written on the unexecuted second side of a sheet of paper, into the duly executed first side. Lord Penzance said that the words on the second page "must be read in the place in which the testator intended they should be read, and therefore preceding the signature."[38] The interpolated words must not of course have been written later in time than the signature.

3. Testator intended by his signature to give effect to the will. Under the amended section 9 a will is invalid unless "it appears that the testator intended by his signature to give effect to the will."

This requirement was not mentioned in the original section 9.[39] Nevertheless, under the original section 9, the signature must have been written with intention to give effect to the will. Hence in *In the Estate of Bean*,[40] where a deceased forgot to sign his will but wrote his name and address on an envelope containing it, the court held that probate must be refused because he wrote his name on the envelope for the purpose of identifying its contents and not as a signature to his will.

Under the amended section 9, must it appear *from the will* that the testator intended by his signature to give effect to the will? Often this appears presumptively from an attestation clause, but such a clause is neither necessary nor conclusive. Very probably the answer to the question is no, because the amended section 9 does not require this mental

---

[34] *In the Goods of Gilbert* (1898) 78 L.T. 762, 763.

[35] *In the Goods of Gee* (1898) 78 L.T. 843: see also *Practice Direction* [1953] 1 W.L.R. 689.

[36] *Royle* v. *Harris* [1895] P. 163. The first page is not duly executed if it was signed merely to authenticate it and prevent interpolation, *Sweetland* v. *Sweetland* (1865) 4 Sw. & T. 6.

[37] (1871) L.R. 2 P. & D. 214: see also *Palin* v. *Ponting* [1930] P. 185 ("See other side for completion" on duly executed first page; "Continuation from the other side" above clauses on unexecuted second page: held these clauses were admissible to probate); *In the Goods of Greenwood* [1892] P. 7.

[38] *In the Goods of Birt, supra*, at p. 215.

[39] But see the Wills Act Amendment Act 1852, quoted *ante*, p. 31.

[40] [1944] P. 83: see also *Re Beadle* [1974] 1 W.L.R. 417 and contrast *In the Goods of Mann* [1942] P. 146 where a testatrix intended her signature on the envelope to be the signature to her will, and probate was granted of the envelope and the unsigned document inside it as together constituting the will of the testatrix. A document inside an envelope may be *incorporated* in a codicil written on the envelope, *Re Almosnino* (1859) 29 L.J.P. 46: see *post*, p. 44.

intention to appear from the will.[41] If so extrinsic evidence as to the words and actions of the testator is admissable (as in the case of a death before 1983) in order to ascertain what the testator intended by his signature.

4. Signature of the testator and the presence of witnesses. The signature of the testator must either be made or acknowledged by the testator in the presence of two witnesses present at the same time.

(1) *Signature made in their presence.* The witnesses need not know that the document is a will.[42] It is sufficient that the witnesses see the testator in the act of writing his signature, although they never see the signature and do not know what he is writing.[43] But if a witness, although present in the same room, is not aware that the testator is writing, this does not suffice.[44] Furthermore if a witness departs before the testator completes his intended signature, this does not suffice.[45]

(2) *Signature acknowledged in their presence.* If the signature on the will was not made in the simultaneous presence of two witnesses, the signature must subsequently be acknowledged by the testator in their simultaneous presence. There are three requisites for a valid acknowledgment—

- (i) The will must already have been signed before acknowledgment.
- (ii) At the time of acknowledgment the witnesses must see the signature or have the opportunity of seeing it. If at that time the signature is covered by the folding of the will,[46] or with blotting paper,[47] there can be no valid acknowledgment: it does not suffice that the testator would have uncovered the signature and allowed the witnesses to see it had he been asked.[48]
- (iii) The testator must acknowledge the signature by his words or conduct.

An express acknowledgment by the testator is desirable[49] but not essential—no particular form of words is required. The testator may acknowledge his signature by gestures.[50] Indeed it is sufficient that he (or someone in his presence and on his behalf) simply requests the witnesses to sign the document before them, without telling them that it is

---

[41] *cf.* the different wording of the Wills Act 1837, s.18(3) and (4) (as amended by the Administration of Justice Act 1982, s.18), which reads "it appears from a will that . . . ": see *post*, p. 61.

[42] *In the Estate of Benjamin* (1934) 150 L.T. 417.

[43] *Smith* v. *Smith* (1866) L.R. 1 P. & D. 143.

[44] *Brown* v. *Skirrow* [1902] P. 3.

[45] *Re Colling* [1972] 1 W.L.R. 1440 (*post*, p. 36).

[46] *Hudson* v. *Parker* (1844) 1 Rob.Ecc. 14: see also *Re Groffman* [1969] 1 W.L.R. 733 (will folded and inside testator's coat pocket).

[47] *In the Goods of Gunstan* (1882) 7 P.D. 102.

[48] *Re Groffman, supra.*

[49] By saying "this is my signature" or words to that effect.

[50] *In the Goods of Davies* (1850) 2 Rob.Ecc. 337.

his will.[51] As Cotton L.J. summed up the position in *Daintree* v. *Butcher*,[52]

"when the paper bearing the signature of the testatrix was put before two persons who were asked by her or in her presence to sign as witnesses that was an acknowledgment of the signature by her. The signature being so placed that they could see it, whether they actually did see it or not, she was in fact asking them to attest that signature as hers."

(3) *Who can be witnesses.* A blind person is incapable of being a witness to a will because it cannot be signed in his "presence" and he cannot be a "witness" to a visible act such as signing for the purposes of section 9.[53] Moreover the requirement that the signature shall be made or acknowledged in the "presence" of two witnesses needs their mental as well as their bodily presence. As Dr. Lushington put it in *Hudson* v. *Parker*,[54] "What could possibly be the object of the Legislature, except that the witnesses should see and be conscious of the act done, and be able to prove it by their own evidence: if the witnesses are not to be mentally, as well as bodily, present, they might be asleep, or intoxicated, or of unsound mind."

Obviously it is desirable to choose literate witnesses of sound mental capacity and of fixed residence, in case they may later be required to give evidence as to the validity of the will.

The Wills Act 1837 contains certain other relevant provisions. Section 15 deprives an attesting witness and his or her spouse of any benefit under the will[55] but allows such an attesting witness to give evidence as to whether or not the will is valid. Thus a beneficiary under a will, or the spouse of a beneficiary, is technically a good attesting witness. Similarly sections 16 and 17 allow a creditor (whose debt is charged on any property by the will) or his or her spouse, and the executor of a will, to give evidence as to whether or not a will is valid.

5. Signatures of witnesses.

(1) *Requirements on death before 1983.* The original section 9 requires the witnesses to *attest, i.e.* bear witness that the signature was made or acknowledged by the testator in their simultaneous presence,[56] and to *subscribe* the will, *i.e.* sign it. Thus the witnesses must intend by their

---

[51] *Daintree* v. *Butcher* (1888) 13 P.D. 102: see also *Gaze* v. *Gaze* (1843) 3 Curt. 451. But if the testator is acknowledging a signature made by another person on his behalf, it appears not to be sufficient for someone in his presence and at his request to ask witnesses to sign whilst the testator remains passive, *In the Goods of Summers* (1850) 2 Rob.Ecc. 295.

[52] (1888) 13 P.D. 102, 103.

[53] *In the Estate of Gibson* [1949] P. 434; however at pp. 437 and 440 Pearce J. left open the possibility that "in peculiar circumstances" a blind man can be a witness to a will: perhaps a blind person can witness a will written and signed in braille if the testator acknowledges his signature, see (1949) 23 A.L.J. 360.

[54] (1844) 1 Rob.Ecc. 14, 24.

[55] *Post*, p. 334.

[56] *Hudson* v. *Parker, supra*, at p. 26.

signatures to attest the due execution of the will by the testator. If a person signs without any intention to attest, his signature is excluded from probate.[57] The witnesses must attest the testator's operative signature. If the testator signs his will both at the top and bottom, and the witnesses see the top signature but not the bottom signature which is covered by blotting paper, the will is invalid.[58]

The section sets out the required order of events. Before either witness signs the testator must first make or acknowledge his signature in their simultaneous presence. If this is not done, the will is invalid.[59] In *Re Colling*[60] the testator, who was in hospital, started to sign his will in the presence of a nurse and another patient as witnesses. Before he had completed his intended signature, the nurse was called away to attend to another patient. During her absence the testator completed his signature and the other witness signed. When the nurse returned both the testator and the other witness acknowledged their signatures and she signed the will. The will was held invalid because the testator neither made nor acknowledged his signature in the presence of both witnesses before both signed. If, after the testator acknowledged his signature in the presence of both of them, the other witness had signed the will again, it would have been valid.

(2) *Requirements on death after 1982.* The amended section 9 requires each witness either (i) to attest and sign the will or (ii) to acknowledge[61] his signature. Thus if the order of events is—one or both witnesses sign the will, the testator makes or acknowledges his signature in their simultaneous presence, and each witness either attests and signs the will or acknowledges his previous signature in the presence of the testator, the will is valid. This amendment to section 9 reverses the effect of *Re Colling* if the testator dies after 1982. The amended section 9 still sets out a required order of events but it makes an acknowledgment by a witness of his previous signature have the same effect as his actual signature.

(3) *Methods of signature by witness.* Instead of signing his name the witness may sign by marking the will in some way intended by him as his signature.[62] The words "Servant to Mr. Sperling" have been held a sufficient signature by a witness, being intended as an identification of himself as the person attesting.[63] The witness must himself sign,[64] though his hand may be guided by another witness or a third person.

---

[57] *In the Goods of Sharman* (1869) L.R. 1 P. & D. 661 (three signatures, two attesting and the third as residuary legatee: the third was excluded from probate).

[58] *In the Estate of Bercovitz* [1962] 1 W.L.R. 321; *Re Beadle* [1974] 1 W.L.R. 417.

[59] *Wyatt* v. *Berry* [1893] P. 5: see also *Hindmarsh* v. *Charlton* (1861) 8 H.L.C. 160; *In the Estate of Davies* [1951] 1 All E.R. 920.

[60] [1972] 1 W.L.R. 1440.

[61] For the nature of an acknowledgment see *ante*, p. 34.

[62] *In the Goods of Ashmore* (1843) 3 Curt. 756; *In the Estate of Bulloch* [1968] N.I. 96 (rubber stamp). A seal is insufficient unless intended as his signature, *In the Estate of Bulloch, supra.*

[63] *In the Goods of Sperling* (1863) 3 Sw. & Tr. 272.

[64] *In the Estate of Bulloch, supra.*

(4) *Position of signatures of witnesses.* The position upon the will of the signatures of the witnesses is immaterial provided they intend by their signatures to attest the testator's operative signature.[65] But their signatures, if not on the same paper as the will, must be on a paper physically connected with it.[66] If the testator signs the will and the witnesses sign a duplicate, the will is invalid.[67]

(5) *Presence of the testator.* The witnesses need not sign in the presence of each other but each witness must sign (or acknowledge his signature, if the testator dies after 1982) "in the presence of the testator." The testator must be mentally, as well as physically, present: if the testator becomes insensible before both witnesses have done this, the will is invalid.[68] If a witness signs, the testator must either see the witness sign, or have the opportunity of doing so if he had chosen to look[69] or had not been blind.[70]

6. Attestation clause. Section 9 provides that no form of attestation is necessary. Nevertheless an attestation clause[71] is highly desirable because it facilitates the grant of probate.

(i) In the absence of an attestation clause a registrar must require the due execution of the will to be established by affidavit evidence before granting probate in common form.[72]

(ii) An attestation clause raises a stronger presumption that the will was duly executed than if no such clause was present.[73] Moreover this presumption *omnia rite esse acta* applies with more force in the case of a formal than an informal attestation clause.[74] The presumption becomes important in cases where, for instance, witnesses are dead or cannot be traced or where the memory of witnesses is defective.

[65] *In the Goods of Braddock* (1876) 1 P.D. 433; *In the Goods of Streatley* [1891] P. 172; *In the Estate of Denning* [1958] 1 W.L.R. 462 (*post*, p. 196). A witness who acknowledges his signature under the amended s.9 is not required to attest.
[66] *In the Goods of Braddock, supra* (witnesses to codicil signed on back of will to which codicil was pinned: codicil held valid).
[67] *In the Goods of Hatton* (1881) 6 P.D. 204.
[68] *Right* v. *Price* (1779) 1 Doug. 241; *In the Goods of Chalcraft* [1948] P. 222.
[69] *Casson* v. *Dade* (1781) 1 Bro.C.C. 99 (testatrix in her carriage able to see witnesses signing in attorney's office through the windows); *Tribe* v. *Tribe* (1849) 1 Rob.Ecc. 775 (testatrix unable to turn herself in bed to see witnesses sign; will held invalid); *Newton* v. *Clarke* (1839) 2 Curt. 320.
[70] *In the Goods of Piercy* (1845) 1 Rob.Ecc. 278. A blind testator's "presence" is different from a blind witness's "presence," see *In the Estate of Gibson* [1949] P. 434 (*ante*, p. 35).
[71] An example reads, "Signed by the above named Testator James Smith as his last Will in the presence of us both present at the same time who in his presence and in the presence of each other have hereunto subscribed our names as witnesses." The words "in the presence of each other" are usual but unnecessary. Other forms of attestation clause are available for illiterate or blind testators and for wills signed by an amanuensis for the testator, see *post*, p. 50, nn. 76 and 77.
[72] N.C.Prob. Rules 1987, r. 12: r. 12 does not apply to wills of privileged testators (r. 17): for probate in common form see *post*, p. 166 and for an affidavit of due execution see *post*, p. 194.
[73] *Post*, p. 195.
[74] *Vinnicombe* v. *Butler* (1864) 3 Sw. & Tr. 580.

7. Reform of formalities' rules.[75] The formalities prescribed for making a will by section 9 of the Wills Act 1837 provide some safeguard not only against forgery and undue influence but also against hasty or ill-considered dispositions[76]: the formalities emphasise the importance of the act of making a will and serve as a check against inconsiderate action. In general, formalities can be justified by the need to provide reliable evidence of a person's testamentary intentions, which may be expressed many years before his death.

Unfortunately some authentic wills, which unquestionably represent the true intention of the testator, fail for non-compliance with the prescribed formalities. The number of wills which are submitted to probate and rejected for non-compliance with these formalities is relatively small; most of them are home-made wills.[77] However, as a result of legal advice, most defectively executed wills are never submitted to probate and there are no reliable statistics to indicate the true extent of the problem.[78]

The Law Reform Committee in their 1980 Report[79] considered two proposals for legislative reform:

(1) *Confer dispensing power on court.* One proposal was to confer on the court a dispensing power to admit a will to probate if the court is satisfied that it was genuine, notwithstanding its defective execution. This has been done, for instance, in South Australia where the court must be satisfied "that there can be no reasonable doubt that the deceased intended the document to constitute his will"[80]: this requirement imposes a high standard of proof but the minimum formality for the exercise by the court of its dispensing power is merely an unsigned document.[81] In Queensland the minimum formality for the exercise of the dispensing power is much stricter—the document must have been executed in "substantial compliance" with the prescribed formalities.[82]

(2) *Relax formalities' rules.* The other proposal was to relax the formalities prescribed for making a will by section 9. The Law Reform Committee suggested two changes—

(i) A will should be admitted to probate if it is apparent "on its face" that the testator intended his signature to validate it,

[75] See generally Miller (1987) I.C.L.Q. 559; Miller, *The Machinery of Succession* (1977), pp. 147 *et. seq.*; Langbein (1975) 88 Harv.L.R. 489; (1981) 125 S.J. 263; Davey [1980] Conv. 64 and 101.
[76] Law Reform Committee, 22nd Report, *The making and revocation of wills*, Cmnd. 7902 (1980), p. 3.
[77] In a three-month survey by the Family Division Principal Registry in 1978, 40,664 wills were admitted to proof and 97 wills were rejected, 93 of them for non-compliance with the s.9 formalities; of the 97 rejected wills, 91 were home-made and six professionally drawn, see Law Reform Committee, 22nd Report, p. 31.
[78] See memorandum submitted to Law Reform Committee in May 1978 on behalf of the Law Society, p. 5.
[79] *Supra*, n. 76.
[80] Wills Act Amendment Act (No. 2) 1975, s.9 inserting a new s.12 in the Wills Act 1936–1975 (S.A.).
[81] *In the Estate of Williams* (1984) 36 S.A.S.R. 423: see Miller (1987) I.C.L.Q. 559 at pp. 567–573.
[82] Queensland Succession Act 1981, s.9: see Miller, *loc. cit.*, at pp. 566–567.

regardless of where on the will the signature was placed.[83] The amendment to section 9 by the Administration of Justice Act 1982 makes this change but very probably does not require the testator's intention to appear on the face of the will.

(ii) An acknowledgment of his signature by an attesting witness should have the same effect as his actual signature.[84] The amendment to section 9 by the Administration of Justice Act 1982 makes this change.

This piecemeal approach will save only a proportion of the genuine wills which have failed in the past for non-compliance with the formalities. However, the Law Reform Committee rejected the first proposal on the ground that a dispensing power might create more problems than it would solve: the Committee considered that, by making it less certain whether a defectively executed will is capable of being admitted to probate, such a power could lead to litigation, expense and delay and this burden would tend to fall on small estates disposed of by home-made wills.[85] On balance the first more radical proposal seems desirable: if its adoption sometimes led to contentious litigation, the county court would have jurisdiction in the case of small estates. At least the contentious litigation would ensure that an authentic will does not fail for non-compliance with the prescribed formalities.

B. Privileged Wills

Section 11 of the Wills Act 1837 provides "that any soldier being in actual military service, or any mariner or seaman being at sea, may dispose of his personal estate" without any formalities whatever. The Wills (Soldiers and Sailors) Act 1918 extended this privilege to realty[86] as well as personalty if the testator died after February 5, 1918, and widened the scope of the privilege in other respects. The Law Reform Committee in its recent report recommended that the privilege should be retained in its present form.[87]

1. Privileged testators. There are three categories of privileged testators:

(1) *A soldier in actual military service.* In this context "soldier" includes a member of the Air Force,[88] a female army nurse,[89] and a member of the W.A.A.F.[90] In the leading case *Re Wingham*[91] Denning L.J. said that

---

[83] Law Reform Committee, 22nd Report, pp. 4–5 and 27.

[84] *Ibid.* at pp. 5–6 and 27.

[85] *Ibid.* at pp. 3–4.

[86] s.3: this section embraces the privileged testator's realty and realty over which he has a general or special power of appointment exercisable by will, *obiter* in *Re Earl of Chichester's W.T.* [1946] Ch. 289.

[87] Law Reform Committee, 22nd Report, p. 9: *cf.* Davey [1980] Conv. 70–72; Cole [1982] Conv. 185.

[88] Wills (Soldiers and Sailors) Act 1918, s.5(2).

[89] *In the Estate of Stanley* [1916] P. 192.

[90] *In the Estate of Rowson* [1944] 2 All E.R. 36.

[91] [1949] P. 187, 196.

it "includes not only the fighting men but also those who serve in the Forces, doctors, nurses, chaplains, W.R.N.S., A.T.S., and so forth."

To be privileged a soldier is required by section 11 to be "in actual military service" when he makes his will. In *Re Wingham* the Court of Appeal held that a member of the Royal Air Force undergoing training as a pilot in Canada in 1943 was privileged and therefore entitled to make an informal will, because he was liable at any time to be ordered to proceed to some area in order to take part in active warfare. The test adopted by the Court of Appeal is that a soldier is in actual military service if he is actually serving with the armed forces "in connection with military operations which are or have been taking place or are believed to be imminent."[92] A soldier employed in internal security operations against terrorists in Northern Ireland in 1978 was held in *Re Jones*[93] to be in actual military service. On the other hand a soldier serving in England or abroad in peacetime when military operations are not imminent is not privileged.[94]

A soldier is in actual military service from the time he receives orders in connection with a war believed to be imminent.[95] Long after fighting has ceased a soldier may still be in actual military service as a member of an army of occupation.[96]

To be privileged, a soldier need not be so circumstanced that he would have been privileged as a legionary who was *in expeditione* under Roman law, or be in danger from enemy action, or be cut off from skilled advice. The privilege was borrowed from Roman law and these factors explain the reasons for its existence but they do not determine its limits, which depend on the construction of section 11 of the Wills Act 1837 and the Wills (Soldiers and Sailors) Act 1918.[97]

(2) *A mariner or seaman being at sea.* Mariner or seaman includes all ranks of Her Majesty's naval or marine forces[98] and of the merchant service, and has been held to extend to a woman typist employed aboard a liner.[99]

The words "being at sea" in section 11 have been liberally construed. The privilege has been held applicable to a seaman who made his will

[92] [1949] P. 187, 196 and see p. 192; at p. 196 Denning L.J. said, "Doubtful cases may arise in peacetime when a soldier is in, or is about to be sent to, a disturbed area or an isolated post, where he may be involved in military operations. As to these cases, all I say is that, in case of doubt, the serving soldier should be given the benefit of the privilege": see also *Re Jones* [1981] Fam. 7, 10.
[93] [1981] Fam. 7 (soldier shot on patrol said, "If I don't make it, make sure Anne gets all my stuff"; held valid will).
[94] *In the Estate of Grey* [1922] P. 140.
[95] *Gattward* v. *Knee* [1902] P. 99; *Re Rippon* [1943] P. 61 (Territorial officer under orders to join unit).
[96] *In the Estate of Colman* [1958] 1 W.L.R. 457 (soldier on leave in England in 1954 from British Army of the Rhine held privileged): see also *Re Limond* [1915] 2 Ch. 240.
[97] *Re Wingham* [1949] P. 187: see also *Re Booth* [1926] P. 118 and *In the Goods of Hiscock* [1901] P. 78, 80.
[98] Wills (Soldiers and Sailors) Act 1918, s.2.
[99] *In the Goods of Hale* [1915] 2 I.R. 362 (typist on the *Lusitania*): see *In the Estate of Knibbs* [1962] 1 W.L.R. 852 (barman on liner); *Re Rapley* [1983] 1 W.L.R. 1069, 1073 (nature of service must be sea service but immaterial in what capacity).

while serving in a ship permanently stationed in Portsmouth harbour.[1] Moreover a seaman is regarded as constructively "at sea" if he makes his will on land in the course of a voyage[2] or whilst under orders to join a ship. In *In the Goods of Newland*[3] a seaman who made his will in England during his leave ashore between voyages, whilst under orders to rejoin his ship a few days later, was held privileged.

(3) *Any member of her Majesty's naval or marine forces so circumstanced that if he were a soldier he would be in actual military service.*[4] Such a person is privileged though not at sea.[5]

2. Extent of the privilege. A testator who falls within one of the above three categories at the time of making his will is privileged in certain respects.

(1) *Informal will.* The testator can make a will without any formalities whatever. It may be written, whether signed or witnessed or not, or it may be nuncupative, *i.e.* oral.[6]

However the testator must intend deliberately to give expression to his wishes in the event of his death, though he need not know that he is making a will: in this respect there is no difference between an informal and a formal will.[7] In *In the Estate of Beech*[8] the testator executed a formal will in 1917 disposing in detail of his property and later, whilst on active service in France in 1918, wrote two letters to his son referring to dispositions which he had already made by his will. The Court of Appeal held that the letters were not admissible to probate as an informal will, because the testator did not intend what he wrote to be remembered as an expression of his wishes in the event of his death— he was merely giving his son a summary of his existing will. Again, in *In the Estate of Knibbs*[9] a barman on a liner (whilst privileged as a mariner at sea) said to the head barman in the course of a conversation about their families' affairs, "If anything ever happens to me, Iris will get anything I have got." The court held that this statement did not

---

[1] *In the Goods of M'Murdo* (1868) L.R. 1 P. & D. 540: see also *In the Goods of Austen* (1853) 2 Rob.Ecc. 611 (Admiral on board ship in Rangoon river on a naval expedition privileged) and *In the Goods of Patterson* (1898) 79 L.T. 123 (master on board ship lying in the Thames before starting ocean voyage held privileged).

[2] *In the Goods of Lay* (1840) 2 Curt. 375 (shore leave).

[3] [1952] P. 71: see also *In the Goods of Wilson* [1952] P. 92 (merchant navy officer in England on leave and whilst under orders to join another ship three days later held privileged); *cf. Re Rapley, supra,* (apprentice seaman on leave and not under orders to join another ship not privileged).

[4] Wills (Soldiers and Sailors) Act 1918, s.2.

[5] See *In the Estate of Anderson* [1916] P. 49, 52; *In the Estate of Yates* [1919] P. 93 (s.2 applies to sailor who made his will before, but died after, the 1918 Act came into operation).

[6] *Re Stable* [1919] P. 7 (oral statement, "If I stop a bullet everything of mine will be yours," by soldier to fiancée; held a valid will): see also *In the Estate of Yates, supra,* (farewell words by Navy officer to son at railway station); *Re Jones* [1981] Fam. 7.

[7] *Re Stable, supra; In the Goods of Spicer* [1949] P. 441.

[8] [1923] P. 46: see also *In the Estate of MacGillivray* [1946] 2 All E.R. 301 and *In the Estate of Donner* [1917] 34 T.L.R. 138 (deceased stated he was content not to make a will owing to his (incorrect) belief that all his estate would pass to his mother on intestacy).

[9] [1962] 1 W.L.R. 852.

constitute an informal will in favour of his sister Iris because it was merely imparted as a matter of interest in an exchange of family gossip.

An informal will made when the testator was privileged remains valid until revoked, notwithstanding that the testator ceases to be privileged.[10]

(2) *Infant.* A person under the age of 18 years can make a will whilst privileged,[11] and, if he does so, can subsequently revoke it whether or not he is still privileged and able to make a will.[12]

As a result of the Wills (Soldiers and Sailors) Act 1918 an infant whilst privileged could make a will disposing of realty as well as personalty. However, section 51(3) of the Administration of Estates Act 1925 provides that where an infant, who dies after 1925 without having been married, is at his death equitably entitled under a settlement[13] to a fee simple estate in land, he is deemed to have had an entailed interest. Probably a privileged testator, who dies after 1925 still an infant and without having been married, cannot dispose by will of a fee simple estate to which he is entitled at his death because he must be deemed to have had an entailed interest[14] which terminates on his death.[15]

C. INCORPORATION OF DOCUMENTS

A testator may incorporate in his will a document which has not been duly executed by him and so make that document part of his will.

1. Requirements for incorporation. This doctrine of incorporation by reference applies if the following three requirements are satisfied. However a document referred to in a will is not incorporated if the testator directs in his will that it is not to form part of the will.[16]

(1) *Document already in existence.* The document must already be in existence when the will is executed.[17] The onus of proving this lies on the person seeking to rely on the doctrine. If the document comes into existence after the will is executed but before a codicil republishing the will is executed, this first requirement is satisfied because the will is treated as having been re-executed at the date of execution of the codicil.[18]

---

[10] *Re Booth* [1926] P. 118 (informal will made in actual military service in 1882 admitted to probate after testator's death in 1924). For revocation or alteration by a privileged testator see *post,* pp. 69–70 and 75.

[11] Wills (Soldiers and Sailors) Act 1918, s.1 (as amended by Family Law Reform Act 1969, s.3(1)(*b*)) which overrode the decision in *Re Wernher* [1918] 1 Ch. 339.

[12] Family Law Reform Act 1969, s.3(3); *semble* an infant who is no longer privileged cannot revoke by an informal instrument.

[13] Defined by the Settled Land Act 1925, ss.1(1) and 117(1)(xxiv); Administration of Estates Act 1925, s.55(1)(xxiv). The settlement may arise under a pre-1926 intestacy, *Re Taylor* [1931] 2 Ch. 242.

[14] An infant cannot bar an entail by will, Law of Property Act 1925, s.176.

[15] See Megarry and Wade, *The Law of Real Property* (5th ed., 1984), pp. 1018–1019.

[16] *Re Louis* (1916) 32 T.L.R. 313.

[17] *Singleton* v. *Tomlinson* (1878) 3 App.Cas. 404.

[18] *In the Goods of Lady Truro* (1866) L.R. 1 P. & D. 201: for republication see *post,* p. 80, and for revival which has the same effect see *post,* p. 77.

(2) *Referred to in the will as already in existence*. The will must refer to the document as being already in existence when the will is executed. If the will refers to "a memorandum *already* written by me" this requirement is satisfied. On the other hand a reference in a will to such articles "as may be described in a paper in my own handwriting,"[19] or to friends "to be named in a letter addressed to X,"[20] does not satisfy this requirement. If a will refers to an already existing document "or any substitution therefor or modification thereof," again this requirement is not satisfied and there is no incorporation even of the existing document.[21]

If the will is republished by a codicil and the document comes into existence between the execution of the will and the codicil, this second requirement is only satisfied if the will refers to the document as being already in existence. In *In the Goods of Smart*[22] the testatrix by her will directed her trustees "to give to such of my friends as I *may* designate in a book or memorandum that will be found with this will" the articles specified for them. Three years later she made the memorandum and afterwards she executed a codicil to her will. The court held that the will (though speaking from the date of execution of the codicil) still referred to a future document and did not refer to the memorandum as being already in existence at the date of execution of the codicil, when the will must be treated as having been re-executed. If instead the will had read "as I *have* designated," this second requirement would have been satisfied.[23]

(3) *Identified in the will*. The document must be sufficiently described in the will to enable it to be identified.[24] If the description in the will is so vague as to be incapable of being applied to any document in particular, it does not suffice.[25] This third requirement applies though both the will and the document are written on the same piece of paper: the document is not incorporated if the will contains no reference to it.[26]

2. Effects of incorporation

(1) *Admissible to probate*. A document incorporated in a duly executed will is admissible to probate as part of the will.[27] The incorporated

---

[19] *In the Goods of Sutherland* (1866) L.R. 1 P. & D. 198.

[20] *In the Goods of Reid* (1868) 38 L.J.P. & M. 1: see *The University College of North Wales* v. *Taylor* [1908] P. 140.

[21] *Re Jones* [1942] Ch. 328, but see p. 331. If an existing settlement is incorporated in a will, a power to vary conferred on the testator by the settlement is invalid when incorporated, *Re Edwards' W.T.* [1948] Ch. 440; *Re Schintz's W.T.* [1951] Ch. 870.

[22] [1902] P. 238: see also *Durham* v. *Northen* [1895] P. 66.

[23] *In the Goods of Lady Truro* (1866) L.R. 1 P. & D. 201.

[24] *In the Goods of Garnett* [1894] P. 90: *In the Estate of Mardon* [1944] P. 109.

[25] *Allen* v. *Maddock* (1858) 11 Moo.P.C. 427, 454: *In the Estate of Saxton* [1939] 2 All E.R. 418 was wrongly decided (will, "I give and bequeath . . . among the following persons": lists found with will held to be incorporated despite absence of any other means of identification in the will).

[26] *In the Goods of Tovey* (1878) 47 L.J.P. 63; *In the Estate of Bercovitz* [1962] 1 W.L.R. 321.

[27] In special circumstances the incorporated document (or an examined copy) will not be required to be filed in the registry, *In the Goods of Balme* [1897] P. 261 (lengthy library catalogue incorporated but filing not required); *In the Goods of Sibthorp* (1866) L.R. 1 P. & D. 106 (third party in possession of incorporated document: filing not required).

document is then open to inspection by the public. If a testator wishes to avoid this he can employ a secret trust.[28]

(2) *Testamentary effect.* The incorporated document operates as part of the will and is subject to the ordinary rules applicable to wills.[29]

(3) *Incorporation of invalid will in duly executed codicil.* If the requirements for incorporation are satisfied, a testator may incorporate an invalidly executed will or codicil in a subsequent duly executed codicil.[30] For instance, a testatrix made an invalid will and later duly executed a codicil describing itself as "a codicil to the last will and testament of me . . . "; on proof that she had made no other will the court held that the invalid will was sufficiently described in the codicil to enable it to be identified and must be admitted to probate as incorporated in the codicil.[31] In another case, a testatrix made an invalid will and placed it in a sealed envelope, on which there was then written a duly executed memorandum stating, "I confirm the contents written in the inclosed document"; the court held that the invalid will was incorporated in this memorandum and both were admissible to probate.[32]

3. Statutory Will Forms 1925.[33] Section 179 of the Law of Property Act 1925 authorises the Lord Chancellor to publish these forms which a testator may incorporate in his will in any manner indicating an intention to do so. By incorporating one or more of these forms in his will a testator may reduce the length of his will. However the forms are seldom used in practice owing to the inconvenience of having to refer to the relevant forms in order to understand the will.

2. THE MIND OF THE TESTATOR

A person under the age of 18 years[34] cannot make a valid will unless he is privileged. Apart from this age limit, capacity to make a will depends on the testator's state of mind. The testator must have testamentary capacity, *i.e.* he must be mentally capable of making a will. Moreover he must know and approve of the contents of his will and he must not make it as a result of the undue influence or fraud of another person.

It is sometimes said that a testator must intend to make a will. Strictly this is inaccurate, though it is often a convenient way of stating the basic requirement that a testator must have a testamentary intention, *i.e.* must intend the wishes he expresses *to take effect only at his death.* If a person intends a duly executed document to take effect only at his

---

[28] See Snell's *Principles of Equity* (28th ed., 1982), pp. 109 *et. seq.*
[29] *Bizzey* v. *Flight* (1876) 3 Ch. 269 (lapse and ademption).
[30] *Allen* v. *Maddock* (1858) 11 Moo.P.C. 427.
[31] *In the Goods of Heathcote* (1881) 6 P.D. 30.
[32] *In the Goods of Almosnino* (1859) 29 L.J.P. 46: see *Re Nicholls* [1921] 2 Ch. 11.
[33] (S.R. & O. 1925, No. 780) (L. 15); see *Hallett's Conveyancing Precedents* (1965), pp. 994 *et. seq.*
[34] Wills Act 1837, s.7 as amended by Family Law Reform Act 1969, s.3(1)(*a*): the age limit is 21 years for wills made before January 1, 1970.

death, it can be admitted to probate as his will, whether or not he intended to make, or was aware that he was making, a will.[35] Similarly a privileged testator must give deliberate expression to his wishes in the event of his death but he need not know that he is making a will.[36]

A. Testamentary Capacity

Test of testamentary capacity.[37] A classic statement of the test to be applied is contained in the judgment of Cockburn C.J. in *Banks* v. *Goodfellow*[38]:

"It is essential . . . that a testator shall understand the nature of the act and its effects; shall understand the extent of the property of which he is disposing; shall be able to comprehend and appreciate the claims to which he ought to give effect; and, with a view to the latter object, that no disorder of the mind shall poison his affections, pervert his sense of right, or prevent the exercise of his natural faculties—that no insane delusion shall influence his will in disposing of his property and bring about a disposal of it which, if the mind had been sound, would not have been made."

This test requires the testator to understand three matters:

(i) the effect of his wishes being carried out at his death, though he need not understand their precise legal effect[39];
(ii) the extent of the property of which he is disposing, though he is not required to carry in his mind a detailed inventory of it[40]; and
(iii) the nature of the claims on him.

The testator must have "a memory to recall the several persons who may be fitting objects of the testator's bounty, and an understanding to comprehend their relationship to himself and their claims upon him."[41] In *Harwood* v. *Baker*[42] a will executed by a testator on his death bed giving all his property to his wife was held invalid because, due to his illness, the testator was unable to comprehend and weigh the claims upon him of his relatives. It did not suffice that the testator knew that he was giving all his property to his wife and excluding all his relatives: he must also be "capable of recollecting who those relatives were, of understanding their respective claims upon his regard and bounty, and of deliberately forming an intelligent purpose of excluding them from any share of his property."[43]

A will is not invalid merely because in making it the testator is moved

---

[35] *Milnes* v. *Foden* (1890) 15 P.D. 105 and see *ante*, pp. 1 *et seq.*
[36] *Re Stable* [1919] P. 7 and see *ante*, pp. 41–42.
[37] For capacity to make a gift *inter vivos* see *Re Beaney* [1978] 1 W.L.R. 770, and to consent to a marriage see *In the Estate of Park* [1954] P. 112, 120–122, 131–133 and 135–136.
[38] (1870) L.R. 5 Q.B. 549, 565.
[39] *Banks* v. *Goodfellow, supra*, at p. 567.
[40] *Waters* v. *Waters* (1848) 2 De G. & Sm. 591, 621 ("*generally* the state of his property and what it consists of"): see *Re Beaney* [1978] 1 W.L.R. 770, 773.
[41] *Per* Sir J. Hannen in *Boughton* v. *Knight* (1873) L.R. 3 P. & D. 64, 65–66.
[42] (1840) 3 Moo.P.C. 282: see *Battan Singh* v. *Amirchand* [1948] A.C. 161.
[43] *Harwood* v. *Baker, supra*, at p. 290.

by capricious, frivolous, mean or even bad motives. If he satisfies this test of testamentary capacity he "may disinherit . . . his children, and leave his property to strangers to gratify his spite, or to charities to gratify his pride."[44]

The same test applies whether the testator has been subnormal from birth or has suffered impairment of the mind during his lifetime, whether through injury, physical or mental illness, senility or addiction.

Effect of delusions. A delusion in the mind of a testator deprives him of testamentary capacity if the delusion influences, or is capable of influencing, the provisions of his will.[45] A testator suffers from a delusion if he holds a belief on any subject which no rational person could hold, and which cannot be permanently eradicated from his mind by reasoning with him.[46] In *Boughton* v. *Knight* Sir J. Hannen told a jury to put to themselves "this question, and answer it; can I understand how any man in possession of his senses could have believed such and such a thing? And if the answer you give is, I cannot understand it, then it is of the necessity of the case that you should say the man is not sane."[47]

In practice it may be difficult to distinguish between grave misjudgment and delusion, particularly in relation to a testator's assessment of the character of a possible beneficiary under his will. Certainly a parent is not incapacitated from making a will because he has formed an unduly harsh view of his child's character. But if the parent's misjudgment really stems from an irrational aversion towards his child, amounting to a delusion, then the parent lacks testamentary capacity.[48]

A delusion in the mind of a testator does not deprive him of testamentary capacity if it cannot have had any influence upon him in making his will. In *Banks* v. *Goodfellow*[49] the testator suffered from the delusion that he was pursued and molested by a certain man, who was already dead and who was in no way connected with the testator, and by devils or evil spirits whom the testator believed to be visibly present. Nevertheless the court held that the testator had testamentary capacity because the delusions were not capable of having had any influence on the provisions of his will.

Time for satisfying the test. The testator must have testamentary capacity at the time when he executes the will. Alternatively it suffices if the testator has testamentary capacity at the time when he gives instructions to a solicitor for the preparation of the will provided (i) the will is prepared in accordance with his instructions and (ii) at the time of

---

[44] *Per* Sir J. Hannen in *Boughton* v. *Knight, supra* at p. 66.

[45] *Dew* v. *Clark* (1826) 3 Add. 79, 5 Russ. 163 (father's insane aversion to only daughter); *Smee* v. *Smee* (1879) 5 P.D. 84 (delusion son of George IV); *Re Belliss* (1929) 141 L.T. 245 (delusion T had already benefited one daughter far more than other); *Battan Singh* v. *Amirchand* [1948] A.C. 161 (delusion T had no relatives); *Re Nightingale* (1974) 119 S.J. 189 (delusion son attempted to shorten his life).

[46] *Dew* v. *Clark* (1826) 3 Add. 79, 90.

[47] (1873) L.R. 3 P. & D. 64, 68.

[48] *Dew* v. *Clark, supra*; *Boughton* v. *Knight*, (1873) L.R. 3 P. & D. 64.

[49] (1870) L.R. 5 Q.B. 549.

execution he is capable of understanding, and does understand, that he is executing a will for which he has given instructions. This alternative is useful in cases where a testator's capacity deteriorates after giving his instructions. This happened to the testatrix in *Parker* v. *Felgate*[50] but her will was upheld because, on being roused from a partial coma at the time of execution, she was capable of understanding, and did understand, that she was executing a will for which she had given instructions. It was immaterial that at the time of execution she was incapable of remembering her instructions, or even of understanding each clause of the will if it had been put to her.

In *Parker* v. *Felgate* the testatrix gave instructions directly to her solicitor. In *Battan Singh* v. *Amirchand*[51] the Privy Council said that the principle enunciated in *Parker* v. *Felgate* should be applied with the greatest caution where the testator gives instructions to a lay intermediary who repeats them to the solicitor:

"the opportunities for error in transmission and of misunderstanding and of deception in such a situation are obvious, and the court ought to be strictly satisfied that there is no ground for suspicion, and that the instructions given to the intermediary were unambiguous and clearly understood, faithfully reported by him and rightly apprehended by the solicitor."[52]

Consequences of incapacity. A will or codicil is wholly invalid if the testator lacked testamentary capacity at the relevant time. But there is a statutory exception to this general rule and possibly another limited exception where part of a will is unaffected by delusion:

(1) *"Statutory" will.* Section 96[53] of the Mental Health Act 1983 empowers the Court of Protection to order the execution of a will for an adult patient who is mentally disordered if the Court has reason to believe that the patient is incapable of making a valid will for himself. Such a "statutory" will may make any provision which could be made by the patient in his will if he were not mentally disordered[54] and has effect, for all purposes, as the patient's will.[55]

A "statutory" will must be executed with the formalities specified in section 97 of the Mental Health Act 1983, which requires a statutory will to be:

(i) expressed to be signed by the patient acting by the person authorised by the Court of Protection to execute the will for the patient (usually the receiver);

(ii) signed by the authorised person with the name of the patient,

---

[50] (1883) 8 P.D. 171: see also *Perera* v. *Perera* [1901] A.C. 354, 361–362.

[51] [1948] A.C. 161.

[52] *Ibid.* at p. 169.

[53] See *Practice Note* [1983] 1 W.L.R. 1077; *Re H.M.F.* [1976] Ch. 33; *Re Davey* [1981] 1 W.L.R. 164 (will made for patient of 93 in poor health, after clandestine marriage); *Re D. (J.)* [1982] Ch. 237 (factors in deciding will's provisions); *Re B* [1987] 1 W.L.R. 552; Sherrin (1983) 13 Fam. Law 135.

[54] A statutory will cannot dispose of immovable property outside England and Wales, Mental Health Act 1983, s.97(4)(*a*).

[55] *Ibid.*, s.97(3); see *Re Davey, supra,* at p. 172 (irrevocable after patient's death).

and with his own name, in the presence of two or more witnesses present at the same time;

(iii) attested and subscribed by those witnesses in the presence of the authorised person; and

(iv) sealed with the official seal of the Court of Protection.

(2) *Part of will unaffected by delusion.* In *In the Estate of Bohrmann*[56] a testator made gifts to certain charities by clause 6 of his will. Later, after developing an insane delusion that the then London County Council was persecuting him, he executed a codicil. Clause 2 of this codicil contained a declaration that clause 6 of his will should be read as if the words "United States of America" were substituted for the word "England." The testator's apparent intention to substitute American for English charities was dictated by his insane delusion. Langton J. decided that the rest of the codicil could not have been affected by the insane delusion and he upheld the validity of the codicil with the exception of clause 2. This is the only reported case in which the court has treated a testator as having testamentary capacity to make part, but not the whole, of a will or codicil. In making this innovation Langton J. relied by way of analogy on the court's settled practice of deleting from testamentary instruments anything not brought to the knowledge and approval of the testator.[57] The scope of this exception to the general rule remains unsettled but it may well prove to be narrow: indeed both the analogy and the exception itself seem to be of doubtful validity.[58]

Burden of proof. The *legal* (or persuasive) burden of proof always lies upon the person propounding a will to prove that the testator had testamentary capacity at the relevant time.[59] If that person fails to discharge this burden the will is not admissible to probate. The *evidential* burden of proof may shift from one party to another in the course of a case.[60]

The following rebuttable presumptions may apply:

(1) *Will rational.* If a duly executed will is rational on the face of it a presumption arises that the testator had testamentary capacity.[61] The person challenging the will may rebut this presumption by evidence to the contrary.

(2) *Continuance of mental illness.* If during a period prior to the execution of his will the testator suffered from serious mental illness, a presumption arises that it continued and the testator lacked testamentary capacity.[62] The person propounding the will may rebut this pre-

[56] [1938] 1 All E.R. 271.

[57] *Post,* p. 54.

[58] See C. A. Wright (1938) 16 Can. Bar Rev. 405, 410–411; R. F. Cross (1950) 24 A.L.J. 12.

[59] *Barry* v. *Butlin* (1838) 2 Moo.P.C. 480, 481.

[60] *Waring* v. *Waring* (1848) 6 Moo.P.C. 341, 355.

[61] *Symes* v. *Green* (1859) 1 Sw. & Tr. 401; *Sutton* v. *Sadler* (1857) 3 C.B.(N.S.) 87, 98. As to a will which appears irrational on its face see *Arbery* v. *Ashe* (1828) 1 Hagg.Ecc. 214; *Austen* v. *Graham* (1854) 8 Moo.P.C. 493.

[62] *Groom* v. *Thomas* (1829) 2 Hagg.Ecc. 433; *Bannatyne* v. *Bannatyne* (1852) 2 Rob. 472; *Banks* v. *Goodfellow* (1870) L.R. 5 Q.B. 549, 570.

sumption by establishing that the testator made the will during a lucid interval[63] or after recovery from the illness.

If there is any reason at all to anticipate that a will about to be executed may be challenged in the future on the ground that the testator lacked testamentary capacity, it is a useful precaution to arrange for the presence of at least one experienced medical practitioner so that he may examine the testator's state of mind at the time when he executes the will and, if he is satisfied, be an attesting witness to the will.[64] This precaution should always be observed in the case of an aged testator or a testator who has suffered a serious illness. In cases of senility there may be marked variations in mental capacity from time to time.

B. KNOWLEDGE AND APPROVAL

A testator must know and approve of the contents of his will. If a testator says to another person, "I will execute any will you draw up for me," and a will is drawn up and the testator executes it in ignorance of its contents, the will is invalid.[65] A will must be the result of a testator's own intelligence and volition, though its contents need not originate from him provided he understands and approves them.[66] There is only one exception—a testator need not know or approve of the contents of a "statutory" will.[67]

Knowledge and approval of legal effect not required. The testator must know and approve of the contents of his will but he need not understand its legal effect. Thus if the testator does know and approve of the contents of his will, it is immaterial that he, or the draftsman employed by him, is mistaken as to its legal effect.[68] Moreover a testator cannot approve the words used in his will subject to a condition that they have the legal effect he desires: if he approves the words, it is immaterial that the condition is not satisfied.[69]

Time of knowledge and approval. The testator must know and approve of the contents of his will at the time when he executes it.[70] Alternatively it suffices if the testator knows and approves of the contents of the instructions which he gives to a solicitor for the preparation of a will, provided (i) the will is prepared in accordance with his instructions and (ii) at the time of execution he is capable of understanding, and does understand, that he is executing a will for which he

[63] *Cartwright* v. *Cartwright* (1793) 1 Phill. 90; *Bannatyne* v. *Bannatyne, supra; Nichols* v. *Binns* (1858) 1 Sw. & Tr. 239.
[64] *Kenward* v. *Adams, The Times,* Nov. 29, 1975 (medical practitioner should record his examination of the testator and his findings); *Re Simpson* (1977) 121 S.J. 224: see Law Reform Committee, 22nd Report, pp. 7–8.
[65] *Hastilow* v. *Stobie* (1865) L.R. 1 P. & D. 64.
[66] *Constable* v. *Tufnell* (1833) 4 Hagg.Ecc. 465, 477.
[67] *Ante,* p. 47.
[68] *In the Estate of Beech* [1923] P. 46, 53; *Collins* v. *Elstone* [1893] P. 1 (mistake as to legal effect of revocation clause in printed will form); *Re Horrocks* [1939] P. 198: see *post,* p. 53.
[69] *In the Estate of Beech, supra.*
[70] *Hastilow* v. *Stobie* (1865) L.R. 1 P. & D. 64; *Guardhouse* v. *Blackburn* (1866) L.R. 1 P.D. 109, 116.

has given instructions. In *In the Estate of Wallace*[71] a testator, when seriously ill, wrote and signed a document headed "Last wish," stating that he wished two named persons to have all his possessions. At that time he knew and approved of the contents of this document. Pursuant to his instructions a solicitor prepared a will which gave effect to this document. On the day before his death the testator executed the will without reading it or having it read to him. At that time the testator did not know or approve of the contents of the will, but he understood that he was executing a will prepared in accordance with his instructions. Devlin J. held the will valid, applying the principle which was laid down in *Parker* v. *Felgate*[72] in relation to testamentary capacity.

Burden of proof. The *legal* (or persuasive) burden of proof always lies upon the person propounding a will to prove that the testator knew and approved of its contents at the relevant time. He must "satisfy the conscience of the Court that the instrument so propounded is the last Will of a free and capable Testator."[73]

(1) *Presumption in ordinary circumstances.* On proof that the testator was of testamentary capacity and that he duly executed the will, in ordinary circumstances a rebuttable presumption arises that he knew and approved of its contents at the time of execution.[74] The *evidential* burden of proof then shifts to the person opposing the will to rebut this presumption. If he does so, or if due to the particular circumstances the presumption is not applicable, the person propounding the will must produce affirmative proof of the testator's knowledge and approval so as to satisfy the legal burden of proof.

(2) *No presumption if testator dumb, blind or illiterate.* If the testator could not speak or read and write and gave instructions for his will by signs, the court requires evidence as to the signs used, establishing that the testator understood and approved of the contents of his will.[75] Similarly the knowledge and approval of a blind or illiterate testator must be proved, *e.g.* by evidence that the will was read over to him before execution.[76] The same rule applies if the will was signed by some other person on the testator's behalf.[77]

---

[71] [1952] 2 T.L.R. 925: see also *Re Flynn* [1982] 1 W.L.R. 310, 319–320.

[72] *Ante*, p. 47. But if the testator gives instructions to a lay intermediary who repeats them to the solicitor, great caution is needed, see *Battan Singh* v. *Amirchand*, *ante*, p. 47.

[73] *Barry* v. *Butlin* (1838) 2 Moo.P.C. 480, 482; *Cleare* v. *Cleare* (1869) L.R. 1 P. & D. 655.

[74] *Barry* v. *Butlin*, *supra*, at p. 484; *Cleare* v. *Cleare*, *supra*, at p. 658.

[75] *In the Goods of Geale* (1864) 3 Sw. & Tr. 431 (testator deaf and dumb and illiterate: detailed evidence as to signs by which testator communicated); *In the Goods of Owston* (1862) 2 Sw. & Tr. 461 (testator deaf and dumb and illiterate); *In the Estate of Holtam* (1913) 108 L.T. 732 (testatrix unable to speak or write due to stroke).

[76] *Fincham* v. *Edwards* (1842) 3 Curt. 63, 4 Moo.P.C. 198 (proof by other evidence than reading over suffices): see N.C.Prob. Rules 1987, r. 13. The attestation clause for the witnesses in the will of a blind or illiterate testator should include a statement that the testator signed the will "after the same had first been read over to him in our presence and had appeared to be perfectly understood and approved by him in the presence of us both. . . ."

[77] See N.C.Prob. Rules 1987, r. 13. The attestation clause in a will signed by an amanuensis for the testator should include a statement similar to that appropriate to the will of a blind or illiterate testator.

(3) *Suspicious circumstances.* The presumption does not apply if a will was prepared and executed under circumstances which raise a well-grounded suspicion that the will (or some provision in it) did not express the mind of the testator. In that event the will (or that provision) is not admissible to probate unless the suspicion is removed by affirmative proof of the testator's knowledge and approval.[78]

In *Barry* v. *Butlin,* Parke B. referred to the classic instance of suspicious circumstances:

"If a party writes or prepares a will, under which he takes a benefit, that is a circumstance that ought generally to excite the suspicion of the Court, and calls upon it to be vigilant and jealous in examining the evidence in support of the instrument, in favour of which it ought not to pronounce unless the suspicion is removed, and it is judicially satisfied that the paper propounded does express the true Will of the deceased."[79]

However, if the benefit taken by the person preparing the will is small in relation to the size of the estate, this does not of itself raise suspicion.[80]

Another example of suspicious circumstances is where a person is active in obtaining a will under which he takes a substantial benefit[81] by, for instance, suggesting the terms of the will to the testator and taking the testator to a solicitor chosen by that person. *Tyrrell* v. *Painton*[82] provides another instance. A testatrix who was ill made a will in favour of her cousin the plaintiff. Two days later the defendant's son brought to her another will prepared by himself in favour of his father. The testatrix executed this will in the presence of the son and a young friend of his. No one else was present and the existence of the will was kept secret until after the death of the testatrix a fortnight later. The Court of Appeal held that the circumstances raised a well-grounded suspicion, and the defendant had failed to remove that suspicion by proving affirmatively that the testatrix knew and approved of the contents of the will in favour of the defendant.

However circumstances only raise a suspicion of want of knowledge and approval if they are "circumstances attending, or at least relevant to, the preparation and execution of the will itself."[83] Thus no suspicion of want of knowledge and approval arose where an executrix learnt of the death of the testatrix but retained possession of her will (under which the daughter of the executrix was the sole beneficiary) until her own death 16 years later, without taking any steps to prove the will.[84]

---

[78] *Per* Davey L.J. in *Tyrrell* v. *Painton* [1894] P. 151, 159: see *In the Estate of Fuld (No. 3)* [1968] P. 675, 712.

[79] (1838) 2 Moo.P.C. 480, 481: see also *Wintle* v. *Nye* [1959] 1 W.L.R. 284 (solicitor took residue). The Law Society sets a very high standard of professional conduct for a solicitor, *Re a Solicitor* [1975] 1 Q.B. 475.

[80] *Ibid.* at pp. 484 and 485.

[81] *Fulton* v. *Andrew* (1875) L.R. 7 H.L. 448, 471–472; *Brown* v. *Fisher* (1890) 63 L.T. 465; *Re Ticehurst, The Times,* March 6, 1973.

[82] [1894] P. 151.

[83] *Per* Willmer J. in *Re R.* [1951] P. 10, 17.

[84] *In the Estate of Musgrove* [1927] P. 264.

Affirmative proof. Affirmative proof of the testator's knowledge and approval may take any form but it must be strong enough to satisfy the court in the particular circumstances.

(1) *Forms of proof.* One form of affirmative proof is to establish that the will was read over by, or to, the testator when he executed it. If a testator merely casts his eye over the will, this may not be sufficient.[85] If it is read over to the testator, this must be done in a proper way so that the testator hears and understands what is read.[86] Another form of affirmative proof is to establish that the testator gave instructions for his will and that the will was drafted in accordance with those instructions.[87]

(2) *Reading over is not conclusive.* There used to be a rule of evidence that a competent testator who had read a will, or had it read over to him, and had executed it, must be taken to have known and approved of its contents unless fraud had been practised on him.[88] Over the years the rigidity of the rule was progressively eroded so that the court was not fettered in ascertaining the truth, and now the rule "does not survive in any shape or form."[89] Of course the fact that the will was read over by, or to, the testator when he executed it must be given the full weight appropriate in all the circumstances of the case, but it is not conclusive.[90]

(3) *Proof where suspicious circumstances exist.* The greater the degree of suspicion, the stronger must be the affirmative proof to remove it.[91] As Viscount Simonds put it in *Wintle* v. *Nye*[92]:

"It is not the law that in no circumstances can a solicitor or other person who has prepared a will for a testator take a benefit under it. But that fact creates a suspicion that must be removed by the person propounding the will. In all cases the court must be vigilant and jealous. The degree of suspicion will vary with the circumstances of the case. It may be slight and easily dispelled. It may, on the other hand, be so grave that it can hardly be removed."

Mistake. A testator's lack of knowledge and approval of the whole, or part, of the contents of a will which he executes may be due to his own inadvertence, or to the fraud of another person—for instance, the draftsman who deliberately inserted his own name instead of that of the intended legatee.[93] Sometimes it is due to a mistake on the part of the testator or the draftsman employed by him.

---

[85] *Re Morris* [1971] P. 62.
[86] *Garnett-Botfield* v. *Garnett-Botfield* [1901] P. 335.
[87] *Fincham* v. *Edwards* (1842) 3 Curt. 63, 4 Moo.P.C. 198.
[88] *Guardhouse* v. *Blackburn* (1866) L.R. 1 P. & D. 109, 116.
[89] *Per* Latey J. in *Re Morris* [1971] P. 62, 79, where the authorities are reviewed at pp. 75–79.
[90] *Per* Sachs J. in *Crerar* v. *Crerar* (1956) 106 L.J. 694: see *Re Morris, supra,* at p. 78.
[91] *Fulton* v. *Andrew* (1875) L.R. 7 H.L. 448, 463 and 472.
[92] [1959] 1 W.L.R. 284, 291 (solicitor took residue under complex will he prepared for elderly lady: grave suspicion and exceptionally heavy burden of proof on solicitor).
[93] *Morrell* v. *Morrell* (1882) 7 P. D. 68, 70.

(1) *Mistake as to whole will.* A testator does not know and approve of a will if he does not intend to execute it as his will. In *In the Goods of Hunt*[94] a lady, who resided with her sister, prepared two wills for their respective execution and by mistake executed the will prepared for her sister. The wills were in similar terms. The court refused probate because the deceased did not know and approve of any part of the contents of the will which she executed—"if she had known of the contents she would not have signed it."[95]

(2) *Mistake as to the words used, not their legal effect.* Whoever makes the mistake, it must relate to the words used in the will and not to their legal effect. If the testator knows and approves of the words used in his will, though he, or the draftsman employed by him, is mistaken as to their legal effect, the words must be admitted to probate.[96] Moreover the testator is deemed to know and approve of technical language used by the draftsman in his will if the testator adopts it as his own after the draftsman has deliberately chosen it: such language must be admitted to probate though the draftsman was mistaken as to its legal effect.[97]

(3) *Mistake by testator as to part of will.* If by mistake a testator includes words in his will, intending to have written other words, he does not know and approve of the words he included.[98] Again, if a testator inadvertently fails to delete a printed clause from a will form, he does not know and approve of the clause. This occurred in *Re Phelan*[99] where the testator executed a home-made will in favour of his landlady and her husband. He then conceived the notion that his three holdings in unit trusts had to be disposed of by separate wills and he executed three more wills in their favour, each will made on a will form at the same time and each disposing of a separate holding. Unfortunately each will contained a printed revocation clause which the testator did not delete. Stirling J. said that "the Court . . . can omit words which have come in by inadvertence or by misunderstanding. . . . "[1] He accordingly admitted all four wills to probate, but with the omission of the revocation clause in the three later wills.

(4) *Mistake by draftsman as to part of will.* If by a slip or a clerical error the draftsman inserts in the will words contrary to the testator's instruc-

[94] (1875) L.R. 3 P. & D. 250: see also *In the Estate of Meyer* [1908] P. 353 (lady executed codicil meant for her sister: probate refused). The Commonwealth courts take a different view, see Hardingham, *The Law of Wills* (1977), p. 64.
[95] (1875) L.R. 3 P. & D. 250, 252.
[96] *In the Estate of Beech* [1923] P. 46, 53; *Collins* v. *Elstone* [1893] P. 1 (T wrongly advised revocation clause in printed will form would not revoke her previous will; held previous will revoked): see *ante*, p. 49.
[97] *Re Morris* [1971] P. 62, 79–81; *Re Horrocks* [1939] P. 198 (use of word "or," instead of "and," in gift of residue to "charitable or benevolent" objects was solicitor's deliberate choice under a mistake as to its legal effect and not typist's error).
[98] See *In the Goods of Swords* [1952] P. 368 (mistake in codicil as to numbering of clauses in will).
[99] [1972] Fam. 33: the revocation clause formed part of each printed will form, see [1971] 3 All E.R. 1256: see also *In the Goods of Moore* [1892] P. 378. Cf. *Collins* v. *Elstone, supra,* n. 96.
[1] [1972] Fam. 33, 35.

tions, the testator does not know and approve of these words unless the discrepancy comes to his notice.[2] The same principle applies if by a slip or a clerical error the draftsman omits words from the will contrary to the testator's instructions, thereby altering the sense of other words in the will.[3] Again the same principle ought to apply if the draftsman misunderstands the testator's instructions and in consequence inserts in the will words contrary to his instructions.[4]

Powers of court to alter words. There are three limited powers to alter the words in a will:

(a) a court of probate can *omit* from the will words of which the testator did not know and approve;

(b) a court of equity can order *rectification* of the will, if the testator dies after December 31, 1982;

(c) a court of construction can *construe* the will as if certain words had been inserted, omitted or changed, if it is clear from the will itself both that an error has been made in the wording and what the substance of the intended wording was. This demanding requirement is considered later.[5]

(1) *Omission of words from probate.*[6] If a testator died before 1983, the court had no power to *add* to a will words intended by the testator when admitting the will to probate.[7] In this respect the court was "enslaved" by the formalities required for a will by the Wills Act 1837.[8] A probate court only had power to *omit* from the will words of which the testator did not know and approve, leaving a blank space in the probate copy.

No problem of severance arose if the omission of the words, of which the testator did not know and approve, did not alter the sense of the rest of the will.[9] Thus the court has ordered the omission of a "self-

---

[2] *In the Goods of Oswald* (1874) 3 P. & D. 162 (revocation clause included *per incuriam* without instructions); *Morrell v. Morrell* (1882) 7 P.D. 68 (T intended to give all his shares; counsel wrote "40" by mistake); *In the Goods of Boehm* [1891] P. 247 (T intended to give legacies to Georgiana and Florence; counsel wrote Georgiana twice and omitted Florence); *In the Goods of Walkeley* (1893) 69 L.T. 419 (error in house number in engrossing will from draft); *Smith v. Thompson* (1931) 47 T.L.R. 603; *Re Morris* [1971] P. 62 (mistake in codicil as to numbering of clause in will).

[3] *Re Reynette-James* [1976] 1 W.L.R. 161 (33 words omitted by typist in engrossing will).

[4] *Re Morris* [1971] P. 62, 79–81 (law not settled). The following appear to be cases of want of knowledge and approval where the draftsman misunderstood his instructions, *Morrell v. Morrell, supra; Brisco v. Baillie-Hamilton* [1902] P. 234: see also Hardingham, *The Law of Wills* (1977), pp. 55 *et seq.*

[5] *Post,* p. 416.

[6] See generally Hardingham, *op. cit.* pp. 65 *et seq.*

[7] *Harter v. Harter* (1873) 3 P. & D. 11, 19; *Morrell v. Morrell* (1882) 7 P.D. 68; *In the Goods of Schott* [1901] P. 190 ("I can strike out words, but I cannot insert anything"); *Re Horrocks* [1939] P. 198, 216 (rule is "elementary"); *In the Goods of Swords* [1952] P. 368; *Re Morris* [1971] P. 62, 75 (rule can possibly be changed by appellate court); *Re Reynette-James* [1976] 1 W.L.R. 161, 166. *Cf. In the Goods of Bushell* (1887) 13 P.D. 7 and *In the Goods of Huddleston* (1890) 63 L.T. 255 (intended words added): but see *In the Goods of Schott, supra* (these decisions "heretical").

[8] *Re Reynette-James, supra:* see also *Harter v. Harter, supra; Re Horrocks, supra.*

[9] *Rhodes v. Rhodes* (1882) 7 App.Cas. 192, 198.

contained" part of the will, such as a revocation clause[10] or the residuary gift in a will.[11] The court has also omitted a house number from the devise of a dwelling-house[12] and the word "forty" from a bequest of "the forty . . . shares . . . in John Morrell & Co. Limited," so that all the testator's 400 shares passed under the bequest as he intended.[13] Again the court has ordered the omission of the name of a legatee on whom a legacy was settled[14]; it was immaterial that the effect of this omission might be to render that clause in the will ambiguous or even meaningless.[15]

Sometimes the court has had to choose the omission which most nearly gave effect to the testator's intentions. In *Re Morris*[16] T by clause 7 of her will gave 20 pecuniary legacies numbered 7(i) to (xx). She wished to revoke the legacy in clause 7(iv). Owing to a slip by her solicitor she executed a codicil revoking clause 7 of the will but did not notice the discrepancy. She died in 1963. Latey J. held that the codicil should be admitted to probate with the omission of the numeral "7" because this omission got nearest to T's intentions: at that date the court had no power to *add* the missing numeral "(iv)" to the codicil, so as to give entire effect to T's intentions.

However, it has been held that the court does not order the omission of words, of which the testator did not know and approve, if this would alter the sense of the rest of the will.[17] In this situation it is impossible to effect severance.

(2) *Rectification of will.* If the testator dies after December 31, 1982, section 20 of the Administration of Justice Act 1982 empowers the court to order that a will shall be rectified so as to carry out the testator's intentions.[18] Such an order may only be made if the court is satisfied that the will is so expressed that it fails to carry out the testator's intentions in consequence (i) of a clerical error,[19] or (ii) of a failure to understand his instructions. If the court orders rectification under section 20, it may of course *add* to the will words intended by the testator. But if the will fails to carry out the testator's intentions in consequence of some other cause

[10] *In the Goods of Oswald* (1874) 3 P. & D. 162; *In the Goods of Moore* [1892] P. 378; *In the Goods of Swords* [1952] P. 368 (words revoking particular clauses in will); *Re Phelan* [1972] Fam. 33, see *ante*, p. 53: see also *Smith* v. *Thompson* (1931) 47 T.L.R. 603.
[11] *In the Goods of Duane* (1862) 2 Sw. & Tr. 590; *Fulton* v. *Andrew* (1875) 7 H.L. 448; *Wintle* v. *Nye* [1959] 1 W.L.R. 284.
[12] *In the Goods of Walkeley* (1893) 69 L.T. 419.
[13] *Morrell* v. *Morrell* (1882) 7 P.D. 68. See also *In the Goods of Schott* [1901] P. 190 (omission in residuary clause preserved the sense); *Brisco* v. *Baillie-Hamilton* [1902] P. 234.
[14] *In the Goods of Boehm* [1891] P. 247.
[15] *Ibid.* at p. 251.
[16] [1971] P. 62: see also *Re Reynette-James* [1976] 1 W.L.R. 161: see Ryder (1976) 40 Conv.(N.S.) 312.
[17] *Re Horrocks* [1939] P. 198; *Rhodes* v. *Rhodes* (1882) 7 App.Cas. 192, 198. For cogent criticism of the latter part of the judgment in *Re Horrocks* (on assumption "or" was inserted by a typist's error) see Hardingham, *op. cit.* pp. 65–67; W. A. Lee (1969) 33 Conv.(N.S.) 322, 329–334.
[18] Administration of Justice Act 1982, ss.73(6) and 76(11); see N.C.Prob. Rules 1987, r. 55; R.S.C., Ord. 76, r. 16. In the High Court rectification is assigned to the Chancery Division, Supreme Court Act 1981, s.61(1) and Sched. I.
[19] *i.e.* an error of a clerical nature, not an error made only by a clerk; *Re Williams* [1985] 1 W.L.R. 905, 912 (a testator can make a clerical error in his home-made will).

(for instance, the draftsman understood his instructions but consciously omitted an intended legacy), section 20 does not apply: in that situation the court only has power to *omit* words, of which the testator did not know and approve, from the probate copy of the will. It seems unfortunate that the new power to rectify only applies where there was a clerical error or a failure to understand instructions[20]: in this respect this power is narrower than the remedy of rectification applicable to other documents.

An application for rectification must not be made later than six months from the date on which a grant of probate or letters of administration to the deceased's estate[21] is first taken out; however the court has an unfettered discretion to extend this time limit.[22] The purpose of this short time limit is to enable the personal representatives safely to distribute the estate to the beneficiaries entitled under the unrectified will as soon as six months have passed without any application being made.[23]

Of course neither the power to rectify nor the power to omit provide any remedy for (i) the testator's failure to appreciate the legal effect of the words used in his will, or (ii) uncertainty as to the meaning of his intended wording, or (iii) a lacuna in the will, because he never had any intention relevant to the events which actually occurred.

C. UNDUE INFLUENCE OR FRAUD

A will must not be made as a result of either the undue influence or the fraud of another person.[24]

1. Undue influence. In a court of probate undue influence means coercion,[25] *i.e.* the testator is coerced into making a will (or part of a will) which he does not want to make.[26] Undue influence takes many forms. At one extreme there may be force, *i.e.* actual violence to the testator. At the other extreme the pressure exerted by talking insistently to a weak and feeble testator in the last days of his life may so fatigue his brain that he may be induced, for quietness' sake, to give way to the pressure.[27]

---

[20] See Law Reform Committee, 19th Report, *Interpretation of Wills*, Cmnd. 5301 (1973), pp. 5–13 and particularly the recommendation at p. 23.

[21] *Post*, pp. 160 *et seq.*

[22] Administration of Justice Act 1982, s.20(2). A grant limited to settled land or trust property is disregarded and so is a grant limited to real or personal estate unless a grant limited to the remainder of the estate has previously been made or is made at the same time, see s.20(4): see *post*, p. 105, n. 13 and n. 14.

[23] For protection of the personal representatives in case the time limit is extended see *ibid.* s.20(3).

[24] Undue influence and fraud are separate pleas—see *Parfitt* v. *Lawless* (1872) L.R. 2 P. & D. 462, 470 and 471; *White* v. *White* (1862) 2 Sw. & Tr. 504, and R.S.C., Ord. 18, rr. 8(1) and 12(1). So is a plea of want of knowledge and approval, *Re Stott* [1980] 1 W.L.R. 246.

[25] *Per* Hannen P. in *Wingrove* v. *Wingrove* (1885) 11 P.D. 81, 82.

[26] *Hall* v. *Hall* (1868) L.R. 1 P. & D. 481, 482.

[27] *Per* Hannen P. in *Wingrove* v. *Wingrove, supra,* at pp. 82–83; *Lamkin* v. *Babb* (1752) 1 Lee 1 (wife's pressure).

Whatever form it takes the test is always the same—was the testator coerced?

"Persuasion, appeals to the affections or ties of kindred, to a sentiment of gratitude for past services, or pity for future destitution, or the like,—these are all legitimate, and may be fairly pressed on a testator. On the other hand, pressure of whatever character, whether acting on the fears or the hopes, if so exerted as to overpower the volition without convincing the judgment, is a species of restraint under which no valid will can be made. . . . In a word, a testator may be led but not driven; and his will must be the offspring of his own volition, and not the record of someone else's."[28]

An immoral influence exercised over the testator by another person does not constitute undue influence in the absence of coercion. A man's mistress may make use of her unbounded influence to induce him to make a will in her favour to the exclusion of his wife and children but in the absence of coercion this does not constitute undue influence. To quote Sir James Hannen in his charge to the jury in *Wingrove* v. *Wingrove*,[29] "It is only when the will of the person who becomes a testator is coerced into doing that which he or she does not desire to do, that it is undue influence."

2. Fraud. Fraud misleads a testator whereas undue influence coerces him. A very plain instance of fraud is a false representation concerning a person's character or conduct, made to the testator for the purpose of inducing him to revoke a gift made to that person in his existing will.[30]

3. Burden of proof. The legal burden of proof of undue influence or fraud always lies on the person alleging it.[31] That person must prove that the will (or such part of it as he alleges to be invalid) was made as a result of the undue influence or fraud of another person.

In equity a rebuttable presumption of undue influence arises where a donee stands in a confidential relationship to a donor, *e.g.* a father benefiting from a gift by his child or a solicitor from his client.[32] This rebuttable presumption applies to *inter vivos* transactions but is not applicable to the making of a will. Thus in *Parfitt* v. *Lawless*[33] no presumption of undue influence arose where a testatrix made a will leaving her residuary estate to a Roman Catholic priest, who resided with her as domestic chaplin and was her confessor.

4. Consequences of undue influence or fraud. A will made by a testator as a result of the undue influence or fraud of another person is invalid. If only part of the will was made as a result of the undue influence or fraud, that part may be rejected and the remainder admit-

[28] *Per* Lord Penzance in *Hall* v. *Hall, supra,* at p. 482.
[29] (1885) 11 P.D. 81, 82.
[30] *Per* Lord Lyndhurst in *Allen* v. *M'Pherson* (1847) 1 H.L.C. 191, 207: see also *In the Estate of Posner* [1953] P. 277 (gift by will to my wife X void if X procured the gift by fraudulently misrepresenting herself as his wife).
[31] *Boyse* v. *Rossborough* (1857) 6 H.L.C. 2, 49; *Craig* v. *Lamoureux* [1920] A.C. 349.
[32] See Snell's *Principles of Equity* (28th ed., 1982), pp. 539 *et seq.*
[33] (1872) L.R. 2 P. & D. 462: see also (1970) 86 L.Q.R. 447.

ted to probate.[34] On the other hand where a beneficiary under the will of a testator prevents him by undue influence or fraud from altering the will, or making a new will, in favour of other persons, probably the court will impose a trust on the beneficiary for those other persons.[35] In that situation an equitable remedy is needed because no remedy is available in a court of probate.

5. Comparison with plea of want of knowledge and approval. The burden of proof of undue influence or fraud lies on the person attacking a will, whereas the burden of proof of the testator's knowledge and approval lies on the person propounding it.[36] Again the practice as to costs in a probate action (which is considered later[37]) is material in making a comparison. A person seeking to attack a will may have little information as to the precise circumstances in which the will was made. Thus he may have no reasonable grounds for pleading undue influence or fraud,[38] but he may nevertheless be able to establish suspicious circumstances relevant to a plea of want of knowledge and approval.[39]

---

[34] *Allen* v. *M'Pherson* (1847) 1 H.L.C. 191, 209; *In the Goods of Boehm* [1891] P. 247, 251 (*obiter* as to effect of fraud on part of a will).

[35] *Betts* v. *Doughty* (1879) 5 P.D. 26; *Allen* v. *M'Pherson, supra*, at p. 214.

[36] *Ante*, p. 50.

[37] *Post*, pp. 200–202.

[38] *Ante*, p. 57.

[39] *Ante*, p. 51: see *Re Stott* [1980] 1 W.L.R. 246.

CHAPTER 3

REVOCATION, ALTERATION, REVIVAL AND REPUBLICATION OF WILLS

1. REVOCATION

A will by its very nature is revocable by the testator until his death.[1] There are four methods of revocation. A will or codicil may be revoked by marriage, destruction, another will or codicil, or duly executed writing declaring an intention to revoke. The *legal* burden of proof of revocation lies on the party alleging it.[2]

The effect of divorce or annulment of marriage on a will is considered later.[3]

A. MARRIAGE

As a general rule, marriage automatically revokes any will made by either party before the marriage. It is immaterial whether the party intends the will to be revoked by the marriage. This rule is enacted both by the original section 18 of the Wills Act 1837 (which, together with section 177 of the Law of Property Act 1925, is applicable if the will was made before January 1, 1983) and by the new section 18 as amended by the Administration of Justice Act 1982 (which is applicable if the will was made after December 31, 1982).[4]

A *voidable* marriage, whether subsequently annulled or not, revokes any will already made by either party: this is so even though the marriage is voidable on the ground of absence of consent,[5] and even though either party lacks testamentary capacity to make a new will at the time of the marriage. On the other hand a *void* marriage, which is treated as never having taken place, does not revoke any will already made by either party.[6]

There are two exceptions to the rule that marriage revokes any will already made by either party. The scope of each exception depends on whether the will was made before 1983 or after 1982.

---

[1] *Ante,* p. 3.

[2] *Harris* v. *Berrall* (1858) 1 Sw. & Tr. 153; *Sprigge* v. *Sprigge* (1868) L.R. 1 P. & D. 608; *Benson* v. *Benson* (1870) L.R. 2 P. & D. 172. For rebuttable presumptions see *post,* p. 65.

[3] *Post,* p. 344.

[4] Administration of Justice Act 1982, ss.18(1), 73(7), 75(1), 76(11) and Sched. 9, Pt. I.

[5] *Re Roberts* [1978] 1 W.L.R. 653: since August 1, 1971 a decree of nullity of a voidable marriage cannot operate retrospectively, Matrimonial Causes Act 1973, s.16. For suggested reform see Law Reform Committee, 22nd Report, *The making and revocation of wills,* Cmnd. 7902 (1980), pp. 16–18; (1981) 125 S.J. 317.

[6] *Mette* v. *Mette* (1859) 1 Sw. & Tr. 416: see also *Warter* v. *Warter* (1890) 15 P.D. 152.

59

1. Will expressed to be made in contemplation of a marriage (will made before 1983). Section 177 of the Law of Property Act 1925 provides that "a will expressed to be made in contemplation of a marriage shall . . . not be revoked by the solemnisation of the marriage contemplated." The section only applies to wills made after 1925 and before 1983. Whether this exception applies depends on the true construction of the will.[7]

(1) *Contemplation of the particular marriage.* The will must be expressed to be made in contemplation of the particular marriage which is later celebrated. If the testator makes a will giving his entire estate to a named beneficiary referred to in the will as "my fiancée" X, or X "my future wife," this suffices and the will is not revoked by his subsequent marriage to her,[8] though it would be revoked by his subsequent marriage to anyone else. On the other hand, if the testator merely declares in his will "that this will is made in contemplation of marriage," this does not suffice to save the will from revocation by his subsequent marriage because it refers to marriage generally and not to a particular marriage.[9]

In *Pilot* v. *Gainfort*[10] a testator made a will by which he gave "to Diana Featherstone Pilot my wife all my worldly goods." At that time he was living with her and later he married her. Lord Merrivale P. decided that the will was not revoked by this marriage because the will "practically" expressed contemplation of his marriage to her. The decision has been questioned on the convincing ground that the will did not express that the marriage was in contemplation but implied that it had already taken place.[11]

(2) *Will expressed to be made.* A clause in a will stating "This will is made in contemplation of my marriage to X" satisfies section 177.[12] But need the *whole* will be expressed to be made in contemplation of the particular marriage? In *Re Coleman*[13] the testator made a will giving his personal chattels, his stamp collection, £5,000 and his dwelling-house to "my fiancée" X, and giving his residuary estate to Y and Z equally. Two months later the testator and X married and a year later the testator died. Megarry J. held that the will had been revoked by the testator's subsequent marriage. He construed section 177 as requiring the will as a whole (and not merely particular gifts in it) to be expressed to be made in contemplation of the particular marriage. He said that if each bene-

---

[7] *Re Coleman* [1976] Ch. 1, 11: for the admission of extrinsic evidence see *post*, pp. 418 *et seq.*

[8] *In the Estate of Langston* [1953] P. 100 ("I give . . . unto my fiancée Maida Edith Beck . . . "); *Re Knight*, unreported but mentioned in *In the Estate of Langston*, p. 103 ("to E.L.B. my future wife"); *Re Coleman* [1976] Ch. 1, 6–8 and 10–11. *Cf. Burton* v. *McGregor* [1953] N.Z.L.R. 487 ("my fiancée" a mere word of description, and no intent will to operate after marriage): followed in *Public Trustee* v. *Crawley* [1973] 1 N.Z.L.R. 695 and *Re Whale* [1977] 2 N.Z.L.R. 1.

[9] *Sallis* v. *Jones* [1936] P. 43.

[10] [1931] P. 103: not followed in *Re Taylor* [1949] V.L.R. 201. See also *In the Estate of Gray* (1963) 107 S.J. 156 and *Re Coleman, supra*, at pp. 5–6.

[11] *Theobald on Wills* (14th ed., 1982), p. 68.

[12] *Re Coleman* [1976] Ch. 1, 8.

[13] [1976] Ch. 1.

ficial disposition made by the will was expressed to be made in contemplation of the testator's marriage to X, this would suffice. But he decided that section 177 did not apply where only some parts of the will were expressed to be made in contemplation of the particular marriage, even if those parts were substantial, unless they amounted to substantially the whole of the beneficial dispositions made by the will.[14]

It seems unlikely that the decision in Re Coleman will be followed. This construction of section 177 by Megarry J. was criticised as "unduly narrow" by the Law Reform Committee,[15] which suggested (i) that the courts in practice usually treat the words "in contemplation of a marriage" as equivalent to "with the intention that the will should survive the impending marriage"[16]; (ii) that if a gift in a will is made in contemplation of a marriage (in the sense of intending that it should survive the marriage), it seems illogical to suppose that the testator did not intend the will to survive the marriage, for the gift cannot survive unless the will survives; and (iii) that the use of the word "fiancée" ought not to be conclusive—for instance, a will ought not to be construed as expressed to be made in contemplation of a marriage if it contains only one trivial gift to "my fiancée" X.[17]

2. Intention will (or disposition) not revoked by particular marriage (will made after 1982). Section 18(3) and (4) of the Wills Act 1837 as amended apply if it appears from a will (i) that at the time it was made the testator was expecting to be married to a particular person, and (ii) that he intended that the will (section 18(3)), or a disposition in the will (section 18(4)), should not be revoked by the marriage. If the two requirements of section 18(3) are satisfied, the will is not revoked by his marriage to that person. If the two requirements of section 18(4) are satisfied, that disposition takes effect notwithstanding the marriage, and so does any other disposition in the will unless it appears from the will that the testator intended the disposition to be revoked by the marriage. Whether these two requirements are satisfied depends on the true construction of the will.

Section 18(3) and (4) give effect to the recommendation of the Law Reform Committee[18] and are a great improvement on the poorly drafted section 177 of the Law of Property Act 1925.

3. Certain appointments by will (will made before 1983). Under section 18 of the Wills Act 1837 an appointment made by will is not revoked by the subsequent marriage of the testator if "the real or personal estate thereby appointed would not in default of such appoint-

---

[14] Ibid. at pp. 8–11 and 12. At p. 10 Megarry J. referred to Re Chase [1951] V.L.R. 477 (gift by will of two-thirds of the testator's estate to X "my fiancée": held will expressed to be made in contemplation of particular marriage) and questioned whether the will as a whole was expressed to have been made in contemplation of the marriage.

[15] Law Reform Committee, 22nd Report, pp. 14–16. See also R. J. Edwards and B. F. J. Langstaff (1975) 39 Conv.(N.S.) 121.

[16] See Burton v. McGregor [1953] N.Z.L.R. 487; Public Trustee v. Crawley [1973] 1 N.Z.L.R. 695; Re Whale [1977] 2 N.Z.L.R. 1: cf. Re Coleman, supra, at p. 10.

[17] See Public Trustee v. Crawley, supra, at p. 700.

[18] Law Reform Committee, 22nd Report, pp. 16 and 27: see also G. M. Bates (1979) 129 New L.J. 547.

ment pass to his or her heir, customary heir, executor, or administrator, or the person entitled as his or her next of kin under the statute of distributions." In order to determine whether this exception applies it is necessary to ascertain who would take in default of the appointment made by the will. The appointment is not revoked by the subsequent marriage if persons taking in the specified capacities would not in all events be entitled in default of the appointment.[19]

(1) *Taking in the specified capacities.* Apart from the testator's executor or administrator, the other specified capacities all refer to succession on a death intestate before 1926 when realty passed to the heir, copyhold land to the customary heir, and personalty to the next of kin under the Statutes of Distribution 1670 and 1685.[20] The underlying purpose was to allow the appointment by will to be revoked by the testator's subsequent marriage only in circumstances where the testator's new family might benefit under the gift in default of appointment.

In *In the Goods of Fitzroy*[21] property was held under a marriage settlement upon trust for such of the children of the marriage as the husband T should appoint, and in default of appointment for the children of the marriage equally. T by will made an appointment in favour of his sons and later remarried. The court held that the appointment by will was not revoked by his remarriage because in default of appointment the children of the first marriage would have taken as the persons named in the settlement. It was immaterial that these children were in fact the persons entitled as T's next of kin under the Statutes of Distribution as they did not take in that capacity. On the other hand, if under the marriage settlement the trust in default of appointment had been for T's heir, or T's executor or administrator, or the persons entitled as T's next of kin under the Statutes of Distribution,[22] the appointment by will would have been revoked by T's remarriage.

Ought the phrase "next of kin under the statute of distributions" in section 18 to be construed since 1925 as referring to the persons entitled on intestacy under the Administration of Estates Act 1925?[23] It seems that the Interpretation Act may have updated section 18 in this way,[24] but the position remains uncertain.

(2) *Remainder of will revoked.* Where this exception applies it saves the appointment, but not the remainder of the will, from revocation by the testator's subsequent marriage.[25]

---

[19] *In the Goods of Fenwick* (1867) L.R. 1 P. & D. 319; *In the Goods of Worthington* (1872) 20 W.R. 260.

[20] As to the rules governing succession on a death intestate before 1926 see Megarry and Wade, *The Law of Real Property* (5th ed., 1984), pp. 539 *et seq.*

[21] (1858) 1 Sw. & Tr. 133: see *In the Goods of McVicar* (1869) 1 P. & D. 671; *In the Goods of Russell* (1890) 15 P.D. 111; *Re Paul* [1921] 2 Ch. 1.

[22] In *In the Goods of Gilligan* [1950] P. 32 "next of kin under the statute of distributions" in s.18 were held to include a widow; *sed quaere*, see J. D. B. Mitchell (1951) 67 L.Q.R. 351 and M. J. Russell (1952) 68 L.Q.R. 455.

[23] For the modern code of intestacy see Chap. 4.

[24] See M. J. Russell (1952) 68 L.Q.R. 455, referring to the Interpretation Act 1889, s.38(1), from which the Interpretation Act 1978, s.17(2) is now derived.

[25] *In the Goods of Russell* (1890) 15 P.D. 111.

4. Certain appointments by will (will made after 1982). Section 18(2) of the Wills Act 1837 as amended provides that "a disposition in a will in exercise of a power of appointment shall take effect notwithstanding the testator's subsequent marriage unless the property so appointed would in default of appointment pass to his personal representatives." The amendment updates this exception, so that it no longer refers to the pre-1926 intestacy rules, and saves an appointment by will from revocation by subsequent marriage unless the property appointed would in default of appointment pass to the testator's estate.[26]

<h2 style="text-align:center">B. DESTRUCTION</h2>

Under section 20 of the Wills Act 1837 the whole or any part of a will or codicil is revoked "by the burning, tearing, or otherwise destroying the same by the testator, or by some person in his presence and by his direction, with the intention of revoking the same." Two distinct elements are required: an act of destruction and an intention to revoke. "All the destroying in the world without intention will not revoke a will, nor all the intention in the world without destroying: there must be the two."[27] Moreover both elements are required for the revocation of each will or codicil. The revocation of a will by destruction does not revoke a codicil to the will.[28]

An actual act of destruction. There must be an actual, and not merely a symbolical, "burning, tearing, or otherwise destroying." Cancelling a will by striking the body of it through with a pen and crossing out the name of the testator is not an act of destruction.[29] In *Cheese* v. *Lovejoy*[30] a testator drew his pen through some lines of his will, wrote on the back of it, "All these are revoked," and threw it among a heap of waste paper in the corner of his sitting room. His housemaid retrieved it and kept it in the kitchen until the testator's death seven years later. The Court of Appeal held that the will was not revoked as the testator had not done any act of destruction.

(1) *Extent of destruction.* In order to revoke it entirely the whole will need not be destroyed, but there must be a destruction of so much of it as to impair the entirety of the will.[31] Accordingly it suffices if the signature of the testator is burnt, torn off or cut out,[32] or so obliterated that

---

[26] See Law Reform Committee, 22nd Report, pp. 13–14.
[27] *Per* James L.J. in *Cheese* v. *Lovejoy* (1877) 2 P.D. 251, 253, quoting Dr. Deane in the court below.
[28] *In the Goods of Savage* (1870) L.R. 2 P. & D. 78; *In the Goods of Turner* (1872) L.R. 2 P. & D. 403 (codicil not revoked by destruction of will, though codicil gave legacy to be held under conditions stated in will). *Cf. In the Goods of Bleckley* (1883) 8 P.D. 169 (both on same piece of paper).
[29] *Stephens* v. *Taprell* (1840) 2 Curt. 459: see also *In the Goods of Brewster* (1859) L.J.P. 69 ("cancelled" written across signature: no revocation).
[30] (1877) 2 P.D. 251. See Law Reform Committee, 22nd Report, pp. 22–23.
[31] *Hobbs* v. *Knight* (1838) 1 Curt. 768, 778.
[32] *Hobbs* v. *Knight, supra,* (signature cut out: *obiter* as to signature burnt or torn out); *In the Goods of Gullan* (1858) 1 Sw. & T. 23.

it cannot be made out,[33] or if the signatures of the attesting witnesses are destroyed by any of these methods.[34]

The testator must complete all he intends to do by way of destruction. In *Doe d. Perkes* v. *Perkes*[35] the testator, being angry with a devisee named in his will, began to tear it up with the intention of revoking it, and tore it into four pieces before he was stopped, partly by a bystander who seized his arms and partly by the apologies of the devisee. The testator then became calm and fitted the pieces together saying, "It is a good job it is no worse." The court held that the will had not been revoked because the testator had not completed all that he originally intended to do by way of destruction. On the other hand, if the testator's original intention had been to tear the will into four pieces, it would have been revoked.

(2) *Destruction by another person.* The act of destruction must be carried out by the testator himself or by another person in his presence[36] and by his direction.[37] If a testator instructs his solicitor by telephone to destroy his will as he wishes to make a new one, and the solicitor does so in the testator's absence, the will is not revoked.[38] A will destroyed by another person in the testator's presence but without the testator's direction to do so is not revoked even if the testator subsequently ratifies the destruction.[39]

Intention to revoke.[40] The testator must have the intention of revoking the whole, or part, of the will whilst the act of destruction is carried out.

(1) *Mental capacity to revoke.* Destruction whilst the testator is of unsound mind does not revoke a will.[41] The same standard of mental capacity is required for revocation by destruction as for the making of a will.[42]

(2) *Accident or mistake.* A will destroyed by accident is not revoked.[43] Again there is no revocation if the act of destruction is done with the intention of destroying but not of revoking the will. Thus a will was not revoked where it was destroyed under the mistaken belief that it was

---

[33] *Hobbs* v. *Knight, supra,* at p. 780; *In the Goods of Morton* (1887) 12 P.D. 141 (signatures of testatrix and attesting witnesses scratched out); *In the Goods of Godfrey* (1893) 69 L.T. 22 (signature of testator scratched but legible: no revocation).

[34] *Hobbs* v. *Knight, supra,* at p. 781 (*obiter* as to erasure); *In the Goods of Dallow* (1862) 31 L.J.P.M. & A. 128 (torn off).

[35] (1820) 3 B. & Ald. 489: see also *Elms* v. *Elms* (1858) 1 Sw. & Tr. 155.

[36] *In the Goods of Dadds* (1857) Dea. & Sw. 290.

[37] *Gill* v. *Gill* [1909] P. 157 (will torn up in testator's presence by his wife in a fit of temper: no revocation as not done by his direction).

[38] *In the Estate of de Kremer* (1965) 110 S.J. 18 ("considerable professional error" of solicitor).

[39] *Mills* v. *Millward* (1890) 15 P.D. 20, 21; *Gill* v. *Gill, supra; Re Booth* [1926] P. 118, 132 and 133.

[40] For conditional revocation see *post,* pp. 70–71.

[41] *Brunt* v. *Brunt* (1873) 3 P. & D. 37 (delirium tremens); *In the Goods of Hine* [1893] P. 282 (softening of the brain); *In the Goods of Brassington* [1902] P. 1 (drunk).

[42] *Re Sabatini* (1969) 114 S.J. 35; see *ante,* pp. 45 *et seq.*

[43] *Burtenshaw* v. *Gilbert* (1774) 1 Cowp. 49, 52; *In the Goods of Taylor* (1890) 63 L.T. 230.

invalid,[44] or that it was useless,[45] or that it had already been revoked.[46] The testator "may have merely torn it up, thinking that it was no longer worth the paper it was written upon. For myself, in those circumstances, I should have thought the right inference to draw was that he did not intend to revoke it at all; he was merely disposing of what he thought was rubbish."[47]

(3) *Whether intention to revoke whole or part.* It is necessary to decide whether the testator intended to revoke the whole or, alternatively, only a particular part of a will. There may be evidence of his expressed intention. If need be, the court infers what the testator intended from the state of the will after the act of destruction. If, for instance, the testator's signature is destroyed this raises an inference that the testator intended to revoke the whole will.[48] If a portion of the will not necessary to its validity as a testamentary instrument is destroyed, the question arises whether the portion destroyed is so important as to raise the inference that the rest cannot have been intended to stand without it.[49] Thus, destruction of a clause at the commencement of a will, or cutting out various legacies, or a clause appointing executors, does not revoke the rest of the will.[50] Again, cutting away half a page, which contained details of the residuary trust, only revoked that part of the will, because sufficient remained to lead to the inference that the testator intended that what remained should be effective.[51] On the other hand it was inferred that the testator intended to revoke the whole will where the first two sheets of a will made on five sheets of paper had been destroyed, because the last three sheets were practically unintelligible and unworkable as a will in the absence of the first two sheets.[52]

Presumptions. Two rebuttable presumptions may apply:

(1) *Will missing at death.* A will last known to be in the testator's possession but which cannot be found at his death is presumed to have been destroyed by the testator with the intention of revoking it.[53] The strength of the presumption varies according to the security of the testator's custody of the will—the safer the security, the stronger is the pre-

---

[44] *Giles* v. *Warren* (1872) 2 P. & D. 401; *In the Goods of Thornton* (1889) 14 P.D. 82.

[45] *Beardsley* v. *Lacey* (1897) 78 L.T. 25; *Stamford* v. *White* [1901] P. 46.

[46] *Scott* v. *Scott* (1859) 1 Sw. & Tr. 258; *Clarkson* v. *Clarkson* (1862) 2 Sw. & Tr. 497 (in both cases mistaken belief that later will had already revoked it).

[47] *Per* Buckley L.J. in *Re Jones* [1976] Ch. 200, 205.

[48] *Hobbs* v. *Knight* (1838) 1 Curt. 768 (T's signature cut out: whole will revoked); *In the Goods of Gullan* (1858) 1 Sw. & Tr. 23; *Bell* v. *Fothergill* (1870) 2 P. & D. 148: *cf. Christmas* v. *Whinyates* (1863) 3 Sw. & Tr. 81 (only part revoked, though signature cut off, due to manner in which cut).

[49] *Clarke* v. *Scripps* (1852) 2 Rob. 563 (part only); *Re White* (1879) 3 L.R.Ir. 413 (whole); *Leonard* v. *Leonard* [1902] P. 243 (whole).

[50] *In the Goods of Woodward* (1871) 2 P. & D. 206; *In the Goods of Nelson* (1872) 6 I.R. Eq. 569; *In the Goods of Maley* (1887) 12 P.D. 134; *In the Goods of Leach* (1890) 63 L.T. 111; *In the Estate of Nunn* (1936) 154 L.T. 498 (strip in middle of will cut out and remainder stitched together: only strip revoked).

[51] *Re Everest* [1975] Fam. 44.

[52] *Leonard* v. *Leonard* [1902] P. 243: see also *Treloar* v. *Lean* (1889) 14 P.D. 49; *In the Estate of Green* (1962) 106 S.J. 1034; *Re White* (1879) 3 L.R.Ir. 413.

[53] *Eckersley* v. *Platt* (1886) L.R. 1 P. & D. 281; *Allan* v. *Morrison* [1900] A.C. 604.

sumption.[54] The presumption may be rebutted by evidence of non-revocation, such as evidence that the will was destroyed by enemy action or accident, or evidence showing the testator's intention to adhere to the will, and the contents of the will may be proved by means of a draft or copy or by oral evidence.[55]

(2) *Will found mutilated at death.* A will, which has been in the testator's possession but which is found to be torn or mutilated at his death, is presumed to have been torn or mutilated by the testator with the intention of revoking it in whole or in part.[56] Again the presumption may be rebutted by evidence to the contrary.[57]

If the testator executed the will whilst of sound mind but was insane during any part of the period when the will was in his possession, there is no presumption that the destruction, or the tearing or mutilation, was carried out by the testator at a time when he was of sound mind. Unless the party alleging revocation proves this, the will is admissible to probate.[58]

C. WILL OR CODICIL

Under section 20 of the Wills Act 1837 the whole or any part of a will may be revoked by another duly executed will or codicil.[59]

Express revocation by will or codicil. Most wills contain a revocation clause in general terms by which the testator expressly revokes "all wills codicils and other testamentary dispositions heretofore made by me." Such a revocation clause normally operates to revoke all previous testamentary instruments[60] just as if they had never existed and it will therefore revoke an appointment made by the testator in a previous will or codicil.[61] The advantage of inserting such a revocation clause is that it makes it unnecessary to consider whether, or to what extent, an earlier will or codicil is revoked by implication. A revocation clause may be much narrower in its ambit—for instance, in a codicil a revocation clause commonly revokes a single clause, or even a single word, in a previous will or codicil. No particular form of words is required for express revocation. However the usual form of commencement of a will,

---

[54] *Sugden v. Lord St. Leonards* (1876) 1 P.D. 154 (will of Lord St. Leonards not kept in close custody).

[55] *Ibid.* (oral evidence of daughter who was a beneficiary); *Re Webb* [1964] 1 W.L.R. 509; *In the Estate of Yule* (1965) 109 S.J. 317: see *post*, pp. 193 *et seq.*

[56] *Lambell v. Lambell* (1831) 3 Hag.Ecc. 568; *Bell v. Fothergill* (1870) L.R. 2 P. & D. 148.

[57] *In the Estate of MacKenzie* [1909] P. 305; *Re Cowling* [1924] P. 113.

[58] *Harris v. Berrall* (1858) 1 Sw. & Tr. 153 (tearing); *Sprigge v. Sprigge* (1868) L.R. 1 P. & D. 608 (destruction).

[59] For conditional revocation see *post*, pp. 67 *et seq.* For the rules of private international law governing revocation by will or codicil see Dicey and Morris, *The Conflict of Laws* (11th ed., 1987), pp. 1037 *et seq.*; Theobald on *Wills* (14th ed., 1982), Chap. 1.

[60] But not statutory nominations, see *ante*, p. 17.

[61] *Sotheran v. Dening* (1881) 20 Ch.D. 99 (general power); *Re Kingdon* (1886) 32 Ch.D. 604 (special power); *Cadell v. Wilcocks* [1898] P. 21, 26.

"This is the last will and testament of me . . . ," is not construed as an express revocation of previous wills.[62]

On its proper construction a revocation clause in general terms may not revoke all previous testamentary instruments. In *Re Wayland*[63] a testator made a will in accordance with the law of Belgium dealing only with his Belgian property. Later he made a will in England which contained a revocation clause but which declared that "this will is intended to deal only with my estate in England." The court construed the revocation clause to mean that the testator revoked all former wills dealing with English property and admitted both the Belgian and the English wills to probate.

A revocation clause does not operate at all if:

(i) the clause is contained in a conditional will which is inoperative owing to the specified condition not being satisfied.[64]

(ii) the clause is rejected for want of knowledge and approval by the testator.[65] The clause is not admitted to probate if the testator did not know and approve of it,[66] though the clause must be admitted if it was included as a result of a mistake as to its legal effect.[67]

(iii) the clause itself is subject to a condition which is not satisfied: this is considered later.[68]

Implied revocation by will or codicil. A prior will or codicil is impliedly revoked by a later will or codicil so far as the latter contains provisions inconsistent with or merely repeating the former. If the provisions of the later will or codicil are wholly inconsistent or repetitive, the prior will or codicil is completely revoked.[69] If they are only partially inconsistent or repetitive, those parts of the prior will or codicil not affected by the inconsistency or repetition remain unrevoked. The question to ask is not which of his wills or codicils did the testator desire to be admitted to probate: the true question is which provisions did the testator intend to take effect at his death.[70] This is a question of construction.[71]

[62] *Cutto* v. *Gilbert* (1854) 9 Moo.P.C. 131; *Lemage* v. *Goodban* (1865) L.R. 1 P. & D. 57; *Simpson* v. *Foxon* [1907] P. 54 ("This is the last and only will and testament of me" not an express revocation); *Kitcat* v. *King* [1930] P. 266.

[63] [1951] 2 All E.R. 1041; *Gladstone* v. *Tempest* (1840) 2 Curt. 650; *Denny* v. *Barton* (1818) 2 Phill. 575.

[64] *In the Goods of Hugo* (1877) 2 P.D. 73; *In the Estate of O'Connor* [1942] 1 All E.R. 546: see *ante*, p. 5.

[65] *Ante*, pp. 49, *et seq.*; see C. H. Sherrin (1972) 122 New L.J. 6.

[66] *Re Phelan* [1972] Fam. 33, see *ante* p. 53; *In the Goods of Oswald* (1874) L.R. 3 P. & D. 162 (included *per incuriam* without instructions); *In the Goods of Moore* [1892] P. 378; *Smith* v. *Thompson* (1931) 47 T.L.R. 603 and *cf. Lowthorpe-Lutwidge* v. *Lowthorpe-Lutwidge* [1935] P. 151 (no evidence of want of knowledge and approval of revocation clause); *In the Goods of Swords* [1952] P. 368.

[67] *Collins* v. *Elstone* [1893] P. 1 (T wrongly advised revocation clause would not revoke her previous will).

[68] *Post*, p. 72.

[69] *In the Estate of Bryan* [1907] P. 125 (wholly inconsistent though later will did not dispose of residue); *In the Goods of Howard* (1869) L.R. 1 P. & D. 636.

[70] *Lemage* v. *Goodban* (1865) L.R. 1 P. & D. 57; *In the Goods of Petchell* (1874) L.R. 3 P. & D. 153.

[71] *Post*, p. 417.

Proof of revocation

(1) *By lost will or codicil.* Revocation of an earlier will or codicil by a later will or codicil takes effect when the latter is executed and it is immaterial that the latter is not forthcoming at the testator's death.[72] But in order to establish revocation by a will or codicil which has been lost or destroyed, it is necessary to prove (i) that it was duly executed and (ii) that by its contents it did expressly or impliedly revoke the earlier will or codicil. The second requirement may be proved by production of a copy or written instructions, or by clear and satisfactory oral evidence.[73]

(2) *By will or codicil inadmissible to probate.* In *Re Howard*[74] a testator first executed a will leaving his estate to his son and later executed two wills on the same day, one in favour of his wife and the other in favour of his son. Each of these two wills contained a revocation clause in general terms. The court held that these two wills were effective to revoke the earlier will. However neither of them could be admitted to probate as they were inconsistent and there was nothing to indicate the order in which they were executed.

D. Duly Executed Writing Declaring an Intention to Revoke

Under section 20 of the Wills Act 1837 the whole or any part of a will may be revoked by "some writing declaring an intention to revoke the same" and duly executed in the same manner as a will.

A statement at the foot of an obliterated codicil, "We are witnesses to the erasure of the above," signed by the testator and attested by two witnesses, was held to be a "writing declaring an intention to revoke."[75] Again, in *Re Spracklan's Estate*[76] the Court of Appeal held this requirement was satisfied by the words, "will you please destroy the will already made out," in a letter signed by the testatrix and duly attested, and addressed to the manager of a bank having custody of her will. The will was therefore revoked as soon as the letter was duly executed.

---

[72] *Brown* v. *Brown* (1858) 8 E. & B. 876; *Wood* v. *Wood* (1867) L.R. 1 P. & D. 309.

[73] *Cutto* v. *Gilbert* (1854) 9 Moo.P.C. 131 ("oral evidence ought to be stringent and conclusive"); the ordinary standard of proof applies, *i.e.* a reasonable balance of probabilities, *Re Wipperman* [1955] P. 59: evidence it was solicitor's usual practice to insert a revocation clause is insufficient by itself; *Re Wyatt* [1952] 1 All E.R. 1030 (contents of later will unknown; it had been drawn by a solicitor whose usual practice was to insert revocation clause: earlier will held not revoked); *Re Rear* [1975] 2 N.Z.L.R. 254, 267; *cf. In the Estate of Hampshire* [1951] W.N. 174.

[74] [1944] P. 39.

[75] *In the Goods of Gosling* (1886) 11 P.D. 79.

[76] [1938] 2 All E.R. 345, following *In the Goods of Durance* (1872) L.R. 2 P. & D. 406, where Lord Penzance said at p. 407, "If a man writes to another 'Go and get my will and burn it,' he shows a strong intention to revoke his will."

E. An Alteration in Circumstances does not Revoke

The general rule that marriage revokes a will ensures that a testator starts married life with a clean slate.[77] Apart from marriage, no other alteration in circumstances, such as the birth of children, revokes a will.[78]

F. Revocation by a Privileged Testator

The four methods of revocation already considered apply to a privileged testator subject only to the differences arising from his ability to make an informal will.[79]

(1) *Marriage.* In *In the Estate of Wardrop*[80] Shearman J. decided that the will of a privileged testator was revoked by his subsequent marriage. He said that section 18 (which provided that *"every* will made by a man or woman shall be revoked by his or her marriage"*) was "a very sweeping enactment and it must be held to apply to soldiers' and sailors' wills." The two exceptions to the rule that marriage revokes a will also apply in the case of a privileged testator.

(2) *Destruction.* This method is applicable to an informal will[81] unless it was made orally so that destruction is impossible.

(3) *Will or codicil.* A privileged testator may revoke any previous will (whether or not made when he was privileged) by an informal will or codicil.[82]

(4) *Writing declaring an intention to revoke.* A privileged testator may revoke any previous will by informal writing declaring an intention to revoke.[83] There is a dictum that such informal writing does not revoke a

---

[77] See Law Reform Committee, 22nd Report, pp. 11–18, recommending no change in the general rule.

[78] See Wills Act 1837, s.19. For the effect of divorce or annulment of marriage see *post*, p. 344.

[79] *In the Estate of Gossage* [1921] P. 194 (the misleading headnote states the *ratio* of Younger L.J., and not that of the majority of the Court of Appeal).

[80] [1917] P. 54: this decision has been doubted on the ground that *In the Estate of Gossage, supra,* by implication overrules it (see Williams, Mortimer and Sunnucks, *Executors, Administrators and Probate* (1982), p. 202, n. 11) but it is only the judgment of Younger L.J. which may carry this implication.

[81] In *In the Estate of Gossage, supra,* at p. 196, Bailhache J. at first instance apparently decided that a privileged will had been revoked by its destruction by another person in the testator's absence: no member of the Court of Appeal relied on this ground and the majority treated s.20 as applicable.

[82] Wills Act 1837, ss.11 and 20: Wills (Soldiers and Sailors) Act 1918: see *In the Goods of Newland* [1952] P. 71.

[83] *In the Estate of Gossage* [1921] P. 194 (letter from privileged soldier in South Africa to sister in England asking her to burn will "for I have already cancelled it": held letter revoked his previous will).

formal will made when not privileged,[84] but it ought to be irrelevant whether the previous will was made when privileged.[85]

G. Conditional Revocation

Revocation of the whole or part of a will or codicil by destruction, or by another will or codicil or by duly executed writing, requires an intention to revoke. The testator's intention to revoke may be absolute or conditional. If it is absolute, revocation takes place immediately. If it is conditional, revocation does not take effect unless the condition is fulfilled. Often the condition makes revocation dependent upon the validity of another will or codicil and this particular type of conditional revocation has in the past been referred to as the doctrine of dependent relative revocation. However, it seems preferable to use the less cumbersome term conditional revocation in all cases.[86]

Question of fact or construction. Whether the testator's intention to revoke was conditional is a question of fact where revocation was by destruction[87] and evidence as to the testator's declarations of intention is therefore admissible.[88] On the other hand it is a question of construction where revocation was by another will or codicil[89] or by duly executed writing: it follows that extrinsic evidence of the testator's intention is only admissible to assist in the interpretation of the document.[90]

Conditional revocation by destruction. The testator's intention to revoke by destruction may be absolute (in the sense that the testator intends the revocation to take effect at once) or conditional (in the sense that he intends the revocation to take effect only if some condition is fulfilled). To consider some instances:

(1) *Conditional upon due execution of new will or codicil.* If T forms the intention of making a new will in favour of B, and T destroys his old will in favour of A, T's intention to revoke his old will may be absolute or conditional. Which it was is a question of fact to be decided after T's death upon all the evidence before the court. Evidence that T had formed the intention of making a new will does not of itself necessarily lead to the conclusion that T's intention to revoke was conditional.[91] For

---

[84] *In the Estate of Gossage, supra,* at pp. 201–202 (writing must be "executed in the manner . . . required for the execution of the will which it is intended to revoke").

[85] Wills Act 1837, s.20 refers to the manner in which "a will," not *the* will, is hereinbefore required to be executed.

[86] "The name of this doctrine seems to me to be somewhat overloaded with unnecessary polysyllables. The resounding adjectives add very little, it seems to me, to any clear idea of what is meant. The whole matter can be quite simply expressed by the word 'conditional,' " *per* Langton J. in *In the Goods of Hope Brown* [1942] P. 136, 138; *Re Jones* [1976] Ch. 200, 212; Law Reform Committee, 22nd Report, p. 24.

[87] *Dixon* v. *Solicitor to the Treasury* [1905] P. 42; *Re Jones, supra,* at pp. 215 and 218.

[88] *Powell* v. *Powell* (1866) L.R. 1 P. & D. 209.

[89] *Att.-Gen.* v. *Lloyd* (1747) 1 Ves.Sen. 32, 34.

[90] *Post,* pp. 418 *et seq.*

[91] *Re Jones* [1976] Ch. 200.

instance, the court may infer that T said to himself, "I cannot get on with making a new will in favour of B until my solicitor returns next week, but at least I will here and now get rid of this one, so that A shall not benefit": if, as in this instance, T's intention to revoke was absolute, T's destruction of his old will revoked it immediately.[92] It is irrelevant that this resulted in an intestacy which it is difficult to believe T intended.[93] On the other hand, the court may infer that T said to himself, "I believe that it is necessary for me to revoke my old will before I can make a new will": if, as in this instance, T's intention to revoke was conditional on his duly executing his new will, T's destruction of his old will did not revoke it unless this condition was fulfilled.[94]

Similarly, if T has already "made" a new will (which fails for want of due execution) and afterwards destroys his old will, T's intention to revoke his old will may be absolute (in which case his old will is revoked immediately)[95] or conditional upon the due execution of his new will (in which case his old will is not revoked unless this condition is fulfilled).[96] Alternatively T may have no intention to revoke, because he mistakenly believes his old will is useless or has already been revoked (in which case his old will is not revoked).[97]

(2) *Conditional upon revival of former will.* A will which has been revoked by a later will cannot be revived by the subsequent revocation of that later will.[98] It follows that if the testator destroys the later will, intending to revoke it conditionally on the revival of the former will, the revocation of the later will is ineffective.[99]

(3) *Conditional upon particular devolution on intestacy.* In *In the Estate of Southerden*[1] a testator made a will giving all his property to his wife. Later he burnt it, intending to revoke it conditionally on his wife being entitled to all his property on his death intestate. This condition was not satisfied and the Court of Appeal held that the will had not been revoked and its contents were admissible to probate.

The doctrine of conditional revocation is not confined to these instances. It is of general application and applies if the testator's intention to revoke is conditional on the existence, or future existence, of a particular fact: if this condition is not satisfied, the will is not revoked by destruction.[2]

---

[92] *Ibid.* at pp. 219–220.

[93] *Ibid.* at pp. 213–214 and 217–218.

[94] *Dixon* v. *Solicitor to the Treasury* [1905] P. 42: see *In the Estate of Bromham* [1952] 1 All E.R. 110. For evidence of conditional revocation of a will missing at death see *post*, p. 194.

[95] See *In the Estate of Green* (1962) 106 S.J. 1034.

[96] *Dancer* v. *Crabb* (1873) L.R. 3 P. & D. 98; *In the Estate of Davies* [1951] 1 All E.R. 920; *Sterling* v. *Bruce* [1973] N.I. 255.

[97] *Ante*, pp. 64–65.

[98] *Post*, p. 77.

[99] *Powell* v. *Powell* (1866) L.R. 1 P. & D. 209; *Cossey* v. *Cossey* (1900) 82 L.T. 203; *In the Estate of Bridgewater* [1965] 1 W.L.R. 416.

[1] [1925] P. 177.

[2] *In the Estate of Southerden* [1925] P. 177; *Re Jones* [1976] Ch. 200, 213 and 216: see *Re Carey* (1977) 121 S.J. 173 (conditional on fact he had nothing to leave by will).

Conditional express revocation by will or codicil. A revocation clause may be subject to an express condition. If, for example, a testator inserts in a codicil a revocation clause expressed to take effect conditionally on his wife predeceasing him, the clause does not operate if she survives him.

Even in the absence of an express condition, a revocation clause may be construed as conditional. An early instance is the decision in *Campbell* v. *French*[3] where the testator by his will gave legacies to his sister's two grandchildren living in America and by a codicil revoked the legacies "they being all dead." In fact they were still alive. Lord Loughborough held that the revocation was ineffective as it was conditional on the legatees being dead. Another instance is *In the Goods of Hope Brown*[4] where a testator made a will prepared by solicitors and carefully disposing of all his property. Some years later he executed a holograph will containing a clause revoking all previous testamentary dispositions. By this later will he gave a life interest to his wife, directed that pecuniary bequests be paid free of duty but in fact made no pecuniary bequests, and directed that after the death of his wife his trustees should divide his estate among "the after-mentioned beneficiaries" but in fact left a blank space instead of naming the beneficiaries. Langton J. held that the revocation clause was inserted conditionally on the testator "concluding" the later will. This condition was not satisfied because the testator did not complete the disposition of all his property in the later will and therefore both wills were admissible to probate, omitting the revocation clause in the later will.

Conditional implied revocation by will or codicil. Where a testator by a will or codicil gives property to X, and by a later will or codicil gives the same property to Y, the gift to X is impliedly revoked. But does this occur if for some reason the gift to Y fails? In that event it is a question of construction whether the testator has shown an intention to revoke the gift to X in any event (in which case X does not take) or conditionally on the gift to Y taking effect (in which case X does take on the failure of the gift to Y).[5] The answer therefore depends on the proper construction of the later will or codicil. The decision in *Re Robinson*[6] is a useful illustration. In that case the testatrix by will gave her estate upon trust to pay an annuity to her son H and after his death to divide her estate equally between her grandchildren who attained 21 years of age. By a later will she gave her whole estate to H absolutely. Unfortunately this disposition was void as H's wife was an attesting witness.[7] The court held that the testatrix had not shown an intention to revoke the earlier will in any event. The only indication in the later will of an intention to revoke was in the different disposition which it contained but

---

[3] (1797) 3 Ves. 321: see also *Doe* d. *Evans* v. *Evans* (1839) 10 Ad. & El. 228; *Re Plunkett* [1964] I.R. 259: contrast *Re Feis* [1964] Ch. 106.

[4] [1942] P. 136: see also *In the Estate of Cocke* [1960] 1 W.L.R. 491; *In the Estate of Crannis* (1978) 122 S.J. 489: see R. G. Henderson (1969) 32 M.L.R. 447: *cf. Re Luck* [1977] WAR 148.

[5] *Ward* v. *Van der Loeff* [1924] A.C. 653 (gift in later codicil void for remoteness: gift in earlier will held not revoked).

[6] [1930] 2 Ch. 332: see also *Re Davies* [1928] Ch. 24.

[7] *Post*, p. 334.

which had failed, and the earlier will had therefore not been revoked. In short her intention to revoke was conditional on the absolute gift to H taking effect and this condition was not satisfied.

2. ALTERATION

Section 21 of the Wills Act 1837 lays down the rule for any alteration in a will:

"no obliteration, interlineation, or other alteration made in any will after the execution thereof shall be valid or have any effect, except so far as the words or effect of the will before such alteration shall not be apparent, unless such alteration shall be executed in like manner as hereinbefore is required for the execution of the will. . . . "

In considering the effect of section 21 three main questions may arise and they should be considered in turn:

A. Was the alteration made before the execution of the will? If so, the alteration is valid and section 21 does not apply.
B. Was the alteration duly executed? If so, it is valid.
C. Has the alteration made any part of the will not "apparent"? If it is not apparent and the testator intended to revoke it, that part is revoked.

A. ALTERATION MADE BEFORE EXECUTION OF WILL

An alteration made in a will before the will is executed by the testator is valid if the testator intends the alteration to form part of the will when it is executed. Thus the alteration is not valid if it was merely deliberative and not final. A rebuttable presumption arises that an alteration in pencil is merely deliberative and that an alteration in ink is intended to be final.[8]

Presumption as to time of alteration. There is a rebuttable presumption that an unattested alteration was made after the execution of the will[9] or any subsequent codicil.[10] This presumption may be rebutted by evidence, which may be internal evidence from the will itself or extrinsic evidence or both. If the alterations are trifling and of little consequence, the presumption may be readily rebutted.[11]

The presumption has been rebutted by internal evidence from the

---

[8] *Hawkes* v. *Hawkes* (1828) 1 Hagg.Ecc. 321 (each presumption is stronger if both ink and pencil alterations); *In the Goods of Adams* (1872) L.R. 2 P. & D. 367.

[9] *Cooper* v. *Bockett* (1846) 4 Moo.P.C. 419; *In the Goods of Adamson* (1875) L.R. 3 P. & D. 253.

[10] *In the Goods of Sykes* (1873) 3 P. & D. 26, 27–28; *Lushington* v. *Onslow* (1848) 6 N. of C. 183.

[11] *In the Goods of Hindmarsh* (1866) 1 P. & D. 307 (testator a lawyer, alterations trifling and apparently written with same pen and ink as rest of will, and not very strong evidence of writing expert: presumption rebutted).

will itself where the alterations were made to supply blanks left in the will by the draftsman,[12] and again where interlineations written with the same ink as the rest of the will completed the otherwise unintelligible sentences of the will.[13] Extrinsic evidence rebutting the presumption may take different forms, for instance evidence from the draftsman of the will[14] or an attesting witness, or declarations by the testator showing that he made the alterations before executing the will.[15] The court considers all the evidence, both internal and extrinsic, in deciding whether the presumption is rebutted.

A different presumption applies if the will was made by the testator whilst privileged. In that case a rebuttable presumption arises that the alteration was made whilst the testator was still privileged and therefore entitled to make informal alterations.[16]

Effect of republication. The republication[17] of a will by its re-execution with the proper formalities validates an alteration made in the will after it was executed but before it was republished, if the testator intends the alteration to form part of the will when it is republished.[18] The same result follows if, after the alteration is made, the will is republished by a duly executed codicil containing some reference to the will.[19] But the alteration is not validated by republication of the will if the alteration was merely deliberative and not final,[20] or if the codicil shows that the testator was treating the will as unaltered.[21]

As already explained, the presumption is that an unattested alteration to the will was made, not only after the execution of the will, but also after the execution of the codicil.[22] Accordingly, unless this presumption is rebutted by evidence showing that the unattested alteration was made before the execution of the codicil,[23] the alteration is not validated by the republication of the will by the codicil.

B. ALTERATION DULY EXECUTED

Formalities. If the alteration was duly executed with the formalities required for the execution of the will, the alteration is valid. In this con-

---

[12] *Birch* v. *Birch* (1848) 1 Rob.Ecc. 675 (blanks left for amounts of legacies); *Greville* v. *Tylee* (1851) 7 Moo.P.C. 320, 327.

[13] *In the Goods of Cadge* (1868) 1 P. & D. 543.

[14] *Keigwin* v. *Keigwin* (1843) 3 Curt. 607.

[15] Until the Civil Evidence Act 1968 such declarations were not admissible if made by the testator after the execution of the will.

[16] *In the Goods of Tweedale* (1874) L.R. 3 P. & D. 204 (soldier's will); *In the Goods of Newland* [1952] P. 71 (seaman's will).

[17] *Post*, p. 80: revival has the same effect, *post*, p. 79.

[18] *In the Goods of Shearn* (1880) 50 L.J.P. 15 (alteration after execution: alteration invalid as will not properly re-executed): *cf. In the Goods of Dewell* (1853) 1 Sp.Ecc. & Ad. 103, which was wrongly decided.

[19] *In the Goods of Sykes* (1873) L.R. 3 P. & D. 26.

[20] *In the Goods of Hall* (1871) L.R. 2 P. & D. 256 (pencil alterations).

[21] *Re Hay* [1904] 1 Ch. 317 (three legacies in will struck out by unattested alteration, later codicil revoked only one of them: held the other two stood, as testatrix was confirming her will without the alterations).

[22] *In the Goods of Sykes, supra*, at pp. 27–28; *Lushington* v. *Onslow* (1848) 6 N. of C. 183.

[23] *In the Goods of Heath* [1892] P. 253 (wording of codicil showed interlineation in will had already been made).

nection section 21 of the Wills Act 1837 provides that the signatures of the testator and the witnesses may be made "in the margin or on some other part of the will opposite or near to such alteration, or at the foot or end of or opposite to a memorandum referring to such alteration, and written at the end or some other part of the will." Accordingly an alteration is valid if the testator signs by writing his initials in the margin against the alteration, and the testator either makes or acknowledges this signature in the simultaneous presence of two witnesses, who then sign in the presence of the testator by writing their initials in the margin.[24] Again an alteration is valid if a duly executed memorandum refers to the alteration.[25]

Two precautions are advisable in practice in connection with alterations:

(i) Unless the testator is *in extremis*, it is advisable to restrict alterations to the correction of small errors, such as the misspelling of a name, and to give effect to all other alterations by the execution of a new will or a codicil.

(ii) All alterations whenever made should be duly executed. This is advisable even though the alteration was made before the execution of the will, because it makes it unnecessary to rebut the presumption that an unattested alteration was made after the execution of the will.

Privileged testator. A testator who has made a will whilst privileged may make alterations to it without any formalities whilst still privileged[26] because no formalities are required for due execution under section 11.

C. PART OF WILL NOT APPARENT

An alteration after execution which makes any part of the will not "apparent" revokes that part if the testator has an intention to revoke it. Probate of the will must be granted with a blank space for the part not apparent.

The test of being not apparent. "Apparent" in section 21 means optically apparent on the face of the will itself.[27] A word in a will is not apparent if an expert cannot decipher it by any "natural" means, such as holding the paper up to the light with a frame of brown paper around the portion attempted to be read[28] or by using magnifying glasses.[29] In determining whether a word is apparent, it is not permissible to ascertain the word by the use of extrinsic evidence,[30] or by physically inter-

---

[24] *In the Goods of Blewitt* (1880) 5 P.D. 116 (initials suffice).

[25] *In the Goods of Treeby* (1875) 3 P. & D. 242.

[26] *In the Goods of Tweedale* (1874) L.R. 3 P. & D. 204.

[27] *Townley* v. *Watson* (1844) 3 Curt. 761, 768; *In the Goods of Itter* [1950] P. 130, 132: see Law Reform Committee, 22nd Report, pp. 23–24 (recommending no change).

[28] *Ffinch* v. *Combe* [1894] P. 191 (slips of paper pasted over words in will after execution).

[29] *In the Goods of Brasier* [1899] P. 36.

[30] *Townley* v. *Watson* (1844) 3 Curt. 761, 768 (evidence of draftsman not admissible to prove what words obliterated were).

fering with the will by using chemicals to remove ink-marks, or remov-
ing a slip of paper pasted over the word,[31] or by making another document, such as an infra-red photograph.[32] If the word can only be
ascertained by these "forbidden" methods it is not apparent.

Intention to revoke. The testator must make the alteration which renders part of the will not apparent with an intention to revoke that part.[33]
A testator who accidently obliterates part of his will by spilling ink over
it does not revoke it.

Conditional obliteration.[34] If the testator's intention to revoke is conditional, revocation does not take place despite the obliteration unless
the condition is fulfilled. If the condition is not fulfilled, the word obliterated must be ascertained so that it can be admitted to probate. For
this purpose the court has recourse to any means of legal proof, including any of the above "forbidden" methods,[35] because the question to be
answered is not, is the word apparent? but rather, can the obliterated
word be ascertained?

Usually the condition relates to the validity of a legacy of a different
amount which the testator attempts to substitute in place of the original
amount which he obliterates. For instance, T by his will gives to X a legacy of "one hundred and fifty pounds": later T obliterates the words
"one hundred and fifty" (making them not apparent) and writes the
words "two hundred" in their place. If, at the time he carries out this
obliteration, T intends to revoke the original amount only if the new
amount is effectually substituted, T's intention to revoke is subject to a
condition which is not fulfilled (unless the alteration is duly executed or
T later republishes his will): accordingly the original amount is admissible to probate.[36] But if T merely obliterates the words "and fifty,"
intending to revoke them but not to substitute any new words, his
intention to revoke is absolute: probate must be granted with a blank
space for the words "and fifty" if these words are not apparent.[37] And
the same result follows even though T later changes his mind and
attempts to substitute new words. Thus if T first obliterates the words
"and fifty," intending to revoke them but not to substitute any new
words, and later changes his mind and writes the words "and ninety"

[31] *In the Goods of Horsford* (1874) L.R. 3 P. & D. 211 (the same will came before the court
in *Ffinch* v. *Combe, supra*). But a slip of paper may be removed in order to ascertain
whether it covers words of revocation which took effect before being covered: *In the Goods
of Gilbert* [1893] P. 183.

[32] *In the Goods of Itter* [1950] P. 130.

[33] *Townley* v. *Watson, supra*, at p. 769.

[34] For conditional revocation by destruction see *ante*, pp. 70–71.

[35] *In the Goods of Horsford, supra*, (strips of paper pasted over amount of legacy in codicil
ordered to be removed as condition of revocation not fulfilled); *In the Goods of Itter, supra;*
Sturton v. *Whetlock* (1883) 52 L.J.P. 29 (evidence of draftsman as to original words).

[36] *In the Goods of Itter* [1950] P. 130; *In the Goods of Horsford, supra.* As to other conditions
see *In the Goods of McCabe* (1873) 3 P. & D. 94 (T gave to niece X, believing X's mother Y
was dying, and later substituted Y for X after Y's recovery: held conditional obliteration of
X, and "X" admitted to probate); *Sturton* v. *Whetlock, supra,* (gifts to grandchildren at age
of twenty one years; "one" erased and "five" substituted: held conditional obliteration).

[37] *In the Goods of Nelson* (1872) 6 I.R. Eq. 569; *In the Goods of Hamer* (1944) 113 L.J.P. 31.

in their place, probate must be granted with a blank space for the words "and fifty."[38]

Whether the testator's intention to revoke was conditional is a question of fact and evidence as to the testator's declarations of intention is therefore admissible.[39] If the testator attempts to substitute a legacy of a different amount, but leaves the name of the legatee untouched, the court may infer from this that his intention to revoke was conditional on the validity of the substituted amount.[40]

3. REVIVAL AND REPUBLICATION

A. REVIVAL

A testator may revive a will or codicil, or any part thereof, which has been revoked. He cannot however revive a will or codicil which is no longer in existence: once it has been destroyed it cannot be revived[41] and the testator must execute a new will or codicil in order to give effect to its provisions.

Two methods of revival.[42] Section 22 of the Wills Act 1837 provides that a will or codicil which has been wholly or partly revoked may only be revived (i) by its re-execution with the proper formalities, or (ii) by a duly executed codicil showing an intention to revive it.

(1) *Revocation of revoking will cannot revive.* No other methods of revival are available. Thus a will which has been revoked by a later will cannot be revived by the subsequent revocation of that later will. In *In the Goods of Hodgkinson*[43] a testator first made a will giving all his property to X and later made a second will giving his realty to Y: the second will impliedly revoked the first will as regards the testator's realty. Subsequently the testator revoked the second will by destruction. The Court of Appeal held that as regards the testator's realty the first will was not revived by the revocation of the second will: the first will disposed of the testator's personalty but his realty passed on intestacy.[44]

(2) *Revival by codicil showing an intention to revive.* The second method of revival requires the testator to execute with the proper formalities a

---

[38] *In the Goods of Itter, supra,* at p. 133.

[39] *In the Goods of McCabe, supra,* at pp. 96–97; *In the Estate of Zimmer* (1924) 40 T.L.R. 502: see conditional revocation by destruction, *ante,* p. 70.

[40] *In the Goods of Itter, supra.*

[41] *Rogers* v. *Goodenough* (1862) 2 Sw. & Tr. 342; *In the Goods of Steele* (1868) L.R. 1 P. & D. 575, 576–577; *In the Goods of Reade* [1902] P. 75. *Quaere* whether a testator may revive a will which has been destroyed without his knowledge.

[42] See Law Reform Committee, 22nd Report, p. 25 (recommending no change).

[43] [1893] P. 339: see also *Major* v. *Williams* (1843) 3 Curt. 432; *In the Goods of Brown* (1858) 1 Sw. & Tr. 32.

[44] The result would have been different if the testator had destroyed his second will, intending to revoke it *conditionally* on the revival of his first will as regards his realty—the condition would not have been fulfilled and the revocation of his second will would not have been effective, see *ante,* p. 71.

codicil showing an intention to revive the revoked will or codicil. Whether a codicil shows the necessary intention to revive is a question of construction. The intention must

> "appear on the face of the codicil, either by express words referring to a will as revoked and importing an intention to revive the same, or by a disposition of the testator's property inconsistent with any other intention, or by some other expressions conveying to the mind of the Court, with reasonable certainty, the existence of the intention in question."[45]

A codicil does not show an intention to revive a revoked will if it is merely attached to it by a piece of tape.[46]

In construing a codicil the normal rules as to the admission of extrinsic evidence apply.[47] For instance, evidence of the surrounding circumstances is admissible under the "armchair principle" so that the court may ascertain the intention of the testator as expressed in the codicil when it is read in the light of the surrounding circumstances in which it was made.[48] *In the Goods of Davis*[49] is a useful illustration. The testator made a will giving all his estate to Ethel Phoebe Horsley. A year later he married her, thereby revoking the will. Subsequently he wrote on the envelope containing the will, "The herein named Ethel Phoebe Horsley is now my lawful wedded wife," and this writing was duly signed and attested. As evidence of the surrounding circumstances an affidavit by Ethel's sister was admitted, proving that shortly before the testator wrote on the envelope the sister pointed out to him that the will had been revoked by his marriage. The court held that the writing on the envelope was a codicil showing the testator's intention to revive the will because it conveyed to the mind of the court with reasonable certainty the existence of this intention, and both the will and the envelope were accordingly admitted to probate.

(3) *Codicil refers to revoked will by its date.* The typical sequence of events to be considered is:

(i) will A dated January 1, 1978;
(ii) will B dated June 30, 1982, which expressly revoked all former wills;
(iii) codicil "to my will dated the lst day of January 1978 . . . ";
(iv) death of testator.

If the codicil is merely described as a codicil to the testator's last will, but giving the date of will A, the codicil does not revive will A or revoke will B: the reference in the codicil to the date of will A does not show an intention to revive will A.[50] These cases may well be supported on the ground that the description of the will by the codicil was ambiguous,

---

[45] *In the Goods of Steele, supra,* at p. 578.
[46] *Marsh* v. *Marsh,* (1860) 1 Sw. & Tr. 528.
[47] *Post,* pp. 418 *et seq.*
[48] *In the Goods of Steele, supra,* at p. 576; *In the Goods of Davis* [1952] P. 279.
[49] [1952] P. 279: see also *In the Goods of Terrible* (1858) 1 Sw. & Tr. 140.
[50] *In the Goods of May* (1868) L.R. 1 P. & D. 575; *In the Goods of Gordon* [1892] P. 228; *Jane* v. *Jane* (1917) 33 T.L.R. 389; *Goldie* v. *Adam* [1938] P. 85.

will A not being the last will of the testator, or, in fact, his will at all, as it had been revoked.[51]

On the other hand, if the codicil not only refers to will A by date but also refers to the provisions of will A, the codicil shows an intention to revive will A.[52] Probate is granted of will A and the codicil, and also of will B unless will B was revoked as a result of the codicil. In doubtful cases the question to what extent will B was revoked may be left to a court of construction. Will B may be revoked expressly by a revocation clause in the codicil or in will A (which operates as if executed at the time of revival),[53] or impliedly by inconsistent or repetitive provisions in the codicil and will A.[54] If the codicil shows an intention to revive part, but not the whole, of will A, probate is granted of that part of will A and the codicil, and also of will B unless will B was revoked as a result of the codicil.[55]

Usually a codicil refers to a revoked will by its date as the result of a blunder.[56] This could have been avoided by proper precautions if:

  (i) after will B was executed, will A had been clearly marked to show it had been revoked by will B, and
  (ii) the draftsman of the codicil had insisted on having the testator's last will before him.

Effects of revival. Under section 34 of the Wills Act 1837 a revived will is deemed for the purposes of the Act to have been made at the time of its revival.[57] A revived will operates as if it had been executed at that time.[58]

(1) *Will revoked in stages.* Section 22 provides that if a will or codicil is first partly revoked and later wholly revoked, but is subsequently revived, the revival does not extend to the part first revoked unless an intention to the contrary is shown.

(2) *Alteration and incorporation.* Revival may validate an unattested alteration made to the will or codicil before its revival.[59] Similarly revival of a will or codicil may incorporate a document which came into

---

[51] *In the Goods of Whatman* (1864) 34 L.J.P.M. & A. 17.

[52] *In the Goods of Stedham* (1881) 6 P.D. 205; *In the Goods of Dyke* (1881) 6 P.D. 207; *In the Goods of Chilcott* [1897] P. 223.

[53] *Re Pearson* [1963] 1 W.L.R. 1358: but see *Re Rear* [1975] 2 N.Z.L.R. 254, 264 (*quaere* from what date revocation clause speaks): for the effect of republication of a will containing a revocation clause see *post*, p. 81.

[54] *Re Baker* [1929] 1 Ch. 668; *In the Goods of Reynolds* (1873) 3 P. & D. 35.

[55] *In the Estate of Mardon* [1944] P. 109.

[56] "If experience had not shown the fact, it would be almost incredible that mistakes should occur so constantly as they do in so simple a matter as reciting the true date of a will," *per* Lord Penzance in *In the Goods of Steele, supra,* at p. 580.

[57] s.34 may on its proper construction merely refer to the commencement of the Act (*Re Elcom* [1894] 1 Ch. 303, 309) but in *Goonewardene* v. *Goonewardene* [1931] A.C. 647 the Privy Council treated it *obiter* as having general application.

[58] Republication generally has the same effect, *post*, pp. 80–81.

[59] *Neate* v. *Pickard* (1843) 2 *Notes of Cases* 406. Revival, like republication, does not validate a merely deliberative alteration; again the reviving codicil may show the testator was treating the revived will or codicil as unaltered; see *ante*, p. 74.

existence prior to its revival, though the document was not in existence when the will or codicil was first executed.[60]

B. REPUBLICATION

A testator may "republish" a will or codicil.[61] The term "republication" has been an anachronism since section 13 of the Wills Act 1837 made publication[62] of a will unnecessary. It might be better if the term "confirmation" came into general use instead, because this is the sense in which republication has been used since 1837.[63]

The difference between revival and republication is that the former revives a revoked will or codicil whereas the latter confirms an unrevoked will or codicil.

Two methods of republication. A will or codicil may only be republished (i) by its re-execution with the proper formalities[64] or (ii) by a duly executed codicil containing some reference to it.[65] The codicil need not show an intention to confirm the previous will or codicil in the sense in which a codicil is required by section 22 to show an intention to revive a revoked will or codicil. In order to republish a will, a codicil need only contain some reference to the will. Thus a will is republished by a codicil which describes itself as "codicil to my will."[66] From such a brief reference the inference is drawn that, when executing the codicil, the testator considered the will as his will and thereby confirmed it. This has been termed constructive republication. It has the same effect as if the testator expressly confirmed the will, *e.g.* by using the phrase usually found at the end of a codicil, "In all other respects I confirm my will."

Effects of republication. Section 34 of the Wills Act 1837 applies to republication as well as to revival.[67] In general a republished will operates as if it had been executed at the time of its republication.[68]

(1) *Republication must not defeat intention.* However the doctrine of republication is not applied so as to defeat the testator's intention by,

---

[60] Republication has the same effect, *ante*, p. 43.
[61] See generally, J. D. B. Mitchell (1954) 70 L.Q.R. 353.
[62] Publication was a declaration by the testator in the presence of witnesses that the instrument produced to them was his will.
[63] *Berkeley* v. *Berkeley* [1946] A.C. 555, 575–576.
[64] *Dunn* v. *Dunn* (1866) L.R. 1 P. & D. 277.
[65] *Re Smith* (1890) 45 Ch.D. 632 (duly executed paper made no reference to previous will: no republication).
[66] *Re Taylor* (1880) 57 L.J.Ch. 430, 434: see also *Skinner* v. *Ogle* (1845) 1 Rob.Ecc. 363; *Serocold* v. *Hemming* (1758) 2 Lee 490 (revival prior to Wills Act 1837, and cited in *Re Smith, supra*); *Re Harvey* [1947] Ch. 285 (where Vaisey J. said "a codicil described as a codicil to a particular will republishes that will").
[67] See *ante*, p. 79, n. 57.
[68] For the effect of republication of a will which contains an appointment under a special power, which becomes exercisable after the will but before republication, see *Re Blackburn* (1890) 43 Ch.D. 75. For the exception relating to an illegitimate child see *post*, pp. 444–445, and for the exception relating to the age of majority see *post*, p. 446.

for instance, invalidating a gift which was valid at the date of the will.[69] As Barton J. put it in the Irish case of *Re Moore*,[70]

"The authorities . . . lead me to the conclusion that the courts have always treated the principle that republication makes the will speak as if it had been re-executed at the date of the codicil not as a rigid formula or technical rule, but as a useful and flexible instrument for effectuating a testator's intentions, by ascertaining them down to the latest date at which they have been expressed."

(2) *Republication of will containing revocation clause.* The sequence of events in *In the Goods of Rawlins*[71] was:

(i) execution of the will which contained a revocation clause in general terms;
(ii) execution of a codicil to the will;
(iii) the testator deleted one clause in the will and re-executed the will.

The court held that the codicil was not revoked by the republication of the will containing the revocation clause. The will was re-executed so as to give effect to the deletion and it was not the testator's intention to revoke the codicil—"prima facie the re-execution of the will is a confirmation and not a revocation of the codicil, which became part of the instrument."[72]

(3) *Alteration and incorporation.* The effect of republication on an unattested alteration already made to the will or codicil,[73] and on the incorporation of a document which came into existence prior to republication,[74] has already been considered.

(4) *Invalid gift to witness or spouse of witness.* Section 15 of the Wills Act 1837 deprives an attesting witness and his or her spouse of any benefit under a gift in the will. But if the will is republished by a codicil not attested by that witness, this validates the gift.[75]

(5) *Lapse and ademption.* The effect of republication on a gift which has lapsed,[76] or been adeemed,[77] is considered later.

(6) *Date from which a will speaks.* Again the effect of republication on the date from which a will speaks is considered later.[78]

---

[69] *Re Moore* [1907] 1 I.R. 315; *Re Heath's W.T.* [1949] Ch. 170; *Re Park* [1910] 2 Ch. 322.

[70] [1907] 1 I.R. 315, 318: see also *Re Hardyman* [1925] Ch. 287, 291.

[71] (1879) 48 L.J.P. 64: see also *Wade* v. *Nazer* (1848) 1 Rob. 627. If a will is republished by codicil, any alteration already made to the will by codicil between the execution and republication of the will stands (*Crosbie* v. *MacDoual* (1799) 4 Ves. 610; *Green* v. *Tribe* (1878) 9 Ch.D. 231) unless the republishing codicil shows an intention to revive a revoked part of the will (*McLeod* v. *McNab* [1891] A.C. 471).

[72] (1879) 48 L.J.P. 64, 65.

[73] *Ante,* p. 74.

[74] *Ante,* p. 43.

[75] *Post,* p. 335.

[76] *Post,* p. 338.

[77] *Post,* pp. 348–349.

[78] *Post,* pp. 427–428.

CHAPTER 4

INTESTACY

Intestacy is either total or partial.[1] There is a total intestacy where the deceased does not effectively dispose of any beneficial interest in any of his property by will.[2] There is a partial intestacy where the deceased effectively disposes of some, but not all, of the beneficial interest in his property by will.[3]

The main rules relating to intestacy are contained in Part IV of the Administration of Estates Act 1925 which has been amended by the Intestates' Estates Act 1952, the Family Provision Act 1966, the Family Law Reform Act 1969, and the Administration of Justice Act 1977. All references in this chapter to the Administration of Estates Act 1925 are to this Act as thus amended. This chapter deals with total or partial intestacy on deaths occurring after June 30, 1972.[4]

1. TOTAL INTESTACY

A. ADMINISTRATION OF ASSETS

Part III of the Administration of Estates Act 1925 deals with the administration of assets before distribution.

Trust for sale and conversion. Section 33(1) provides that the personal representatives of an intestate shall hold all his property, whether real or personal, which does not consist of money upon trust for sale and conversion into money. The personal representatives have power to postpone sale and conversion for so long as they think proper. This duty to sell and convert is qualified by section 33(1) in two respects:

---

[1] For the rules of private international law governing intestate succession see Dicey and Morris, *The Conflict of Laws* (11th ed., 1987), pp. 1005 *et seq.*; Theobald on *Wills* (14th ed., 1982), pp. 7–8; *Re Collens* [1986] 2 W.L.R. 919.

[2] *Re Skeats* [1936] Ch. 683 (total intestacy where will appointed an executrix but made no disposition of property: intestacy rules applied).

[3] *Post,* p. 96.

[4] The rules of inheritance applicable to realty under the general law in force before 1926 still apply (i) to an unbarred entail (Law of Property Act 1925, s.130(4); Administration of Estates Act 1925, ss.45(2) and 51(4)), and (ii) on the death of a person who was a lunatic of full age at the end of 1925, and who dies without recovering testamentary capacity, as regards realty as to which he died intestate (Administration of Estates Act 1925, s.51(2) and see *Re Bradshaw* [1950] Ch. 582 and *Re Sirett* [1969] 1 W.L.R. 60). For these rules of inheritance see Megarry and Wade, *The Law of Real Property* (5th ed., 1984), pp. 539 *et. seq.*

(i) Any reversionary interest of the intestate must not be sold until it falls into possession, unless the personal representatives see "special reason" for sale. A reversionary interest means "a future interest vested in the intestate at the moment of his death in some specific property, which at that moment is in the possession or enjoyment of some other person."[5] For instance, if at his death the intestate is entitled to his deceased father's estate subject to the prior life interest of his mother who is still living, the intestate's reversionary interest must not be sold until it falls into possession on the death of his mother, unless the personal representatives see special reason for sale.

(ii) Personal chattels[6] of the intestate must not be sold except for special reason, unless required for purposes of administration owing to want of other assets.

The provisions of section 33(1) correspond to the trust for sale and conversion inserted in many wills. The only unusual feature is the second qualification dealing with personal chattels, but of course in a will the testator can insert a specific gift disposing of such of his personal chattels as he wishes to exclude from the trust for sale and conversion in his will.

Payment of debts and expenses. The personal representatives must pay the intestate's funeral, testamentary and administration expenses, debts and other liabilities out of the net money arising from the sale and conversion of his property and his ready money.[7] They have power during the minority of any beneficiary or the subsistence of any life interest to invest any money held by them.[8]

Residuary estate defined. The "residuary estate of the intestate," which is distributable among the persons beneficially entitled on intestacy under Part IV of the Act, means (i) the residue of such money and any investments for the time being representing it, and (ii) any part of the intestate's estate retained unsold and not required for administration purposes.[9]

B. THE SURVIVING SPOUSE

Spouse must survive. The intestate's spouse[10] must survive the intestate in order to take any beneficial interests on intestacy: it is immaterial that the spouse only survives the intestate for a very short time.

Where the intestate and his or her spouse die in circumstances ren-

---

[5] *Re Fisher* [1943] Ch. 377, 383 (moneys payable by instalments after the intestate's death under an insurance policy are not a reversionary interest).

[6] Defined in Administration of Estates Act 1925, s.55(1)(x); for definition, and entitlement of surviving spouse, see *post*, pp. 84 *et seq.*; for enjoyment by infant contingently entitled see s.47(1)(iv).

[7] Administration of Estates Act 1925, s.33(2); s.33(5) does not exclude the application of the rule in *Allhusen* v. *Whittell* (1867) L.R. 4 Eq. 295, for which see *post*, p. 330.

[8] Administration of Estates Act 1925, s.33(3).

[9] *Ibid.* s.33(4).

[10] See *Re Seaford* [1968] P. 53 (no divorce after death).

dering it uncertain which of them survived the other, the general presumption in section 184 of the Law of Property Act 1925[11] that the younger survived the elder does not apply on an intestacy if the spouse is the younger. Instead the younger spouse is presumed not to have survived the older intestate.[12] It follows that, if an old husband and his young wife both die intestate in circumstances rendering it uncertain which of them survived the other, neither of them takes on the intestacy of the other. This is the only exception to the general presumption, which otherwise is applicable where, after 1925, two or more persons have died in circumstances rendering it uncertain which of them survived the other or others. Thus if their child also dies and it is uncertain whether he survived them, the child being younger is presumed to have survived each of them.

Effect of judicial separation. If either spouse dies intestate while a decree of judicial separation is in force and the separation is continuing, the surviving spouse is treated as already dead and takes no beneficial interests on intestacy.[13]

Beneficial interest if intestate leaves issue. The beneficial interest of a surviving spouse (whether a widow or widower) in the residuary estate varies considerably in extent according to the state of the intestate's family at or after his death. Three different situations are dealt with in section 46 of the Act. The first is where the intestate leaves any issue (*i.e.* children, grandchildren or remoter descendants) who attain the age of 18 years or marry under that age.[14] Under this head a surviving spouse takes the following interests:

(1) *The personal chattels absolutely.* The detailed definition of this expression in section 55(1)(x) of the Act reads as follows:

" 'Personal chattels' mean carriages, horses, stable furniture and effects (not used for business purposes), motor cars and accessories (not used for business purposes), garden effects, domestic animals, plate, plated articles, linen, china, glass, books, pictures, prints, furniture, jewellery, articles of household or personal use or ornament, musical and scientific instruments and apparatus, wines, liquors and consumable stores, but do not include any chattels used at the death of the intestate for business purposes nor money or securities for money."

Broadly this definition includes all articles of personal use or ornament and all the contents of the home, but excludes money, securities for money, and chattels used at the death of the intestate for business purposes. A motor car used for both business and private purposes by, for instance, a doctor or solicitor appears to fall outside the definition of personal chattels.

[11] See *post*, pp. 338–340.
[12] Administration of Estates Act 1925, s.46(3).
[13] Matrimonial Causes Act 1973, s.18(2). The surviving spouse may nevertheless apply to the court for reasonable provision under the Inheritance (Provision for Family and Dependants) Act 1975, see Chap. 5.
[14] *Ibid.* s.46(1)(i) and (4) and s.47(1)(i) and (2)(c).

Usually in applying this definition the only question is whether an article comes within the ordinary meaning of the word used[15]—*e.g.* horses,[16] furniture,[17] and jewellery.[18] But user is sometimes relevant because the article must not be used for business purposes[19] and because articles of household or personal use or ornament fall within the definition.[20] The phrase "articles of . . . personal use" has been held to include a 60-foot motor-yacht used by the deceased for pleasure,[21] a stamp collection made by the deceased as a hobby,[22] and a collection of watches[23]: referring to this collection of watches, Russell L.J. in delivering the judgment of the Court of Appeal said,[24] "A watch is in its nature an article of personal use: and in the present case we regard the cherishing [by the deceased] by eye and hand of the collection as well as the wearing of selected items from time to time as bringing them within the definition of articles of personal use."

The statutory definition of "personal chattels" has been criticised[25]: obviously the opening reference to "carriages, horses, stable furniture and effects" has less relevance now than in 1926. However on the whole the definition works reasonably well and it is quite common for a testator by his will to make a gift of "all my personal chattels as defined by section 55(1)(x) of the Administration of Estates Act 1925."

(2) *The fixed net sum with interest.* The fixed net sum is (i) £15,000 if the intestate died after June 30, 1972, (ii) £25,000 if the intestate died after March 14, 1977, (iii) £40,000 if the intestate died after February 28, 1981, or (iv) £75,000 if the intestate died after May 31, 1987.[26] It is payable free of death duties and costs with interest thereon at the specified rate (4 per cent. per annum until September 14, 1977, 7 per cent. per annum until September 30, 1983, and thereafter 6 per cent. per annum[27]) from the date of death until it is paid or appropriated. The payment of both

---

[15] *Re Crispin's W.T.* [1975] Ch. 245, 251.
[16] *Re Hutchinson* [1955] Ch. 255 ("horses" included 12 racehorses used by intestate for recreation by racing them).
[17] *Re Crispin's W.T.* [1975] Ch. 245 ("furniture" included collection of clocks, whether used or stored or on loan to a museum, and whether bought or inherited).
[18] *Re Whitby* [1944] Ch. 210 ("jewellery" included unmounted cut diamonds).
[19] *Re Ogilby* [1942] Ch. 288 (intestate's herd of cattle held not to be personal chattels as used for farming purposes, though at a loss): see R.E.M. (1966) 82 L.Q.R. 18.
[20] *Re Crispin's W.T.* [1975] Ch. 245, 251.
[21] *Re Chaplin* [1950] Ch. 507: see *Re White* [1916] 1 Ch. 172.
[22] *Re Reynold's W.T.* [1966] 1 W.L.R. 19: as to a bought collection see p. 22 and *cf. Re Crispin's W.T.* [1975] Ch. 245, 251–252 and R.E.M. (1966) 82 L.Q.R. 18.
[23] *Re Crispin's W.T., supra,* (collection of clocks and watches worth £50.000).
[24] [1975] Ch. 245, 252.
[25] *Re Chaplin, supra,* ("an omnium gatherum . . . The enumeration of specific articles in the definition is neither happy nor clear"); *Re Reynolds' W.T., supra,* ("the curious collection of terms I find in the definition"). As to chattels subject to hire-purchase agreements see Bicknell (1966) 116 New L.J. 1287.
[26] Family Provision (Intestate Succession) Orders 1972 (No. 916), 1977 (No. 415), 1981 (No. 255), 1987 (No. 799). These orders were made by the Lord Chancellor pursuant to his power to fix the amount of the fixed net sum from time to time by statutory instrument under s.1 of the Family Provision Act 1966.
[27] Intestate Succession (Interest and Capitalisation) Order 1977 (No. 1491), para. 2 and Intestate Succession (Interest and Capitalisation) Order 1977 (Amendment) Order 1983 (No. 1374), para. 2. The Lord Chancellor has power to specify the rate by statutory instrument under s.46(1)(i) and (1A) of the Administration of Estates Act 1925.

the fixed net sum and the interest is charged on the residuary estate but the interest is primarily payable out of the income of the residuary estate. The fixed net sum is often referred to as the statutory legacy: it bears a close resemblance to a general pecuniary legacy given to a surviving spouse by will, with a direction in the will that it is to be paid immediately after the testator's death.

(3) *A life interest in one-half of the balance of the residuary estate, i.e.* the balance after withdrawing the personal chattels and providing for the fixed net sum with interest.[28]

Beneficial interest if intestate leaves no issue but specified relative. This head applies if the intestate leaves no issue who attain the age of 18 years or marry under that age, but leaves one or more of the following specified relatives, *i.e.* a parent, or a brother or sister of the whole blood, or issue of a brother or sister of the whole blood who (in the case of the brother or sister or issue) attain the age of 18 years or marry under that age.[29] Under this head a surviving spouse takes the following interests:

(1) *The personal chattels absolutely.*

(2) *The fixed net sum with interest.* In this case the fixed net sum is (i) £40,000 if the intestate died after June 30, 1972, (ii) £55,000 if the intestate died after March 14, 1977, (iii) £85,000 if the intestate died after February 28, 1981, or (iv) £125,000 if the intestate died after May 31, 1987[30]: the same interest is payable as under head 1 above.

(3) *One-half of the balance absolutely.* Under head 1 the surviving spouse is entitled for life to the *income* from one-half of the balance of the residuary estate whereas under this head the surviving spouse is entitled to the *capital* of one-half of that balance.[31]

Beneficial interest if intestate leaves no issue and no specified relative. If the intestate leaves no issue who attain the age of 18 years or marry under that age and no specified relative (as described above), the surviving spouse takes *the entire residuary estate absolutely.*[32]

The extent of the beneficial interest of a surviving spouse may depend on future events after the intestate's death. If the intestate leaves at his death an only child aged six years and an only nephew (the son of the intestate's deceased brother of the whole blood) aged four

---

[28] Subject to the beneficial interest of the surviving spouse the residuary estate is held on the statutory trusts for the issue of the intestate, see *post*, p. 90.

[29] Administration of Estates Act 1925, ss.46(1)(i) and 47(2)(*a*), (*b*) and (4).

[30] *Supra*, n. 26.

[31] The specified relatives are entitled to the other half in the order set out, *post*, pp. 93–94.

[32] Administration of Estates Act 1925, ss.46(1)(i) and 47(2)(*b*) and (4).

years, but no other relatives, whether head 1, 2 or 3 applies depends on future events. At the least the surviving spouse must take the interests set out under head 1. If the child dies unmarried under the age of 18 years, the surviving spouse takes the larger interests set out under head 2. If the nephew also dies unmarried under the age of 18 years, the surviving spouse takes the entire residuary estate absolutely under head 3.

Often the statutory legacy under heads 1 or 2 exhausts the residuary estate of the intestate and in consequence the surviving spouse alone benefits on intestacy, even though head 3 is not applicable.

Election to have life interest redeemed. A surviving spouse who is entitled to a life interest in part of the residuary estate under head 1 may elect to have it redeemed and to receive its capital value instead from the personal representatives.[33] If that part of the residuary estate includes any property not in possession, the right to elect for redemption is only exercisable in respect of the life interest in the property in possession.[34] The capital value is to be reckoned by reference to published tables, which take into account the age of the surviving spouse and the prevailing yield on medium-term Government Stocks.[35]

The surviving spouse must elect for redemption within 12 months from the first general grant of representation[36] to the intestate's estate (unless the court extends this time limit)[37] by giving written notice to the personal representatives[38] or, if the surviving spouse is the sole personal representative, to the Senior Registrar of the Family Division of the High Court.[39]

Redemption frees the residuary estate from the surviving spouse's life interest but diminishes the residuary estate by the capital value of the life interest and the costs of the transaction. The surviving spouse receives capital instead of income.[40] The same result can be achieved by agreement between the surviving spouse and the intestate's issue (assuming that all parties are *sui juris*) without observing the statutory requirements.

Acquisition of the matrimonial home. The Second Schedule to the Intestates' Estates Act 1952 contains three different provisions which make it easier for the surviving spouse of an intestate to acquire "the

---

[33] Administration of Estates Act 1925, s.47A: the personal representatives also pay the costs of the transaction. For the effect of election on inheritance tax see Inheritance Tax Act 1984, s.145.

[34] s.47A(3) and see s.49(4).

[35] s.47A(3A) and (3B); Intestate Succession (Interest and Capitalisation) Order 1977 (No. 1491).

[36] s.47A(9).

[37] s.47A(5).

[38] s.47A(6).

[39] s.47A(7) as amended by Administration of Justice Act 1970, Sched. 2, para. 4 and Supreme Court Act 1981, Sched. 5. In this case the form of notice is prescribed and must be filed in the Principal Registry or in the district probate registry from which the grant issued (N.C.Prob. Rules 1987, r. 56).

[40] A surviving spouse who is an infant may elect but the capital value is not to be paid to the infant, s.47A(8): see *post*, p. 363.

matrimonial home."[41] The Act uses this expression in an unusually
wide sense. All three provisions apply to the intestate's interest in a
dwelling-house[42] in which the surviving spouse was resident at the
intestate's death, without any requirement as to residence by the intestate.

(1) *Power of appropriation enlarged.* Personal representatives have a
statutory power to appropriate any asset of a deceased's estate in or
towards satisfaction of any interest in his estate.[43] This statutory power
cannot, however, be used if the value of the asset to be appropriated
exceeds the beneficiary's interest in the estate. The Second Schedule
creates a limited exception by permitting the appropriation of an interest in a dwelling-house in which the surviving spouse was resident at
the intestate's death, partly in satisfaction of an interest of the surviving
spouse in the intestate's estate, and partly in return for the payment of
"equality money" by the surviving spouse to the personal representatives.[44]

(2) *Right to appropriation of matrimonial home.* Normally a beneficiary
who wishes to take a particular asset of the estate cannot require the
personal representatives to exercise this statutory power in his favour.
The Second Schedule gives the surviving spouse a special right to
require the personal representatives to appropriate the intestate's interest in a dwelling-house in which the surviving spouse was resident at
the intestate's death: the appropriation is to be made in or towards
satisfaction of any absolute interest[45] of the surviving spouse in the
intestate's estate, or partly in satisfaction of that interest and partly in
return for the payment of equality money by the surviving spouse.[46]
Thus this special right applies, whether the value of the intestate's
interest in the dwelling-house is equal to, or is worth less, or more, than
that absolute interest of the surviving spouse.[47]

(a) INTEREST IN DWELLING-HOUSE. The intestate's interest in the dwelling-house may be freehold or leasehold. However this special right
does not apply to a tenancy which would expire, or be determinable by
the landlord by notice, within two years from the intestate's death
unless the surviving spouse would thereby be entitled to acquire the
freehold or an extended lease under the Leasehold Reform Act 1967.[48]

---

[41] Intestates' Estates Act 1952, s.5.
[42] This includes part of a building occupied as a separate dwelling, Sched. 2, para. 1(5);
see also Sched. 2, para. 7(1).
[43] Administration of Estates Act 1925, s.41: see *post*, p. 365.
[44] Sched. 2, para. 5(2): see *Re Phelps* [1980] Ch. 275, 278 ("a transaction which in essence
is partly appropriation and partly sale becomes an appropriation").
[45] This includes the fixed net sum and the capital value of a life interest which the surviving spouse has elected under s.47A to have redeemed, Sched. 2, para. 1(4).
[46] *Re Phelps* [1980] Ch. 275.
[47] *Ibid.* at p. 279.
[48] Sched. 2, para. 1(2); Leasehold Reform Act 1967, s.7(8). The personal representatives
may appropriate a short tenancy to which this special right does not apply, but cannot be
required to do so.

Normally the consent of the court to the exercise of this special right is not required.[49]

(b) TIME LIMIT AND MODE OF EXERCISE. This special right must be exercised within 12 months from the first general grant of representation to the intestate's estate (unless the court extends this time limit)[50] by giving written notice to the personal representatives.[51] It cannot be exercised after the death of the surviving spouse.[52] During this period of 12 months the personal representatives must not without the written consent of the surviving spouse sell or otherwise dispose of the intestate's interest in the dwelling-house, unless this is necessary for the purposes of administration owing to want of other assets.[53] However, prior to appropriation this special right does not give the surviving spouse any equitable interest in the dwelling-house.[54]

(c) VALUATION. Before deciding whether to exercise this special right the surviving spouse may require the personal representatives to have the intestate's interest in the dwelling-house valued and to inform the surviving spouse of the result of the valuation.[55] It is the normal practice to have such a valuation made for the purposes of an appropriation. The intestate's interest in the dwelling-house is to be appropriated at its value at the time of appropriation, and not at the time of the intestate's death.[56]

(3) *Purchase of matrimonial home.* Normally a purchase of an asset from the estate by a personal representative is voidable at the instance of any beneficiary.[57] The Second Schedule creates a limited exception by providing that this rule shall not prevent a surviving spouse, who is one of two or more personal representatives, from purchasing from the estate an interest in a dwelling-house in which the surviving spouse was resi-

---

[49] In four cases the surviving spouse may not exercise the special right without an order of the court, which must be satisfied that its exercise is not likely to diminish the value of the other assets in the residuary estate or make them more difficult to dispose of—*viz.* if the dwelling-house (i) forms part of a building the whole of which is comprised in the residuary estate, or (ii) is held with agricultural land which is so comprised, or (iii) as to the whole or part was at the intestate's death used as a hotel or lodging house, or (iv) as to part was at the intestate's death used for non-domestic purposes; Sched. 2, paras. 2 and 4(2).

[50] Sched. 2, para. 3(1)(*a*) and (3).

[51] Sched. 2, para. 3(1)(*c*). If the surviving spouse is one of the personal representatives, notice must be given to the other personal representatives: if the surviving spouse is the sole personal representative no notice is required.

[52] Sched. 2, para. 3(1)(*b*).

[53] Sched. 2, para. 4(1), (3) and (5). The restriction on sale does not apply if the surviving spouse is a personal representative.

[54] *Lall* v. *Lall* [1965] 1 W.L.R. 1249: see also Sched. 2, para. 4(5) which protects a purchaser from the personal representatives though no such consent has been given.

[55] Sched. 2, para. 3(2): see also Administration of Estates Act 1925, s.41(3).

[56] *Re Collins* [1975] 1 W.L.R. 309 (value of house was £4,2000 at intestate's death in 1972 and £8,000 at hearing of case in 1974).

[57] See Snell's *Principles of Equity* (28th ed., 1982), pp. 247 *et seq.*

dent at the intestate's death.[58] The exception does not apply if the surviving spouse is the sole personal representative.[59]

C. The Issue

Subject to the beneficial interests of the surviving spouse (if any), the residuary estate is held on the "statutory trusts" for the issue of the intestate.[60]

The statutory trusts. Under the statutory trusts such of the children of the intestate as are living[61] at the intestate's death are beneficially entitled, if more than one in equal shares, subject to three qualifications:

(i) *subject to representation, i.e.* subject to the rule that such of the issue of a deceased child as are living[61] at the intestate's death take that child's share, if more than one in equal shares, *per stirpes*[62]; and

(ii) *subject to the rule that no child or other issue is entitled to a vested interest until he or she attains the age of 18 years or marries under that age;* and

(iii) *subject to hotchpot.*[63]

To consider an example:

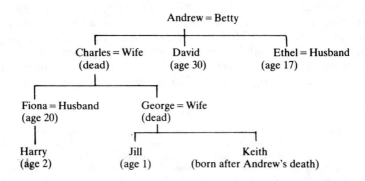

Andrew died intestate on January 1, 1988, leaving his widow Betty. His

---

[58] Sched. 2, para. 5(1).

[59] Where the exception is not applicable the surviving spouse needs the leave of the court for his purchase: alternatively the surviving spouse may purchase the interests of the other beneficiaries from them if they are *sui juris*. The surviving spouse may well prefer to exercise the power of, or the right to, appropriation.

[60] ss.46(1) and 47(1).

[61] References to a child (or issue) living at the intestate's death include a child (or issue) *en ventre sa mère* at the death, s.55(2).

[62] *Per stirpes* means through each stock of descent. No issue take whose parent is living at the intestate's death and so capable of taking, s.47(1)(i).

[63] *Post,* p. 91.

son Charles and his grandson George predeceased him. His great-grandson Keith was *en ventre sa mère* at Andrew's death and is accordingly treated as then living.[64] Under the intestacy rules Andrew's residuary estate is distributed or held in trust as follows:

(i) His surviving spouse Betty takes the personal chattels absolutely, £75,000 with interest, and a life interest in one-half of the balance of the residuary estate. Unless Betty's life interest is redeemed, one-half of the balance of the residuary estate must be held by the personal representatives upon trust for Betty during her life. Subject to Betty's life interest, the balance of the residuary estate is held on the statutory trusts for Andrew's issue.

(ii) Under the statutory trusts David (having attained 18 years) and Ethel (having married) each take vested one-third shares. Fiona, Jill and Keith take Charles' one-third share *per stirpes*, with the result that Fiona takes a vested one-sixth share, and Jill and Keith (taking in place of George) will each take a vested one-twelfth share if each attains the age of 18 years or marries under that age.[65] If Jill and Keith both die unmarried under that age, Fiona will take the whole of Charles' one-third share. Harry takes nothing because his mother Fiona is living at Andrew's death and so is capable of taking.[66]

Hotchpot. The hotchpot rule in section 47(1)(iii) requires certain benefits conferred on his *child* by the intestate during his lifetime to be brought into account on the division of his residuary estate into shares under the statutory trusts. For example, if during his lifetime the deceased gave £4,000 to his elder child on marriage, and later the deceased dies intestate, a widower, leaving a residuary estate worth £16,000 which is divisible between his two children (both of full age) under the statutory trusts, under section 47(1)(iii) the elder child receives £6,000 and the younger child £10,000. The benefit is to be "brought into account" but there is no obligation to refund it to the estate. If the deceased had given £20,000 to his elder child on marriage, the younger child would receive the entire £16,000 on intestacy but the elder child would be entitled to retain the £20,000.

(1) *Benefits to be brought into hotchpot.* Section 47(1)(iii) applies to "any money or property[67] which, by way of advancement or on the marriage of a child of the intestate, has been paid to such child by the intestate or settled by the intestate for the benefit of such child (including any life or less interest and including property covenanted to be paid or settled)."

---

[64] See *supra*, n. 61.

[65] Subject to Betty's prior life interest in one-half, the income and half the capital of the respective shares of Jill and Keith may be applied during infancy for their respective benefit under the statutory powers of maintenance and advancement; s.47(1)(ii); Trustee Act 1925, ss.31 and 32 (s.31 as amended by Family Law Reform Act 1969, s.1(3) and (4), Sched. 1, Pt. I and Sched. 3, para. 5(1)): for these powers see Snell's *Principles of Equity* (28th ed., 1982), pp. 273 *et. seq.*

[66] *Ante*, n. 62.

[67] "Property" includes a thing in action and any interest in real or personal property, Administration of Estates Act 1925, s.55(1)(xvii).

Property transferred directly to a child by the intestate (*e.g.* a gift of a house on marriage) falls within this definition despite the omission of any reference to property being "transferred" to the child.[68]

To satisfy this definition the payment or settlement must be made by the intestate on the marriage of his child or "by way of advancement," *i.e.* for the purpose of establishing his child in life or of making a permanent provision for him. Payments made for establishing a child in a profession or in business are made by way of advancement.[69] On the other hand payments made for education, or maintenance, or by way of temporary assistance are not so made.[70] In the absence of evidence as to the purpose for which a payment was made, a gift to a child of a sum sufficiently substantial in itself to be in the nature of a permanent provision is prima facie an advancement.[71] Again a transfer by a mother of valuable company shares to two of her adult children, giving them effective control of the family business, constituted an advancement because it made permanent provision for them and it was immaterial that they were already well established in the family business and were not in any particular need.[72] The onus of proving that a payment or transfer was "by way of advancement" lies on the party who asserts this.[73]

In the case of a settlement for the benefit of a child, the benefit to be brought into hotchpot depends on the interests arising under the settlement. If the settlement is on the child for life, with remainder to that child's children absolutely, the capital of the settled property (and not merely the child's life interest) must be brought into hotchpot.[74]

(2) *Against what share on intestacy.* Such benefits are brought into account against the child's share "or the share which such child would have taken if living at the death of the intestate."[75] A deceased child's issue must therefore bring into hotchpot benefits conferred on the child by the intestate. If, for instance, in the example already considered[76] the elder child had predeceased the intestate, the elder child's issue[77] would have received £6,000 and the younger child £10,000.

---

[68] *Hardy* v. *Shaw* [1976] Ch. 82 (gift of company shares by mother to two of her adult children: "it is common ground that a transfer of [company] shares is within the expression 'money or property . . . paid' ": see also E. C. Ryder (1973) 26 C.L.P. 208, 209; *Re Reeve* [1935] Ch. 110, 117, *Re Young* [1951] Ch. 185, 188.

[69] *Taylor* v. *Taylor* (1875) L.R. 20 Eq. 155 (payment of admission fee to Inn of Court for intending barrister and for purchase of mining plant for son's business held advancements).

[70] *Taylor* v. *Taylor, supra,* (payment of fee to special pleader for intending barrister to read in chambers, payments made to curate to assist him in his living expenses, and payment of army officer's debts held not advancements); *Hatfield* v. *Minet* (1878) 8 Ch.D. 136 (annuities paid to daughters for maintenance held not advancements).

[71] *Re Hayward* [1957] Ch. 528 (nominations amounting to £507 in favour of son aged 43; held not prima facie an advancement).

[72] *Hardy* v. *Shaw, supra.*

[73] *Hardy* v. *Shaw, supra* at p. 87.

[74] *Re Grover's W.T.* [1971] Ch. 169, 174.

[75] s.47(1)(iii).

[76] *Ante,* p. 91.

[77] *i.e.* issue entitled who attained the age of 18 years or married under that age.

(3) *At what valuation.* The value of such benefits is "to be reckoned as at the death of the intestate."[78] Probably the intestate's residuary estate is also to be valued for this purpose as at the death of the intestate, for the sake of consistency: the amount actually available at distribution can then be distributed in the proportions calculated by reference to a notional distribution at death.[79]

(4) *Contrary intention.* This hotchpot rule is excluded by "any contrary intention (on the part of the intestate) expressed or appearing from the circumstances of the case."[80] The test of contrary intention "is not objective—that is, if the intestate had thought of everything, what would her intention be likely to have been—but *subjective*, that is, looking at all the circumstances, do they require an inference that her intention was that the gift should not be brought into hotchpot" on her death?[81] The onus of proving a contrary intention on the part of the intestate lies on the party who asserts it.[82]

D. The Other Relatives

If no issue of the intestate attains a vested interest, then, subject to the beneficial interests of the surviving spouse (if any), the residuary estate of the intestate is held in trust for the relatives of the intestate in the order set out below.[83] Any person who takes a vested interest under a particular paragraph excludes any person falling within a subsequent paragraph.

1. Parents who survive the intestate take in equal shares absolutely; if only one survives the intestate, that parent takes absolutely.

2. Brothers and sisters of the whole blood of the intestate, on the statutory trusts. The statutory trusts applicable under this paragraph (and also under paragraphs 3, 5 and 6 below) are the same as those for the intestate's issue[84] except that the hotchpot rule does not apply.[85] The result under this paragraph is (i) that such of the issue of a deceased brother or sister as are living at the intestate's death take the deceased brother's or sister's share, if more than one in equal shares, *per stirpes,* and (ii) that no brother or sister, or issue of a deceased brother or sister, is entitled to a vested interest until he or she attains the age of 18 years or marries under that age.

The specified relatives[86] end at this point. Relatives within para-

---

[78] s.47(1)(iii): see *Re Reeve* [1935] Ch. 110 (intestate's life interest surrendered to children: its value at his death was nil): J. T. Farrand (1961) 25 Conv.(N.S.) 468, 478.

[79] See *Re Hargreaves* (1903) 88 L.T. 100; J. T. Farrand, *ibid.* at pp. 480–489 (giving examples).

[80] s.47(1)(iii).

[81] *Per* Goff J. in *Hardy* v. *Shaw* [1976] Ch. 82, 89.

[82] *Hardy* v. *Shaw, supra,* at p. 87.

[83] s.46(1).

[84] s.47(3); *ante* p. 90.

[85] *Ante,* p. 91.

[86] *Ante,* p. 86.

graphs 1 or 2 may take even though the intestate left a surviving spouse,[87] but relatives within any of the later paragraphs take nothing if the intestate left a surviving spouse.

3. Brothers and sisters of the half blood of the intestate, on the statutory trusts.

4. Grandparents who survive the intestate take in equal shares absolutely; if only one survives the intestate that grandparent takes absolutely.

5. Uncles and aunts of the whole blood, on the statutory trusts. Such an uncle or aunt must be a brother or sister of the whole blood of a parent of the intestate: thus an uncle's, or aunt's, spouse is excluded, although usually called aunt or uncle.

6. Uncles and aunts of the half blood, on the statutory trusts. Such an uncle or aunt must be a brother or sister of the half blood of a parent of the intestate.

E. BONA VACANTIA

If the intestate leaves no surviving spouse, and no issue or other relative of the intestate attains a vested interest under the rules set out above, the Crown[88] takes the residuary estate of the intestate as *bona vacantia*.[89] The Crown in its discretion may provide thereout for dependants of the intestate, whether or not related to him, and for other persons for whom the intestate might reasonably have been expected to make provision.[90]

F. ADOPTED, LEGITIMATED AND ILLEGITIMATE CHILDREN

Adopted child. Under the Adoption Act 1976 an adopted child is treated for purposes of intestacy as the legitimate child of the married couple who adopted him (or, in any other case, as the legitimate child of his adopter), and not as the child of his natural parents.[91] A child adopted by a married couple is therefore treated as the brother or sister of the whole blood of any other child, or adopted child, of both the spouses. In any other case, the adopted child is treated as the brother or sister of the half blood of any other child, or adopted child, of the adopter. The Act applies to an adoption order made by a court in any

---

[87] If the intestate left a surviving spouse the other half of the balance of the residuary estate (*ante,* p. 86) is held in trust for relatives within paras. 1 or 2 in that order.

[88] Or Duchy of Lancaster or Duke of Cornwall.

[89] s.46(1)(vi).

[90] s.46(1)(vi): see generally, Ing, *Bona Vacantia*; Chatterton (1987) 84 L.S.Gaz. 3315.

[91] s.39: as to adoption by one of the child's natural parents see s.39(3), and as to protection of personal representatives see s.45. In the case of a death intestate before January 1, 1976, the Adoption Act 1958, ss.16 and 17 and provisions containing references to those sections continue to apply, Sched. 2, para. 6.

part of the United Kingdom, the Isle of Man or the Channel Islands,[92] and to certain overseas adoptions.[93]

Legitimated child. Under the Legitimacy Act 1976 a legitimated person (and any other person) is entitled to take any interest on intestacy as if the legitimated person had been born legitimate.[94]

Illegitimate child. Of course an illegitimate child takes on the intestacy of his spouse or issue and similarly his spouse or issue take on his intestacy. But, at common law, as regards ancestors and collaterals an illegitimate child was not put on the same footing on intestacy as a legitimate child.[95] Exceptionally under section 14 of the Family Law Reform Act 1969, on a death intestate after 1969:

(i) An illegitimate child (or his legitimate issue if he is dead) takes on the intestacy of each of his parents as if he had been born legitimate.[96] For this purpose he is put on an equal footing with the legitimate issue of each of his parents.
(ii) Each of his parents takes on the intestacy of the illegitimate child as if he had been born legitimate.

Both these rights of intestate succession depend solely on proof of parentage[97] and it is, for instance, immaterial that the father never supported or recognised the illegitimate child as his before either of them died. These rights of intestate succession under section 14 are limited in their scope. Thus an illegitimate child does not take on the intestacy of his "brothers or sisters," "grandparents," or "uncles or aunts," and likewise none of them takes on the intestacy of the illegitimate child: if an illegitimate child dies intestate without leaving a surviving spouse, issue or parent, his estate passes as *bona vacantia* to the Crown.[98]

Section 18 of the Family Law Reform Act 1987 reverses the common law rule if the intestate dies after April 3, 1988.[99] Under section 18 references to any relationship between two persons are to be construed without regard to whether the father and mother of either of them (or of any person through whom the relationship is deduced)

---

[92] The Adoption Act 1958, ss.16 and 17 only applied to an adoption order made in the Isle of Man or Channel Islands on a death intestate after July 15, 1964.

[93] ss.38(1) and 72(2): for the relevant rules of private international law see Dicey and Morris, *The Conflict of Laws* (11th ed. 1987), pp. 881 *et seq.*

[94] Legitimacy Act 1976, ss.5(1)–(4) and 10(1): as to posthumous legitimation see s.5(6) and as to protection of personal representatives see s.7. In the case of a death intestate before January 1, 1976, the Legitimacy Act 1926, ss.3–5 continues to have effect, Legitimacy Act 1976, Sched. 1, para. 2(1). For the relevant rules of private international law see Dicey and Morris, *op. cit.* pp. 860 *et seq.*

[95] Legitimacy Act 1926, s.9 (now repealed) gave limited rights of intestate succession between a mother and her illegitimate child on deaths before 1970.

[96] For succession to an entail see *post*, pp. 445–446.

[97] Family Law Reform Act 1969, s.14(4) raises a presumption that an illegitimate child was not survived by his father unless the father proves the contrary: see also s.17 for special protection of personal representatives. For proof of parentage see *Re Trott* [1980] C.L.Y. 1259.

[98] *Ante*, p. 94.

[99] Family Law Reform Act 1987 (Commencement No. 1) Order 1988 (S.I. 1988 No. 425).

were married to each other at any time. Thus, on a death after April 3, 1988, an illegitimate child is entitled to take on the intestacy of his brothers or sisters, grandparents, or uncles or aunts, and likewise they are entitled to take on the intestacy of the illegitimate child.[1]

2. PARTIAL INTESTACY

A partial intestacy arises where the deceased effectively disposes of some, but not all, of the beneficial interest in his property by will. A partial intestacy differs from a total intestacy in two main respects:

A. The intestacy rules take effect subject to the provisions contained in the will. Thus the will prevails over the intestacy rules.
B. Two more hotchpot rules apply on a partial intestacy. These hotchpot rules require a surviving spouse and any issue of the deceased to bring into hotchpot beneficial interests acquired under his will.

A. The Will Prevails over the Intestacy Rules

1. Rules as to administration on intestacy. Section 33(7) of the Administration of Estates Act 1925 provides that section 33 "has effect subject to the provisions contained in the will."

(1) *Trust for sale and conversion.* Section 33(1) enacts that "on the death of a person intestate as to any real or personal estate" such estate shall be held by his personal representatives upon trust for sale and conversion into money.[2] The section imposes an immediate trust for sale at the death of the deceased.

Section 33(1) does not apply to an asset of the deceased's estate if the deceased effectively disposes of some beneficial interest (*e.g.* a life interest) in the whole of that asset by his will.[3] Again section 33(1) does not apply to an asset held upon an express trust for sale imposed by the deceased's will: this express trust for sale excludes the statutory trust for sale imposed by section 33(1) because there cannot be two subsisting trusts for sale at the same time.[4]

On the other hand, section 33(1) applies to an asset if the deceased dies wholly intestate as to that asset. Section 33(1) also applies to a share in an asset of the deceased's estate if the deceased dies wholly intestate

---

[1] Family Law Reform Act 1987, s.18(2) raises a presumption that an illegitimate child was not survived by his father, or by any person related to the child only through his father, unless the contrary is shown: see also s.20 (no special protection for personal representatives).

[2] For the sale of reversionary interests and personal chattels see *ante*, pp. 82–83.

[3] *Re McKee* [1931] 2 Ch. 145, 159, 160 and 165; *Re Plowman* [1943] Ch. 269.

[4] *Re McKee, supra,* esp. at pp. 159 and 165–166; *Re Taylor's Estate* [1969] 2 Ch. 245: see *post*, pp. 312–313.

as to that share and no trust for sale is imposed on that asset by the will.[5]

In *Re McKee*[6] the deceased by his will made certain bequests and gave his residuary estate to his trustee upon trust for sale and conversion, and after payment of his funeral and testamentary expenses, debts and legacies, to stand possessed of the net residue upon trust for his wife for life and after her death for his brothers and sisters who survived his wife. None of his brothers or sisters did so and there was a partial intestacy. The Court of Appeal held that section 33 did not apply to any asset of the deceased's estate because the deceased had by his will effectively disposed of a life interest for his wife in his entire estate. Alternatively, the express trust for sale in the will excluded the statutory trust for sale imposed by section 33(1).

(2) *Payment of debts, expenses and legacies.* Section 33(2) directs the personal representatives out of the net money arising from the sale and conversion directed by section 33(1) and the deceased's ready money to pay all such funeral, testamentary and administration expenses, debts and other liabilities as are properly payable thereout under the rules of administration contained in Part III of the Act, and out of the residue of the money to set aside a fund sufficient to provide for any pecuniary legacies given by the will. The provisions of the will may exclude or vary this rule. The effect of this rule is considered later.[7]

2. Rules as to distribution on intestacy. Where there is a partial intestacy section 49(1) makes Part IV of the Act applicable to any of the deceased's property (or interest in that property[8]) not effectively disposed of by his will, subject (i) to the provisions contained in the will[9] and (ii) to the two additional hotchpot rules.

Part IV of course includes sections 46 and 47,[10] which specify the persons beneficially entitled on a total or partial intestacy. The personal representative of the deceased, subject to his rights and powers for purposes of administration, is a trustee of such undisposed of property for the persons beneficially entitled on intestacy.[11]

Section 49(1) operates as if the Legislature had inserted at the end of every deceased's will an ultimate gift of any undisposed of property (or interest in property) in favour of the persons beneficially entitled on

---

[5] *Re Berrey's W.T.* [1959] 1 W.L.R. 30 (gift of residue by T to A, B, C and D equally; B predeceased T, causing B's share to lapse and go as on T's intestacy: held s.33(1) applied to B's share). A gift of land by will to persons as tenants in common imposes a statutory trust for sale, Law of Property Act 1925, s.34(3).

[6] [1931] 2 Ch. 145.

[7] As to expenses, debts and liabilities see *post*, pp. 251 *et seq.* and as to legacies see *post*, p. 310.

[8] "Property" in s.49(1) includes any interest in real or personal property, s.55(1)(xvii): see *Re McKee, supra*, at pp. 161 and 163.

[9] *Post*, p. 98.

[10] The references to "intestate" in ss.46 and 47 include a person who leaves a will but dies intestate as to some beneficial interest in his real or personal estate, s.55(1)(vi).

[11] s.49(1)(*b*), which adds the qualification "unless it appears by the will that the personal representative is intended to take such part beneficially." The word "expressly" in s.49(1)(*b*) may be a misprint for "effectively."

intestacy.[12] Section 49(1) is always applicable on a partial intestacy, whether the deceased dies wholly intestate as to a particular asset or intestate as to some beneficial interest in that asset. Thus section 49(1) applies irrespective of whether section 33(1) imposes a statutory trust for sale.

In *Re Bowen-Buscarlet's Will Trusts*[13] the deceased by his will directed his trustees to hold his residuary estate upon trust for his widow during her life, but failed to direct what was to happen thereafter. Accordingly there was a partial intestacy. The deceased died in 1967 leaving his widow and a married daughter. As the deceased left issue, under the intestacy rules the widow was entitled to the personal chattels absolutely, the statutory legacy with interest, and a life interest in one-half of the balance of the residuary estate.[14] However, this life interest under the intestacy rules failed because the widow could not enjoy it after her own death when her life interest under the will would end.[15] Disregarding the personal chattels,[16] the deceased's residuary estate was therefore held:

(i) *under the will,* upon trust for the widow during her life, and, subject to her life interest,

(ii) *under the intestacy rules,* subject to providing for the payment of the statutory legacy[17] with interest to the widow, on trust for the daughter who was absolutely entitled under the statutory trusts for the intestate's issue.

Goff J. held that the widow was entitled to *immediate* payment of the statutory legacy[17] with interest, because her interests in it under (i) and (ii) merged.[18] Subject to this payment, the income of the remainder of the residuary estate was payable under the will to the widow during her life. Subject to the widow's life interest, the daughter was absolutely entitled under the intestacy rules to the remainder of the residuary estate.

Re Bowen-Buscarlet's Will Trusts shows how capital undisposed of by the will passes to the persons beneficially entitled on intestacy. Income undisposed of by the will similarly passes to those persons.[19]

3. Subject to the provisions contained in the will. Both section 33 and section 49(1) take effect "subject to the provisions contained in the will." This qualification refers to effective provisions and not to provisions which become inoperative for any reason.[20]

---

[12] *Re Mckee, supra,* at p. 161.
[13] [1972] Ch. 463: see *Re Buttle's W.T.* [1977] 1 W.L.R. 1200.
[14] *Ante,* pp. 84–86.
[15] *Re McKee, supra,* at p. 162.
[16] The report does not state whether the deceased specifically disposed of his personal chattels by his will. If he did, the personal chattels would not pass under the intestacy rules, *ibid.* If he did not, the wife in *Re Bowen-Buscarlet's W.T.* would be entitled to immediate delivery of the personal chattels, see *Re Douglas' W.T.* [1959] 1 W.L.R. 744, 748.
[17] As reduced (under the hotchpot rule) by the actuarial value of her life interest in the residuary estate, valued as at the date of the deceased's death, *post,* p. 100.
[18] Goff J. followed *Re Douglas' W.T., supra,* and rightly rejected the unsatisfactory decision of the C.A. on this point in *Re McKee, supra,* where the point was not argued.
[19] *Re Plowman* [1943] Ch. 269 (undisposed of income of residuary estate).
[20] *Re Thornber* [1937] Ch. 29.

(1) *Inoperative provision.* A provision in a will does not take effect if the gift in the will to which it is ancillary fails. In *Re Thornber*[21] the deceased by his will directed his trustees to pay an annuity to his wife out of the income of his residuary estate, and to accumulate any surplus income for 21 years from his death or until his wife's earlier death, and at the expiration of the accumulation period to hold his residuary estate and the accumulations upon trust for his children. The deceased died childless in 1933. The Court of Appeal held that the direction to accumulate surplus income was inoperative because the trust of the accumulations for the children had failed. Under section 49(1) the surplus income passed to the persons beneficially entitled on intestacy free from the inoperative provision for accumulation.

A provision may become inoperative by disclaimer. In *Re Sullivan*[22] the deceased by his will gave his residuary estate to his trustees upon trust to pay the income to his widow during her life and after her death upon trust for his children. The deceased owned the musical copyrights of Sir Arthur Sullivan and the will contained a provision that any royalties received by his trustees should be treated as capital and not income. The deceased died childless in 1928. Under the intestacy rules then in force the widow was entitled to the personal chattels absolutely, a statutory legacy with interest, and a life interest in the whole of the balance of the residuary estate. Moreover under the intestacy rules royalties are treated as income and not capital.[23] Maugham J. decided that, if the widow disclaimed her life interest under the will, the provision in the will as to royalties would become inoperative as the deceased had died childless. He said, "In the present case the provision as to royalties was inserted in the will in order to diminish the widow's life interest for the benefit of children who, in the event, do not exist. It was clearly not inserted in order to determine the nature of interests to be taken in property in respect of which he died or might die intestate."[24] The provision as to royalties would therefore not apply to the life interest taken by the widow on intestacy under section 49(1) if she disclaimed her life interest under the will.

(2) *Provision intended to operate on intestacy.* A deceased may insert in his will a provision intended to operate on his intestacy. Romer L.J. suggested a suitable clause in *Re Thornber*,[25] "In the event of any of my property being undisposed of by this my will and the provisions of section 49 taking effect I direct that any such property shall be dealt with" as follows. . . . In *Re Sullivan* the deceased could have inserted such a clause in his will so as to make the provision as to royalties applicable on his intestacy, irrespective of whether he left any children benefiting under the will.

---

[21] *Ibid.*

[22] [1930] 1 Ch. 84.

[23] Administration of Estates Act 1925, s.33(5), which excludes apportionment of income under the rule in *Howe* v. *Earl of Dartmouth* (1802) 7 Ves. 137, but see *Re Fisher* [1943] Ch. 377.

[24] *Re Sullivan, supra,* at p. 87.

[25] [1937] Ch. 29, 36–37.

B. Hotchpot on a Partial Intestacy

In addition to the hotchpot rule in section 47(1)(iii), which applies to
certain benefits conferred on his *child* by the intestate during his lifetime,[26] two more hotchpot rules apply on a partial intestacy.

1. The surviving spouse. Under section 49(1)(*aa*) of the Administration of Estates Act 1925 a surviving spouse who acquires any beneficial
interests under the deceased's will[27] (other than personal chattels specifically bequeathed[28]) is not entitled to the full amount of the fixed net
sum with interest thereon under the intestacy rules.[29] Instead the surviving spouse takes the fixed net sum *less* the value at the deceased's
death of such beneficial interests, with interest on this reduced sum.
Two examples will illustrate the rather arbitrary operation of this hotchpot rule.

(i) Firstly, the case of a general or specific legacy[30] to a surviving
spouse. The deceased by his will gives to his widow his personal chattels as defined in section 55(1)(x) and a general legacy of £50,000 payable
immediately after his death (or, alternatively, a specific legacy of company shares which are valued at £50,000 at his death). The deceased dies
intestate as to his residuary estate on January 1, 1988, leaving children
of full age. Under the intestacy rules, instead of taking £75,000 with
interest thereon, the widow takes £25,000 with interest thereon. If the
will had given her a legacy of £90,000, the widow would not have taken
any fixed net sum with interest, but she would still have been entitled
to a life interest in one-half of the residuary estate under the intestacy
rules. This hotchpot rule reduces the amount of the fixed net sum with
interest, but not the other beneficial interests of a surviving spouse
under the intestacy rules.

(ii) Next the case of a residuary gift. The deceased by his will gives to
his widow his personal chattels as defined in section 55(1)(x) and a life
interest in one-half of his residuary estate, and gives the other half of
his residuary estate to his children absolutely. The will does not dispose
of the beneficial interest in remainder in the first half of his residuary
estate. Again the deceased dies on January 1, 1988, leaving children of
full age. The widow's fixed net sum of £75,000 must be reduced by the
value at the deceased's death of her life interest in one-half of his residuary estate under the will. On a *total* intestacy the widow would have
taken both the fixed net sum of £75,000 *and* a life interest in one-half of
the balance of the residuary estate. In some circumstances it may be
better for the widow to disclaim[31] her life interest under the will.

---

[26] *Ante*, pp. 91–93.
[27] Including any acquired by virtue of the exercise by the will of a general power of
appointment (including the statutory power to dispose of entailed interests), but not of a
special power of appointment, s.49(2). s.49(1) applies to beneficial interests in *foreign*
property, *Re Osoba* [1978] 1 W.L.R. 791, 796–797; [1979] 1 W.L.R. 247, 255.
[28] *Ante*, p. 84.
[29] *Ante*, pp. 85–86.
[30] *Post*, pp. 294 *et seq.*
[31] *Post*, p. 352.

2. Issue. Section 49(1)(*a*) requires beneficial interests acquired by any *issue* of the deceased under his will[32] to be brought into hotchpot on a partial intestacy.[33] Unfortunately the section was poorly drafted.[34] It provides that the requirements of section 47(1)(iii)[35] "as to bringing property into account shall apply to any beneficial interest acquired by any issue of the deceased under the will of the deceased, but not to beneficial interests so acquired by any other persons." Thus section 49(1)(*a*) defines another subject matter which is to be brought into account under section 47(1)(iii), but on the face of it makes no other change.

It is useful to analyse the basic structure of section 47(1)(iii) and section 49(1)(*a*).

	What subject matter is to be brought into hotchpot?	Against what share on intestacy?
Section 47(1)(iii)	certain benefits (as defined) conferred on "*a child* of the intestate" by the intestate during his lifetime.	"the share of *such child* or the share which such child would have taken if living at the death of the intestate."
Section 49(1)(a)	"any beneficial interests acquired by *any issue* of the deceased under the will of the deceased."	"the share of *such child* . . ." (as above). Section 49(1)(*a*) on the face of it made no change.

The definition in section 49(1)(*a*) of the subject matter to be brought into hotchpot did not refer to "a child," though this was necessary to make the reference in section 47(1)(iii) to "the share of such child" meaningful.

(1) *Construction.* Two different constructions of section 49(1)(*a*) have been suggested. The first is the *stirpital* construction, which reads section 49(1)(*a*) as follows:

Stirpital construction of section 49(1)(a)	"any beneficial interests acquired by [*a child of the deceased or any issue of that child*] under the will of the deceased."	"the share of *such child* . . ." (as above).

In *Re Young*[36] Harman J. construed section 49(1)(*a*) as if it had been worded in this way, saying that "'issue' must mean children or remoter issue," and that "any member of the family belonging to a certain

[32] *Ante,* n. 27.
[33] See generally, E. C. Ryder (1973) 26 C.L.P. 208.
[34] "As bad a piece of draftsmanship as one could conceive, in many respects," *per* Danckwerts J. in *Re Morton* [1956] Ch. 644, 647: "great difficulties of language," *per* Pennycuick J. in *Re Grover's W.T.* [1971] Ch. 168, 174.
[35] *Ante,* pp. 91 *et seq.*
[36] [1951] Ch. 185.

branch must bring in everything that has been taken or acquired under
the will by that branch."[37] In *Re Young* the deceased by his will gave his
widow a life interest in his residuary estate, and after her death gave
one-seventh of his residuary estate to each of his children A, B, C, D,
and E, and another one-seventh on trust to apply the income or capital
at the discretion of the trustees for the maintenance of his son F and his
children during his life, and after his death on trust for F's children
absolutely. Subject to the widow's life interest the deceased died intestate as to the remaining one-seventh. Under section 49(1)(*a*) the one-
seventh shares of A, B, C, D and E had to be brought into hotchpot
against their respective shares on intestacy. Harman J. decided that the
capital of the one-seventh share which was settled by the will on F and
his children must also be brought into hotchpot against F's share on
intestacy. He rejected the argument that only the very limited interest of
F himself in this one-seventh share was liable to be brought into hotchpot. Thus, under the stirpital construction, the intestate's child taking
on a partial intestacy brings into hotchpot beneficial interests acquired
by that child *or any issue of that child* under the will.

Re Young has been followed at first instance in the Chancery Division
in two other cases, *Re Morton*[38] and *Re Grover's Will Trusts*,[39] and in all
probability the stirpital construction will continue to be adopted, at any
rate at first instance.

In deciding *Re Grover's Will Trusts* Pennycuick J. followed *Re Young*
and *Re Morton*, but confessed that another construction (which may be
called the *distributive* construction) appealed to him: under this other
construction, he said,

"any descendant of the testator who acquires a beneficial interest
under his will brings that interest, and nothing more, into account
against his share under the partial intestacy. So, for instance, a child
of the testator would bring into account any beneficial interest
acquired by that child under the will, but nothing more, and similarly
a grandchild of the testator would bring into account any beneficial
interest taken by that grandchild."[40]

The stirpital construction appears to be more consistent with the
basic structure of section 49(1)(*a*) and 47(1)(iii). Certainly section
47(1)(iii) was not worded so as to require a particular grandchild to
bring certain property into hotchpot against his share as a grandchild
on intestacy. On the contrary, section 47(1)(iii) requires the same property to be brought into hotchpot against a child's share, irrespective of
whether the child or the child's issue representing him take that share
on intestacy.[41]

[37] *Ibid.* at pp. 189–190: see also *Re Grover's W.T., supra,* at p. 176 where Pennycuick J.
referred to this statement of Harman J. as being "in extremely wide terms."
[38] [1956] Ch. 644 (declare "each child ought to bring into hotchpot the value of the interest actually taken by such child or his or her issue" under the will; order of Danckwerts J.,
at p. 649).
[39] [1971] Ch. 168.
[40] *Per* Pennycuick J. in *Re Grover's W.T., supra,* at p. 174.
[41] *Ante,* p. 92.

(2) *At what valuation.* Section 49(1)(*a*) does not alter the rule in section 47(1)(iii) that the value of interests brought into hotchpot is "to be reckoned as at the death of the intestate."[42] In order to produce equality so far as possible, the method of valuation to be used depends on the circumstances, and events occurring after the intestate's death may be considered in deciding which method of valuation to adopt.[43]

In *Re Young*, where a one-seventh share of residue was settled by the will on a protective trust for F during his life and after his death on trust for F's children absolutely, the beneficial interests were brought into hotchpot at the capital value of this one-seventh share. On the other hand in *Re Morton*, where the will gave a share of residue to a son S for life and after his death to S's son for life, Danckwerts J. directed their life interests to be brought into hotchpot at a valuation made according to relevant actuarial considerations—as he put it, "To value the interest as being equivalent to a gift of capital in a case where a person takes no more than a life interest seems to me contrary to fairness, common sense and everything else."[44] In each of these cases the court adopted the method of valuation which was most appropriate to produce equality in the particular circumstances.

(3) *Contrary intention.* The application of this hotchpot rule is excluded by a contrary intention on the part of the deceased, "expressed or appearing from the circumstances of the case."[45]

---

[42] In *Re Grover's W.T., supra*, at p. 179 Pennycuick J. suggested *obiter* that "in certain circumstances" it may be necessary to depart from this rule. As to valuation of the intestate estate, see *ante*, p. 93.

[43] *Re Young, supra*, at p. 190.

[44] *Re Morton, supra*, at p. 649: see *Re Grover's W.T., supra* at pp. 178 and 179.

[45] s.47(1)(iii); see *ante*, p. 93.

CHAPTER 5

PROVISION FOR THE DECEASED'S FAMILY AND DEPENDANTS

By his will a testator may dispose of all his property in whatever way he pleases.[1] Under English law a testator's spouse and children have no legal right to inherit a fixed proportion of his estate. But, whether the deceased dies testate or wholly or partly intestate, after his death the court has power to order provision to be made out of the deceased's net estate[2] for certain applicants, namely (a) the deceased's wife or husband, (b) a former wife or husband of the deceased who has not remarried, (c) a child of the deceased, (d) a person treated by the deceased as a child of the family in relation to any marriage of the deceased, and (e) a dependant of the deceased.[3] This power is conferred on the court by the Inheritance (Provision for Family and Dependants) Act 1975, which applies on the death of any person after March 31, 1976.[4] This Act was passed as a result of a Law Commission report[5] in order to make "fresh provision"[6] for empowering the court to make such an order. The Act made some important changes but it forms part of a continuum and the body of case law built up under the Inheritance (Family Provision) Act 1938[7] (which applied on a death before April 1, 1976) is not to be put on one side and ignored.[8]

A. Domicile, Jurisdiction and Time Limit

Domicile. The 1975 Act only applies if the deceased died domiciled in England and Wales.[9] The legal burden of proof that the deceased died so domiciled lies on the applicant.[10]

---

[1] *Re Coventry* [1980] Ch. 461, 474–475 (but subject to fiscal demands). For a comparative study see Sherrin (1980) 31 N.I.L.Q. 21. [2] *Post*, p. 126.

[3] Each category of applicant is considered more fully, *post*, pp. 115 *et seq.*

[4] 1975 Act, ss.1(1) and 27(3): for variation of a periodical payments order whenever made see *post*, p. 132.

[5] Second Report on Family Property: *Family Provision on Death* (1974), Law Com. No. 61.

[6] Long title of 1975 Act.

[7] The 1938 Act (as amended) governed applications by the deceased's spouse and children; Matrimonial Causes Act 1965, ss.26–28A (as amended), applications by the deceased's former spouse; and Law Reform (Miscellaneous Provisions) Act 1970, s.6, applications by a person who in good faith entered into a void marriage with the deceased.

[8] *Re Coventry* [1980] Ch. 461, 474 and 487.

[9] 1975 Act, ss.1(1) and 27(2): for domicile see Dicey and Morris, *The Conflict of Laws* (11th ed., 1987), pp. 116 *et seq.*; Theobald on *Wills* (14th ed., 1982), pp. 3–7. For forceful criticism of domicile as the sole basis of jurisdiction see J. H. C. Morris (1946) 62 L.Q.R. 170, 178–179; see also Law Com. No. 61, paras. 258–262, which recommended no change.

[10] *Mastaka* v. *Midland Bank Executor and Trustee Co. Ltd.* [1941] Ch. 192 (now under the Domicile and Matrimonial Proceedings Act 1973 a married woman can acquire a domicile independent of her husband).

Jurisdiction. An application under the Act may be made (i) to the Chancery Division or the Family Division of the High Court,[11] which has unlimited jurisdiction, *or* (ii) to the county court, which has jurisdiction where it is shown to the satisfaction of the court that the value at the deceased's death of all the property of which he had power to dispose by his will (otherwise than by virtue of a special power of appointment), after deducting the amount of his funeral, testamentary and administration expenses, debts and liabilities, including any inheritance tax payable out of his estate on his death, does not exceed £30,000.[12]

Time limit for application. An application under the Act must not be made later than six months from the date on which a valid grant of probate or letters of administration to the deceased's estate[13] is first taken out.[14] However the court has an unfettered discretion to extend this time limit.[15]

Protection of personal representatives. The personal representatives may safely pay the deceased's funeral, testamentary and administration expenses, debts and liabilities before the six months' time limit has expired, irrespective of whether any application under the Act has been made.[16]

After this time limit has expired, if no application under the Act has been made, the personal representatives may safely distribute the estate

[11] s.25(1); R.S.C., Ord. 99, r. 2. For the code of procedure, which is common to both Divisions, see R.S.C., Ord. 99; *Practice Note (Inheritance: Family Provision)* [1976] 1 W.L.R. 418; *Practice Direction (Family Provision: Application)* [1978] 1 W.L.R. 585; *Practice Direction (Grants of Representation: Endorsement of Order)* [1979] 1 W.L.R. 1.

[12] County Courts Act 1984, s.25: the limit was increased to £30,000 from December 1, 1981; S.I. 1981 No. 1636. For the procedure see C.C.R. 1981, Ord. 48.

[13] See *post*, pp. 160 *et seq.* A grant limited to settled land or trust property is disregarded, and so is a grant limited to real or personal estate unless a grant limited to the remainder of the estate has previously been made or is made at the same time, s.23; *Re Miller* [1969] 1 W.L.R. 583 (representation is first taken out on grant in common form, though affirmed in solemn form later); *Re Freeman* [1984] 1 W.L.R. 1419 (time only runs from a valid grant of representation).

[14] s.4. An application is made when the summons is issued, and not when it is served: *Re Chittenden* [1970] 1 W.L.R. 1618. For a standing search for a grant see *post*, p. 188.

[15] s.4: as to property of which the deceased was a beneficial joint tenant see *post*, p. 127. As to exercise of this discretion see *Re Salmon* [1981] Ch. 167 ((i) the discretion is to be exercised judicially, (ii) the onus lies on the applicant to make out a substantial case for it being just and proper for the court to exercise its discretion, and the court should consider (iii) how promptly, and in what circumstances, the applicant applied to the court for an extension and also warned the defendant of the proposed application, (iv) whether negotiations commenced within the time limit (if so, and time ran out while they were proceeding, this is likely to encourage the court to extend the time), (v) whether the estate had been distributed before a claim under the Act was made or notified, and (vi) whether a refusal to extend the time would leave the applicant without redress against anybody or, alternatively, with a claim against his own solicitors for negligence); *Re Dennis* [1981] 2 All E.R. 140 (applicant must show he has arguable case); *Escritt* v. *Escritt* (1982) 3 F.L.R. 280 (conscious decision not to claim); *Smith* v. *Loosley* (1986) Transcript on Lexis (no guidelines, just factors to consider); *Perry* v. *Horlick* (1987) Transcript on Lexis (applicant also claiming equitable interest in deceased's house).

[16] See definition of the deceased's net estate, *post*, p. 126: as to the power of a personal representative to postpone performance of a contract which the personal representative has reason to believe the deceased entered into with the intention of defeating an application for financial provision under the Act, see *post*, p. 138.

to the beneficiaries under the deceased's will or intestacy. The time limit is short so as not unduly to impede distribution by the personal representatives. The Act provides that after this time limit has expired they can distribute without taking into account the possibility that the court might (i) extend this time limit or (ii) vary its original order for the making of periodical payments to an applicant,[17] but this protection for the personal representatives does not prejudice any power to recover, by reason of the making of an order under the Act, any part of the estate so distributed.[18]

If an applicant does apply to the court, there is no rigid rule that the personal representatives must preserve the entire net estate intact until the pending application has been heard by the court. Whether it is safe for the personal representatives to make any distribution depends on the circumstances. It may be safe, for instance, for them to pay a legacy to the applicant who is seeking more provision under the Act, or to some other legatee if there is no risk of the court directing that any part of any provision ordered for the applicant should fall on the legacy because (say) the legacy is trifling in comparison with the size of the residuary estate, or because the legatee has a high claim on the testator and is in need of the money. If in doubt personal representatives can seek the consent of the interested parties to such a payment being made and, if consent is not forthcoming, apply to the court for leave to make the payment.[19]

B. The Test of Reasonable Financial Provision

The court may only order provision to be made under the Act for an applicant if the court "is satisfied that the disposition of the deceased's estate effected by his will or the law relating to intestacy, or the combination of his will and that law, is not such as to make reasonable financial provision for the applicant."[20] Exactly the same test applies whether the deceased died testate or wholly or partly intestate.[21]

Two standards of reasonable financial provision. Section 1(2) of the 1975 Act sets two different standards of reasonable financial provision, which may be called "the surviving spouse standard" and "the maintenance standard."

(1) *The surviving spouse standard.* Reasonable financial provision at the surviving spouse standard means "such financial provision as it would be reasonable in all the circumstances of the case for a husband or wife to receive, whether or not that provision is required for his or her maintenance."[22] In short the standard is reasonable provision *in all the cir-*

---

[17] *Post*, p. 132.
[18] s.20(1).
[19] *Re Ralphs* [1968] 1 W.L.R. 1522, 1525 where Cross J. gave helpful guidance.
[20] s.2(1): see *Rajabally* v. *Rajabally* (1987) Transcript on Lexis (widow's application not defeated by unenforceable assurances by beneficiaries not to insist on their rights under will).
[21] *Re Coventry* [1980] Ch. 461, 488–489: see also s.24.
[22] s.1(2)(*a*).

cumstances, and not (as it was under the 1938 Act) reasonable provision for the *maintenance* of the husband or wife.[23] In setting this new surviving spouse standard "the legislature had in mind a very much wider approach" than under the 1938 Act.[24] The Law Commission justified the introduction of this new standard on the ground that the claim of a surviving spouse upon the family assets should be at least equal to that of a divorced spouse, and the court's powers to order provision for a surviving spouse should be as wide as its powers to order financial provision on a divorce.[25]

This surviving spouse standard is applicable on any application by the deceased's wife or husband,[26] including a person who in good faith entered into a void marriage with the deceased,[27] but excluding a spouse who is judicially separated from the deceased at the latter's death.[28]

(2) *Discretion to apply surviving spouse standard.* The court may in its discretion apply the surviving spouse standard on an application by a judicially separated spouse[28] or a former spouse who has not remarried[29] if (i) the deceased died within 12 months from the decree of judicial separation, or from the decree absolute of divorce or nullity of marriage (as the case may be), and (ii) at the deceased's death no order making (or refusing) provision for such spouse had been made in the matrimonial proceedings.[30] In this exceptional situation the court has a discretion to apply the surviving spouse standard. The Law Commission recommended this in order to cope with cases where the death of the deceased has caused the judicially separated or former spouse to miss the opportunity to obtain a fair share of the family assets in the matrimonial proceedings.[31] This is the only situation in which the court has any discretion as to which standard of reasonable financial provision to apply.

(3) *The maintenance standard.* Reasonable financial provision at the maintenance standard means "such financial provision as it would be reasonable in all the circumstances of the case for the applicant to receive for his maintenance."[32] The same standard was applicable on all applications under the 1938 Act.

Reasonable provision for maintenance does not mean, on the one hand, merely the provision of the bare necessities of life so as to keep an

---

[23] *Re Besterman* [1984] Ch. 458, 465–466 and 470: see *post,* p. 117.

[24] *Re Coventry* [1980] Ch. 461, 468 and 484–485.

[25] Law Com. No. 61, paras. 12–18 and 26–30.

[26] s.1(2)(a): see *post,* p. 115.

[27] s.25(4): see *post,* p. 115.

[28] *i.e.* a spouse whose marriage with the deceased was the subject of a decree of judicial separation and at the date of death of the deceased the decree was in force and the separation was continuing, s.1(2)(a).

[29] s.1(1)(b): see *post,* p. 118.

[30] s.14: no financial provision order or property adjustment order under ss.23 and 24 of the Matrimonial Causes Act 1973 must have been made or refused; it is immaterial that maintenance pending suit under s.22 has been ordered or refused.

[31] Law Com. No. 61, paras. 59–63.

[32] s.1(2)(b).

applicant at subsistence level[33]; "on the other hand, it does not mean anything which may be regarded as reasonably desirable for his general benefit or welfare."[34] In *Re Coventry*[35] Buckley L.J. suggested it means "such financial provision as would be reasonable in all the circumstances of the case to enable the applicant to maintain himself in a manner suitable to those circumstances." Maintenance connotes provision which, directly or indirectly, enables the applicant "to discharge the cost of his daily living at whatever standard of living is appropriate to him."[36]

This maintenance standard is applicable on an application by a judicially separated spouse or a former spouse who has not remarried, unless the court has, and exercises, the discretion to apply the surviving spouse standard. It is always applicable on an application by a child of the deceased or a person treated by the deceased as a child of the family,[37] or by a dependant of the deceased.[38]

No provision ordered unless test satisfied. The court cannot order provision to be made under the Act for an applicant unless it is satisfied that the disposition of the deceased's estate is not such as to make reasonable financial provision for the applicant, measured by the surviving spouse or maintenance standard as is appropriate.[39] "It clearly cannot be enough to say that the circumstances are such that if the deceased had made a particular provision for the applicant, that would not have been an unreasonable thing for him to do and therefore it now ought to be done. The court has no carte blanche to reform the deceased's dispositions or those which statute makes of his estate [on his intestacy] to accord with what the court itself might have thought would be sensible if it had been in the deceased's position."[40] Again, it is not the proper test to ask "how the available assets should be fairly divided?"[41]

---

[33] *Re Coventry* [1980] Ch. 461, 485 and 494; *Re E.* [1966] 1 W.L.R. 709, 715 (the purpose of the 1938 Act was not to require the deceased to keep applicants "above the breadline").

[34] *Per* Goff L.J. in *Re Coventry* [1980] Ch. 461, 485. In *Re Christie* [1979] Ch. 168, 174 the deputy judge said that maintenance "refers to no more and no less than the applicant's way of life and well-being, his health, financial security and allied matters such as the well-being, health and financial security of his immediate family for whom he is responsible": but in *Re Coventry, supra,* at p. 471 Oliver J. expressed reservations as regards this "very broad interpretation of the word 'maintenance' which seems to me to come dangerously near to equating it simply with 'wellbeing' or 'benefit' ": see also *Re Coventry, supra,* at p. 490.

[35] *Re Coventry, supra,* at p. 494: see also *Re Borthwick* [1949] Ch. 395, 401 (a widow's application to which the surviving spouse standard would now be applicable); *Millward* v. *Shenton* [1972] 1 W.L.R. 711, 715 (married son a hopeless invalid: a television set, or a car, or even a better house); *Malone* v. *Harrison* [1979] 1 W.L.R. 1353, 1361.

[36] *Per* Browne-Wilkinson J. in *Re Dennis* [1981] 2 All E.R. 140 (payment of his debts to enable him to carry on a profit-making profession or business may be for maintenance).

[37] s.1(1)(c) and (d): see *post,* pp. 120 *et seq.*

[38] s.1(1)(e): see *post,* p. 123.

[39] s.2(1); *Re Coventry* [1980] Ch. 461, 474–475 and 494–495; *Re Fullard* [1982] Fam. 42, 46 and 50 ("condition precedent").

[40] *Re Coventry, supra,* at p. 475.

[41] *Re Coventry, supra,* at pp. 486 and 493.

The test is objective. The vital question whether the disposition of the deceased's estate is not such as to make reasonable financial provision for the applicant (measured by whichever standard is appropriate) is to be answered objectively from the point of view of the court and not subjectively from the point of view of the deceased.[42] As Megarry J. put it in *Re Goodwin*,[43] "The statutory language is . . . wholly impersonal." Accordingly it is irrelevant to consider whether the deceased acted unreasonably in making no provision, or no larger provision, for the applicant.[44] The question whether the deceased stands convicted of unreasonableness does not arise.[45]

This objective approach makes it irrelevant to consider whether the deceased knew of all the material facts. On an application by a former wife, for instance, there may well be some material fact which is proved in evidence but which was not known to the deceased—unknown to the deceased his former wife may have fallen on ill-health or other ill-fortune and be no longer capable of self-support.[46] The court has regard to all the material facts irrespective of whether they were known to the deceased. Indeed the court even takes into account material facts which occurred after the death of the deceased before the court hears the application.[47]

Two stages of an application. The court considers an application under the Act in two stages because the court has to decide two key questions in turn.[48]

(1) *First stage.* The court first decides whether it is satisfied that the disposition of the deceased's estate effected by his will or the law relating to intestacy, or the combination of his will and that law, is not such as to make reasonable financial provision for the applicant, measured by the surviving spouse or the maintenance standard as is appropriate. If the court decides that the disposition does make reasonable financial provision, the application fails at the first hurdle.[49] Thus if the will,[50] or the law relating to intestacy,[51] makes no provision at all for the applicant, but the court decides that reasonable financial provision is nil, the application fails. On the other hand, if the court is satisfied that the disposition is not such as to make reasonable financial provision for the

---

[42] ss.1(1) and 2(1): *Re Coventry, supra,* at pp. 474–475 and 488–489 ("any view expressed by a deceased person that he wishes a particular person to benefit will generally be of little significance, because the question is not subjective but objective"): *cf. Re Christie* [1979] Ch. 168, 174.

[43] [1969] 1 Ch. 283, 287 (on the similar language of the 1938 Act): see also *Re Shanahan* [1973] Fam. 1, 8.

[44] *Re Coventry* [1980] Ch. 461, 474.

[45] *Re Goodwin* [1969] 1 Ch. 283, 288.

[46] *Re Shanahan, supra,* at p. 4. See also *Re Franks* [1948] Ch. 62 (son born two days before death of mother who had no chance to change her will and provide for him: held provision should be made for son).

[47] s.3(5).

[48] ss.2(1) and 3(1): *Re Coventry, supra,* at pp. 469 and 486–487; *Re Sivyer* [1967] 1 W.L.R. 1482, 1486–1487.

[49] *Re Coventry, supra; Re Fullard* [1982] Fam. 42.

[50] *Re Fullard* [1982] Fam. 42 (former wife): see *post,* p. 119.

[51] *Re Coventry, supra,* (adult child): see *post,* p. 121.

applicant, the court proceeds to the second stage. This first stage involves a "value judgment, or a qualitative decision" by the trial judge.[52]

(2) *Second stage.* If the application passes the first hurdle, the court next decides, in the exercise of its discretion, whether, and in what manner, it shall order provision to be made for the applicant.[53] This is a question of discretion.[54] At this second stage the court quantifies the provision to be ordered for the applicant by reference to the test of reasonable financial provision, measured by the surviving spouse or the maintenance standard as is appropriate.[55]

Facts as known to the court at the date of hearing. At both these stages section 3(5) of the Act directs the court to take into account the facts as known to the court at the date of the hearing.[56] Thus the court must take into account events which occurred after the death of the deceased before the hearing of the application. For instance, the value of the deceased's net estate may rise or fall after his death: at both these stages the court considers the value of the deceased's net estate at the date of the hearing and not at the date of death. Again, if an applicant, who at the deceased's death was poor and had good prospects of making a successful application, shortly afterwards wins a huge fortune in a football pool, the court takes this into account at the hearing and the application must fail because reasonable provision for the applicant is nil.[57]

The general guidelines.[58] At both stages of an application section 3 of the Act requires the court to have regard to (i) general guidelines, which are applicable on any application, and (ii) particular guidelines, which are specified for each different category of applicant. The particular guidelines are considered later.[59]

Financial resources and needs. The first three general guidelines are the financial resources and financial needs which (a) the applicant, (b) any other applicant for an order under the Act, and (c) any beneficiary[60] has or is likely to have in the foreseeable future.

In considering any person's financial resources the court must take

---

[52] *Re Coventry, supra,* at pp. 487 and 495.
[53] s.2(1) and 3(1); *Re Coventry, supra,* at p. 469 and 486; *Re Rowlands* (1984) 5 F.L.R. 813 (whether and in what manner poses two questions): for the orders which the court may make see *post,* p. 127.
[54] *Re Coventry, supra,* at p. 487.
[55] *Re Besterman* [1984] Ch. 458: see *post,* p. 117.
[56] See *Re Coventry, supra,* at pp. 491 and 493.
[57] *Quaere* whether the court will extend the six months' time limit in a case where the applicant relies for his success on an event which occurred after this time limit had expired—for instance, the sudden onset of a disability which made the applicant permanently unfit for work: see *post,* p. 113.
[58] The term guidelines was used in Law Com. No. 61, paras. 31–36, 52–54, 81–84, and 96–98: the 1975 Act does not use this term but refers to them as "matters."
[59] *Post,* pp. 115 *et seq.*
[60] *i.e.* a person beneficially interested under the deceased's will or intestacy, or a person who takes under a statutory nomination or a *donatio mortis causa* made by the deceased, s.25(1).

into account his earning capacity,[61] and not just his, perhaps low, current earnings.[62] Again, the court takes into account a person's pension, whether from the state or the deceased's employers.[63] Other forms of state aid may also be relevant.[64]

A person's financial resources include his capital assets, such as his house or flat, company shares and money in the bank, and also the damages received by that person for personal injuries.[65] However, generally it would not be right to treat the value of a person's home as expendable capital which he should spend in maintaining himself.[66] The reference in the guideline to the financial resources which a person is likely to have in the foreseeable future covers, for instance, assets which that person is likely to inherit under the will of an elderly testator.[67]

In considering any person's financial needs the court must take into account his financial obligations and responsibilities.[68] Again the guideline refers both to present financial needs and needs which a person is likely to have in the foreseeable future.[69]

Obligations and responsibilities of the deceased. The fourth general guideline is "(d) any obligations and responsibilities which the deceased had towards any applicant . . . or towards any beneficiary."[70] Whether the deceased had any obligations and responsibilities towards an applicant or a beneficiary depends on all the circumstances.[71] Before the 1975 Act these obligations and responsibilities were sometimes referred to as a moral claim on the deceased's bounty.

The deceased's estate may be large enough to satisfy all his obli-

---

[61] s.3(6).

[62] *Re Ducksbury* [1966] 1 W.L.R. 1226, 1233: see also *Malone* v. *Harrison* [1979] 1 W.L.R. 1353, 1359 and 1364–1365 (woman's earning capacity until age of 60).

[63] *Re Catmull* [1943] Ch. 262 (widow's pension); *Re Charman* [1951] 2 T.L.R. 1095 (bank's voluntary pension unlikely to be withdrawn); *Re Clayton* [1966] 1 W.L.R. 969 (prospect of future pension from employer); *Re Crawford* (1983) 4 F.L.R. 273 (widow's pension).

[64] *Re E.* [1966] 1 W.L.R. 709; *Re Clayton* [1966] 1 W.L.R. 969: see *post,* p. 112.

[65] *Daubney* v. *Daubney* [1976] Fam. 267.

[66] *Malone* v. *Harrison* [1979] 1 W.L.R. 1353, 1365. A house may yield income from lodgers, *Re E., supra.*

[67] See *Morgan* v. *Morgan* [1977] Fam. 122.

[68] s.3(6).

[69] *Re Clayton, supra,* (provision for crippled widow as employment might end); *Re Ducksbury* [1966] 1 W.L.R. 1226, 1233 (future needs when no longer able to earn her living).

[70] *Ante,* n. 60.

[71] See cases cited *infra,* nn. 73–74; *Re Simson* [1950] Ch. 38, 40 (housekeeper, as beneficiary); *Re Andrews* [1955] 1 W.L.R. 1105 (father owed no moral obligation to daughter incapable of maintaining herself, who left home 42 years before to live as common law wife): *cf. Millward* v. *Shenton* [1972] 1 W.L.R. 711 (son aged 52 incapacitated from earning by progressive illness); *Re Clarke* [1968] 1 W.L.R. 415 (moral claims of applicant wife, and deceased's elderly mother as beneficiary, on his bounty: distant relatives no such claims); *Re Coventry* [1980] Ch. 461, 475–477, 487–490 and 494–495 (father owed no moral obligations to adult son); *Re Fullard* [1982] Fam. 42 (no obligations to former wife); *Re Besterman* [1984] Ch. 458 (duty to wife but not to main beneficiary Oxford University); *Re Rowlands* (1984) 5 F.L.R. 813 (some small moral obligation owed to wife despite 43 years' separation); *Re Debenham* (1986) 7 F.L.R. 404 (mother's moral obligation to unwanted daughter, aged 58 and epileptic). See also *Re Harker-Thomas* [1969] P. 28, 31 where Latey J. said "the ties of blood and, indeed, the rights and benefits which the law itself provides on intestacy . . . amount to a claim": *sed quaere* in what sense: *cf. Re Clarke, supra.*

gations and responsibilities.[72] But if it is not, the court may have to weigh in the balance the respective obligations which the deceased had towards each applicant and beneficiary in order to adjudicate on the conflicting claims of, for instance, a widow and a common law wife,[73] or a widow and a former wife,[74] or a wife and the children of another marriage.[75] In doing so, the court considers all the circumstances, including such factors as each person's resources and needs,[76] and the source of the deceased's assets—it may be material that one of the claimants had helped the deceased build up his business,[77] or that most of the deceased's assets had been inherited by him from the mother of one of the claimants.[78]

Two of the particular guidelines, which apply where an application is made under the Act by a person treated by the deceased as a child of the family or by a dependant of the deceased, refer specifically to the assumption by the deceased of responsibility for the applicant's maintenance. These particular guidelines are considered later.[79]

Size and nature of the estate. The fifth general guideline is "(e) the size and nature of the net estate[80] of the deceased." If the deceased left a large net estate, reasonable financial provision for an applicant may well be considerably more than would be appropriate, or indeed possible, from a smaller net estate.[81]

The 1975 Act does not impose any minimum limit on the value of the net estate in respect of which an application may be made. "The smallness of the estate neither excludes jurisdiction nor full consideration."[82] Nevertheless the smallness of the estate may be significant in three different ways: ·

(i) It may be reasonable to make no provision for a needy applicant out of a small estate if the only effect of making provision would be to relieve the state from having to pay means tested benefits.[83]

(ii) Again it may be reasonable to make no provision if the maintenance standard is applicable and the estate is too small to make an effective contribution to the applicant's maintenance, having

---

[72] *Malone v. Harrison* [1979] 1 W.L.R. 1353, 1364.

[73] *Re Joslin* [1941] Ch. 201 (T's moral obligation to common law wife and children by her, as beneficiaries); *Re E.* [1966] 1 W.L.R. 709; *Re Thornley* [1969] 1 W.L.R. 1037.

[74] *Re Talbot* [1962] 1 W.L.R. 1113; *Roberts v. Roberts* [1965] 1 W.L.R. 560 (moral claims of applicant first wife, and widow as beneficiary, on T's bounty).

[75] *Re Sivyer* [1967] 1 W.L.R. 1482 (applicant child, and third wife entitled on intestacy, had calls upon deceased's bounty); *Re Bellman* [1963] P. 239 (claims of applicant former wife, and sons as beneficiaries, on T's bounty); *Re Ducksbury* [1966] 1 W.L.R. 1226 (applicant daughter aged 29, and second wife as beneficiary).

[76] *Re Joslin, supra,* (applicant widow of small means; common law wife and children by her penniless); *Re Sivyer, supra; Re Bellman, supra: Re E., supra.*

[77] *Re Thornley, supra:* see also *Re E., supra,* at p. 714.

[78] *Re Sivyer, supra,* at pp. 1488–1489; *Re Styler* [1942] Ch. 387, 390: see *Re Canderton* (1970) 114 S.J. 208; *Jelley v. Iliffe* [1981] Fam. 128: see *post,* p. 114.

[79] *Post,* pp. 122 and 123.

[80] For the meaning of net estate see *post,* p. 126.

[81] *Re Inns* [1947] Ch. 576, 581; *Re Borthwick* [1949] Ch. 395; *Malone v. Harrison* [1979] 1 W.L.R. 1353, 1364; *Re Besterman* [1984] Ch. 458 (£378,000 provision ordered for widow of millionaire).

[82] Per Ungoed-Thomas J. in *Re Clayton* [1966] 1 W.L.R. 969, 971.

[83] *Re E.* [1966] 1 W.L.R. 709, 715; *Re Clayton, supra,* at pp. 971 and 974.

regard to his means and standard of living. Where the maintenance standard is applicable, the purpose of the 1975 Act is to provide maintenance and not just a small windfall legacy for an
applicant.[84] However, it may be appropriate for maintenance to
be ordered by way of a small lump sum payment to an applicant.[85]

(iii) "Claims in cases where the costs of establishing claims leave virtually nothing significant for the claimant deprive the claim of
substance, and are to be discouraged."[86] One form of discourage-
ment is for the court to make an order for costs against the
claimant.[87]

Disability of any applicant or beneficiary. The sixth general guideline is
"(f) any physical or mental disability" of any applicant or any beneficiary.[88] Such a disability may reduce the earning capacity and increase
the financial needs of an applicant[89] or beneficiary (which is relevant
under general guidelines (a), (b) and (c)). Again such a disability may
give rise to, or strengthen, the obligations and responsibilities which
the deceased had towards an applicant[90] or beneficiary (which is relevant under general guideline (d)). Thus in *Millward* v. *Shenton*[91] the
Court of Appeal held that a mother's will giving her whole estate to
cancer research did not make reasonable provision for the maintenance
of her married son, who was aged 52, and incapacitated from earning by
a progressive illness.

The availability of state aid, such as free hospital accommodation, is a
factor to be taken into account. It has been held reasonable to make only
limited provision for a daughter incapable of maintaining herself by
reason of mental disability, because the daughter could be maintained
free of charge in a state mental hospital.[92] However, in such a case it
may be unreasonable to make no provision for pocket money, so as to
enable the applicant to buy extra "comforts" not provided by the
state.[93]

Conduct and any other matter. The last general guideline is "(g) any
other matter, including the conduct of the applicant or any other

---

[84] *Re Clayton, supra*, at pp. 971–972; see also *Re Vrint* [1940] Ch. 920, 925–926.

[85] *Re Clayton, supra*, (£400 lump sum from £1,271 estate).

[86] Per Ungoed-Thomas J. in *Re Clayton, supra*, at p. 972; see *Re Coventry* [1980] Ch. 461,
486.

[87] *Re Vrint, supra*, (net estate £138: widow's application dismissed with costs): see *Re
Fullard* (1982) Fam. 42, 46.

[88] *i.e.* a person beneficially interested under the deceased's will or intestacy, or a person
who takes under a statutory nomination or a *donatio mortis causa* made by the deceased,
s.25(1).

[89] *Re Clayton* [1966] 1 W.L.R. 969 (widower crippled in both legs); *Millward* v. *Shenton*
[1972] 1 W.L.R. 711.

[90] *Re Clayton, supra*; *Millward* v. *Shenton, supra*: *cf. Re Andrews* [1955] 1 W.L.R. 1105.

[91] [1972] 1 W.L.R. 711 (estate £3,144: lump sum of eleven-twelfths of estate awarded to
son): see also *Re Pointer* [1941] Ch. 60.

[92] *Re Watkins* [1949] 1 All E.R. 695; *Re E.* [1966] 1 W.L.R. 709, 714–715 ("something might
have been provided for comforts").

[93] *Re Pringle* [1956] C.L.Y. 9248 (£2,291 net estate: 10s. per week ordered for mentally
defective son resident in state mental hospital).

person, which in the circumstances of the case the court may consider relevant."

This reference to conduct is in wide terms.[94] It covers the conduct of the deceased[95] as well as that of an applicant or beneficiary. The court has considered, for instance, whether an applicant was a good and loving wife,[96] a deeply affectionate mistress,[97] or a dutiful child.[98] Again the court has considered to what extent an applicant widow and a mistress (who was a beneficiary under the will) each helped the deceased in his business.[99]

Another matter which the court may consider relevant is the source of the deceased's assets. Thus it was material that the deceased earnt a death grant (the main asset in his estate) whilst living with his common law wife, to whom he gave the whole of his estate by his will.[1]

The deceased's reasons. The 1975 Act, unlike the 1938 Act, does not specifically require the court to have regard to the deceased's own reasons for not making any provision, or any more provision, for an applicant. This is logical because it is irrelevant to consider whether the deceased acted, or believed himself to have acted, reasonably: it is the disposition of the deceased's estate which has to be judged and not the deceased himself.[2] If the deceased's reasons are good reasons based on truth, the court has regard to them under guideline (g) or possibly one of the other guidelines. If they are bad or false reasons, the court disregards them.[3]

The 1975 Act makes a statement made by the deceased, whether orally or in a document or otherwise, admissible under the Civil Evidence Act 1968 as evidence of any fact stated in it.[4]

The deceased's state of mind. The deceased's testamentary capacity is determined in probate proceedings and cannot be put in issue in an application under the 1975 Act.[5] However the deceased's state of mind may be a relevant matter to be considered—*e.g.* it may be relevant to the deceased's obligations that an applicant, or beneficiary, cared for the deceased during a long period of mental illness.[6]

---

[94] *Per* Hollings J. in *Malone* v. *Harrison* [1979] 1 W.L.R. 1353, 1364.

[95] *Re Thornley* [1969] 1 W.L.R. 1037, 1042 (deceased manic-depressive and violent in drink: "human behaviour (and particularly the domestic variety) is contrapuntal. It is impossible to form a fair or intelligent view of the conduct of either party in a domestic or social relationship without also considering how the other behaved").

[96] *Re Morris* [1967] C.L.Y. 4114 (applicant did not intend to carry out her responsibilities as a wife when she married and never did so); *Re Borthwick* [1949] Ch. 395 (wife not at fault); *Re Blanch* [1967] 1 W.L.R. 987; *Re Thornley, supra,* (gravely wronged wife); *Re Snoek* (1983) 13 Fam. Law 18 (wife's atrocious and vicious behaviour): see *post,* p. 117.

[97] *Malone* v. *Harrison* [1979] 1 W.L.R. 1353.

[98] *Re Cook* (1956) unreported but referred to in 106 L.J. 466; *Re Ducksbury* [1966] 1 W.L.R. 1226, 1233.

[99] *Re Thornley* [1969] 1 W.L.R. 1037.

[1] *Re E.* [1966] 1 W.L.R. 709 (widow's application dismissed): for other instances see *ante,* p. 112.

[2] See Law Com. No. 61, para. 105 and *ante,* p. 109.

[3] *Re Borthwick* [1949] Ch. 395; *Re Clarke* [1968] 1 W.L.R. 415; *Re Coventry* [1980] Ch. 461, 488–489.

[4] s.21.

[5] *Re Blanch* [1967] 1 W.L.R. 987.

[6] *Ibid.* at pp. 991–992.

C. Persons Who May Apply and the Particular Guidelines

Each of the following persons who survived the deceased[7] may apply to the court for an order under the 1975 Act.[8]

1. The deceased's wife or husband.[9] The burden of proof lies upon an applicant under this head to prove that at the deceased's death the applicant was the deceased's spouse by a subsisting marriage.[10] A judicially separated spouse falls within this category,[11] and so does a party to a voidable marriage which has not been annulled prior to the deceased's death. A wife of a polygamous marriage also falls within this category.[12]

Exceptionally a person who in good faith entered into a void marriage with the deceased also falls within this category unless during the deceased's lifetime (i) the marriage was dissolved or annulled[13] or (ii) that person entered into a later marriage.[14] Such a person cannot now recover damages for breach of promise of marriage against the deceased's estate,[15] but instead is treated as the deceased's wife or husband for the purpose of an application under the 1975 Act.

The surviving spouse standard is applicable on any application by the deceased's wife or husband, including a person who in good faith entered into a void marriage with the deceased, but excluding a spouse who is judicially separated from the deceased at the latter's death to whom the maintenance standard is applicable (unless the court has, and exercises, the discretion to apply the surviving spouse standard).[16]

The particular guidelines to which the court must have regard on an application by the deceased's wife or husband are[17]:

(a) the age of the applicant and the duration of the marriage[18];
(b) the contribution made by the applicant to the welfare of the

---

[7] If the applicant dies before an order is made, the application cannot proceed, *Whytte* v. *Ticehurst* [1986] Fam. 64 (widow); *Re R (Deceased)* (1986) 16 Fam. Law 58 (former wife).

[8] s.1(1).

[9] See Miller (1986) 102 L.Q.R. 445.

[10] *Re Peete* [1952] 2 All E.R. 599; *Re Watkins* [1953] 1 W.L.R. 1323.

[11] But a judicially separated spouse may be barred from applying for provision by an order of the court made on the application of the other spouse on or after the decree of judicial separation, s.15(1) and (4), as amended by Matrimonial and Family Proceedings Act 1984, s.8: for similar order following overseas legal separation see s.15A as amended by 1984 Act, s.25(3).

[12] *Re Sehota* [1978] 1 W.L.R. 1506.

[13] The dissolution or annulment must be recognised by English law, s.25(4).

[14] s.25(4).

[15] Law Reform (Miscellaneous Provisions) Act 1970, s.1 (agreement to marry not enforceable).

[16] *Ante*, pp. 106 *et seq.*

[17] s.3(2).

[18] See *Re Pugh* [1943] Ch. 387 (two-and-a-half years' marriage); *Re Clarke* [1968] 1 W.L.R. 415, 421 (seven months together): a period of pre-marital cohabitation does not lengthen the duration of a marriage, *Campbell* v. *Campbell* [1976] Fam. 347, 352, but see *Kokosinski* v. *Kokosinski* [1980] Fam. 72, 83–88; *Foley* v. *Foley* [1981] Fam. 160: and for applications by a dependant mistress see *post*, pp. 123 *et seq.*

deceased's family, including any contribution made by looking after the home or caring for the family[19]; and

(c) the provision which the applicant might reasonably have expected to receive if on the day on which the deceased died the marriage, instead of being terminated by death, had been terminated by a decree of divorce. This is the "imaginary divorce" guideline.

This last guideline (c) does not apply on an application by a spouse who is judicially separated from the deceased at the latter's death unless the court has, and exercises, the discretion to apply the surviving spouse standard.[20]

The imaginary divorce guideline. Guidelines (a) and (b) set out factors to which the court must also have regard in applications under the Matrimonial Causes Act 1973.[21] The introduction of the imaginary divorce guideline (c) was recommended by the Law Commission so as to enable the court "to adopt an approach similar to that adopted in divorce proceedings."[22] Unfortunately the guideline did not set out all the hypothetical circumstances of the imaginary divorce. In *Re Bunning*[23] the court assessed the provision which the applicant wife would have received in the imaginary divorce on the day of her husband's death by taking into account his likely future needs, assuming no foreknowledge of his imminent death. Presumably, if the deceased was not of retiring age at his death, the court would similarly take into account his likely future earnings, again assuming no foreknowledge of his imminent death. The imaginary divorce guideline is open to the criticism that it ignores the vital distinction between real divorce proceedings and family provision proceedings—in the latter the deceased is dead and has no future needs or future earnings. The court is required to assess the imaginary divorce provision in hypothetical circumstances (often a difficult task) before the court turns to reality and tackles the key questions[24] which arise in an application under the 1975 Act.

The 1975 Act does not require the court to treat the imaginary divorce guideline as decisive, or as laying down a minimum, or maximum[25] provision for the applicant. It is one guideline out of a number of general and particular guidelines, to all of which the court must have regard[26] and which are not ranked in any order of priority. The key questions must be decided by applying the test of reasonable financial

[19] See *H.* v. *H.* [1975] Fam. 9, 16 (contribution made but job unfinished); *Re Rowlands* (1984) 5 F.L.R. 813.
[20] s.14: see *ante*, p. 108.
[21] Matrimonial Causes Act 1973, s.25(1)(*d*) and (*f*) as amended by 1984 Act: for the case law on these guidelines under the Matrimonial Causes Act 1973 see Cretney, *Principles of Family Law* (4th ed., 1984), pp. 790 *et seq.*
[22] Law Com. No. 61, paras. 33–34: see also paras. 16–18.
[23] [1984] Ch. 480, 496.
[24] *Ante*, p. 109.
[25] *Re Bunning* [1984] Ch. 480 (£36,000 for wife under imaginary divorce guideline: £60,000 ordered under 1975 Act): but see *Stephens* v. *Stephens* (1985) Transcript on Lexis.
[26] *Per* Oliver L.J. in *Re Besterman* [1984] Ch. 458, 469.

provision, measured by the surviving spouse standard. Thus "the overriding consideration is what is 'reasonable' in all the circumstances."[27]

Provision measured by the surviving spouse standard. In *Re Besterman*[28] a wife W applied for provision to be made for her out of the estate of her deceased husband H. They had been married for 18 years and W had been a faithful and dutiful wife. W was 66 years of age and she only had a widow's pension of £400 per annum. By his will H gave W his personal chattels and a yearly income of £3,500 for life. H left a net estate of over £1.4 million. Oxford University, the major beneficiary under his will, acknowledged that H's provision for W was not a reasonable provision for a millionaire's widow accustomed to a high standard of living. The key question for the court was the amount of the provision to be ordered for W. The trial judge treated the maintenance of W as the paramount factor in fixing this amount, referring to the cost of purchasing an annuity sufficient to maintain W's standard of living, and awarded W a lump sum of £238,000 from H's estate. The Court of Appeal increased the lump sum to £378,000 because reasonable financial provision for W had to be measured by the surviving spouse standard (*i.e.* reasonable provision for W in all the circumstances) and not by the maintenance standard (*i.e.* reasonable provision for W's maintenance). Moreover the sum awarded by the trial judge bore little relation to the sum of £350,000 which W might reasonably have expected to receive on divorce under the imaginary divorce guideline and took no real account of the need to cushion W against possible future contingencies, such as ill health.

In the case of an estate of more modest size there is inevitably less available from which the court is able to make provision over and above what is required for the maintenance of the applicant spouse.[29]

Relevance of conduct. In what circumstances is the conduct of the applicant, or of the deceased, likely to be considered "relevant" by the court under general guideline (g)?[30] Under the 1938 Act the court was required to have regard to the conduct of the applicant in every case.[31] Under general guideline (g) of the 1975 Act the court is to have regard to "any other matter, including the conduct of the applicant or any other person which in the circumstances of the case the court may consider relevant." The court may also need to consider conduct under other guidelines. The conduct of an applicant or beneficiary may be relevant to the deceased's obligations and responsibilities under general guideline (d). Again some aspects of an applicant's conduct may be relevant in considering the applicant's contribution to the welfare of the deceased's family under particular guideline (b).[32]

If at the deceased's death the marriage with the applicant had broken down, the court usually considers that the conduct of the parties which

---

[27] *Ibid.*

[28] [1984] Ch. 458; see also *Re Bunning, supra; Stephens v. Stephens, supra; Stead v. Stead* [1985] 6 F.L.R. 16.

[29] *Stead v. Stead, supra.*

[30] *Ante*, p. 113.

[31] Inheritance (Family Provision) Act 1938, s.1(6).

[32] See *H. v. H.* [1975] Fam. 9, 16.

led to the breakdown is irrelevant.[33] This is the view adopted by the court in applications for financial provision in divorce proceedings[34] and a lengthy post-mortem to ascertain who was responsible for the breakdown of the marriage seems even less appropriate in family provision proceedings after one party to the marriage has died.[35] It is open to the court to take the same view in family provision proceedings because general guideline (g) (unlike the other guidelines) only requires the court to have regard to conduct if the court considers it a relevant matter in the circumstances of the case. But, as in divorce proceedings,[36] there will still be a minority of cases where the applicant's conduct is relevant because it would be inequitable to disregard it, so that reasonable financial provision for the applicant is either nothing at all or a reduced amount. Thus in *Re Snoek*,[37] where the wife's atrocious and vicious conduct towards her husband during the latter part of the marriage did not quite cancel out her contribution to the welfare of the family in the early part of the marriage when she managed the home and brought up their children, the court awarded her only a "modest" lump sum of £5,000 out of her husband's £34,000 net estate.

Again it is possible for the deceased's conduct to be relevant—for instance, the deceased may have attacked and injured the applicant, disabling the applicant from working again, and this may justify an increased amount of financial provision.[38]

Application by husband. The same standard of provision and the same guidelines apply whether the applicant is a man or a woman. In *Re Clayton*[39] Ungoed-Thomas J. (referring to the 1938 Act) said, "I certainly do not see in the Act a greater onus of proof on the surviving husband than on the surviving wife."

2. The deceased's former wife or husband who has not remarried.[40]

A former wife or husband means a person whose marriage with the deceased was dissolved or annulled during the deceased's lifetime *either* (i) by a decree of divorce or nullity granted under the law of any

[33] The Law Commission hoped the court would take this view, see Law Com. No. 61, paras. 35–36. For applications under the 1938 Act see *Re Borthwick* [1949] Ch. 395 (husband deserted wife); *Re Thornley* [1969] 1 W.L.R. 1037 (husband's cruelty); *Re Clarke* [1968] 1 W.L.R. 415 (husband's desertion); *Re Gregory* [1970] 1 W.L.R. 1455 (husband's desertion; 42 years' separation and virtually no payment of maintenance: wife's application failed).

[34] *Wachtel* v. *Wachtel* [1973] Fam. 72: see generally Cretney, *op. cit.* pp. 797 *et seq.*

[35] *Re Bunning* [1984] Ch. 480, 489.

[36] Matrimonial Causes Act 1973, s.25(2)(g), as amended by 1984 Act; *Wachtel* v. *Wachtel, supra,* at p. 90: *per* Cairns L.J. in *Harnett* v. *Harnett* [1974] 1 W.L.R. 219, 224, "Where there is something in the conduct of one party which would make it quite inequitable to leave that out of account having regard to the conduct of the other party as well in the course of the marriage"; *Bateman* v. *Bateman* [1979] Fam. 25; *Robinson* v. *Robinson* [1983] Fam. 42; *Kyte* v. *Kyte* (1987) Transcript on Lexis.

[37] (1982) Transcript on Lexis.

[38] See *Jones (M.A.)* v. *Jones (W.)* [1976] Fam. 8 (divorce: "conduct of such a gross kind that it would be offensive to a sense of justice that it should not be taken into account").

[39] [1966] 1 W.L.R. 969, 972 (widower crippled); *Re Wilson* [1969] 113 S.J. 794: provision for a widower was also ordered in *Re Lawes* (1946) 62 T.L.R. 231 and *Re Bonham* (1962) 112 L.J. 634.

[40] Remarriage includes a marriage which is by law void or voidable and it is immaterial that the previous marriage was void or voidable, s.25(5).

part of the British Islands *or* (ii) overseas by a divorce or annulment recognised as valid by English law.[41] The deceased must however have died domiciled in England and Wales.[42]

A former wife or husband may be barred from applying under the 1975 Act by an order of the court made on the application of the other spouse on or after the decree of divorce or nullity.[43]

The maintenance standard is applicable on an application by the deceased's former wife or husband unless the court has, and exercises, the discretion to apply the surviving spouse standard.[44] *The particular guidelines* to which the court must have regard are those applicable on an application by the deceased's wife or husband, except that the imaginary divorce guideline (c) does not apply unless the court has, and exercises, the discretion to apply the surviving spouse standard.[45]

Relevance of financial provision in matrimonial proceedings. Any financial provision made in the matrimonial proceedings, whether by order of the court or by agreement between the parties,[46] is a matter to which the court must have regard under the general guideline (g).[47] In view of the court's powers to make appropriate capital adjustments between spouses in matrimonial proceedings, the Court of Appeal has indicated in *Re Fullard*[48] that there will be comparatively few cases where a former wife or husband will succeed in an application under the 1975 Act. But such an application may succeed, for instance, where the deceased made periodical payments to the former spouse for a long time and leaves a reasonable amount of capital,[49] or where a substantial capital fund is unlocked by the death of the deceased, such as insurance or pension policies.[50] It has been doubted whether the mere accretion of wealth by the deceased after the dissolution of the marriage would of itself justify such an application.[51] Again an application succeeded where the deceased died intestate less than a year after an order in divorce proceedings to make periodical payments to his former spouse. The court decided that the nil provision for the former spouse under the intestacy rules did not make reasonable financial provision for her,

[41] s.25(1) as amended by 1984 Act, s.25(1) and (2): British Islands means the U.K., Channel Islands and Isle of Man, Interpretation Act 1978, s. 5 and Sched. 1.

[42] *Ante*, p. 104.

[43] s.15 as amended by 1984 Act, s.8: for similar order following overseas divorce or annulment see s.15A as amended by 1984 Act, s.25(3). For an instance see *Kokosinski* v. *Kokosinski* [1980] Fam. 72, 88: see also *Re Fullard* [1982] Fam. 42, 49–50. Apart from s.15, *semble* the court's jurisdiction under the 1975 Act cannot be ousted by agreement with the deceased during his lifetime, see *Re M.* [1968] P. 174.

[44] *Ante*, p. 107.

[45] ss.3(2) and 14: see *ante* p. 107.

[46] *Re Fullard* [1982] Fam. 42 (agreement by which W purchased H's share in matrimonial home settled financial affairs on divorce).

[47] *Ibid.*

[48] *Ibid.* at pp. 45–46; in the case of a small estate the onus on the applicant of satisfying s.2(1) is "very heavy indeed," p. 46: see also *Brill* v. *Proud* [1984] Fam. Law 19.

[49] *Ibid.* at pp. 49 and 52; *Re Crawford* (1983) 4 F.L.R. 273; *cf. Cumming Burns* v. *Burns* (1985) Transcript on Lexis. For the relevance of a secured periodical payments order see *Re Eyre* [1968] 1 W.L.R. 530: for the court's powers to vary or discharge such an order see *post*, p. 130, n. 50.

[50] *Re Fullard, supra,* at pp. 49 and 52.

[51] *Ibid.* at p. 52: but see *Re Eyre, supra,* at p. 543.

having regard to the fact that the periodical payments order ran for such a short time.[52]

Relevance of conduct. Probably the court will consider the conduct of the parties which led to the breakdown of the marriage to be irrelevant except in a minority of cases where it would have been relevant in an application for financial provision in divorce proceedings.[53]

3. A child of the deceased. This category includes a child of the deceased *en ventre sa mère* at the deceased's death,[54] an illegitimate child,[55] and a child adopted by the deceased.[56]

The maintenance standard is applicable on an application by a child of the deceased.[57] *The particular guideline* to which the court must have regard is (d) "the manner in which the applicant was being or in which he might expect to be educated or trained."[58]

Application by adult son or daughter. Under the 1938 Act, a son who had attained the age of 21 years and a daughter who had been married were not eligible to apply for provision to be made for their maintenance out of the deceased's estate unless, by reason of some mental or physical disability, they were incapable of maintaining themselves.[59] Under the 1975 Act, there is no age limit or requirement that an applicant must not have been married.[60] In what circumstances is an application by an adult son or daughter appropriate under the 1975 Act?

The particular guideline points to one such situation—the deceased dies whilst supporting his adult son or daughter in the process of acquiring some educational or occupational qualification.[61] General guideline (f)[62] points to another—by reason of physical or mental disability the applicant cannot maintain him or herself,[63] or, perhaps, is seriously handicapped in earning capacity.[64] Again the deceased may have obligations and responsibilities under general guideline (d) towards an applicant who gives up work in order to care for the

---

[52] *Re Farrow* [1987] 1 F.L.R. 205.
[53] *Ante*, p. 117.
[54] s.25(1).
[55] *Ibid.*
[56] Adoption Act 1976, s.39.
[57] *Ante*, p. 107. For an instance see *Re Chatterton,* unreported but referred to in [1980] Conv. 150 (daughter aged five, whom deceased had never seen).
[58] s.3(3).
[59] 1938 Act, s.1(1).
[60] See Law. Com. No. 61, paras. 71–79.
[61] *Re Coventry* [1980] Ch. 461, 469–470 and 476; see *Re Snoek* (1982) Transcript on Lexis.
[62] *Ante*, p. 113.
[63] *Re Wood* (1982) Transcript on Lexis (daughter mentally disabled, residing in hospital: £15,000 ordered for extra comforts such as electric wheelchair, outings and holidays); *Re Debenham* (1986) 7 F.L.R. 404 (married daughter, 58, sick with epilepsy); *Re Pointer* [1941] Ch. 60; *Milward* v. *Shenton* [1972] 1 W.L.R. 711 (see *ante*, p. 113): *cf. Re Andrews* [1955] 1 W.L.R. 1105 (father owed no moral obligation to daughter incapable of maintaining herself, who left home 42 years before to live as common law wife).
[64] See *Re Clayton* [1966] 1 W.L.R. 969 (widower crippled in both legs: maintained himself but handicapped in earning capacity and in looking after himself).

deceased during illness or old age,[65] or to a daughter who is a widow with young children and who has not been provided for by her deceased husband.[66]

In *Re Coventry*[67] Oliver J. commented that applications for maintenance under the 1975 Act "by able-bodied and comparatively young men in employment and able to maintain themselves must be relatively rare and need to be approached . . . with a degree of circumspection."[68] In that case a son who was 46 years old, in good health and working as a chauffeur, applied for provision to be made for him out of his father's £7,000 net estate. His financial resources left him little or no margin for expenditure on anything other than the necessities of life. The father had died intestate, leaving his widow, who was 74 years old, solely entitled under the intestacy rules. She had lived apart from the deceased without any maintenance from him for the last 19 years. During that period the son had lived rent free with his father but had provided his father's food and contributed to the household outgoings. The Court of Appeal, affirming the decision of Oliver J., held that it was reasonable that the disposition of the deceased's estate effected by the intestacy rules made no provision for the son's maintenance and the son's application therefore failed at the first hurdle.[69] There was no "special circumstance" (such as a moral obligation upon the deceased to make such provision for the son) which made this unreasonable.[70]

In all probability an application by an adult daughter, who has no disability and is in employment and able to maintain herself, will similarly fail at the first hurdle in the absence of any special circumstance.[71] The same is true of an application by a married daughter whose husband is supporting her.[72]

---

[65] *Re Coventry* [1980] Ch. 461, 476–477: see *Re Cook* (1956) unreported but referred to in 106 L.J. 466.
[66] Law Com. No. 61, para. 78.
[67] [1980] Ch. 461.
[68] *Ibid.* at p. 465. But there is no "especially heavy burden on a male applicant of full age beyond that which must, as a practical matter, necessarily exist when a person who applies to be maintained by somebody else is already capable of adequately maintaining himself," *ibid.* at p. 474: see also *Re Dennis* [1981] 2 All E.R. 140, 145.
[69] *Ante,* p. 109.
[70] [1980] Ch. 461, 487–489 and 494–495. *Cf. Re Christie* [1979] Ch. 168 (adult son took half T's £13,000 estate, under T's will: held not reasonable provision and T's £9,000 house should be transferred to son): this was a hard case but the decision was unsatisfactory because (i) no evidence son was in any need (he already owned £14,000 house subject to £6,000 mortgage), (ii) deputy judge defined maintenance too widely, *ante,* p. 108, n. 34, and (iii) applied subjective test and relied on T's non-testamentary intention to give house to son, *ante,* p. 109: for criticism see *Re Coventry* [1980] Ch. 461, 471–472 and 490.
[71] Applications under the 1938 Act succeeded in *Re Borthwick* [1949] Ch. 395 (modest salary; £130,000 net estate); *Re Ducksbury* [1966] 1 W.L.R. 1226 (daughter, part-time art student aged 30, earned meagre living in part-time employment: order to help provide for future needs when no longer able to earn own living); *Re Sivyer* [1967] 1 W.L.R. 1482 (daughter aged 13 living with foster parents): and failed in *Mastaka* v. *Midland Bank Executor and Trustee Co. Ltd.* [1941] Ch. 192 (daughter aged 19; ordinary relationship of mother and daughter did not exist); *Re Andrews* [1955] 1 W.L.R. 1105 (see *ante,* n. 63). The applicant succeeded in *Re Leach* [1986] Ch. 226 (adult child of the family, employed but near retirement, and had relied on deceased's stated intention to make provision by will).
[72] *Re Rowlands* (1984) 5 F.L.R. 813: see Law Com. No. 61, paras. 74 and 78; *Re Andrews* [1955] 1 W.L.R. 1105.

4. A person treated by the deceased as a child of the family in relation to any marriage to which the deceased was at any time a party (not being the deceased's child).

The maintenance standard is applicable on an application by such a person.[73] *The particular guidelines* to which the court must have regard are the same guideline (d) (as to education or training) as is applicable on an application by a child of the deceased,[74] and also the following three guidelines[75]:

(e) whether the deceased had assumed any responsibility for the applicant's maintenance and, if so, the extent to which and the basis upon which the deceased assumed that responsibility and the length of time for which the deceased discharged that responsibility[76];

(f) whether in assuming and discharging that responsibility the deceased did so knowing that the applicant was not his own child; and

(g) the liability[77] of any other person to maintain the applicant.

Application by adult stepchild. Obviously this category covers a young step-child whose mother or father married the deceased and who was brought up by the deceased as a child of the family after the marriage. However this category is not restricted to minor or dependant children. In *Re Callaghan*[78] the successful applicant was 35 years of age and living with his wife in their own home when his mother married the deceased. The deceased treated the applicant as a child (albeit an adult child) of the family in relation to this marriage by acknowledging his own role of grandfather to the applicant's children, placing confidences as to his property and financial affairs in the applicant, and depending upon the applicant to care for him in his last illness.[79] The deceased died intestate and the court held that the nil provision for the applicant under the intestacy rules did not make reasonable financial provision for his maintenance, especially as the deceased's assets were derived from the applicant's mother and ultimately from a gift to her by his paternal grandfather after his father was killed on active service.[80] Treatment of a person as a child of the family refers to the behaviour

---

[73] *Ante*, p. 107.

[74] *Ante*, p. 120.

[75] s.3(3): these three guidelines correspond to those applicable on an application by such a child in matrimonial proceedings, Matrimonial Causes Act 1973, s.25(4) as amended by 1984 Act.

[76] Under this guideline the assumption by the deceased of responsibility for the applicant's maintenance is not essential for success, *Re Beaumont* [1980] Ch. 444, 454–455; *Re Leach* [1986] Ch. 226, 231: *cf.* the wording of the particular guideline applicable on an application by a dependant, *post*, p. 123.

[77] This means any liability enforceable at law, whether or not an order has been made, *Roberts* v. *Roberts* [1962] P. 212.

[78] [1985] Fam. 1: see *Re Leach* [1986] Ch. 226 (step-daughter was 32 when her father married the deceased).

[79] *Per* Booth J. in *Re Callaghan, ibid.* at p. 6. *Quaere* whether treatment of the applicant as a child of the family *before* the marriage suffices, *ibid.*

[80] *Ibid.* at p. 7 (lump sum payment of £15,000 ordered from £31,000 estate to enable applicant to buy his council house).

of the deceased towards that person. The mere display of affection, kindness, or hospitality by a step-parent towards a step-child does not by itself constitute such treatment.[81] The deceased must, as wife or husband (or widow or widower[82]) under the relevant marriage, expressly or impliedly, assume the position of a parent towards the applicant, with the attendant responsibilities and privileges of that relationship.[83] Normally the privileges of the quasi-parent tend to increase and the responsibilities to diminish as the years go by. In *Re Callaghan* the privileges of the elderly quasi-parent were more important than the responsibilities.[84]

5. A dependant of the deceased. This category covers any person (not falling within the preceding categories) "who immediately before the death of the deceased was being maintained, either wholly or partly, by the deceased."[85] Section 1(3) provides that a person shall be treated as being so maintained by the deceased only[86] "if the deceased, otherwise than for full valuable consideration, was making a substantial contribution in money or money's worth towards the reasonable needs of that person." The Law Commission recommended the introduction of this new category of applicant,[87] whom it is convenient to call a dependant of the deceased. Obviously this new category is not confined to relatives of the deceased or to members of the deceased's household, and it covers persons who had no right to maintenance enforceable against the deceased during his lifetime.[88]

The maintenance standard is applicable on an application by a dependant.[89] *The particular guideline* to which the court must have regard is (h) "the extent to which and the basis upon which the deceased assumed responsibility for the maintenance of the applicant and . . . the length of time for which the deceased discharged that responsibility."[90] No minimum period of dependence on the deceased is prescribed but the length of this period is a matter to which the court must have regard.

---

[81] *Re Leach* [1986] Ch. 226, 235.

[82] Treatment of the applicant as a child of the family *after* the marriage has ended by the death of the other spouse is a relevant factor if the treatment stems from the marriage, *ibid.* at pp. 233–235 (giving an example). If treatment occurs, it need not continue until the deceased dies, *ibid.* at p. 233.

[83] *Ibid.* at p. 237.

[84] *Ibid.*

[85] s.1(1)(e). See generally Cadwallader [1980] Conv. 46; *Naresh* (1980) 96 L.Q.R. 534.

[86] s.1(3) is to be construed as if the word "only" was inserted in it, so that s.1(3) qualifies s.1(1)(e) and does not provide an alternative to it, *Re Beaumont* [1980] Ch. 444, 450–451; *Jelley* v. *Iliffe* [1981] Fam. 128.

[87] Law Com. No. 61, paras. 85–98.

[88] See *Re Wilkinson* [1978] Fam. 22 (sister acting as companion); *Re Viner* [1978] C.L.Y. 3091 (poor widowed sister); *Malone* v. *Harrison* [1979] 1 W.L.R. 1353 (mistress); *Re C.* (1979) 123 S.J. 35 (common law wife); *Jelley* v. *Iliffe, supra* (common law husband); *Harrington* v. *Gill* (1983) 4 F.L.R. 265 (common law wife); *Williams* v. *Roberts* (1984) Transcript on Lexis (common law wife).

[89] *Ante,* p. 107.

[90] s.3(4).

Burden of proof. The burden of proof lies upon an applicant[91] under this category to prove that immediately before the death of the deceased:

(i) the deceased was making a substantial contribution in money or money's worth towards the reasonable needs of the applicant,[92] and

(ii) the deceased was doing so otherwise than for full valuable consideration.[93]

In *Re Wilkinson*[94] the deceased provided board and lodging for her sister, the applicant, who did a share of the light housework and cooking, helped the deceased to dress, and acted as companion to her. Arnold J. held that requirements (i) and (ii) were satisfied because the sister did not do enough to provide full valuable consideration for her board and lodging.

Does requirement (ii) mean full valuable consideration *under a contract*? Arnold J. answered no—the applicant's services had to be valued in order to decide whether they constituted full valuable consideration, irrespective of whether there was a contractual duty to provide those services.[95] And in *Re Beaumont*[96] Megarry V.-C. took the same view and so did the Court of Appeal in *Jelley v. Iliffe.*[97]

Deceased's assumption of responsibility. In *Re Beaumont*[98] Megarry V.-C. held that an applicant must also prove that before his death the deceased had assumed responsibility for the applicant's maintenance. He arrived at this conclusion because the particular guideline (h) applicable to a dependant makes an implicit assumption that the deceased had done so, unlike the particular guideline (e) applicable to a person treated by the deceased as a child of the family.[99] An applicant does not, however, need to prove that the deceased had assumed responsibility for the applicant's maintenance *after the death of the deceased.*[1]

In *Jelley v. Iliffe* the Court of Appeal decided that, as a general rule, proof that the deceased was maintaining the applicant raises a presumption that the deceased had assumed responsibility for the applicant's maintenance.[2] There need be no other overt act to demonstrate the deceased's assumption of responsibility[3]: by making a substantial

[91] *Re Wilkinson, supra,* at p. 23.
[92] *Re Wilkinson, supra,* (board and lodging); *Re Viner, supra,* (£5 per week); *Malone* v. *Harrison, supra,* (all living expenses paid; also flats in England and Malta in joint names, a car, £15,000 shares, and £5,500 furs and jewellery); *Re C., supra,* (lived as his wife); *Jelley* v. *Iliffe* [1981] Fam. 128 (rent-free accommodation); *Harrington* v. *Gill, supra,* (lived as his wife).
[93] Valuable consideration does not include marriage or a promise of marriage, s.25(1).
[94] [1978] Fam. 22.
[95] *Ibid.* at p. 25: this view was criticised in (1978) 94 L.Q.R. 175 and (1978) 41 M.L.R. 352.
[96] [1980] Ch. 444, 453–454 and 456–457.
[97] [1981] Fam. 128.
[98] [1980] Ch. 444.
[99] *Ibid.* at pp. 454–456: see *ante,* p. 122.
[1] *Jelley* v. *Iliffe* [1981] Fam. 128.
[2] [1981] Fam. 128: *Re Beaumont* [1980] Ch. 444, 457–458 is overruled on this point. It may be that the presumption can be rebutted by circumstances, including a disclaimer of any intention to maintain, *per* Stephenson L.J. in *Jelley* v. *Iliffe, supra,* at p. 137.
[3] *Per* Griffiths L.J. in *Jelley* v. *Iliffe, supra,* at p. 142.

contribution in money or money's worth towards the reasonable needs of the applicant the deceased both assumed, and discharged, responsibility for the applicant's maintenance. Thus the requirement that before his death the deceased had assumed responsibility for the applicant's maintenance does not in general increase the burden of proof upon an applicant.

Under the particular guideline (h) it is obviously material for the court to have regard to the extent to which and the basis upon which the deceased assumed responsibility for the applicant's maintenance. At one extreme the deceased may have assumed this responsibility for the rest of the applicant's life,[4] and at the other the deceased may have disclaimed any further responsibility beyond the contribution he made.[5] Again the deceased may have assumed responsibility for the applicant's complete maintenance on a generous scale,[6] or (on the other hand) grudgingly assumed responsibility for the applicant's partial maintenance.[7]

Immediately before the death of the deceased. Requirements (i) and (ii) of the burden of proof must be satisfied "immediately before the death of the deceased."[8] What if the situation immediately before the death differs from normal? For instance, C, who normally lives with and is fully maintained by D, falls ill and enters a N.H.S. hospital for investigation: D dies whilst C is still in hospital. If only the abnormal situation at the instant before D's death is to be considered, C is not a dependant of D.[9] In *Re Beaumont* Megarry V.-C. held that the court should consider the settled basis or arrangement at D's death, under which C was fully maintained by D, rather than any temporary variation due to C being in hospital.[10] And in *Jelley* v. *Iliffe*[11] the Court of Appeal took the same view: if, for example, D has been making regular payments to the support of C an old friend, C's claim to be a dependant is not defeated if those payments cease during D's terminal illness because D is too ill to make them.[12]

---

[4] *Malone* v. *Harrison* [1979] 1 W.L.R. 1353, 1358 and 1364–1365 (cable to mistress, "I say to you you will have happiness and contentment with security for ever").
[5] See *Re Beaumont* [1980] Ch. 444, 458 ("it may be that would-be benefactors who wish to protect their families ought to obtain from anyone to whose maintenance they propose to contribute an acknowledgment that they are undertaking no responsibility for his or her [future] maintenance"): Law Com. No. 61, para. 97.
[6] *Malone* v. *Harrison, supra,* (at least £4,000 per annum, plus furs and jewellery and two flats in joint names).
[7] *Re Viner* [1978] C.L.Y. 3091 (£5 per week paid for six months before death: provision ordered restricted to that made by deceased).
[8] s.1(1)(e): see *Kourkey* v. *Lusher, The Times,* December 9, 1981 (responsibility abandoned before death for maintenance of mistress); *Layton* v. *Martin* (1985) Transcript on Lexis (common law wife dismissed two years before death of deceased: not dependant at death).
[9] For this and other examples see *Re Beaumont* [1980] Ch. 444, 451–453.
[10] [1980] Ch. 444, 452–453: similarly, services rendered temporarily by C to D, such as nursing D during D's last illness, do not debar C from being a dependant because the court considers the settled arrangement, *ibid.*
[11] [1981] Fam. 128.
[12] *Per* Griffiths L.J. in *Jelley* v. *Iliffe, supra,* at p. 141.

Weighing the contribution of each to the other's needs. If C and D live together and each of them makes some contribution towards the other's reasonable needs, on D's death C can claim as a dependant if D's contribution was substantially greater than C's.[13] But if the contributions were broadly equal, or C's contribution was greater than D's, C cannot claim.[14]

The court takes a broad common sense view of the issue whether C was a dependant of D: the right question to ask is whether C was dependent on D for maintenance during D's lifetime, or did C give as good as C got?[15] In striking a balance between their respective contributions "the court must use common sense and remember that the object of Parliament in creating this extra class of persons who may claim benefit from an estate was to provide relief for persons of whom it could truly be said that they were wholly or partially dependent on the deceased. It cannot be an exact exercise of evaluating services in pounds and pence. By way of example, if a man was living with a woman as his wife providing the house and all the money for their living expenses, she would clearly be dependent upon him, and it would not be right to deprive her of her claim by arguing that she was in fact performing the services that a housekeeper would perform and it would cost more to employ a housekeeper than was spent on her and indeed perhaps more than the deceased had available to spend upon her."[16]

D. Orders which the Court May Make

The deceased's net estate. The deceased's "net estate," from which the court may order provision to be made for an applicant, is widely defined in the 1975 Act.

Property always included in the net estate. The deceased's net estate always includes the following property[17]:

(a) All property of which the deceased had power to dispose by his will[18] (except by virtue of a special power of appointment) *less* the amount of his funeral, testamentary and administration expenses, debts and liabilities, including any inheritance tax payable out of his estate on his death. This category does not include benefits arising under assurance policies on the life of the deceased if the benefits are payable direct to a beneficiary and not to the deceased's estate.[19]

(b) Any property in respect of which the deceased held a general

---

[13] *Ibid.*

[14] *Per* Stephenson L.J. in *Jelley* v. *Iliffe, supra* at pp. 138–139: see *Re Kirby* (1981) 11 Fam. Law 210.

[15] *Per* Stephenson L.J. in *Jelley* v. *Iliffe, supra* at p. 139.

[16] *Per* Griffiths L.J. in *Jelley* v. *Iliffe, supra,* at p. 141.

[17] s.25(1): "property" includes any chose in action, *ibid. Cf.* the property which constitutes assets for the payment of the deceased's debts and liabilities, see *post,* pp. 251 *et seq.*

[18] Or would have had power to dispose by will if he had been of full age and capacity, s.25(2): it is immaterial that the estate passes as *bona vacantia* on the death of the deceased intestate, s.24. Probably property, or a debt, subject to the Rule in *Strong* v. *Bird (ante,* p. 25) falls within category (a).

[19] But category (e) may be applicable, see *post,* p. 127. For occupational pension benefits see *Re Cairnes* (1983) 4 F.L.R. 225; Rosettenstein (1979) 123 S.J. 661.

power of appointment (not exercisable by will) which has not been exercised. This category does not apply if it has been exercised.[20] If the general power was exercisable by will, the property falls within category (a), whether or not the deceased exercised the power.

(c) Any sum of money or other property nominated to any person by the deceased under a statutory nomination[21] or received by any person from the deceased as a *donatio mortis causa, less* any inheritance tax payable in respect thereof and borne by the nominee or donee.[22]

Property included if court so orders. The deceased's net estate also includes the property in each of the following two categories if the court so orders:

(d) The deceased's severable share of any property of which he was a beneficial joint tenant immediately before his death.[23] If the deceased and X were beneficial joint tenants of (say) a house or a chose in action (such as an account with a bank) immediately before the deceased's death, X becomes absolutely entitled by operation of the right of survivorship at the deceased's death. But the court nevertheless has power to order that the deceased's severable share shall, to such extent as appears just in all the circumstances and having regard to any inheritance tax payable in respect of that share, be treated as part of the deceased's net estate.[24] Such an order may only be made if an application is made to the court for an order under the 1975 Act within the six months' time limit[25]: if no application is made within this time limit, X cannot be deprived in this way of the benefit of the right of survivorship because this category of property is not available on an application made out of time with the court's permission.

Of course, if the deceased and X were beneficial tenants in common, the deceased's undivided share falls within category (a).

(e) Any sum of money or other property which the court directs to be provided by any person under its powers to prevent evasion of the 1975 Act.[26] These powers are considered later.[27]

Forms of provision ordered for applicant. If the court is satisfied that the disposition of the deceased's estate is not such as to make reasonable financial provision for the applicant, measured by the surviving spouse or maintenance standard as is appropriate, the court may, in the

[20] Again category (e) may be applicable.

[21] For statutory nominations see *ante,* p. 15.

[22] ss.8 and 25(1): s.8 protects a person who pays money or transfers property in accordance with the nomination or *donatio mortis causa.* If any such inheritance tax is repaid in consequence of an order making provision for an applicant, it forms part of the deceased's net estate, Inheritance Tax Act 1984, s.146(1), (4), (5) and (7): see *post,* p. 131.

[23] ss.9 and 25(1). For an instance see *Re Crawford* (1983) 4 F.L.R. 273 (building society and bank accounts held jointly by deceased and second wife).

[24] Valuation is to be made as at immediately before the death of the deceased, s.9(1). Any person is protected for anything done by him before an order is made, s.9(3); *e.g.* the bank is protected if it pays the surviving joint tenant. If any such inheritance tax borne by the surviving joint tenant is repaid in consequence of the order, it forms part of the deceased's net estate, Inheritance Tax Act 1984, s.146(1), (4), (5) and (7): see *post,* p. 131.

[25] s.9(1): see *ante,* p. 105.

[26] ss.10, 11 and 25(1).

[27] *Post,* pp. 134 *et seq.*

exercise of its discretion, make any one or more of the following orders.[28]

(1) *Periodical payments, i.e.* an order for the making of periodical payments to the applicant out of the deceased's net estate. Such an order may provide for periodical payments:

   (i) of a specified amount[29] (*e.g.* £10 per week), *or*
  (ii) equal to the whole, or a specified part, of the income of the net estate (*e.g.* one-half of the income of the net estate), *or*
 (iii) equal to the whole of the income of such part of the net estate as the court directs to be set aside or appropriated.[30]

Alternatively such an order may provide for the amount of the periodical payments to be determined in any other way the court thinks fit.[31] The 1975 Act does not limit the maximum amount which may be awarded by way of periodical payments by reference to the estimated income of the net estate.[32] In practice the court has regard to the amount of this estimated income, but the court has power to order periodical payments in excess of this amount so that some capital has to be used.

Periodical payments are payable for the period specified by the court in the order.[33] Usually such payments are ordered to run from the death of the deceased (the court fixes the commencing date at its discretion)[34] and invariably the payments are ordered to terminate at the latest at the death of the applicant. An order for the making of periodical payments to a judicially separated spouse or former spouse of the deceased terminates automatically on the remarriage of that spouse.[35] However, the 1975 Act does not specify any other event on which an order for periodical payments terminates. It follows that periodical payments continue to be payable to the widow or widower of the deceased[36] despite remarriage, unless the court has otherwise ordered.[37] Similarly, periodical payments continue to be payable to a child of the deceased despite attainment of full age or marriage, unless the court has otherwise ordered.[37]

---

[28] s.2(1).
[29] In that case the court may direct that a sufficient, but not excessive, part of the net estate be set aside or appropriated to meet the payments by its income, s.2(3).
[30] s.2(2).
[31] *Ibid.*
[32] See *Re Blanch* [1967] 1 W.L.R. 987, 992.
[33] s.2(1)(*a*): *Re Blanch, supra,* at pp. 992–993.
[34] See *Askew* v. *Askew* [1961] 1 W.L.R. 725 (former wife had received national assistance payments since death of former husband: order ran from death despite possible repayment); *Re Goodwin* [1969] 1 Ch. 283, 292: *cf. Re Lecoche* (1967) 111 S.J. 136 (order from date of judgment to avoid sale of house); *Re Eyre* [1968] 1 W.L.R. 530, 544 (date of summons); *Lusternik* v. *Lusternik* [1972] Fam. 125 (late application and proceedings over four years); *Re Debenham* (1986) 7 F.L.R. 404 (date of order, plus small lump sum to obviate need to backdate order as applicant had received social security).
[35] s.19(2); but any arrears are still payable, *ibid.*
[36] And also to a person who in good faith entered into a void marriage with the deceased, see *ante*, p. 115.
[37] Or unless the court varies its order, see *post*, p. 132. See generally Law Com. No. 61, paras. 37–43.

(2) *Lump sum payment.* The court may order a lump sum to be paid to the applicant out of the deceased's net estate. The amount of the lump sum is specified in the order and may extend to the entire net estate.[38] The lump sum may be made payable by instalments and the court may subsequently vary the number of instalments payable, and the amount, and date of payment, of any instalment but not the amount of the lump sum itself.[39] In the case of a small estate a lump sum payment may well be the only practicable order.

(3) *Transfer of property.* The court may order the transfer to the applicant of specified property comprised in the deceased's net estate.[40] This may be preferable to an order for a lump sum payment if the latter would necessitate an improvident sale of assets.

(4) *Settlement of property.* Again the court may order the settlement for the applicant's benefit of specified property comprised in the deceased's net estate.[41]

(5) *Acquisition of property for transfer or settlement.* The court may also order the acquisition of specified property (for instance, a house) out of assets comprised in the deceased's net estate, and either the transfer of the acquired property to the applicant or the settlement of it for his benefit.

(6) *Variation of marriage settlement.* Finally the court may order a variation of any ante-nuptial or post-nuptial settlement (including one made by will) made on the parties to a marriage of the deceased.[42] The variation must be for the benefit of the surviving spouse of that marriage, or any child of that marriage, or any person who was treated by the deceased as a child of the family in relation to that marriage. This form of provision, unlike all the others, is restricted to these particular applicants.

Quantum of provision ordered. If an application passes the first hurdle, the court determines whether, and in what manner, it shall order provision to be made for an applicant. The only express requirement is that in doing so the court must have regard to the general and particular guidelines.[43] But it seems implicit that the court should use the surviv-

---

[38] s.25(3).

[39] s.7; see *Re Besterman* [1984] Ch. 458, 478 (if lump sum, court should take account of contingencies and inflation). Application for variation may be made by the person to whom the lump sum is payable, the personal representatives of the deceased, or the trustees of the property out of which the lump sum is payable, s.7(2).

[40] *e.g.* a house, *Re Christie* [1979] Ch. 168. A weekly contractual tenancy is "property," *Hale* v. *Hale* [1975] 1 W.L.R. 931 (private landlord); *Thompson* v. *Thompson* [1976] Fam. 25 (local authority landlord).

[41] And confer on the trustees of the property such powers as appear to the court to be necessary or expedient, s.2(4)(*c*): see *e.g. Harrington* v. *Gill* (1983) 4 F.L.R. 265 (house to be settled on applicant for life).

[42] Settlement has a wide meaning in this context but does not cover an absolute, unqualified and immediate transfer of property, see *Prinsep* v. *Prinsep* [1929] P. 225, 232; *Prescott* v. *Fellowes* [1958] P. 260.

[43] s.3(1).

ing spouse, or maintenance, standard of reasonable financial provision (applicable at the first stage of the application) as a measure of the provision to be ordered for the applicant at the second stage.[44]

If the surviving spouse standard is applicable and the court orders a lump sum payment, in fixing the amount of that payment the court does not start with a bias against making a provision which may, ultimately, enable the applicant to make provision for somebody else who is not an applicant. That possibility is inherent in a lump sum order under the surviving spouse standard.[45] But the position is different if the maintenance standard is applicable because maintenance of the applicant is then a limiting factor.[46] In fixing the amount of a lump sum payment under the maintenance standard the court assumes that the applicant will have to spend capital as well as income on maintenance during the period for which provision is being made.[47] However generally it would not be right to treat the value of an applicant's home as expendable capital.[48] The possibility of marriage may also be a relevant factor in fixing this amount.[49]

Consequential and supplemental provisions. An order of the court may contain such consequential and supplemental provisions as the court thinks necessary or expedient for the purpose of (1) giving effect to the order, or (2) securing that it operates fairly as between the beneficiaries.[50]

(1) *Giving effect to the order.* In particular the court has power to order any person who holds any property which forms part of the deceased's net estate to make such payment, or to transfer such property, as is specified in the order.[51] This power is useful because the deceased's net estate may include property held by persons other than the deceased's personal representatives—for instance, property nominated by the deceased under a statutory nomination and (if the court so orders) the deceased's severable share of property of which he was a beneficial joint tenant.[52]

---

[44] See *Malone* v. *Harrison* [1979] 1 W.L.R. 1353, 1365 (maintenance standard); *Re Besterman* [1984] Ch. 458 (surviving spouse standard).

[45] *Re Besterman, ibid.* at pp. 466 and 470.

[46] *Ibid.*: see *Re Debenham* (1986) 7 F.L.R. 404 (periodical payments for applicant but not her husband).

[47] *Malone* v. *Harrison, supra,* (period of applicant's actuarial expectation of life, with possibility of marriage; "it is not my duty to provide for the beneficiaries under her will": estate large and multiplier calculation used to fix amount): for criticism of the multiplier calculation see Bryan (1980) 96 L.Q.R. 165 and *cf. Re Brown* (1955) 105 L.J. 169 ("a judge . . . should not condescend to an analytical statement of how he has arrived at that figure").

[48] *Ibid.*

[49] *Ibid:* see also *Re Sivyer* [1967] 1 W.L.R. 1482, 1487–1488 (under 1938 Act).

[50] *Ibid.* s.2(4). For the court's powers to vary or discharge a secured periodical payments order made under the Matrimonial Causes Act 1973, and to vary or revoke a maintenance agreement, see 1975 Act, ss.16 and 17: see also Matrimonial Causes Act 1973, ss.31 (as amended by Administration of Justice Act 1982, s.51 and 1984 Act, s.6) and 36 (as amended by 1975 Act, s.26(1)) and 1975 Act, s.18. See generally Law Com. No. 61, paras. 263–276.

[51] s.2(4)(a). But it appears that the court has no power to order a settlement of the applicant's *own* property, *Malone* v. *Harrison* [1979] 1 W.L.R. 1353, 1366.

[52] *Ante,* p. 127.

(2) *Incidence as between the beneficiaries.* The incidence of the provision ordered is of vital importance to the beneficiaries.[53] The court has power to vary the disposition of the deceased's estate effected by his will or the law relating to intestacy in such manner as the court thinks fair and reasonable, having regard to the provisions of the order and all the circumstances of the case.[54] Thus, if the court makes an order for the transfer to the applicant of property which was specifically given to a beneficiary by the will, the court may vary the disposition of the deceased's estate so as to make some other provision for that beneficiary. Again, if the court makes an order for periodical payments or a lump sum payment to an applicant, the court may direct from which part of the net estate this provision is to be made and which of the beneficiaries are to bear the burden of it. For example, the court may throw the burden of an order for periodical payments on to specific gifts and pecuniary legacies as well as on to residuary gifts,[55] or the burden of a lump sum payment on to the residuary beneficiaries in proportions different from their respective shares of residue.[56] The court has an unfettered discretion and is not bound by a direction in a will as to the incidence of any provision which may be ordered.[57]

Effect of an order. If the court makes an order making provision for an applicant, then for all purposes (including the inheritance tax legislation) the deceased's will or the law relating to intestacy (or both) are deemed to have had effect as from the deceased's death subject to the provisions of the order.[58] An order for a lump sum payment therefore makes the applicant "the equivalent of a beneficiary under the will"[59] or intestacy, and entitled to enforce the order by administration proceedings.[60]

Interim order. The court has power to make an interim order in favour of an applicant.

Two requirements. There are two requirements. It must appear to the court:

(i) that the applicant is in immediate need of financial assistance, but it is not yet possible to determine what final order (if any) should be made; and

(ii) that property forming part of the deceased's net estate is or can be made available to meet the need of the applicant.[61]

In determining what interim order (if any) to make the court must have

---

[53] *i.e.* a person beneficially interested under the deceased's will or intestacy, or a person who takes under a statutory nomination or a *donatio mortis causa* made by the deceased, s.25(1).

[54] s.2(4)(*b*): see also s.24.

[55] *Re Simson* [1950] Ch. 38: see also *Re Jackson* [1952] 2 T.L.R. 90.

[56] *Re Preston* [1969] 1 W.L.R. 317.

[57] *Ibid.*

[58] s.19(1): see also as to inheritance tax, Inheritance Tax Act 1984, s.146.

[59] *Re Jennery* [1967] Ch. 280, 286: see also *Re Pointer* [1946] Ch. 324.

[60] *Ibid.* For administration proceedings see *post*, pp. 396 *et seq.*

[61] s.5(1).

regard, so far as the urgency of the case admits, to the general and particular guidelines.[62]

Form of interim order. By an interim order the court orders payment to the applicant out of the deceased's net estate of such sum or sums, and (if more than one) at such intervals, as the court thinks reasonable.[63] Such an order may impose conditions or restrictions[64] and may contain consequential and supplemental provisions.[65]

By its final order making provision for the applicant the court may direct to what extent any sum paid to the applicant under the interim order is to be treated as having been paid on account of any payment provided for by the final order.[66]

Protection of personal representative. A personal representative who makes a payment under an interim order does not incur any liability by reason of the net estate not being sufficient to make that payment unless at the time of the payment he has reasonable cause to believe that the estate is not sufficient.[67] This protection for the personal representative is necessary in case a payment made by him under an interim order leaves insufficient assets (as events turn out) to pay the deceased's funeral, testamentary and administration expenses, debts and liabilities in full.

E. VARIATION OR DISCHARGE OF A PERIODICAL PAYMENTS ORDER

Under section 6 of the 1975 Act the court has a wide power to vary or discharge any order already made for the making of periodical payments to an applicant.[68] The court exercises this power by making a new order, which it is convenient to call a variation order. On the other hand, apart from its power to vary the instalments by which a lump sum has been made payable,[69] the court has no power to vary an order making any other form of provision for an applicant. This is in the interests of finality and certainty in the administration of an estate.

The relevant property. A variation order may only affect "relevant property."[70] There are two alternatives to consider:

---

[62] s.5(3).

[63] s.5(1). For instances see *Re Besterman* [1984] Ch. 458 (£75,000 capital for widow to buy house and £11,500 income for her maintenance); *Stead* v. *Stead* (1985) 6 F.L.R. 16.

[64] *Ibid.* see *Re Ralphs* [1968] 1 W.L.R. 1522, 1524 (interim order directed payment of £10 per week to widow, to be brought into account against income to which entitled under will).

[65] s.5(2); see *ante*, p. 130: the provisions as to periodical payments in s.2(2) and (3) are also applicable.

[66] s.5(4).

[67] s.20(2).

[68] This power to vary applies to a periodical payments order made under the 1938 or 1965 Act, as well as one made under the 1975 Act, s.26(4): see *Re Fricker* (1981) 11 Fam. Law 188.

[69] *Ante*, p. 129.

[70] s.6(6).

(i) The variation order is made *before* the periodical payments have ceased to be payable under the original order. In that case the relevant property means property the income of which is applicable wholly or in part for the making of the periodical payments at the date of the variation order.[71] The extent of this property depends on the terms of the original order. For instance, the original order may have directed part of the deceased's net estate to be set aside or appropriated and the periodical payments made out of its income: in that case the relevant property is that part of the deceased's net estate which has been set aside or appropriated.

(ii) The variation order is made *after* the periodical payments have ceased to be payable under the original order, *i.e.* after the occurrence of a terminating event specified in the original order[72] (*e.g.* the death of the applicant), or after the expiration of the period of payment so specified (*e.g.* the period during which the applicant was receiving full-time instruction at an educational establishment). In that case the relevant property means property the income of which was applicable wholly or in part for the making of periodical payments immediately before the occurrence of that event or the expiration of that period.[73] But this alternative only applies if application for a variation order is made within six months from the date of the occurrence of that event[74] or the expiration of that period.[75]

This rule that a variation order may only affect relevant property imposes a time limit beyond which a variation order either cannot be made (in alternative (i)), or cannot be applied for (in alternative (ii)).

Applicants for variation order. Any of the following persons may apply for a variation order:

(a) a person who either did apply (whether successfully or not), or would but for the time limit be entitled to apply, for an original order[76];

(b) the deceased's personal representatives;

(c) the trustees of any relevant property; and

(d) any beneficiary[77] of the deceased's estate.[78]

The applicant to whom the periodical payments are payable under the original order may apply for a variation order under category (a): such a person is referred to as "the original recipient."

Powers of the court. In exercising its powers the court must have regard to all the circumstances of the case, including any change affect-

---

[71] s.6(6)(*a*).

[72] Other than the remarriage of a former wife or former husband, s.6(3): for the meaning of former wife or former husband see s.25(1) and *ante*, p. 118.

[73] s.6(6)(*b*).

[74] Other than the remarriage of a former wife or former husband, s.6(3): the remarriage of a judicially separated spouse is not referred to in s.6(3), though it is in s.19(2).

[75] s.6(3).

[76] s.6(5)(*a*): see also s.26(4) for an order made under the 1938 or 1965 Act.

[77] *i.e.* a person beneficially interested under the deceased's will or intestacy, or a person who takes under a statutory nomination or a *donatio mortis causa* made by the deceased, s.25(1).

[78] s.6(5).

ing any of the general and particular guidelines which were applicable when the original order was made.[79]

By making a variation order the court may vary or discharge the original order, or suspend any provision of it temporarily, or revive the operation of any suspended provision.[80] The court may also provide for the making of periodical payments after the occurrence of a terminating event specified in the original order (other than the remarriage of the deceased's former wife or husband) or after the expiration of a period so specified.[81]

Instead of (or in addition to) ordering periodical payments to be made, a variation order may direct the payment of a lump sum or the transfer of all or a specified part of the relevant property.[82] Moreover, a variation order is not restricted to making provision for the original recipient: it may provide for any person who either applied (whether successfully or not), or would but for the time limit be entitled to apply, for an original order.[83] But, whatever new provision is ordered, a variation order may only affect the relevant property.[84]

Prior to the variation order the periodical payments may already have ceased to be payable to the original recipient: in that case any new provision made by the variation order cuts down the interest of the beneficiaries in the relevant property. On the other hand, if the periodical payments had not ceased to be payable to the original recipient but the variation order makes new provision for another person, both the original recipient and the beneficiaries may be adversely affected.

Subsequent variation. The court has power subsequently to vary a variation order in so far as it provides for the making of periodical payments.[85]

F. PREVENTION OF EVASION

By taking action in his lifetime a person could easily defeat applications to the court for provision to be made under the 1938 Act after his death. Under the 1938 Act the court might order provision to be made for an applicant out of the deceased's net estate.[86] In order to avoid the Act a person need only reduce the value of his net estate at his death—the smaller the value of his net estate, the less the provision which could be

---

[79] s.6(7): see also s.26(4) for an order made under the 1938 or 1965 Act.
[80] s.6(1): for the power to give consequential directions see s.6(8).
[81] s.6(10): for the meaning of former wife or former husband see s.25(1) and *ante*, p. 118: again the remarriage of a judicially separated spouse is not referred to in s.6(10), though it is in s.19(2).
[82] s.6(2): see also s.6(9).
[83] s.6(2).
[84] s.6(2) and (6).
[85] s.6(4).
[86] Under the 1938 Act (and also the 1965 Act) the deceased's net estate meant all the property of which the deceased had power to dispose by his will (except by virtue of a special power of appointment) *less* the amount of his funeral, testamentary and administration expenses, debts and liabilities and estate duty (or capital transfer tax) payable out of his estate on his death, 1938 Act, s.5(1) and 1965 Act. s.26(6).

ordered by the court. Basically there were two methods of reducing the value of his net estate at his death:

(i) to reduce the property of which he had power to dispose by his will. This could be done by means of dispositions made during his lifetime. For instance, he might make a gift of property to a donee whom he wished to benefit, or settle property on the donee, retaining for himself the income from the settled property until his own death.[87]

(ii) to increase the debts and liabilities payable out of his estate on his death. This could be done by means of contracts made during his lifetime. For instance, he might enter into a contract under seal with a "donee" to pay to the donee at his own death a sum of money large enough to exhaust his assets. Alternatively, he might enter into a contract with the "donee" to leave by his will a particular asset, or a pecuniary legacy, to the donee. If he failed to do so, the donee was entitled to damages for breach of contract against his estate.[88] If he duly did so, in all probability the court had no power to throw the burden of a family provision order on to that particular asset.[89]

The 1975 Act confers powers on the court in order to stop the evasion of just claims for provision by either of these methods. An applicant, who applies to the court for an order making provision for him, may also apply in the same proceedings for an anti-evasion order compelling the "donee" under such a disposition or contract to provide money or other property for the purpose of making financial provision for the applicant.[90] Such an anti-evasion order may also be made against the donee's personal representative or a trustee.

Before the court may make an anti-evasion order the court must be satisfied on four matters[91] and these are considered first.

Four requirements for making of anti-evasion order

(1) *Disposition or contract made by the deceased.* First, a disposition or contract must have been made by the deceased since the Act came into force: the Act does not apply to any disposition or contract made before April 1, 1976.[92]

(a) DISPOSITION. A disposition means any *inter vivos* disposition of property made by the deceased except an appointment made under a special power of appointment. The disposition may be a payment of

---

[87] But *possibly* a fraudulent transfer of property might be set aside so far as necessary to give relief against damage suffered from loss of a chance of obtaining relief under the 1938 Act, *Cadogan* v. *Cadogan* [1977] 1 W.L.R. 1041.

[88] Or specific performance in appropriate circumstances, see *ante*, p. 9.

[89] *Schaefer* v. *Schuhmann* [1972] A.C. 572, esp. at pp. 585 and 587 (P.C. in N.S.W. appeal), not following *Dillon* v. *Public Trustee of New Zealand* [1941] A.C. 294 (P.C. in N.Z. appeal): see also *Re Brown* (1955) 105 L.J. 169.

[90] ss.10–13: an application for such an order against a donee cannot be made in proceedings for variation of a periodical payments order. If an application for an anti-evasion order is made in relation to a disposition, the donee under that disposition (or his personal representative) or any applicant for provision may seek an anti-evasion order in relation to any other disposition made by the deceased, ss.10(5) and 12(4). See generally Sherrin [1978] Conv. 13.

[91] ss.10(2) and 11(2).

[92] ss.10(8), 11(6) and 27(3).

money, including the payment of a premium under an assurance policy, and it is immaterial whether it was made by any instrument or not.[93]

(b) CONTRACT. The Act applies to any contract by which the deceased agreed either to leave by his will a sum of money or other property to any person, or that a sum of money or other property would be paid or transferred to any person out of his estate.[94]

A disposition must have been made less than six years before the deceased's death[95] but no such time limit is applicable to a contract. It follows that a disposition (but not a contract) made at least six years before death remains an effective means of avoiding the 1975 Act. For example, a settlement made at least six years before death effectively avoids the 1975 Act even though the settlor retains for himself both the income from the settled property until his death and a special power of appointment exercisable by deed or will over the settled property.[96] Such a settlement needs to contain an ultimate trust for one or more beneficiaries absolutely in default of appointment: any beneficial interest retained by the settlor which continues after his death falls within his net estate.

(2) *Intention of defeating an application for provision.* The deceased must have made the disposition or contract with the intention of defeating an application for financial provision under the Act.[97] This requirement is satisfied if the court is of the opinion that, on a balance of probabilities, the deceased's intention (though not necessarily his sole intention) was to prevent an order for financial provision being made or to reduce the amount of the provision which might otherwise be ordered.[98]

A special rule applies to a contract made by the deceased for which no valuable consideration was provided by any person, *e.g.* a contract under seal or a contract where the only consideration provided was marriage or a promise of marriage, which is not valuable consideration for this purpose.[99] In that case a rebuttable presumption arises that the deceased made the contract with the required intention of defeating an application for financial provision under the Act.[1]

(3) *Full valuable consideration not given.* The third requirement is that full valuable consideration for the disposition or contract must not have

---

[93] s.10(7): a statutory nomination or a *donatio mortis causa* do not constitute a disposition, *ibid.*: see *Clifford* v. *Tanner* (1986) Transcript on Lexis (husband released daughter from her covenant to permit his wife to live in house: held release was a disposition).

[94] s.11(2)(*a*).

[95] s.10(2)(*a*). See Law Com. No. 61, para. 211 (which recommended this time limit so that the court would not need "to investigate a man's intentions at remote periods of time") and *cf.* para. 237 (no time limit for contract).

[96] For special powers see definition of net estate in s.25(1) and definition of disposition in s.10(7). But for the position at common law see *Cadogan* v. *Cadogan* [1977] 1 W.L.R. 1041.

[97] ss.10(2) and 11(2)(*b*).

[98] s.12(1): see *Re Kennedy* [1980] C.L.Y. 2820.

[99] s.25(1).

[1] s.12(2).

been given by the "donee" or any other person.[2] "The donee" means the person to whom the disposition, or with whom the contract, was made or for whose benefit the disposition, or contract, was made.[3] Marriage or a promise of marriage is not regarded as valuable consideration for this purpose.[4]

(4) *Facilitate financial provision for applicant.* The last requirement is that an anti-evasion order would facilitate the making of financial provision for the applicant.[5]

A disposition is widely defined in the first requirement but the second and third requirements are demanding and very much restrict the number of dispositions open to review after the deceased's death. The class of contracts is narrowly defined in the first requirement and is further restricted by the second and third requirements.

Anti-evasion order against the donee. If the court is satisfied as to these four requirements, the court in the exercise of its discretion may make an anti-evasion order against the donee. In deciding what order (if any) to make the court must have regard to the circumstances in which the disposition or contract was made, any valuable consideration which was given for the disposition, the relationship (if any) of the donee to the deceased, the conduct and financial resources of the donee and all the other circumstances of the case.[6]

(1) *Donee under a disposition.* The court may order the donee under a disposition to provide a specified sum of money or other property for the purpose of making financial provision for the applicant.[7] But the amount of the sum of money, or the value of the property, which the donee is ordered to provide must not exceed the statutory limit on the donee's liability. This statutory limit is:

(i) if the disposition consisted of the payment of money to or for the benefit of the donee, the amount of the payment made by the deceased *less* any inheritance tax borne by the donee in respect of the payment[8];

(ii) if the disposition consisted of the transfer of other property to or for the benefit of the donee, the value at the deceased's death of such property *less* any inheritance tax borne by the donee in respect of the transfer.[9]

---

[2] ss.10(2)(*b*) and 11(2)(*c*): s.11(2)(*c*) provides that when the contract was made full valuable consideration for that contract must not have been "given or promised" by the donee or any other person. See, *e.g. Re Dawkins* (1986) 7 F.L.R. 360, *post*, p. 138.

[3] *Ibid.*

[4] s.25(1).

[5] ss.10(2)(*c*) and 11(2)(*d*).

[6] ss.10(6) and 11(4): valuable consideration does not include marriage or a promise of marriage, s.25(1). For the effect of valuable consideration given for the contract see *post*, p. 138.

[7] s.10(2).

[8] s.10(3). If any such inheritance tax is repaid in consequence of the order it forms part of the deceased's net estate, Inheritance Tax Act 1984, s.146(1)–(3), (5) and (7).

[9] s.10(4); if such property has been disposed of, the value is taken at the date of disposal and not at the deceased's death, *ibid.* As to inheritance tax, see *supra*, n. 8.

The payment by the deceased of a premium due under an assurance policy on his life (of which the benefits are payable to another person X) is an example of a disposition consisting of the payment of money for the benefit of X. Say the deceased pays the premiums due under this policy during the last 10 years of his life. Assuming that the four requisites are satisfied in respect of each of the premiums paid by the deceased less than six years before his death, the statutory limit on X's liability is the amount of these premiums less any inheritance tax borne by X in respect of these payments.[10]

Re Dawkins[11] is an example of a disposition by the transfer of property. The deceased died insolvent having sold his house worth £27,000 to the daughter of his previous marriage for £100. He did this 15 months before his death with the intention of defeating an application under the 1975 Act. His second wife applied under the 1975 Act and the court ordered the daughter to provide £10,000 for the purpose of providing a lump sum for the applicant.

The donee does not escape liability if before the deceased's death he spends all the money paid to him, or the proceeds of sale of other property transferred to him, by the deceased.[12] However, in deciding what order (if any) to make, the court has to consider the donee's financial resources and the court is unlikely to make any order against a donee who has meagre financial resources when the application is heard.

(2) *Donee under a contract.* By the time the application is heard the deceased's personal representatives may already have paid or transferred money or other property to or for the benefit of the donee in accordance with the contract. If so, the court may order the donee to provide a specified sum of money or other property for the purpose of making financial provision for the applicant.[13] The court may also order the personal representatives to make no, or no further, payment or transfer of property or only a reduced payment or transfer[14]: of course such an order increases the value of the deceased's net estate from which provision may be directed for the applicant.

Again there is a statutory limit. The court may only exercise its powers to the extent of the gift element in the contract, *i.e.* to the extent that the court considers that the amount of any money or the value of any property payable or transferable in accordance with the contract exceeds the value of any valuable consideration given or to be given for the contract.[15]

If the personal representatives have reason to believe that the deceased entered into such a contract with the intention of defeating an application for financial provision under the Act, the personal representatives have power to postpone the payment or transfer of money or property under the contract until the six months' time limit for the mak-

---

[10] See Law Com. No. 61, paras. 203–206 and, as to a policy disposed of less than six years before death, see Ross Martyn, *The Modern Law of Family Provision* (1978), p. 35.

[11] (1986) 7 F.L.R. 360.

[12] s.10(2).

[13] s.11(2).

[14] *Ibid.*

[15] s.11(3): property must be valued as at the date of the hearing, *ibid.*

ing of an application has expired or until any application made within that time limit has been determined.[16]

(3) *Consequential directions.* The court has a wide power to give consequential directions for the purpose of giving effect to its order or securing a fair adjustment of the rights of the persons affected by it.[17] For example, if the court orders the personal representatives to make no transfer of property to the donee in accordance with the contract, the court may direct a smaller money payment to be made to the donee out of the net estate by way of fair adjustment.

Anti-evasion order against donee's personal representative. If the donee has died, instead of making an order against the donee the court may make an order against the donee's personal representative. However the court must not make an order in respect of any property forming part of the donee's estate which has been distributed by the personal representative.[18]

Anti-evasion order against trustee. The deceased may have settled property less than six years before his death with the intention of defeating an application for financial provision under the Act: in that case an order may be made against the trustees for the time being of the settlement in respect of the disposition to the original trustees.[19] But any order against a trustee (whether or not he was an original trustee under the disposition) is subject to a special limit. A trustee is only liable to the extent of the value of the relevant assets in his hands at the date of the order, *i.e.* the assets which consist of, or represent or are derived from the money or other property paid or transferred under the disposition.[20] Similar provisions apply in respect of any payment made or property transferred to trustees in accordance with a contract made by the deceased.[21]

---

[16] s.20(3).
[17] ss.11(5) and 12(3).
[18] s.12(4): the donee's personal representative is not liable for having distributed before he has notice of the making of an application on the ground that he ought to have taken into account the possibility that such an application would be made, *ibid.*
[19] s.13(1) and (3).
[20] s.13(1): a trustee is not liable for having distributed on the ground that he ought to have taken into account the possibility that such an application would be made, s.13(2).
[21] s.13.

CHAPTER 6

EXECUTORS AND ADMINISTRATORS

The personal representatives of a deceased person are either executors or administrators.[1] On the other hand executors *de son tort* are not personal representatives but are liable to creditors and beneficiaries of the deceased as if they were the lawful executors.[2]

1. EXECUTORS

A. APPOINTMENT OF EXECUTORS

Executors may be appointed:

1. By the testator in his will. This is by far the most common method of appointment of executors.
2. Under a power conferred by the testator in his will. This method is rarely used.
3. By the court which has statutory powers to appoint executors in certain circumstances.

1. By the testator in his will. The appointment of executors by the testator in his will may be express or implied or, in the case of settled land, statutory.

(1) *Express appointment*. Most wills contain an express appointment of one or more named, or otherwise identified, persons as the "executors" of the will. A typical clause reads "I appoint AB of (address and description) and CD of (address and description) to be the executors of this will."[3]

The appointment of an executor may be absolute, or may be qualified in one or more respects, for instance:

---

[1] Or, if female, executrices or administratrices. See Administration of Estates Act 1925, s.55(1)(i), (ii) and (xi).

[2] Administration of Estates Act 1925, ss.28 and 55(1)(xi): *post*, pp. 408 *et seq*.

[3] This form is suitable for a will which only contains absolute immediate gifts. For a will containing any other gifts, where trustees will be needed, it is usual to appoint the same persons "to be the executors *and trustees* of this will." A suitable clause for the appointment of the partners in a firm of solicitors reads, "I appoint the partners at the date of my death in the firm of XY & Co. of (address) or the firm which at that date has succeeded to and carries on its practice to be the executors and trustees of this my will (and I express the wish that two and only two of them shall prove my will and act initially in its trusts)"; the words in brackets are precatory: see *Re Horgan* [1971] P. 50, 61.

(i) By a condition precedent or subsequent, *e.g.* "I appoint my nephew EF and also my son GH *if he shall have attained the age of 25 years at the time of my death* to be the executors of this will."[4]

(ii) As to the subject matter of the office, *e.g.* "I appoint my brother IJ to be the executor of this will *as to the business of grocer carried on by me at the date of this Will at* (address)." Usually the testator first appoints general executors, *i.e.* appoints persons to be "the executors of this will except as to my business as hereinafter defined."

(iii) As to the time when the person appointed shall begin, or shall cease, to be executor, *e.g.* "I appoint my sister KL to be the executrix of this will *during the minority of my son* MN."

The testator may appoint one or more substituted executors to take office on a specified event in place of the first named executors, *e.g.* "I appoint my wife PQ to be the executrix of this will *but if she shall die in my lifetime or renounce probate* then I appoint my son RQ to be executor in her place." The event on which the substitution is to take place should be clearly specified.[5]

(2) *Implied appointment.* A person impliedly appointed executor by the testator in his will is usually called "an executor according to the tenor" of the will. A person is an executor according to the tenor if the testator has shown by his will an intention that he should act as executor of the will, without expressly nominating him as "executor." Whether the testator has shown such an intention by his will is a question of construction. The following are examples of the appointment of an executor according to the tenor[6]:

(i) "I appoint my sister AB my executrix, only requesting that my nephews, CD and EF, will kindly act for or with this dear sister." Held CD and EF were executors according to the tenor[7]—"they can only act for or with her in the same character as was conferred on her, namely, as executors."[8]

(ii) "I desire GH to pay all my just debts." Held GH was an executor according to the tenor.[9] "The essential duties of an executor are to collect the assets of the deceased, to pay his funeral expenses

---

[4] A condition precedent. As to an infant who is appointed executor see *post*, p. 145.

[5] *Cf. In the Goods of Foster* (1871) L.R. 2 P. & D. 304 (wife appointed executrix "and in default of her" JK and RF appointed executors; wife took probate and died: held substitution intended in event of wife's death, whether before or after probate); *In the Goods of Betts* (1861) 30 L.J.P.M. & A. 167 (JJ appointed executor "but should he decline or consider himself incapable of acting" EJ appointed executor; JJ died before testatrix: held EJ entitled to probate); *In the Goods of Lane* (1864) 33 L.J.P.M. & A. 185.

[6] For a summary of the case law see Williams, Mortimer and Sunnucks, *Executors, Administrators and Probate* (1982), pp. 27 *et seq.*

[7] *In the Goods of Brown* (1877) 2 P.D. 110 (a combination of express and implied appointments).

[8] *Ibid.* at p. 111.

[9] *In the Goods of Cook* [1902] P. 115: see also *In the Estate of Fawcett* [1941] P. 85 ("All else be sold and proceeds after debts, etc., Barclays Bank will do this to Emily Thompson": held Bank was executor according to the tenor).

and debts, and to discharge the legacies"[10] and other gifts made by his will.

(iii) "I nominate as trustees to carry out this will JK and LM." Held they were executors according to the tenor[11]—the case fell "within the principle that where the direction is to carry out the general provisions of the will, and not to execute a specific trust, the trustees are executors according to the tenor."[12] On the other hand, "I wish PQ to act as trustee to this estate," was not enough to make him executor according to the tenor—the will did not require him to pay the debts and generally to administer the estate.[13]

A person who is the universal devisee and legatee under a will (*i.e.* sole beneficiary of the entire estate) is not entitled to probate as an executor according to the tenor unless the will shows an intention that he should act as executor.[14]

As in the case of an express appointment, the appointment of an executor according to the tenor may be absolute or qualified, or substitutional.

(3) *Settled land.* Section 22 of the Administration of Estates Act 1925 deals with settled land vested in the testator at his death, which was settled previously to his death and not by his will, and which remains settled land after his death.[15] The section provides that,

"a testator may appoint, and in default of such express appointment shall be deemed to have appointed, as his special executors in regard to settled land, the persons, if any, who are at his death the trustees of the settlement thereof, and probate may be granted to such trustees specially limited to the settled land."[16]

Thus, in the case of settled land, there is either an *express* appointment or a *deemed* appointment by the testator of the trustees of the settlement as his special executors in regard to settled land. The testator is of course free to appoint persons of his own choice to be his general executors in regard to his other assets.[17]

2. Under a power conferred by the testator in his will. The testator may by his will authorise another person to appoint executors of the will after the testator's death. For instance, the testator may by his will

---

[10] *In the Goods of Adamson* (1875) L.R. 3 P. & D. 253, 254.

[11] *In the Goods of Russell* [1892] P. 380: see also *In the Goods of Laird* [1892] P. 381; *In the Goods of Way* [1901] P. 345; *In the Goods of Baylis* (1865) L.R. 1 P. & D. 21, where Lord Penzance said at p. 22, "the persons appointed trustees are to get in and receive the whole estate, to pay the debts, and to divide the residue. Now that is the very office of an executor, and therefore it is clear that the trustees are executors according to the tenor."

[12] *In the Goods of Laird, supra,* at p. 381.

[13] *In the Goods of Punchard* (1872) L.R. 2 P. & D. 369: see also *In the Estate of Mackenzie* [1909] P. 305; *In the Goods of Wilkinson* [1892] P. 227; *In the Goods of Jones* (1861) 2 Sw. & Tr. 155.

[14] *Re Pryse* [1904] P. 301; *In the Goods of Oliphant* (1860) 1 Sw. & Tr. 525.

[15] *Re Bridgett and Hayes' Contract* [1928] Ch. 163.

[16] See *post,* p. 176.

[17] Administration of Estates Act 1925, s.22(2).

authorise his legatees to appoint two executors,[18] or direct that on the death of one of two executors expressly appointed in his will the surviving executor may appoint another executor.[19]

3. By the court. The court has power to appoint executors[20] in the following circumstances:

(1) *Substituted personal representative.* The court has a wide power to appoint a substituted personal representative in place of all or any of the existing personal representatives of the deceased. As from the date of appointment the substituted personal representative becomes an executor if he is appointed to act with one or more existing executors but otherwise he becomes an administrator. The power is exercisable by the court on an application relating to the deceased's estate made by a personal representative of the deceased or a beneficiary under the deceased's will or intestacy.[21]

(2) *Minority or life interest.* If at any time during the minority of a beneficiary or the subsistence of a life interest under a will or intestacy there is only one personal representative (not being a trust corporation), the court has power to appoint one or more additional personal representatives to act while the minority or life interest subsists and until the estate is fully administered.[22] The power is exercisable on the application of any person interested or the guardian or receiver of any such person.[23]

(3) *Settled land.* The court has power to appoint a special or additional personal representative in respect of settled land on the application of the trustees of the settlement or any person beneficially interested thereunder.[24]

B. TRANSMISSION OF THE OFFICE

In general an executor cannot assign his office because it is an office of personal trust.[25] However section 7 of the Administration of Estates Act

---

[18] *In the Goods of Cringan* (1828) 1 Hagg.Ecc. 548.

[19] *In the Goods of Deichman* (1842) 3 Curt. 123: see also *In the Goods of Ryder* (1861) 2 Sw. & Tr. 127 (will concluded, "I must beg EC to appoint someone to see this my will executed," EC appointed himself as executor: probate granted to EC); *Jackson & Gill v. Paulet* (1851) 2 Rob. 344.

[20] In both (2) and (3) below the relevant legislation uses the generic term "personal representative"; see Williams, Mortimer and Sunnucks, *Executors, Administrators and Probate* (1982), p. 31, n. 65 (not strictly executors).

[21] Administration of Justice Act 1985, s.50: for remuneration of the substituted personal representative see *post*, p. 248, and for appointment instead of a judicial trustee see s.50(4) and *post*, p. 399.

[22] Supreme Court Act 1981, s.114(4): for trust corporation see *post*, p. 146, and for the rules governing the number of personal representatives see *post*, pp. 145 and 156.

[23] *Ibid.* See also N.C. Prob. Rules 1987, r. 26.

[24] Administration of Estates Act 1925, s.23(2)–(5) (as amended by Administration of Justice Act 1970, s.1 and Sched. 2, para. 3): for an instance see *In the Estate of Clifton* [1931] P. 222.

[25] *In the Estate of Skinner* [1958] 1 W.L.R. 1043.

1925 provides for the automatic transmission of the office on death through proving executors. This important provision must now be considered.[26]

Executor by representation. X is the sole, or last surviving, executor of a testator T. X has obtained probate of T's will. X dies, having by his will appointed Y to be his executor, and Y obtains probate of X's will. Y is the executor of X and *the executor by representation of* T. As section 7(1) puts it, "An executor of a sole or last surviving executor of a testator is the executor of that testator"—subject to the proviso that each executor must have proved the will of his testator.[27]

If Y is unwilling to act as the executor by representation of T, he should renounce probate of X's will. Y cannot both accept office as executor of X and renounce office as executor by representation of T.[28]

The chain of representation. The last executor in an unbroken chain of representation is the executor of every preceding testator.[29] So if Y obtains probate of X's will and later dies, having by his will appointed Z to be his executor, and Z obtains probate of Y's will, Z is the executor of Y and *the executor by representation of both X and T.*

But the chain of representation is broken by:

  (a) an intestacy, *i.e.* if Y dies intestate in the above example; or
  (b) the failure of a testator to appoint an executor, *i.e.* if Y does not appoint an executor; or,
  (c) the failure to obtain probate of a will, *i.e.* if Y appoints Z to be his executor but Z does not obtain probate of Y's will.[30]

On the other hand the chain of representation is not broken by a temporary grant of administration to Y's estate if Z subsequently obtains probate of Y's will.[31]

Effect of representation. Section 7(4) provides that every executor in the chain of representation to a testator—

  (a) has the same rights in respect of the testator's estate as the original executor would have had if living; and

[26] For another statutory transmission see Public Trustee Act 1906, s.6(2), which permits transfer of the estate by an executor or administrator to the Public Trustee with the sanction of the court.
[27] It suffices that the original executor obtained probate limited to certain property, *In the Goods of Beer* (1851) 2 Rob. 349: for limited probate see *post*, p. 180. There is no chain of representation through a grant of probate limited to settled land, *Registrar's Direction*, July 21, 1936; or through an additional personal representative appointed under Supreme Court Act 1981, s.114(4), *ibid.* s.114(5); or through a substituted personal representative appointed under Administration of Justice Act 1985, s.50(1) and (2). For Scottish confirmations and Northern Irish grants see *post*, p. 164.
[28] *In the Goods of Perry* (1840) 2 Curt. 655; *Brooke* v. *Haymes* (1868) L.R. 6 Eq. 25. For possible reform see Law Reform Committee, 23rd Report, *The powers and duties of trustees*, Cmnd. 8733 (1982), pp. 53–54 and 67.
[29] Administration of Estates Act 1925, s.7(2).
[30] *Ibid.* s.7(3). If the chain of representation is broken, and X's or T's estate has not been fully administered, a grant of letters of administration *de bonis non administratis* with the will annexed is needed to each estate, see *post*, p. 180.
[31] *Ibid.* s.7(3).

(b) is, to the extent to which the testator's estate has come to his hands, answerable as if he were an original executor.

Double probate. Finally to consider the position if T by his will appoints (say) two executors, P and Q, and P alone obtains probate of T's will, power to prove being reserved to Q. P dies, having by his will appointed R to be his executor, and R obtains probate of P's will. R is the executor of P and the executor by representation of T. But if Q later obtains probate of T's will (called double probate[32]) R will thereupon cease to be the executor by representation of T. A grant of double probate terminates an executorship by representation.[33]

C. NUMBER AND CAPACITY OF EXECUTORS

Number of executors. By his will a testator may appoint any number of executors as he pleases. What rules govern the number of executors to whom probate may be granted?

(1) *Maximum number*. Section 114(1) of the Supreme Court Act 1981 provides that probate or administration shall not be granted to more than four persons in respect of the same part of the deceased's estate. If a testator appoints six executors of the same property, probate can be granted to not more than four of them, though power will be reserved to the others (if they have not renounced) to apply on the occurrence of any vacancy. However, section 114(1) does not prohibit probate being granted to four executors in respect of a particular part of the deceased's estate and to four different executors in respect of the remainder of the estate.

(2) *No minimum number*. Probate may be granted to one executor, whether or not there is a minority or a life interest arises under the deceased's will or intestacy.[34] The rule is different for grants of administration.[35]

Capacity of executors. By his will a testator is free to appoint any persons[36] as his executors, irrespective of their infancy, mental or physical incapacity, insolvency, criminal record, foreign nationality,[37] marital status, [38] or anything else. What rules govern the capacity of a person so appointed to act as executor after the testator's death and take probate?

(1) *Minor*. A minor who is appointed an executor cannot obtain probate until he attains the age of 18 years.[39] The testator's estate does not

---

[32] See *post*, p. 176.
[33] *Ibid*. s.7(1).
[34] For the court's power to appoint additional personal representatives see *ante*, p. 143.
[35] *Post*, p. 156.
[36] Including a corporation and members of a particular firm, *Re Horgan* [1971] P. 50 (partners in firm of solicitors), *ante*, p. 140.
[37] Status of Aliens Act 1914, s.17, as amended by British Nationality Act 1948, s.34 and Sched. 4, Pt. II.
[38] For married women see Law Reform (Married Women and Tortfeasors) Act 1935, s.1.
[39] N.C. Prob. Rules 1987, rr. 32 and 33; Family Law Reform Act 1969, s.1(3) and Sched. I. For grants of administration for the use and benefit of a minor see *post*, p. 181.

vest in the minor and he cannot act as an executor for any purpose until he obtains probate.[40]

(2) *Mental or physical incapacity.* A person who is incapable of managing his affairs by reason of mental or physical incapacity cannot act as executor or take probate so long as his incapacity continues.[41]

(3) *Corporation.* Three types of corporation must be considered. A corporation sole may act as executor and take probate in his own name.[42] Again under section 115(1) of the Supreme Court Act 1981 a trust corporation[43] may act as executor and obtain probate in its own name, either alone or jointly with another person. On the other hand a corporation aggregate which is not a trust corporation cannot take probate in its own name.[44] Instead letters of administration (with the will annexed)[45] for its use and benefit may be granted to a nominee or attorney appointed by the corporation.[46]

D. PASSING OVER AN EXECUTOR

Other factors, such as the insolvency or the criminal record of an executor, do not disqualify him from acting as executor and taking probate.[47] But under section 116 of the Supreme Court Act 1981 the court has power to pass over an executor and appoint as administrator such other person as it thinks expedient if "by reason of any special circum-

---

[40] Supreme Court Act 1981, s.118.

[41] *Evans* v. *Tyler* (1849) 2 Rob. 128: see also *In the Goods of Galbraith* [1951] P. 422 (probate granted to two executors revoked, as both had become unfit to act in old age due to physical and mental infirmity); *In the Estate of Shaw* [1905] P. 92; N.C. Prob. Rules 1987, r. 35.

[42] *In the Goods of Haynes* (1842) 3 Curt. 75 (Archbishop of Tuam for the time being): as to the effect of a vacancy in the office see Law of Property Act 1925, s.180(3).

[43] See Supreme Court Act 1981, s.128; Law of Property (Amendment) Act 1926, s.3. Trust corporations include the Public Trustee, the Treasury Solicitor, and a corporation authorised by rules made under Public Trustee Act 1906, s.4(3) to act as custodian trustee: see Public Trustee Rules 1912, (S.R. & O. 1912 No. 348, r. 30) (as amended); N.C. Prob. Rules 1987, r. 36; *Practice Direction* [1981] 2 All E.R. 1104: see also *Re Bigger* [1977] Fam. 203 (Bank of Ireland). A trust corporation can also act as administrator, Supreme Court Act 1981, s.115(1).

[44] *In the Estate of Rankine* [1918] P. 134, 139; *In the Goods of Darke* (1859) 1 Sw. & Tr. 516. For a brief period it could do so under the Administration of Justice Act 1920, s.17 which was repealed by the Administration of Estates Act 1925, s.56 and Sched. 2, Pt. II.

[45] *Post,* p. 151.

[46] If the corporation is appointed executor jointly with an individual, the latter must be cleared off, see N.C. Prob. Rules 1987, r. 36(4).

[47] *Smethurst* v. *Tomlin & Bankes* (1861) 2 Sw. & Tr. 143 (conviction for felony did not disqualify executor). The court has no power of selection among executors not appointed by the court, as it has among administrators entitled in the same degree, *post,* p. 154. The court does of course refuse probate to any executor who lacks capacity. It is not clear whether the murder or manslaughter of the testator by a sane executor automatically disqualifies him; in practice the court may pass over such an executor, and the issue of automatic disqualification does not arise.

stances" this appears to be necessary or expedient.[48] The grant of administration may be limited in any way the court thinks fit. Probably the "special circumstances" need not relate to the estate itself or the administration of it but extend to any other circumstances which the court thinks relevant.[49]

This useful power enables the court to pass over an executor where special circumstances exist. For instance, in *In the Estate of S.*[50] the court passed over an executrix who was serving a sentence of life imprisonment for the manslaughter of the testator, her husband—this made it in a practical sense "quite impossible for her to act as executrix."[51] Again in *In the Estate of Biggs*[52] the court passed over two executors, a husband and wife, both elderly and infirm, and both of whom had steadfastly refused to take out a grant of probate. The husband had intermeddled with the testator's estate and had been cited to take probate,[53] but he had ignored an order of the registrar to do so: he was so violently aggrieved that it was possible that he might go to the length of suffering imprisonment rather than obey this order. The wife had not been cited but she shared the hostility of her husband to undertaking the duty of an executor. It was probable that even if the executors took a grant of probate they would still cause a great deal of difficulty and expense which the testator's small estate would have to bear. In these special circumstances the court exercised its power to pass over the executors and appointed another person as administratrix of the estate, with the will annexed.

E. ACCEPTANCE AND RENUNCIATION

Executor may accept or renounce. A person who has been appointed executor is free to accept or renounce the office as he pleases.[54] "No man has a right to make another an executor without his consent; and even if in the lifetime of the testator he has agreed to accept the office, it is still

---

[48] See N.C. Prob. Rules 1987, r. 52, under which applications for passing over may be made to a registrar. In the case of deaths before 1926 the court had power to pass over an executor under the Court of Probate Act 1857, s.73; before 1982 the court had this power under Judicature Act 1925, s.162(1), as amended by Administration of Justice Act 1928, s.9.

[49] *Re Clore* [1982] Fam. 113, [1982] Ch. 456 (conduct of executors so far in administration and both executors abroad: passed over): *cf. In the Goods of Edwards-Taylor* [1951] P. 24, 27: both cases were decided under the 1925 Act: *Re Mathew* [1984] 1 W.L.R. 1011.

[50] [1968] P. 302: see also the following cases decided under the 1857 Act; *In the Estate of Crippen* [1911] P. 108; *In the Estate of Drawmer* (1913) 108 L.T. 732 (executor serving 12 months' prison sentence for conspiracy: passed over); *In the Goods of Wright* (1898) 79 L.T. 473 (executor disappeared and warrant for arrest issued on embezzlement charge: passed over) and *In the Goods of Clayton* (1886) 11 P.D. 76.

[51] *In the Estate of S., supra,* at p. 305.

[52] [1966] P. 118: see also *In the Estate of Potticary* [1927] P. 202 (intermeddling and misfeasance: executors passed over under 1857 Act); *In the Goods of Ray* (1927) 96 L.J.P. 37; *In the Estate of Leguia* [1934] P. 80; (1936) 105 L.J.P. 72; *Re D. and B.* (1979) 10 Fam. Law 55.

[53] *Post,* p. 149.

[54] This does not apply to personal representatives after their appointment by the court, see *ante,* p. 143. But see N.C. Prob. Rules 1987, r. 26(1) for prior consent of the person proposed for appointment by the court under Supreme Court Act 1981, s.114(4); Administration of Estates Act 1925, s.23(3). The Public Trustee is free to accept or renounce, subject to restrictions imposed by the Public Trustee Act 1906, ss.2 and 5.

in his power to recede."[55] Even persons deemed to have been appointed as special executors in regard to settled land are free to accept or renounce.[56]

Citation to accept or refuse probate. However an executor can be compelled to decide whether he will accept office by taking probate. The court has power to summon any person named as executor in a will to prove, or renounce probate of, the will.[57] The court exercises this power by issuing a citation at the instance of any person who would himself be entitled to a grant of letters of administration if the executor renounced.[58] The citation calls on the executor to enter an appearance and accept or refuse probate of the will. If the executor does not appear to the citation or renounces probate, his rights as executor wholly cease.[59] Thus the issue of the citation compels the executor to decide whether to take probate.

In *Re Stevens* Vaughan Williams L.J. said that he thought "no action would lie for neglect to take out probate—no such action appears ever to have been brought; and I think that plaintiff's only remedy is by citing the executor."[60]

Acceptance of office. An executor accepts office (1) by taking probate or (2) by acting as executor.

(1) *By taking probate*. An executor accepts office by taking probate—he has made his choice and cannot renounce after he has taken probate.[61] "By taking probate an executor takes upon himself duties and liabilities which he cannot afterwards shake off."[62] But an executor who has sworn the executor's oath[63] may still renounce if probate has not yet been granted to him.[64]

(2) *By acting as executor*. An executor also accepts office if he does any act or acts in relation to the testator's assets which indicate an intention to take upon himself the executorship. Examples of such acts of inter-meddling include taking possession of the testator's goods, receiving or releasing debts due to the testator,[65] writing to request payment of money due upon an insurance policy on the testator's life,[66] and insert-

[55] *Per* Lord Redesdale in *Doyle* v. *Blake* (1804) 2 Sch. & Lef. 231, 239; *Hargreaves* v. *Wood* (1862) 2 Sw. & Tr. 602.
[56] See the words "if willing to act" in Administration of Estates Act 1925, s.23(3)
[57] Supreme Court Act 1981, s.112.
[58] N.C. Prob. Rules 1987, r. 47; see *post*, p. 158.
[59] Administration of Estates Act 1925, s.5. If the executor appears, but does not apply for probate, the citor may apply for a grant of administration to himself, N.C. Prob. Rules 1987, r. 47(7).
[60] [1898] 1 Ch. 162, 177; Chitty L.J. expressed the same view, at p. 174.
[61] *In the Goods of Veiga* (1862) 32 L.J.P.M. & A. 9 ("once an executor, always an executor").
[62] *Ibid.* at p. 10.
[63] *Post*, p. 191.
[64] *Jackson & Wallington* v. *Whitehead* (1821) 3 Phill. 577; *M'Donnell* v. *Prendergast* (1830) 3 Hagg.Ecc. 212.
[65] *Pytt* v. *Fendall* (1754) 1 Lee 553 (executor had released debt due to the testator: held he had accepted office and could not renounce).
[66] *Re Stevens* [1897] 1 Ch. 422.

ing an advertisement calling upon all persons who had any claim on the testator's estate to send in their accounts and to pay all money due to the estate to X and Y "his executors in trust."[67] However, whether the executor's acts indicate an intention to take upon himself the executorship depends on all the circumstances. An executor does not accept office if he deals with the testator's assets solely as the agent of another executor to whom probate has been granted.[68] Again the executor's acts, though technically acts of administration, may be too trivial to indicate an intention on his part to take upon himself the executorship.[69] And section 36(5) of the Trustee Act 1925 provides that a sole or last surviving executor intending to renounce, or all the executors where they all intend to renounce, may appoint new trustees before renouncing probate without thereby accepting the office of executor.

An executor who accepts office by acting as executor cannot thereafter renounce.[70]

Citation to take probate. Any person interested in the estate may cite an executor to take probate if he has accepted office by acting as executor. Such a citation may be issued at any time after the expiration of six months from the testator's death unless proceedings as to the validity of the will are pending.[71] After the executor has been cited, the citor may apply for an order requiring the executor to take probate within a specified time,[72] and if the executor fails to do so he becomes liable to a fine and committal to prison for his contempt of court.[73] Alternatively the citor may apply for a grant to himself or some other person, pursuant to the court's power under section 116 of the Supreme Court Act 1981 to pass over an executor where special circumstances exist.[74] By adopting this latter course the citor may avoid the difficulty and expense which is likely to be incurred in compelling an unwilling executor to take probate.

Renunciation. An executor who has not accepted office is free to renounce probate. Once he has done so he may only retract his renunciation with the leave of the court.

Form of renunciation. An executor renounces probate in writing signed by him[75] and filed in a probate registry. A renunciation becomes binding on being filed: until it has been filed the executor is free to withdraw it and take probate.[76]

---

[67] *Long & Feaver* v. *Symes & Hannam* (1832) 3 Hagg.Ecc. 771.
[68] *Rayner* v. *Green* (1839) 2 Curt. 248.
[69] *Holder* v. *Holder* [1968] Ch. 353, 392, 397 and 401.
[70] *In the Goods of Badenach* (1864) 3 Sw. & Tr. 465; *Re Stevens* [1897] 1 Ch. 422; *Long & Feaver* v. *Symes & Hannam, supra*, (executors who intermeddled compelled to take probate); *Pytt* v. *Fendall, supra*: see also *Holder* v. *Holder, supra*.
[71] N.C. Prob. Rules 1987, r. 47(3).
[72] N.C. Prob. Rules 1987, r. 47(5)(c) and (7)(c).
[73] *Mordaunt* v. *Clarke* (1868) L.R. 1 P. & D. 592: see Contempt of Court Act 1981, s.14.
[74] N.C. Prob. Rules 1987, r. 47(5)(c) and (7)(c); *In the Estate of Biggs* [1966] P. 118 and see *ante*, p. 147.
[75] Or under seal if a trust corporation.
[76] *In the Goods of Morant* (1874) L.R. 3 P. & D. 151.

An executor cannot renounce in part. An executor cannot renounce part of his office and accept the other part. " The principle is very plain that a person cannot accept one part of the duties of an executor and refuse the rest."[77] For instance, after the death of X, who is the sole or last surviving executor of T, X's executor Y cannot both accept office as executor of X and renounce office as executor by representation of T.[78] There is a single statutory exception to the rule that an executor cannot renounce in part; an executor, who is not a trustee of a settlement which was created before the testator's death and not by his will, may renounce his office in regard to the settled land without renouncing it in regard to other property.[79]

Effect of renunciation. If an executor renounces probate his rights in respect of the executorship wholly cease.[80] But any right which the executor may have to a grant of administration in some other capacity (whether as a beneficiary or creditor) does not cease unless he expressly renounces that right as well.[81]

Retracting a renunciation. An executor who has renounced probate may with the leave of the court retract his renunciation and take probate.[82]

Grounds for obtaining leave. The court only grants leave to an executor to retract his renunciation if this will be for the benefit of the estate, or of those interested under the testator's will. Leave was refused where an executor renounced probate as a result of his solicitor's erroneous advice that he would be put to great trouble in proving the will, and later the executor changed his mind.[83] In another case leave was granted to an executor to retract his renunciation and take probate because his co-executor had absconded after taking probate.[84]

Effect of retractation. Section 6 of the Administration of Estates Act 1925 provides that if an executor is permitted to retract his renunciation and prove the will, the probate shall take effect without prejudice to the previous acts and dealings of, and notices to, any other personal representative who has previously proved the will or taken out letters of administration.

---

[77] *Per* Romilly M.R. in *Brooke* v. *Haymes* (1868) L.R. 6 Eq. 25, 30.
[78] See *ante.* p. 144. Similarly an executor cannot refuse a worthless leasehold interest of the deceased; see *post*, p. 229.
[79] Administration of Estates Act 1925, s.23(1); see *post*, p. 178.
[80] *Ibid.* s.5. See *Crawford* v. *Forshaw* [1891] 2 Ch. 261 (executor who renounces is not entitled to exercise powers conferred on executors as such and not as individuals).
[81] N.C. Prob. Rules 1987, r. 37(1); *cf.* effect of renouncing administration, *post*, p. 159.
[82] *In the Goods of Stiles* [1898] P. 12 (on Court of Probate Act 1857, s.79, the predecessor of Administration of Estates Act 1925, s.5): Administration of Estates Act 1925, s.6, now assumes that an executor may retract. See also N.C. Prob. Rules 1987, r. 37(3); a registrar may give leave, but only "in exceptional circumstances" may leave be given to an executor to retract after a grant has been made to some other person entitled in a lower degree: *ibid.*
[83] *In the Goods of Gill* (1873) 3 P. & D. 113.
[84] *In the Goods of Stiles, supra.*

2. ADMINISTRATORS

An administrator is a person to whom the court has granted letters of administration of a deceased's estate.[85] He can only be appointed to his office by the court. There is no transmission of the office on the death of a sole, or last surviving, administrator[86]; if by then the original deceased's estate has not been fully administered, one or more new administrators may be appointed by a grant of letters of administration *de bonis non administratis.*[87]

A. ORDER OF PRIORITY TO ADMINISTRATION

The Non-Contentious Probate Rules 1987 regulate the classes of persons entitled to a grant of letters of administration in particular circumstances and the order of priority between them.[88] Two main heads need to be considered:

1. Where the deceased left a will. In this case, if no executor takes probate, the court makes a grant of letters of administration with the will annexed.[89]
2. Where the deceased died wholly intestate. In this case the court makes a grant of letters of administration (or "simple" administration).[90]

However the court has power to pass over the person who would otherwise have been entitled to the grant of administration under the normal order of priority: this power is considered later.[91]

1. Where the deceased left a will. Rule 20 of the Non-Contentious Probate Rules 1987 specifies the order of priority to a grant of probate or administration with the will annexed. The order is as follows:

(a) *The executor.* The executor is of course entitled to a grant of probate: a person who falls within any of the later classes is entitled to a grant of administration with the will annexed. The later

---

[85] See *Administration of Estates Act* 1925, s.55(1)(i) and (ii): for a substituted personal representative see *post,* p. 399.
[86] *Cf.* the automatic transmission of office on death through proving executors, *ante,* p. 143; and see *ante,* n. 26, for statutory transmission to the Public Trustee.
[87] *Post,* p. 180.
[88] See Supreme Court Act 1981, s.127: the N.C. Prob. Rules 1954 were made under s.100 of the Judicature Act 1925 (now repealed). For the rebuttable presumption that the deceased left no surviving relatives who are illegitimate, or whose relationship is traced through illegitimacy, see Family Law Reform Act 1987, s.21 (not applicable on death before April 4, 1988). For the special rules applicable where the deceased died domiciled outside England see N.C. Prob. Rules 1987, rr. 28(2) and 30.
[89] Supreme Court Act 1981, s.119.
[90] *Post,* p. 154.
[91] *Post,* p. 157. For settled land and other limited grants see *post,* pp. 176 *et seq.*

classes become relevant if, for instance, no executor was appointed, or the executor appointed has died,[92] or has renounced probate, or has not appeared to a citation to accept or refuse probate.[93]

If T appoints P and Q to be executors of his will and P alone applies for a grant of probate, with power to prove being reserved to Q (who has not renounced), P must give notice of his application to Q.[94]

(b) *Any residuary legatee or devisee holding in trust for any other person,* i.e. any person to whom the residuary personal or real estate is given by the will upon trust.

(c) *Any other residuary legatee or devisee*[95] *(including one for life) or where the residue is not wholly disposed of by the will, any person entitled to share in the undisposed of residue under the intestacy rules.*[96]

For example, if T by his will gave his residuary real and personal estate to X and Y upon trust for his widow W for life and after her death upon trust for his three nephews A, B and C absolutely in equal shares, then X and Y fall within class (b) and W, A, B and C fall within class (c). If A predeceased T so that the gift to A lapsed and A's share passed on T's intestacy, the persons entitled to it under the intestacy rules fall within class (c).

(d) *The personal representative of any residuary legatee or devisee (but not one for life, or one holding in trust for any other person), or of any person entitled to share in any residue not disposed of by the will.*

For example, if C died soon after T's death, C's personal representative falls within class (d).

(e) *Any other legatee or devisee (including one for life or one holding in trust for any other person) or any creditor of the deceased.*[97]

Class (e) covers all beneficiaries under the will other than residuary beneficiaries who fall within the earlier classes.

A creditor is entitled to a grant notwithstanding that his debt is

---

[92] Unless he took probate before his death and the chain of representation continues; *ante,* p. 143.

[93] *Ante,* p. 148.

[94] N.C. Prob. Rules 1987, r. 27(1); a registrar may dispense with the giving of notice if this is impracticable or would result in unreasonable delay or expense, r. 27(3); see *Practice Direction (Probate: Executor, Notice to)* [1988] 1 W.L.R. 195.

[95] Unless a registrar otherwise directs, a residuary legatee or devisee whose legacy or devise is vested in interest is preferred to one entitled on the happening of a contingency, r. 20(c), proviso (i).

[96] Including the Treasury Solicitor (or Solicitor for the affairs of the Duchy of Lancaster and the Solicitor of the Duchy of Cornwall) when claiming *bona vacantia* on behalf of the Crown (or Duchy of Lancaster or Duke of Cornwall). For the power of the registrar to disregard the persons entitled as on intestacy where the testator has disposed of the whole or substantially the whole of the known estate see r. 20(c), proviso (ii).

[97] Unless a registrar otherwise directs, a legatee or devisee whose legacy or devise is vested in interest is preferred to one entitled on the happening of a contingency, r. 20(e), proviso.

barred by limitation[98] or was assigned to him after the death of the debtor.[99]

(f) *The personal representative of any other legatee or devisee (but not one for life or one holding in trust for any other person) or of any creditor of the deceased.*

Where a gift by will to a beneficiary is void by reason of him (or his spouse) having attested the will, the beneficiary has no right to a grant of administration as a beneficiary named in the will, though this does not prejudice his right to a grant in any other capacity, such as a person taking on intestacy or a creditor.[1] Again a sane person who commits murder or manslaughter is generally debarred by public policy from taking any benefit under the will or intestacy of his victim[2]: if so debarred, the killer is not entitled to a grant of administration of his victim's estate as a person beneficially interested.[3]

Clearing off. Any applicant for a grant of administration with the will annexed must "clear off" all persons who have a prior right to a grant.[4] To consider again T's will, which gave his residuary real and personal estate to X and Y upon trust for his widow W for life and after her death upon trust for his three nephews A, B and C absolutely in equal shares. If A and B, who fall within class (c), wish to apply for a grant of administration with the will annexed, they must first clear off all persons who fall within classes (a) or (b). If no executor was appointed by or under T's will, no one falls within class (a). If X predeceased T, this clears him off. A and B must also clear off Y, who falls within class (b). Y must either renounce his right to administration[5] (if Y is willing to do so) or A and B must cite Y to accept or refuse a grant of administration. If Y does not appear to the citation, or appears but does not apply for a grant to himself, A and B may apply for a grant of administration with the will annexed to themselves.[6]

Persons entitled in the same degree. W, A, B and C all fall within class (c) and are therefore entitled to a grant in the same degree. A grant of administration may be made to any person entitled without any notice being given to other persons entitled in the same degree.[7] Thus A and B do not need to give any notice to C or W. However it is open to C or W

---

[98] *Coombs* v. *Coombs* (1866) L.R. 1 P. & D 193 and 288.

[99] *In the Goods of Cosh* (1909) 25 T.L.R. 785 (statutory assignment), but see *Macnin* v. *Coles* (1863) 33 L.J.P.M. & A. 175. See also Companies Act 1985, ss.539(2)(*f*) and 610 for power of liquidator of company to take a grant of administration to a deceased contributory.

[1] N.C. Prob. Rules 1987, r. 21.

[2] *Post,* p. 352. For proof of the crime see Civil Evidence Act 1968, s.11; *Re Raphael* [1973] 1 W.L.R. 998; for relief against forfeiture see Forfeiture Act 1982, *post,* p. 352.

[3] *In the Estate of G.* [1946] P. 183.

[4] N.C. Prob. Rules 1987, r. 8(4). Alternatively persons having a prior right may be passed over by the court, *post,* p. 157.

[5] *Post,* p. 159.

[6] N.C. Prob. Rules 1987, r. 47: see *post,* p. 158.

[7] N.C. Prob. Rules 1987, r. 27(4): *cf.* the requirement of notice to another executor, see *ante,* p. 152.

to enter a caveat which ensures that no grant is sealed without notice to the person entering the caveat.[8]

Unless a registrar otherwise directs, administration must be granted:

(i) to a living person in preference to the personal representative of a deceased person, and

(ii) to a person of full age in preference to a guardian of a minor.[9]

If a dispute arises among persons entitled in the same degree as to which of them shall take a grant of letters of administration, the court[10] in its discretion selects the person or persons who are most likely to administer the estate to the best advantage in the interests of the creditors and beneficiaries.[11] Grounds of objection to an applicant include his bad character, bankruptcy or insolvency,[12] or ineptitude for business: again an applicant who has an interest which conflicts with the proper administration of the estate will not be selected.[13] If no specific ground of objection to an applicant exists, the court's usual practice is to select the applicant with the largest interest or who is supported by those with the largest interest.[14] However, this practice is not binding on the court.[15]

2. Where the deceased died wholly intestate. Rule 22 of the Non-Contentious Probate Rules 1987 specifies the following order of priority[16] to a grant of administration where the deceased died wholly intestate after 1925:

(1) *The person or persons[17] having a beneficial interest in the estate, in the following order of priority:*

(a) *The surviving husband or wife.*

(b) *The children of the deceased and the issue of any deceased child who died before the deceased.*

(c) *The father and mother of the deceased.*

(d) *Brothers and sisters of the whole blood and the issue of any deceased brother or sister of the whole blood who died before the deceased.*

(e) *Brothers and sisters of the half blood and the issue of any deceased brother or sister of the half blood who died before the deceased.*

(f) *Grandparents.*

(g) *Uncles and aunts of the whole blood and the issue of any deceased uncle or aunt of the whole blood who died before the deceased.*

---

[8] *Post,* p. 187.

[9] N.C. Prob. Rules 1987, r. 27(5). For grants on behalf of minors see *post.* pp. 157 and 181.

[10] On a summons before a registrar, N.C. Prob. Rules 1987, rr. 27(6)–(8).

[11] *Warwick* v. *Greville* (1809) 1 Phill. 123, 125.

[12] *Bell* v. *Timiswood* (1812) 2 Phill. 22.

[13] *Budd* v. *Silver* (1813) 2 Phill. 115; *In the Goods of Carr* (1867) 1 P. & D. 291.

[14] *Dampier* v. *Colson* (1812) 2 Phill. 54 (applicant beneficiary); *In the Goods of Smith* (1892) 67 L.T. 503 (applicant creditor).

[15] *Cardale* v. *Harvey* (1752) 1 Lee 177, 179 and 180; *In the Goods of Stainton* (1871) L.R. 2 P. & D. 212.

[16] But subject to the court's power to pass over the person entitled under this order of priority, see *post,* p. 157.

[17] For illegitimacy see *supra,* n. 88.

(h) *Uncles and aunts of the half blood and the issue of any deceased uncle or aunt of the half blood who died before the deceased.*

The personal representative of any person has the same right to a grant as the person whom he represents.[18]

A person must have a beneficial interest in the estate in order to be entitled to a grant under paragraph (1) of this order of priority. For instance, if under the intestacy rules the surviving spouse is beneficially entitled to the whole estate, then the surviving spouse (or his or her personal representative) is the only person entitled to a grant under these paragraphs because no other person has a beneficial interest in the estate. In order to ascertain the person or persons who are entitled to a grant of administration, it is therefore necessary to apply the intestacy rules.[19]

(2) *In default of any person having a beneficial interest in the estate, the Treasury Solicitor[20] if he claims bona vacantia on behalf of the Crown.*

(3) *If all prior persons entitled to a grant have been cleared off, a creditor of the deceased, or the personal representative of such a creditor,[21] or any person who may have a beneficial interest in the event of an accretion to the estate.*

Clearing off. Any applicant for a grant of "simple" administration to the estate of a deceased who died wholly intestate must clear off all persons who have a prior right to a grant.[22] For example, a creditor who applies for a grant of administration must establish that each of the persons beneficially interested in the estate under the intestacy rules has either renounced his right to administration or has been cited to accept or refuse a grant of administration.[23]

Persons entitled in the same degree. The rules and practice already considered in connection with grants of administration with the will annexed also apply where two or more persons are entitled in the same degree to a grant of simple administration.[24]

3. Grants to assignees. If all the persons entitled to the deceased's estate under his will or intestacy have assigned their whole interest in the estate, the assignees replace the assignor (or, if more than one, the

---

[18] Subject to (i) the preference of a living person over the personal representative of a deceased person (*ante,* p. 154), and (ii) the preference of the persons mentioned in classes (b) to (h) over the personal representative of a spouse who has died without taking a beneficial interest in the deceased's whole estate as ascertained at the time of the application for the grant, see r. 22(4).

[19] See *ante,* pp. 83 *et seq.*

[20] Including the Solicitor for the affairs of the Duchy of Lancaster and the Solicitor of the Duchy of Cornwall, N.C. Prob. Rules 1987, r. 2(1).

[21] Subject to the preference of a living person over the personal representative of a deceased person, r. 27(5).

[22] N.C. Prob. Rules 1987, r. 8(4). Alternatively persons having a prior right may be passed over by the court, *post,* p. 157.

[23] If no persons are beneficially interested in the estate under the intestacy rules, the creditor must clear off the Treasury Solicitor who has a prior right to a grant.

[24] *Ante,* p. 153.

assignor with the highest priority) in the relevant order of priority for a grant of administration.[25] If there are two or more assignees, administration may be granted with the consent of the others to any one or more (not exceeding four) of them.[26]

4. Foreign domicile. Rules 20 and 22 of the Non-Contentious Probate Rules 1987 do not normally apply if the deceased died domiciled outside England and Wales.[27]

B. NUMBER AND CAPACITY OF ADMINISTRATORS

Number of administrators

(1) *Maximum number.* Section 114(1) of the Supreme Court Act 1981 provides that probate or administration shall not be granted to more than four persons in respect of the same part of the deceased's estate. This provision has already been considered.[28]

(2) *Minimum number.* Section 114(2) also lays down the important "minimum number" rule—if under a will or intestacy any beneficiary is a minor or a life interest arises, administration must be granted *either* to a trust corporation (with or without an individual) *or* to not less than two individuals, *unless* it appears to the court to be expedient in all the circumstances to appoint an individual as sole administrator.[29] For instance, in order to comply with the rule on an intestacy under which there is a minority or a life interest arises, a grant of administration may be made to the deceased's spouse and child of full age, or (if the deceased's spouse has been cleared off) to two of the deceased's children of full age.[30] The rule of course applies to a grant of administration with the will annexed as well as to a grant of simple administration.[31]

On the other hand the rule does not apply:

   (i) in the case of a grant to an administrator pending suit under section 117 of the Supreme Court Act 1981, which refers to "an administrator" in the singular[32]: and

   (ii) in the case of a grant of administration (whether or not with the will annexed) limited to settled land.[33]

---

[25] N.C. Prob. Rules 1987, r. 24.

[26] *Ibid.* r. 24(2).

[27] *Ibid.* r. 28(2): instead r. 30 regulates grants where the deceased died domiciled outside England and Wales.

[28] *Ante,* p. 145.

[29] On an application for administration the oath must state whether any minority or life interest arises under the will or intestacy, N.C. Prob. Rules 1987, r. 8(4), and the court may act on the prescribed evidence, Supreme Court Act 1981, s.114(3).

[30] As to joinder of a second administrator with the person entitled to administration see N.C. Prob. Rules 1987, r. 25.

[31] The rule applies to an insolvent estate, *Re White* [1928] P. 75; and where the court passes over the person otherwise entitled to a grant, *Re Hall* [1950] P. 156: but it may appear expedient to appoint a sole administrator in such circumstances under s.114(2).

[32] *In the Estate of Lindley* [1953] P. 203; *In the Estate of Haslip* [1958] 1 W.L.R. 583 (decided on similar wording in Judicature Act 1925, s.163): for administration pending suit see *post,* p. 185.

[33] *Post,* p. 176.

(3) *Power to appoint additional personal representatives.* If, pursuant to the minimum number rule, administration is granted to two individuals and one of them subsequently dies, there is no requirement that a replacement must be appointed and the survivor can continue to act alone. However, if at any time during the minority of a beneficiary or the subsistence of a life interest there is only one administrator (not being a trust corporation), the court has power to appoint one or more additional personal representatives to act while the minority or life interest subsists and until the estate is fully administered.[34] The power is exercisable on the application of any person interested or the guardian or receiver of any such person.[35]

Capacity of administrators. A minor[36] or a person who is incapable of managing his affairs by reason of mental or physical incapacity[37] cannot take a grant of administration. A trust corporation may take a grant of administration in its own name, either alone or jointly with another person.[38] Any other corporation aggregate cannot take a grant of administration: instead letters of administration for its use and benefit may be granted to a nominee or attorney appointed by the corporation.[39] These rules are the same as those governing the capacity of executors.

C. PASSING OVER A PERSON ENTITLED TO ADMINISTRATION

The power of the court under section 116 of the Supreme Court Act 1981 to pass over an executor has already been considered.[40] The court has power under the same provision to pass over the person who would otherwise have been entitled to the grant of administration and appoint as administrator such other person as it thinks expedient if "by reason of any special circumstances" this appears to be necessary or expedient.[41] The grant of administration may be limited in any way the court thinks fit. Probably the "special circumstances" need not relate to the estate itself or the administration of it but extend to any other circumstances which the court thinks relevant.[42]

The court has used its power to pass over a person entitled to administration in a wide variety of special circumstances[43] of which the following are merely examples.

---

[34] Supreme Court Act 1981, s.114(4), which also applies if there is only one executor, *ante*, p. 143.

[35] *Ibid.* See also N.C. Prob. Rules 1987, r. 26.

[36] For grants of administration for the use and benefit of a minor see *post*, p. 181.

[37] N.C. Prob. Rules 1987, r. 35 (mental incapacity).

[38] Supreme Court Act 1981, s.115(1): for trust corporation see *ante*, p. 146, n. 43.

[39] N.C. Prob. Rules 1987, r. 36(4); see *ante*, p. 146.

[40] *Ante*, p. 146.

[41] See N.C. Prob. Rules 1987, r. 52, under which applications for passing over may be made to a registrar: see *ante*, p. 147, n. 48.

[42] *Re Clore* [1982] Fam. 113, [1982] Ch. 456: *cf. In the Goods of Edwards-Taylor* [1951] P. 24, 27; *Re Mathew* [1984] 1 W.L.R. 1011.

[43] For the extensive case law see Williams, Mortimer and Sunnucks, *Executors, Administrators and Probate* (1982), pp. 319 *et seq.*

(1) *Bad character or otherwise unfit to act.* The deceased's husband has been passed over because he was a man of drunken habits and was mismanaging a public house which was an asset of the estate.[44] A person serving a prison sentence may be passed over on the ground that it is impracticable to carry out the duties of an administrator from a prison cell.[45]

(2) *Person missing.* If the person entitled has been missing for a number of years, he may be passed over.[46]

(3) *Person entitled abroad.* If the person entitled is abroad he may be passed over, particularly in urgent cases.[47]

(4) *Death of sole solicitor.* If a solicitor in practice on his own dies, the interests of his former clients may be jeopardised if no grant of representation to his estate is obtained within a reasonable time after his death. In these circumstances the court may pass over the persons entitled and make a grant to a nominee of the Law Society.[48]

On the other hand, in *In the Goods of Edwards-Taylor*[49] the court refused to pass over a daughter of 21 years of age, who was entitled to administration of her mother's estate as the residuary legatee under her will. The daughter was alleged to be immature and therefore unfit freely to enjoy the estate but the court refused to pass her over merely in order to protect her from herself.

D. ACCEPTANCE AND RENUNCIATION

Person entitled to administration may accept or renounce. A person entitled to administration, like an executor, is free to accept or renounce office as he pleases. He cannot be compelled to take a grant of administration.[50]

Citation to accept or refuse administration. Again, like an executor, a person entitled to administration may be cited by the court to accept or refuse a grant of administration: such a citation is issued at the instance of any person who would himself be entitled to a grant if the person cited renounced. If the person cited does not appear to the citation, or appears but does not apply for a grant, the citor may apply for a grant to himself.[51]

---

[44] *In the Goods of Ardern* [1898] P. 147: see also *In the Estate of Paine* (1916) 115 L.T. 935 (widow who had propounded will found to be forged and had made claims against the estate passed over).

[45] See *In the Estate of S.* [1968] P. 302 (executor passed over); see *ante*, p. 147.

[46] *In the Goods of Callicott* [1899] P.189; *In the Goods of Chapman* [1903] P. 192: see also *In the Goods of Peck* (1860) 2 Sw. & Tr. 506 (uncertain order of deaths); *In the Goods of Harling* [1900] P. 59.

[47] *In the Goods of Cholwill* (1866) 1 P. & D. 192 (deceased a farmer: son in New Zealand passed over and administration granted to deceased's sister limited until son or his attorney obtained administration).

[48] *Practice Direction* [1965] 1 W.L.R. 552.

[49] [1951] P. 24: *cf. Re Clore* [1982] 2 W.L.R. 314, 318; [1982] 3 W.L.R. 228.

[50] *In the Goods of Davis* (1860) 4 Sw. & Tr. 213.

[51] N.C. Prob. Rules 1987, r. 47.

Acceptance of office. A person entitled to administration accepts office by taking a grant of letters of administration. But, unlike an executor, he does not accept office as administrator by doing acts in relation to the deceased's assets which indicate an intention to take upon himself the office.[52] "An executor who has intermeddled can be compelled to take probate, but an administrator who has intermeddled cannot be compelled to take a grant."[53] The court has never issued citations to take administration.

In *In the Goods of Davis*[54] administration with the will annexed was granted to X. Afterwards a later will of the deceased was discovered and X was cited to, and did, bring in her grant to the registry so that it might be revoked. The court refused to issue a citation against X to take a grant of administration with this later will annexed, because the court does not compel anyone (even intermeddlers) to take a grant of administration.

Renunciation. *Form of renunciation.* Like an executor renouncing probate, a person renounces his right to administration in writing signed by him and filed in a probate registry.[55] Unlike an executor, he need not declare that he has not intermeddled in the deceased's estate.[56]

Effect of renunciation. Renunciation by a person of administration in one capacity (*e.g.* as a residuary legatee) precludes him from obtaining administration in some other capacity (*e.g.* as creditor) unless a registrar otherwise directs.[57] But renunciation by a person of administration does not bind that person's personal representatives and after his death they are free to take a grant of administration to the original deceased.

Retracting a renunciation. A renunciation of administration may be retracted with the leave of the court.[58] Retractation is permitted if necessary or expedient.[59]

---

[52] *In the Goods of Davis* (1860) 4 Sw. & Tr. 213; *In the Goods of Fell* (1861) 2 Sw. & Tr. 126: *cf. ante*, p. 148.

[53] *In the Goods of Davis, supra.*

[54] *Ibid.*

[55] *Ante*, p. 149. Again, like an executor, he cannot renounce in part except under Administration of Estates Act 1925, s.23(1); see *ante*, p. 150.

[56] *In the Goods of Fell, supra.*

[57] N.C. Prob. Rules 1987, r. 37(2): *cf.* effect of renouncing probate, *ante*, p. 150.

[58] N.C. Prob. Rules 1987, r. 37(3); a registrar may give leave, *ibid.*

[59] *In the Goods of Thacker* [1900] P. 15 is an instance.

CHAPTER 7

GRANTS OF PROBATE AND LETTERS OF ADMINISTRATION

1. JURISDICTION OVER GRANTS

A. The Courts

A grant of probate or letters of administration is an order under seal of the Family Division of the High Court of Justice, which has exclusive jurisdiction in England and Wales to issue a grant.[1] The High Court also has authority to determine all questions relating to the grant or revocation of probate or administration.[2] The county court has jurisdiction (limited in amount) over any contentious matter arising in connection with the grant or revocation of probate or administration but does not itself issue such a grant.

1. The High Court. Since 1971 the probate jurisdiction[3] of the High Court has been split between the Family Division and the Chancery Division:

(1) non-contentious or common form probate business is assigned to the Family Division, and
(2) all other probate business (termed contentious or solemn form probate business) is assigned to the Chancery Division.[4]

For over 100 years previously probate business had been dealt with in the same court (the Court of Probate from 1858 to 1875) or in the same division of the High Court (the Probate, Divorce and Admiralty Division from 1875 to 1971).

(1) *Non-contentious or common form probate business,* assigned to the Family Division. This expression has a technical meaning[5] which is defined in section 128 of the Supreme Court Act 1981:

" 'non-contentious or common form probate business' means the

---

[1] Supreme Court Act 1981, ss.25, 61(1) and 128, and Sched. 1, para. 3. For recognition of Scottish confirmations and Northern Irish grants of representation see *post,* p. 164.

[2] *Ibid.* ss.19(2), 25 and 128; Judicature Act 1925, ss.20 and 175(1).

[3] "Probate jurisdiction" includes jurisdiction in relation to letters of administration as well as probates, Supreme Court Act 1981, s.25(1).

[4] *Ibid.* ss.61(1) and 128, and Sched. 1, paras. 1 and 3.

[5] *Re Clore* [1982] Fam. 113, 116 (matter categorised as non-contentious "could hardly be more contentious").

business of obtaining probate and administration where there is no
contention as to the right thereto, including—

(i) the passing of probates and administrations through the High
Court in contentious cases where the contest has been terminated,
(ii) all business of a non-contentious nature in matters of testacy and
intestacy not being proceedings in any action, and
(iii) the business of lodging caveats[6] against the grant of probate or
administration."

The great majority of grants of probate or letters of administration are
issued "in common form" without any contention as to the applicants'
right to the grant.[7] Thus a very high proportion of probate business is
non-contentious or common form. Moreover, even in contentious cases,
once the contest as to (say) the validity of an alleged will has been terminated by an order of the Chancery Division (or the county court) pronouncing for or against the validity of the will, any consequent grant of
probate or letters of administration is non-contentious business. It follows that every grant of probate or letters of administration is made by
the Family Divison of the High Court.

Non-contentious or common form probate business is regulated by
the Non-Contentious Probate Rules 1987.[8] Most of this business is dealt
with in the Principal Registry of the Family Division in London or in
one of the district probate registries.[9] However a small part of it may
come before a judge of the Family Division by summons or on motion—
for instance, an appeal from any decision or requirement of a registrar
of the principal or a district probate registry,[10] or a reference to a judge
by a registrar who is doubtful whether a will was duly executed.[11]

(2) *Contentious or solemn form probate business,* assigned to the Chancery Division. A probate action in the Chancery Division begins with
the issue of a writ.[12] Probate actions are usually classified in three categories:

(i) actions seeking a decree pronouncing for or against the validity
of an alleged will (if the court pronounces for its validity, the will
is said to be proved "in solemn form");
(ii) "interest actions" in which the interest alleged by a claimant to a
grant of letters of administration is disputed (*e.g.* the dispute
may be as to whether the claimant is the child of the intestate);
and

[6] For caveats see *post,* p. 187.
[7] A dispute between persons entitled to a grant in the same degree is determined by a
registrar and is technically non-contentious, N.C. Prob. Rules 1987, r. 27(6). So is a dispute
as to passing over, *Re Clore* [1982] Fam. 113, [1982] Ch. 456.
[8] See Supreme Court Act 1981, s.127.
[9] Supreme Court Act 1981, ss.104–106; District Probate Registries Order 1982, (S.I. 1982
No. 379). There are at present 11 district probate registries; all except one have one or
more sub-registries attached.
[10] N.C. Prob. Rules 1987, r. 65(1); *Re Clore, supra,* is an instance.
[11] *Ibid.* r. 61; *Re Bigger* [1977] Fam. 203 is an instance.
[12] R.S.C., Ord. 76.

(iii) actions for the revocation of a previous grant of probate or letters of administration.

These three categories are not mutually exclusive. A plaintiff may bring a probate action claiming, as the son and only person entitled on intestacy to the deceased's estate, (i) to have the probate of an alleged will of the deceased granted in common form to the defendant as executor revoked, (ii) to have the alleged will pronounced against (*e.g.* on the ground that the deceased lacked testamentary capacity), and (iii) to have a grant of letters of administration of the estate of the deceased. If the defendant denies that the plaintiff is the son of the deceased and seeks to uphold the validity of the will, the action falls within all three categories.

2. The county court. The county court has jurisdiction over any contentious matter arising in connection with the grant or revocation of probate or administration[13] if the value of the deceased's estate at the time of his death was less than £30,000, exclusive of property of which he was a trustee and after making allowance for funeral expenses, debts and incumbrances.[14] Within this monetary limit the county court has the same function as the Chancery Division in contentious or solemn form probate business.

B. Jurisdiction to Make a Grant

Property in England and Wales. Until 1932 the court only had jurisdiction to make a grant of probate or letters of administration to a deceased's estate if there was property to be administered within England and Wales.[15] The object of the court in making grants was "to enable the executor or administrator to administer property in this country."[16] It was, however, immaterial whether the property to be administered was situated in England and Wales at the death of the deceased or was brought to this country after his death.[17] This object still remains the primary purpose of most grants and the court generally makes a grant for this purpose as a matter of course.[18]

Discretion of the court. Section 2(1) of the Administration of Justice Act 1932[19] gave the court jurisdiction to make a grant notwithstanding that the deceased left no estate. Thus it is no longer a bar to a grant of representation that there is no property of the deceased to be adminis-

---

[13] *In the Estate of Thomas* [1949] P. 336 (county court may pronounce on validity of a will).

[14] County Courts Act 1984, s.32 as amended by Administration of Justice Act 1985, s.51; County Courts Jurisdiction Order 1981, (S.I. 1981 No. 1123).

[15] *In the Goods of Fittock* (1863) 32 L.J.P.M. & A. 157 (letters of administration refused); *In the Goods of Tucker* (1864) 3 Sw. & Tr. 585.

[16] *In the Goods of Coode* (1867) L.R. 1 P. & D. 449 (will disposing only of property in Chile not entitled to probate).

[17] *In the Goods of Coode, supra; Stubbings* v. *Clunies-Ross* (1911) 27 T.L.R. 127.

[18] *Cf. In the Goods of Ewing* (1881) 6 P.D. 19.

[19] Now repealed but its effect is preserved by Supreme Court Act 1981, ss.19(2), 25(2) and 152(4), and Sched. 7.

tered within England and Wales and the court in its discretion may nevertheless make a grant.[20] There must be sufficient reason for the court to make a grant in such circumstances.[21]

Proof of a will. The jurisdiction of the court to admit a will to proof by granting probate of the will, or letters of administration with the will annexed, needs fuller consideration under these two heads.

(1) *Property in England and Wales.* Under this head, assuming that there is property to be administered within England and Wales, a will is admissible to proof:

(i) if it appoints one or more executors, even though the appointed executor renounces probate[22]; or

(ii) if it contains a disposition of property within England and Wales.[23]

In *In the Goods of Coode*[24] the deceased left two wills, one of which disposed of his property in England and the other of his property in Chile. The court admitted the will of his English property to probate but refused probate of the other will because it did not dispose of any property within England and Wales. On the other hand, if in this case either will had incorporated the other will by confirming it, both would have been admitted to probate because together they would have constituted the deceased's will.[25] A later will which merely confirms an earlier will is admissible to probate.[26]

A will or codicil, the whole of which is subject to a condition which has not been satisfied, is not admissible to proof.[27] Again an instrument which does no more than completely revoke the previous will of the deceased is not admissible to proof[28]: of course such a revoking instrument is effective for its purpose and is admissible in evidence in a probate action in order to establish the revocation of the will. On the other hand an instrument which only effected a partial revocation of the deceased's previous will is admissible to proof.

A will which merely appoints a guardian of the testator's children,

[20] *Re Wayland* [1951] 2 All E.R. 1041.

[21] See *Aldrich* v. *Att.-Gen.* [1968] P. 281, 295 ("contrary to principle" for court to make grant to estate of person domiciled abroad, who left no assets in England): but s.2(1) did not fetter court's discretion by any requirement as to the deceased's domicile.

[22] *In the Goods of Jordan* (1868) L.R. 1 P. & D. 555; *In the Goods of Leese* (1862) 2 Sw. & Tr. 442.

[23] The will need not *effectively* dispose—a will may be admitted to proof though all the dispositions have failed by lapse, *Re Cuffe* [1908] 2 Ch. 500.

[24] (1867) L.R. 1 P. & D. 449.

[25] *In the Goods of Howden* (1874) 43 L.J.P. & M. 26. If the foreign will is independent of the English will and is not admitted to probate, an attested copy of it is filed and its existence is noted on the probate, *In the Goods of Astor* (1876) 1 P.D. 150.

[26] *Weddall* v. *Nixon* (1853) 17 Beav. 160.

[27] *In the Estate of Thomas* [1939] 2 All E.R. 567 (codicil inadmissible as conditional on testator surviving his wife, which did not occur); *In the Estate of O'Connor* [1942] 1 All E.R. 546: see *ante*, p. 5.

[28] *In the Goods of Fraser* (1870) L.R. 2 P. & D. 40; *Toomer* v. *Sobinska* [1907] P. 106: see also *Re Howard* [1944] P. 39. The revoking instrument must be filed in the registry and its existence is noted on the grant of letters of administration.

but does not appoint any executor or dispose of any property within England and Wales, is not admissible to proof under this head.[29]

(2) *Discretion of the court.* Since the Administration of Justice Act 1932[30] the court may in its discretion admit a will to proof which does not appoint any executor or dispose of any property within England and Wales. Thus in *Re Wayland*[31] the court granted probate both of the deceased's English will and codicil (which dealt with his estate in England) and of his two Belgian wills (which dealt only with his Belgian property). The Belgian wills were admitted to probate under the discretion of the court in order to obviate "an injustice to the estate in respect of the Belgian property"[32]: if the Belgian wills had not been admitted to probate, duty would have become payable under Belgian law on the whole of the deceased's English and Belgian assets.

Probably, since the Administration of Justice Act 1932, the court may in its discretion admit to proof a will which merely appoints a guardian of the testator's children.

C. Recognition and Resealing of Grants

Recognition of Scottish confirmations and Northern Irish grants. The Administration of Estates Act 1971 provides for the direct recognition in England and Wales of Scottish confirmations or Northern Irish grants of representation if the deceased died domiciled[33] in the country where the grant was issued.[34] Thus if the deceased died domiciled in Scotland or Northern Ireland leaving assets in England and Wales, the normal practice is for a grant of representation to be taken only in the country where he was domiciled.

A Scottish confirmation is equivalent to an English grant of probate or letters of administration: a Scottish executor nominate is equivalent to an English executor and an executor dative to an administrator. In Northern Ireland (as in England and Wales) a grant of representation is either a grant of probate or of letters of administration.

(1) *Scottish confirmation.* Where a person dies domiciled in Scotland, a Scottish confirmation[35] which notes his Scottish domicile is treated (i) under section 1(2)(*a*) as a grant of probate to the executors named in the

---

[29] *In the Goods of Morton* (1864) 3 Sw. & Tr. 422. For the appointment of guardians by will see *ante*, p. 7.

[30] *Ante*, n. 19.

[31] [1951] 2 All E.R. 1041.

[32] *Ibid.* at p. 1044.

[33] For domicile see Dicey and Morris, *The Conflict of Laws* (11th ed., 1987), pp. 116 *et seq.*; Theobald on *Wills* (14th ed., 1982), pp. 3–7.

[34] Administration of Estates Act 1971, s.1. Under ss.2 and 3 English grants of representation are similarly recognised in Northern Ireland and Scotland if the deceased died domiciled in England.

[35] Or certificate of confirmation. As to the noting of property outside Scotland of which the deceased was a trustee, and the inclusion of real estate situate in any part of the U.K. in the inventory of the deceased's estate, see ss.5 and 6.

confirmation where it appears from the confirmation that they are executors nominate, and (ii) under section 1(2)(*b*) as a grant of letters of administration in any other case.[36]

(2) *Northern Irish grants of representation.* Where a person dies domiciled in Northern Ireland, a grant of probate or letters of administration made by the High Court in Northern Ireland and which notes his domicile there is treated as if it had been originally made by the High Court in England and Wales.[37]

(3) *Effect of recognition on chain of representation.* The chain of representation through proving executors under section 7 of the Administration of Estates Act 1925[38] continues through an executor who obtains a Northern Irish grant of probate if the grant is recognised in England and Wales.[39] Does the chain of representation continue through an executor nominate named in a Scottish confirmation which is recognised in England and Wales? Section 1(3) of the 1971 Act provides that section 7 of the Administration of Estates Act 1925 shall not, by virtue of section 1(2)(*a*), apply on the death of an executor named in a confirmation. To consider the effect of this:

(i) T dies domiciled in Scotland and confirmation is granted in respect of his estate to his executor nominate X, noting T's Scottish domicile: the confirmation is recognised in England and Wales. However, on X's death section 1(3) of the 1971 Act applies and X's executor, who obtains probate in England of X's will, does not become the executor by representation of T.

(ii) T dies domiciled in England and probate is granted in England to Y, the sole executor of T's will. Y dies domiciled in Scotland and confirmation is granted in respect of his estate to his executor nominate Z, noting Y's Scottish domicile. The confirmation is recognised in England and Wales and presumably Z becomes the executor by representation of T. But on Z's death section 1(3) applies and the chain of representation ends.

Resealing of Commonwealth and Colonial grants. A grant of representation made in any country to which the Colonial Probates Act 1892 has been applied may be resealed with the seal of the Family Division of the High Court and thereafter has the same effect as an English grant.[40] The Act has been applied by Order in Council to the great

---

[36] *Ibid.* s.1(1) and (2): s.1 applies to confirmations, probates and letters of administration granted before, as well as after, the 1971 Act, s.1(6).

[37] *Ibid.* s.1(4): see *supra* n. 36.

[38] *Ante,* p. 143.

[39] *i.e.* if the deceased (whether the original testator or an executor in the chain) died domiciled in Northern Ireland and the grant notes his domicile there.

[40] Colonial Probates Act 1892, ss.1 and 2 (as to s.2 see Administration of Estates Act 1971, s.11), and Colonial Probates (Protected States and Mandated Territories) Act 1927: see also N.C. Prob. Rules 1987, r. 39. There is a chain of representation through a resealed probate.

majority of the countries within the Commonwealth.[41] The Act still applies to South Africa[42] but does not apply to Eire.

The court has a discretion whether to reseal such grants whereas Scottish confirmations and Northern Irish grants receive direct recognition without being resealed. However, the Colonial Probates Act 1892 does not require the deceased to have been domiciled in the country where the grant was made.[43]

2. THE NATURE OF A GRANT

A. Proof of a Will in Common or Solemn Form

Proof in common form. A will may be proved in common form or in solemn form. A will is proved in solemn form when the court pronounces for the validity of the will in a probate action. Unless the court has done so, a will can only be proved in common form.

If a will is proved in common form, a grant of probate or letters of administration with the will annexed is made in the absence of the interested parties. Indeed if a will contains a proper attestation clause and does not on the face of it give rise to any doubt,[44] the executors need only support their application for probate by their own oath[45] in order to obtain a grant of probate in common form. The executors are not required to give notice of their application for probate to the deceased's next of kin entitled under the intestacy rules.

(1) *Revocation of grant in common form.* Any grant made in common form may later be challenged in an action for revocation of the grant brought by an interested party.[46] Thus one of the next of kin entitled under the intestacy rules may bring an action for revocation of the probate of a will granted in common form to the executors, alleging that the will is invalid for some reason, such as want of due execution, the testator's incapacity, or want of knowledge or approval. If the court decides that the will is invalid, the probate is revoked. It is sometimes said that the next of kin as interested parties have a right to have a will proved in solemn form, notwithstanding a previous grant of probate in common form. It seems preferable to say that the next of kin, by bringing an action for revocation, may insist on the validity of such a will

---

[41] Colonial Probates Act Application Order 1965 (S.I. 1965 No. 1530); as to Aden see S.I. 1968 No. 465 and as to Tanganyika see S.I. 1969 No. 1685. As to Zimbabwe see *Practice Direction* [1980] 1 W.L.R. 553. As to New Zealand see *Practice Direction*, March 2, 1982.

[42] South Africa Act 1962, s.2(1) and Sched. 2, para. 1; S.R. & O. 1914 No. 144.

[43] But see N.C. Prob. Rules 1987, r. 39(3).

[44] See N.C. Prob. Rules 1987, rr. 12 (doubt as to due execution), 13 (doubt as to testator's knowledge of contents of will at time of execution), 14 (terms, conditions and date of execution of will), and 15 (appearance of attempted revocation); see *post*, pp. 194 *et seq.*

[45] *Post*, p. 191. A personal applicant must also produce a certificate of death, N.C. Prob. Rules, r. 4(5).

[46] Interested parties include any person entitled as on an intestacy and an executor or beneficiary under any other will of the deceased. Only a creditor to whom administration has already been granted may oppose an application for probate, *Menzies* v. *Pulbrook* (1841) 2 Curt. 845, 851.

being determined by the court in contentious proceedings. The next of kin cannot compel executors, who have obtained probate of a will in common form, to start an action to establish the validity of the will in solemn form,[47] although the executors are at liberty to do so.

If there is any doubt as to the validity of a will or any possibility of its validity being challenged in the future, it is advisable for the executors (or the persons entitled to a grant of administration with the will annexed) to prove the will in solemn form, rather than take a grant in common form. Of course proof in solemn form costs more but, if this is not done, there is a risk that the validity of the will may be challenged years later when material witnesses have died or cannot be traced.

(2) *Effect of delay or acquiescence.* An interested party is not barred from bringing an action for revocation of a grant made in common form by lapse of time,[48] or his acquiescence in the making of the grant,[49] or his acceptance of a legacy under the will he seeks to challenge.[50]

Proof in solemn form. It is necessary to consider (1) what persons are bound by an order of the court pronouncing a will valid in a probate action, and (2) on what grounds a person bound by such an order may nevertheless have it set aside.

(1) *Persons bound.* Such an order of the court pronouncing a will valid is of course binding on the parties to the action.[51] The order is also binding on any person who, being *sui juris*, was aware (i) of the probate action and (ii) of his own interest, which would have enabled him to apply to the court to be added as a defendant.[52] Thus in *Newell v. Weeks*[53] two of the deceased's next of kin, who were aware of (i) a previous suit, in which the deceased's will had been unsuccessfully contested by other next of kin, and (ii) of their own interest as next of kin,

---

[47] *Re Jolley* [1964] P. 262.

[48] *Re Flynn* [1982] 1 W.L.R. 310 (*obiter*): an action for revocation may be struck out by the court if the claim is frivolous or vexatious or otherwise an abuse of the process of the court, *ibid.* p. 318.

[49] *Bell v. Armstrong* (1822) 1 Add. 365, 373; *Goddard v. Smith* (1873) L.R. 3 P. & D. 7: see also *Williams v. Evans* [1911] P. 175 (next of kin, who as executor of will had obtained probate in common form, may bring action for revocation of probate). Acquiescence in a Chancery inquiry for next of kin has defeated an application for letters of administration made useless by the acquiescence, *Mohan v. Broughton* [1899] P. 211, [1900] P. 56: *cf. Re Coghlan* [1948] 2 All E.R. 68.

[50] *Bell v. Armstrong, supra,* at p. 374 (but the party challenging the will must bring the legacy into court); *Goddard v. Norton* (1846) 5 N.C. 76 (legacy paid to infant).

[51] Under R.S.C., Ord. 35, r. 2 the court has a discretion to set aside an order obtained where one party does not appear at the trial, see *Re Barraclough* [1967] P. 1, 11 (for instance, by unavoidable accident): as to compromise of a probate action see Administration of Justice Act 1985, s.49; Sunnucks (1987) 137 N.L.J. 721.

[52] This is the modern equivalent of the old right of intervention, under which such a person might apply to the court for leave to "intervene" in the action.

[53] (1814) 2 Phill. 224 (the report refers to citations to see proceedings which are no longer issued; instead a person not joined as a defendant may be served with notice of proceedings, in order that he may be bound by the court's decision): see also *Ratcliffe v. Barnes* (1862) 2 Sw. & Tr. 486, *In the Estate of Langston* [1964] P. 163. As to the effect of a compromise, see *Wytcherley v. Andrews* (1871) 2 P. & D. 327; *Re West* [1948] W.N. 432.

were held bound by the previous decision of the court pronouncing for the validity of the will. As Sir John Nicholl pointed out,[54]

> "if they had been dissatisfied, they might have intervened at any moment of the proceedings . . . they had not only a right, but it was their duty to intervene if they meant not to abide by the decision— their interests were directly affected; if the will had been set aside, they would have established their claim. The *lis pendens* served as a public notice on which they were bound to act."

On the other hand, a person who is aware of the probate action but is not aware of his own interest in it is not bound by the order of the court.[55]

The rule applied in *Newell* v. *Weeks* is a rule of substantive law peculiar to the probate jurisdiction of the court and is derived directly from the law and practice of the Prerogative Court of Canterbury.[56]

(2) *Grounds for setting aside.* A person bound by such an order of the court in a probate action may nevertheless have that order set aside on any of the following grounds:

  (i) that the order was obtained by fraud[57]—for instance, a "beneficiary" propounded a will which he had forged;
 (ii) the discovery, after the order was made, of a will or of a later will than that previously pronounced for;
(iii) the discovery, after the order was made, that the will previously pronounced for had been revoked by the marriage of the testator.

A person not bound by such an order of the court in a probate action is not restricted to these narrow grounds of attack and may re-open issues already decided in that action. If such an order of the court is subsequently set aside at the instance of a person not bound by it, this enures to the benefit of those persons bound by it who were adversely affected by it because "the will is either good or bad against all the world."[58]

B. Different Effects of Probate and Letters of Administration

An executor derives his title from the testator's will, whereas an administrator derives his title from the grant to him of letters of administration. This basic distinction explains the differences which exist between the effects of probate and of letters of administration.

1. Source of authority. A grant of probate *confirms* the authority of an executor, whereas a grant of letters of administration *confers* authority on an administrator.

---

[54] (1814) 2 Phill. 224, 233.
[55] *Young* v. *Holloway* [1895] P. 87 (unaware of own interest under another will).
[56] *In the Estate of Langston* [1964] P. 163, 178 and 179.
[57] *Birch* v. *Birch* [1902] P. 62 and 130.
[58] *Ibid.* at p. 138.

(1) *Executor.* An executor who is expressly or impliedly appointed by the testator in his will derives his authority from the will and not from any grant of probate.[59] Similarly a special executor in regard to settled land derives his authority from the will by express or deemed appointment by the testator.[60] Again an executor appointed under a power conferred by the testator in his will derives his authority from the combined effect of the will and the appointment made under it.[61] In all these cases a grant of probate merely confirms the authority of the executor.[62]

(2) *Administrator.* On the other hand an administrator derives his authority from the letters of administration which appoint him to his office.[63] This is so whether the letters of administration are granted with the deceased's will annexed or on intestacy.

(3) *Proof of authority.* In order to prove his title in any court, any personal representative must produce a grant of probate or letters of administration (as the case may be).[64] Even an executor is not permitted to prove his title in any other way.[65]

2. Time at which property vests. (1) *Executor.* At his death the deceased's real and personal property vests in an executor appointed by him in his will if the executor is of full age.[66] A subsequent grant of probate enables the executor to prove that this has occurred.[67]

(2) *Administrator.* Section 9 of the Administration of Estates Act 1925 provides that "where a person dies intestate, his real and personal estate, until administration is granted in respect thereof, shall vest in the Probate Judge," *i.e.* in the President of the Family Division of the High Court.[68] This section certainly applies if the deceased dies intestate leaving no executor. But the deceased may die:

(i) wholly or partially intestate, but leaving an executor of full age appointed by him in his will. In this case the deceased's estate ought to vest at death in the executor.

(ii) wholly testate, but leaving no executor of full age (because, for instance, the deceased appointed no executor by his will, or the

---

[59] *Chetty* v. *Chetty* [1916] 1 A.C. 603, 608; *Biles* v. *Caesar* [1957] 1 W.L.R. 156, 159–160.

[60] *Ante*, p. 142.

[61] *Ante*, p. 142.

[62] By way of exception, an executor appointed by the court under its statutory powers does not derive his authority from the will; see *ante*, p. 143.

[63] *Chetty* v. *Chetty* [1916] 1 A.C. 603, 609.

[64] For recognition of Scottish confirmations and Northern Irish grants of representation and resealing of Commonwealth and Colonial grants see *ante*, p. 164.

[65] *Chetty* v. *Chetty, supra*, at pp. 608–609. *Cf. Re Crowhurst Park* [1974] 1 W.L.R. 583, 594 (unproved will of realty on death prior to Land Transfer Act 1897 admissible) and *Whitmore* v. *Lambert* [1955] 1 W.L.R. 495 (unproved will admissible in Rent Act case).

[66] *Woolley* v. *Clark* (1822) 5 B. & Ald. 744; *Chetty* v. *Chetty, supra*, (as to personalty); Administration of Estates Act 1925, ss.1(1) and 3 (as to realty). As to devolution of property on death see *post*, pp. 209 *et seq.*

[67] *Whitehead* v. *Taylor* (1839) 10 A. & E. 210, 212.

[68] Administration of Estates Act 1925, ss.9 and 55(1)(xv) as amended by Administration of Justice Act 1970, s.1(6) and Sched. 2: see also s.55(1) (vi).

executor appointed is an infant or predeceased him). In this case the deceased's estate ought to vest at death in the President.

In order to achieve these results the court will probably construe the word "intestate" in section 9 as meaning in this context "leaving no executor in whom his estate vests." Section 9 refers to the deceased's estate vesting in the President "until administration is granted" and administration is defined in section 55(1) so as to include administration with the will annexed as well as simple administration.[69]

The President has no duties to perform in respect of property vested in him by section 9,[70] but if the deceased held leasehold property, notice to quit the premises may be served by the landlord upon the President.[71] The deceased's property vests in an administrator when letters of administration are granted to him in respect of that property.[72]

(3) *Relation back.* A doctrine (or fiction) of relation back has been adopted by the courts for the limited purpose of protecting the deceased's estate from wrongful injury in the interval between his death and the grant of letters of administration to his estate. Under this doctrine the letters of administration relate back to the death of the deceased.

"It is clear that the title of an administrator, though it does not exist until the grant of administration, relates back to the time of the death of the intestate; and that he may recover against a wrongdoer who has seized or converted the goods of the intestate after his death, in an action of trespass or trover."[73]

The administrator may sue in respect of any wrongdoing to an asset of the deceased's estate during this interval between death and the grant of letters of administration—for instance, in respect of trespass to the deceased's land[74] or breaches of covenant by a lessee of the deceased's land.[75]

This doctrine of relation back does not apply outside the limits of the purpose for which it was created—namely, protecting the deceased's estate from wrongful injury during this interval. Administrators cannot invoke the doctrine in order to bring to life the deceased's tenancy which has been lawfully determined by notice to quit served by the

[69] *Harper* v. *Taylor* (1950) 100 L.J. 108 (deceased tenant died wholly testate, but failed to appoint any executor by his will: held by Judge Sir Gerald Hurst in the county court that tenancy vested in the President).
[70] *Re Deans* [1954] 1 W.L.R. 332, 334: see also *Fred Long & Son Ltd.* v. *Burgess* [1950] 1 K.B. 115, 119 (power of President to give directions about the property in case of necessity).
[71] *Fred Long & Son Ltd.* v. *Burgess, supra; Wirral Borough Council* v. *Smith* (1982) 43 P. & C.R. 312: as to the mode of service on the President see *Practice Direction* [1985] 1 W.L.R. 310.
[72] *Woolley* v. *Clark, supra* (as to personalty), Administration of Estates Act 1925, ss.1(1) and 3 (as to realty).
[73] *Per* Parke B, in *Foster* v. *Bates* (1843) 12 M. & W. 226, 233; *Thorpe* v. *Stallwood* (1843) 5 M. & Gr. 760; *Re Pryse* [1904] P. 301, 305.
[74] *R.* v. *Inhabitants of Horsley* (1807) 8 East 405, 410 (trespass to leaseholds); *Re Pryse, supra*, (trespass to freehold land).
[75] *Fred Long & Son Ltd.* v. *Burgess, supra*, at p. 121.

landlord on the President during this interval.[76] "The doctrine of 'relation back' cannot breathe new life into a corpse."[77]

An executor appointed by the deceased in his will does not need to rely on this doctrine of relation back because the deceased's property vests in the executor at death.

3. **Litigation before grant.** (1) *Executor.* An executor may commence an action in his representative character before obtaining probate and continue it until such time as he needs to prove his title, but at that stage he must produce a grant of probate.[78] It is immaterial that the defendant to the action is willing to admit the plaintiff's title as executor—the court nevertheless insists that the plaintiff must prove his title by producing a grant of probate, so as to protect the interests of the deceased's creditors and the beneficiaries under his will or intestacy.[79] If the executor brings an action against a defendant, who is willing to pay a debt due to the deceased as soon as the executor can prove his title to receive it, the court does not dismiss the action but stays proceedings in the action until the executor obtains probate.[80]

(2) *Administrator.* On the other hand an administrator cannot commence any action in his representative character before obtaining letters of administration. In *Ingall* v. *Moran*[81] the plaintiff issued a writ "as administrator of his son's estate" claiming damages in respect of the son's death intestate in a motor accident caused by the defendant's negligence. The plaintiff did not take out letters of administration to his son's estate until nearly two months after the issue of the writ. The Court of Appeal held that the action must fail because the plaintiff had no title to sue when he issued the writ. The son's cause of action for negligence was vested in the President[82] when the writ was issued and only became vested in the father when he took out letters of administration to his son's estate. The doctrine of relation back did not apply for the purpose of validating the invalid writ.

If in *Ingall* v. *Moran* the son had made a will by which he appointed the plaintiff his executor, the son's cause of action would have vested in the plaintiff at the son's death and the plaintiff would have been

---

[76] *Fred Long & Son Ltd.* v. *Burgess, supra.*

[77] *Per* Asquith L.J. in *Fred Long & Son Ltd.* v. *Burgess, supra,* at p. 121.

[78] *Easton* v. *Carter* (1850) 5 Exch. 8, 14; *Chetty* v. *Chetty* [1916] 1 A.C. 603, 608; *Re Crowhurst Park* [1974] 1 W.L.R. 583: see also *Biles* v. *Caesar* [1957] 1 W.L.R. 156.

[79] *Re Crowhurst Park, supra,* at pp. 590–592.

[80] *Webb* v. *Adkins* (1854) 14 C.B. 401 (if the defendant "pays money into court, he may be paying it to a person who may never acquire the title of executor; and so he may be forced to pay it over again"); *Tarn* v. *Commercial Banking Company of Sydney* (1884) 12 Q.B.D. 294.

[81] [1944] K.B. 160: see also *Chetty* v. *Chetty, supra; Hilton* v. *Sutton Steam Laundry* [1946] K.B. 65, and *Finnegan* v. *Cementation Co. Ltd.* [1953] 1 Q.B. 688 (plaintiff had obtained letters of administration in Eire but had no title to sue in England) and *cf. Stebbings* v. *Holst & Co. Ltd.* [1953] 1 W.L.R. 603 and *Bowler* v. *John Mowlem & Co.* [1954] 1 W.L.R. 1445. An administrator with the will annexed, like an administrator on intestacy, cannot commence any action in his representative character before obtaining letters of administration, *Phillips* v. *Hartley* (1827) 3 Car. & P. 121.

[82] Of the then Probate, Divorce and Admiralty Division.

entitled to issue the writ as executor of his son's estate before obtaining probate.[83]

(3) *Effect of actual possession.* If a plaintiff, whether an executor or an intending administrator, has had actual possession of the property which is the subject of the action before it came to the defendant's hands, the plaintiff may bring an action founded upon his possession—for instance, an action of trespass. In such an action the plaintiff does not need to rely upon his title as personal representative and therefore it is immaterial whether the plaintiff has obtained any grant of probate or letters of administration.[84]

4. Acts of administration before grant. (1) *Executor.* Before obtaining probate an executor[85] has power to do all the acts which are incident to his office, except those acts for which he needs a grant of probate in order to prove his title.[86] For instance, before obtaining probate an executor may do the following acts:

- (i) take possession of any of the assets of the testator's estate and receive, or release, debts owing to the estate.[87] But if the holder of any asset refuses to hand it over, or any debtor refuses to pay, the executor cannot prove his title in an action against him without producing a grant of probate.[88] In practice many debtors are unwilling to pay their debts before probate is obtained because meanwhile they cannot be certain that the person claiming to be the executor has been duly appointed.[89]
- (ii) pay, or take releases of, debts owing from the estate.[90]
- (iii) sell and transfer to a purchaser any of the assets of the testator's estate. A conveyance of the testator's unregistered land by an executor to a purchaser therefore vests the legal title to the land in the purchaser, but the purchaser can only establish the executor's authority to sell and convey by proving that the executor subsequently obtained probate.[91] Accordingly a purchaser of land is entitled to (and invariably does) insist on the production by the executor of a grant of probate before completion of the sale to the

---

[83] *Ingall* v. *Moran* [1944] 1 K.B. 160, 167–168 and 170.

[84] *Oughton* v. *Seppings* (1830) 1 B. & Ad. 241 (money had and received, waiving the trespass).

[85] The executor must be of full age at the testator's death, *ante*, p. 145.

[86] *Re Stevens* [1897] 1 Ch. 422, 429–430, citing *Williams on Executors* (9th ed.), p. 249; *Kelsey* v. *Kelsey* (1922) 91 L.J.Ch. 382, 384 (notice to be served on "personal representatives" validly served on executors before probate). For appointment of new trustees by an executor before probate see *Re Crowhurst Park* [1974] 1 W.L.R. 583, 593–594: see *post*, p. 237, n. 28.

[87] *Re Stevens, supra.* He may also distrain for rent due to the testator, *Whitehead* v. *Taylor* (1839) 10 A. & E. 210.

[88] Revenue Act 1884, s.11 as amended by Revenue Act 1889, s.19; Administration of Estates Act 1925, s.2(1).

[89] For the protection of persons making payments in good faith to an executor who has obtained probate see *post*, p. 207.

[90] *Re Stevens, supra.*

[91] Or, if (say) the executor died without obtaining probate, by means of a grant to some other person of letters of administration with the will annexed, which establishes the appointment of the executor.

purchaser.[92] A transfer of the testator's registered land cannot be registered before probate is granted.[93]

(iv) pay legacies or transfer property given by the will to the person entitled.[94] Again the latter can only establish the executor's authority to do so by proving that the executor subsequently obtained probate.[95]

If an executor does any of these acts incident to his office and dies without obtaining probate such acts "stand firm and good."[96] The death of the executor without obtaining probate determines his executorship,[97] but does not invalidate acts done by him before his death whilst his authority as executor subsisted.[98]

(2) *Administrator.* A person entitled to administration has no power to do anything as administrator before letters of administration are granted to him.[99] He derives his authority solely from his appointment as administrator by the court.

(3) *Protection of the estate before grant.* In order to protect the assets of the estate before a grant of probate or letters of administration is made, the court may appoint a receiver pending the grant.[1] An application to the Chancery Division for the appointment of such a receiver may be made by any person interested, whether a creditor[2] or a beneficiary.[3] For example, the court has appointed a receiver where an executor carried on the deceased's practice as a solicitor for three years after his death without taking probate.[4]

5. Period after grant. These differences between the effects of probate and of letters of administration relate to the period between the death of the deceased and the grant of representation to his estate. There is one important difference which relates to the period *after* a grant of representation has been made—the chain of representation through executors is continued by a grant of probate, but is not continued by a grant

---

[92] *Newton* v. *Metropolitan Railway Co.* (1861) 1 Dr. & Sm. 583: for the indorsement on the probate or letters of administration of a notice of an assent or conveyance by a personal representative see Administration of Estates Act 1925, s.36(5).

[93] Land Registration Rules 1925, r. 170(4).

[94] *Re Stevens, supra; Re Crowhurst Park* [1974] 1 W.L.R. 583, 594.

[95] *Johnson* v. *Warwick* (1856) 17 C.B. 516 (*per* Jervis C.J., when a will has been proved (by a grant of probate or letters of administration with the will annexed) "the court has the legal optics through which to look at it"); see, *supra,* n. 91.

[96] *Re Stevens, supra.*

[97] Administration of Estates Act 1925, s.5.

[98] *Wankford* v. *Wankford* (1704) 1 Salk. 299, 309.

[99] *Wankford* v. *Wankford, supra,* at p. 301; *Doe d. Hornby* v. *Glenn* (1834) 1 A. & E. 49; *Morgan* v. *Thomas* (1853) 8 Exch. 302; *Holland* v. *King* (1848) 6 C.B. 727 (notice to be served by administrator of deceased partner: intending administatrix cannot give notice before grant) and *cf. Kelsey* v. *Kelsey, ante,* n. 86; *Mills* v. *Anderson* [1984] Q.B. 704 (settlement of claim on behalf of deceased's estate prior to letters of administration not binding).

[1] For grants of administration *pendente lite* and *ad colligenda bona* see *post,* pp. 184–186.

[2] *Re Sutcliffe* [1942] Ch. 453.

[3] *Steer* v. *Steer* (1864) 2 Dr. & Sm. 311 (receiver and manager of deceased's business appointed); *Re Oakes* [1917] 1 Ch. 230; *Ingall* v. *Moran* [1944] K.B. 160, 169, 171–172.

[4] *Re Sutcliffe, supra.*

of letters of administration.[5] Apart from this single difference, section 21 of the Administration of Estates Act 1925 provides that every person to whom letters of administration are granted has[6] the same rights and liabilities, and is accountable in like manner, as if he was the executor of the deceased. Moreover, if letters of administration are granted in respect of a deceased's estate, section 15 of the Act provides that no person shall have power to bring any action or otherwise act as executor of the deceased in respect of that estate so long as the grant has not been recalled or revoked.

C. Payments for Which a Grant May Not be Needed

The general rule is that a grant of probate or letters of administration must be produced in order to establish the right to recover or receive any part of the deceased's estate situated in the United Kingdom.[7] There are, however, a large number of provisions, made by statute or statutory instrument, under which payment of particular sums otherwise due to the deceased's estate may be made to persons entitled without the production of any grant of representation to the deceased's estate.[8] Obviously the scope and effect of each of these provisions depends on its own particular wording but some characteristics are common to most, if not all, of them.[9]

1. Sum must not exceed £5,000. Almost every such provision specifies that the sum payable must not exceed £5,000 in amount. The Administration of Estates (Small Payments) Act 1965 made a £500 limit generally applicable by inserting this £500 limit in almost 50 such provisions listed in the First Schedule to the Act.[10] The Treasury has power to fix a higher limit. In 1975 the Treasury fixed a £1,500 limit on the sum payable and in 1984 increased this limit to £5,000.[11]

---

[5] *Ante*, p. 143.

[6] But subject to any limitations contained in the grant: for limited grants see *post*, p. 179.

[7] Revenue Act 1884, s.11 (personalty) and extended to realty by Land Transfer Act 1897, s.2(2), now replaced by Administration of Estates Act 1925, s.2(1).

[8] Instances are: (a) Friendly Societies Act 1974, s.68: (b) Trade Union and Labour Relations Act 1974, Sched. I, para. 31 (as amended by Employment Protection Act 1975, Sched. 16, Pt. III, para. 32); Trade Union (Nominations) Regulations 1977 (S.I. 1977 No. 789), reg. 6 (as amended by S.I. 1984 No. 1290): (c) National Savings Bank Act 1971, s.9; National Savings Bank Regulations 1972 (S.I. 1972 No. 764), reg. 40 (as amended by S.I. 1984 No. 602): (d) National Debt Act 1972, s.11; Savings Certificates Regulations 1972 (S.I. 1972 No. 641), reg. 20 (as amended by S.I. 1984 No. 603): (e) Building Societies Act 1986, s.32 and Sched. 7.

[9] The provision contained in the Revenue Act 1884, s.11 (as amended by Revenue Act 1889, s.19) is exceptional: it provides that the production of a grant of representation from a U.K. court shall not be necessary to establish the right to receive money payable in respect of a life assurance policy effected with any insurance company by a person who dies domiciled outside the U.K.; there is no maximum limit on the money payable and payment is obligatory, see *Haas* v. *Atlas Assurance Co.* [1913] 2 K.B. 209 (foreign executor entitled to judgment for policy money less estate duty).

[10] Administration of Estates (Small Payments) Act 1965, s.1(1).

[11] *Ibid.* s.6; Administration of Estates (Small Payments) (Increase of Limit) Orders 1975 (S.I. 1975 No. 1137), para. 3, and 1984 (S.I. 1984 No. 539), paras. 2 and 3.

2. Payment is permissive. These provisions authorise the payer to make the payment without the production of any grant of representation to the deceased's estate, but do not compel the payer to do so. The payer may insist on making his payment to the deceased's personal representatives after they have proved their title by production of a grant of representation. For instance, under section 25(1)[12] of the Industrial and Provident Societies Act 1965, if any member of a registered society dies and his property in the society in respect of shares, loans or deposits does not exceed £5,000 and is not the subject of any nomination, the committee of the society *may*, without letters of administration or probate of any will having been obtained, distribute that property among such persons as appear to the committee on such evidence as they deem satisfactory to be entitled by law to receive it. The committee's power to distribute under this provision is entirely discretionary.[13]

By way of contrast, on the death of a nominator payment to his nominee entitled under a valid statutory nomination[14] is obligatory, subject to satisfactory proof of the nominator's death.[15]

3. The payer is protected. Many of these provisions expressly protect the payer against the risk of making a payment to a person who turns out not to be entitled. For instance, section 27 of the Industrial and Provident Societies Act 1965 provides that all payments made by the committee under section 25 to any person appearing to the committee at the time of the payment to be entitled thereunder shall be valid and effectual against any demand made upon the committee or society by any other person.

3. FORMS OF GRANT

There are three basic types of grant of representation: (i) probate (which is granted when an executor proves a will), (ii) administration with the will annexed (which is granted when a person other than an executor proves a will), and (iii) administration or "simple" administration (which is granted when the deceased died wholly intestate). Each of these basic types of grant may be general or limited—for instance limited as to the property to which the grant extends or as to the duration of the grant.[16]

A. General Grants

Most grants of probate or administration (whether or not with the will annexed) are general in the sense that the grant is not by its terms

---

[12] As amended by Administration of Estates (Small Payments) Act 1965; S.I. 1984 No. 539, para. 2.

[13] *Escritt* v. *Todmorden Co-operative Society* [1896] 1 Q.B. 461.

[14] For statutory nominations see *ante*, p. 15.

[15] See *e.g.* Industrial and Provident Societies Act 1965, s.24.

[16] Supreme Court Act 1981, s.113.

limited in any way. A grant may be general though it was preceded by another grant in respect of the same estate:

1. Double probate. When probate of a will is granted to some but not all of the executors, it is the practice to reserve power to the other executors who have not renounced to apply later for probate. If such an executor later applies for probate, he receives a grant called double probate.[17] If he was a minor when the original grant was made, he must attain 18 years of age before he applies, and if the original grant was made to four executors (the maximum number permitted), he must wait for the occurrence of a vacancy.

A grant of double probate is a general grant which runs concurrently with the original grant. Until the grant of double probate is made, the executors to whom probate was originally granted may exercise all the powers conferred by law on a personal representative.[18]

2. Cessate grant. A grant of probate or administration which is limited as to its duration terminates at the end of its allotted span. For instance, where a minor is the sole executor of a will, administration with the will annexed may be granted to his guardian, limited until the minor attains the age of 18 years[19]: when this event occurs the grant automatically terminates. On the termination of any grant by the occurrence of the event which limited its duration, a further grant called a *cessate* grant may be made. In this instance, on attaining full age, the executor may apply for a *cessate* grant of probate, which is a general grant.

B. Grant to Settled Land

Settled land grant. A special form of grant known as a settled land grant may be made on the death of a person after 1925 in whom settled land was vested at his death. The land must have been settled previously to his death and not by his will, and must remain settled land notwithstanding his death.[20] Such a grant is made to the deceased's special personal representatives. To consider an example. Land is settled on A for life, remainder to B for life, remainder to C in fee simple, and the legal estate in the land is vested in A (who is of full age) as tenant for life.[21] At A's death the land remains settled land because it is still limited in trust for B and C by way of succession. Accordingly, on the death of A a settled land grant may be made to A's special personal representatives. B (who is of full age) is the next tenant for life and A's

---

[17] Such an executor may be cited to accept or refuse a grant at the instance of the executors who have proved, or the executors of the last survivor of them, N.C. Prob. Rules 1987, r. 47(2).

[18] Administration of Estates Act 1925, s.8.

[19] *Post*, pp. 181–183.

[20] Administration of Estates Act 1925, s.22(1); N.C. Prob. Rules 1987, r. 29. "Settled land" has the same meaning as in the Settled Land Act 1925, see Administration of Estates Act 1925, s.55(1)(xxiv): for the requirement that the land must remain settled land notwithstanding his death see *Re Bridgett & Hayes' Contract* [1928] Ch. 163.

[21] Settled Land Act 1925, ss.1(1) and 19(1).

special personal representatives convey the land to B.[22] However, at B's death the land ceases to be settled land if C is then of full age and has not in the meantime settled his interest in remainder. If at B's death the land ceases to be settled land, it vests in B's general personal representatives[23] and they in turn convey the land to C.[24]

Special personal representatives. Special personal representatives are either special executors or special administrators.

(1) *Special executors.* Section 22(1) of the Administration of Estates Act 1925 provides that a testator may appoint, and if he does not do so, is deemed to have appointed, as his special executors in regard to settled land, the persons (if any) who are the trustees of the settlement at his death, and probate may be granted to such trustees limited to the settled land. To consider more fully the situation at the death of A in the above example, if A leaves a will and at his death S and T are the trustees of the settlement of the land,[25] then S and T are by express, or deemed, appointment the special executors of his will in regard to the settled land. S and T may therefore obtain a grant of probate limited to the settled land.

(2) *Special administrators.* Rule 29 of the Non-Contentious Probate Rules 1987 provides for a grant of administration limited to settled land to be made to the persons who are the trustees of the settlement at the time of their application for a grant.[26] Unlike special executors the applicants need not be the trustees of the settlement at the death of the deceased. To continue with the above example, if S and T die without obtaining a grant of probate and new trustees of the settlement are appointed after A's death, the new trustees may obtain a grant of administration with A's will annexed, limited to the settled land. If A leaves no will at his death, the trustees of the settlement may obtain a grant of simple administration limited to the settled land.

(3) *General grant excluding settled land.* A grant of probate or administration made in respect of the deceased's free estate alone must expressly exclude the settled land.[27] However, if the persons entitled to a grant in respect of the free estate are also entitled to a grant of the same nature in respect of settled land, a grant expressly including the settled land may issue to them.[28] This only applies if the applicants are entitled either to probate or administration in both cases. If the applicants are

---

[22] *Ibid.* s.7(1). The conveyance to B is made by vesting assent or vesting deed, *ibid.* s.8(1) and (4).

[23] Administration of Estates Act 1925, s.1(1) and (3); *Re Bridgett & Hayes' Contract, supra;* see *post*, p. 206.

[24] Settled Land Act 1925, s.7(5). The conveyance to C is made by ordinary assent or conveyance. Conversely, if the land continues to be settled land at B's death, it vests in B's special personal representatives, *In the Estate of Taylor* [1929] P. 260 (settlement by C); *Re Norton* [1929] 1 Ch. 84 (subsisting voluntary rentcharges).

[25] Settled Land Act 1925, s.30.

[26] For powers to make limited grants see Supreme Court Act 1981, ss.113 and 116; *post*, p. 179.

[27] N.C. Prob. Rules 1987, r. 29(5).

[28] *Ibid.* r. 29(4).

entitled to probate in one case and administration in the other, separate grants to them are necessary.

Order of priority to settled land grant. The order of priority to a settled land grant is as follows[29]:

(i) *The special executors* who take a grant of probate limited to the settled land.

(ii) *The trustees of the settlement at the time of the application for the grant.*

(iii) *The personal representatives of the deceased.* The persons in classes (ii) or (iii) take a grant of administration with the will annexed (if the deceased left a will) or simple administration (if the deceased left no will), in each case limited to the settled land. If the personal representatives of the deceased apply for such a grant, they must clear off the persons who fall within classes (i) or (ii) unless these persons are passed over by the court.[30]

A personal representative of the deceased (not being a trustee of the settlement) is not bound to act in regard to settled land as well as the deceased's free estate. If he is not a trustee of the settlement, he may, before representation has been granted, renounce his office in regard to settled land without renouncing it in regard to other property, and he may, after representation has been granted, apply to the court for revocation of the grant in regard to settled land without applying in regard to other property.[31]

Land ceasing to be settled land. The provisions authorising a settled land grant do not apply if the land ceases to be settled land at the death of the deceased. In that event the land vests in the deceased's general personal representatives.[32] To consider two common situations:

(i) Land is settled on D for life with remainder to E and F in fee simple upon an express trust for sale. The legal estate in the land is vested in D (who is of full age) as tenant for life. At D's death the land ceases to be settled land because it becomes subject to an express trust for sale[33] and therefore it vests in D's general personal representatives.[34] E and F are entitled to require D's general personal representatives to convey the land to E and F.[35]

(ii) Land is settled on G for life with remainder to H and J in fee sim-

---

[29] *Ibid.* r. 29(2) and (3).

[30] *Cf. In the Estate of Powell* [1935] P. 114.

[31] Administration of Estates Act 1925, s.23(1). For the power of the court to appoint a special or additional personal representative in respect of settled land see Administration of Estates Act 1925, s.23(2)–(5) (as amended by Administration of Justice Act 1970, s.1 and Sched. 2, para. 3); *In the Estate of Clifton* [1931] P. 222; *In the Estate of James* (1926) 162 L.T.J. 498.

[32] *Re Bridgett & Hayes' Contract* [1928] Ch. 163 (see *post*, p. 206) followed in *In the Estate of Bordass* [1929] P. 107. For grants where the deceased died intestate without known next of kin see *In the Estate of Birch* [1929] P. 164 and *In the Estate of Mortifee* [1948] P. 274.

[33] Settled Land Act 1925, s.1(7) (as amended by Law of Property (Amendment) Act 1926, s.7 and Sched.).

[34] *Re Bridgett & Hayes' Contract, supra.*

[35] Settled Land Act 1925, s.7(5). The conveyance to E and F is made by ordinary assent or conveyance.

ple as tenants in common. The legal estate in the land is vested in G (who is of full age) as tenant for life. At G's death the land ceases to be settled land because it becomes subject to a statutory trust for sale, of which the trustees of the former settlement are trustees.[36] The land therefore vests in G's general personal representatives. The trustees of the former settlement are entitled to require G's general personal representatives to convey the land to them.[37]

Position of purchaser. Section 24 of the Administration of Estates Act 1925 provides that the special personal representatives may dispose of the settled land without the concurrence of the general personal representatives, who may likewise dispose of the other property of the deceased without the concurrence of the special personal representatives.

The Settled Land Act 1925 requires every vesting instrument to describe the settled land,[38] so that a purchaser may identify the land without reference to the trust instrument. Unfortunately there is no similar requirement for a settled land grant, which is just as much a document of title to the legal estate. An example will illustrate the consequent difficulty which faces a purchaser. By a Settlement, both Blackacre and Whiteacre are settled on A for life, with remainder as to Blackacre to trustees upon an express trust for sale, and as to Whiteacre to B for life, remainder to C in fee simple. The legal estate in both Blackacre and Whiteacre is vested in A (who is of full age) as tenant for life. On A's death intestate his general administrators obtain a grant of administration save and except settled land, and his special administrators (*i.e.* the trustees of the settlement) obtain a grant of administration limited to land vested in A at his death under the Settlement and remaining settled notwithstanding his death. In order to ascertain that Blackacre passed to A's general administrators and Whiteacre passed to A's special administrators, a purchaser of either property would need to investigate the equitable title because it is not apparent on the face of the grant of administration limited to settled land that it applies to Whiteacre but not to Blackacre.[39]

C. Limited Grants

Powers to make limited grants. Under section 113 of the Supreme Court Act 1981 the court has power to grant probate or administration in respect of any part of the deceased's estate, limited in any way the court thinks fit.[40] This wide power to make limited grants is subject to only one restriction: where the deceased's estate is known to be insol-

---

[36] *Ibid.* s.36(1), (2) and (6).

[37] *Ibid.* s.36(1); *Re Cugny's W.T.* [1931] 1 Ch. 305; *Re Thomas* [1939] Ch. 513. The conveyance is made by ordinary assent or conveyance (the reference to "vesting" assent in *Re Cugny's W.T.,* 309 is a slip).

[38] ss.5(1) and (2) and 8(4).

[39] See A. H. Withers (1946) 62 L.Q.R. 167, 168 and Settled Land Act 1925, s.110.

[40] See N.C. Prob. Rules 1987, r. 51.

vent,[41] the section forbids severance of the grant of representation to it, except as regards a trust estate in which the deceased had no beneficial interest. Thus if the deceased D dies insolvent, holding land on trust for B, a separate grant may be made limited to this land as a trust estate.

Again, if the court exercises its powers under section 116 of the Act to pass over an executor or a person who would otherwise have been entitled to the grant of administration, and appoint some other person as administrator,[42] the court may limit its grant of administration in any way the court thinks fit.[43] Thus, on passing over, the power to make a limited grant is not subject to any restriction.

If a grant is first made limited to particular property or a particular purpose, a grant may later be made *caeterorum, i.e.* of all the rest of the estate. If the grants are made in the reverse order, a grant is first made *save and except* the particular property or particular purpose, and a grant limited to that property or purpose may be made later.

Limited probate. The appointment by a testator of an executor may be qualified as to the subject matter of his office (an appointment "to be the executor of this will as to the business of grocer carried on by me at the date of this Will"), or as to time (an appointment of an executor "during the minority of my son James").[44] Such an executor may only take a grant of probate limited to the property, or the time, specified in the will.[45]

Administration de bonis non. A grant of administration *de bonis non administratis* (usually known as a grant *de bonis non*) is made in respect of a deceased's unadministered estate. Such a grant, like a settled land grant, is by its nature limited as to the property to which the grant extends. The purpose of such a grant is to enable the administration of the estate to be completed.

1) *When made.* A grant *de bonis non* is made following the death of a sole, or last surviving, personal representative who died without having fully administered the deceased's estate. Two requirements apply:

(i) There must have been a prior grant of probate or letters of administration to the personal representative who has died. If, for instance, a sole executor starts to administer the deceased's estate but dies before taking probate, an original grant of administration with the will annexed is made, and not a grant *de bonis non*. Again the prior grant must not have terminated by the occurrence of the event which limited its duration—if this occurs a *cessate* grant[46] is made and not a grant *de bonis non*.

(ii) Any chain of representation through proving executors must

---

[41] *Post,* p. 285.

[42] See *ante,* pp. 146 and 157.

[43] For an instance see *In the Goods of Baldwin* [1903] P. 61 (will only made specific gift to X: next-of-kin passed over and letters of administration (with will annexed) granted to X limited to property specifically given to X by will).

[44] *Ante,* pp. 140–141.

[45] *In the Estate of Falkner* (1915) 113 L.T. 927.

[46] *Ante,* p. 176.

have been broken.[47] A grant *de bonis non* cannot be made so long as the chain of representation through proving executors continues. In *In the Goods of Reid*[48] T died, having by his will appointed X and Y to be his executors. X alone obtained probate of T's will, power to prove being reserved to Y. X died, not having fully administered T's estate. By his will X appointed Z to be his executor and Z proved X's will. Accordingly Z was the executor by representation of T.[49] The court therefore refused the application of T's daughter for a grant to herself of letters of administration *de bonis non* with T's will annexed. Of course the chain of representation would have been broken if Z had not proved X's will; in that event, assuming Y was either cleared off or passed over, a grant of letters of administration *de bonis non* with T's will annexed would have been made.

A grant *de bonis non* is also made following the revocation by the court of a previous grant of probate or administration. For example, in *In the Goods of Galbraith*[50] two elderly executors, to whom probate had been granted six years previously, became unfit to act due to their physical and mental infirmity. As they had not fully administered the estate of the testatrix, the court revoked the probate and granted letters of administration *de bonis non* with the will annexed to another person.

(2) *To whom made.* The rules of priority which govern applications for original grants apply equally to applications for *de bonis non* grants. Thus rule 20 of the Non-Contentious Probate Rules applies to an application for administration *de bonis non* with the will annexed, and rule 22 to an application for simple administration *de bonis non*.[51] An applicant for a *de bonis non* grant must clear off all persons who have a prior right to a grant: alternatively the court may pass them over pursuant to its power under section 116 of the Supreme Court Act 1981.

Administration for the use and benefit of a minor. A minor cannot take a grant of probate or letters of administration.[52] If the person to whom a grant of probate or administration would otherwise be made is a minor, administration is granted for the use and benefit of the minor until he attains the age of 18 years.[53] If a grant of probate or administration with the will annexed would otherwise be made, it is a grant of administration with the will annexed: if the deceased left no will, it is a grant of simple administration. This form of grant, formerly known as a

---

[47] *Ante,* p. 143.

[48] [1896] P. 129.

[49] Z may cite Y to accept or refuse probate of T's will, N.C. Prob. Rules 1987, r. 47(2): if Y does not appear to the citation, his rights in respect of the executorship wholly cease, Administration of Estates Act 1925, s.5.

[50] [1951] P. 422; see also *In the Goods of Loveday* [1900] P. 154 (grant to administratrix who could not be traced revoked, and grant *de bonis non* made); *In the Estate of French* [1910] P. 169.

[51] *Ante,* pp. 151 and 154.

[52] *Ante,* pp. 145 and 157. An infant is usually referred to as a minor in probate practice.

[53] N.C. Prob. Rules 1987, r. 32. As an alternative to a grant for the use and benefit of a minor, a trust corporation may sometimes take a grant limited until the minor applies for and obtains a grant, see r. 36(3).

grant *durante minore aetate,* is by its nature limited as to its duration and terminates automatically when the minor attains the age of 18 years or dies under this age. When the minor attains this age, probate or administration may be granted to him.

(1) *When made.* If the sole executor is a minor, a grant of administration for his use and benefit is made. But if there are two or more executors of whom at least one is not under disability, probate may be granted to any executor not under disability, with power reserved to the executor who is a minor to take probate on attaining full age[54]: in such a case a grant for the use and benefit of the minor cannot be made unless the executors not under disability either renounce or fail to take probate on being cited to accept or refuse a grant.[55]

In determining whether a minor is the person to whom a grant of administration would otherwise be made, rule 27(5) of the Non-Contentious Probate Rules requires administration to be granted to a person of full age entitled thereto in preference to a guardian of a minor, unless a registrar otherwise directs.

(2) *To whom made.* Under rule 32 a grant for the use and benefit of a minor is made to:

(i) *the parents[56] of the minor jointly, or the surviving parent (as the statutory guardian[57]) or the guardian appointed by a deceased parent by deed or will (as the testamentary guardian[58]), or any guardian appointed by a court of competent jurisdiction.[59]* Under this head both parents (if living) must jointly apply for a grant.

There is a single exception to this head (i). If a minor who is sole executor has no interest in the deceased's residuary estate, such a grant is made to the person entitled to the residuary estate, unless a registrar otherwise directs.[60]

(ii) *assigned guardians, i.e. any person assigned as guardian by order of a registrar.[61]*

The assigned guardian may obtain administration for the use and benefit of the minor in default of, or jointly with, or even to the exclusion of, any person falling under head (i). Thus any person falling under head (i) may be passed over.

If any beneficiary is a minor or a life interest arises under a will or

---

[54] N.C. Prob. Rules 1987, r. 33(1).

[55] *Ibid.* r. 33(2).

[56] Including adoptive parents and the parents of a legitimated child.

[57] N.C. Prob. Rules 1987, r. 2(1); Guardianship of Minors Act 1971, s.3(1) and (2). The survivor of two adoptive parents is a statutory guardian. The mother of an illegitimate child is not a statutory guardian, but the father may be, see s.14(3) (as amended by Domestic Proceedings and Magistrates' Courts Act 1978, s.36(1)). The 1971 Act is to be amended by Family Law Reform Act 1987, ss.2, 4, 6 and 32 and Sched. I (not yet in force on April 4, 1988).

[58] N.C. Prob. Rules 1987, r. 2(1); Guardianship of Minors Act 1971, s.4. The mother of an illegitimate child may appoint a testamentary guardian, *Re A.* (1940) 164 L.T. 230; as to the father see s.14(3) (as amended). See *supra,* n. 57.

[59] *Ibid.* ss.3–6 and 15.

[60] N.C. Prob. Rules 1987, r. 32(1), proviso.

[61] *e.g.* a local authority assigned as guardian to a child in its care, see Child Care Act 1980, ss.2–5.

intestacy, administration must be granted either to a trust corporation (with or without an individual) or to not less than two individuals unless it appears to the court to be expedient to appoint an individual as sole administrator.[62] If there is only one person competent and willing to take a grant under heads (i) and (ii), that person may nominate a suitable person as co-administrator unless a registrar otherwise directs.[63]

(3) *Renunciation.* A minor's right to administration may be renounced only by an assigned guardian who is authorised to renounce by a registrar.[64] On the other hand a minor's right to take probate as executor on attaining the age of 18 years may not be renounced by any person on his behalf.[65]

(4) *Accountability of administrator.* An administrator who takes a grant for the use and benefit of a minor has the same rights and liabilities as an ordinary administrator.[66] "The limit to this administration is no doubt the minority of the person, but there is no other limit. He is an ordinary administrator: he is appointed for the very purpose of getting in the estate, paying the debts . . . "[67] and otherwise carrying out the due administration of the estate.[68] After his grant has terminated he must account to the person who subsequently obtains a grant of representation to the deceased—often this person is the former minor who takes probate or administration after attaining full age.[69]

Administration during mental incapacity. A person who is incapable of managing his affairs by reason of mental incapacity cannot take a grant of probate or letters of administration. Instead administration may be granted for his use and benefit, limited until further representation is granted or in such other way as the registrar may direct.[70] If the deceased left a will it is a grant of administration with the will annexed—otherwise it is a grant of simple administration.

(1) *When made.* Unless a registrar otherwise directs, no such grant is made unless all the persons equally entitled with the incapable person have been cleared off.[71] As in the case of an infant executor, probate may be granted to any other executor not under disability, with power reserved to the incapable executor to take probate on his disability ceasing.

---

[62] Supreme Court Act 1981, s.114(2).
[63] N.C. Prob. Rules 1987, r. 32(3).
[64] *Ibid.* r. 34(2).
[65] *Ibid.* r. 34(1).
[66] Administration of Estates Act 1925, s.21.
[67] *Per* Jessel M.R. in *Re Cope* (1880) 16 Ch.D. 49, 52.
[68] *Harvell* v. *Foster* [1954] 2 Q.B. 367.
[69] *Fotherby* v. *Pate* (1747) 3 Atk. 603; *Taylor* v. *Newton* (1752) 1 Lee 15 (accounting to creditor administrator).
[70] N.C. Prob. Rules 1987, r. 35(2): such a grant was formerly known as a grant *durante dementia.*
[71] *Ibid.* r. 35(1).

Notice of an intended application for such a grant must be given to the Court of Protection.[72]

(2) *To whom made.* Under rule 35 such a grant is made:

  (i) to the person authorised by the Court of Protection to apply for a grant;
  (ii) where there is no person so authorised, to the lawful attorney of the incapable person acting under a registered enduring power of attorney[73];
  (iii) where there is no such attorney entitled to act, or if the attorney renounces administration, to the person entitled to the deceased's residuary estate.

If there is only one person competent and willing to take a grant under heads (i), (ii) and (iii), and a grant is required to be made to not less than two administrators, that person may nominate a co-administrator unless a registrar otherwise directs.[74]

A registrar may override this order of priority by ordering administration for the use and benefit of the incapable person to be granted to such two or more other persons as the registrar may direct.[75]

Administration ad colligenda bona. A grant of administration *ad colligenda bona* is made to any suitable person for the purpose of preserving the assets of the estate until a general grant is made. Such a grant is useful, for instance, where urgent action is needed and the person entitled to a general grant cannot readily apply for it.[76] A grant *ad colligenda bona* is usually limited to the purpose of collecting, getting in and receiving the estate and doing acts necessary for its preservation, and is always limited until a further grant of representation is made. The grant is one of administration, and the will (if any) of the deceased is not annexed because no distribution to beneficiaries is authorised. A grant *ad colligenda bona* may specifically confer any wider power (such as a power to sell the deceased's farming stock) needed by the administrator. But if wider powers are needed, or it is not clear what action the administrator may have to take, it is preferable to apply for a grant to be made, limited as may be appropriate, under section 116 of the Supreme Court Act 1981.[77]

---

[72] *Ibid.* r. 35(5). For proof of mental incapacity see *Practice Note* [1962] 2 All E.R. 613; *Practice Direction* [1969] 1 All E.R. 494.

[73] For enduring power of attorney see *Practice Direction (Powers of Attorney)* [1986] 1 W.L.R. 419.

[74] N.C. Prob. Rules 1987, r. 35(3).

[75] *Ibid.* r. 35(4).

[76] *In the Goods of Bolton* [1899] P. 186 (next of kin in South America, goodwill of deceased's business as a newsagent needed to be sold before it became valueless; grant *ad colligendum* made to deceased's friend); see also *In the Goods of Stewart* (1869) L.R. 1 P. & D. 727; *In the Goods of Schwerdtfeger* (1876) 1 P.D. 424; *In the Goods of Ashley* (1890) 15 P.D. 120; *In the Goods of Roberts* [1898] P. 149; *Re Clore* [1982] Fam. 113, [1982] Ch. 456 (capital transfer tax dispute: Official Solicitor, not executors, appointed): N.C. Prob. Rules 1987, r. 52.

[77] *Ante,* pp. 147 and 157: see *In the Goods of Wyckoff* (1862) 32 L.J.P.M. & A. 214; *In the Goods of Suarez* [1897] P. 82.

Administration pending suit. After a probate action has begun[78] the court has power under section 117 of the Supreme Court Act 1981 to grant administration of the deceased's estate to an administrator. Such a grant of administration pending suit is limited to the duration of the probate action and terminates at its conclusion.[79] The person entitled may then take a grant of probate or administration as appropriate.

(1) *When made.* A grant of administration pending suit is made if this is proper in all the circumstances. In general a grant is justified if there are assets of the estate to be collected and safeguarded.[80] On the other hand, the court refused to make such a grant where a probate action had been begun to try the validity of a codicil, but the appointment of executors by the deceased's will was not challenged.[81] An application for the appointment of an administrator pending suit may be made by any party to the probate action or by any other interested person, such as a creditor.[82]

(2) *To whom made.* Usually such a grant is made to a person unconnected with the action,[83] such as an accountant, and not to a party to the action unless all parties consent.[84] A sole administrator pending suit may be appointed, although there is the possibility of a minority or a life interest arising, because section 117 refers to the appointment of "an administrator" in the singular and an administrator pending suit is under the constant supervision of the court.[85]

(3) *Function of administrator pending suit.* Section 117 provides that an administrator pending suit shall have all the rights, duties and powers of a general administrator,[86] subject to an important restriction—he must not make any distribution of the deceased's estate to any beneficiary without the leave of the court.[87] The administrator is subject to the

---

[78] *Salter* v. *Salter* [1896] P. 291 (caveator appearing to warning but no writ issued: no jurisdiction to grant administration *pendente lite*).

[79] *Weiland* v. *Bird* [1894] P. 262 (probate action terminates with decree); *Taylor* v. *Taylor* (1881) 3 P.D. 29 (appeal extends probate action).

[80] *Re Bevan* [1948] 1 All E.R. 271.

[81] *Mortimer* v. *Paull* (1870) L.R. 2 P. & D. 85: see also *Horrell* v. *Witts* (1866) L.R. 1 P. & D. 103 and *In the Estate of Day* [1940] 2 All E.R. 544 (only second codicil disputed: court pronounced for will appointing executors and first codicil, the executors undertaking not to dispose of property dealt with in second codicil pending the probate action).

[82] *In the Goods of Evans* (1890) 15 P.D. 215; *In the Estate of Cleaver* [1905] P. 319. Application is made in the Chancery Division, R.S.C., Ord. 76, r. 15, and after appointment by the Chancery Division the administrator applies to the Principal Registry of the Family Division for a grant.

[83] *Stratton* v. *Ford* (1755) 2 Lee 216; *Whittle* v. *Keats* (1866) 35 L.J.P. & M. 54.

[84] *Re Griffin* [1925] P. 38 (plaintiff appointed without defendant's consent as appointment was clearly desirable).

[85] *In the Estate of Lindley* [1953] P. 203; *In the Estate of Haslip* [1958] 1 W.L.R. 583; see *ante*, p. 156.

[86] *Re Toleman* [1897] 1 Ch. 866 (administrator *pendente lite* may be sued by a creditor of the deceased without any leave of the court).

[87] *Or* in such circumstances as may be prescribed by rules of court, Supreme Court Act 1981, ss.117(2) and 151(1).

immediate control of the court and acts under its direction[88]: he should, for instance, obtain the directions of the court as to any disputed debt.[89]

The administrator, like a receiver, must lodge his accounts for passing by the court[90] and he is entitled to such reasonable remuneration as the court thinks fit out of the deceased's estate.[91]

Representation in legal proceedings. If there is no personal representative of the deceased and it is necessary for the estate to be represented in legal proceedings, a grant of administration limited to an action (or *ad litem*) may be made under section 116 of the Supreme Court Act 1981.[92] Such a grant is limited to bringing, defending or being a party to particular legal proceedings. Thus an intending plaintiff, who wishes to bring an action for damages against the deceased's estate in respect of the deceased's negligence in a motor accident, may apply for a grant to be made to the plaintiff's nominee limited to defending the action.[93]

Since 1971 the Rules of the Supreme Court have provided a simpler alternative procedure, which is applicable where any person against whom an action would have lain has died but the cause of action survives.[94] If no grant of probate or administration has been made, the plaintiff may bring his action against the estate of the deceased (*e.g.* against "the personal representatives of A.B. deceased") and then apply in the action for an order appointing a person to represent the deceased's estate for the purpose of the proceedings.[95] This procedure is likely to be adopted in preference to a grant of administration *ad litem* but it is not applicable to an action to be brought by (and not against) the deceased's estate, or to an action which would not have lain against the deceased, such as an application for family provision on death.

---

[88] *Ibid.* s.117(2).

[89] *Charlton* v. *Hindmarsh* (1860) 1 Sw. & Tr. 519.

[90] R.S.C., Ord. 30, rr. 2–4 and 6 and Ord. 76, r. 15(2); *Practice Direction* [1973] 1 W.L.R. 627.

[91] Supreme Court Act 1981, s.117(3): see also *Re Howlett* [1950] P. 177. See *post,* p. 249.

[92] *Ante,* pp. 146 and 157.

[93] *In the Estate of Simpson; In the Estate of Gunning* [1936] P. 40; *In the Goods of Knight* [1939] 3 All E.R. 928 (grant *ad litem* to Treasury Solicitor);*In the Estate of Newsham* [1967] P. 230.

[94] R.S.C., Ord. 15, r. 6A: Supreme Court Act 1981, s.87(2) (replacing Proceedings Against Estates Act 1970, s.2, as amended by Administration of Justice Act 1977, s.27). As to the County Court, see C.C.R. 1981, Ord. 5, r. 8.

[95] R.S.C., Ord. 15, r. 6A: the deceased driver's insurers may be appointed in a running-down action. As to the appointment of the Official Solicitor see r. 6A(5A); *Re Amirteymour* [1979] 1 W.L.R. 63. See also R.S.C., Order 15, r. 15; *Lean* v. *Alston* [1947] 1 K.B. 467.

Chapter 8

THE MAKING AND REVOCATION OF GRANTS

1. THE MAKING OF GRANTS

A. Caveats and Citations

Caveats. A caveat is a notice in writing to the Family Division of the High Court that no grant is to be sealed in the deceased's estate without notice to the caveator who enters the caveat.[1] An index of caveats entered in any registry is kept and is searched on any application for a grant being made in any registry.[2] A registrar must not allow any grant to be sealed if he has knowledge of an effective caveat.[3] Thus the entry of a caveat stops the issue of any grant in the deceased's estate (except to the caveator himself) until the caveat ceases to be effective. It gives the caveator time to take legal advice, or collect evidence, so that he may decide whether to oppose an application by another person for a grant.

(1) *Warning of caveat.* When an applicant for a grant finds that a caveat has been entered, he may issue a warning in the prescribed form to the caveator.[4] A warning states the interest of the applicant (*e.g.* that he is the executor of the will of the deceased, or interested on intestacy as the lawful brother of the whole blood) and sets out two alternative courses of action open to the caveator:

(i) to enter an appearance to the warning in the Registry, stating the caveator's contrary interest (*e.g.* that he is the executor of a different will of the deceased).[5] If the caveator enters an appearance, no grant can be issued without an order of the court.[6] Often the applicant or the caveator commences a probate action at this point in order to obtain the decision of the court as to the person entitled to a grant.

(ii) to issue a summons for directions if the caveator has no contrary

---

[1] Caveats are regulated by N.C. Prob. Rules 1987, r. 44.

[2] Supreme Court Act 1981, s.108; N.C.Prob. Rules 1987, r. 44(4).

[3] *Ibid.* r. 44(1): a caveat does not prevent a grant being sealed on the day the caveat is entered. A caveat is effective against the resealing of Commonwealth or Colonial grants, but does not stop the issue of a grant *ad colligenda bona*, *Re Clore* [1982] Fam. 113, [1982] Ch. 456.

[4] *Ibid.* r. 44(5): any person interested may issue a warning.

[5] *Ibid.* r. 44(10).

[6] *Ibid.* rr. 44(13) and 45(3): for the caveator's position in a consequent probate action see *Rose* v. *Epstein* [1974] 1 W.L.R. 1565: for caveats entered by a vexatious litigant see *Re Hancock* [1978] C.L.Y. 1443.

interest but wishes to show cause against the sealing of a grant to the applicant.[7] The caveator and the applicant may, for instance, be entitled to a grant in the same degree.

If the caveator does not follow either of these courses of action the caveat ceases to be effective[8] and a grant of probate or administration may be issued to the applicant.

(2) *Duration of caveat.* A caveat also ceases to be effective at the expiration of six months beginning with the date on which it was entered.[9] A caveator may lodge a written application for its extension during the last month of this six months' period: each time the caveator does so, the caveat remains in force for an additional six months.[10]

Needless to say a caveat ceases to be effective if the caveator withdraws it before he enters an appearance to a warning.[11]

(3) *Standing search for a grant.* A person who wishes to commence family provision or other proceedings need not enter a caveat in order to ascertain when a grant is issued. Instead application may be made for a standing search to be made for any grant of representation to the deceased's estate issued within the previous 12 months or within the following six months.[12]

Citations. There are three types of citation.[13] Two have already been considered, namely a citation to accept or refuse a grant[14] and a citation to take probate.[15] The third type now to be considered is a citation to propound a will.

A person who is interested on intestacy, or (alternatively) under an earlier will of the deceased, may cite the executors and beneficiaries under an alleged will, or (alternatively) an alleged later will, to propound it. If they fail to enter an appearance and propound the alleged will, the citor may apply for an order for a grant in common form as if the alleged will were invalid.[16] A citation to propound a will is not, however, appropriate if the will in question has already been proved in common form—instead the person challenging the will may bring a probate action for the revocation of the previous grant.[17]

This procedure by citation is useful where there is doubt as to the validity of a will. However, the procedure cannot be invoked by an executor of a will who doubts the validity of a later codicil. In *In the Estate of Muirhead*[18] the executrix of a will cited the beneficiary under a later

---

[7] *Ibid.* r. 44(6).
[8] *Ibid.* r. 44(12); the caveator has at least eight days to do so, see r. 44(10) and (6).
[9] *Ibid.* r. 44(3a); but see r. 48(8) and (13).
[10] *Ibid.* r. 44(3); but see r. 44(4).
[11] *Ibid.* r. 44(11).
[12] *Ibid.* r. 43: for exclusion see r. 43(3).
[13] For the issue of citations see N.C. Prob. Rules 1987, r. 46.
[14] *Ante,* p. 148 (probate) and p. 158 (administration).
[15] *Ante,* p. 149.
[16] N.C. Prob. Rules 1987, r. 48: see also *In the Goods of Morton* (1863) 3 Sw. & Tr. 179; *In the Goods of Dennis* [1899] P. 191; *In the Goods of Bootle* (1901) 84 L.T. 570.
[17] *Re Jolley* [1964] P. 262.
[18] [1971] P. 263, following *In the Goods of Benbow* (1862) 2 Sw. & Tr. 488.

codicil (which named no executor) to propound the codicil. The beneficiary failed to enter an appearance to the citation. Cairns J. refused the application of the executrix for a grant of probate of the will without the codicil. He held that the citation to propound the codicil was not appropriate—if the beneficiary did propound the codicil, Cairns J. questioned whether separate grants could be made to the executrix (in respect of the will) and to the beneficiary (in respect of the codicil). The executrix should have applied for a grant of probate in solemn form and, if she had reason to believe that the codicil was invalid, should have adduced evidence of the invalidity of the codicil.[19]

B. Time Limit for Issuing a Grant

Minimum time. Normally no grant of probate or letters of administration with the will annexed may be issued within seven days and no grant of simple administration within 14 days of the deceased's death. An earlier grant may be issued with the leave of a registrar.[20]

No maximum time. There is no maximum limit of time within which a grant must be obtained. However penalties are laid down for administering an estate without obtaining a grant of representation.[21]

C. Liability of Personal Representatives for Inheritance Tax

On the death of any person inheritance tax is charged as if, immediately before his death, the deceased had made a chargeable transfer by which he transferred the value of his estate.[22] Thus inheritance tax becomes payable in respect of the value of the deceased's estate, subject of course to certain exemptions and reliefs. The value is ascertained after taking into account the deceased's debts and liabilities (so far as deductible)[23] and after making an allowance for reasonable funeral expenses.[24]

The liability of the deceased's personal representatives for this inheritance tax must now be considered. The incidence of this tax on the beneficial interests under the deceased's will or intestacy is considered later.[25]

Liability of the personal representatives. Under section 200(1) of the Inheritance Tax Act 1984 the deceased's personal representatives are liable for the inheritance tax charged on his death on the value of:

---

[19] *In the Estate of Muirhead, supra,* at p. 270. Cairns J. also suggested *obiter* that his decision might apply in a case where there were two wills with the same executors, the later will if valid revoking the earlier.

[20] N.C. Prob. Rules 1987, r. 6(2); see also r. 6(1) (registrar's inquiries to be answered before grant issued).

[21] Stamp Act 1815, s.37 as amended by Finance Act 1975, s.59(5) and Sched. 13 Pt. I; Customs and Inland Revenue Act 1881, s.40.

[22] Inheritance Tax Act 1984, s.4(1): for the definition of estate see s.5.

[23] *Ibid.,* s.5(5); Finance Act 1986, s.103.

[24] Inheritance Tax Act 1984, s.172.

[25] *Post,* p. 279.

(i) any property which was not immediately before his death comprised in a settlement; and

(ii) any land in the United Kingdom which immediately before his
death was comprised in a settlement and which devolves upon or
vests in the personal representatives.[26]

Head (ii) is relatively narrow in its ambit whereas head (i) is very wide,
including, not only the deceased's property which vests in his personal
representatives, but also the deceased's severable share of property held
jointly and the deceased's foreign property which does not vest in
them. Thus the personal representatives are liable for inheritance tax on
the deceased's foreign property—otherwise the Revenue might well
experience difficulty in securing payment of the tax.

This liability of a personal representative for inheritance tax under
section 200(1) is a *personal* liability—his own assets are liable to be
taken in execution to satisfy the tax due to the Crown.[27]

Limit on extent of liability. In order to protect a personal representative section 204(1) imposes a limit on the extent of his personal liability—he is not liable for tax under head (i) except to the extent of the
assets which he has received as personal representative or might have
so received but for his own neglect or default. This upper limit becomes
operative in a case where the tax payable on the deceased's death
(including the tax payable on his foreign property) exceeds the amount
of the assets which the personal representative either received or ought
to have received. The personal representative is not personally liable for
tax in excess of the amount of these assets.[28] There is a similar upper
limit on the extent of the personal representative's liability under head
(ii).

Delivery of Inland Revenue Account. The personal representatives[29]
must deliver an account to the Commissioners of Inland Revenue
within 12 months from the end of the month in which the death occurs
or (if this is later) within three months from the date on which they first
acted.[30] However normally no account need be delivered if the value of
the deceased's estate does not exceed £70,000.[31] The account specifies to
the best of their knowledge and belief[32] all property which formed part
of the deceased's estate immediately before his death and the value of

---

[26] For exceptions to the personal representatives' liability under s.200(1) see ss.30–35 (as
amended), 125–130, and 207–208; the exceptions include heritage property and woodlands
to which special accountability rules apply: for the definition of settlement see s.43. For
the contingent secondary liability of personal representatives to tax in respect of lifetime
transfers see s.199(2), as amended by Finance Act 1986, Sched. 19, para. 26.

[27] *I.R.C.* v. *Stannard* [1984] 1 W.L.R. 1039 (order is in *de bonis propriis* form).

[28] See *Re Clore* [1982] Fam. 113, [1982] Ch. 456.

[29] This means executors, any person by whom or on whose behalf an application for a
grant of administration or for the resealing of a grant made outside the U.K. is made, and
an executor *de son tort*, see s.272: as to an executor *de son tort* see *post*, pp. 408 *et seq.*

[30] ss.216(1) and (6) and 257. For delivery of the account to a probate registry instead see
s.257(3).

[31] Capital Transfer Tax (Delivery of Accounts) Regulations 1981 (S.I. 1981 No. 880) and
1983 (S.I. 1983 No. 1039) and Inheritance Tax (Delivery of Accounts) Regulations 1987 (S.I.
1987 No. 1127); *Practice Direction (Probate: Representation Grant)* [1981] 1 W.L.R. 1185.

[32] *I.R.C.* v. *Stype Trustees (Jersey) Ltd.* [1985] 1 W.L.R. 1290.

that property.[33] They may submit a provisional estimate of value if they are unable to ascertain the exact value of any property and undertake to deliver a further account as soon as its value is ascertained. If the personal representatives discover that the account delivered by them is defective in a material respect, they must deliver a corrective or supplementary account within six months of this discovery.[34] Personal representatives often discover other assets or liabilities of the deceased in the course of administration

No grant before payment of tax. Personal representatives must pay all the tax for which they are liable on delivery of their account, unless they are entitled to, and do, elect to pay by instalments.[35] Though they have 12 months from the end of the month in which the death occurs to deliver their account, interest at the rate of 6 per cent. per annum is charged on unpaid tax as soon as six months have passed from the end of the month in which the death occurs.[36] If the personal representatives wish to avoid the payment of any interest, they need to deliver their account and pay the tax before the end of this six months' period.

The High Court cannot make any grant of probate or letters of administration, or reseal any grant made outside the United Kingdom, until the personal representatives have paid any inheritance tax payable on delivery of their account.[37] The personal representatives may well be obliged to borrow money in order to pay this inheritance tax—the deceased's property only vests in an administrator when letters of administration are granted to him and even an executor needs a grant of probate in order to prove his title.[38]

D. Oath and Other Evidence

Every application for a grant must be supported by an oath sworn by the applicant and by such other papers as the registrar may require.[39]

The oath. The oath of the applicant is contained in an affidavit sworn by him. The form of oath varies according to the circumstances of the case. For instance, if the application for a grant is made after judgment has been given in a probate action, the oath refers to the judgment. An oath normally includes the following:

---

[33] s.216(3); see also s.5(1) and (2). A special executor delivers an account specifying the settled land and its value, s.216(3) and (4). The Revenue may restrict the property to be specified by any class of personal representatives, s.216(3)(b).

[34] s.217. For penalties in connection with accounts see ss.245–253.

[35] s.226(2). For their election to pay tax by 10 yearly instalments in the case of land, certain company shares or securities, a business or interest in a business, see ss.227–234.

[36] s.233: Inheritance Tax and Capital Transfer Tax (Interest on Unpaid Tax) Order 1987 (S.I. 1987 No. 887). Interest payable is not deductible for tax purposes, s.233(3).

[37] Supreme Court Act 1981, s.109 as amended by Inheritance Tax Act 1984, Sched. 8: this requirement may be dispensed with by arrangement between the President of the Family Division and the Revenue, s.109(2): see *Re Clore* [1982] Fam. 113, 117.

[38] *Ante*, pp. 168–170.

[39] N.C. Prob. Rules 1987, r. 8(1): the applicant may affirm instead of swearing the oath.

(1) *Death of the deceased.* The applicant swears to the death of the deceased, stating the date of death if this is known. If the applicant cannot swear to the death of the deceased but there is evidence from which his death may be presumed (*e.g.* he was on board a missing aircraft), application may be made for an order giving him leave to swear to the death.[40]

(2) *Domicile at death.* The oath states where the deceased died domiciled[41] and this is noted in the grant. If the deceased died domiciled in England and Wales, a grant of probate or letters of administration made by the High Court and noting his domicile there is recognised in Scotland and Northern Ireland.[42]

(3) *Will or intestacy.* The applicant swears that he believes "the paper writing now produced to and marked[43] by me to contain the true and original last will and testament" of the deceased (on an application for probate or administration with the will annexed), *or* that the deceased died intestate (on an application for simple administration).

(4) *Title of applicant to grant.* In his oath the applicant shows his title to the grant for which he is applying—for instance, that he is the sole executor of the will (on an application for probate), the residuary legatee and devisee named in the will (on an application for administration with the will annexed), or the lawful son and one of the persons entitled to share in the estate (on an application for simple administration). On any application for administration (whether or not with the will annexed), the oath must state in what manner, all persons having a prior right to a grant have been cleared off, and whether any minority or life interest arises under the will or intestacy.[44]

(5) *Settled land.* The oath must state whether, to the best of the applicant's knowledge, information and belief, there was land vested in the deceased which was settled previously to his death and not by his will and which remained settled land notwithstanding his death.[45]

(6) *Duties of personal representative.* Section 25 of the Administration of Estates Act 1925[46] summarises the duties of a personal representative as being "to—

    (a) collect and get in the real and personal estate of the deceased and administer it according to law;

    (b) when required to do so by the court, exhibit on oath in the court

[40] *Ibid.* r. 53.
[41] *Ibid.* r. 8(2).
[42] Administration of Estates Act 1971, ss.2(1) and 3(1); see *ante*, p. 164.
[43] The will is "marked" by the signatures of the applicant and the person before whom the oath is sworn, N.C. Prob. Rules 1987, r. 10.
[44] N.C. Prob. Rules 1987, r. 8(4). For the minimum number of administrators see *ante*, p. 156.
[45] *Ibid.* r. 8(3) (applicable if the deceased died after 1925); for grants to settled land see *ante*, pp. 176, *et seq.*
[46] As amended by Administration of Estates Act 1971, s.9; see also Report on Administration Bonds, etc., Law. Com. No. 31, pp. 5–6.

a full inventory of the estate and when so required render an account of the administration of the estate to the court;

(c) when required to do so by the High Court, deliver up the grant of probate or administration to that court."

The applicant swears that he will carry out these duties which are set out in the oath. Unfortunately the duty in paragraph (a) to "administer it according to law" is expressed in such general terms that it probably has little meaning to most applicants.

(7) *Value of the estate.* In his oath the applicant states the gross value and net value of the estate passing under the grant to the best of his knowledge, information and belief.[47]

Will not available. Normally on an application for probate or administration with the will annexed the applicant lodges the original will in the registry,[48] where a photostat copy of it is made and annexed to the grant.[49] Sometimes the original will is not available. It may be in the custody of a foreign court or official, in which case a duly authenticated copy of the will may be admitted to proof.[50] It may have been lost or destroyed, either during the testator's lifetime (without being revoked) or since his death. In that case a registrar may make an order admitting to proof the will as contained in a copy or a reconstruction its contents.[51] The registrar may require application to be made to a judge,[52] who in turn may make such an order or, if there is opposition from persons entitled under an intestacy or an earlier will, require the will to be propounded in a probate action. Usually the grant made is limited until the original will or a more authentic copy of it be proved.[53]

An applicant who seeks to prove a will which has been lost or destroyed needs to establish:

(i) that the will was duly executed. This may be proved, for instance, by the evidence of one or more of the attesting witnesses or any other person who was present when the will was executed, or by proof that the will contained a proper attestation clause.[54]

---

[47] The fee payable for a grant of probate or administration is assessed on the net value shown in the Inland Revenue account or oath, N.C. Prob. Fees Order 1981 (S.I. 1981 No. 861) as amended by S.I. 1981 No. 1103, S.I. 1983 No. 1180, S.I. 1986 No. 705 and S.I. 1986 No. 2185; *Practice Direction (Probate: Representation Grant)* [1981] 1 W.L.R. 1185.

[48] The original will is then preserved in a place of deposit, Supreme Court Act 1981, s.124; *Re Greer* (1929) 45 T.L.R. 362 and *cf. In the Estate of White Todd* [1926] P. 173.

[49] For the lodging of an engrossment of the original will where a photographic copy would not be satisfactory, or where the will contains alterations not admissible to proof or has been ordered to be rectified, see N.C. Prob. Rules 1987, r. 11.

[50] N.C. Prob. Rules 1987, r. 54(2).

[51] *Ibid.* r. 54(1): the rule also applies to a nuncupative will of a privileged testator.

[52] *Ibid.* r. 61(1) and see *In the Estate of Nuttall (Practice Note)* [1955] 1 W.L.R. 847.

[53] *In the Goods of Lemme* [1892] P. 89 (French notary forbidden to part with original will); *In the Goods of Von Linden* [1896] P. 148.

[54] *In the Estate of Phibbs* [1917] P. 93 (proof that will contained a proper attestation clause sufficed though identity of attesting witnesses not known); *Re Webb* [1964] 1 W.L.R. 509 (attestation clause in completed draft); *Harris v. Knight* (1890) 15 P.D. 170 (no attestation clause, will signed by testator and two others, maxim *"omnia praesumuntur rite esse acta"* applied).

(ii) what the contents of the will were. There may, for instance, be a copy or draft of the will in existence, or the contents of the will may be proved by the evidence of a person who read the will before it was lost.[55]

In addition, if the will was last known to be in the testator's possession but could not be found at his death so that a presumption of revocation arises, the applicant needs to rebut this presumption by evidence of non-revocation, such as evidence showing the testator's intention to adhere to the will[56] or to revoke subject to a condition which is not fulfilled,[57] or proving that the will was destroyed by enemy action or accident. Of course, if the will was in existence at the testator's death but was lost or destroyed afterwards, no presumption of revocation arises.

Re Webb[58] is a useful illustration. Shortly before the death of the testatrix her sister unearthed a completed draft of her will from a tin trunk and the testatrix told her, "Don't throw that away; it's my will." After her death the original will could not be found and the sister (a beneficiary) propounded the completed draft in a probate action. Faulks J. held that the presumption of revocation was rebutted by what the testatrix said to her sister, which was incompatible with an intention to revoke. He found that the original will had been destroyed by enemy action in 1940[59] and the completed draft was admissible as secondary evidence to prove its contents. But had the original will been duly executed? The completed draft contained an attestation clause. A witness (named as attesting witness in the draft) testified that she did not remember signing the will but she did remember being called by the testatrix to her shop for some purpose and that "a little man in a homburg hat" was there. This was a solicitor who was named in the draft as the other attesting witness. Faulks J. held, applying the maxim *omnia praesumuntur rite esse acta*, that this attestation clause, which spoke to the regularity of the execution of the will, was, in the absence of cogent negative evidence, sufficient evidence of due execution. He therefore admitted the completed draft to probate.

Evidence of due execution. An attestation clause raises a presumption that the will was duly executed.[60] If a will contains no attestation clause or the clause is insufficient, or if it appears to the registrar that there is some doubt about the due execution of a will, he must require

---

[55] *Re Webb, supra,* (completed draft); *In the Goods of Leigh* [1892] P. 82 (will torn into pieces and some lost, copy will supplied the missing words); *Sugden* v. *Lord St. Leonards* (1876) 1 P.D. 154 (oral evidence of daughter who was a beneficiary); *In the Estate of Phibbs, supra; In the Estate of Lintott* [1941] L.T.Jo. 115 (copy will: original destroyed by enemy action after death of testatrix); *Re Yelland,* (1975) 119 S.J. 562.

[56] *Sugden* v. *Lord St. Leonards, supra; Re Webb, supra; In the Estate of Wilson* (1961) 105 S.J. 531.

[57] *In the Estate of Botting* [1951] 2 All E.R. 997 (conditional revocation, though no direct evidence of destruction of will), explaining *Homerton* v. *Hewitt* (1872) 25 L.T. 854; *In the Estate of Bridgewater* [1965] 1 W.L.R. 416; *Sterling* v. *Bruce* [1973] N.I. 255: for conditional destruction see *ante,* p. 70.

[58] *Supra;* see also [1964] 2 All E.R. 91.

[59] The court might have decided that the presumption was also rebutted by the will's destruction by enemy action.

[60] *Ante,* p. 37.

an affidavit as to its due execution before admitting the will to probate in common form.[61] For instance, if the signature of the testator appears below the signatures of the witnesses, the registrar may consider that there is some doubt about due execution despite the presence of an attestation clause.

The affidavit of due execution is to be from one or more of the attesting witnesses[62] or, if no attesting witness is conveniently available, from any other person who was present when the will was executed.[63] Sometimes both the attesting witnesses are dead or cannot be traced, and so far as is known no other person was present when the will was executed. If no such affidavit can be obtained, the registrar may accept evidence on affidavit from any person to show that the signature on the will is in the handwriting of the deceased, or of any other matter which may raise a presumption in favour of due execution and he may require notice of the application to be given to any person prejudiced by the will.[64] Normally evidence on affidavit as to the deceased's handwriting is accepted if accompanied by the consent of the persons prejudiced (if all are *sui juris*) or by evidence on affidavit as to the handwriting of the witnesses. If after considering the evidence the registrar is doubtful whether the will was duly executed, he may refer the matter to a judge on motion, and if he is satisfied that the will was not duly executed he must refuse probate and mark the will "Probate Refused."[65]

The maxim *omnia praesumuntur rite esse acta* may apply if the observance of all the formalities required for due execution is not proved by the evidence of witnesses. To quote Lindley L.J. in *Harris* v. *Knight*,[66]

"The maxim, '*omnia praesumuntur rite esse acta*,' is an expression, in a short form, of a reasonable probability, and of the propriety in point of law of acting on such probability. The maxim expresses an inference which may reasonably be drawn when an intention to do some formal act is established; when the evidence is consistent with that intention having been carried into effect in a proper way; but where the actual observance of all due formalities can only be inferred as a matter of probability."

The maxim applies with more or less force according to the circumstances of each case—for example, a formal attestation clause in a will regular in form raises a strong presumption, but an informal clause,[67] or a formal clause in a will irregular in form,[68] raises a weaker presumption. In *Re Webb*[69] the maxim was applied where the completed draft of

---

[61] N.C. Prob. Rules 1987, r. 12(1): see also r. 16. For proof of a privileged will see rr. 17 and 18.

[62] An attesting witness who refuses to make an affidavit may be required to attend for examination in open court, Supreme Court Act 1981, s.122; N.C. Prob. Rules 1987, r. 50(1): see *In the Goods of Sweet* [1891] P. 400.

[63] N.C. Prob. Rules 1987, r. 10(2).

[64] *Ibid.* r. 12(2).

[65] *Ibid.* r. 12(1).

[66] (1890) 15 P.D. 170, 179.

[67] *Vinnicombe* v. *Butler* (1864) 3 Sw. & Tr. 580.

[68] *In the Estate of Bercovitz* [1961] 1 W.L.R. 892, 896.

[69] [1964] 1 W.L.R. 509; see *ante*, p. 194.

a will destroyed by enemy action contained an attestation clause and the will was held to have been duly executed, although the surviving attesting witness did not remember signing the will.

The maxim may apply in the absence of any attestation clause. In *In the Estate of Denning*[70] the will consisted of a small sheet of writing paper. On one side (and occupying the whole of it) was written, "Sept. 3rd. Year of our Lord 1939. I give all I possess to my cousins Mary Jane and John Harnett in Parish of St. Feock, County of Cornwall" followed by the signature of the testatrix. On the other side (turning the paper upside down) two names were written in different hands, "Edith Freeman" and "Dorothy Edwards," one below the other. No person of either of these names could be traced. During her lifetime the testatrix had told John Harnett that she had made a will in favour of him and his sister: at her death no other will had been found. In a probate action Sachs J. held the maxim applicable and declared the will to be duly executed. He said that it seemed to him "that there is no other practical reason why these names should be on the back of the document unless it was for the purpose of attesting the will." The decision illustrates how useful the maxim is when the attesting witnesses (and any other person present) are dead, or cannot be traced, or cannot remember what occurred when the will was executed, perhaps many years previously. Of course the maxim is not needed if the observance of all the formalities required for due execution is proved by the evidence of witnesses. On the other hand the maxim is not applicable if such observance is disproved by the evidence.[71]

Doubt as to knowledge and approval. If a will appears to have been signed by a blind or illiterate testator, or by another person by the testator's direction, or for any other reason gives rise to doubt as to the testator having had knowledge of the contents of the will at the time of its execution, the registrar must satisfy himself that the testator had such knowledge before admitting the will to proof[72] and may require affidavit evidence for this purpose.

Condition, alteration or attempted revocation of will. (1) *Condition.* If a will contains any reference to another document in such terms as to suggest that it ought to be incorporated in the will, the registrar must require the document to be produced and accounted for by evidence.[73]

(2) *Alteration.* The registrar must require evidence to show whether an unattested alteration was present in a will when it was executed[74]: if

---

[70] [1958] 1 W.L.R. 462: see also *In the Goods of Peverett* [1902] P. 205; *Harris* v. *Knight* (1890) 15 P.D. 170; *Trott* v. *Skidmore* (1860) 2 Sw. & Tr. 12: cf. *In the Estate of Early* [1980] I.R. 223.

[71] *In the Estate of Bercovitz* [1961] 1 W.L.R. 892, [1962] 1 W.L.R. 321.

[72] N.C. Prob. Rules 1987, r. 13; for the burden of proof of the testator's knowledge and approval see *ante*, pp. 50–51.

[73] *Ibid.* r. 14(3); see also r. 14(4) if there is doubt as to the date on which the will was executed.

[74] *Ibid.* r. 14(1).

it was present at that time, the alteration is valid. There is of course a rebuttable presumption that an unattested alteration was made after the execution of the will.[75] The registrar also has a useful time-saving power to disregard any alteration which appears to him to be of no practical importance[76]—for instance, an alteration to a gift which has lapsed.

(3) *Attempted revocation.* Any appearance of attempted revocation of a will by burning, tearing or otherwise must be accounted for to the registrar's satisfaction.[77] The person who found the will may swear an affidavit as to its plight and condition when found.

E. The Surety's Guarantee

Until 1972 an administrator was normally required to enter into an administration bond, usually with one or more sureties, for the due performance of his duties. This requirement has been abolished. Instead since 1971 the court may require a guarantee from one or more sureties as a condition of granting letters of administration.[78] An executor was never required to enter into an administration bond and cannot now be required to provide a surety's guarantee on taking probate.

When guarantee required. Normally a surety's guarantee is not required as a condition of granting administration. Indeed the Non-Contentious Probate Rules no longer make any provision for requiring a guarantee as a condition of granting letters of administration. In future it seems likely that the court will only require a guarantee in special circumstances.

The guarantee and its effect. (1) *Form of guarantee.* In the form of guarantee formerly prescribed a surety entered into a guarantee under seal that he would make good any loss which any person interested in the administration of the deceased's estate might suffer in consequence of the breach by the administrator of his duties.[79] These duties were set out in the guarantee in the same way as in the oath.[80]

(2) *Effect of guarantee.* Section 120(2) of the Supreme Court Act 1981 provides that a guarantee shall enure for the benefit of every person interested in the administration of the deceased's estate as if contained in a contract under seal made by the surety with every such person. However, no action to enforce a guarantee may be brought without the

---

[75] *Ante,* p. 73.
[76] *Ibid.* r. 14(2).
[77] *Ibid.* r. 15.
[78] Supreme Court Act 1981, s.120: for the power of the court to require a surety's guarantee as a condition of resealing letters of administration see Administration of Estates Act 1971, s.11 (as amended by Supreme Court Act 1981, s.152(1) and Sched. 5). See generally Report on Administration Bonds, etc., Law. Com. No. 31.
[79] Supreme Court Act 1981, s.120(1); N.C. Prob. Rules 1954, r. 38(3) and Sched. I, Form I.
[80] *Ante,* p. 193.

leave of the court.[81] Thus a creditor or beneficiary who has suffered loss in consequence of a breach by the administrator of his duties has a remedy, not only against the administrator, but also (with the leave of the court) against a surety under his guarantee.

For a surety to be liable under his guarantee there must be a breach by the administrator of his duties *as administrator* and not of his duties as trustee. The same rule governed the liability of sureties under an administration bond. In *Harvell* v. *Foster*[82] a testator by his will gave all his estate to his daughter D absolutely and appointed her sole executrix. At his death she was a minor and letters of administration with the will annexed were granted to her husband for her use and benefit until she should attain full age. The husband entered into an administration bond with two solicitors as sureties. The solicitors, acting for the husband, got in the testator's estate, paid his debts and funeral and testamentary expenses, and paid the balance to the husband, who disappeared with most of it and failed to pay D when she attained full age. The Court of Appeal held the sureties liable to D for the missing sum, stating that,[83]

> "the duty of an administrator, as such, must at least extend to paying the funeral and testamentary expenses and debts and legacies (if any) and where, as here, immediate distribution is impossible owing to the infancy of the person beneficially entitled, retaining the net residue in trust for the infant. At least until the administrator can show that he has done this, it cannot, in our judgment, be said of him that he has duly administered the estate according to law."

Section 42 of the Administration of Estates Act 1925 provides that where an infant is absolutely entitled, either under a will (in which no trustees are appointed of the gift to the infant) or an intestacy,[84] the personal representatives may appoint a trust corporation or two or more individuals not exceeding four (whether or not including the personal representatives) to be trustees for the infant. On such an appointment being made the personal representatives are discharged from all further liability. It follows that the sureties would not have been liable in *Harvell* v. *Foster* if (say) the husband had appointed himself and Y to be trustees of the net residuary estate, and the husband and Y had later misappropriated it: in that case the husband would have committed a breach of his duties as trustee but not of his duties as administrator.[85]

F. OMITTING WORDS FROM PROBATE

A particular passage or word in an otherwise valid will or codicil is omitted from probate if it was inserted:

[81] Supreme Court Act 1981, s.120(3): leave may be given by a registrar, N.C. Prob. Rules 1987, r. 40.

[82] [1954] 2 Q.B. 367; *cf. Re Cockburn's W.T.* [1957] Ch. 438.

[83] [1954] 2 Q.B. 367, 383.

[84] On a death intestate after 1925 an infant is absolutely entitled in the capacity of surviving spouse, but only a married infant is absolutely entitled under the statutory trusts for the issue of the intestate, see *ante*, p. 90.

[85] [1954] 2 Q.B. 367, 384.

   (i)   owing to an insane delusion on the part of the testator[86];
   (ii) without the testator's knowledge and approval[87];
 (iii) as a result of undue influence or fraud[88]; or
 (iv) as an alteration which was not duly executed by the testator.[89]

The court may also exclude from probate words which have no testamentary value[90] but which are offensive,[91] defamatory[92] or blasphemous. Such words are not expunged from the will itself but are omitted from the probate copy.[93]

G. Probate Actions

In general the same practice and rules of evidence are applicable in a probate action as in other actions. However, a few significant differences may be mentioned.

Administration pending suit. After a probate action has begun a grant of administration pending suit limited to the duration of the probate action may be made. This type of grant has already been considered.[94] If the probate action is for the revocation of a previous grant of probate or letters of administration, the previous grant must be lodged in court after the commencement of the action.[95]

Affidavit of testamentary scripts. At an early stage in a probate action each party must swear and file an affidavit of testamentary scripts of the deceased.[96] A testamentary script means a will or draft will of the deceased, written instructions for a will (*e.g.* a solicitor's attendance note recording the deceased's instructions), and any document purporting to be evidence of the contents, or to be a copy, of a will which is alleged to have been lost or destroyed. The affidavit must describe any testamentary script of which the party has any knowledge. If he has any such script in his possession, he must lodge it in court with his affidavit: if any such script is not in his possession, he must state its whereabouts if known to him. The court has wide powers for compelling the production of testamentary documents.[97]

---

[86] *In the Estate of Bohrmann* [1938] 1 All E.R. 271; see *ante*, p. 48.

[87] *Ante*, p. 54: for rectification see *ante*, p. 55.

[88] *Ante*, p. 57.

[89] *Ante*, pp. 73 *seq.*

[90] *In the Estate of Rawlings* (1934) 78 S.J. 338 ("that rascal" her husband relevant to construction).

[91] *In the Goods of Bowker* [1932] P. 93 (offensive directions as to disposal of testator's remains and funeral excluded): *cf. In the Estate of Caie* (1927) 43 T.L.R. 697 (exhortation to become a Freemason not excluded).

[92] *In the Estate of White* [1914] P. 153; *In the Goods of Wortnaly* (1846) 1 Rob. 423; *Marsh v. Marsh* (1860) 1 Sw. & Tr. 528; *In the Goods of Honywood* (1871) L.R. 2 P. & D. 251.

[93] *Re Maxwell* (1929) 45 T.L.R. 215: for the procedure see *Practice Direction* [1968] 1 W.L.R. 987.

[94] *Ante*, p. 185.

[95] R.S.C., Ord. 76, r. 4.

[96] *Ibid.* r. 5.

[97] Supreme Court Act 1981, ss.122 and 123.

This special procedure ensures that at an early stage in a probate action any testamentary scripts in the possession of the parties are lodged in the safe custody of the court, where the parties may inspect them. The procedure is different from discovery of documents, which takes place at a later stage in a probate action, as in other actions.

Evidence of attesting witnesses. The party propounding a will in a probate action must call one of the attesting witnesses to give evidence as to its due execution unless they are all unavailable,[98] *e.g.* dead, insane, beyond the jurisdiction or untraceable. If the first attesting witness to be called does not prove its due execution, the party propounding the will must call the other attesting witness (if available) to give evidence as to its due execution.[99]

(1) *Witness of the court.* An attesting witness is regarded as the witness of the court. Accordingly (and contrary to the general rule) he may be cross-examined by the party calling him on matters relating to the execution of the will[1] and on other issues,[2] and no claim of professional privilege may be made in respect of his previous statements to solicitors concerning execution.[3]

(2) *Not conclusive.* The evidence of the attesting witnesses is not conclusive for, or against, the due execution of the will. A formal attestation clause in a will raises a presumption of due execution[4] and the party propounding a will is free to call other evidence that it was duly executed.[5] The court decides whether the will was duly executed having regard to all the circumstances of the case.[6]

Costs. Costs in a probate action, as in other proceedings in the High Court and civil division of the Court of Appeal, are in the discretion of the court.[7] Generally costs follow the event,[8] *i.e.* the losing party is ordered to pay the costs of the successful party.

(1) *Notice to cross-examine.* Order 62, rule 4(3) of the Rules of the Supreme Court imposes a single restriction on the court's discretion in a probate action. A party who opposes a will in a probate action may give notice with his defence to the party setting up the will that he merely insists upon the will being proved in solemn form and only intends to cross-examine the witnesses produced in support of the will.

---

[98] *Bowman* v. *Hodgson* (1867) L.R. 1 P. & D. 362: see Evidence Act 1938, s.3. The rules in this section doubtless apply to a witness who acknowledges his signature under the amended s.9 of the Wills Act 1837, *ante,* p. 36.

[99] *Owen* v. *Williams* (1863) 4 Sw. & Tr. 202; *Coles* v. *Coles* (1866) L.R. 1 P. & D. 70.

[1] *Oakes* v. *Uzzell* [1932] P. 19; *Re Brock; Jones* v. *Jones* [1908] 24 T.L.R. 839.

[2] *Re Webster* [1974] 1 W.L.R. 1641 (party calling attesting witness may cross-examine him on other issues, as well as due execution).

[3] *In the Estate of Fuld* [1965] P. 405.

[4] *Ante,* p. 195.

[5] *Re Vere-Wardale* [1949] P. 395.

[6] *Wright* v. *Rogers* (1869) L.R. 1 P. & D. 678 (formal attestation clause; memory of attesting witness unreliable).

[7] Supreme Court Act 1981, s.51.

[8] R.S.C., Ord. 62, r. 3(3); *Twist* v. *Tye* [1902] P. 92.

No order may then be made for him to pay the costs of the other side unless the court is of opinion that there was no reasonable ground for opposing the will.[9] This protection may be relied on if the party opposing the will pleads want of due execution, incapacity, or want of knowledge and approval,[10] but not if he pleads undue influence or fraud[11] or claims revocation of probate already granted in common form.[12]

(2) *Exceptions to general rule.* Apart from this single restriction the court has an unfettered discretion as to costs. The general rule of practice is that costs follow the event but in special circumstances a different order may be made. The special circumstances justifying a different order may be classified under two heads,[13] *i.e.* (a) fault of testator or residuary beneficiary—costs out of the estate, (b) case for inquiry—no order as to costs.[14]

(a) COSTS OUT OF THE ESTATE. If the litigation has been caused by the conduct of the deceased, or of the residuary beneficiaries, the costs of both parties may be ordered to be paid out of the estate. Such an order was made where the litigation was caused by the confusion in which the deceased left his testamentary papers,[15] or by the deceased's habits and mode of life which gave grounds for questioning his testamentary capacity.[16] Again, such an order was made where the residuary beneficiaries were active in the preparation of a will in their own favour, thereby raising suspicions by their conduct,[17] and where the residuary beneficiary despite inquiries failed to produce the will after administration had been granted to the next of kin.[18]

(b) NO ORDER AS TO COSTS. If the circumstances led reasonably to an inquiry into the issues raised, the losing party is left to pay his own costs but is not ordered to pay the costs of the successful party. It is therefore necessary to consider whether the losing party had reasonable grounds, looking to his knowledge and means of knowledge, for the issues he raised.[19] Thus no order for costs was made where the next of kin unsuccessfully opposed a will because the deceased's doctor, who

---

[9] *Davies* v. *Jones* [1899] P. 161 (reasonable ground for opposing though opposition failed: no order as to costs); *Spicer* v. *Spicer* [1899] P. 38 (no reasonable ground: costs follow event).

[10] *Cleare* v. *Cleare* (1869) 1 P. & D. 655.

[11] *Ireland* v. *Rendall* (1866) 1 P. & D. 194; *Harrington* v. *Bowyer* (1871) 2 P. & D. 264.

[12] *Tomalin* v. *Smart* [1904] P. 141.

[13] *Spiers* v. *English* [1907] P. 122; *Mitchell* v. *Gard* (1863) 3 Sw. & Tr. 275.

[14] *Re Cutcliffe's Estate* [1959] P. 6, 13.

[15] *Jenner* v. *Ffinch* (1879) 5 P.D. 106 (doubt as to deceased's intention to revoke former will); *Lemage* v. *Goodban* (1865) L.R. 1 P. & D. 57; *Orton* v. *Smith* (1873) L.R. 3 P. & D. 23 (testator had patched up his signature); *cf. Re Wynn* [1983] 3 All E.R. 310, 315.

[16] *Davies* v. *Gregory* (1873) 3 P. & D. 28 (deceased a recluse of strange habits); *Roe* v. *Nix* [1893] P. 55 (testatrix of unsound mind); see also *Boughton* v. *Knight* (1873) L.R. 3 P. & D. 64 (testator outwardly capable of managing his affairs); *Larke* v. *Nugus* (1979) 123 S.J. 337 (solicitor draftsman ought to provide full information as to execution and surrounding circumstances).

[17] *Goodacre* v. *Smith* (1867) L.R. 1 P.& D. 359; *Orton* v. *Smith* (1873) L.R. 3 P. & D. 23; *In the Estate of Osment* [1914] P. 129 (conduct of legatees).

[18] *Smith* v. *Smith* (1865) 4 Sw. & Tr. 3.

[19] *Mitchell* v. *Gard* (1863) 3 Sw. & Tr. 275, 278.

was an attesting witness, stated that when the will was read over the testator approved it by gesture only and that he could not swear that the testator was in full possession of his mental faculties.[20]

(3) *Pleas of undue influence or fraud.* A party ought never to put forward a plea of undue influence or fraud unless he has reasonable grounds upon which to support it.[21] If he does plead undue influence or fraud, and loses the action, the same rule of practice as to costs applies— costs follow the event[22] unless the special circumstances justify a different order. There are a few reported cases where head (a) or (b) has been held applicable[23] but usually a party who makes an unsuccessful plea of undue influence or fraud has to pay the costs of the successful party.

(4) *Executor's right to costs out of the estate.* An executor who proves a will in solemn form is entitled, unless the court orders otherwise, to take his costs of the probate action out of the estate.[24] He does not need an order of the court for this purpose.[25] The court may order otherwise if the executor has acted unreasonably—for instance, by carelessly losing the original will.[26] If the executor unsuccessfully propounds a will the rules of practice already considered apply—costs follow the event[27] unless head (a) or (b) applies.[28] To protect himself against the risk of being condemned in costs, a person appointed executor may find it advisable to insist on an indemnity from the beneficiaries interested in upholding the will before he propounds it.

2. THE REVOCATION OF GRANTS

A. GROUNDS FOR REVOCATION

A personal representative may be removed *either* by the revocation of his grant (which is considered in this section) *or* by the appointment of a substituted personal representative or the termination of the appointment of the personal representative (which is considered later[29]).

The jurisdiction of the High Court to revoke a grant of probate or

---

[20] *Tippett* v. *Tippett* (1865) 1 P. & D. 54: see also *Ferrey* v. *King* (1861) 3 Sw. & Tr. 51 (conflicting evidence of attesting witnesses); *Re Fanshawe's Estate* (1983) Transcript on Lexis.

[21] *Spiers* v. *English* [1907] P. 122, 124.

[22] *Spiers* v. *English, ibid.*; *Re Cutcliffe's Estate* [1959] P. 6 (not special circumstances if T misled persons into false hopes of benefiting by his will).

[23] *e.g.* costs out of the estate in *Mitchell* v. *Gard* (1863) 3 Sw. & Tr. 75 and 275 (undue influence and three other pleas failed); *Orton* v. *Smith* (1873) L.R. 3 P. & D. 23 (undue influence, fraud, and other pleas failed): no order as to costs in *Smith* v. *Smith* (1866) L.R. 1 P. & D. 239 (undue influence and two other pleas failed).

[24] Ord. 62, r. 6(2): see *In the Estate of Plant* [1926] P. 139 (executors proved will but failed on codicil); *Re Barton* [1977] C.L.Y. 3182.

[25] He is better off without an order, which necessitates taxation of his costs. *In the Estate of Cole* (1962) 106 S.J. 837.

[26] *Burls* v. *Burls* (1868) 1 P. & D. 472.

[27] *Twist* v. *Tye* [1902] P. 92.

[28] *e.g.* costs out of the estate in *Boughton* v. *Knight* (1873) L.R. 3 P. & D. 64.

[29] *Post,* p. 399.

letters of administration is exercised by the Family Division as regards non-contentious or common form business, and by the Chancery Division as regards revocation actions.[30] The county court also has jurisdiction (limited in amount) over revocation actions.[31] In the Family Division a registrar may order a grant to be revoked or amended, but only on the application or with the consent of the person to whom the grant was made unless there are exceptional circumstances.[32] An instance of special circumstances is where the grant was wrongly made as a result of an official error: the court has power to revoke a grant of its own volition where the grant ought not to have been made or contains an error.[33] However, if the person to whom the grant was made opposes revocation, a revocation action is normally necessary.

The main grounds for revocation of a grant may be classified in two categories:

1. Grant wrongly made. Usually a grant is wrongly made as a result of a false statement by the grantee, whether made fraudulently or in ignorance of the truth. For example, revocation is ordered where the "deceased" is found to be still alive[34]; where a will is discovered after a grant of simple administration has been made, or a later will is discovered after an earlier will has been proved; where an invalid or revoked will has been proved; where a grant has been made to an infant on the basis that he is of full age; where administration has been granted to a person who falsely claimed to be the deceased's surviving spouse,[35] or the next of kin entitled to the grant[36]; or where administration has been granted to the Treasury Solicitor on behalf of the Crown and next of kin are discovered. Occasionally a grant is wrongly made as a result of an official error. For example, revocation is ordered where a grant has been made without special leave before the minimum time has elapsed from the deceased's death,[37] or where a grant has been made whilst a caveat was in force.[38]

The effects of proving a will in common or, alternatively, in solemn form have already been considered. If a will has been proved in solemn form, persons bound by the order of the court pronouncing the will valid in a probate action are seldom entitled to challenge the grant made as a result of the order.[39]

---

[30] *Ante*, p. 160.

[31] *Ante*, p. 162.

[32] N.C. Prob. Rules 1987, r. 41; see also r. 26(2).

[33] Supreme Court Act 1981, s.121: the court may also cancel the resealing of a grant, s.121(3); for resealing see *ante*. p. 165.

[34] *In the Goods of Napier* (1809) 1 Phill. 83 (left for dead on the field of battle and appeared personally in court on revocation of probate).

[35] *In the Goods of Moore* (1845) 3 N.C. 601 ("widow" not married to deceased); *In the Estate of Evon* (1963) 107 S.J. 893.

[36] *In the Goods of Bergman* (1842) 2 N. of C. 22: see also *In the Goods of Morris* (1862) 2 Sw. & Tr. 360 (grant to elected guardian of minors revoked as there was testamentary guardian).

[37] *Ante*, p. 189.

[38] See *Re Davies* [1978] C.L.Y. 3095.

[39] *Ante*, pp. 167–168.

2. Subsequent events. A grant which was properly made may be revoked by reason of the occurrence of subsequent events.

(1) *Grantee becomes incapable.* If there are at least two executors and one or more of them becomes incapable of managing his affairs by reason of mental or physical incapacity, the grant of probate is revoked. In *In the Goods of Galbraith*[40] a grant of probate made six years previously to two executors was revoked because both had become unfit to act in their old age, due to their physical and mental infirmity. Instead the court made a grant of letters of administration *de bonis non* with the will annexed. If only one of the executors had become incapable, the court would have revoked the original grant and made a fresh grant of probate to the other executor, with power for the incapable executor to take probate if he recovered.[41]

Similarly, if there are at least two administrators and one or more of them becomes incapable, the grant of administration is revoked and a new grant made.[42]

However, if there is a sole, or sole surviving, executor or administrator and he becomes incapable, the grant to him is not revoked. Instead a grant of letters of administration *de bonis non* and for the use and benefit of the incapable grantee, limited during his incapacity, is made and the court impounds the original grant so that it does not remain at large.[43]

(2) *Grantee wishes to be relieved of duties.* A grant may be revoked if a grantee wishes to be relieved of his duties for some good reason, such as advanced age.[44]

(3) *Grantee disappears.* If a grantee disappears and the estate is not fully administered, the grant is revoked and a new grant made.[45] As Sir Francis Jeune P. put it in *In the Goods of Loveday*[46] where the administratrix had disappeared,

"the real object which the Court must always keep in view is the due and proper administration of the estate and the interests of the parties beneficially entitled thereto; and I can see no good reason why the Court should not take fresh action in regard to an estate where it is made clear that its previous grant has turned out abortive or

---

[40] [1951] P. 422.

[41] *In the Estate of Shaw* [1905] P. 92.

[42] *In the Goods of Newton* (1843) 3 Curt. 428.

[43] *In the Goods of Cooke* [1895] P. 68; the original grant is not impounded if the new grant is made to a person authorised by the Court of Protection; see *ante*, p. 184. For enduring powers of attorney see *Practice Direction (Powers of Attorney)* [1986] 1 W.L.R. 419.

[44] *In the Goods of Thacker* [1900] P. 15 (grant to receiver in bankruptcy revoked after debts paid); *In the Goods of Hoare* (1833) 2 Sw. & Tr. 361 and *cf. In the Goods of Heslop* (1846) 1 Rob.Eccl. 457. For reform to allow personal representative to retire for good cause see Law Reform Committee, 23rd Report, *The powers and duties of trustees*, Cmnd. 8733 (1982), pp. 53 and 67.

[45] *In the Goods of Loveday* [1900] P. 154 (widow obtained administration and later disappeared); *In the Goods of Covell* (1890) 15 P.D. 8; *In the Goods of Bradshaw* (1888) 13 P.D. 18 (creditor administrator absconded): see also *In the Estate of Thomas* [1912] P. 177 (administrator emigrated to New Zealand but his address was ascertainable: grant revoked).

[46] [1900] P. 154, 156.

inefficient. If the Court has in certain circumstances made a grant in the belief and hope that the person appointed will properly and fully administer the estate, and if it turns out that the person so appointed will not or cannot administer, I do not see why the Court should not revoke an inoperative grant and make a fresh grant."

(4) *Grantee commits breach of duty.* If the grantee commits a serious breach of his duties, probably his grant may be revoked and a new grant made where this is appropriate so as to secure the proper administration of the estate. This ground for revocation appears to be supported by the words already quoted of Sir Francis Jeune in *In the Goods of Loveday.*[47] On the other hand the decision in *In the Estate of Cope*[48] must be mentioned. In that case revocation of a grant of administration was sought on the ground that the administrators had failed to submit an accurate estate duty account, having omitted certain assets and having included a disputed debt from the deceased to one of them. Collingwood J. decided that it was "not a case in which the court can order revocation of the grant," though there might be a case for ordering the administrators to bring into court an inventory of the estate and an account of its administration.[49] Perhaps *In the Estate of Cope* is best regarded as a case where the breach of duty was not such as to make revocation of the grant appropriate as a means of securing the proper administration of the estate.

B. Effect of Revocation

A grant of probate or letters of administration is in a sense a precarious title because the grant is liable to be revoked at some later date. The deceased may die apparently intestate so that a grant of simple administration is made, and years later a will appointing executors may be found. Or the deceased may die leaving a "will" which is proved by the executors, but which years later is discovered to have been a forgery. In the meantime, before the revocation of the first grant, the personal representative may have wholly or partly administered the estate.

Purchaser from the former personal representative. A purchaser from a personal representative to whom a grant has been made is protected by two statutory provisions:

(1) *Conveyance valid despite revocation of grant.* Section 37 of the Administration of Estates Act 1925 provides that a conveyance of any interest in real or personal estate made to a purchaser by a person to whom probate or letters of administration have been granted is valid, notwithstanding any subsequent revocation or variation of the grant.[50]

---

[47] But see *In the Estate of Cope* [1954] 1 W.L.R. 608, 609, where Collingwood J. said that "those words must be read with regard to the facts" of *In the Goods of Loveday.*
[48] [1954] 1 W.L.R. 608, [1954] 1 All E.R. 698.
[49] [1954] 1 W.L.R. 608, 700.
[50] s.37 applies whenever the conveyance was made, or the grant was revoked or varied, or the testator or intestate died, but without prejudice to any order of the court made before 1926, s.37(1) and (2). As to contracts made by a personal representative see Administration of Estates Act 1925, s.39(1).

The section has a wide application because "conveyance" is so widely defined by the Act—the expression includes "a mortgage, charge by way of legal mortgage, lease, assent, vesting declaration, vesting instrument, disclaimer, release and every other assurance of property or of an interest therein by any instrument, except a will."[51] However, to be protected under section 37, a purchaser must have acquired the interest in the property in good faith and for valuable consideration, which includes marriage but not a nominal consideration in money.[52]

In so far as there are any dispositions of property to a purchaser by a personal representative which are not made by a "conveyance," so that section 37 does not apply, the similar principle laid down in 1914 by the Court of Appeal in *Hewson* v. *Shelley*[53] remains applicable. In that case a widow took a grant of simple administration to her husband's estate, believing that he had died intestate as no will could be found despite a diligent search. The administratrix sold and conveyed the deceased's land to a purchaser. Eleven years later a will of the deceased was found in the back of a bureau, the letters of administration were revoked, and probate was granted to the plaintiffs as executors. The plaintiffs sued the purchaser for the return of the land, but the Court of Appeal held that the purchaser had a good title because he had bought the land in good faith. Probably most sales of goods by a personal representative fall outside section 37 as the property in the goods is usually transferred to the buyer without any written instrument: if so, the principle in *Hewson* v. *Shelley* applies and the purchaser has a good title if he bought the goods in good faith.

(2) *Grant conclusive as an order of the court.* A purchaser is also protected by section 204(1) of the Law of Property Act 1925 which reads, "An order of the court under any statutory or other jurisdiction shall not, as against a purchaser, be invalidated on the ground of want of jurisdiction, or of want of any concurrence, consent, notice, or service, whether the purchaser has notice of any such want or not." A grant of probate[54] or letters of administration[55] is of course an order of the court and is therefore conclusive. Again, section 204(1) only protects a purchaser in good faith and for valuable consideration, which (as before) includes marriage but not a nominal consideration in money.[56]

These two statutory provisions were considered in *Re Bridgett & Hayes' Contract*.[57] In that case land was settled on B for life and after her death upon trust for sale. At B's death in 1926 the legal estate was vested in her as tenant for life and T was the sole trustee of the settlement. A general grant of probate was made to B's executor C, who contracted to sell the land to a purchaser. The purchaser objected to C's title on the ground that the legal estate was vested in T as B's special executor.

---

[51] s.55(1)(ii).

[52] s.55(1)(xviii).

[53] [1914] 2 Ch. 13.

[54] *Re Bridgett & Hayes' Contract* [1928] Ch. 163.

[55] *Hewson* v. *Shelley* [1914] 2 Ch. 13, 29–30 and 33.

[56] Law of Property Act 1925, s.205(1)(xxi), which also provides that "purchaser" includes a lessee, mortgagee, or other person who acquires an interest in property.

[57] *Supra*: see also *In the Estate of Taylor* [1929] P. 260, 263.

Romer J. held that C could make a good title. Even assuming that the legal estate vested in T at B's death, the legal estate vested in C as from the date of the general grant of probate, and the purchaser was protected by section 204(1) of the Law of Property Act 1925. Romer J. added that if this grant of probate was subsequently revoked, the purchaser would be protected by section 37 of the Administration of Estates Act 1925—it could hardly be doubted that if the purchaser took a conveyance from C he would be acting in good faith.[58]

Payments made to the former personal representative. Section 27(2) of the Administration of Estates Act 1925 provides that, where a grant of probate or letters of administration is revoked, all payments and dispositions made in good faith to a personal representative under the grant before its revocation are a valid discharge to the person making them. Thus, if a debtor of the deceased pays his debt in good faith to the deceased's personal representative under a grant before it is revoked, the debtor is discharged.

Payments made by the former personal representative. Section 27(2) of the Act also enacts that a personal representative who acted under a grant before its revocation may retain and reimburse himself in respect of any payments or dispositions made by him, which the person to whom representation is afterwards granted might have properly made. The former personal representative should reimburse himself in this way before delivering the balance of the assets to the new personal representative.

Indemnity of former personal representative. Section 27(1) of the Administration of Estates Act 1925 reads, "Every person making or permitting to be made any payment or disposition in good faith under a representation shall be indemnified and protected in so doing, notwithstanding any defect or circumstance whatsoever affecting the validity of the representation." Presumably the section applies to any payment or disposition made in good faith by the former personal representative before his grant was revoked, whether in discharging the deceased's funeral, testamentary and administration expenses, debts and liabilities, or in distributing the deceased's estate to the beneficiaries entitled under the former grant. In *In the Estate of Bloch*[59] a grant of letters of administration made to X and Y in 1952 was revoked by the court in 1959 because the "deceased" was still alive. Y was held entitled to an indemnity under section 27(1), but the court refused an indemnity to X who had not acted in good faith, having withheld material evidence when application was made for leave to swear death prior to the grant.

Apart from any protection afforded by section 27(1), a personal representative who receives notice of a claim which casts doubt on the validity of the grant made to him, and subsequently makes payments in

---

[58] Romer J. also decided that anyway T was not entitled to a grant of probate limited to settled land, because the land ceased to be settled land at B's death, see *ante*. pp. 176–177.

[59] *The Times*, July 2, 1959: the report does not state the nature of the payments made by X and Y.

disregard of that claim, is liable to the deceased's estate if his grant is later revoked. Thus in a New Zealand case an executor, who obtained probate of a will and, knowing that next of kin were contemplating an action for revocation on the ground that the testatrix lacked testamentary capacity, paid pecuniary legacies to beneficiaries under the will, was held liable by the Privy Council to the deceased's estate for the sums so paid, after probate had been revoked.[60] The same result would follow under English law unless an honest belief by the executor that the testatrix had testamentary capacity and the action for revocation would fail suffices for "good faith," so that the executor is protected by section 27(1).

Distribution to wrong beneficiary. If the former personal representative made a distribution to a beneficiary entitled under the former grant but not under the new grant, the beneficiary is not protected. The remedies available against him are considered later.[61]

---

[60] *Guardian Trust & Executors Company of New Zealand Ltd.* v. *Public Trustee of New Zealand* [1942] A.C. 115; see p. 123 where the Privy Council referred to "what befell another executor who paid the legacies given by a will that was afterwards declared to be invalid, and whose sad story was told by him to Sam Weller when they were fellow inmates of the Fleet prison," (*Pickwick Papers*, Chap. XLIV).

[61] *Post*, pp. 403 *et seq.*

CHAPTER 9

COLLECTION, REALISATION AND MANAGEMENT OF THE ESTATE

A personal representative has a statutory duty to "collect and get in the real and personal estate of the deceased and administer it according to law."[1] This chapter explains part of this process of administration. The next chapter deals with the payment of the deceased's funeral, testamentary and administration expenses, debts and liabilities, and Chapter 13 deals with the distribution of the estate to the persons entitled under the deceased's will or intestacy. Normally the administration of the deceased's estate is carried out by the personal representatives out of court. If need be, the personal representatives may ask the court to decide any matters of difficulty which arise.[2] Very occasionally the general administration of the estate is carried out under the directions of the court in an administration action.[3]

A. DEVOLUTION ON PERSONAL REPRESENTATIVES

Devolution of property on death before 1926. At common law a deceased's entire personal estate (including leaseholds) devolved on his personal representatives. This included personalty held on trust by the deceased, unless the deceased was survived by one or more co-trustees who held the personalty jointly with the deceased, and who therefore took on his death by operation of the right of survivorship. However, at common law a deceased's realty did not vest in his personal representatives but passed directly to the devisee under his will or his heir entitled on intestacy. But if the deceased died after 1897, the Land Transfer Act 1897 made the deceased's realty (including realty over which he exercised a general power of appointment by his will) vest in his personal representatives.[4] After 1897 the *personal* representatives also became the *real* representatives of the deceased.

Devolution of property on death after 1925. On a death after 1925 the deceased's entire personal estate continues to devolve on his personal

---

[1] Administration of Estates Act 1925, s.25 as amended by Administration of Estates Act 1971, s.9.

[2] *Post*, pp. 400 *et seq.*

[3] *Post*, pp. 396 *et seq.*

[4] s.1: s.1 did not apply to legal estates in copyholds or customary freeholds but it did apply to equitable interests therein, *Re Somerville & Turner's Contract* [1903] 2 Ch. 583. On a death after 1881 real estate held by the deceased on trust or by way of mortgage vested in his personal representative. Conveyancing Act 1881, s.30.

representatives. As to the deceased's land, section 1(1) of the Administration of Estates Act 1925 provides that "real estate to which a deceased person was entitled for an interest not ceasing on his death shall on his death . . . devolve from time to time on the personal representative of the deceased" in the same manner as chattels real (*i.e.* leaseholds) devolved before 1926. The personal representatives represent the deceased in regard to this real estate as well as in regard to his personal estate,[5] though they are still called *personal* representatives.

(1) *"Real estate" which devolves.* The "real estate" which devolves is defined to include chattels real (*i.e.* leaseholds), and land in possession, remainder, or reversion, and every interest in or over land to which the deceased was entitled at his death.[6] It includes:

   (i) land held on trust by the deceased, including settled land.[7] This head is only applicable where the deceased held the land at his death as the sole trustee, *e.g.* as the last surviving trustee of land held on trust for sale or as the sole tenant for life of settled land. It is not applicable where the deceased is survived by one or more co-trustees who held the land jointly with the deceased and who therefore take on his death by operation of the right of survivorship. Again it is not applicable where the deceased held the land at his death in his capacity as a personal representative and not as a trustee.[8]

   (ii) land held by the deceased by way of mortgage or security.[9]

   (iii) land appointed by the deceased in his will under a general power of appointment.[10] By way of contrast, pure personalty appointed by the deceased in his will under a general power of appointment has never devolved on his personal representatives, either at common law or in equity, or under the Administration of Estates Act 1925.[11]

   (iv) land in which the deceased held an entailed interest which was barred by his will and which passes under a gift contained in the deceased's will: if not, the entailed interest does not devolve on the deceased's personal representatives.[12]

(2) *Interest ceasing on death.* An interest of the deceased which ceases on his death does not devolve on his personal representatives: thus the deceased's interest for his own life does not devolve. Again, the interest of the deceased under a joint tenancy does not devolve where another joint tenant survives the deceased and takes on his death by operation

[5] Administration of Estates Act 1925, s.1(3).
[6] *Ibid.* ss.3(1)(i) and 55(1)(xxiv).
[7] *Ibid.* s.3(1)(ii).
[8] *Ante*, p. 180.
[9] *Ibid.* s.3(1)(ii).
[10] *Ibid.* s.3(2). For the exercise by will of a general power of appointment see *post*, p. 428.
[11] *O'Grady* v. *Wilmot* [1916] 2 A.C. 231. But both real and personal estate appointed by the deceased in his will under a general power of appointment are assets for payment of his debts, *post*, p. 252.
[12] Administration of Estates Act 1925, s.3(2) and (3); Law of Property Act 1925, s.176; see *post*, p. 431.

of the right of survivorship.[13] On the other hand, the interest of the deceased as a tenant in common devolves unless it was an interest for the deceased's own life. It is therefore necessary to ascertain the interests of the deceased and his co-owner, both at law and in equity, at the death of the deceased.[14] The deceased may have been a legal joint tenant and equitable tenant in common: in that case his co-owner takes at law by operation of the right of survivorship but the deceased's equitable undivided share devolves on his personal representatives. For instance, the deceased and his wife may have held the legal fee simple in Blackacre as joint tenants upon an express (or statutory[15]) trust for sale and to stand possessed of the proceeds of sale and the income until sale upon trust for the deceased and his wife absolutely as tenants in common in equal shares. At the death of the deceased his wife takes the legal fee simple estate by operation of the right of survivorship, but the deceased's equitable half-share as tenant in common devolves on the deceased's personal representatives. This equitable half-share, being an interest under a trust for sale of land, devolves on the deceased's personal representatives as personalty, not as realty.[16]

(3) *Statutory tenancy.* A statutory tenancy under the Rent Acts does not devolve on the tenant's death on his personal representatives and cannot be given by will.[17] It is not really a tenancy at all but rather "a status of irremovability." On the death of a protected or statutory tenant of a dwelling-house under the Rent Acts, the surviving spouse, if residing there immediately before his death, or otherwise any member of his family who has resided with him for not less than six months immediately before his death, becomes statutory tenant in his place. Such a statutory transmission can occur twice.[18]

(4) *Corporation sole.* On the death of a corporator sole (such as a bishop) his interest in the corporation's real and personal estate devolves on his successor and not on the deceased's personal representatives.[19]

Devolution on personal representatives for the time being. The deceased's estate, both real and personal, devolves on the personal representatives for the time being of the deceased.[20] If any change occurs in the representation of the deceased, the deceased's estate automatically devolves on the new personal representatives. For instance, if a grant of

[13] Administration of Estates Act 1925, s.3(4).
[14] See Snell's *Principles of Equity* (28th ed., 1982), pp. 37–39; *Re Caines* [1978] 1 W.L.R. 540 (possible severance of equitable joint tenancy).
[15] Law of Property Act 1925, ss.34(2) and 35.
[16] Administration of Estates Act 1925, s.3(1)(ii).
[17] *Lovibond* v. *Vincent* [1929] 1 K.B. 687.
[18] Rent Act 1977, s.2(1)(*b*) and Sched. I, Pt. I, as amended by Housing Act 1980, s.76(1) and (2): see also Rent (Agriculture) Act 1976, ss.3 and 4 as amended by Housing Act 1980, s.76(3); Housing Act 1985, ss.87–90 (public sector tenancies, only one transmission); Gray, *Elements of Land Law* (1987), pp. 1059 *et seq.* See *Moodie* v. *Hosegood* [1952] A.C. 61 (a contractual tenancy vests in personal representatives and is suspended during statutory transmission).
[19] Administration of Estates Act 1925, s.3(5).
[20] *Ibid.* ss.1(1) and 55(1)(xi).

letters of administration is revoked and a new grant made in its place, the deceased's estate formerly vested in the old administrators automatically vests in the new administrators.

Of course, if there are different personal representatives for different parts of the deceased's estate, the deceased's estate devolves in separate parts on the appropriate personal representatives. There may be special administrators (under a settled land grant) on whom the deceased's settled land devolves and general administrators (under a general grant excluding settled land) on whom all the deceased's estate apart from settled land devolves.[21]

Causes of action. The general rule laid down by the Law Reform (Miscellaneous Provisions) Act 1934 is that any causes of action vested in the deceased at his death survive for the benefit of his estate—and similarly any causes of action subsisting against him survive against his estate.[22] Where a cause of action survives for the benefit of the deceased's estate two special rules as to damages apply—(i) the damages recoverable never include any exemplary damages or any damages for loss of income in respect of the "lost years" after death,[23] and (ii) where the deceased's death has been caused by the act or omission which gives rise to the cause of action, the damages recoverable must be calculated without reference to any loss or gain to his estate consequent on his death, except that a sum in respect of funeral expenses may be included.[24] Thus the damages recoverable must be calculated without reference to the *loss* arising in respect of the cost of administration of his estate or the liability of his estate to inheritance tax, or the *gain* arising from the proceeds of an insurance policy on his life.[25]

(1) *Contract.*[26] The deceased's personal representatives may therefore enforce a contract made by the deceased with X in his lifetime and obtain damages for X's breach[27] or, if appropriate, an injunction or specific performance.[28] The personal representatives may also carry out the performance of such a contract and then recover the contract price

---

[21] *Ante*, p. 176. As to timber, emblements and fixtures see Williams, Mortimer and Sunnucks, *Executors, Administrators and Probate* (1982), pp. 476–481 and 484–488.

[22] Law Reform (Miscellaneous Provisions) Act 1934, s.1(1): a cause of action is treated as subsisting against the deceased at his death though the damage necessary to complete the cause of action occurs at or after death, s.1(4): see *R. v. Criminal Injuries Compensation Board, ex p. Tong* [1976] 1 W.L.R. 1237; *Ronex Properties Ltd. v. John Laing Construction Ltd.* [1983] Q.B. 398 (contribution); *Re Lanc* [1986] 1 F.L.R. 283 (order on divorce). For claims under the Inheritance (Provision for Family and Dependants) Act 1975 see *ante*, p. 115, n. 7.

[23] *Ibid.* s.1(2)(*a*), as amended by Administration of Justice Act 1982, s.4(2).

[24] *Ibid.* s.1(2)(*c*); *Hart v. Griffiths-Jones* [1948] 2 All E.R. 729 (funeral expenses include embalming of the body but not monument costing £225); *Stanton v. Ewart F. Youldon Ltd.* [1960] 1 W.L.R. 543 (funeral expenses include simple gravestone but not marble memorial set up as a sign of love and affection); *Gammell v. Wilson* [1982] A.C. 27 (funeral expenses include £595 headstone).

[25] *Gammell v. Wilson* [1982] A.C. 27, 46–47, 69, 74 and 77–78.

[26] See P. M. North (1966) 116 N.L.J. 1364–1366.

[27] *Otter v. Church, Adams, Tatham & Co.* [1953] Ch. 280.

[28] *Beswick v. Beswick* [1968] A.C. 58.

from X.[29] Conversely the personal representatives are liable to X (to the extent of the deceased's assets) for any breach of contract committed before or after the death of the deceased.[30] For example, if during his lifetime the deceased made a contract with X for building work to be carried out by X, the deceased's personal representatives are under a duty to carry out the deceased's obligations under the contract and pay the agreed price to the builder, unless an opportunity presents itself of coming to some arrangement with the builder that will be of advantage to the deceased's estate.[31]

A contract for personal services is exceptional because it comes to an end by an implied condition on the death of either party. As Willes J. put it in *Farrow* v. *Wilson*,[32] where a farm bailiff's contract of employment was held to have come to an end on his master's death,

"Generally speaking, contracts bind the executor or administrator, though not named. Where, however, personal considerations are of the foundation of the contract, as in cases of principal and agent, and master and servant, the death of either party puts an end to the relation; and, in respect of service after the death, the contract is dissolved, unless there be a stipulation express or implied to the contrary. It is obvious that, in this case, if the servant had died, his master could not have compelled his representatives to perform the service in his stead, or pay damages, and equally by the death of the master the servant is discharged of his service, not in breach of the contract, but by implied condition."

However, even in the case of a contract for personal services, any causes of action subsisting at the death of either party survive for the benefit of, or against, the deceased's estate. The master's personal representatives are therefore liable to the servant (to the extent of the master's assets) for any arrears of wages due from the master at his death.[33]

(2) *Tort.* The general rule that any causes of action vested in, or subsisting against, the deceased survive for the benefit of, or against, his estate is applicable to all torts with the exception of defamation.[34] The damages recovered by the personal representatives in respect of any cause of action vested in the deceased form part of his estate for all pur-

[29] *Marshall* v. *Broadhurst* (1831) 1 Cr. & J. 403 (executors carried out contract for construction work).
[30] *Wantworth* v. *Cock* (1839) 10 Ad. & El. 42 ("like any ordinary case of goods ordered by a testator, which the executor must receive and pay for"); *Cooper* v. *Jarman* (1866) L.R. 3 Eq. 98 (administrators liable on intestate's contract). For special defences of personal representatives see *post*, p. 401.
[31] *Ahmed Angullia Bin Hadjee Mohamed Salleh Angullia* v. *Estate and Trust Agencies (1927) Ltd.* [1938] A.C. 624.
[32] (1869) L.R. 4 C.P. 744, 746; see also *Graves* v. *Cohen* (1930) 46 T.L.R. 121 (contract by jockey to ride owner's horses discharged by owner's death).
[33] *Stubbs* v. *The Hollywell Railway Co.* (1867) L.R. 2 Ex. 311 (engineer's personal representative entitled to recover arrears of salary due at engineer's death).
[34] Law Reform (Miscellaneous Provisions) Act 1934, s.1(1); Law Reform (Miscellaneous Provisions) Act 1970, ss.4–5: a claim for bereavement under Fatal Accidents Act 1976, s.1A does not survive for the benefit of a person's estate on his death, Law Reform (Miscellaneous Provisions) Act 1934, s.1(1A), as amended by Administration of Justice Act 1982, s.4(1).

poses. The special rules as to the damages recoverable have already been mentioned.[35]

Such a cause of action, which was vested in the deceased and survives for the benefit of his estate, must be sharply distinguished from a cause of action for damages under the Fatal Accidents Act 1976. Under this Act the personal representatives may recover damages on behalf of certain dependants of the deceased where the death of the deceased was caused by a wrongful act in respect of which the deceased could have sued if he had not died.[36] The damages belong to the dependants for whose benefit they are awarded—the damages are to compensate the dependants for the loss of their "breadwinner."[37] Under this Act the personal representatives may also recover £3,500 damages for bereavement for the benefit of the deceased's wife or husband, or the deceased's parents if the deceased was an unmarried minor.[38] Any damages recovered under the Fatal Accidents Act do not form part of the deceased's estate for any purpose.[39]

(3) *Tax.* The personal representatives are liable for income tax and capital gains tax chargeable on the deceased.[40]

B. COLLECTION AND PRESERVATION OF THE ESTATE

Collection of the estate. The personal representatives must carry out their statutory duty to "collect and get in the real and personal estate of the deceased" with reasonable diligence.[41]

(1) *Unsecured debts.* Personal representatives should therefore require payment of any unsecured debts due to the deceased and, if need be, bring legal proceedings in order to recover payment. In *Caney* v. *Bond*[42] the testator died, having lent £500 to X on a promissory note. His executor failed to call in the debt, saying that the money was as safe as if it

[35] *Ante,* p. 212. Damages for loss of expectation of life are never recoverable, but damages for pain and suffering take account of suffering caused to the injured person by awareness of his reduced expectation, Administration of Justice Act 1982, s.1.
[36] Fatal Accidents Act 1976, ss.1 and 2–4, as amended by Administration of Justice Act, 1982, s.3(1).
[37] Damages may also be awarded in respect of the deceased's funeral expenses if incurred by the dependants: Fatal Accidents Act 1976, s.3(5), as amended.
[38] *Ibid.* s.1A: the specified sum of £3,500 damages may be varied by the Lord Chancellor by statutory instrument, s.1A(5).
[39] In assessing damages under the Fatal Accidents Act 1976, benefits accruing to any person from the deceased's estate or otherwise as a result of his death are disregarded, *ibid.* s.4, as amended.
[40] Taxes Management Act 1970, ss.74(1) and 77(1).
[41] Administration of Estates Act 1925, s.25, as amended by Administration of Estates Act 1971, s.9; *Re Tankard* [1942] Ch. 69 (personal representatives' duty to pay debts with "due diligence"): see *post*, p. 257.
[42] (1843) 6 Beav. 486: see also *Lowson* v. *Copeland* (1787) 2 Bro.C.C. 156 (sum due on bond); *Powell* v. *Evans* (1801) 5 Ves. 839 (sums due on bond: "debts due upon personal security are what executors without great reason ought not to permit to remain longer than is absolutely necessary"); *Tebbs* v. *Carpenter* (1816) 1 Madd. 290 (executor failed to collect rents); *Stiles* v. *Guy* (1848) 16 Sim. 230, 1 M. & G. 422 (executors failed to compel their co-executor to account and pay the balance he owed).

were in the Bank of England. X repaid £100 to the executor and would have repaid the whole debt if he had been pressed to do so. The executor did not press him and the balance of £400 was lost when X died insolvent two years after the testator's death. The court held that the executor was personally liable to make good the loss. Again, a personal representative is personally liable if, by his delay in commencing an action against a debtor of the deceased, he enables the debtor to escape payment by pleading limitation.[43] However, a personal representative who has taken no steps to enforce a debt is not liable if he can prove that there were reasonable grounds for believing that the debtor could not pay.[44]

(2) *Secured debts.* On the other hand personal representatives are not under a similar duty to call in and realise loans made by the deceased on mortgages of land which are authorised investments under the deceased's will, if the money is not needed for the payment of funeral and testamentary expenses, debts and pecuniary legacies.[45]

(3) *Statutory powers.* Under section 15 of the Trustee Act 1925 a personal representative has power to allow any time of payment of any debt, to accept any composition or any real or personal security for any debt or any property claimed, and to compromise, abandon or otherwise settle any debt or claim relating to the deceased's estate.[46] If the personal representative exercises this wide power[47] in good faith, he is not responsible for any consequential loss. But the personal representative is only protected by section 15 if he exercises an active discretion. In *Re Greenwood*[48] the testator died, having lent £1,000 to X during his lifetime. By his will the testator gave his estate to his executors upon the usual trusts for conversion and investment. The executors did not collect this debt of £1,000, though it was unsecured and ought to have been got in at an early stage. Seven years later, at the instance of the beneficiaries, the executors issued a writ for the debt, but by then X was insolvent and part of the debt could not be recovered. Eve J. held the executors liable to the beneficiaries for the loss. The executors would have been protected by section 21 of the Trustee Act 1893 (the predecessor of section 15 of the Trustee Act 1925) if they had given time to the debtor after a full consideration by them of all the circumstances. But here the giving of time resulted from the passive inactivity of the executors, who let the matter drift. An executor is not protected if "the loss has arisen from the neglect or carelessness or supineness of the [executor], and not from a mistaken but bona fide exercise by him of the statutory powers vested in him."[49]

---

[43] *Hayward* v. *Kinsey* (1701) 12 Mod.Rep. 568, 573: for nature of a *devastavit* see *post*, pp. 386 *et seq.*

[44] *Clack* v. *Holland* (1854) 19 Beav. 262, 271–272; *Stiles* v. *Guy*, *supra*, (onus on executors to prove debtor could not pay); *Re Brogden* (1888) 38 Ch.D. 546.

[45] *Re Chapman* [1896] 2 Ch. 763, esp. at pp. 773 and 778.

[46] For the statutory powers in relation to reversionary interests, see Trustee Act 1925, ss.22 and 68(1)(17).

[47] See *Re Earl of Strafford* [1980] Ch. 28.

[48] (1911) 105 L.T. 509.

[49] *Ibid.* at p. 514.

Section 26 of the Administration of Estates Act 1925 also confers on a personal representative statutory powers to distrain for arrears of a rentcharge due to the deceased, and for arrears of rent due to the deceased, in like manner as the deceased might have done had he been living. Arrears of rent due to the deceased form part of his personal estate. Under this statutory power the deceased's general personal representatives may distrain for arrears of rent due to the deceased, even though the reversion has devolved on the deceased's special representatives. If the latter in fact recover such arrears (as they are entitled to do as reversioners), they must account to the general representatives.

The inventory and account. If required to do so by the court, the personal representative has a statutory duty to "exhibit on oath in the court a full inventory of the estate and when so required render an account of the administration of the estate to the court."[50] Any person interested[51] in the deceased's estate may apply to the court[52] for an order requiring such an inventory and account from the personal representative. An order may be made against a former administrator whose grant has been revoked by the court in a probate action.[53] Lapse of time is not in itself a bar but the court has a discretion to refuse such an order.[54]

Compared with an administration action[55] an application for an inventory and account is a relatively cheap procedure but the scope of the remedy is limited. In essence it enables the applicant to obtain information from the personal representative as to the property comprised in the estate (the inventory) and the manner in which the administration has been carried out (the account).

Time for realisation of unauthorised investments. Personal representatives have a duty to realise any investments, which it is not proper for them to retain, within a reasonable time, which prima facie means within the executor's year, i.e. within a year from the date of death. In *Grayburn* v. *Clarkson*[56] the testator held company shares with unlimited liability and by his will he directed his executors to convert his estate with all convenient speed. The court held that the executors were liable for the loss caused by their failure to sell the shares within the executor's year. The executors were entitled to exercise a reasonable dis-

---

[50] Administration of Estates Act 1925, s.25, as amended by Administration of Estates Act 1971, s.9.

[51] *Myddleton* v. *Rushout* (1797) 1 Phillim. 244 ("any kind of interest" suffices); *Hackman* v. *Black* (1755) 2 Lee 251 (creditor); *Kenny* v. *Jackson* (1827) 1 Hag.Ecc. 105 (residuary legatee).

[52] Application is made to a registrar, N.C. Prob. Rules 1987, r. 61(2).

[53] *In the Estate of Thomas* [1956] 1 W.L.R. 1516; *Taylor* v. *Newton* (1752) 1 Lee 15 (order made against former administrator whose grant had expired). Apparently an order may be made against the executors of a deceased administrator with the will annexed, *Ritchie* v. *Rees* (1822) 1 Add. 144, 153, and against the executor of a deceased executor though the other original executor is still alive, *Gale* v. *Luttrell* (1824) 2 Add. 234.

[54] *Burgess* v. *Marriott* (1843) 3 Curt. 424, 426; *Ritchie* v. *Rees, supra,* (administration granted in 1777: application in 1822 for inventory and account refused as estate fully administered); *Scurrah* v. *Scurrah* (1841) 2 Curt. 919; *Pitt* v. *Woodham* (1828) 1 Hag.Ecc. 247; *Bowles* v. *Harvey* (1832) 4 Hag.Ecc. 241.

[55] See *post*, pp. 396 *et seq.*

[56] (1868) 3 Ch.App. 605: see also *Hughes* v. *Empson* (1856) 22 Beav. 181.

cretion as to when they sold, but they had failed to show any reason why they had not sold within the executor's year. "It certainly was the duty of the executors with all convenient speed, and, indeed, as early as possible, to sell shares involving such [an unlimited] liability."[57] However the executors are not liable if, in the honest exercise of the reasonable discretion allowed them, they decide to postpone the sale beyond the end of the executor's year.[58]

Preservation of the estate. Personal representatives are under a duty to take reasonable care in preserving the deceased's estate.[59] If they do take reasonable care, they are not liable for the loss of the testator's goods which are destroyed by an accidental fire,[60] or which are taken by a thief from the possession of the personal representatives or their agent, such as their solicitor or banker.[61]

(1) *Power to insure.* A personal representative has power under the Trustee Act 1925 to insure any building or other insurable property[62] against loss or damage by fire to any amount not exceeding three-quarters of its value. The premiums may be paid out of the income of the insured property or of any other property subject to the same trusts without obtaining the consent of any person entitled to the income.[63] This power is not applicable if the deceased's will expresses a contrary intention,[64] or if the personal representative is bound forthwith to convey the property absolutely to any beneficiary upon being requested to do so[65]—in that case it is left to the beneficiary to insure if he chooses.

However a personal representative is not under any duty to insure unless the deceased's will imposes such a duty on him.[66]

(2) *Deposit of documents.* If a personal representative (not being a trust corporation) retains, or invests in, any securities payable to bearer, such securities *must*, until they are sold, be deposited for safe custody and collection of income with a banker or banking company.[67] The personal

---

[57] *Ibid.* at p. 608: see also *Sculthorpe* v. *Tipper* (1871) L.R. 13 Eq. 232: *cf. Re Norrington* (1879) 13 Ch.D. 654.

[58] *Buxton* v. *Buxton* (1835) 1 My. & Cr. 80 (Mexican bonds sold 19 months after death); *Marsden* v. *Kent* (1877) 5 Ch.D. 598; *Re Chapman* [1896] 2 Ch. 763.

[59] *Job* v. *Job* (1877) 6 Ch.D. 562 (*per* Jessel M.R., "an executor or administrator is in the position of a gratuitous bailee"); *Re Gunning* [1918] 1 Ir.R. 221.

[60] *Executors of the Lady Croft* v. *Lyndsey* (1676) 2 Freem.Ch. 1.

[61] *Jones* v. *Lewis* (1751) 2 Ves.Sen. 240 (administratrix not liable for loss of assets taken by robbery from her solicitor).

[62] *Re Earl of Egmont's Trusts* [1908] 1 Ch. 821 (heirlooms are insurable property).

[63] Trustee Act 1925, ss.19(1) and 68(1)(17): as to the application of insurance money see s.20.

[64] *Ibid.* s.69(2).

[65] *Ibid.* s.19(2).

[66] *Re McEacharn* (1911) 103 L.T. 900 (no duty to exercise the statutory power); *Bailey* v. *Gould* (1840) 4 Y. & C.Ex. 221 (uninsured factory burnt down: executors not liable); *Fry* v. *Fry* (1859) 27 Beav. 144: but see *Garner* v. *Moore* (1855) 3 Drew. 277 and Williams, Mortimer and Sunnucks, *Executors, Administrators and Probate* (1982), p. 713. For possible reform see Law Reform Committee, 23rd Report, *The powers and duties of trustees*, Cmnd. 8733 (1982), pp. 41–43 and 66.

[67] Trustees Act 1925, ss.7(1) and 68(17): for the power to retain or invest in such securities see s.7(1).

representative is not responsible for any loss incurred by reason of the deposit and any cost incurred is payable out of the income of the trust property.[68] Apart from this duty to deposit securities payable to bearer, any documents held by a personal representative *may* be deposited with any banker or banking company or any other company whose business includes the undertaking of the safe custody of documents and any cost incurred is payable in the same way.[69] Such documents may also be deposited with the personal representative's solicitor or other agent for the purpose of transacting business required in the administration of the deceased's estate.[70]

C. Realisation of the Estate

Personal representatives often hold either the whole, or part, of the deceased's estate upon trust for sale. If the deceased died wholly or partly intestate, section 33 of the Administration of Estates Act 1925 imposes a trust for sale on each asset (other than money) as to which the deceased died wholly intestate.[71] Again, it is quite common for a testator by his will to direct his executors to hold his residuary estate upon trust for sale. However generally personal representatives do not make title to a purchaser under such a trust for sale. Instead the personal representatives sell and make title under the ample powers which attach to the office of personal representative.[72] These powers to sell, mortgage and lease must now be considered.

Powers to sell. Powers of sale are conferred both (1) at common law and in equity, and (2) by statute.

(1) *Common law.* Both at common law and in equity a personal representative has power to sell the deceased's personal estate (including leaseholds) for the purpose of carrying out the administration of the deceased's estate. An unpaid creditor of the deceased,[73] or a beneficiary under his will or intestacy,[74] cannot reclaim the property sold from the purchaser—if this were not the rule, no one would ever buy from a personal representative.

Under section 2(1) of the Administration of Estates Act 1925 a personal representative has the same powers with respect to real estate[75] as were in force before 1926 with respect to leaseholds.[76] Thus the personal representative's common law power of selling the deceased's leaseholds

---

[68] *Ibid.* s.7(2).

[69] *Ibid.* ss.21 and 68(17): see *Re Sisson's Settlement* [1903] 1 Ch. 262.

[70] *Field* v. *Field* [1894] 1 Ch. 425 (deeds in custody of trustees' solicitors): see also Trustee Act 1925, ss.23 and 30 and *Re Vickery* [1931] 1 Ch. 572, *post*, pp. 238 *et seq.*

[71] *Ante*, pp. 82 (total intestacy) and 96 (partial intestacy).

[72] As to the powers exercisable under a grant of administration *ad colligenda bona* or limited to an action see *ante*, pp. 184 and 186.

[73] *Nugent* v. *Gifford* (1738) 1 Atk. 463; *Whale* v. *Booth* (1784) 4 T.R. 625.

[74] *Ewer* v. *Corbet* (1723) 2 P.Wms. 148.

[75] See Administration of Estates Act 1925, s.3, and *ante*, p. 210.

[76] The Land Transfer Act 1897, s.2(2) had the same effect on a death after 1897.

is now exercisable by a personal representative as respects the deceased's real estate.[77]

(2) *Statute.* A personal representative also has a statutory power of sale under section 39(1) of the Administration of Estates Act 1925. This section provides that in dealing with the deceased's real and personal estate his personal representatives shall have all the powers conferred on trustees for sale of land. These include all the powers of a tenant for life and the trustees of a settlement under the Settled Land Act 1925[78]; for instance, power to sell or exchange land, or any part thereof, or any easement right or privilege of any kind over or in relation to the land,[79] and power to sell or exchange the surface and the minerals separately.[80] Personal representatives have power to enter into a contract to make such a sale or exchange[81] and any contract is binding on, and enforceable by, the personal representatives for the time being of the deceased.[82] The powers conferred by section 39(1) apply even though the deceased died prior to 1926.[83]

The powers conferred by section 39(1) are exercisable for purposes of administration (as was the case at common law) and also "during a minority of any beneficiary or the subsistence of any life interest, or until the period of distribution arrives."[84] The reference to a minority of any beneficiary or the subsistence of any life interest appears to have been inserted to cover the case of the deceased dying intestate leaving a widow or infant next of kin.[85] Certainly the period of distribution arrives when the personal representatives assent to the vesting of property in any person entitled, such as the trustees of the deceased's will (who are often the same persons as the personal representatives).[86] But if the personal representatives do not vest the deceased's land in the person entitled but merely permit that person to take possession of it, this does not prejudice the right of the personal representatives to resume possession or convey the land[87] or to exercise their powers under section 39(1).

Powers to mortgage. (1) *Common law.* At common law and in equity a personal representative has power to raise money required for purposes

---

[77] *Re Chaplin & Staffordshire Potteries Waterworks Co. Ltd's Contract* [1922] 2 Ch. 824 (personal representatives may sell the surface and minerals of the deceased's freehold land separately).
[78] Law of Property Act 1925, s.28(1) (as amended by Law of Property (Amendment) Act 1926).
[79] Settled Land Act 1925, s.38; for the regulations respecting sales and exchanges see ss.39 and 40.
[80] *Ibid.* s.50: see also Trustee Act 1925, s.12(2).
[81] *Ibid.* s.90(1): see also Trustee Act 1925, s.12(1).
[82] Administration of Estates Act 1925, s.39(1)(iii): for power to raise capital money see Trustee Act 1925, s.16.
[83] *Ibid.* s.39(3).
[84] *Ibid.* s.39(1): for the meaning of minority see Family Law Reform Act 1969, s.1 and Sched. 3, para. 6.
[85] *Re Trollope's W.T.* [1927] 1 Ch. 596, 603–605.
[86] *Ibid.*
[87] Administration of Estates Act 1925, s.43(1): see also *Williams* v. *Holland* [1965] 1 W.L.R. 739 (executor entitled to recover possession of deceased's house from beneficiary under will in order to sell it for purposes of administration).

of administration by mortgaging[88] or pledging[89] (as may be appropriate) any of the deceased's personal estate. Such a mortgage may confer a power of sale on the mortgagee.[90]

(2) *Statute.* Under section 39(1) of the Administration of Estates Act 1925 this common law power "including power to raise money by mortgage or charge (whether or not by deposit of documents)" may be exercised by personal representatives over both the real and personal estate of the deceased. Again, because under section 39(1) personal representatives have all the powers conferred on trustees for sale of land, they have all the powers to raise money by legal mortgage of a tenant for life under the Settled Land Act 1925.[91] As explained above, these powers under section 39(1) are exercisable for purposes of administration and also during a minority of any beneficiary or the subsistence of any life interest, or until the period of distribution arrives.

Personal representatives also have power, for the purpose of paying inheritance tax for which they are liable on any property (or raising the amount of it when paid), to raise the amount of the tax by sale or mortgage of, or a terminable charge on, the property.[92]

Powers to lease. (1) *Common law.* At common law and in equity a personal representative has power to grant a lease for purposes of administration.[93] For instance, if the deceased's estate includes a leasehold interest for which the personal representative cannot find a purchaser or negotiate a surrender to the landlord, he may grant an underlease. This common law power now applies to the deceased's real estate as well as to the deceased's leaseholds.[94]

(2) *Statute.* As already mentioned, under section 39(1) of the Administration of Estates Act 1925 personal representatives have all the powers of a tenant for life under the Settled Land Act 1925, which include powers to lease[95] and to accept a surrender of a lease.[96]

---

[88] *Mead* v. *Orrery* (1745) 3 Atk. 235, 239–240; *Scott* v. *Tyler* (1788) Dick. 712, 725; *M'Leod* v. *Drummond* (1810) 17 Ves. 152, 154; *Earl Vane* v. *Rigden* (1870) L.R. 5 Ch. 663 ("it is a very common practice for an executor to obtain an advance from a banker for the immediate wants of the estate by depositing securities. It would be a strange thing if that could not be done").

[89] *Russell* v. *Plaice* (1854) 18 Beav. 21, 28–29.

[90] *Ibid.*

[91] Law of Property Act 1925, s.28(1) (as amended); Settled Land Act 1925, ss.49(1)(c), 69–71 and 90. For extensions of s.71 see *inter alia* Landlord and Tenant Act 1927, s.13(1); Landlord and Tenant Act 1954, s.8(5) and Sched. 2, para. 6, and Leasehold Reform Act 1967, s.6(5) and Sched. 2, para. 9(1). For the power of personal representatives to demise land for a term to trustees to raise money for giving effect to beneficial interests see Administration of Estates Act 1925, s.40: see also Trustee Act 1925, s.16.

[92] Inheritance Tax Act 1984, s.212(1) and (4) (tax includes interest and costs properly incurred in respect of tax).

[93] *Oceanic Steam Navigation Co.* v. *Sutherberry* (1880) 16 Ch.D. 236, 243.

[94] Administration of Estates Act 1925, s.2(1).

[95] Settled Land Act 1925, ss.41 and 43; for the regulations see ss.42 and 44–48, and for the grant of an option see s.51.

[96] *Ibid.* s.52: for the power to enter into contracts see s.90(1) and Administration of Estates Act 1925, s.39(1)(iii).

Protection of purchaser. (1) *Propriety of the disposition.* At common law a purchaser or mortgagee was entitled to presume that the sale or mortgage to him by the personal representative was made for purposes of administration. Thus the purchaser or mortgagee was not concerned to inquire into the propriety of the disposition, even if 20 years or more had elapsed since the death of the deceased.[97] But the purchaser or mortgagee was not protected if he knew that the disposition was made by the personal representative other than for purposes of administration.[98]

Section 36(8) of the Administration of Estates Act 1925 now provides greater protection for a purchaser of a legal estate in land. It provides that "a conveyance[99] of a legal estate by a personal representative to a purchaser shall not be invalidated by reason only that the purchaser may have notice that all the debts, liabilities, funeral and testamentary or administration expenses, duties, and legacies of the deceased have been discharged or provided for." However, for section 36(8) to apply, the purchaser (or mortgagee or lessee[1]) must have acquired a legal estate in land[2] in good faith[3] and for money or money's worth.[4] At common law the powers of personal representatives were only exercisable for purposes of administration. The powers conferred by section 39 of the Act on personal representatives are not confined to purposes of administration but are exercisable during the minority of any beneficiary or the subsistence of any life interest, or until the period of distribution arrives. If a purchaser has notice that the personal representatives' disposition is not made for purposes of administration, section 36(8) makes it unnecessary for the purchaser to inquire whether the power is exercisable owing to the minority of a beneficiary or the subsistence of a life interest, or the non-arrival of the period of distribution.[5]

(2) *Application of the purchase-money.* Again, at common law a purchaser or mortgagee was not concerned to ensure that the personal representative applied the purchase, or mortgage, money properly. As Lord Thurlow put it in *Scott* v. *Tyler,*[6]

> "It is of great consequence that no rules should be laid down here, which may impede executors in their administration, or render their disposition of the testator's effects unsafe, or uncertain to the purchaser; his title is complete by sale and delivery; what becomes of the price, is no concern of the purchaser: This observation applies equally to mortgages or pledges. . . . "

This common law rule has now been enacted in section 14 of the Trustee

---

[97] *Re Venn & Furze's Contract* [1894] 2 Ch. 101.

[98] *Re Verrell's Contract* [1903] 1 Ch. 65; *Wilson* v. *Moore* (1834) 1 M. & K. 337.

[99] "Conveyance" includes *inter alia* a mortgage, charge by way of legal mortgage, and a lease: see Administration of Estates Act 1925, s.55(1)(iii).

[1] *Ibid.* s.55(1)(xviii): s.36(8) applies to conveyances made after 1925, whenever the deceased died, s.36(12).

[2] *Ibid.* s.55(1)(vii).

[3] *Ibid.* s.55(1)(xviii).

[4] *Ibid.* s.36(11): *quaere* whether a nominal consideration in money suffices, see s.55(1)(xviii); *Midland Bank Trust Co. Ltd.* v. *Green* [1981] A.C. 513, 531–532.

[5] *Re Spencer and Hauser's Contract* [1928] Ch. 598, 605–606.

[6] (1788) Dick. 712, 725: see also *M'Leod* v. *Drummond* (1810) 17 Ves. 152, 154.

Act 1925 which provides that the receipt in writing of a personal representative[7] for any money, securities or other personal property payable or transferable to him under any trust or power shall be a sufficient discharge to the person paying or transferring the same and "shall effectually exonerate him from seeing to the application or being answerable for any loss or misapplication thereof." The statutory protection of the purchaser cannot be excluded by a contrary direction in the deceased's will.[8]

(3) *Good faith essential.* Good faith on the part of the purchaser is always essential, whether the conveyance is of a legal estate in land (so that section 36(8) applies) or of an equitable interest in land or any interest in pure personalty (to which section 36(8) is not applicable). If the purchaser knows that the disposition to him is a breach of duty on the part of the personal representative, the purchaser's bad faith vitiates the disposition. In *Doe* v. *Fallows*[9] a widow owed £300 to an attorney. She was the administratrix of her deceased husband's estate and in order to secure her personal debt she executed a mortgage of the deceased's leasehold property to the attorney. The mortgage falsely stated that the attorney had lent £300 to the administratrix, and the deceased's next of kin executed the mortgage in ignorance of the fact that the attorney had paid nothing to the deceased's estate. The court held that the mortgage was invalid because the attorney had assisted the administratrix in misapplying the assets of the deceased's estate. In *Scott* v. *Tyler*[10] Lord Thurlow gave some instances of bad faith on the part of a purchaser—he said that the transaction was vitiated if the purchaser "concerts with an executor . . . by obtaining the testator's effects at a nominal price, or at a fraudulent under value,[11] or by applying the real value to the purchase of other objects for his own behoof, or in extinguishing the private debt of the executor." If the transaction is vitiated by bad faith on the part of the purchaser, a creditor or a beneficiary entitled under the deceased's will[12] or intestacy may have the transaction set aside unless the creditor or beneficiary is barred by laches.[13]

(4) *Previous assent.* A personal representative's powers are exercisable over the property for the time being vested in him in his capacity as personal representative. He cannot exercise his powers over property which he has already transferred to the trustees or the beneficiary entitled under the deceased's will or intestacy.[14] Prior to 1926 this principle sometimes gave rise to difficulty, particularly in a case where the deceased had settled property by his will and the trustees were the

---

[7] Trustee Act 1925, s.68(1)(17).

[8] *Ibid.* s.14(3): see also ss.17 and 68(1), (7) and (17).

[9] *Doe* d. *Woodhead* v. *Fallows* (1832) 2 Cr. & J. 481.

[10] (1788) Dick 712, 725.

[11] See *Rice* v. *Gordon* (1848) 11 Beav. 265 (fraudulent sale by administrator to his brother of deceased's leasehold property at gross undervalue held void).

[12] *Hill* v. *Simpson* (1802) 7 Ves. 152; *M'Leod* v. *Drummond* (1810) 17 Ves. 152, 169–170; *Wilson* v. *Moore* (1834) 1 M. & K. 337.

[13] *Elliot* v. *Merriman* (1740) 2 Atk. 41; *Andrew* v. *Wrigley* (1792) 4 Bro.C.C. 125.

[14] *Attenborough* v. *Solomon* [1913] A.C. 76 (see *post*, p. 234).

same persons as the executors. If the executors had assented expressly or by implication[15] to the gift in the will to themselves as trustees, then they ceased to hold the subject-matter of the gift as personal representatives and henceforth could only make title pursuant to their powers (if any) as trustees.[16] "The effect of the assent was to strip the executors of their title as executors and to clothe them with a title as trustees."[17]

Since 1925 section 36(6) of the Administration of Estates Act 1925 provides some protection for a purchaser (or mortgagee or lessee[18]) of a legal estate in land[19] in good faith[20] and for money or money's worth.[21] To consider an example where P contracts to purchase the legal estate in Blackacre from a personal representative V. If V has previously made an assent or conveyance of Blackacre to the trustees or the beneficiary entitled under the deceased's will or intestacy, the latter may require that notice of the assent or conveyance be placed on or annexed to the probate or letters of administration.[22] If this has been done, P will ascertain from his inspection of the probate or letters of administration that V cannot make title to Blackacre as personal representative. But if this has not been done, section 36(6) protects P by providing:

(i) that a statement in writing by a personal representative V that he has not given or made an assent or conveyance in respect of a legal estate in Blackacre shall, in favour of P, be sufficient evidence[23] of this (in practice such a statement is invariably inserted in a conveyance of unregistered land by a personal representative); and

(ii) that a conveyance by V of a legal estate in Blackacre to P accepted on the faith of such a statement "shall . . . operate to transfer or create the legal estate expressed to be conveyed in like manner as if no previous assent or conveyance had been made by the personal representative."

Thus, where section 36(6) applies, P acquires the legal estate in Blackacre, despite the previous assent or conveyance made by V in favour of the trustees or the beneficiary entitled under the deceased's will or intestacy. However section 36(6) operates "without prejudice to any previous disposition made in favour of another purchaser deriving title mediately or immediately under the personal representative." It follows that section 36(6) does not protect P as against a previous purchaser for money or money's worth,[24] whether the latter took directly from the personal representative, or took from the trustees or beneficiary in

[15] For assents see *post*, pp. 368 *et seq.*
[16] *Attenborough* v. *Solomon, supra; Wise* v. *Whitburn* [1924] 1 Ch. 460.
[17] *Per* Eve J. in *Wise* v. *Whitburn, supra,* at p. 468.
[18] Administration of Estates Act 1925, s.55(1)(xviii): s.36(6) applies to assents and conveyances made after 1925, whenever the deceased died, s.36(12).
[19] *Ibid.* s.55(1)(vii).
[20] *Ibid.* s.55(1)(xviii).
[21] *Ibid.* s.36(11). See generally on section 36(6). *Williams on Assents* (1947), Appendix V.
[22] *Ibid.* s.36(5). In the case of registered land this precaution appears unnecessary, see Ruoff & Roper, *Registered Conveyancing* (5th ed., 1986), p. 670.
[23] Sufficient but not conclusive evidence, see *Re Duce & Boots Cash Chemists (Southern) Ltd.'s Contract* [1937] Ch. 642 (on the construction of s.36(7)).
[24] *Ibid.* ss.36(11) and 55(1)(xviii).

whose favour the personal representative made a previous assent or conveyance.

(5) *Revocation of grant*. The protection of a purchaser from a personal representative against any subsequent revocation of the latter's grant has already been considered.[25]

D. Carrying On the Deceased's Business

On the death of the sole proprietor of a business, the assets of the business which were vested in the deceased devolve on his personal representatives. Similarly, on the death of a partner, the assets of the partnership which were vested in the deceased (other than as a joint tenant[26]) devolve on his personal representatives: such assets nevertheless remain partnership assets and the surviving partner or partners may deal with them for the purposes of the partnership.[27] On the other hand, if the deceased was a shareholder in an incorporated company which owned the business, the deceased's shares, but not the assets of the business, devolve on his personal representatives. If the shares are unauthorised investments, the personal representatives should sell them within a reasonable time.[28]

Authority to carry on business. The general rule is that personal representatives have no authority to carry on the deceased's business.[29] Similarly on the death of a partner, his personal representatives are generally under a duty to call in the deceased's share in the partnership business and they ought not to permit the deceased's share to be left outstanding in the business.[30] For instance, if under the partnership agreement (or under a contract made with the personal representatives after the deceased's death) the surviving partners are bound to purchase the deceased's share, the personal representatives should require payment of the price due to the deceased's estate: if the surviving partners are not so bound, the personal representatives should require the business of the partnership to be wound up.[31]

There are certain exceptions to the general rule that personal representatives have no authority to carry on the deceased's business.

(1) *Proper realisation*. Personal representatives have authority to carry on the deceased's business with a view to the proper realisation of his

---

[25] *Ante*, pp. 205 *et seq.*

[26] Land vested in the partners is held by them as legal joint tenants, Law of Property Act 1925, s.34, but in equity the partners are presumed to be tenants in common, *Re Fuller's Contract* [1933] Ch. 652.

[27] *Re Bourne* [1906] 2 Ch. 427.

[28] *Ante*, p. 216. For the duty of personal representatives who are majority shareholders see *Re Lucking's W.T.* [1968] 1 W.L.R. 866, 874–875; *Bartlett* v. *Barclays Bank Trust Co. Ltd.* (No. 1) [1980] Ch. 515, 530–535 (trust corporation has higher duty of care).

[29] *Barker* v. *Parker* (1786) 1 T.R. 287, 295; *Kirkman* v. *Booth* (1848) 11 Beav. 273.

[30] *Kirkman* v. *Booth, supra.*

[31] Partnership Act 1890, ss.33(1), 38–39 and 42: see *Barclays Bank Trust Co. Ltd.* v. *Bluff* [1982] Ch. 172.

estate—for example, so as to carry out the deceased's obligations under any contract made by him,[32] or so as to enable the business to be sold as a going concern.[33] Thus, if selling the deceased's business as a going concern is a proper method of realisation, his personal representatives may carry on the business for such a reasonable period of time as is necessary to enable them to effect the sale. Normally this period is not much longer than the executor's year.[34]

(2) *Authority in the will.* The personal representatives have authority to carry on the deceased's business if they are directed, or empowered, to do so by the deceased in his will. If a testator wishes to direct, or empower, his personal representatives to do so, it is desirable that he should insert a suitable express provision in his will. However, if the personal representatives are empowered to postpone the sale of the deceased's business, they have by implication authority to carry on the business during the period of postponement. When the proceeds of the business become distributable, the power to postpone, and with it the power to carry on the business, come to an end. In *Re Crowther*[35] the testator by his will gave his real and personal estate to trustees upon trust for sale and conversion, with power to postpone such sale and conversion "for such period as to them shall seem expedient." At his death the testator carried on two businesses, one as sole proprietor and the other in partnership with his son (who was one of the trustees of the will). The trustees carried on both businesses for 22 years after the testator's death, not with a view to their sale but for the benefit of his widow as the life tenant under his will. Chitty J. decided that the trustees had authority to carry on both the businesses in this way under their power to postpone sale—"a power to postpone the sale of a business involves a power of continuing the business in the meantime."[36]

Again it is desirable that a testator should specify in his will which assets of his estate may be employed by his personal representatives in carrying on his business.[37] If a testator directs his personal representatives to carry on his business but does not specify which assets they may employ in so doing, his will is likely to be construed as authorising the personal representatives to use only the assets employed in the business at the testator's death.[38]

Section 33(1) of the Administration of Estates Act 1925, in imposing a trust for sale and conversion on an intestacy, confers on the personal representatives power to postpone such sale and conversion for such a period as they may think proper. Probably, applying the reasoning in

---

[32] *Marshall* v. *Broadhurst* (1831) 1 Cr. & J. 403 ("if a man makes half a wheelbarrow or a pair of shoes, and die, the executors may complete them"); *Edwards* v. *Grace* (1836) 2 M. & W. 190.

[33] *Dowse* v. *Gorton* [1891] A.C. 190, 199; *Garrett* v. *Noble* (1834) 6 Sim. 504.

[34] *Re Crowther* [1895] 2 Ch. 56, 60.

[35] [1895] 2 Ch. 56: *cf. Re Smith* [1896] 1 Ch. 171; *Re Chancellor* (1884) 26 Ch.D. 42, 46.

[36] *Re Crowther, supra,* at p. 60.

[37] *e.g. Cutbush* v. *Cutbush* (1839) 1 Beav. 184 (assets employed in the business at the testator's death); *Re Slater* (1915) 113 L.T. 691 (power to employ a sufficient amount of deceased's other capital not employed in the business).

[38] *M'Neillie* v. *Acton* (1853) 4 De G.M. & G. 744.

Re Crowther, the personal representatives have by implication authority to carry on the deceased's business during the period of postponement.

Personal representatives who carry on the deceased's business without authority are liable to make good any losses they incur. If personal representatives consider it expedient to carry on the deceased's business but lack the authority to do so, it may be advisable for them to apply to the court for an order authorising them to do so,[39] or to seek an indemnity from the beneficiaries (if they are ascertained and *sui juris*).

Liability of personal representative for debts incurred. A personal representative is personally liable on every contract which he makes in carrying on the deceased's business—"he is liable for every shilling on every contract he enters into."[40] It is immaterial that he is expressed to make the contract as personal representative[41]—he is still personally liable. Thus, if the personal representative incurs a debt in carrying on the deceased's business, the creditor may sue the personal representative personally and enforce the judgment against the latter's assets. The creditor is not entitled at common law to payment out of the deceased's assets because the debt was not due from the deceased.[42] However, the creditor may be entitled in equity to payment out of the deceased's assets by subrogation to the personal representative's own right of indemnity out of those assets.

Indemnity of personal representative. To what extent is a personal representative who incurs liabilities in carrying on the deceased's business entitled to be indemnified out of the assets of the deceased's estate? The personal representative may be entitled to such an indemnity (1) because he had authority to carry on the business, or (2) because one or more creditors of the deceased have assented to the carrying on of the business by the personal representative.

(1) *Effect of authority to carry on the business.* Under this head the extent of the personal representative's right of indemnity depends on the nature of the authority he exercised to carry on the business.

(a) PROPER REALISATION. If the personal representative carried on the business with a view to the proper realisation of the deceased's estate, his right of indemnity may be exercised against both the creditors and the beneficiaries of the deceased.[43] In this case his right of indemnity takes priority over the claims of the creditors of the deceased.

(b) OTHER AUTHORITY. On the other hand, if the personal representative carried on the business under an authority in the will but not with a view to proper realisation, his right of indemnity may be exercised

---

[39] See Trustee Act 1925, s.57.

[40] *Owen* v. *Delamere* (1872) L.R. 15 Eq. 134, 139.

[41] *Labouchere* v. *Tupper* (1857) 11 Moo.P.C. 198; *Liverpool Borough Bank* v. *Walker* (1859) 4 De G. & J. 24.

[42] *Re Morgan* (1881) 18 Ch.D. 93, 99: see also *Farhall* v. *Farhall* (1871) 7 Ch.App. 123.

[43] *Dowse* v. *Gorton* [1891] A.C. 190, 199 (realisation by selling the deceased's business as a going concern).

against the beneficiaries but not against the creditors of the deceased.[44] The reason for this distinction is that the beneficiaries are bound by the terms of the will but the creditors are not. Of course under this right of indemnity the personal representative may only resort to assets which the will authorised him to employ in carrying on the business.[45]

A personal representative may be in default (*i.e.* "in debt"[46]) to the deceased's assets which he is authorised to employ in carrying on the business—for instance, he may have wrongfully taken money out of such assets for his own purposes. If so, the personal representative loses his right of indemnity to the extent of his own debt to such assets.[47] In effect the personal representative must first indemnify himself out of the debt he owes.

(2) *Effect of assent by creditor.* If a creditor of the deceased has assented to the carrying on of the business, the personal representative is entitled to be indemnified out of the assets of the deceased's estate in priority to that creditor.[48] This rule applies whether or not the personal representative had authority under the will to carry on the business.[49] On the other hand, if a creditor of the deceased has not assented to the carrying on of the business, and the business has not been carried on with a view to proper realisation, that creditor may treat the continuance of the business as improper: if he does so, he is entitled to be paid out of the value of the assets which existed at the death of the deceased and the personal representative has no right to be indemnified in priority to him.[50]

A creditor does not assent to the carrying on of the business if he merely knows of it and does nothing to stop it.[51] "It is necessary . . . to show an active affirmative assent. Mere standing by with knowledge and doing nothing is not sufficient."[52]

Under this head, as in the case where he is entitled to an indemnity because he had authority to carry on the business, a personal representative loses his right of indemnity to the extent of his own debt to the deceased's estate.

Creditor's right of subrogation. If in carrying on the deceased's business the personal representative incurs a debt[53] in respect of which he is entitled to indemnity out of the assets, then, by subrogation to the personal representative, his creditor is entitled to claim the benefit of

---

[44] *Dowse* v. *Gorton, supra; Re Millard, ex p. Yates* (1895) 72 L.T. 823; *Re East* (1914) 111 L.T. 101.

[45] *Ex p. Garland* (1804) 10 Ves. 110; *Cutbush* v. *Cutbush* (1839) 1 Beav. 184.

[46] *Re Kidd* (1894) 70 L.T. 648 (default in rendering accounts does not preclude indemnity).

[47] *Re Johnson* (1880) 15 Ch.D. 548.

[48] *Dowse* v. *Gorton* [1891] A.C. 190. The assets out of which the personal representative is entitled to be indemnified include any assets acquired in carrying on the business.

[49] *Re Brooke* [1894] 2 Ch. 600.

[50] *Re Oxley* [1914] 1 Ch. 604; *Re East* (1914) 111 L.T. 101.

[51] *Re Oxley, supra.*

[52] *Re Oxley, supra,* at p. 616.

[53] Or a liability for damages for a tort, *Re Raybould* [1900] 1 Ch. 199 (letting down the surface in the course of carrying on the deceased's colliery business in a reasonable manner).

his right of indemnity. The creditor is therefore entitled in equity to stand in the shoes of the personal representative and obtain payment out of the assets.[54]

The creditor may obtain payment out of the assets to exactly the same extent as the personal representative is entitled to be indemnified out of the assets. To consider a few instances:

(i) If the personal representative carried on the business with a view to proper realisation, his creditor may obtain payment out of the assets as against both the creditors and the beneficiaries of the deceased.

(ii) If the personal representative carried on the business under an authority in the will but not with a view to proper realisation, his creditor may obtain payment out of the authorised assets as against the beneficiaries of the deceased.[55] But a creditor of the deceased who did not assent to the carrying on of the business is entitled to be paid first out of the value of the assets which existed at the death of the deceased.[56]

(iii) If the personal representative owes a larger debt to the authorised assets than to his own creditor, the latter has no right to obtain payment out of these assets unless the personal representative's default is made good.[57] But if only one of three executors is in debt to the authorised assets, their creditors may rely on the right of indemnity of each of the other two executors.[58]

This right of subrogation is most important to the creditor if the personal representative becomes insolvent. In that event, by invoking his right of subrogation, the creditor may be able to obtain payment in full out of the deceased's assets.

Assets and profits of the business. Any assets acquired and any profits made by the personal representative in carrying on the deceased's business belong to the deceased's estate.[59] However, a creditor of the deceased who is entitled to treat the continuance of the business as improper may not be entitled to invoke this principle. Such a creditor has a choice:

(i) If he treats the continuance of the business as improper, he may only make the personal representative accountable for the value of the assets which existed at the death of the deceased: in that

---

[54] *Ex p. Edmonds* (1862) 4 De G.F. & J. 488, 498; *Re Johnson* (1880) 15 Ch.D. 548; *Re Evans* (1887) 34 Ch.D. 597. As to interest on a debt due to the creditor see *Re Bracey* [1936] Ch. 690 (R.S.C., Ord. 44, r. 18 only applies to a debt of the deceased).

[55] *Re Johnson, supra.*

[56] *Re Owen* (1892) 66 L.T. 718 (deceased's creditors assented to carrying on of business: order of priority was (i) executors for administration expenses, (ii) business creditors of executors under right of subrogation, and (iii) deceased's creditors).

[57] *Re Johnson, supra.*

[58] *Re Frith* [1902] 1 Ch. 342.

[59] *Abbott v. Parfitt* (1871) L.R. 6 Q.B. 346 (price due for bread sold by personal representatives carrying on deceased's bakery business was asset of deceased's estate); *Moseley v. Rendell* (1871) L.R. 6 Q.B. 338; *Gibblett v. Read* (1744) 9 Mod. 459.

event the personal representative has no right to be indemnified in priority to him.[60]

(ii) Conversely, if he treats the business as properly continued, the personal representative is accountable to him for assets acquired and profits made in carrying on the business, but the personal representative is entitled to be indemnified in priority to him against liabilities incurred in carrying on the business. Such a creditor "cannot approbate and reprobate in one breath"[61]: if he chooses to adopt the action of the personal representative in continuing the business, he cannot claim priority over the personal representative's right to indemnity.

E. The Deceased's Leaseholds

On the death of a lessee his leasehold interest devolves on his personal representatives[62] without any entry by them.[63] The personal representatives cannot refuse the leasehold interest, even though it is worthless as the rent exceeds the value of the land, because they cannot renounce part of their office.[64] If the lease contains a covenant prohibiting any assignment by the lessee without the lessor's consent, there is no breach of covenant when the leasehold interest devolves by operation of law on the lessee's personal representatives.[65]

When considering the liability of a personal representative for rent or breach of the other covenants in a lease, it is vital to distinguish between two types of liability:

1. Liability as personal representative (or representative liability), which arises from his office; and
2. Personal liability as assignee of the deceased's leasehold interest, which arises if the personal representative enters into possession of the demised premises.

1. Liability as personal representative. The personal representative is liable as such for rent due from the deceased at his death and for any subsisting breach of the other covenants in the lease which were binding on the deceased.[66] Similarly, the personal representative is liable as

---

[60] *Per* Lord Macnaghten in *Dowse* v. *Gorton* [1891] A.C. 190, 203–204 (such creditors may "make the executors accountable for the value of the assets used in carrying on the business, and they may also follow the assets and obtain a charge on the business in the hands of the executors for the value of the assets misapplied, with interest thereon; and they may enforce the charge, if necessary, by means of a receiver and a sale").

[61] *Ibid.* at p. 204.

[62] *Ante*, p. 209.

[63] *Wollaston* v. *Hakewill* (1841) M. & G. 297.

[64] *Billinghurst* v. *Speerman* (1695) 1 Salk. 297; *Rubery* v. *Stevens* (1832) 4 B. & Ad. 241, 244. For renunciation by a personal representative of his office in regard to settled land if he is not a trustee of the settlement, see Administration of Estates Act 1925, s.23(1), and *ante*, p. 178.

[65] *Parry* v. *Harbert* (1539) 1 Dyer 45b.

[66] If the deceased was the original lessee, under privity of contract all the covenants in the lease were binding on him, but if he was an assignee of the lease, under privity of estate only covenants which touched and concerned the land were binding on him: see Megarry and Wade, *The Law of Real Property* (5th ed., 1984), pp. 742 *et seq.*

such for rent falling due and for any breach of these other covenants committed during the period for which he is liable after the death of the deceased.[67] This "liability period" ends, of course, with the determination of the lease. If the deceased was an assignee of the lease (and thus liable under privity of estate but not privity of contract), this liability period also ends with an assignment of the lease by the personal representative. However, if the deceased was the original lessee, his personal representative remains liable as such for rent and any breach of the other covenants during the entire unexpired term of the lease, despite any assignment of the lease by the personal representative.[68]

(1) *Extent of representative liability.* In his representative capacity the personal representative is only liable to the extent of the deceased's assets.[69] He does not incur any personal liability unless he enters into possession of the demised premises.[70]

(2) *Protection against representative liability.* If the deceased was an assignee of the lease, the personal representative may end the liability period by assigning the lease. Indeed, if the lease is onerous (the rent exceeding the value of the land), the personal representative should try to end the liability period as soon as possible by negotiating a surrender of the lease to the lessor or an assignment of the lease to a third party.[71] But if the deceased was the original lessee, an assignment by the personal representative does not end the liability period. However, section 26 of the Trustee Act 1925 provides protection for the personal representative against any representative liability after he has assigned the lease to a purchaser or a beneficiary entitled to it. This protection cannot be excluded by the testator in his will. Section 26[72] provides that if the personal representative (i) satisfies all existing liabilities under the lease which have accrued and have been claimed, (ii) where necessary, sets apart a fund to answer any future claim which may be made in respect of any fixed and ascertained sum which the lessee agreed to lay out on the demised premises, although the period for so doing may not have arrived, and (iii) assigns the lease to a purchaser or beneficiary,[73] thereafter the personal representative may distribute the deceased's residuary estate without setting aside a fund to meet any other future

---

[67] *Youngmin* v. *Heath* [1974] 1 W.L.R. 135 (weekly tenancy of furnished rooms).

[68] *Coghil* v. *Freelove* (1690) 3 Mod. 325; *Pitcher* v. *Tovey* (1692) 4 Mod. 71, 76: and despite any assignment of the lease by the deceased during his lifetime, *Brett* v. *Cumberland* (1619) Cro.Jac. 521.

[69] *Wilson* v. *Wigg* (1808) 10 East 315 (personal representative may plead *plene administravit*, whether breach of covenant was by the deceased or after his death); *Helier* v. *Casebert* (1665) 1 Lev. 127; *Lydall* v. *Dunlapp* (1743) 1 Wils. 4.

[70] *Rendall* v. *Andreae* (1892) 61 L.J.Q.B. 630; *Wollaston* v. *Hakewill* (1841) 3 M. & G. 297, 320–321.

[71] *Rowley* v. *Adams* (1839) 4 My. & Cr. 534: *cf. Rendall* v. *Andreae, supra,* at p. 631.

[72] As amended by Law of Property (Amendment) Act 1926, ss.7 and 8 and Sched.

[73] s.26(1) reads "to a purchaser, legatee, devisee, or other person entitled to call for a conveyance" of the demised premises: s.26 replaced s.27 of the Law of Property Amendment Act 1859, which read "to a purchaser" of the lease: in *Re Lawley* [1911] 2 Ch. 530 this was construed to mean a person who pays a price in money for the lease and not a person who was paid £500 by the personal representative for taking an assignment of the lease. s.26 does not apply to a lease assigned by the deceased, *Re Nixon* [1904] 1 Ch. 638 and see *post,* p. 261.

liability under the lease and the personal representative is not personally liable in respect of any subsequent claim under the lease.[74]

2. Personal liability. If the personal representative[75] (as is usual)
enters into possession of the demised premises, he becomes personally
liable as an assignee of the deceased's leasehold interest.[76] A constructive entry into possession suffices: for example, a personal representative enters into possession if he accepts rent from a sub-tenant.[77] A
personal representative who enters is personally liable for rent falling
due and any breach of the other covenants[78] committed after his entry
into possession so long as the lease is vested in him.[79] He is not personally liable as assignee for breaches committed after he has assigned the
lease.

(1) *Extent of personal liability.* There is a most unusual upper limit on
his personal liability for rent. The personal representative may, by
proper pleading, limit his liability for rent to the actual value of the
premises, *i.e.* the amount he received or might by the exercise of reasonable diligence have received from the premises during his period of
liability as assignee.[80] Presumably this upper limit is meant to prevent
hardship to the personal representative in a case where the rent
reserved exceeds the actual value of the premises. Rather illogically, this
upper limit appears not to be applicable to his personal liability for
breach of other covenants, so that a personal representative who enters
is apparently fully liable for breach of a repairing covenant in the lease,
even though the lease is onerous.[81]

(2) *Protection against personal liability.* Section 26 of the Trustee Act
1925 provides protection for a personal representative against his representative liability but not against his personal liability.[82] A personal
representative who incurs personal liability by entering into possession

---

[74] s.26 does not prejudice the right of the lessor to follow the deceased's assets into the
hands of persons amongst whom they have been distributed, s.26(2): for this remedy see
post, pp. 403 *et seq.* The section also protects the personal representative against representative liability for a rentcharge or under an indemnity covenant, see s.26(1) and (3).
[75] The rule does not apply to an executor *de son tort* because the deceased's leasehold
interest does not devolve on him. *Mayor, Aldermen & Burgesses of Stratford-upon-Avon* v.
Parker [1914] 2 K.B. 562; see *post* p. 410, n. 9.
[76] *Mayor, Aldermen & Burgesses of Stratford-upon-Avon* v. *Parker, ibid.* at p. 567; *Tilney* v.
Norris (1700) 1 Ld.Raym. 553.
[77] *Ibid.* at p. 569.
[78] If they touch and concern the land, so as to be binding on him as assignee under
privity of estate.
[79] *Whitehead* v. *Palmer* [1908] 1 K.B. 151.
[80] *Rendall* v. *Andreae* (1892) 61 L.J.Q.B. 630, 633; *Re Bowes* (1887) 37 Ch.D. 128 (for form of
pleading see *ibid.* at p. 132); *Hornidge* v. *Wilson* (1841) 11 Ad. & E. 645 (executor liable for
value he might have received if he had complied with covenant to repair); *Hopwood* v.
Whaley (1848) 6 C.B. 744. See also *Minford* v. *Carse* [1912] 2 Ir.R. 245 (receiver in possession:
executors not liable for rent).
[81] *Rendall* v. *Andreae, supra,* at p. 633; *Tremeere* v. *Morison* (1834) 1 Bing.N.C. 89; *Sleap* v.
Newman (1862) 12 C.B.(N.S.) 116: but see *Reid* v. *Lord Tenterden* (1833) 4 Tyr. 111, 118 and
120.
[82] *Re Owers* [1941] Ch. 389.

is entitled (i) to have a proper indemnity from the beneficiaries[83] (*e.g.* the beneficiaries may give security) or (ii) to set aside an indemnity fund out of the deceased's estate.[84] The indemnity fund is for the protection of the personal representative and not of the lessor.[85] It is distributable to the beneficiaries when all possible claims against the personal representative have either been satisfied, or become statute-barred by lapse of time since the determination, or assignment by the personal representative, of the lease.[86] If the personal representative assigns the lease to the beneficiary entitled without taking a proper indemnity from him, the personal representative is not then entitled to set aside an indemnity fund out of the deceased's estate.[87]

F. EXERCISE OF POWERS BY PERSONAL REPRESENTATIVES

Sole personal representative. A sole personal representative has the same powers as two or more personal representatives. This is so where a single personal representative was appointed initially or where only one of several personal representatives survives.[88] In particular a sole personal representative, acting as such, may give a valid receipt for, or direct the application of, the proceeds of sale of land[89]: by way of contrast a sole trustee may not do so unless the sole trustee is a trust corporation.[90]

A sole personal representative may contract in his representative capacity with himself as an individual[91]: normally a person cannot make a contract with himself.

Joint personal representatives. The general rule is that joint executors have joint *and several* authority: the act of one of them in exercise of their powers is therefore binding on the other executors and the deceased's estate.[92] This general rule may well apply to joint administrators though there is no decisive authority.[93] To take a few instances:

(i) A sale or other disposition of a chattel comprised in the

---

[83] *Simmons* v. *Bolland* (1817) 3 Mer. 547; *Dobson* v. *Carpenter* (1850) 12 Beav. 370; *Hickling* v. *Boyer* (1851) 3 Mac. & G. 635; *Dean* v. *Allen* (1855) 20 Beav. 1.

[84] *Re Owers, supra.*

[85] *King* v. *Malcott* (1852) 9 Hare 692.

[86] *Re Lewis* [1939] Ch. 232.

[87] *Re Bennett* [1943] 1 All E.R. 467; *Shadbolt* v. *Woodfall* (1845) 2 Coll. 30; *Smith* v. *Smith* (1861) 1 Dr. & Sm. 384.

[88] Administration of Estates Act 1925, s.2(1) and (2). For survivorship of powers see *post,* p. 235.

[89] Law of Property Act 1925, s.27(2) as amended by Law of Property (Amendment) Act 1926, Sched.

[90] *Ibid.*; Settled Land Act 1925, s.18(1); Trustee Act 1925, s.14.

[91] *Rowley, Holmes & Co.* v. *Barber* [1977] 1 W.L.R. 371 (executor of solicitor employed himself as legal executive).

[92] *Jacomb* v. *Harwood* (1751) 2 Ves.Sen. 265, 267; *Attenborough* v. *Solomon* [1913] A.C. 76. For possible reform see Law Reform Committee, 23rd Report, *The powers and duties of trustees,* Cmnd. 8733 (1982), pp. 55–56 and 68.

[93] *Fountain Forestry Ltd.* v. *Edwards* [1975] Ch. 1, 10–14 (where Brightman J. reviewed the case law).

deceased's estate by one of the executors is valid.[94] So, too, is a contract made by one of the executors to sell such a chattel.[95]

(ii) Again one executor may pay a debt due from the deceased,[96] or accept payment of[97] or release[98] a debt due to the estate, or settle an account with a person liable to the estate[99]: in each case the act of the one executor binds them all.

(1) *Statutory exceptions.* This general rule is subject to important statutory exceptions.

(a) CONVEYANCE OF LAND. The rule does not apply to any "conveyance"[1] of freehold or leasehold land[2]: such a conveyance must not be made without the concurrence of all the personal representatives (still living) to whom a grant has been made in respect of the land conveyed, or without an order of the court.[3] A contract to sell land is not a "conveyance": probably, under the general rule, one of two or more executors may enter into a contract binding on the deceased's estate to sell land to a purchaser, although he cannot convey the land to the purchaser without the concurrence of his co-executors or an order of the court.[4] However, there is no contract binding on the deceased's estate if one of two executors, acting without any authority from his co-executor, purports to sign the contract on behalf of himself and as agent of his co-executor[5]: "to put the matter shortly, a contract purporting to be made by two executors jointly cannot be enforced as if it were a contract by one executor severally when it transpires that the other executor did not contract."[6]

(b) SHARES AND STOCK. If personal representatives are registered as the holders of shares or stock in a company incorporated under the Companies Clauses Acts, a transfer is invalid unless executed by all of them.[7] Again, if the company is regulated by the Companies Acts, the

[94] *Kelsack* v. *Nicholson* (1596) Cro.Eliz. 478 and 496; *Jacomb* v. *Harwood, supra.*

[95] *Fountain Forestry Ltd.* v. *Edwards, supra*, at p. 11. Probably one executor cannot validly vary the terms of a contract for sale which all the executors had previously made; see *ibid.* and *Turner* v. *Hardey* (1842) 9 M. & W. 770.

[96] *Jacomb* v. *Harwood, supra*, at pp. 267–268.

[97] *Charlton* v. *Earl of Durham* (1869) 4 Ch.App. 433.

[98] *Herbert* v. *Pigott* (1834) 2 Cr. & M. 384.

[99] *Smith* v. *Everett* (1859) 27 Beav. 446.

[1] "Conveyance" is defined to include "a mortgage, charge by way of legal mortgage, lease, assent, vesting declaration, vesting instrument, disclaimer, release and every other assurance of property or of an interest therein by any instrument, except a will," Administration of Estates Act 1925, s.55(1)(iii). A denial of their landlord's title in a pleading on behalf of one of two executors is not a "conveyance" within this definition, *Warner* v. *Sampson* [1958] 1 Q.B. 404 (reversed on other grounds [1959] 1 Q.B. 297).

[2] Administration of Estates Act 1925, s.3(1). If the deceased died before 1926 the general rule applies to his leasehold land, see *ibid.* s.54; Land Transfer Act 1897, s.2(2) and *Anon.* (1536) 1 Dyer 23(b).

[3] Administration of Estates Act 1925, ss.2(2) and 24.

[4] *Fountain Forestry Ltd.* v. *Edwards* [1975] Ch. 1, 11–12.

[5] *Ibid.; Sneesby* v. *Thorne* (1855) 7 De G.M. & G. 399: the executor who signed is liable in damages for breach of his warranty of authority.

[6] *Ibid.* at p. 15.

[7] *Barton* v. *North Staffordshire Railway Co.* (1888) 38 Ch.D. 458; *Barton* v. *London and North Western Railway Co.* (1889) 24 Q.B.D. 77.

articles of the company usually require a transfer to be executed by all the personal representatives.[8] As to government stock, the Bank of England may decline to give effect to a transfer unless the transfer is executed by all the personal representatives.[9]

(2) *Authority of trustees.* By way of contrast, trustees, unlike executors, must always act jointly. This difference between the authority of executors and trustees may make it essential to decide whether persons appointed to be executors and trustees held particular property as executors or as trustees at the time when one of them sold or otherwise disposed of it. In *Attenborough* v. *Solomon*[10] T by his will appointed his sons X and Y to be executors and trustees and, after bequeathing certain pecuniary legacies, gave his residuary estate to X and Y upon trust for sale and distribution as directed by the will. Within one year of T's death X and Y paid all the debts and expenses and legacies and settled the estate accounts. Fourteen years after T's death X (unknown to Y) pledged certain silver plate comprised in the residuary estate with a pawnbroker A, who did not know that X was not the absolute owner of the plate. X misapplied the money raised by the pledge. After X's death Y discovered the pledge and sued A for the return of the plate. The House of Lords held that the pledge was invalid. Long before the date of the pledge X and Y had assented to the dispositions of the will taking effect, so that at the date of the pledge X and Y held the residuary estate (including the plate) as trustees and not as executors. It followed that X had no power to make a valid pledge because trustees must always act jointly. Of course, if at the date of the pledge X and Y had held the residuary estate as executors, the pledge would have been binding on T's estate under the general rule that executors have joint and several authority.

Powers in the will annexed to an office. By his will a testator may confer powers on the persons who are appointed by him as his executors or his trustees. It is a question of construction of the will whether such a power is intended to be (i) a bare power personal to those persons,[11] or (ii) a power annexed to their office, so as to be exercisable by the holders or holder of the office for the time being.[12]

In *Re Smith*, where the testator conferred a power by his will on "my

---

[8] Companies Act 1985, ss.8, 182 and 183(3); Companies (Alteration of Table A etc.) Regulations 1984 (S.I. 1984 No. 1717), Table A, arts. 29–31.

[9] Government Stock Regulations 1965 (S.I. 1965 No. 1420), reg. 6(2); Finance Act 1942, s.47(2) and Sched. 11, Pt. III.

[10] [1913] A.C. 76.

[11] *Down* v. *Worrall* (1833) 1 M. & K. 561; *Forbes* v. *Forbes* (1854) 18 Beav. 552 (bequest of £2,000 to executors in trust to build a bridge over the river Don, the site "to be chosen by them": Romilly M.R. said power to choose site seemed to have been personal to original executors, who had died without choosing).

[12] *Crawford* v. *Forshaw* [1891] 2 Ch. 261 (power for "my executors herein named" to select charities held annexed to office of executor: two executors who proved could, but renouncing executor could not, exercise power): see also *Lambert* v. *Rendle* (1863) 3 New Rep. 247 (power for executor acting under his will to carry on testator's business; executor renounced: held power not exercisable by administratrix with will annexed).

said trustees," Farwell J. summed up the relevant rule of construction as follows[13]:

> "Every power given to trustees which enables them to deal with or affect the trust property is prima facie given them *ex officio* as an incident of their office, and passes with the office to the holders or holder thereof for the time being: whether a power is so given *ex officio* or not depends in each case on the construction of the document giving it, but the mere fact that the power is one requiring the exercise of a very wide personal discretion is not enough to exclude the prima facie presumption, and little regard is now paid to such minute differences as those between 'my trustees,' 'my trustees A and B,' and 'A and B my trustees': the testator's reliance on the individuals to the exclusion of the holders of the office for the time being must be expressed in clear and apt language."

This rule of construction is equally applicable to a power conferred by will on executors.

Survivorship of powers. Under section 18(1) of the Trustee Act 1925,[14] where a trust or power is imposed on, or given to, personal representatives jointly, it may be performed, or exercised, by the survivors or survivor of them for the time being. In the absence of any contrary direction in the will,[15] this provision applies to all the statutory and common law powers of personal representatives and to all the powers conferred by will which are annexed to their office.[16]

Effect of order for general administration. If in an administration action the court makes an order for general administration (*i.e.* an order for the administration of the deceased's estate under the direction of the court[17]), the personal representatives must not exercise their powers without first obtaining the sanction of the court.[18] Thus if the personal representatives desire to sell, deal with, or distribute any assets of the deceased's estate, they must first apply for the sanction of the court, which is readily given if the court is satisfied that the proposed transaction is a proper one. Such an order does not deprive the personal representatives of their powers but they commit a breach of duty if they exercise them without the sanction of the court.[19]

---

[13] [1904] 1 Ch. 139, 144.

[14] Applicable to personal representatives, Trustee Act 1925, ss.68(1)(17) and 69(1).

[15] *Ibid.* s.69(2).

[16] But not to a bare power given to persons by name and not annexed to an office, *Re Harding* [1923] 1 Ch. 182. See also Williams, Mortimer and Sunnucks, *Executors, Administrators and Probate* (1982), pp. 690–691.

[17] For administration proceedings see *post*, pp. 396 *et seq.*

[18] *Re Viscount Furness* [1943] Ch. 415 (sanction is needed even if the accounts and inquiries ordered are not to be proceeded with except with the leave of the judge in person); *Minors* v. *Battison* (1876) 1 App.Cas. 428.

[19] *Berry* v. *Gibbons* (1873) L.R. 8 Ch.App. 747 (executrix deposited picture as security with bank which had no notice of general administration order: held security was valid); *Re Viscount Furness, supra,* at p. 421: see generally A. J. Hawkins (1968) 84 L.Q.R. 64, 68–73.

G. Deceased a Sole Trustee

If at his death the deceased held property as a sole or last surviving trustee, the property devolves on his personal representatives.[20] To meet this situation section 18(2) of the Trustee Act 1925 provides as follows:

"Until the appointment of new trustees, the personal representatives or representative[21] for the time being of a sole trustee, or, where there were two or more trustees of the last surviving or continuing trustee, shall be capable of exercising or performing any power or trust which was given to, or capable of being exercised by, the sole or last surviving or continuing trustee, or other the trustees or trustee for the time being of the trust."

This provision applies to any trust unless a contrary intention is expressed in the trust instrument.[22]

Personal representative not bound to act as trustee. The personal representative of such a deceased trustee is not bound to perform the trust—he has "an absolute right to decline to accept the position and duties of trustee if he chooses so to do."[23] He is only bound, in his capacity as personal representative, to collect and preserve the property of which the deceased was trustee[24]: he is not bound, for instance, to pay the income of that property to the beneficiary entitled to it under the trust. However under section 18(2) the personal representative may, if he chooses, perform the trust or exercise the power. There is only one restriction—under section 18(2) a sole personal representative (who is not a trust corporation) cannot give a valid receipt for the proceeds of sale or other capital money arising under a trust for sale of land or for capital money arising under the Settled Land Act 1925.[25]

Appointment of new trustees. The personal representative may only perform the trust or exercise the power under section 18(2) "until the appointment of new trustees." An appointment of new trustees may be made under section 36 of the Trustee Act 1925[26]:

(i) by the person or persons nominated for the purpose of appointing new trustees by the trust instrument. (If the persons nominated make an appointment of new trustees but do not include

---

[20] Ante, pp. 209 et seq.: for grants to settled land see ante, pp. 176 et seq.

[21] This does not include an executor who has renounced or has not proved, Trustee Act 1925, s.18(4).

[22] Ibid. s.69(1) and (2).

[23] Re Benett [1906] 1 Ch. 216, 225: see also Legg v. Mackrell (1860) 2 De G.F. & J. 551, Re Ridley [1904] 2 Ch. 774. But as to the personal representative of a Settled Land Act trustee appointed by the court see Settled Land Act 1925, s.34(2).

[24] Re Benett, supra, at pp. 227–228: see also Administration of Estates Act 1925, s.25 as amended by Administration of Estates Act 1971, s.9.

[25] Trustee Act 1925, ss.18(3) and 14(2) (as amended by Law of Property (Amendment) Act 1926, ss.7, 8(2) and Sched.).

[26] Subject to any contrary intention expressed in the trust instrument, ibid. s.69(1) and (2).

the personal representative among the new trustees, this operates to displace the personal representative for all purposes from
the trust.[27])

(ii) if there is no person nominated able and willing to act, by the
personal representative.[28] (The personal representative may
include himself among the new trustees he appoints[29]: if he does
not do so, his own appointment of new trustees displaces him for
all purposes from the trust.)

The personal representative cannot be compelled to exercise his
power to appoint new trustees.[30] If need be, an appointment of new
trustees may be made by the court.[31]

H. Delegation by a Personal Representative

The basic rule is that a personal representative cannot delegate unless
he has authority to do so.[32] The same rule applies to a trustee.[33] There
are several statutory provisions which confer authority on a personal
representative to delegate to an agent. Taken together these statutory
provisions have a wide ambit, but they do not authorise a personal representative to delegate everything to his agent on every occasion. It is
necessary to consider each of the three main statutory provisions in
turn, with a view to ascertaining in each case:

(1) the extent of the personal representative's power to delegate (for
instance, is the personal representative permitted to delegate the
exercise of his powers to the agent?); and

(2) in what circumstances liability is imposed on the personal representative in case loss occurs (for instance, in case the agent disappears, taking with him assets of the deceased's estate).

The three main statutory provisions[34] are all contained in the Trustee
Act 1925. They are:

1. section 23(1), which confers a general power to employ an agent;
2. section 23(2), which confers a power to appoint an agent in
respect of any property forming part of the deceased's estate in
any place outside the United Kingdom; and

[27] *Re Routledge's Trusts* [1909] 1 Ch. 280.

[28] Trustee Act 1925, s.36(1) and (4): for appointment by a renouncing executor see
s.36(5). An executor who has not proved may appoint under section 36(1), but his title to
appoint can only be proved by production of a grant of probate or letters of administration with the will annexed, *Re Crowhurst Park* [1974] 1 W.L.R. 583, 593–594.

[29] *Ibid.* s.36(1).

[30] *Re Knight's Will* (1884) 26 Ch.D. 82.

[31] Trustee Act 1925, s.41(1) and Settled Land Act 1925, s.34.

[32] See generally on delegation, G. H. Jones (1959) 22 M.L.R. 381; W. S. H. (1931) 47
L.Q.R. 463; Law Reform Committee, 23rd Report, *The powers and duties of trustees,*
Cmnd. 8733 (1982), pp. 34–41 and 65–66.

[33] *Pilkington* v. *Inland Revenue Commissioners* [1964] A.C. 612, 639; *Turner* v. *Corney*
(1841) 5 Beav. 515, 517.

[34] Other provisions include (i) Trustee Act 1925, s.8 (employment of valuer when lending money on mortgage), (ii) s.22(4) (audit of accounts by independent accountant), and
(iii) Law of Property Act 1925, s.29 (delegation of powers of management) and Administration of Estates Act 1925, s.39(1).

3. section 25, which confers a power of temporary delegation by power of attorney.

1. General power to employ an agent. Section 23(1) of the Trustee Act 1925 contains the power which is most commonly exercised by personal representatives. It reads as follows:

"Trustees or personal representatives may, instead of acting personally, employ and pay an agent, whether a solicitor, banker, stockbroker or other person, to transact any business or do any act required to be transacted or done in the execution of the trust, or the administration of the testator's or intestate's estate, including the receipt and payment of money, and shall be entitled to be allowed and paid all charges and expenses so incurred, and shall not be responsible for the default of any such agent if employed in good faith."

(1) *Extent of the power.* Under this provision the personal representative may delegate to the agent any business required to be transacted or any act required to be done in the administration of the estate. There is no further requirement (as there was before 1926[35]) that delegation to the agent should be reasonably necessary or in accordance with ordinary business practice. A personal representative "is no longer required to do any actual work himself, but he may employ a solicitor or other agent to do it, whether there is any real necessity for the employment or not."[36] However, there is one significant limit on the extent of the personal representative's power to delegate under section 23(1)—the personal representative may not delegate to the agent the execution of any duty or the exercise of any power or discretion vested in the personal representative. Thus the personal representative may employ a solicitor to carry out the conveyancing work required on a sale of land, or a stockbroker to sell (say) government stock, but under section 23(1) the personal representative has no power to delegate to his agent the decision whether to sell the land or the stock. By way of sharp contrast, both the other main statutory provisions (yet to be considered) expressly authorise delegation of any duty, power or discretion vested in the personal representative.

The general power to employ an agent conferred by section 23(1) is in effect supplemented by section 23(3), which deals with the delegation to an agent of the receipt of money (or other valuable consideration) in certain transactions.[37] Section 23(3) authorises a personal representative to appoint a solicitor[38] to be his agent to receive (say) the price due from a purchaser of land, or money payable under an insurance policy, by producing a deed containing a receipt and executed by the personal representative, or the policy of insurance with a receipt signed by the personal representative.

---

[35] *Ex p. Belchier* (1754) Amb. 218; *Speight* v. *Gaunt* (1883) 22 Ch.D. 727, C.A., (1883) 9 App.Cas. 1, H.L.
[36] *Per* Maugham J. in *Re Vickery* [1931] 1 Ch. 572, 581.
[37] s.23(3) applies to a personal representative, ss.68(1)(17) and 69(1).
[38] Or banker in the case of money payable under an insurance policy, s.23(3)(*c*).

(2) *Liability of the personal representative for loss.* Unfortunately it is not certain what rules govern the liability of the personal representative in case loss occurs following delegation to an agent under section 23(1).

(a) THE RULES BEFORE 1926. The rules in force before 1926 were clear and well settled. A personal representative or trustee had a duty to act as a prudent man of business, both in selecting and in supervising his agent.[39] Thus a personal representative had to employ an agent appropriate to the work to be done[40]—*e.g.* a stockbroker to do stockbrokers' work—and had to take proper care in selecting his agent—selecting a stockbroker who stood in good credit and whose fitness he had no reason to doubt.[41] Again a personal representative had to take proper care in supervising his agent—thus, if anything occurred which would have aroused the suspicions of a prudent man as to the stockbroker's solvency or honesty, the personal representative had to take active steps to protect the assets of the estate.[42] Moreover the personal representative must not leave money or other assets of the estate in the hands of his agent for an unreasonable length of time.[43] But if the personal representative carried out his duty to act as a prudent man of business in the selection and supervision of his agent, the personal representative was not liable for loss caused by the agent.[44]

The question arises whether these rules have been changed since 1925 (i) by section 23(1) and (3), and (ii) by section 30(1) of the Trustee Act 1925.

(b) EFFECT ON LIABILITY OF SECTION 23(1) AND (3). The final words of section 23(1) state that a personal representative "shall not be responsible for the default of any such agent if employed in good faith." On one construction of these words the personal representative's duty has been reduced from the objective standard of proper care in selection and supervision to the subjective level of employment of the agent in good faith.[45]

However it remains uncertain whether section 23(1) has this effect. It may be that these final words in section 23(1) exempt the personal representative who employs in good faith from any possible *vicarious* liability for his agent's default, but leave intact the personal representative's *own duty* to take proper care in the selection and supervision of his agent.[46] The reference in these final words to responsibility for the *agent's default* are appropriate to the exemption of a principal from vicarious responsibility for his agent's default. If before 1926 the per-

[39] *Speight* v. *Gaunt, supra.*
[40] *Fry* v. *Tapson* (1884) 28 Ch.D. 268.
[41] *Speight* v. *Gaunt* (1883) 22 Ch.D. 727, 740, 745, 747 and 762.
[42] *Speight* v. *Gaunt* (1883) 9 App.Cas. 1, 13–15.
[43] *Matthews* v. *Brise* (1843) 6 Beav. 239 (stockbroker sold Exchequer bills left in his hands and misapplied proceeds: trustee held liable to beneficiaries); *Rowland* v. *Witherden* (1851) 3 Mac. & G. 568; *Wyman* v. *Paterson* [1900] A.C. 271.
[44] *Speight* v. *Gaunt, supra.*
[45] Snell's *Principles of Equity* (28th ed., 1982), p. 264 (it seems the liability of trustees "no longer depends on reasonableness but merely on good faith"): *cf.* the wording of the Trustee Act 1925, s.15, see *ante*, p. 215.
[46] G. H. Jones (1959) 22 M.L.R. 381, 394–395, Hanbury and Maudsley, *Modern Equity* (12th ed., 1985), pp. 545–553.

sonal representative committed a breach of his own duty to take proper care in selection and supervision, the personal representative was liable for the loss arising from the breach: probably these final words in section 23(1) do not refer to this liability of the personal representative for breach of his own duty.

In the absence of any decision on the effect of section 23(1) on the liability of a personal representative, a dictum of Maugham J. in *Re Vickery* provides the only judicial guidance available. Referring to section 23(1) Maugham J. said, "No doubt [the personal representative] should use his discretion in selecting an agent, and should employ him only to do acts within the scope of the usual business of the agent. . . ."[47] But which construction of section 23(1) does this dictum support?

A proviso to the supplementary power in section 23(3) expressly preserves the pre-1926 liability of a personal representative in case he permits any money (or other valuable consideration) to remain in the hands of the solicitor for a period longer than is reasonably necessary to enable the solicitor to pay it to the personal representative. This proviso is applicable where the personal representative delegates under this supplementary power.[48] If section 23(1) really does reduce a personal representative's duty to the subjective level of employment of the agent in good faith, it is open to a personal representative to minimise his liability by appointing his agent whenever possible under section 23(1) rather than under 23(3).

(c) EFFECT ON LIABILITY OF SECTION 30(1). Section 30(1) of the Trustee Act 1925 provides as follows:

"A trustee shall be chargeable only for money and securities actually received by him notwithstanding his signing any receipt for the sake of conformity, and shall be answerable and accountable only for his own acts, receipts, neglects, or defaults, and not for those of any other trustee, nor for any banker, broker, or other person with whom any trust money or securities may be deposited, nor for the insufficiency or deficiency of any securities, nor for any other loss, unless the same happens through his own wilful default."

Section 30(1) certainly applies to a personal representative because "trustee" is defined to include a personal representative.[49]

Section 30(1) was not new in 1925. An almost identical statutory provision had been in force since 1859.[50] Moreover the provision in the 1859 Act itself reproduced an indemnity clause commonly inserted by draftsmen in trust instruments before 1859.[51] What effect did this statutory provision have before 1926? Lord Selborne L.C. gave the answer in

---

[47] [1931] 1 Ch. 572, 581.

[48] *Re Vickery, ibid.* at p. 581. The personal representative is not liable under the proviso unless he knew or ought to have known of the solicitor's receipt of the money, *Re Sheppard* [1911] 1 Ch. 50.

[49] Trustee Act 1925, ss.68(1)(17) and 69(1).

[50] Law of Property Amendment Act (or Lord Cranworth's Act) 1859, s.31 repealed and re-enacted by Trustee Act 1893, s.24.

[51] *Re Brier* (1884) 26 Ch.D. 238, 243. For an instance of such an indemnity clause in a will see *Buxton* v. *Buxton* (1835) 1 My. & Cr. 80.

1884 in *Re Brier*,[52] "It does not substantially alter the law as it was administered by Courts of Equity, but gives it the authority and force of statute law, and appears to me to throw the *onus probandi* on those who seek to charge an executor or trustee with a loss arising from the default of an agent, when the propriety of employing an agent has been established." In *Re Brier* a coal merchant was owed a number of small debts at his death. His executors (acting properly) employed an agent to collect the debts but the money collected was lost owing to the agent's insolvency. The Court of Appeal held that the executors were not liable for this loss unless it occurred due to their wilful default (for instance, because "the executors were negligent"[53]), and the burden of proving this lay on the persons who sought to charge the executors with the loss. "Wilful default" was (and still is) a technical expression of equity. A personal representative or trustee normally has to account only for assets which he has actually received. But he may be ordered to account upon the footing of wilful default, *i.e.* to account in addition for assets which he would have received but for his own wilful default.[54] In this context wilful default means a breach of duty by the accounting party which caused a loss of assets.[55] Before 1926 the words "wilful default" at the end of this statutory provision were construed in the same sense. In *Re Chapman*[56] (decided in 1896) the testator held a number of mortgage securities on different freehold farms. The trustees of his will retained these mortgage securities (which were authorised investments) for 13 years after his death. During this period the farms gradually fell in value owing to the agricultural depression, and by the end of this period the securities were insufficient and could only be realised at a considerable loss. The Court of Appeal held that the trustees were not liable for this loss. As Lindley L.J. put it,[57]

"Trustees acting honestly, with ordinary prudence and within the limits of their trust, are not liable for mere errors of judgment. . . . To throw on the trustees the loss sustained by the fall in value of securities authorised by the trust, wilful default, which includes want of ordinary prudence on the part of the trustees, must be proved; but it is not proved in this case."

To sum up the effect of this statutory provision before 1926, (i) the burden of proving wilful default lay on the persons who sought to charge the personal representative with any loss which had arisen following delegation to any agent, and (ii) wilful default meant a breach of duty by the personal representative which caused the loss—for instance, a breach of his duty to use proper prudence.

[52] *Re Brier, supra*, at p. 243. But *cf.* Romer J.'s explanation of *Re Brier* in *Re City Equitable Fire Insurance Co. Ltd.* [1925] Ch. 407, 438–439.
[53] *Ibid.* at p. 243 (an interjection of Lord Selborne L.C. in argument).
[54] *Post*, pp. 388–389.
[55] *Re Stevens* [1898] 1 Ch. 162, 170 and 175; *Job* v. *Job* (1877) 6 Ch.D. 562, 564–565; *Re Tebbs* [1976] 1 W.L.R. 924 (*post*, p. 389); *Bartlett* v. *Barclays Bank Trust Co. Ltd. (No. 2)* [1980] Ch. 515, 545–546 (wilful default does not require conscious wrongdoing): see generally J. E. Stannard [1979] Conv. 345: *cf.* J. A. Andrews (1981) 1 Legal Studies, 303, 310–311 and 322.
[56] [1896] 2 Ch. 763: see also *Speight* v. *Gaunt* (1883) 9 App.Cas. 1, 13–14.
[57] *Ibid.* at p. 776.

In 1931 in *Re Vickery*[58] Maugham J. put a radically different meaning on the words "wilful default" in section 30(1) of the Trustee Act 1925. The defendant S, as sole executor of the deceased, employed J, a local solicitor, to wind up her estate. The plaintiffs were the beneficiaries entitled to her residuary estate, which included £214 in the Post Office Savings Bank and £62 in Savings Certificates. J obtained a grant of probate to S and with S's authority collected these sums of £214 and £62. In September S learnt for the first time that J had a tarnished reputation for dishonesty, having in the past been suspended for five years by the Law Society, and one of the plaintiffs pressed S to change his solicitor but S did not do so as J was promising to complete the matter in a very few days. S continued to press J for an immediate settlement and J promised this repeatedly. Early in December S instructed another solicitor and thereafter obtained from the court an order against J for an account, but J absconded and these sums were lost. Maugham J. held that S was not liable for this loss because he was guilty only of an error of judgment in not changing his solicitor in September, and this did not amount to wilful default within section 30(1). To quote from his judgment[59]:

> "I think that, where an executor employs a solicitor or other agent to receive money belonging to the estate in reliance on s.23, sub-s. 1, of the Trustee Act 1925, he will not be liable for a loss of the money occasioned by the misconduct of the agent unless the loss happens through the wilful default of the executor, using those words as implying . . . either a consciousness of negligence or breach of duty, or a recklessness in the performance of a duty."

Maugham J. took this meaning of "wilful default" from a decision of the Court of Appeal in *Re City Equitable Fire Insurance Company, Limited*[60] where a clause in the company's articles exempted the directors and auditors from liability for loss unless it happened through their own "wilful neglect or default." In this case Warrington L.J. warned against the "great danger of being misled" if one attempted to apply decisions on the duties of trustees in order to determine the liability of auditors under a clause in a company's articles.[61] Maugham J. reversed this process and applied this decision on the duties of auditors under a clause in a company's articles in order to determine the liability of an executor under section 30(1) of the Trustee Act 1925.

If Maugham J.'s construction of "wilful default" in section 30(1) is good law, then a personal representative is not liable for the loss of assets received by an agent appointed under section 23(1) unless the personal representative was conscious that, in doing the act which is complained of or in omitting to do the act which it is said he ought to have done, he was committing a breach of duty, or he was recklessly careless whether it was a breach of his duty or not. However, Maugham J.'s construction is unlikely to be followed because it is not compatible

---

[58] [1931] 1 Ch. 572: see also *Re Munton* [1927] 1 Ch. 262, 274–275.
[59] *Ibid.* at pp. 583–584.
[60] [1925] 1 Ch. 407, esp. pp. 430–442 (and note Romer J. never referred to *Re Chapman* or *Speight* v. *Gaunt*) and 516–518, 521–525, and 528–529.
[61] *Ibid.* at pp. 523–524.

with the pre-1926 authorities and it does not set an objective standard of prudent conduct for personal representatives. This is not to say that S would have been held liable in *Re Vickery* if Maugham J. had applied the pre-1926 rule that a personal representative must take proper care in supervising his agent: if a personal representative took proper care, he was not liable for "mere errors of judgment."[62]

(d) WHEN IS WILFUL DEFAULT MATERIAL? On what occasions does section 30(1) require wilful default (whatever its meaning) to be established in order to make a personal representative liable? Maugham J. in *Re Vickery* gave a list—losses occasioned by his signing receipts for the sake of conformity, or by reason of the wrongful acts or defaults of another personal representative or of an agent with whom trust money or securities have been deposited, or by the insufficiency or deficiency of any securities, or "some other analogous loss."[63]

In *Re Lucking's Will Trusts*[64] Cross J. discussed the liability of a trustee who employs a manager for an unincorporated business owned by the trust. He rejected the argument that such a trustee would only be liable for his negligence in supervising the manager if wilful default by the trustee was established: section 30(1) was not applicable because the manager was not a person with whom trust money or securities were deposited. This indicates that the category of "some other analogous loss" is a narrow one.

2. Property outside the United Kingdom. Section 23(2) of the Trustee Act 1925 confers on a personal representative power to appoint any person to act as his agent or attorney in respect of any property forming part of the deceased's estate in any place outside the United Kingdom.

(1) *Extent of the power.* Under this provision the personal representative may delegate to the agent the collection, sale, or management of this foreign property,[65] and also the execution of any trust (or any duty incident to the office of personal representative[66]) or the exercise of any power or discretion vested in the personal representative in relation to it.

(2) *Liability of the personal representative for loss.* Section 23(2) concludes with the cryptic statement that the personal representatives "shall not, by reason only of their having made such appointment, be responsible for any loss arising thereby." This appears to leave intact the personal representative's duty to take proper care in the selection and supervision of the agent. The effect (if any) of section 30(1) on this duty has already been discussed.

---

[62] *Ante*, p. 241.
[63] [1931] 1 Ch. 572, 582.
[64] [1968] 1 W.L.R. 866, 873–874.
[65] And also "executing and perfecting insurances" of it—the word "insurances" being "obviously a misprint for assurances," *per* Eve J. in *Green* v. *Whitehead* [1930] 1 Ch. 38, 45.
[66] Trustee Act 1925, s.68(1)(17).

3. Temporary delegation by power of attorney. Under section 25 of the Trustee Act 1925[67] a personal representative has a wide power of temporary delegation by power of attorney. In practice a personal representative is most likely to delegate by this means on the occasion of his absence abroad but the exercise of the power is not restricted to any particular occasion.

(1) *Extent of the power.* By power of attorney the personal representative may delegate the execution of any trust (or any duty incident to the office of personal representative[66]) or the exercise of any power or discretion vested in him as personal representative, either alone or jointly with any other person. The delegation must be for a period not exceeding 12 months and, if there are only two personal representatives, must not be made to the other personal representative, unless a trust corporation.

(2) *Liability of the personal representative for loss.* Section 25(5) makes the personal representative liable for the attorney's acts or defaults in the same manner as if they were his own. This obviously makes it important for the personal representative to select a suitable attorney.

Direction in will. These statutory powers of a personal representative to delegate to an agent apply subject to any contrary intention expressed in the deceased's will,[68] but such a contrary intention is rarely, if ever, expressed. Sometimes a will contains an express indemnity clause protecting an executor against any liability for loss unless (to quote the widest form of clause) the loss has been caused by his own actual fraud. This form of clause confers an extremely wide protection and many draftsmen would regard it as inappropriate for any executor who is to be paid for his services.

A direction by a testator in his will that a named solicitor shall be "the solicitor to my estate and to my said trustees in the management and carrying out the provisions of this my will" is not binding on the executors and trustees of his will.[69] They may choose their own agents.

I. REMUNERATION OF PERSONAL REPRESENTATIVES

The fundamental principle is that a personal representative, like a trustee, is not entitled to any remuneration for the work he does[70] unless he is in some way authorised to receive remuneration. If he accepts the office, then, in so far as he is not authorised to receive remuneration, he must give his services gratuitously, though he is

---

[67] As amended by Powers of Attorney Act 1971, s.9. Beware of the now misleading marginal note referring to delegation during absence abroad. A power of attorney under s.25 cannot be an enduring power, Enduring Powers of Attorney Act 1985, s.2(8).

[68] Trustee Act 1925, s.69(2).

[69] *Foster* v. *Elsley* (1881) 19 Ch.D. 518: see also *Shaw* v. *Lawless* (1838) 5 Cl. & F. 129.

[70] *Robinson* v. *Pett* (1734) 3 P.Wms. 249 ("It is an established rule, that a trustee, executor, or administrator, shall have no allowance for his care and trouble"); *Brocksopp* v. *Barnes* (1820) 5 Madd. 90; *Re White* [1898] 2 Ch. 217.

entitled to reimburse himself out of the deceased's estate for his out-of-pocket expenses.[71] However there are several different ways in which a personal representative may acquire authority to receive remuneration for his services. These must now be considered in turn.

1. Legacy given to proving executors. The most obvious way is by the testator making a gift by will to each of his executors who proves his will or, alternatively (a wider form) who accepts office.[72] Such a gift encourages an executor to prove the will and not renounce. Usually such a gift takes the form of a pecuniary legacy.

There is a presumption that any specific or general legacy given to a person appointed executor is meant to be conditional on his accepting the office.[73] This presumption may of course be rebutted—for instance, by the testator expressing some other motive for giving the legacy[74]— and the presumption does not apply to a gift of residue[75] or a gift of a legacy in remainder after a life interest.[76] In order to avoid doubt as to whether the presumption is applicable, any gift made by will to a person appointed executor should either be expressed as conditional (*e.g.* "if he shall prove this will") or as unconditional (*e.g.* "whether or not he shall prove this will").

2. Charging clause in will. By his will the testator may authorise his executors to charge and be paid remuneration for their services. Such a "charging clause" is a form of gift which is commonly inserted in a will because otherwise a professional person, such as a solicitor or account-ant, is unlikely to be willing to act as executor.

(1) *Construction of charging clause.* Which executors may charge? At what rate? And for what services? The answers to these questions depend on the proper construction of the particular charging clause. Often a charging clause authorises any executor engaged in any pro-fession[77] or business to charge his usual professional or proper charges.[78] But for what services may he charge? The charging clause may authorise him to charge only for work which could not have been done by a layman: if so, an executor who is a solicitor is not entitled to charge for work which a layman could have done for himself.[79] On the other hand, the charging clause may (and in current practice usually does) authorise the executor to charge both for professional services and

---

[71] *Post,* p. 256.

[72] *Ante,* p. 148.

[73] *Re Appleton* (1885) 29 Ch.D. 893; *Stackpoole* v. *Howell* (1807) 13 Ves. 417. See generally Hawkins and Ryder on *The Construction of Wills* (1965), pp. 398–400.

[74] *Bubb* v. *Yelverton* (1871) 13 Eq. 131 (gift of £1,000 to each executor "as a remem-brance": held executor who did not act was entitled); *Cockerell* v. *Barber* (1826) 2 Russ. 585.

[75] *Griffiths* v. *Pruen* (1840) 11 Sim. 202; *Christian* v. *Devereux* (1841) 12 Sim. 264; *Re Max-well* [1906] 1 I.R. 386: but see *Barber* v. *Barber* (1838) 3 My. & Cr. 688.

[76] *Re Reeve's Trusts* (1877) 4 Ch.D. 841.

[77] *Re Wertheimer* (1912) 106 L.T. 590 (executor who was British Museum keeper of anti-quities entitled to charge for professional services in selling testator's works of art).

[78] *Re Fish* [1893] 2 Ch. 413 (one trustee cannot settle charges of other solicitor-trustee so as to bind beneficiaries); *Willis* v. *Kibble* (1839) 1 Beav. 559; *Re Wells* [1962] 1 W.L.R. 874.

[79] *Re Chapple* (1884) 27 Ch.D. 584; *Re Chalinder & Herington* [1907] 1 Ch. 58; *Harbin* v. *Darby* (1860) 28 Beav. 325: see also *Clarkson* v. *Robinson* [1900] 2 Ch. 722.

for work which a layman could have done for himself: if so, a solicitor-executor may charge for all the work he does.[80] It has been said that a charging clause "has always received a strict interpretation from the courts"[81]: certainly, in so far as a charging clause on its proper construction does not authorise remuneration, a personal representative must (in accordance with the general principle) give his services gratuitously.

This form of charging clause, which is appropriate to an executor engaged in any profession or business, does not empower a trust corporation (such as a bank appointed to be an executor) to charge its scale fees.[82] For this purpose a charging clause appropriate to a trust corporation is needed.[83]

(2) *A charging clause is a legacy.* A charging clause in a will constitutes a conditional legacy to the executor, just as a gift by will of £100 to the executor for his trouble if he proves the will is a conditional legacy. A charging clause is therefore subject to the rules which govern legacies in a will.[84]

(a) EXECUTOR OR SPOUSE AN ATTESTING WITNESS. Section 15 of the Wills Act 1837 deprives an attesting witness, and his or her spouse, of any benefit under a legacy in the will.[85] It follows that if a solicitor-executor (or the solicitor's spouse) attests the will, the solicitor is not entitled to any remuneration for his services under a charging clause in the will.[86] Of course the solicitor-executor's attestation of the will does not disqualify his co-executor (not being the solicitor's spouse) from taking remuneration for his services under the charging clause.

(b) INSOLVENT ESTATE. If the deceased's estate is insolvent, his funeral, testamentary and administration expenses, debts and liabilities must be paid so far as possible.[87] No legacy can be paid because no part of the estate is left after payment of expenses, debts and liabilities. Thus, if the

---

[80] *Re Ames* (1883) 25 Ch.D. 72; *Re Fish, supra.* An example (from *Hallet's Conveyancing Precedents* (1965), p. 1044) reads, "Any of my Executors or my Trustees who shall be an individual engaged in any profession or business may be employed by my Executors or my Trustees and shall be entitled to charge and be paid all professional or other reasonable and proper charges for any business done or services rendered or time spent by him or his firm in connection with the administration of my estate or the trusts powers or provisions of this Will or any codicil hereto whether or not within the usual scope of his profession or business and although not of a nature requiring the employment of a professional or business person."

[81] *Per* Harman J. in *Re Gee* [1948] Ch. 284, 292; *Re Orwell's W.T.* [1982] 3 All E.R. 177, 179. A clause authorising an executor to retain directors' fees may also be advisable: see *Re Llewellin's W.T.* [1949] Ch. 225.

[82] *Re Cooper* (1939) 160 L.T. 453; *In the Estate of Campbell* [1954] 1 W.L.R. 516.

[83] Each bank or insurance company undertaking such business is ready to supply its own recommended current form of charging clause. Usually the charges include both an acceptance fee and a withdrawal fee (payable out of capital) and an income fee. For an instance see *Re Waterman's W.T.* [1952] 2 All E.R. 1054.

[84] But remuneration under a charging clause may be "earned" for tax purposes, *Dale* v. *I.R.C.* [1954] A.C. 11.

[85] *Post,* p. 334.

[86] *Re Pooley* (1888) 40 Ch.D. 1: *cf. Re Royce's W.T.* [1959] Ch. 626 (solicitor appointed trustee of will after testator's death may rely on charging clause though an attesting witness).

[87] *Post,* pp. 285 *et seq.*

deceased's estate turns out to be insolvent, an executor is not entitled to any remuneration for his services under a charging clause in the will.[88]

(c) ABATES AS A PECUNIARY LEGACY. If the deceased's estate is solvent but there are insufficient assets available to pay his pecuniary legacies in full, then the pecuniary legacies abate rateably.[89] For instance, if there are only sufficient assets available to pay one-third of the total amount of the pecuniary legacies, then each legatee receives only one-third of the amount of his pecuniary legacy. The sum payable to an executor as remuneration under a charging clause is a pecuniary legacy[90] and abates rateably with the other pecuniary legacies,[91] unless (exceptionally) there is a provision in the will giving the executor priority over the other pecuniary legatees.

If an executor is disqualified under these rules from relying on a charging clause, he is nevertheless entitled by virtue of his office of personal representative to reimbursement out of the estate for his out-of-pocket expenses.

(3) *Solicitor-executor with no charging clause.* In the absence of a charging clause on which he can rely or any other authority to receive remuneration, a solicitor-executor, like any other executor, is not entitled to remuneration for his services, but only to reimbursement for his out-of-pocket expenses.[92] The rule is just as much applicable if the solicitor-executor employs his own firm, of which he is a partner, to perform the services: the firm is not entitled to remuneration for its services because the solicitor-executor is in effect acting as his own solicitor.[93]

Of course a solicitor-executor may employ another solicitor to act for him and may reimburse himself out of the estate for his out-of-pocket expenses, including the amount properly paid to the other solicitor. A solicitor-executor may therefore employ his partner (as opposed to the firm which includes himself) to act for him and pay his partner's proper charges, provided that it has been expressly agreed between him and his partner that he shall not derive any benefit from the charges.[94]

---

[88] *Re White* [1898] 1 Ch. 297, [1898] 2 Ch. 217; *Re Salmen* (1912) 107 L.T. 108. But the court may authorise remuneration in a proper case, *post*, p. 248. For possible reform see Law Reform Committee, 23rd Report, *The powers and duties of trustees*, Cmnd. 8733 (1982), pp. 27 and 64.

[89] For the abatement of pecuniary legacies see *post*, pp. 271 and 299.

[90] Administration of Estates Act 1925, s.55(1)(ix).

[91] *Re Brown* [1918] W.N. 118 (amount due to solicitor under charging clause to be ascertained when work done and to abate rateably); *Commissioner of Stamp Duties of New South Wales* v. *Pearse* [1954] A.C. 91, 113. For possible reform see Law Reform Committee, 23rd Report, *supra*.

[92] *Moore* v. *Frowd* (1837) 3 My. & Cr. 45; *Todd* v. *Wilson* (1849) 9 Beav. 486.

[93] *Re Corsellis* (1887) 34 Ch.D. 675; *Re Gates* [1933] Ch. 913 (rule applies though solicitor-executor agrees with partners not to share in profit costs); *Re Hill* [1934] Ch. 623 (rule applies though solicitor-executor is a salaried partner); *Christophers* v. *White* (1847) 10 Beav. 523 (rule applies though other partners do the work).

[94] *Clack* v. *Carlon* (1861) 30 L.J.Ch. 639 (*quoad* the transaction the solicitor-executor and his partner must not be in partnership); *Re Doody* [1893] 1 Ch. 129, 134; *Re Hill, supra*, at pp. 631 and 633–634.

3. Contract with beneficiaries. A personal representative may contract with beneficiaries entitled under the deceased's will or intestacy (and who are *sui juris*) for remuneration to be paid to him for his services out of the assets to which they are entitled. Again, a personal representative may presumably make a similar contract with creditors of the deceased. To be valid such a contract must not be made as a result of undue influence by the personal representative.[95] Moreover, unless the contract is made under seal, it must be supported by valuable consideration: if (say) letters of administration have already been granted to the personal representative he may well not furnish consideration by promising to perform, or performing, his existing duty to administer the estate according to law.[96]

4. Order of the court. The court may authorise remuneration for a personal representative (or a trustee) in the exercise of its inherent jurisdiction to secure the competent administration of the estate.[97] Remuneration may be authorised for his past[98] and future[99] services, and the remuneration authorised by a charging clause in the will may be increased, whether or not he has already accepted office.[1] The court only authorises remuneration in a proper case,[2] where it is in the interests of the creditors[3] or the beneficiaries[4] to do so.

The court has a statutory jurisdiction to authorise remuneration for a corporation (other than the Public Trustee[5]) where the court appoints the corporation to be a personal representative, either solely or jointly with another person.[6] Thus, on granting letters of administration to a bank, the court may authorise the bank to charge for its services.[7] The court may also authorise a person appointed as a substituted personal

---

[95] *Gould v. Fleetwood* (1732) 3 P.Wms. 251, n. [A] (executor agreed with residuary legatees to act in return for 100 guineas but died before completing his task; held not entitled and the court said, "all bargains of this kind ought to be discouraged, as tending to eat up the trust"); *Aycliffe v. Murray* (1740) 2 Atk. 58 (court would be "extremely cautious and wary" in upholding such a contract).

[96] See A. L. Goodhart (1956) 72 L.Q.R. 490.

[97] *Re Duke of Norfolk's S.T.* [1982] Ch. 61 (reviewing the cases): see also *Forster v. Ridley* (1864) 4 De G.J. & S. 452 (executors remunerated for managing deceased's leaseholds and carrying on business); *Re Freeman's S.T.* (1887) 37 Ch.D. 148 (remuneration for trustee). For possible reform see Law Reform Committee, 23rd Report, *The powers and duties of trustees*, Cmnd. 8733 (1982), pp. 29–30 and 64 (professional persons acting as administrators).

[98] *Re Macadam* [1946] Ch. 73 (trustees holding company shares remunerated for exceptional work as directors); *Re Masters* [1953] 1 W.L.R. 81 (bank remunerated for acting as administrator and trustee); *Re Keeler's S.T.* [1981] Ch. 157: see also *Boardman v. Phipps* [1967] 2 A.C. 46, 104 and 112.

[99] *Re Duke of Norfolk's S.T.*, *supra*, (future services of trust corporation).

[1] *Ibid.*

[2] *Re Worthington* [1954] 1 W.L.R. 526 (remuneration refused to solicitor-administrator in absence of exceptional circumstances); *Re Barbour's S.T.* [1974] 1 W.L.R. 1198, 1203.

[3] *Re Duke of Norfolk's S.T. supra*, at p. 77 (order of court authorising remuneration binds creditors of insolvent estate); *Re Worthington, supra*.

[4] *Re Duke of Norfolk's S.T. supra*, at p. 79.

[5] The Public Trustee has statutory authority to charge fees, Public Trustee Act 1906, s.9, as amended by Public Trustee (Fees) Act 1957 and fees orders made thereunder.

[6] Trustee Act 1925, ss.42, 68(1), (17) and 69(1).

[7] *In the Estates of Young* [1934] W.N. 106; *Re Masters, supra*.

representative to charge remuneration for his services.[8] Again, if the court appoints a judicial trustee under the Judicial Trustees Act 1896, the court may assign remuneration to him.[9] The court may in its discretion appoint a judicial trustee so as to provide a remedy in a case where the administration of the deceased's estate by his executor or administrator has broken down and it is not desired to put the estate to the expense of a general administration by the court.[10] Similarly, the court may assign reasonable remuneration to an administrator pending suit.[11]

5. The Rule in Cradock v. Piper. Under the Rule in *Cradock v. Piper*[12] a solicitor who is a personal representative (or his firm) is entitled to profit costs for work done in connection with litigation on behalf of the personal representatives jointly, except so far as the costs have been increased by his being one of the parties. The Rule applies whether the litigation is hostile (*e.g.* an action by or against the personal representatives) or friendly (*e.g.* an application in chambers for the maintenance of an infant[13]). But the Rule does not apply to work done on behalf of the solicitor alone[14]—he must have acted on behalf of himself and his co-executor or co-administrator jointly. Moreover the Rule has no application at all to non-litigious work[15] and is therefore of relatively narrow ambit. The Rule "must be taken as settled but it is exceptional and anomalous and not to be extended."[16]

6. Foreign remuneration received without volition. In *Re Northcote's Will Trusts*[17] the deceased died domiciled in England and his executors took an English grant of probate. Then, in accordance with an undertaking given by them to the Inland Revenue, they obtained a grant in New York State in respect of the deceased's American assets. Under the law of that state they were entitled to a commission on the American assets got in by them. Harman J. held that the executors might keep this commission, which never formed part of the English assets, and which came to them without their volition because they were under an obligation to carry out their undertaking. The ambit of this rule appears to be very narrow indeed.

The Committee of Enquiry into the Public Trustee Office recommended legislation enabling all professional or corporate trustees to charge for their services, whether or not the will includes a charging

---

[8] Administration of Justice Act 1985, s.50(3): see *post*, p. 399.
[9] Judicial Trustees Act 1896, s.1(5); Judicial Trustee Rules 1983 (S.I. 1983 No. 370), reg. 11.
[10] *Re Ridsdel* [1947] Ch. 597, 605: see also *Re Ratcliff* [1898] 2 Ch. 352 and *Re Wells* [1968] 1 W.L.R. 44: see *post*, p. 399.
[11] Supreme Court Act 1981, s.117(3): see also *Re Howlett* [1950] P. 177: see *ante*, p. 186.
[12] (1850) 1 Mac. & G. 664.
[13] *Re Corsellis* (1887) 34 Ch.D. 675.
[14] *Lyon v. Baker* (1852) 5 De G. & Sm. 622.
[15] *Re Corsellis, supra; Broughton* v. *Broughton* (1855) 5 De G.M. & G. 160.
[16] *Re Worthington* [1954] 1 W.L.R. 526, 529; see also *Re Corsellis, supra,* at pp. 682–683, 687–688 and 689; *Re Doody* [1893] 1 Ch. 129, 141–142.
[17] [1949] 1 All E.R. 442. See also *Denton v. Davy* (1836) 1 Moo.P.C. 15 and *Campbell v. Campbell* (1842) 13 Sim. 168.

clause.[18] If implemented this recommendation would confer on those personal representatives who are members of a profession, such as solicitors or accountants, or who are corporations, a general authority to charge for their services. At present only the Public Trustee enjoys such a general authority.

CHAPTER 10

PAYMENT OF EXPENSES AND DEBTS

1. ASSETS, EXPENSES AND DEBTS

A. WHAT ARE ASSETS?

The question what property devolves on personal representatives has already been considered.[1] Now a different question arises—what property constitutes assets for the payment of the deceased's debts and liabilities? Section 32(1) of the Administration of Estates Act 1925 defines two categories of property which constitute assets as follows:

> "The real and personal estate, whether legal or equitable, of a deceased person, to the extent of his beneficial interest therein, and the real and personal estate of which a deceased person in pursuance of any general power (including the statutory power to dispose of entailed interests) disposes by his will, are assets for payment of his debts (whether by specialty or simple contract) and liabilities, and any disposition by will inconsistent with this enactment is void as against the creditors. . . . "

This is not an exhaustive definition of assets and other categories of property which constitute assets must also be considered.[2]

1. Deceased's estate to the extent of his beneficial interest. The first category mentioned in section 32(1) is "the real and personal estate, whether legal or equitable, of a deceased person, to the extent of his beneficial interest therein." Thus the entire real[3] and personal estate of the deceased constitutes assets to the extent of the deceased's beneficial interest in it. If at his death the deceased held property as a sole or last surviving trustee so that the property devolves on his personal representatives, this trust property is not assets,[4] though any beneficial interest of the deceased therein (not ceasing on his death) constitutes assets.

The following property constitutes assets in the hands of a personal representative, whether or not it falls within section 32(1).

---

[1] *Ante*, pp. 209 *et seq.*
[2] For foreign property of the deceased see Dicey and Morris. *The Conflict of Laws* (11th ed., 1987), pp. 993 *et seq.*
[3] Real estate means real estate, including chattels real, which devolves on the personal representative, Administration of Estates Act 1925, s.55(1)(xix) and see *ante*, p. 210.
[4] *Re Webb* [1941] Ch. 225; *Re Gordon* [1940] Ch. 851; *Hassall* v. *Smithers* (1806) 12 Ves. 119.

(1) *Transactions defrauding creditors.* If the deceased during his lifetime entered into a transaction which is set aside after his death as defrauding his creditors,[5] any property recovered by his personal representatives constitutes assets in their hands.[6]

(2) *Income and assets arising after death.* Income arising after death from the deceased's beneficial interest in his real and personal estate is assets. Thus the income of the deceased's residuary estate arising after his death is assets.[7] So, too, are assets "by increase," such as the lambs born to the deceased's sheep after his death.[8] Again, any property acquired and any profits made by the personal representative in carrying on the deceased's business after his death are assets.[9]

(3) *Benefits for which personal representative is accountable.* A personal representative, like a trustee, is accountable for benefits received by him by virtue of his position as personal representative and such benefits constitute assets for the payment of the deceased's debts and liabilities. For instance, under the Rule in *Keech* v. *Sandford*,[10] if a personal representative obtains a renewal of a lease of property which was vested in him as personal representative, he holds the new lease for the benefit of the deceased's estate[11] and the new lease therefore constitutes assets.

2. Property appointed by will under a general power. The second category of property mentioned in section 32(1) is realty and personalty of which the deceased "in pursuance of any general power[12] (including the statutory power to dispose of entailed interests) disposes by his will."

(1) *Entailed interest.* If at his death the deceased is tenant in tail in possession of Blackacre and disposes by will of the fee simple in Blackacre pursuant to his statutory power,[13] then under section 32(1) the fee simple in Blackacre constitutes assets and (as has already been noted)

---

[5] Insolvency Act 1986, ss.423–425.
[6] For the operation of Law of Property Act 1925, s.172 (now repealed) see *Re Eichholz* [1959] Ch. 708, 723–724; *Shears* v. *Rogers* (1832) 3 B. & Ad. 362: see also *Cadogan* v. *Cadogan* [1977] 1 W.L.R. 1041.
[7] *Re Tong* [1931] 1 Ch. 202.
[8] *Re Tong* [1930] 2 Ch. 400, 404.
[9] For this rule and its limits see *ante*, p. 228.
[10] (1726) Sel.Cas. t. King 61: see generally Cretney (1969) 33 Conv.(N.S.) 161. The Rule in *Keech* v. *Sandford* applies to an executor *de son tort*, *Mulvany* v. *Dillon* (1810) 1 Ball & B. 409. For another instance see *Re Edwards' W.T.* [1982] Ch. 30.
[11] *Bromfield* v. *Chichester* (1773) 2 Dick. 480 (executrix renewed leases held by deceased: court declared she held renewed leases for benefit of deceased's estate: *James* v. *Dean* (1805) 11 Ves. 392; *Re Thompson* [1930] 1 Ch. 203: *cf Re Biss* [1903] 2 Ch. 40 (landlord refused renewal to administratrix of deceased tenant and granted new lease to one of next of kin: latter was held entitled to retain lease).
[12] *Re Phillips* [1931] 1 Ch. 347: see A. D. Hughes (1962) 26 Conv.(N.S.) 25, esp. at pp. 32–34; Williams, Mortimer and Sunnucks, *Executors, Administrators and Probate* (1982), pp. 551–552.
[13] Law of Property Act 1925, s.176: the will must refer specifically to Blackacre, or to the instrument under which it was acquired, or to entailed property generally: see *post*, p. 431.

devolves on the deceased's personal representatives.[14] On the other hand an unbarred entail is not assets for the payment of the debts of the deceased tenant in tail.[15]

(2) *Appointment by will.* To consider an example:

By a settlement land and company shares are settled on trust for D for life and after his death on trust for such person or persons as D shall by deed or will appoint and in default of appointment for E absolutely.

If by his will D exercises his general power of appointment in favour of F absolutely, then under section 32(1) both the land and the company shares constitute assets for the payment of D's debts and liabilities.[16] Land appointed by will under a general power devolves on the deceased's personal representatives but, by an anomaly, pure personalty so appointed does not do so.[17] Thus the company shares do not vest in D's personal representatives but nevertheless D's personal representatives are entitled on the ground of practical convenience to receive the company shares from the settlement trustees, and then to pay the debts and liabilities out of them.[18] After the debts and liabilities have been paid, F is entitled to any surplus of the land and the company shares appointed to him.

It is immaterial that during his lifetime D borrowed money from F and contracted for value with F to exercise by will his general power of appointment in F's favour. If by his will D appoints in favour of F, then under section 32(1) the appointed property is made assets for the payment of *all* D's creditors: D cannot prefer F to his other creditors by this means.[19]

Section 32(1) only applies if by his will D exercises his general power of appointment.[20] If D does not do so, E takes in default of appointment and the settled property does not constitute assets for the payment of D's debts and liabilities.[21] Of course, if D does not do so but under the settlement D takes in default of appointment, then the settled property does constitute assets.

3. **Property appointed by deed under a general power.** Before 1926 a creditor was entitled in equity to resort, not only to property appointed by will under a general power, but also, in the last instance, to property appointed by the deceased by deed under a general power, provided

[14] *Ante*, p. 210.
[15] *Ibid.* s.176(2).
[16] The same result would follow though F predeceases D, so that the appointment to F fails. *Re Khan's Settlement* [1966] Ch. 567, 577.
[17] *Ante*, p. 210.
[18] *O'Grady* v. *Wilmot* [1916] 2 A.C. 231, 248–251; *Re Hoskin's Trusts* (1876) 5 Ch.D. 229, (1877) 6 Ch.D. 281, 283; *Re Peacock's Settlement* [1902] 1 Ch. 552.
[19] *Beyfus* v. *Lawley* [1903] A.C. 411.
[20] As to the exercise by will of a general power of appointment see Wills Act 1837, s.27, *post*, pp. 428 *et seq.*
[21] *Holmes* v. *Coghill* (1802) 7 Ves. 499, (1806) 12 Ves. 206. But it forms part of D's net estate under Inheritance (Provision for Family and Dependants) Act 1975, s.25(1): see *ante*, p. 126.

the appointment was made in favour of a volunteer and only took effect at the deceased's death.[22] "The basis of this rule was that the appointor could have exercised the power in favour of his creditors, and that the claims of creditors were regarded in equity as paramount to the claims of a volunteer. It was inequitable that the appointor should confer a benefit upon a volunteer whilst his creditors remained unsatisfied."[23]

Section 32(1) does not mention property appointed by deed and the pre-1926 law remains applicable. On a death after 1925 a creditor is still entitled to resort, in the last instance, to property appointed by the deceased by deed under a general power provided:

   (i) the appointment was made in favour of a volunteer (*i.e.* an appointee who did not provide valuable consideration for the appointment); and
  (ii) the appointment only took effect at the deceased's death.[24] For instance, this requirement would clearly be satisfied if (in the example already considered) D appointed by deed "to F absolutely if F shall survive D" because the appointment would only operate to transfer the appointed property on the death of D.[25]

Such property appointed by the deceased by deed under a general power does not devolve on his personal representatives. A creditor may bring proceedings to "intercept" the appointed property.[26]

Property appointed by the deceased by will or deed under a special power is never assets[27] unless the deceased makes a valid appointment of it to himself.[28]

4. Donatio mortis causa. Property given by *donatio mortis causa* is liable for the debts of the donor but only in the last resort on a deficiency of the assets of his estate.[29] If the donor makes the *donatio* by an "incomplete" delivery or transfer, the legal title to the property remains vested in the donor's personal representatives. On the other hand, if the *donatio* vests the donor's title in the donee, presumably a creditor may bring proceedings against the donee for payment of his debt out of the property. Probably property to which the Rule in *Strong* v. *Bird* would otherwise apply is liable for the debts of the donor.[30]

---

[22] *O'Grady* v. *Wilmot, supra; Townshend* v. *Windham* (1750) 2 Ves.Sen. 1; *George* v. *Milbanke* (1803) 9 Ves. 190; *Pack* v. *Bathurst* (1745) 3 Atk. 269; *Troughton* v. *Troughton* (1747) 3 Atk. 656.

[23] *Williams on Executors and Administrators* (12th ed. 1930), p. 1083 quoted with approval in *Re Phillips* [1931] 1 Ch. 347, 351.

[24] *Re Phillips* [1931] 1 Ch. 347.

[25] *Ibid.* at p. 351, commenting on *Townshend* v. *Windham, supra;* (1928) 72 S.J. 771.

[26] *Re Phillips, supra.*

[27] *Townshend* v. *Windham* (1750) 2 Ves.Sen. 1, 9–10.

[28] *Re Penrose* [1933] Ch. 793. If the deceased may make a valid appointment to himself, it may be classifiable as a general power.

[29] *Smith* v. *Casen* (1718) 1 P.Wms. 406; *Ward* v. *Turner* (1752) 2 Ves.Sen. 431, 434; *Tate* v. *Leithead* (1854) Kay 658, 659; *Re Korvine's Trust* [1921] 1 Ch. 343, 348: *cf.* Warnock-Smith [1978] Conv. 130. See *ante,* p. 25.

[30] *Ante,* p. 28. As to property subject to a statutory nomination see *Bennett* v. *Slater* [1899] 1 Q.B. 45, 52.

B. Funeral, Testamentary and Administration Expenses

Funeral expenses. The law relating to the corpse of a testator has already been discussed.[31] Now two matters must be considered—(1) when is a personal representative personally liable for the deceased's funeral expenses? and (2) what funeral expenses are payable out of the deceased's estate?

(1) *Personal liability of personal representative*. The personal liability of a personal representative for funeral expenses may arise under contract or quasi-contract:

(i) A personal representative who orders the funeral is personally liable in contract to the undertaker for the contract price or, if no price is fixed, on a *quantum meruit* for a reasonable price for the funeral which is ordered.[32] If another person orders the funeral and the undertaker gives credit to that person, the latter is liable in contract to the undertaker but the personal representative is not liable at all to the undertaker.[33]

(ii) If no other person is liable in contract to the undertaker, a personal representative is personally liable in quasi-contract to the undertaker for reasonable funeral expenses. It is immaterial that another person ordered the funeral; if no other person is liable in contract, the law imposes an obligation on the personal representative to pay the reasonable expenses of a funeral conducted in a manner suitable to the deceased's position and circumstances.[34] However, the personal representative is only liable so far as he has available assets of the deceased to meet the expenses.[35]

(2) *Funeral expenses payable out of the deceased's estate*. Reasonable funeral expenses are payable out of the deceased's estate to the personal representative if he incurs liability in contract or quasi-contract to the undertaker. Similarly, another person who orders and pays for the funeral may recover reasonable funeral expenses from the personal representative out of the deceased's estate[36] unless that person paid for the funeral as an act of bounty.[37] But if the personal representative (or another person) incurs funeral expenses in excess of what is reasonable, he must bear the excess himself.

What funeral expenses are reasonable is a question of fact to be

---

[31] *Ante*, p. 6.

[32] *Corner* v. *Shaw* (1838) 3 M. & W. 350, 356; *Brice* v. *Wilson* (1834) 8 Ad. & E. 349, n.(c) (executor ratified contract with undertaker).

[33] *Green* v. *Salmon* (1838) 8 Ad. & E. 348, 350, explaining *Brice* v. *Wilson, supra.*

[34] *Rogers* v. *Price* (1829) 3 Y. & J. 28; *Tugwell* v. *Heyman* (1812) 3 Campb. 298 ("the dead body could not remain on the surface of the earth"); *Corner* v. *Shaw, supra*, at pp. 355–356; *Rees* v. *Hughes* [1946] K.B. 517, 524–525 and 528.

[35] In *Sharp* v. *Lush* (1879) 10 Ch.D. 468, 472 Jessel M.R. said *obiter*, "Even if the executor never receives assets to the amount of the funeral expenses, he is liable to pay, although he did not order the funeral"; *Re Walter* [1929] 1 Ch. 647, 655. Probably the personal representative is liable to pay to the extent of the assets.

[36] *Green* v. *Salmon, supra.*

[37] *Colely* v. *Colely* (1866) 12 Jur.(N.S.) 496; *cf. Williams* v. *Williams* (1882) 20 Ch.D. 659. See also *Shallcross* v. *Wright* (1850) 12 Beav. 505.

decided having regard to all the circumstances of the particular case.[38]
The following factors may be material:

(i) the insolvency of the deceased's estate which makes a lower scale
of expenses appropriate, at any rate if the personal representative
knows of or has reason to anticipate the insolvency[39];

(ii) the deceased's position in life[40]; and

(iii) the deceased's religious belief[41] and any wishes expressed by
him as to his funeral.

Social fund payments to meet funeral expenses are recoverable by the
D.H.S.S. out of the deceased's estate, as if they were funeral expenses.[42]

Testamentary and administration expenses. The Administration of
Estates Act 1925 uses the expression "testamentary and administration
expenses" in connection with the administration of solvent estates[43]
but does not define its meaning. The same expression is used in connection with the administration of insolvent estates without defining
its meaning.[44] Recourse must therefore be had to the decided cases
which are mainly concerned with the meaning of similar expressions in
wills.

The expression "testamentary and administration expenses" means,
in general, expenses incident to the proper performance of the duties of
an executor or administrator.[45] By way of example the expression
includes the following, if properly incurred:

(i) the expense of obtaining probate or letters of administration,
whether in common or solemn form[46];

(ii) the costs of obtaining the advice of solicitors or counsel as to the
administration of the estate[47];

(iii) the costs of an administration action or other proceedings insti-

---

[38] *Goldstein* v. *Salvation Army Assurance Society* [1917] 2 K.B. 291 (funeral expenses recoverable under assurance policy may include tombstone): see also *Hart* v. *Griffiths-Jones*
[1948] 2 All E.R. 729 (embalming of body but not monument costing £225); *Stanton* v.
Ewart F. Youldon Ltd. [1960] 1 W.L.R. 543 (simple gravestone but not marble memorial set
up as a sign of love and affection); *Gammell* v. *Wilson* [1982] A.C. 27 (£595 headstone)—all
cases decided under Law Reform (Miscellaneous Provisions) Act 1934.

[39] *Edwards* v. *Edwards* (1834) 2 Cr. & M. 612; *Hancock* v. *Podmore* (1830) 1 B. & Ad. 260;
Bissett v. *Antrobus* (1831) 4 Sim. 512; *Stag* v. *Punter* (1744) 3 Atk. 119.

[40] *Stag* v. *Punter, supra; Re Walter* [1929] 1 Ch. 647, 655.

[41] *Gammell* v. *Wilson* [1982] A.C. 27, 43.

[42] Social Security Act 1986, s.32(4): for these payments see Social Fund (General Regulations) 1987 (S.I. 1987 No. 481), para. 7).

[43] Administration of Estates Act 1925, s.34(3): see *post*, p. 285.

[44] Administration of Insolvent Estates of Deceased Persons Order 1986 (S.I. 1986
No. 1999), paras. 4(2) and 5(2): see *post*, p. 286.

[45] *Sharp* v. *Lush* (1879) 10 Ch.D. 468 (in a will "executorship expenses" are "expenses
incident to the proper performance of the duty of the executor in the same way as testamentary expenses are, neither more nor less"); *Re Taylor's Estate* [1969] 2 Ch. 245 (in the
construction of wills "testamentary expenses" and "administration expenses" are prima
facie synonymous).

[46] *Re Clemow* [1900] 2 Ch. 182 and *cf. Re Prince* [1898] 2 Ch. 225. For costs of a probate
action see *ante*, p. 202.

[47] *Sharp* v. *Lush, supra*.

tuted for a proper purpose, such as deciding any matters of difficulty which arise in the administration of the estate[48];
(iv) the expense incurred in collecting and preserving the assets of
the deceased's estate,[49] other than property specifically devised
or bequeathed[50]; and
(v) the expense incurred in ascertaining the deceased's debts and
liabilities (for instance, the cost of advertisements).

Testamentary and administration expenses also include, in general, any
inheritance tax payable in respect of the deceased's death on his property situated in the United Kingdom which vests in his personal representatives. This is considered more fully later.[51]

C. DEBTS AND LIABILITIES

The general rule that causes of action subsisting against the deceased at
his death survive against his estate has already been dealt with.[52] So,
too, has the liability of personal representatives for rent or breach of the
other covenants in a lease held by the deceased.[53] The personal representatives' duty to pay the debts and liabilities of the deceased must
now be considered. This is one of the main duties of personal representatives in the administration of the deceased's estate.

Personal representatives' duty to pay debts. Personal representatives
must carry out their duty to pay the debts of the deceased with due diligence, having regard to the assets in their hands which are properly
applicable for that purpose.

(1) *Nature of the duty.* To quote the classic statement of this duty by
Uthwatt J. in *Re Tankard*[54]:

"it is the duty of executors, as a matter of the due administration of
the estate, to pay the debts of their testator with due diligence having
regard to the assets in their hands which are properly applicable for
that purpose, and in determining whether due diligence has been
shown regard must be had to all the circumstances of the case. . . .
The duty is owed not only to creditors, but also to beneficiaries, for
the ultimate object of the administration of an estate is to place the
beneficiaries in possession of their interest and that object cannot be
fully achieved unless all debts are satisfied."

Thus if personal representatives fail to pay a debt of the deceased with
due diligence, though they have assets in hand properly applicable for

---

[48] *Sharp* v. *Lush, supra; Miles* v. *Harrison* (1874) L.R. 9 Ch.App. 316; *Harloe* v. *Harloe*
(1875) L.R. 20 Eq. 471; *Re Hall-Dare* [1916] 1 Ch. 272.
[49] *Peter* v. *Stirling* (1878) 10 Ch.D. 279, 284; *Re Goetze* [1953] Ch. 96, 111–113; *Re Sebba*
[1959] Ch. 166.
[50] For property specifically devised or bequeathed see *post*, p. 300.
[51] *Post*, p. 279.
[52] *Ante*, p. 212.
[53] *Ante*, pp. 229 *et seq.*
[54] [1942] Ch. 69, 72.

that purpose, they are liable not only to creditors but also to the beneficiaries for any consequent loss. To take two examples of loss to the beneficiaries—(i) in the case of a debt which bears interest, the assets in hand may be earning a lower rate of interest than the rate due on the debt,[55] and (ii) in the case of any debt which they fail to pay, whether it is interest-bearing or not, the costs incurred by them in proceedings brought by the creditor to obtain payment of his debt constitute loss.[56]

(2) *Time for payment.* To quote Uthwatt J. again in *Re Tankard*[57]:

"there is, in my opinion, no rule of law that it is the duty of executors to pay . . . debts within a year from the testator's death. The duty is to pay with due diligence. Due diligence may, indeed, require that payment should be made before the expiration of the year, but the circumstances affecting the estate and the assets comprised in it may justify non-payment within the year, but, if debts are not paid within the year, the onus is thrown on the executors to justify the delay."

The personal representatives may well be able to justify non-payment of a debt within the executor's year. For example, the personal representatives may never have had assets in their hands properly applicable for payment of the debt.[58] Again, if the deceased's estate either is insolvent (the assets being insufficient to pay the funeral, testamentary and administration expenses, debts and liabilities in full), or may turn out to be insolvent, the personal representatives may need more than one year in order to ascertain the assets and the extent of the debts, and to determine which debts are payable under the order of priority applicable to an insolvent estate.[59]

In this last quotation Uthwatt J. was referring to debts due from the deceased at his death. If the debt does not fall due for payment until (say) two years after the deceased's death, the personal representatives' duty (assuming the estate is solvent) is to pay the debt with due diligence once it has become due.

(3) *Modification of the duty by will.* Quoting from this judgment of Uthwatt J. yet again[60]:

"As against creditors, the provisions of the testator's will which relate to the realisation of his assets or otherwise bear on the payment of debts are irrelevant. As against beneficiaries, the position is different. Beneficiaries take their interest under the will only on the terms of the will. As respects them full effect has to be given to any provisions which, either in express terms or by implication, modify the executor's duty of paying debts with due diligence."

In *Re Tankard* T by his will gave his residuary estate to his executor (a trust company) upon the usual trust for sale and, after payment of his debts, funeral and testamentary expenses, to hold the balance for the

[55] *Ibid.* at pp. 72–73; *Hall* v. *Hallett* (1784) 1 Cox. 134; *Re Stevens* [1898] 1 Ch. 162, 168–169.
[56] *Ibid.* at p. 73.
[57] *Ibid.*
[58] *Re Stevens, supra.*
[59] *Post,* pp. 288 *et seq.*
[60] [1942] Ch. 69, 74.

beneficiaries. The will empowered the executor to retain any part of T's estate in the form of investment existing at his death for so long as the executor in its absolute discretion might think fit, without being responsible for any loss occasioned thereby. At his death T owed over £9,000 to a creditor. The executor did not sell sufficient of T's assets to clear this debt during the executor's year. After the end of the executor's year the assets fell in value and the executor had to sell more of the assets to clear this debt than would have been necessary on a sale during the executor's year. Uthwatt J. held that the beneficiaries' action for damages against the executor failed, because the executor had duly exercised the power to retain assets conferred on him by the will: as against the beneficiaries, the will had modified the executor's duty to pay the deceased's debts with due diligence.

Of course, if the creditor had suffered loss from any breach by the executor of this duty to pay the deceased's debts with due diligence, the power to retain assets conferred by the will would have been irrelevant in an action for damages by the creditor against the executor.

Debts unknown to personal representatives. Personal representatives who distribute assets to the beneficiaries remain liable for the unpaid debts and liabilities of the deceased to the extent of the assets which would have been properly applicable for their payment, even though the personal representatives had no notice of such debts and liabilities when they made the distribution to the beneficiaries.[61] Fortunately personal representatives may readily protect themselves against this onerous liability by (1) advertising for claims in accordance with section 27 of the Trustee Act 1925, *or* (2) obtaining the leave of the court to distribute on the footing that all the deceased's debts and liabilities have been ascertained.

(1) *Advertising for claims.* Under section 27 of the Trustee Act 1925[62] personal representatives may give notice of their intention to distribute, requiring any person interested to send in particulars of his claim[63] to the personal representatives within a stated time, not being less than two months. The notice is to be given:

   (i) by advertisement in the *London Gazette,* and
  (ii) by advertisement in a newspaper circulating in the district in which land to be distributed is situated (this requirement is not applicable if no land is to be distributed), and
  (iii) by "such other like notices, including notices elsewhere than in England and Wales,[64] as would, in any special case, have been directed by a court of competent jurisdiction in an action for

---

[61] *Knatchbull* v. *Fearnhead* (1837) 3 My. & Cr. 122 (executors distributed without notice of deceased's liability for his breach of trust); *Norman* v. *Baldry* (1834) 6 Sim. 621. For the defence of limitation see *post,* p. 392.

[62] As amended by Law of Property (Amendment) Act 1926, ss.7, 8(2) and Sched.

[63] This includes a claim to be a beneficiary under the deceased's will or intestacy as well as a claim to be a creditor, *Re Aldhous* [1955] 1 W.L.R. 459, see *post,* pp. 359–360: it is desirable for the notice to refer to both a creditor and a beneficiary (*e.g.* "any person having any claim against or any interest in" the deceased's estate), *ibid.* at p. 462.

[64] *Re Holden* [1935] W.N. 52: *cf. Re Achillopoulos* [1928] Ch. 433.

administration."[65] This requirement refers to the advertisements which the court would direct in an administration action—normally the court directs an advertisement for creditors in such local or national newspapers as may be appropriate having regard to the circumstances of the case.[66] If the personal representatives are in any doubt as to what advertisements are needed to satisfy this requirement, they may ask the court to certify what advertisements the court would direct in an administration action.[67] It is important for the personal representatives to satisfy this requirement because otherwise they lose the protection of section 27.

Section 27(2) provides that nothing in the section "frees the . . . personal representatives from any obligation to make searches or obtain official certificates of search similar to those which an intending purchaser would be advised to make or obtain." The meaning of this provision is not clear. Personal representatives are only under "any obligation" to make searches in the sense that the registration of any registrable matter under the Land Charges Acts is deemed to constitute actual notice to all persons for all purposes connected with the land affected.[68] Probably, in order to be certain of the protection of section 27, before distributing land personal representatives should carry out the same searches as an intending purchaser of land would be advised to make in the Land Charges Register (or, in the case of registered land, in the Land Registry) and the local land charges registry. Possibly, before distributing any asset, personal representatives should search in bankruptcy against the deceased and against any beneficiary to whom the distribution is to be made.

After the expiration of the stated time for claims to be sent in, the personal representatives may distribute to the persons entitled having regard only to the claims (whether formal or not) of which the personal representatives then have notice. Thus, if the personal representatives first satisfy the requirements as to advertising and making searches, and then distribute the deceased's assets, the personal representatives are not, in respect of the distributed assets, liable for any debt or liability of the deceased[69] of which the personal representatives have not had notice at the time of distribution.[70] It is advisable for personal representatives to advertise and make searches at an early stage in the

---

[65] Trustee Act 1925, s.27(1).

[66] See R.S.C., Ord. 44, r. 5; *Re Bracken* (1889) 43 Ch.D. 1. For advertisement for beneficiaries under the deceased's will or intestacy see *Newton* v. *Sherry* (1876) 1 C.P.D. 246, 256 (advertise in foreign country if claimant may be residing there).

[67] *Re Holden, supra:* see also *Re Letherbrow* [1935] W.N. 34 and 48 (advertisement for next of kin under s.27).

[68] Law of Property Act 1925, s.198(1). For the similar effect of certain land charges created by a company and registered under the Companies Acts see Land Charges Act 1972, s.3(7) and (8). For registered land see Land Registration Act 1925, s.20.

[69] Or to an unknown beneficiary under the deceased's will or intestacy, *Re Aldhous* [1955] 1 W.L.R. 459: see *post*, pp. 359–360.

[70] Trustee Act 1925, s.27(2); *Clegg* v. *Rowland* (1866) L.R. 3 Eq. 368 (executor has the same protection as if he had distributed under an order of the court); *Re Frewen* (1889) 60 L.T. 953. For notice where a personal representative is acting for the purpose of more than one estate see Trustee Act 1925, s.28.

administration of the deceased's estate, because section 27 does not protect them in respect of assets which they have already distributed before these requirements are satisfied[71]: "a prudent and reasonable executor ought to advertise . . . as soon as possible after his testator's death"[72] and an administrator as soon as possible after the grant of letters of administration.[73]

Section 27 does not protect personal representatives against any debt or liability of which they have had notice at the time of distribution, though the claimant did not respond to the advertisement.[74] Nor does section 27 protect personal representatives against a person who claims that they have "no right to administer the estate at all"[75]—for instance, against the next of kin entitled on intestacy, who claim that the grant of probate of the deceased's will to the executors should be revoked on the ground that the deceased lacked testamentary capacity.

A testator cannot by his will deprive his personal representatives of their protection under section 27.[76]

(2) *Leave of the court to distribute.* If the court gives personal representatives leave to distribute on the footing that all the deceased's debts and liabilities have been ascertained, this protects the personal representatives against any unknown debts and liabilities. In *Re Gess*[77] the deceased, who was of Polish nationality, died domiciled in England in 1939 and the administrators of his estate were unable to advertise for creditors in Poland owing to the wartime occupation of Poland by Germany. The court gave them leave to distribute without advertising in Poland and on the footing that all the debts and liabilities of the estate had been ascertained.

Neither section 27 of the Trustee Act 1925 nor the leave of the court to distribute prejudices the remedy of an unpaid creditor against a recipient of the deceased's assets.[78] This remedy is considered later.[79]

Future debts and liabilities. A debt or liability of the deceased may not fall due for payment until long after the deceased's death. For example, during his lifetime the deceased may have covenanted to pay an annuity to X for life: if X survives the deceased, the covenanted sum will continue to fall due from the deceased's estate at regular intervals until X's death. Again, to take an example of a remote contingent liability, the deceased may have been the original lessee of a 99 years' lease,

[71] *Re Kay* [1897] 2 Ch. 518 (some assets distributed before advertisement to widow in need: personal representatives not protected, but relief against liability granted under Judicial Trustees Act 1896, s.3—now Trustee Act 1925, s.61): see *post*, p. 395.

[72] *Ibid.* at p. 522.

[73] An executor (but not an administrator) may give this notice before obtaining a grant of representation; see Trustee Act 1925, s.68(1)(9) and *ante*, pp. 172–173.

[74] *Re Land Credit Company of Ireland* (1872) 21 W.R. 1351.

[75] *Guardian Trust & Executors Company of New Zealand Ltd.* v. *Public Trustee of New Zealand* [1942] A.C. 115, 125 (a Privy Council decision on the New Zealand equivalent to s.27): see *ante*, p. 208.

[76] s.27(3).

[77] [1942] Ch. 37: see also *Re Benjamin* [1902] 1 Ch. 723 (missing beneficiary) and *post*, p. 360.

[78] Trustee Act 1925, s.27(2); *Re Gess, supra*, at p. 39.

[79] *Post*, pp. 403 *et seq.*

which he assigned to TA long before his death: his personal representatives will remain liable as such for rent and any breach of the other covenants during the entire unexpired term of the lease, though, if the lease is valuable, it is very likely that TA and his assigns will continue to pay the rent and perform the covenants in order to avoid forfeiture of the lease. Of course, in the case of a possible future debt or liability arising under a lease, which was not assigned by the deceased but which devolved on the personal representatives, they should for their own protection satisfy the requirements of section 26 of the Trustee Act 1925, which have already been considered.[80] If there is any possible future debt or liability of which the personal representatives have notice (so that they are not protected by advertising for claims in accordance with section 27 of the Trustee Act 1925), and to which section 26 does not apply, what courses of action are open to the personal representatives?

(1) *Order of the court.* The safest course is for the personal representatives to apply to the court for directions. If the personal representatives make a full disclosure of all the information they have, and act in accordance with the order of the court, the personal representatives are fully protected.[81] The court generally authorises the estate to be distributed without making any provision for future contingent liabilities.[82] This protects the personal representatives and leaves the unpaid creditor (if the contingent liability arises) to pursue his remedy against a recipient of the deceased's assets.[83] However, this practice is not appropriate if there is a reasonable probability that the contingent liability will arise—for instance, in the case of a covenant by the deceased to pay an annuity to X, the court has directed the personal representatives not to distribute without retaining such a sum as, when invested, would produce the amount of the annuity.[84]

(2) *Distribution without an order of the court.* If the personal representatives distribute the assets of the estate without first applying to the court and acting in accordance with its order, and later the contingent liability arises, the personal representatives are liable to the unpaid creditor to the extent of the assets they distributed.[85] If this occurs, the personal representatives may claim repayment from a beneficiary of the capital value of the assets which they distributed to him, unless at the time of distribution the personal representatives knew that the claim

---

[80] *Ante,* pp. 229–231: s.26 does not apply to a lease assigned by the deceased, *Re Nixon* [1904] 1 Ch. 638.

[81] *Re King* [1907] 1 Ch. 72 where Neville J. reviewed the case law (possible future liability on deceased's company shares not fully paid up: order of the court directing distribution to residuary beneficiaries exonerates personal representatives from liability to company); *Re Nixon, supra,* (leases formerly held by deceased: distribution directed and personal representatives not liable on leases thereafter).

[82] *Re King, supra; Re Johnson* [1940] W.N. 195; *Re Sales* [1920] W.N. 54.

[83] *Post,* pp. 403 *et seq.*

[84] *Re Arnold* [1942] Ch. 272: *cf. Re Johnson, supra.*

[85] *Taylor* v. *Taylor* (1870) L.R. 10 Eq. 477 (executors liable for unexpected calls on company shares made after death); *Knatchbull* v. *Fearnhead* (1837) 3 M. & C. 122; *Re Bewley's Estate* (1871) 24 L.T. 177. For the defence of limitation see *post,* p. 392.

had already fallen due for payment.[86] This right to claim repayment encourages the personal representatives to distribute the assets of the estate in a case where the contingent liability is remote: if no such right to claim repayment existed, personal representatives would be tempted to keep sufficient assets of the estate in hand until every possible known liability of the estate, however remote, had been satisfied.[87]

In order to secure more protection without incurring the expense of an application to the court, personal representatives:

(i) may obtain a proper indemnity fron the beneficiaries before distributing the assets (*e.g.* a beneficiary may give security[88] to repay his share of the assets if the contingent liability arises); or

(ii) may set aside an indemnity fund out of the deceased's estate.[89] In practice it may well be difficult to quantify the indemnity fund needed for complete protection.

Which of these different courses of action should be chosen by the personal representatives may depend on several factors, including the nature and extent of the possible future debt or liability, the value of the deceased's estate and the financial position of each beneficiary. Of course, the personal representatives are only faced with this choice of different courses of action if the deceased's estate is solvent and assets are available for distribution to beneficiaries. If the deceased's estate is insolvent, future debts and liabilities are provable against the estate in accordance with the law of bankruptcy.[90]

Statute-barred debts. Personal representatives commit a breach of duty (or *devastavit*) if they pay a debt which need not be paid.[91] They have a duty to rely on all proper defences, including the defence that the claim is unenforceable under the Statute of Frauds 1677[92] or section 40 of the Law of Property Act 1925. To this general rule there is a single well-established exception—personal representatives may plead the Limitation Acts as a defence, but they are not under any duty to do so if the Acts have only barred the claimant's remedy and not extinguished his claim. Thus, if they think fit, personal representatives may pay a statute-barred debt of the deceased.[93] But this exception is anomalous

---

[86] *Jervis* v. *Wolferstan* (1874) L.R. 18 Eq. 18 (repayment of capital but not of intermediate income received by beneficiary); *Whittaker* v. *Kershaw* (1890) 45 Ch.D. 320.

[87] *Jervis* v. *Wolferstan, supra,* at pp. 25–26; *Whittaker* v. *Kershaw, supra,* at pp. 326 and 329.

[88] A personal representative may, as a condition of giving an assent, require security for the discharge of a liability: Administration of Estates Act 1925, s.36(10).

[89] *Simmons* v. *Bolland* (1817) 3 Mer. 547; *Fletcher* v. *Stevenson* (1844) 3 Hare 360; *Dobson* v. *Carpenter* (1850) 12 Beav. 370; *Hickling* v. *Boyer* (1851) 3 Mac. & G. 635; *Dean* v. *Allen* (1855) 20 Beav. 1.

[90] *Post,* p. 287.

[91] *Re Rownson* (1885) 29 Ch.D. 358, 363–364; *Midgley* v. *Midgley* [1893] 3 Ch. 282, 289, 299 and 304. For their statutory powers in relation to debts (including power to pay or allow any debt or claim on any evidence that they think sufficient) see Trustee Act 1925, s.15 and *ante,* p. 215.

[92] *Re Rownson, supra*: see Law Reform (Enforcement of Contracts) Act 1954.

[93] *Norton* v. *Frecker* (1737) 1 Atk. 524, 526; *Stahlschmidt* v. *Lett* (1853) 1 Sm. & G. 415; *Hill* v. *Walker* (1858) 4 K. & J. 166; *Midgley* v. *Midgley, supra,* at pp. 289, 297 and 304. See Limitation Act 1980 ss.5, 8 and 20 (debt not extinguished) and *cf.* s.17 (title to land extinguished).

and is not to be extended.[94] There are limits to the scope of the exception:

(1) *Debt already declared statute-barred.* If the court has already declared the debt to be statute-barred, the personal representatives have a duty to rely on the defence of *res judicata* and they must not pay the debt.[95] In short, the general rule applies and not the anomalous exception.

(2) *Order for administration.* If the court makes an order for the administration of the estate, any creditor or beneficiary is entitled to raise the defence of limitation against a creditor who comes in under the order to prove his debt, notwithstanding the refusal of the personal representatives to raise this defence.[96] But, exceptionally, they are not permitted to raise this defence against a creditor who was himself the plaintiff in the administration proceedings. The personal representatives did not raise this defence against the plaintiff, and another creditor or beneficiary, who has got the benefit of the administration order, cannot be permitted to raise this defence against the plaintiff whose debt was the foundation of the order.[97]

Again, if application is made to the court to determine whether a claimant is a creditor of the deceased (without an administration order being made[98]), any creditor or beneficiary is entitled to raise the defence of limitation against the claimant because the parties must be treated as standing in the same position as if an administration order had been made.[99]

(3) *Insolvent estate.* If the deceased's estate is insolvent only debts provable in bankruptcy may be claimed and a statute-barred debt is not provable in bankruptcy.[1] Accordingly in this case the anomalous exception appears not to be applicable.

If a claimant sues for his debt and one of the personal representatives pleads limitation in his defence, but the other personal representative does not, the court acts on the former defence as being more for the advantage of the deceased's estate.[2] Whether one personal representative may pay a statute-barred debt of the deceased if the other personal representative objects has never been decided[3]; perhaps one executor

---

[94] *Re Rownson, supra,* at pp. 363–365; *Midgley* v. *Midgley supra,* at p. 299 (this anomalous exception "is to be confined within the limits of its own anomaly").

[95] *Midgley* v. *Midgley, supra.*

[96] *Shewn* v. *Vanderhorst* (1831) 1 Russ. & M. 347 (residuary legatee raised defence of limitation); *Moodie* v. *Bannister* (1859) 4 Drew. 432; *Fuller* v. *Redman (No. 2)* (1859) 26 Beav. 614 (creditor raised defence of limitation). But the court does not raise this defence on behalf of an absent beneficiary, *Alson* v. *Trollope* (1866) L.R. 2 Eq. 205.

[97] *Briggs* v. *Wilson* (1835) 5 De G.M. & G. 12, 21; *Fuller* v. *Redman (No. 2)* (1859) 26 Beav. 614, 617–619.

[98] See R.S.C., Ord. 85, r. 2.

[99] *Re Wenham* [1892] 3 Ch. 59.

[1] Administration of Insolvent Estates of Deceased Persons Order 1986 (S.I. 1986 No. 1999); *Ex p. Dewdney, ex p. Seaman* (1809) 15 Ves. 479, (1815) 19 Ves. 467.

[2] *Midgley* v. *Midgley* [1893] 3 Ch. 282, 298 and 302.

[3] *Ibid,* at pp. 297 and 301–302.

may do so under the rule that executors have joint and several authority.[4]

Interest on debts. If a debt of the deceased carries interest, any interest due is payable by the personal representatives as part of the sum due from the estate. If a debt does not carry interest but the court directs an account of the deceased's debts to be taken, then, unless the court orders otherwise, interest is allowed on the debt at the rate payable on judgment debts from the date of the judgment directing the account.[5] But if the estate is insolvent, the bankruptcy rules as to interest on debts are applicable.[6]

2. SOLVENT ESTATE

The deceased's estate is solvent if the assets are sufficient to pay all his funeral, testamentary and administration expenses, debts and liabilities.[7] In that event these expenses, debts and liabilities are payable in full and any balance of the deceased's estate is distributable to the beneficiaries entitled under his will or intestacy. The beneficiaries are therefore concerned as to which assets of the deceased's estate are liable to bear the burden of these expenses, debts and liabilities. It is in the interest of each beneficiary to claim that this burden should not fall on the assets to which he is entitled. Accordingly rules are needed to regulate the burden of the deceased's expenses, debts and liabilities. In essence these rules as to incidence regulate "competition" between the beneficiaries as to which assets of the estate should bear this burden. The creditors are not concerned with these rules regulating the burden of the deceased's expenses, debts and liabilities: indeed a creditor is not bound by them and may obtain payment out of any of the assets regardless of these rules.[8] If a creditor is paid out of an asset which is not liable to bear the burden of his debt under these rules, the matter can be adjusted between the beneficiaries in the personal representatives' final accounts and, if need be, the doctrine of marshalling (which is explained later[9]) provides a remedy for the disappointed beneficiary.

All the rules as to incidence now to be considered have one common feature—they may be varied by a contrary intention on the part of the deceased. However it is necessary to consider the expression of such a contrary intention separately in relation to each of the incidence rules.

A. The Statutory Order of Application of Assets

Section 34(3) of the Administration of Estates Act 1925 provides that where the deceased's estate is solvent his real and personal estate shall,

[4] *Ibid.* p. 297: see *ante,* p. 232.
[5] R.S.C., Ord. 44, r. 9. See also Supreme Court Act 1981, s.35A, as amended by Administration of Justice Act 1982, s.15(1) and Sched. I, Pt. I.
[6] *Post,* pp. 288 and 291–292.
[7] *Re Leng* [1895] 1 Ch. 652, 658: see *post,* p. 285.
[8] *Re Tong* [1931] 1 Ch. 202, 212; Administration of Estates Act 1925, s.35(3).
[9] *Post,* pp. 284–285.

subject to any provisions contained in his will, be applicable towards the discharge of the funeral, testamentary and administration expenses, debts and liabilities payable thereout in the order mentioned in Part II of the First Schedule to the Act. Special rules are applicable to debts charged on the deceased's property and to the incidence of inheritance tax payable in respect of his death: these special rules are considered later.[10]

The statutory order of application of assets set out in Part II of the First Schedule is as follows:

"1. *Property of the deceased undisposed of by will, subject to the retention thereout of a fund sufficient to meet any pecuniary legacies.*[11]
2. *Property of the deceased not specifically devised or bequeathed but included (either by a specific or general description) in a residuary gift, subject to the retention out of such property of a fund sufficient to meet any pecuniary legacies, so far as not provided for as aforesaid.*[11]
3. *Property of the deceased specifically appropriated or devised or bequeathed (either by a specific or general description) for the payment of debts.*
4. *Property of the deceased charged with, or devised or bequeathed (either by a specific or general description) subject to a charge for the payment of debts.*
5. *The fund, if any, retained to meet pecuniary legacies.*
6. *Property specifically devised or bequeathed, rateably according to value.*
7. *Property appointed by will under a general power, including the statutory power to dispose of entailed interests, rateably according to value.*
8. *The following provisions shall also apply—*
   (a) *The order of application may be varied by the will of the deceased.*
   (b) . . . . "

This statutory order applies on the death of any person after 1925[12] unless the order is varied by the deceased's will.

In this statutory order no distinction is made between realty and personalty. The Schedule refers repeatedly to "property," which is defined in the Administration of Estates Act 1925 as including any interest in real or personal property.[13] All the real and personal property falling within a particular paragraph is therefore liable rateably for the expenses, debts and liabilities.[14] To take an example of the operation of the statutory order:

By his will T gave his freehold house Blackacre to A, his shares in Tilley & Co. Ltd. to B, legacies of £5,000 to C and £2,000 to D (which lega-

---

[10] *Post*, pp. 274 and 279.

[11] For the incidence of general pecuniary legacies, see *post*, pp. 308 *et seq.*

[12] Administration of Estates Act 1925, s.54; *Re Gates* [1930] 1 Ch. 199 (order applies on death intestate after 1925 of pre-1926 lunatic).

[13] s.55(1)(xvii).

[14] *Re Harland-Peck* [1941] Ch. 182, 187–189; *Re Anstead* [1943] Ch. 161 (the headnote is wrong).

cies T directed to be paid out of his residuary personal estate), and his residuary real estate to E and his residuary personal estate to F.

T died in 1988 and all the beneficiaries survived him. None of T's property is undisposed of by his will so paragraph 1 of the statutory order is not applicable. The first step to take is to set aside out of the residuary personal estate a fund to satisfy the general pecuniary legacies of £5,000 and £2,000.[15] T's estate is applicable towards the discharge of expenses, debts and liabilities in the following order:

   (i) Both T's residuary real estate (given to E) and his residuary personal estate (given to F) fall within paragraph 2. This property is primarily liable for expenses, debts and liabilities and it must be exhausted before any other property is touched. The residuary real estate and residuary personal estate bear this burden rateably in proportion to their respective values. Thus, if the residuary real estate is valued at £30,000 and the residuary personal estate at £10,000, the residuary real estate bears three-quarters and the residuary personal estate bears one-quarter of the burden of the expenses, debts and liabilities.

  (ii) None of T's property falls within paragraphs 3 or 4 so the pecuniary legacy fund is liable next under paragraph 5. If (say) one-half of the pecuniary legacy fund is needed to meet expenses, debts and liabilities, then each pecuniary legacy abates proportionally: in that event C and D each receive only one-half of their respective legacies.

 (iii) Both Blackacre (realty specifically devised to A) and T's shares in Tilley & Co. Ltd. (personalty specifically bequeathed to B) fall within paragraph 6 and bear expenses, debts and liabilities rateably according to their respective values. Thus if Blackacre is valued at £20,000 and the company shares at £10,000, Blackacre bears two-thirds and the company shares one-third of the burden of any expenses, debts and liabilities falling on paragraph 6 property.

In this example T did not by his will vary the statutory order or give priority to a particular pecuniary legacy. T might, for instance, have directed that the legacy to C should be payable in priority to the legacy to D: in that event D's legacy would have abated first before C's legacy.[16]

Paragraph 1—property undisposed of by will. It is necessary to consider (1) what property of the deceased falls within paragraph 1, and (2) what provisions in a will vary the statutory order so that property falling within paragraph 1 is not primarily liable.

(1) *Property not effectively disposed of by will falls within this paragraph.* Property of the deceased falls within paragraph 1 so far as it is not effec-

---

[15] *Re Anstead, supra,* (unlike the example in the text, the will did not contain a direction to pay legacies out of residuary personalty); *Re Wilson* [1967] Ch. 53, 70. For the classification of legacies and devises, see *post,* pp. 294 *et seq.*

[16] But C would not have been entitled to interest on his legacy in priority to the legacy to D, in the absence of express direction to this effect; *Re Wyles* [1938] Ch. 313.

tively disposed of by the deceased's will. Paragraph 1 is not confined to property which the deceased does not attempt to dispose of by will, but includes property which he does attempt, albeit unsuccessfully, to dispose of by will. In *Re Lamb*[17] T by his will directed his debts and expenses to be paid by his executors as soon as possible after his death and, after making certain gifts, directed the residue of his estate to be equally divided between W, X, Y and Z. The words of severance in this direction created a tenancy in common. W predeceased T and his quarter share of T's residue lapsed[18] and went to T's next-of-kin entitled under the intestacy rules. The court held that this quarter share of T's residue was "property of the deceased undisposed of by will" and therefore was primarily liable under paragraph 1 for T's expenses and debts. If W, X, Y and Z had all survived T and each had taken his quarter share, T's residue as a whole would have been primarily liable under paragraph 2 for T's expenses and debts.

Again, if a testator by his will gives his residuary estate upon trusts which do not effectively dispose of all the income arising after his death, any undisposed of income is "property of the deceased undisposed of by will" and therefore is primarily liable under paragraph 1 for the testator's expenses and debts.[19]

(2) *Variation of the statutory order.* The testator may vary the statutory order by his will, either by express provision or by implication, so that property falling within paragraph 1 is not primarily liable. Most of the decided cases deal with lapsed shares of residue and they fall into two distinct groups:

(i) In one group of cases the testator varies the statutory order *by directing expenses and debts to be paid out of residue as a whole*, thereby charging residue as a whole with their payment. *Re Harland-Peck*[20] is an instance. T made certain gifts by her will and then provided as follows: "Subject to the payment of my funeral and testamentary expenses . . . and debts . . . I devise and bequeath all the rest and residue of my property" to X and Y in equal shares as tenants in common. Y predeceased T and his half share lapsed and went to Z, T's next-of-kin entitled on intestacy. The Court of Appeal held that this provision in the will varied the statutory order and that expenses and debts were payable out of residue as a whole, and not primarily out of Y's lapsed share under paragraph 1. The result was that X and Z each suffered part of the burden of the expenses and debts.

---

[17] [1929] 1 Ch. 723: see also *Re Tong* [1931] 1 Ch. 202; *Re Worthington* [1933] Ch. 771; *Re Sanger* [1939] Ch. 238.

[18] For the doctrine of lapse (and the exceptions to it), see *post*, pp. 336 *et seq.*

[19] *Re Tong, supra,* (gift of income to X failed as X's spouse attested the will: income liable under para. 1): *cf.* the earlier decision in *Re Cruse* [1930] W.N. 206 (gift of income effective but gift in remainder partially failed: debts held payable out of residue as a whole).

[20] [1941] Ch. 182: see also *Re Petty* [1929] 1 Ch. 726 (gift of residue to trustees upon trust for sale and out of the proceeds to pay expenses and debts); *Re Kempthorne* [1930] 1 Ch. 268 (personal estate subject to and after payment of expenses and debts to be divided among residuary legatees); *Re Berrey's W.T.* [1959] 1 W.L.R. 30 ("after all my debts, and funeral, and expenses are paid I give" residue to named beneficiaries). See also *Re Atkinson* [1930] 1 Ch. 47 and *Re Martin* [1955] Ch. 698.

(ii) In the other group of cases the testator directs expenses and debts to be paid *but does not specify out of what property they are to be paid*. This is construed as a direction to pay them in due course of administration pursuant to the statutory order. Expenses and debts are therefore payable primarily out of any lapsed shares of residue under paragraph 1. *Re Lamb*[21] (which has already been considered) falls within this group of cases. The result in *Re Lamb* was that T's next-of-kin suffered the primary burden of the expenses and debts.

It has been suggested[22] that it is difficult to distinguish between a gift of residue subject to and after payment of expenses and debts (which falls within the first group of cases) and, on the other hand, a direction to pay expenses and debts followed by a gift of residue (which falls within the second group of cases). However, there appears to be a clear distinction to be drawn—in the first group of cases the testator directs expenses and debts to be paid out of residue as a whole, whereas in the second group of cases the testator does not direct out of what property they are to be paid.

Paragraph 2—property included in a residuary gift. Paragraph 2 is worded so that property of the deceased falls within it if the property is not specifically devised or bequeathed but is included (either by a specific or general description) in a residuary gift. As explained already, gifts by T's will of "my freehold house Blackacre" to A and "my shares in Tilley & Co. Ltd." to B (followed by gifts of T's residuary real estate to E and residuary personal estate to F) are examples of a specific devise and a specific bequest. Blackacre and the company shares both fall within paragraph 6 and T's residuary real and residuary personal estate both fall within paragraph 2. On the other hand if, after making these gifts of Blackacre and his shares in this company, T had given "my residuary real estate including my freehold house Whiteacre" to E and "my residuary personal estate including my Rover car" to F, both Whiteacre and the Rover car would have fallen within paragraph 2, being property included in a residuary gift by a specific description.

A general gift by the testator in his will of all his real estate, or of all his personal estate, may be a residuary gift within paragraph 2. In *Re Wilson*[23] T by her will, after giving a number of specific and pecuniary legacies, gave "all my real estate and the residue of my personal estate" to D absolutely. Pennycuick J. held that T's real estate (as well as her residuary personal estate) fell within paragraph 2, though there was no previous devise of any other realty in the will. He said that "in ordinary language today lawyers would, I think, not inaptly describe such a gift as a residuary devise. They would certainly not describe it as a specific devise."[24]

[21] [1929] 1 Ch. 723: see also *Re Tong, supra, Re Worthington, supra; Re Sanger, supra.*
[22] *Per* Simonds J. in *Re Sanger, supra,* at pp. 248–249.
[23] [1967] Ch. 53: *cf* dicta in *Re Rowe* [1941] Ch. 343, 348 and *Re Ridley* [1950] Ch. 415, 420–422: for the pre-1926 rule that "all devises were by their nature specific" see *Hensman* v. *Fryer* (1867) 3 Ch.App. 420 and *Lancefield* v. *Iggulden* (1874) 10 Ch.App. 136, and *post,* p. 296.
[24] *Ibid.* at p. 68.

Paragraphs 3 and 4—property specifically appropriated and property charged

(1) *Property falling within paragraphs 3 and 4.* Paragraphs 3 and 4 are similar. Property of the deceased falling within each of these paragraphs is liable for the deceased's expenses, debts and liabilities, either (under paragraph 3) because the property was specifically appropriated or devised or bequeathed (either by a specific or general description) for the payment of debts, or (under paragraph 4) because the property was charged with, or devised or bequeathed (either by a specific or general description) subject to a charge for the payment of debts.

By his will a testator often appropriates his residuary estate for the payment of debts or charges his residuary estate with the payment of debts. However paragraphs 3 and 4 do not apply to property included in a residuary gift (either by a specific or general description), because under the statutory order such property falls within the earlier paragraph 2.[25]

(2) *Variation of the statutory order.* Assuming that the statutory order applies, property falling within paragraph 3 or 4 is only liable after property undisposed of by the will (paragraph 1) and property included in a residuary gift (paragraph 2) has been exhausted. But the statutory order may of course be varied by the testator's will. Thus if a will appropriates, or charges, property for, or with, the payment of expenses and debts, it is necessary to decide (i) whether the will varies the statutory order so as to make that property primarily liable for expenses and debts, or (ii) whether that property merely falls within paragraph 3 or 4. It is useful to consider two contrasting cases:

(i) In *Re Meldrum*[26] T by his will gave to A "the sum of £500 for her immediate expenses . . . and the residue of my deposit account at Lloyds Bank Dartmouth after all legacies debts funeral and other expenses have been liquidated but excluding death duties and testamentary expenses." T gave the residue of his property to trustees upon certain trusts and there was no property undisposed of by the will. If the statutory order was applicable, T's residuary estate was primarily liable for debts and expenses under paragraph 2—ranking before the deposit account which fell within paragraph 4. However, Upjohn J. held that the statutory order had been varied by T's will because T had shown a clear intention that his debts and funeral and other expenses (but not death duties and testamentary expenses) should be paid out of his deposit account: this necessarily involved an intention on T's part to exonerate his residuary estate from these items so far as the deposit account was adequate to meet them. He said that it is "essentially a matter of construction of the will in each case whether the provisions of the schedule apply, or whether they have been varied by the terms of the will."[27]

If in *Re Meldrum* the trusts applicable to T's residuary estate under his

---

[25] *Re Kempthorne* [1930] 1 Ch. 268.

[26] [1952] Ch. 208: see also *Re Littlewood* [1931] 1 Ch. 443; *Re James* [1947] Ch. 256 and *cf. Re Kempthorne* [1930] 1 Ch. 268, 278–279 (reversed by C.A. on another ground).

[27] [1952] Ch. 208, 212.

will had wholly, or partly, failed (*e.g.* because all, or some of, the residuary beneficiaries had predeceased T), the court would still have held that the statutory order had been varied by T's will and that these items should be paid out of the deposit account in exoneration of the residuary estate.[28]

(ii) On the other hand, the statutory order was held applicable in *Re Gordon*.[29] By her will T gave to her executors the sum of £50 upon trust to pay thereout her debts, funeral and testamentary expenses, any balance of the £50 remaining to be paid to the Rationalist Press Association for its general purposes. There was no residuary gift in the will. The court held that there was no indication in the will that T intended to vary the statutory order. The sum of £50 therefore fell within paragraph 3 or 4 (it did not matter which), and T's property undisposed of by her will was primarily liable under paragraph 1 for debts and expenses. The absence of any residuary gift in the will was crucial. T's will would have varied the statutory order so as to make the sum of £50 primarily liable for debts and expenses (a) if T had attempted to dispose of residue, thereby showing an intention to exonerate residue from debts and expenses so far as the £50 was adequate to meet them, or (b) if T had in some other manner shown an intention to vary the statutory order[30]— for instance, by directing that her debts and expenses were to be paid out of this sum of £50 "in exoneration of any property of mine undisposed of by my will."

Paragraph 5—the pecuniary legacy fund. The expression "pecuniary legacy" is widely defined in section 55(1)(ix) of the Administration of Estates Act 1925—it "includes an annuity, a general legacy, a demonstrative legacy so far as it is not discharged out of the designated property, and any other general direction by a testator for the payment of money, including all death duties free from which any devise, bequest, or payment is made to take effect." The distinction between a general legacy, a demonstrative legacy, and a specific devise or specific legacy is important in applying paragraphs 5 and 6 of the statutory order: this is considered in the next chapter.[31]

If part of the pecuniary legacy fund is needed to meet expenses and debts, all the pecuniary legacies abate rateably unless by his will the testator has shown an intention that one or more pecuniary legacies are to have priority.

Paragraph 6—property specifically devised or bequeathed. Under paragraph 6 property specifically devised or bequeathed bears the burden of expenses and debts "rateably according to value."

(1) *Rateably according to value.* In applying paragraph 6 the relevant value is the value of each property to the testator at his death. *Re John*[32]

---

[28] For the analogous situation where part of residue is expressly charged with debts see *Re Atkinson* [1930] 1 Ch. 47; *Re Martin* [1955] Ch. 698; *Re Feis* [1964] Ch. 106.

[29] [1940] Ch. 769: see also *Re Kempthorne, supra.*

[30] *Re James* [1947] Ch. 256, 261–262.

[31] *Post*, pp. 294 *et seq.* As to abatement of annuities see *post*, pp. 305 *et seq.*

[32] [1933] Ch. 370: see also *Re Cohen* [1960] Ch. 179 (probate values and not later sale values).

provides a classic illustration. By his will T gave Blackacre (subject to a mortgage created by T during his lifetime) to X and Whiteacre (subject to certain legacies given by T's will) to Y. Farwell J. held that Blackacre and Whiteacre were liable to bear the burden of expenses and debts rateably according to the value of each property to the testator at his death. In the case of Blackacre this was the probate value of T's equity of redemption (*i.e.* the value of Blackacre less the mortgage debt), and in the case of Whiteacre the probate value of Whiteacre but without making any deduction for the legacies to be paid thereout.[33]

(2) *Option given by will.* By his will T may give X an option to purchase particular property comprised in T's estate at a stated price from T's personal representatives. For instance, in *Re Eve*[34] T by his will gave X an option to acquire 1,000 of T's ordinary shares in a particular company at the price of £1 per share, which was less than the market value. X duly gave notice of his intention to exercise the option. T's residue was insufficient to pay expenses and debts in full and the question arose whether these shares had to bear any part of the expenses and debts. Roxburgh J. said that, "The shares are not bequeathed subject to a charge or condition. An option to purchase cannot be a specific bequest of shares"[35] and the benefit given to X (*i.e.* the difference between the stated price and the market value) was not a specific bequest. He decided that property subject to an option given by will did not fall anywhere within the statutory order. He concluded that—

> "the property subject to an option is the last to be available for the payment of debts. For, indeed, in so far as the property subject to the option is required for the payment of debts, the option over that property cannot be exercised at all, and the benefit of it is totally destroyed by operation of law. But so long as the purchase price stated in the will is, with the other available assets, sufficient for the payment of debts, it, and not the shares, constitutes the fund available for that purpose."[36]

If the principles enunciated in *Re Eve* are good law, an option is destroyed if any sum, however small, is required from the property (in addition to the option price) for the payment of expenses and debts. The destruction of the option frees the option property to meet expenses and debts (normally as part of the residuary estate), and thereby benefits a beneficiary under the will who was given other property which was liable for expenses and debts before the option property. In essence the decision in *Re Eve* treats X as a person with a right to purchase the shares if available for sale, and not as a beneficiary whose benefit under the will is liable to abatement.[37] But of course

---

[33] Subject to the provisions of the will, the legatees take priority over Y and the legacies only abate if Whiteacre (after bearing its share of expenses and debts) is insufficient to pay them in full, *Re Saunders-Davies* (1887) 34 Ch.D. 482; *Re Bawden* [1894] 1 Ch. 693.

[34] [1956] Ch. 479.

[35] *Ibid.* at p. 482.

[36] *Ibid.* at p. 483; but *cf. Re Kerry* [1889] W.N. 3.

[37] *Cf. Re Fison's W.T.* [1950] Ch. 394, esp. at p. 407 (effect of Administration of Estates Act 1925, s.35(1) on option) and see *post*, p. 277; *Re Lander* [1951] Ch. 546 (incidence of estate duty on an option) and see *post*, p. 282.

X acquired his right to purchase the shares by virtue of the gift of the option to X in the will: it is arguable that X is really a beneficiary and as such his benefit ought to be liable to abatement.

If X takes as a beneficiary under a conditional specific gift in the will, the property falls within paragraph 6 and the gift abates with the other specific devises or bequests. Thus if by his will T gives his property Blackacre to X if X pays £1,000 to Y, Blackacre is property specifically devised and falls within paragraph 6. Does it make any difference if X is required to pay the £1,000 to T's estate and not to Y? If on the true construction of T's will X takes as a beneficiary, it makes no difference and Blackacre falls within paragraph 6.[38]

Paragraph 7—property appointed by will under a general power. Paragraph 7 is the last paragraph in the statutory order. "Property appointed by will under a general power, including the statutory power to dispose of entailed interests"[39] falls within paragraph 7 and is liable for expenses and debts rateably according to value.

Under section 27 of the Wills Act 1837 a general gift includes property over which the testator has a general power of appointment, unless the will shows a contrary intention.[40] Accordingly such property passes under a residuary gift without any express appointment, unless the will shows a contrary intention. Alternatively the testator may make a gift of his residuary estate "including any property over which I have a general power of appointment." Before 1926, if a residuary bequest in a will included personal property over which the testator had a general power of appointment (either by virtue of section 27 or by such express inclusion), the appointed property was liable for expenses and debts as if it formed part of the testator's residuary personalty.[41] It has been suggested that since 1925, if a residuary gift includes real or personal property over which the testator has a general power of appointment (either by virtue of section 27 or by express inclusion), the appointed property is liable for expenses and debts under paragraph 2, and not under paragraph 7, of the statutory order.[42] If this is so, it must be because the will has thereby varied the statutory order, as paragraph 2 only applies to property of the deceased.

Assets not included in the statutory order. As already explained, property which is subject to an option given by the testator's will was held in Re Eve to fall outside the statutory order. Again, property appointed by deed under a general power and property given by donatio mortis causa are liable for the deceased's debts in the last resort,[43] though neither is mentioned in the statutory order: the order of application of these assets inter se remains to be decided.

---

[38] Probably, if X is required to pay the £1,000 to T's estate, the burden of debts and expenses falling on Blackacre ought to be borne so far as possible by the £1,000 paid by X: cf. ante, n. 33.
[39] Ante. p. 252.
[40] Post, pp. 428–430.
[41] Re Hartley [1900] 1 Ch. 152.
[42] Hawkins and Ryder on the Construction of Wills (1965), p. 361.
[43] Ante, pp. 253 and 254.

B. Debts Charged on the Deceased's Property

Under section 35 of the Administration of Estates Act 1925 a special rule applies to any debt charged on property of the deceased. A common instance is a mortgage debt due from the deceased to a building society and charged on the deceased's freehold or leasehold house. Under this rule the property charged is primarily liable for the payment of the debt unless the deceased has shown a contrary intention. If by his will the deceased gives his house to his widow in fee simple, she takes it subject to the mortgage debt due to the building society and is not entitled to have the mortgage debt discharged out of other assets of the deceased's estate not taken by her, unless the deceased has shown a contrary intention.

Section 35(1), which is applicable on the death of any person after 1925,[44] provides as follows:

"Where a person dies possessed of, or entitled to, or, under a general power of appointment (including the statutory power to dispose of entailed interests) by his will disposes of, an interest in property, which at the time of his death is charged with the payment of money, whether by way of legal mortgage, equitable charge or otherwise (including a lien for unpaid purchase money), and the deceased has not by will deed or other document signified a contrary or other intention, the interest so charged shall, as between the different persons claiming through the deceased, be primarily liable for the payment of the charge; and every part of the said interest, according to its value, shall bear a proportionate part of the charge on the whole thereof."

Property charged at death. For section 35(1) to apply there must be an interest in property which is charged with the payment of money at the time of the deceased's death.

(1) *Interest in property.* Section 35(1) applies to any interest in any property, whether real or personal,[45] (i) if the deceased is possessed of or entitled to it at his death,[46] or (ii) if by his will the deceased disposes of it under a general power of appointment (including the statutory power to dispose of entailed interests).[47] Usually the property charged is an interest in land but section 35(1) also applies to pure personalty— for instance, to the deceased's company shares which under the articles of association are subject to an equitable charge for money owing to the company by the deceased at his death.[48]

---

[44] Administration of Estates Act 1925, s.54. On a death before 1926 the Real Estate Charges Act 1854 (Locke King's Act) and the Real Estate Charges Acts 1867 and 1877 (all together called Locke King's Acts) applied this special rule to any debt charged on realty or leaseholds, but not on pure personalty.

[45] *Ibid.* s.55(1)(xvii).

[46] *Re Coxen* [1948] 2 All E.R. 492 (motor car ordered by but no particular car appropriated to deceased: s.35 not applicable to unpaid price as deceased not entitled at death).

[47] *Ante*, p. 252. On a death before 1926 the Acts did not apply to entails, *Re Anthony* [1893] 3 Ch. 398.

[48] *Re Turner* [1938] Ch. 593: see also *Re Coxen, supra*, at p. 496.

(2) *Charged with the payment of money at death.* The section applies to any charge "whether by way of legal mortgage, equitable charge or otherwise (including a lien for unpaid purchase money)." It is not confined to charges created by act of parties[49] but extends to charges created by statute, such as the charge on realty and foreign property for estate duty,[50] the Inland Revenue charge for inheritance tax,[51] and the charge imposed by a court on property of a judgment debtor.[52]

But the interest in property must be charged with the payment of money at the time of the deceased's death. In *Re Birmingham*[53] T contracted to buy Blackacre from V at the price of £3,500 and paid to V a deposit of £350. Before completion of the purchase T died. After T's death her solicitors completed their work in connection with the purchase and became entitled to their costs. By her will T gave Blackacre to her daughter D and her residuary estate to E and F. The court held that under section 35(1) D took Blackacre subject to V's lien for the unpaid balance of the purchase price: V's lien arose when the contract was made and therefore Blackacre was already charged with the payment of this unpaid balance at T's death. Thus, if the market value of Blackacre was £3,500, D only benefited to the extent of the £350 deposit. On the other hand, the court held that the solicitors' costs did not fall within section 35(1), but were payable out of T's residue as an ordinary debt, because at T's death Blackacre was not charged with the payment of these costs.[54]

Incidence of the charge under section 35. Assuming that the deceased has not shown a contrary intention then "as between the different persons claiming through the deceased" the charged property is made primarily liable for the payment of the charge. The section regulates the incidence of the charge as between the different beneficiaries claiming through the deceased.[55]

(1) *Two properties (charged together) given to different beneficiaries.* To consider an example. At his death T is entitled to the Whiteacre Estate (which comprises Greater Whiteacre and Lesser Whiteacre) in fee simple subject to a mortgage securing a loan of £25,000 by M to T. By his will T gives Greater Whiteacre to X and his residuary estate (including Lesser Whiteacre) to Y. Under section 35(1) each part of the property charged, according to its value, must bear a proportionate part of the

---

[49] *Pembrooke* v. *Friend* (1860) 1 J. & H. 132 (equitable mortgage by deposit of title deeds); *Re Hawkes* [1912] 2 Ch. 251 (memorandum of charge securing an overdraft; *Re Kidd* [1894] 3 Ch. 558 and *Re Fraser* [1904] 1 Ch. 726 (vendor's lien).

[50] *Re Bowerman* [1908] 2 Ch. 340 (A died intestate leaving realty; B, who was A's heir and next of kin, died intestate: held B's heir took the realty subject to the statutory charge for estate duty payable on it in respect of A's death).

[51] Inheritance Tax Act 1984, s.237.

[52] Charging Orders Act 1979, ss.1–3: see *Re Anthony* [1892] 1 Ch. 450 (charge created by Judgments Act 1838, s.13).

[53] [1959] Ch. 523.

[54] *Ibid.* at p. 531: the court pointed out that, if the conveyance had been completed in T's lifetime, the solicitors would have received the title deeds in the normal course and at T's death would have had an equitable lien on the deeds for their unpaid costs.

[55] Including the Crown taking property as *bona vacantia* on an intestacy, Administration of Estates Act 1925, ss.46(1)(vi) and 57(1).

charge. Thus X takes Greater Whiteacre and Y takes Lesser Whiteacre subject (in each case) to a rateable proportion of the mortgage debt. In *Re Neeld*[56] the Court of Appeal held that the fact that part of the mortgaged property is specifically devised and the other part falls into residue does not signify a contrary intention so as to exclude the application of section 35(1).

(2) *Two properties (charged separately) given to the same beneficiary.* Next a different situation involving two charges, each on a different property. At his death T is entitled in fee simple to (i) Blackacre subject to a mortgage securing a loan of £10,000 to T, and (ii) Greenacre subject to another mortgage securing a loan of £6,000 to T. By his will T gives Blackacre and Greenacre by two separate gifts to B and his residuary estate to C. Under section 35(1) B takes Blackacre subject to the £10,000 mortgage and Greenacre subject to the £6,000 mortgage. If Blackacre is worth less than the mortgage debt secured on it, the amount of the deficiency falls on the fund liable for T's unsecured debts (in this example T's residuary estate); section 35(1) does not saddle B with an obligation to make up the deficiency out of the equity of redemption of Greenacre.[57]

However, T by his will may show an intention that B is to take Blackacre and Greenacre as a whole subject to the burden of both the mortgages: in that event under the will the amount of the deficiency in respect of Blackacre falls primarily on the equity of redemption of Greenacre.[58]

Section 35 confined to regulating incidence between beneficiaries. Section 35 is solely concerned with regulating the incidence of the charge as between the different beneficiaries.

(1) *Chargee's rights remain the same.* Section 35(3) makes it clear that the rights of the chargee (*i.e.* the person entitled to the charge) are not affected in any way. If the deceased was personally liable to the chargee for the debt, the chargee may obtain payment out of other assets of the deceased: if he does so, the doctrine of marshalling applies so that the debt falls ultimately on the charged property.[59] Again a beneficiary entitled to the charged property under the deceased's will or intestacy does not become personally liable to the chargee for the debt,[60] but if the beneficiary fails to make the payments due under the charge, the chargee is likely to enforce his remedies against the property.

(2) *Debt not falling on property charged with it.* If the charged property of the deceased is not primarily liable for the debt, section 35 is only rel-

---

[56] [1962] Ch. 643, where the authorities are reviewed and *Re Biss* [1956] Ch. 243 is overruled. In *Re Biss* it was held that Lesser Whiteacre which fell into residue was primarily liable for the whole mortgage debt.

[57] *Re Holt* (1916) 115 L.T. 73 (pre-1926 intestacy under which B took Blackacre and Greenacre as heir: the balance of the mortgage debt secured on Blackacre fell on the deceased's personalty as the fund then liable for unsecured debts, and not on Greenacre).

[58] *Frewen* v. *Law Life Assurance Society* [1896] 2 Ch. 511; *Re Baron Kensington* [1902] 1 Ch. 203.

[59] *Post*, pp. 284–285.

[60] *Syer* v. *Gladstone* (1885) 30 Ch.D. 614 (the headnote is misleading).

evant so far as the debt cannot be discharged by the person, or from the property, primarily liable and therefore falls on the charged property. In *Re Ritson*[61] T, who carried on a business in partnership with his brother, charged his own freehold property to secure a partnership debt to the bank. At T's death the partnership assets were sufficient to pay all the partnership debts in full, including the debt to the bank. The Court of Appeal held that the debt to the bank must be paid out of the partnership assets and that T's executors were only entitled to T's share of any surplus partnership assets after payment of all the partnership debts. The debt to the bank did not fall on T's freehold property or any other asset of his estate, and therefore no question arose as to the incidence of this debt as between the different beneficiaries entitled to T's estate.

(3) *Option given by will.* Does section 35(1) apply if by his will T gives X an option to purchase particular property comprised in T's estate at a stated price from T's personal representatives and the property is charged with a debt at T's death? The answer depends on the construction of T's will. If X is to be regarded as a person with a right to purchase (even though on favourable terms), then section 35(1) does not apply and if X exercises the option he is entitled to a transfer of the property free from incumbrances. On the other hand, if X is to be regarded as a beneficiary under the will, then under section 35(1) X can only take the property subject to the charge.[62]

Contrary intention. The deceased's contrary or other intention (excluding or modifying the operation of section 35(1)) may be shown by will, deed or other document. In practice, if a testator wishes to give particular property free from charges, it is desirable for him to show his intention clearly in his will, rather than by letter or in some other document.

(1) *Direction in will for payment from personal or residuary estate.* Under section 35(2) a general direction by a testator for the payment of debts (or all his debts) out of his general personal estate, or his residuary real and personal estate, or his residuary real estate (or a charge of debts on any such estate) is not enough to exclude the operation of section 35(1). There must, in addition, be words expressly or by necessary implication referring to all or some part of the charge. For example, by his will T makes a specific devise of Whiteacre to X, and at T's death Whiteacre is charged with a mortgage debt due from T. Whiteacre will be relieved of the primary burden of the mortgage debt if by his will T directs payment out of residue of all his debts, "including the mortgage debt charged on Whiteacre" *or* "including all my mortgage debts." Similarly Whiteacre will be relieved of this burden if by his will T directs payment out of residue of all his debts "except mortgage debts, if any, charged on Brownacre": these words by necessary implication show T's

---

[61] [1899] 1 Ch. 128: see also *Re Holland* [1907] 2 Ch. 88 and *Re Hawkes* [1912] 2 Ch. 251, 255 (if T charges his property as surety, and after T's death the principal debtor pays off the debt, no question arises as to its incidence between T's beneficiaries).

[62] *Re Fison's W.T.* [1950] Ch. 394, esp. 407 (reviewing previous authorities): see also *Re Biss* [1956] Ch. 243 (devise subject to right of pre-emption).

intention that the mortgage debt on Whiteacre is to be paid out of residue.[63]

(2) *Direction in will for payment from special fund.* On the other hand a direction by T for the payment of his debts out of a special fund (not being his general personal estate, residuary real and personal estate, or residuary real estate) is sufficient to show his intention that any debt charged on Whiteacre is to be paid out of the special fund—in this case there need be no express or implied reference to the charge on Whiteacre. Thus, if T directs payment of his debts out of his Barclays Bank account *or* out of the proceeds of sale of his property Greenacre, this shows his intention that any debt charged on Whiteacre is to be paid out of this account or out of these proceeds.[64]

However, if the special fund is inadequate to pay off the whole of the debt charged on Whiteacre, Whiteacre remains primarily liable under section 35(1) for the payment of the unsatisfied balance.[65] Thus in *Re Birch*[66] T made a specific devise of Whiteacre (which at his death was subject to a mortgage debt of £500), directed that this mortgage debt should be paid out of the proceeds of sale of Blackacre, and disposed of his residuary estate. The net proceeds of sale of Blackacre amounted to only £285. The court held that Whiteacre remained primarily liable for the payment of the balance of the mortgage debt. T had shown an intention to exonerate Whiteacre to the extent of the proceeds of sale of Blackacre, but had not shown any intention to exonerate Whiteacre out of his residuary estate.

(3) *Document other than deceased's will.* In order to show a contrary intention (excluding or modifying the operation of section 35(1)) in a non-testamentary document, the deceased must indicate how he intends the burden of the charge to be borne as between the beneficiaries after his death. Thus, if T contracts to buy Blackacre from V and sends to his solicitors a letter enclosing a cheque and stating "Cheque enclosed for balance of purchase money," this letter merely indicates T's intention as to the payment of the unpaid balance of the purchase price in his lifetime. If T dies before completion of the purchase, the letter does not indicate how the burden of V's lien for the unpaid balance of the purchase price is to be borne as between the beneficiaries under T's will.[67] Again in *Re Birmingham* (which has already been discussed[68]) T, having contracted to buy Blackacre from V, wrote to her solicitors stating that she wished to leave Blackacre to her daughter D, and T subsequently executed a codicil to this effect. The court held that

---

[63] *Re Valpy* [1906] 1 Ch. 531. See also *Re Fleck* (1888) 37 Ch.D. 677 ("trade debts" to be paid from residuary personalty included trade debt secured by equitable mortgage); *Re Nevill* (1889) 59 L.J.Ch. 511. *Cf. Re Beirnstein* [1925] Ch. 12 (direction to pay sums secured on mortgage does not apply to unpaid purchase money secured by vendor's lien).

[64] *Re Fegan* [1928] Ch. 45.

[65] *Ibid.*

[66] [1909] 1 Ch. 787.

[67] *Re Wakefield* [1943] 2 All E.R. 29: see also *Re Nicholson* [1923] W.N. 251 (T served six months' notice on mortgagee of her intention to pay off mortgage but died before doing so: held letter showed no contrary intention excluding s.35(1)).

[68] *Ante*, p. 275.

T had not signified a contrary intention because neither the letter nor the codicil indicated how the burden of V's lien was to be borne as between the beneficiaries under T's will.

C. Incidence of Inheritance Tax

Rules are needed to determine the incidence of inheritance tax payable by personal representatives in respect of the deceased's death. There are two basic rules:

1. Inheritance tax on the deceased's free real and personal estate in the United Kingdom is a testamentary and administration expense[69] and is payable in accordance with the statutory order of application of assets.
2. Inheritance tax on any other property falls on that property and must be borne by the beneficiary who takes it.[70]

Both these rules apply subject to any contrary intention shown by the deceased in his will. It is convenient to refer to such a contrary direction as a "free of inheritance tax" provision.

The Inheritance Tax Act 1984 includes detailed rules as to the incidence on gifts by will of the exemptions from inheritance tax, such as the exemption for a transfer by the deceased to his spouse. These detailed rules are set out in the Inheritance Tax Act[71] and are not discussed here.[72]

1. Inheritance tax as a testamentary expense. Inheritance tax payable by personal representatives is a testamentary and administration expense if it is payable in respect of the deceased's death on his free real and personal estate in the United Kingdom, *i.e.* on "the value of property in the United Kingdom which (a) vests in the deceased's personal representatives, and (b) was not immediately before the death comprised in a settlement."[73] Thus, if by his will T makes specific gifts of his freehold house Blackacre situated in Yorkshire and his shares in BP to his son, any inheritance tax payable in respect of T's death on the value of these assets is a testamentary expense and is payable in accordance with the statutory order of application of assets, unless there is a contrary direction in the will. As these gifts are specific, Blackacre and T's shares in BP fall within paragraph 6 of the statutory order and are only liable for expenses and debts after property falling within paragraphs 1 to 5 has been exhausted.

Certain items of property are conditionally exempted from inheritance tax on death. For instance such pictures, prints, books, manuscripts, works of art, scientific collections or other things not yielding income as appear to the Treasury to be of national, scientific, historic or

---

[69] Inheritance Tax Act 1984, s.211(1).
[70] *Ibid.* s.211(3).
[71] ss.36–42, as amended by Finance Act 1986, s.105 and Sched. 19, para. 13.
[72] See Whitehouse & Stuart-Buttle, *Revenue Law* (5th ed., 1987), pp. 358 *et seq.*
[73] Inheritance Tax Act 1984, s.211(1).

artistic interest are exempted from inheritance tax if an undertaking is given to keep each such object in the United Kingdom and to take steps agreed with the Treasury for its preservation and for securing reasonable access to the public.[74] If this undertaking is broken, or if the object is disposed of, a charge to inheritance tax arises.[75] However, this inheritance tax is not a testamentary expense because otherwise personal representatives would need to retain assets indefinitely in order to cover any charge to inheritance tax arising on any future breach of this undertaking or on any future disposal. Instead, for the sake of convenience, this inheritance tax is to be borne by the persons who would be interested in the proceeds of sale of the object,[76] or who disposed of the object.[77] Similar provisions apply to land which in the opinion of the Treasury is of outstanding scenic or historic or scientific interest, to a building for the preservation of which special steps should in the opinion of the Treasury be taken by reason of its outstanding historic or architectural interest, to any area of land which in the opinion of the Treasury is essential for the protection of the character and amenities of such a building, and to an object which in the opinion of the Treasury is historically associated with such a building.[78]

2. **Inheritance tax borne by the beneficiary**. Inheritance tax which is payable in respect of the deceased's death on any property other than the deceased's free real and personal estate in the United Kingdom falls on that property and must be borne by the beneficiary who takes it. This second rule arises from section 211(3) of the Inheritance Tax Act 1984 which provides that, where personal representatives have paid tax which is not a testamentary expense, it shall where occasion requires, be repaid to them by the person in whom the property is vested.[79]

Section 211(3) applies to all property movable or immovable outside the United Kingdom. It also applies to property which does not vest in the deceased's personal representatives, such as property given by *donatio mortis causa*[80] or statutory nomination,[81] and the deceased's severable share of property held jointly (which vests by survivorship in the other joint tenant). In each case under this second rule the personal representatives are entitled to claim repayment of the inheritance tax which they have paid from the person in whom the property is vested. In practice, in the case of property outside the United Kingdom, the personal representatives may experience difficulty in obtaining repay-

---

[74] *Ibid.* ss.30–31, as amended by Finance Act 1985, Sched. 26.

[75] *Ibid.* ss.32 and 33: certain disposals do not make tax chargeable, s.32(4) and (5).

[76] *Ibid.* s.207(1) (breach of undertaking).

[77] *Ibid.* s.207(2) (disposal).

[78] *Ibid.* ss.31–33, as amended by Finance Act 1985, Sched. 26.

[79] Repayment may be made by instalments if the personal representatives had an option to pay by instalments, s.213; a certificate by the Revenue specifying the tax paid is conclusive, s.214.

[80] *Re Hudson* [1911] 1 Ch. 206 (estate duty on a *d.m.c.* is not a testamentary expense): the bare legal title to the subject matter of a *d.m.c.* may vest in the personal representatives but the equitable interest vests in the donee, see *ante*, p. 24.

[81] *Re Walley* [1972] 1 W.L.R. 257 (estate duty on a statutory nomination not a testamentary expense).

ment if the foreign executors and beneficiary remain out of the jurisdiction.

Section 211(3) also applies to any land (whether freehold or leasehold) which was settled land at the death of the deceased. This is so whether the land vests in the deceased's special personal representatives or whether, ceasing to be settled at the deceased's death, it vests in his general personal representatives.

Incidence of inheritance tax on a pecuniary legacy. In the absence of any contrary direction in T's will, these two basic rules regulate the incidence of inheritance tax on any immediate pecuniary legacy given by T's will.

(1) *Property from which immediate pecuniary legacy is payable.* The incidence of inheritance tax on an immediate pecuniary legacy therefore depends on the nature of the property from which it is payable. This is determined by the provisions of T's will, or by the general rules as to the incidence of pecuniary legacies.[82] If under the provisions of T's will, or these general rules, the pecuniary legacy is payable out of T's free real and personal estate in the United Kingdom, any inheritance tax is a testamentary expense. On the other hand, so far as the pecuniary legacy is payable out of T's property outside the United Kingdom, the pecuniary legacy bears its own inheritance tax.

A pecuniary legacy may be made payable out of a mixed fund of (i) real and personal property in the United Kingdom and (ii) property outside the United Kingdom, the mixed fund being held on trust for sale. Say T by his will gives to C a legacy of £50,000 and gives his residuary real and personal estate to his trustees upon trust for sale and out of the proceeds of sale to pay his funeral and testamentary expenses, debts and legacies. This has the effect of charging C's legacy rateably on all the assets comprised in T's residuary estate. If his residuary estate includes property outside the United Kingdom then, so far as C's legacy is payable out of this property, the legacy bears its own inheritance tax.[83] This is a trap into which testators fall—a testator does not intend a legacy to be reduced by being forced to contribute to the inheritance tax payable on foreign property comprised in his residuary estate. In order to avoid this trap, T needs to insert in his will a suitable free of inheritance tax provision stating that C's legacy is to be free of inheritance tax. Alternatively, T may direct by his will that C's legacy is to be paid out of T's real and personal estate in the United Kingdom.

(2) *Deferred pecuniary legacy.* The position is different in the case of a deferred pecuniary legacy given by T's will. Say T by his will gives property on trust for P for life, and after P's death on trust to pay a pecuniary legacy to Q and subject thereto for R absolutely. When P dies Q and R must bear the inheritance tax payable on the property in respect of P's death rateably according to the respective values of Q's legacy and

---

[82] *Post,* pp. 308 *et seq.*
[83] See *Re Owers* [1941] Ch. 17 (estate duty on pecuniary legacy); *Re Spencer Cooper* [1908] 1 Ch. 130.

R's residue, and this is so even though the property is situated in the United Kingdom.[84]

Incidence of inheritance tax on an option. If T by his will gives X an option to purchase particular property comprised in T's estate at a stated price from T's personal representatives, how is the inheritance tax to be borne? If the option property is real or personal estate in the United Kingdom, the inheritance tax is payable as a testamentary expense in accordance with the statutory order of application of assets, subject of course to any contrary direction by T in his will. If the option property is situated outside the United Kingdom, the decision in *Re Lander*[85] (on the incidence of estate duty) provides some guidance on the incidence of inheritance tax. In that case T by his will gave X an option to purchase Redacre (which, like property outside the United Kingdom, bore its own estate duty) for £14,000 from T's executors. X duly exercised the option. Assuming (for purposes of explanation) that at T's death the value of Redacre was £21,000,[86] the court held that X must bear one-third of the estate duty on Redacre and T's residue must bear the other two-thirds. In effect X was treated as taking Redacre as a beneficiary as to one-third of its value, and as a purchaser as to two-thirds of its value.[87]

Free of inheritance tax provisions

(1) *The need for variation*. The rules which govern the incidence of inheritance tax payable in respect of a deceased's death are unsatisfactory because they do not carry out the likely intentions of the deceased. How many testators would wish inheritance tax to be borne by one beneficiary who takes a specific gift of shares in a foreign company, but not by another beneficiary who takes a specific gift of shares in an English company? Again, how many testators would wish inheritance tax to be borne by a pecuniary legatee in so far as his legacy is payable from property outside the United Kingdom, but not otherwise? No doubt incidence rules as to tax are bound to be technical but they ought not to constitute a trap for testators.[88]

While these unsatisfactory incidence rules remain in force a testator needs to consider very carefully what free of inheritance tax provisions he wishes to insert in his will. A testator may vary these incidence rules by his will as he chooses.[89] Of course if the testator wishes to relieve one beneficiary of the burden of the tax which he would otherwise be liable to bear, the testator needs to consider which other beneficiary is

---

[84] See *Berry* v. *Gaukroger* [1903] 2 Ch. 116. Probably Q's legacy does not bear inheritance tax payable in respect of T's death even though it falls on the property, see *Re McNeill* [1958] Ch. 259 and *Re Maryon-Wilson's W.T.* [1968] Ch. 268.

[85] [1951] Ch. 546: *cf. Re Jolley* (1901) 17 T.L.R. 244.

[86] In fact the value was £21,645 so that X bore 7645/21645ths of the estate duty.

[87] *Cf.* the incidence on an option of expenses and debts, and of a charged debt falling within the Administration of Estates Act 1925, s.35: see *ante*, pp. 272 and 277.

[88] *Re Owers* [1941] Ch. 17, 19.

[89] Administration of Estates Act 1925, s.34(3) and Sched. 1, Pt. II, para. 8(*a*) (as to testamentary expenses); Inheritance Tax Act 1984, s.211(2) and (3).

to bear the burden of that tax. A free of inheritance tax provision shifts the burden from one beneficiary to another.[90]

(2) *Construction.* The Inheritance Tax Act 1984 provides that so far as any provision in any document, whenever executed, refers (in whatever terms) to estate duty or death duties, it shall have effect, so far as may be, as if it also referred to inheritance tax chargeable on death.[91] Similarly any reference to capital transfer tax in any document has effect as a reference to inheritance tax.[92]

The construction of a free of inheritance tax provision always depends on the precise words of the particular provision, which must be read in the context of the will as a whole so as to ascertain the testator's intention. However the existing case law on free of duty (*i.e.* free of estate duty) provisions gives some guidance to the likely construction of free of inheritance tax provisions. On the basis of this case law the court will probably adopt the following approach:

(i) The court will presume that a free of inheritance tax provision is only intended by the testator to apply to tax payable in respect of his own death and not to tax payable in respect of any other event, such as the subsequent death of a beneficiary who takes a life interest under the testator's will.[93] In order to rebut this presumption the testator needs to show an intention to provide for tax payable in respect of that other event.[94] If the testator does so, the personal representatives will be obliged to retain sufficient assets to meet an unknown amount of tax payable in the future on the occurrence of that other event. This is very inconvenient—hence the presumption against this being the testator's intention.

(ii) A direction in a will to pay "testamentary expenses" out of residue will only apply to inheritance tax so far as it is a testamentary expense, and not to inheritance tax payable on property outside the United Kingdom.[95] On the other hand, a direction in a will to pay "all inheritance tax" out of residue will include tax payable on property outside the United Kingdom[96] in respect of the dispositions made by the will.[97] But such a direction must always be read in the context of the will as a whole. Thus if the will includes a number of specific gifts of property outside the United Kingdom, some stated to be free of inheritance tax and others silent as to tax, a subsequent direction to pay all inheritance tax out of residue may be construed as an administrative provision inserted in order to give effect to the earlier provisions relieving certain specific gifts from the burden of bearing their own tax, and not

---

[90] But an exempt gift of a share of residue can never bear inheritance tax attributable to a non-exempt share of residue, Inheritance Tax Act 1984, s.41.

[91] Sched. 6, para. 1; Finance Act 1986, s.100(1).

[92] Finance Act 1986, s.100(1).

[93] *Re Shepherd* [1949] Ch. 117; *Re Embleton's W.T.* [1965] 1 W.L.R. 840.

[94] *Re Jones* [1928] W.N. 227; *Re Paterson's W.T.* [1963] 1 W.L.R. 623.

[95] *Re Owers* [1941] Ch. 17.

[96] *Re Pimm* [1904] 2 Ch. 345; *Re Neeld (No. 2)* [1965] 1 W.L.R. 73, 76.

[97] *Re Walley* [1972] 1 W.L.R. 257 (on construction of will estate duty direction extended to statutory nomination but not *inter vivos* gifts).

as a general direction relieving the other specific gifts from this burden.[98]

D. Marshalling as Between Beneficiaries

Need for marshalling. A creditor of the deceased may obtain payment out of any of the assets, regardless of the rules as to the incidence of the deceased's expenses and debts as between the beneficiaries entitled under his will or intestacy or any variation of these rules by the deceased.[99] If a creditor is paid out of an asset which, as between the beneficiaries, is not liable to bear the burden of his debt, the doctrine of marshalling provides a remedy for the disappointed beneficiary. The doctrine ensures that the incidence rules, and not the choice of a creditor or of the personal representatives, finally prevail as between the beneficiaries.[1]

Effect of marshalling. Under the doctrine of marshalling equity adjusts the remaining assets so as to compensate B, the disappointed beneficiary. Say the creditor has obtained payment out of Blackacre, which was specifically devised to B by the deceased in his will and which therefore falls within paragraph 6 of the statutory order of application of assets. Assuming that the deceased did not vary the statutory order by his will, any property falling within paragraphs 1 to 5 of the statutory order is liable for expenses and debts before Blackacre. Accordingly B is entitled to compensation out of any property falling within paragraphs 1 to 5.

"The general principle of marshalling is that if any beneficiary is disappointed of his benefit under the will through a creditor being paid out of the property intended for the beneficiary, then to the extent of the disappointment the beneficiary may recoup or compensate himself by going against any property which ought to have been used to pay the debts before resorting to his property."[2]

Again, if other property was specifically devised or bequeathed by the deceased in his will, B is entitled to insist that it must contribute rateably to the payment of the debt.[3]

If B obtains compensation out of property included in the deceased's residuary gift (falling within paragraph 2), but property not effectively disposed of by the deceased's will (falling within paragraph 1) is available to meet expenses and debts, the residuary beneficiary is in turn entitled to compensation out of the property not effectively disposed of. In this way the debt is ultimately borne by the property which, as between the beneficiaries, is liable to bear its burden.

---

[98] *Re King* [1942] Ch. 413; *Re Neeld (No. 2), supra; Re Phuler's W.T.* [1965] 1 W.L.R. 68; *cf. Re Williams* [1974] 1 W.L.R. 754.

[99] *Ante,* p. 265.

[1] *Aldrich* v. *Cooper* (1803) 8 Ves. 382, 396; *Re Cohen* [1960] Ch. 179, 190. See also Administration of Estates Act 1925, s.2(3).

[2] Snell's *Principles of Equity* (25th ed., 1960), p. 337, quoted in *Re Matthews' W.T.* [1961] 1 W.L.R. 1415, 1419. See also *Re Wilson* [1967] Ch. 53, 72.

[3] *Tombs* v. *Roch* (1846) 2 Coll. 490; *Gervis* v. *Gervis* (1847) 14 Sim. 654: see also *Re Cohen, supra.*

Assessment of compensation. Compensation is assessed so as to make good to the disappointed beneficiary what he has lost. In *Re Broadwood*[4] T by his will gave all his shares in a particular company to T's son if he attained the age of 21 years. T's executors sold some of the shares at the price of 17s. 6d. per share for the purpose of paying T's debts. Later T's son attained 21 years and under the doctrine of marshalling became entitled to compensation (from the fund retained to meet T's pecuniary legacies) for his disappointment in not receiving the shares which had been sold. When T's son attained 21 years the shares were worth only 5s. per share. The court held that the compensation must be measured by the loss to the son at the date when he attained 21 years and became entitled to a transfer of the shares—*i.e.* by the loss of the value of 5s., and not 17s. 6d., per share.[5]

3. INSOLVENT ESTATE

The deceased's estate is insolvent if the assets, when realised, will be insufficient to meet in full all his funeral, testamentary and administration expenses, debts and liabilities.[6] Solvency or insolvency is a question of fact.[7] For instance, if during his lifetime the deceased covenanted to pay an annuity to X for life, and X survives the deceased, the capital value of the annuity at the deceased's death is treated as a debt due from the deceased in order to test whether the deceased's estate is solvent or insolvent.[8] If there is doubt as to the solvency of the deceased's estate, the prudent course is for the personal representatives to administer the estate in accordance with the rules applicable to an insolvent estate and make no distribution to the beneficiaries, until it becomes certain that the estate is solvent.

If the deceased's estate is insolvent but is not being administered in bankruptcy, certain provisions of the law of bankruptcy are applicable in the administration of the deceased's estate. These provisions are specified in the Administration of Insolvent Estates of Deceased Persons Order 1986[9] and, unlike the incidence rules applicable in the case of a solvent estate, they cannot be varied by a contrary intention on the part of the deceased.[10] The provisions regulate "competition" between the creditors as to which of them shall be paid—the creditors cannot all be paid in full and of course nothing is distributable to the beneficiaries.

Under the Administration of Insolvent Estates of Deceased Persons Order 1986:

---

[4] [1911] 1 Ch. 277.

[5] Plus any dividends paid in respect of the period since T's death.

[6] Insolvency Act 1986, s.421(4); see *Re Leng* [1895] 1 Ch. 652, 658.

[7] *Re Pink* [1927] 1 Ch. 237, 241–242: see also *Re Smith* (1883) 22 Ch.D. 586, 592 (the court may direct an inquiry whether the estate is insolvent) and *George Lee & Sons (Builders) Ltd.* v. *Olink* [1972] 1 W.L.R. 214 (inquiry ordered).

[8] *Re Pink, supra.*

[9] S.I. 1986 No. 1999, made under the Insolvency Act 1986, s.421.

[10] *Re Rothermere* [1943] 1 All E.R. 307; *Turner* v. *Cox* (1853) 8 Moo.P.C. 288.

(i) The reasonable funeral, testamentary, and administration expenses have priority over preferential debts.[11]

(ii) The bankruptcy rules apply to the administration of the estate "with respect to the respective rights of secured and unsecured creditors, to debts and liabilities provable, to the valuation of future and contingent liabilities and to the priorities of debts and other payments."

Thus some, but by no means all, of the bankruptcy rules are applicable to the administration of the deceased's insolvent estate by personal representatives.

The administration of a deceased's insolvent estate may be carried out in three different ways—*i.e.* (i) by the personal representatives out of court (this is the usual method), (ii) under the directions of the court in an administration action,[12] or (iii) in bankruptcy, after an insolvency administration order has been made by the bankruptcy court for the administration in bankruptcy of the deceased's estate. Under the Insolvency Act 1986 such an order may be made upon the petition of the personal representatives or of a creditor whose debt would have been sufficient to support a bankruptcy petition against the deceased if still alive.[13] If such an order is made, the official receiver acts as receiver of the deceased's estate[14] until the appointment of a trustee in bankruptcy,[15] in whom the deceased's estate vests on his appointment.[16] The trustee carries out the administration in bankruptcy of the deceased's estate. However the same rules as to payment of funeral, testamentary and administration expenses and debts apply, irrespective of the way in which the administration of the deceased's insolvent estate is carried out.[17]

A. Assets, Expenses and Debts

What are assets? The question what property constitutes assets for the payment of the deceased's debts and liabilities was considered at the beginning of this chapter.[18] The special rules of bankruptcy, which

---

[11] *Post*, pp. 289 *et seq.*

[12] *Post*, p. 396 *et seq.* The court in which proceedings for administration have been commenced may, if satisfied the estate is insolvent, transfer proceedings to the bankruptcy court, Insolvency Act 1986, s.271, as modified by the Order (S.I. 1986 No. 1999), para. 3 and Sched. 1. Referenced to this Act "as modified" mean as modified by this Order.

[13] ss.264, 267, 269, and 271–273, as modified; for other persons who may petition see s.264(1)(c) and (d).

[14] ss.287–289 and 291, as modified.

[15] ss.292–297, as modified: the official receiver may become the trustee, *ibid.*

[16] s.306.

[17] ss.305, 328–329 and 386–387 and Sched. 6, as modified. Exceptionally s.347(1) (right of landlord to distrain for only six months' rent accrued due before the date of the insolvency administration order) applies in an administration in bankruptcy of the deceased's estate, but not otherwise, *Re Fryman's Estate* (1888) 38 Ch.D. 468; *Re Wells* [1929] 2 Ch. 269.

[18] *Ante*, pp. 251 *et seq.* On an administration of the deceased's estate in bankruptcy, such clothing, bedding, furniture, household equipment and provisions as are necessary for satisfying the basic domestic needs of the deceased's family are excluded from the deceased's estate, Insolvency Act 1986, s.283(2), as modified; see also ss.308–309. As to the deceased's dwelling-house see ss.313 and 336–337.

in certain circumstances add the property of third persons to a bankrupt's assets for the benefit of his creditors, only apply if an insolvency administration order has been made by the bankruptcy court for the administration in bankruptcy of the deceased's estate: these special rules cover, for instance, transactions entered into by the deceased at an undervalue,[19] preferences by the deceased,[20] and extortionate credit transactions between the deceased and a creditor.[21]

Funeral, testamentary and administration expenses. These expenses (so far as they are reasonable) take priority over the deceased's preferential debts.[22] In all probability the deceased's funeral expenses[23] retain their long-established priority over the testamentary and administration expenses.[24]

Debts and liabilities. The bankruptcy rules apply with respect to the debts and liabilities provable in the administration of the deceased's insolvent estate:

(1) *Debts and liabilities provable at their value.* All debts and liabilities of the deceased, present or future, certain or contingent, are provable against his insolvent estate. It is immaterial whether the amount of a debt or liability is fixed or liquidated, or is capable of being ascertained by fixed rules or as a matter of opinion.[25] Again it is immaterial whether the liability arises under an enactment, a breach of trust, a contract, a tort,[26] a bailment, or out of an obligation to make restitution.[27]

If a debt or liability of the deceased does not bear a certain value, by reason of its being subject to any contingency or for any other reason, its value must be estimated.[28] The estimation of value is made as at the death of the deceased, but taking into account any subsequent events which occur prior to the estimation being made. For instance, if during his lifetime the deceased covenanted to pay an annuity to Miss Y for life, and she survives the deceased, she may prove against the deceased's insolvent estate for the estimated capital value of her annuity as at the death of the deceased, having regard to Miss Y's age and expectation of life.[29] If Miss Y dies before the estimation is made, the value of her annuity as at the death of the deceased (but taking into

---

[19] ss.339 and 341–342, as modified.

[20] ss.340–342, as modified.

[21] s.343, as modified.

[22] *Post*, p. 289 *et seq.*

[23] *Ante*, pp. 255–256.

[24] *R* v. *Wade* (1818) 5 Price 621, 627; *Re Walter* [1929] 1 Ch. 647 (funeral expenses of bankrupt).

[25] Insolvency Act 1986, s.382(1) and (3). A statute-barred debt is not provable, *Ex p. Dewdney, ex p. Seaman* (1809) 15 Ves. 479, (1815) 19 Ves. 467: and counsel's fees are not provable against a deceased solicitor's insolvent estate, *Re Sandiford (No. 2)* [1935] Ch. 681.

[26] *Ante*, pp. 213–214.

[27] Insolvency Act 1986, s.382(2) and (4).

[28] Insolvency Act 1986, s.322(3): any person dissatisfied with the estimate may apply to the court, which may assess its value, s.303. As to the value of contingent debts or liabilities see *Hardy* v. *Fothergill* (1888) 13 App.Cas. 351; *Re Bridges* (1881) 17 Ch.D. 342; *Re McMahon* [1900] 1 Ch. 173 (company may prove for estimated value of liability of deceased insolvent shareholder for future calls).

[29] *Re Viscount Rothermere* [1945] Ch. 72 (valuation of "tax-free" annuity).

account the subsequent event of her death) is the amount of the payments falling due to Miss Y up to the date of her death.[30] If the annuity is terminable on the remarriage of the annuitant, or on her ceasing to lead a chaste life, these "apparently imponderable risks"[31] are taken into account in the valuation.[32]

(2) *Set-off.* Where there have been mutual dealings between the deceased and another person, an account must be taken and the sum due from the one party must be set off against that due from the other, and only the balance of the account is to be claimed.[33]

(3) *Interest on debts.* If a debt bears interest, that interest is provable as part of the debt for any period up to the date of the insolvency administration order.[34] Probably, in an administration out of court or under the directions of the court in an administration action, interest borne by a debt ought to be calculated up to the date of death of the deceased.[35]

B. ORDER OF PRIORITY OF DEBTS

The order of priority of debts in the administration of a deceased's insolvent estate is governed by the bankruptcy rules.

1. Debts of secured creditors. A secured creditor holds some security for his debt (whether a mortgage, charge, lien or other security) over property of the deceased.[36] A typical instance is a building society holding a mortgage on the deceased's house as a security for the repayment by the deceased of money lent to him. Under the bankruptcy rules the rights of a secured creditor are as follows:

   (i) He may rely on his security and not prove for his debt.[37] This is a safe course if his security is adequate and ultimately realises sufficient to pay his debt in full.
   (ii) He may realise his security and prove for the balance of his debt.[38] This is a possible course if his security is inadequate: of course he proves for the balance of his debt as an unsecured creditor.

---

[30] *Re Dodds* (1890) 25 Q.B.D. 529.

[31] [1945] Ch. 72, 75.

[32] *Ex p. Blakemore* (1877) 5 Ch.D. 372 ("like every other contingency affecting human life or human conduct, it [*i.e.* remarriage by a widow] is, I think, capable of estimation"); *Ex p. Neal* (1880) 14 Ch.D. 579.

[33] Insolvency Act 1986, s.323; *Watkins* v. *Lindsay & Co.* (1898) 67 L.J.Q.B. 362; *Re D. H. Curtis (Builders) Ltd.* [1978] Ch. 162.

[34] *Ibid.* s.322(2), as modified. This reference to the date of the insolvency administration order is a drafting error: it should refer to the date of death of the deceased debtor, so as to be consistent with ss.328(4) and 329(2), as modified, which provide for interest since the date of death, see *post*, pp. 291–292.

[35] The bankruptcy rule applies (*Re Bush* [1930] 2 Ch. 202; *Re Theo. Garvin Ltd.* [1969] 1 Ch. 624) but cannot be applied literally: see also *Re Sagor* [1930] W.N. 149 (interest allowed to date of order by court for administration).

[36] Insolvency Act 1986, s.383(2): a lien on documents is disregarded unless the documents are held as giving a title to property, s.383(4).

[37] *Ibid.* s.285(4).

[38] *Ibid.* s.322(1); Insolvency Rules 1986 (S.I. 1986 No. 1925), rr. 6.109 and 6.119.

(iii) He may set a value on his security and prove for the balance of his debt as an unsecured creditor.[39] Again this is a possible course if his security is inadequate but he values it at his own risk. If he values it too low, the personal representatives (or trustee in bankruptcy) will exercise their right to redeem the security at his value.[40] If he values it too high, he will prove for too small a balance.[41]

(iv) He may surrender his security and prove for the whole debt.[42] This course is not advisable if his security has any value, unless there are sufficient assets to pay his particular debt in full under the order of priority applicable to unsecured creditors.

In so far as a secured creditor obtains the payment of his debt by realising his security, he enjoys priority over the deceased's funeral, testamentary and administration expenses and unsecured creditors. On the other hand, in so far as a secured creditor proves for his debt, he is in the same position, and entitled to the same priority, as an unsecured creditor.

The deceased's reasonable funeral, testamentary and administration expenses take priority over the debts of unsecured creditors. The latter are payable according to the following order of priority, under which four classes of debts exist, *i.e.* specially preferred, preferential, ordinary and deferred debts.

2. Specially preferred debts. The first class is specially preferred debts. These are:

(i) *money or property belonging to any friendly society*, which was in the possession of the deceased as an officer of the society,[43] even though at his death he had ceased to be such an officer[44]:

(ii) *proper expenses incurred by the trustee under a deed of arrangement* which has subsequently been avoided by the bankruptcy of the debtor,[45] or incurred as expenses of the administration of a voluntary arrangement under the Insolvency Act 1986, which has been superceded by a bankruptcy order on the debtor's default.[46]

These specially preferred debts[47] must be met out of the deceased's insolvent estate before any other of his debts are paid.[48]

---

[39] Insolvency Rules 1986, rr. 6.96 and 6.98. The creditor has a limited power to alter his valuation, r. 6.115; *Re Becher* [1944] Ch. 78.

[40] *Ibid.* r. 6.117: alternatively they may insist on sale, r. 6.118. The creditor may require them to elect within six months whether they will redeem, failing which they lose their equity of redemption to the creditor, r. 6.117(4).

[41] *Re Hopkins* (1881) 18 Ch.D. 370 ("The creditor values for himself, and so he values at his own risk . . . he can gain nothing by valuing too high or too low").

[42] Insolvency Rules 1986, r. 6.109(2).

[43] Friendly Societies Act 1974, s.59.

[44] *Re Eilbeck* [1910] 1 K.B. 136.

[45] Deeds of Arrangement Act 1914, s.21; see *Re Geen* [1917] 1 K.B. 183.

[46] Insolvency Act 1986, ss.264(1)(c) and 276.

[47] See also Regimental Debts Act 1893, s.2 (preferential debts of persons dying while subject to military law); Ley (1971) 35 Conv.(N.S.) 420.

[48] Insolvency Act 1986, s.328(6).

3. Preferential debts. The preferential debts are next payable, ranking equally between themselves, so that if there are insufficient assets to pay them all in full they must all abate proportionately.[49] The preferential debts are listed in Schedule 6 to the Insolvency Act 1986.[50] The categories of preferential debts are as follows:

(i) *Money owed to the Inland Revenue for income tax deducted at source*: this category covers sums due at death[51] from the deceased on account of PAYE income tax deductions from his employees' remuneration paid during the period of 12 months before his death.[52]

(ii) *VAT, car tax, betting and gaming duties*: this category of debts due to the Customs and Excise covers VAT referable to the period of six months before death[53]; car tax due at death from the deceased and which became due within the period of 12 months before his death; and any amount due at death from the deceased, and which became due within this 12 months' period, by way of general betting duty or bingo duty, or general betting duty and pool betting duty recoverable from an agent collecting stakes,[54] or gaming licence duty.[55]

(iii) *Social security contributions*: this category covers sums due at death from the deceased and which became due within this 12 months' period on account of Class 1 or 2 contributions[56]; and sums which at death have been assessed on and are due to the Inland Revenue Commissioners from the deceased on account of Class 4 contributions,[57] and are assessed on the deceased up to April 5 next before death, but not exceeding, in the whole, any one year's assessment.[58]

(iv) *Pension scheme contributions*: any sum owed by the deceased on account of contributions to occupational pension schemes and state scheme premiums.[59]

(v) *Remuneration of employees*: any amount owed by the deceased to his employee or former employee by way of remuneration[60] in

[49] Insolvency Act 1986, s.328(1) and (2).
[50] *Ibid.* s.386.
[51] *Ibid.* 387(6), as modified. If at death an interim receiver has been appointed under s.286, the date on which the interim receiver was first appointed is the relevant date, and not the date of death, throughout Sched. 6.
[52] And in respect of deductions required to be made by the deceased for that period under Finance (No. 2) Act 1975, s.69 (sub-contractors in the construction industry).
[53] See Insolvency Act 1986, Sched. 6, para. 3.
[54] Under Betting and Gaming Duties Act 1981, s.12(1).
[55] Under *ibid.* s.14 or Sched. 2.
[56] Under Social Security Act 1975 or Social Security (Northern Ireland) Act 1975.
[57] *Ibid.*
[58] The I.R.C. need not select the last fiscal year before death for their preferential claim, *Re Pratt* [1951] Ch. 225.
[59] Being a sum to which Social Security Pensions Act 1975, Sched. 3 applies (imposing 4 or 12 months' time limits).
[60] This is widely defined in Insolvency Act 1986, Sched. 6, paras. 13–15 so as to include certain sums due under the Employment Protection (Consolidation) Act 1978 and the Employment Protection Act 1975.

respect of the period of four months before his death, but not exceeding £800 (being the limit currently prescribed by order by the Secretary of State[61]); and any amount owed by way of accrued holiday remuneration in respect of any period of employment before death to an employee whose employment by the deceased has been terminated.[62]

If any person has distrained on the goods of the deceased within three months before an insolvency administration order is made, the distrained goods, or their proceeds of sale, are charged for the benefit of the deceased's estate with the specially preferred and preferential debts of the deceased to the extent that the deceased's estate is insufficient to meet these debts.[63]

4. Ordinary debts. Next in order of priority come the ordinary debts, *i.e.* all other debts except the deferred debts (which are considered next). For example, the ordinary debts include all remuneration owed to employees by the deceased, except in so far as any of it constitutes a preferential debt.

All the ordinary debts rank equally between themselves and if they cannot be paid in full they must all abate proportionately.[64] A creditor does not obtain any priority over the other creditors by obtaining judgment for his debt against the personal representatives.[65]

5. Interest on preferential and ordinary debts since death. Next in order of priority interest is payable on all the preferential and ordinary debts in respect of the periods during which they have been outstanding since the death of the deceased. Interest on these debts ranks equally, irrespective of the priority accorded to the debts themselves.[66] The rate of interest payable on a debt is whichever is the greater of (i) the rate specified in section 17 of the Judgments Act 1838[67] at the death (currently 15 per cent.[68]), and (ii) the rate applicable to that debt apart from the bankruptcy.[69]

6. Deferred debts. Deferred debts come last in the order of priority. They are debts owed in respect of credit provided by a person who was the spouse of the deceased at the latter's death: it is immaterial whether this was so at the time the credit was provided.[70] The same interest is

[61] Insolvency Proceedings (Monetary Limits) Order 1986 (S.I. 1986 No. 1996), para. 4.
[62] Any sum owed in respect of money advanced for the purpose of, and applied for, the payment of a debt which, if not paid, would have been preferential under this category is a preferential debt, Insolvency Act 1986, Sched. 6, para. 11. Also any amount ordered to be paid by the deceased under the Reserve Forces (Safeguard of Employment) Act 1985 in respect of the deceased's default, but not exceeding £800, is a preferential debt, *ibid.* para. 12.
[63] Insolvency Act 1986, s.347(3): the person distraining ranks as a preferential creditor to the extent that the charge operates, *ibid.* s.347(4).
[64] *Ibid.* s.328(3).
[65] *Pritchard* v. *Westminster Bank Ltd.* [1969] 1 W.L.R. 547.
[66] Insolvency Act 1986, s.328(4), as modified.
[67] As amended by Administration of Justice Act 1970, s.44.
[68] Judgment Debts (Rate of Interest) Order 1985 (S.I. 1985 No. 437).
[69] Insolvency Act 1986, s.328(5), as modified.
[70] *Ibid.* s.329, as modified.

payable on these debts and this interest has the same priority as the debts on which it is payable.[71]

C. FAILURE TO OBSERVE THE ORDER OF PRIORITY OF DEBTS

Liability for payment of inferior debt. A personal representative is under a duty to administer a deceased's insolvent estate in accordance with the statutory rules as to the payment of debts.[72] He is therefore liable for a breach of this duty (constituting a *devastavit*) if he fails to observe the order of priority of debts. Thus the personal representative incurs liability if he applies the deceased's assets in paying an inferior debt (*e.g.* a deferred debt) which he ought not to have paid, and leaves unpaid a superior debt (*e.g.* a preferential or ordinary debt) which he ought to have paid because he had notice of it. His payment of the inferior debt constitutes an admission by him that he has assets sufficient to satisfy all debts of which he then has notice and which have priority over the inferior debt: if the deceased's assets are not sufficient, the personal representative is personally liable to pay all such debts.[73] But the personal representative does not incur liability if, acting in good faith and without undue haste, he pays an inferior debt without notice of a superior debt.[74]

Duty to pay debts of the same class pari passu. Formerly a personal representative had a right of preference, *i.e.* a right to prefer one creditor of the same class to another, and a right of retainer, *i.e.* a right to pay his own debt in full in preference to other creditors of the same class as himself. These ancient common law rights of preference and retainer were abolished by section 10(1) of the Administration of Estates Act 1971 as from January 1, 1972,[75] because they were regarded as anomalous and incompatible with the fiduciary position of a personal representative.[76] Accordingly a personal representative is generally under a duty to pay all debts of the same class *pari passu*, at any rate if the personal representative has notice of them.

Personal representative having no reason to believe estate insolvent. However section 10(2) of the Administration of Estates Act 1971 provides *partial* protection for a personal representative who pays a debt

---

[71] *Ibid.* s.329(2), as modified.

[72] Administration of Estates Act 1925, s.25 as amended by Administration of Estates Act 1971, s.9; Insolvency Act 1986, s.421; Administration of Insolvent Estates of Deceased Persons Order 1986 (S.I. 1986 No. 1999).

[73] 2 Bl.Comm. 511: see *Britton* v. *Batthurst* (1683) 3 Lev. 113; *Rock* v. *Layton* (1700) 1 Ld.Raym. 589.

[74] *Harman* v. *Harman* (1686) 2 Show. 492; *Re Fludyer* [1898] 2 Ch. 562 ("Since the case of *Harman* v. *Harman* it has been considered settled law that an executor who pays creditors without notice of the existence of a creditor of higher degree is not liable to account for the sums so paid at the instance of that creditor"). Contrast the position of a personal representative who distributes to *beneficiaries* without notice of an unpaid debt of the deceased, *ante*, p. 259.

[75] s.14(2).

[76] See Law Com. No. 31, paras. 5 and 7–9: for criticism see Sunnucks (1972) 122 New L.J. 26.

when he has no reason to believe that the deceased's estate is insolvent. Under section 10(2) a personal representative who, in good faith and at a time when he has no reason to believe that the deceased's estate is insolvent, pays the debt of any creditor (including himself, unless he took letters of administration in his capacity as creditor) is not liable to account to creditors of the same class as the paid creditor if it subsequently appears that the estate is insolvent. This does not protect the personal representative against creditors of a superior class, to whom the personal representative is certainly liable to account if he had notice of them.[77] Section 10(2) was introduced to enable a personal representative to pay tradesmen's bills at an early stage in the administration.[78] But it does not provide any protection to a personal representative if he has any reason to believe that the deceased's estate is insolvent because, for instance, a particular asset is of dubious value or a particular liability is of dubious extent.[79]

---

[77] Cf. Law Com. No. 31, para. 8, esp. n. 16.

[78] Law Com. No. 31, para. 8.

[79] For the court's power to relieve a personal representative from liability see Trustee Act 1925, ss.61, 68(1)(17) and 69(1), post, pp. 394–395.

CHAPTER 11

GIFTS BY WILL

The rules applicable on a total or partial intestacy have already been considered in Chapter 4. Now the effect of gifts by will must be considered. Some of the rules of construction applicable to wills are discussed later in Chapter 15.

1. LEGACIES AND DEVISES

A. CLASSIFICATION OF LEGACIES AND DEVISES

Classification of legacies. Legacies in wills may be classified under three heads—(1) specific legacies, (2) general legacies, and (3) demonstrative legacies.[1] This classification is important because the effect of each type of legacy is different.

(1) *Specific legacies.* A specific legacy is a gift by will of specified personal estate: *e.g.* "I give my 200 shares in Marks & Spencer plc to A" or "I give to my wife B all my personal chattels as defined by section 55(1)(x) of the Administration of Estates Act 1925."[2] The thing given:

(i) must itself be a part of the testator's personal property, and
(ii) must be a specified part, so that it is severed or distinguished by the testator from the general mass of his estate.[3]

If the testator uses the word "my" ("*my* 200 shares in Marks & Spencer plc"), or any other possessive word, this shows that the subject matter of the gift is itself a part of the testator's property. So, too, does a reference to the acquisition by the testator of the subject of the gift, *e.g.* "I give to C the diamond ring which my husband gave me." The thing given may be specified in any way which distinguishes it from the remainder of his estate,[4] and it is immaterial whether the time for ascer-

---

[1] See generally *Jarman on Wills* (8th ed., 1951), pp. 1036 *et seq.*
[2] See *ante*, pp. 84–85.
[3] *Bothamley* v. *Sherson* (1875) L.R. 20 Eq. 304 (a gift of "all my shares or stock in the Midland Railway Company" held specific: a specific legacy must be "what has been sometimes called a severed or distinguished part" of the testator's personal estate); *Robertson* v. *Broadbent* (1883) 8 App.Cas. 812, 815; *Re Rose* [1949] Ch. 78 (reviewing some of the case law). As to the nature of an option see *ante*, p. 272.
[4] Apart from other identical things, *Re Cheadle* [1900] 2 Ch. 620 (gift of "my 140 shares" in C Co.; T had 40 fully paid and 240 partly paid shares: held legatee no right to select but entitled to 140 partly paid shares): see also *Re Tetsall* [1961] 1 W.L.R. 938, 943.

taining it is the date of the will ("the cars which I own at the date of my will") or the date of death ("the cars which I own at the date of my death").[5]

Whether a legacy is specific, general, or demonstrative depends on the construction of the particular will. However "the court leans against specific legacies, and is inclined, if it can, to construe a legacy as general rather than specific; so that if there is any doubt it should, on the whole, be resolved in favour of the view that the legacy is general."[6]

(2) *General legacies.* A general legacy is a gift of something to be provided out of the testator's general estate. It is irrelevant whether its subject matter forms part of the testator's property at his death.

"A general bequest may or may not be a part of the testator's property. A man who gives £100 money or £100 stock may not have either the money or the stock, in which case the testator's executors must raise the money or buy the stock; or he may have money or stock sufficient to discharge the legacy, in which case the executors would probably discharge it out of the actual money or stock. But in the case of a general legacy, it has no reference to the actual state of the testator's property, it being only supposed that the testator has sufficient property which on being realised will procure for the legatee that which is given to him."[7]

Usually a general legacy takes the form of a gift of a sum of money, *e.g.* "I give £3,000 to D." Of course a gift of a sum of money may be (but in practice seldom is) specific, *e.g.* 'I give all the money in my wallet to E'[8] or "I give to F the money now owing to me from G.'"[9]

A gift of some particular thing—such as shares in a particular company—is a general legacy if there is nothing on the face of the will to show that the testator is referring to shares belonging to him. Thus "I give 500 shares in ICI plc to H" is a general legacy unless there are sufficient indications in the will, construed as a whole in the light of relevant circumstances, that the testator intended to refer to shares belonging to him.[10] However, if at the date of his will the testator held exactly 500 shares in ICI, this, standing by itself, is not a sufficient indication that the testator intended to give the particular shares which then belonged to him. In *Re Willcocks*[11] T by her will gave to her father £948 3s. 11d. Queensland 3½ per cent. Inscribed Stock: at the date of her will T held exactly this sum of stock. The court held that this was a general

---

[5] *Bothamley v. Sherson, supra,* at pp. 309–312. For the effect of Wills Act 1837, s.24 see *post,* pp. 424 *et seq.*

[6] *Re Rose, supra.* at p. 82.

[7] *Per* Jessel M.R. in *Bothamley v. Sherson, supra* at p. 308.

[8] *Lawson v. Stitch* (1738) 1 Atk. 507 (legacy of sum of money in a particular bag is specific).

[9] *Ashburner v. Macguire* (1786) 2 Bro.C.C. 108; *Chaworth v. Beech* (1799) 4 Ves. 555; *Nelson v. Carter* (1832) 5 Sim. 530; *Davies v. Morgan* (1839) 1 Beav. 405. See also *Re Wedmore* [1907] 2 Ch. 277 ("I forgive my child all debts . . . due from him to me on my death . . . ": held a specific legacy—"it really is a gift to the child of what he owes"); *Commissioner of Stamp Duties v. Bone* [1977] A.C. 511, 519–520.

[10] *Re Rose* [1949] Ch. 78.

[11] [1921] 2 Ch. 327: see also *Re Gage* [1934] Ch. 536; *Re O'Connor's W.T.* [1948] Ch. 628; *Re Rose, supra.*

legacy in the absence of anything else in the will indicating that T intended to give a specific legacy: T's possession of that exact sum of stock may have been her motive for fixing the amount of the legacy, but yet T may have intended to give it in the form of a general legacy.[12]

(3) *Demonstrative legacies.* A demonstrative legacy is a gift which is in its nature a general legacy, but which is directed to be satisfied primarily out of a specified fund or specified part of the testator's property.[13] Examples include "I give £1,000 to J out of my current account with Lloyds Bank plc" or "out of my 2½ per cent. Consols."[14] But if the gift is directed to be satisfied *only* out of the specified fund or property, it cannot be demonstrative because an essential characteristic of a demonstrative legacy is that it should operate as a general legacy so far as it cannot be satisfied out of the specified fund or property.[15]

As the examples already considered indicate, a legacy of money (or pecuniary legacy) may be specific, general or demonstrative. Sometimes the term "pecuniary legacy" is used synonymously with the term "general legacy." If the term "pecuniary legacy" is used without stating whether it is specific, general, or demonstrative, it is necessary to ascertain the sense in which the term is used from its context.[16] The term "pecuniary legacy" is used in the Administration of Estates Act 1925,[17] which provides its own wide definition of the meaning of this term when used in the Act.[18]

Specific devises. A specific devise is a gift by will of specified real estate: *e.g.* "I give to L in fee simple my farm Blackacre situated near High Top in the County of Durham," or "all my farms in the County of Durham," or "such of my houses at Sutton in the County of Norfolk as L shall select."[19] As in the case of a specific legacy, the thing given:

    (i) must itself be a part of the testator's real property, and
    (ii) must be a specified part, so that it is severed or distinguished by the testator from the general mass of his estate.

It used to be said that all devises were by their nature specific: that was a loose and inaccurate way of stating that specific and residuary devises ranked *pari passu* for the purpose of the payment of the testator's debts before 1926.[20] Since 1925 a general or a residuary devise falls within

---

[12] *Re Willcocks, supra,* at p. 329.

[13] *Per* Lord Thurlow L.C. in *Ashburner* v. *Macguire* (1786) 2 Bro.C.C. 108, 109, "a demonstrative legacy, that is, a legacy in its nature a general legacy, but where a particular fund is pointed out to satisfy it."

[14] *Kirby* v. *Potter* (1799) 4 Ves. 748; *Re Webster* [1937] 1 All E.R. 602 (I bequeath to K the sum of £3,000 to be paid to him out of my partnership share: held a demonstrative legacy).

[15] *Re O'Connor* [1970] N.I. 159; *Re Culbertson* (1967) 62 D.L.R. (2d) 134.

[16] See, *e.g. Re O'Connor's W.T.* [1948] Ch. 628.

[17] s.33(2) and Sched. 1, Pt. II: see *post,* p. 298 (abatement) and *post,* p. 310 (incidence of general legacies).

[18] s.55(1)(ix), which is quoted *ante,* p. 271.

[19] *Springett* v. *Jenings* (1871) L.R. 6 Ch.App. 333, 335–336 (gift of particular property in parish of Hawkhurst to X followed by gift of "the rest of my freehold hereditaments situate in the parish of Hawkhurst" to Y: both gifts were specific devises). For the effect of the Wills Act 1837, s.24 see *post,* pp. 424 *et seq.*

[20] *Hensman* v. *Fryer* (1867) 3 Ch.App. 420; *Lancefield* v. *Iggulden* (1874) 10 Ch.App. 136.

paragraph 2 and a specific devise falls within paragraph 6 of the statutory order of application of assets.[21]

B. Different Effects of Legacies and Devises

The main differences in the effects of specific legacies and devises, general legacies, and demonstrative legacies relate to 1. ademption, and 2. abatement. The other differences relate to 3. income and interest, and 4. expenses. These are explained in turn.

1. Ademption of a specific legacy or specific devise. A specific legacy or specific devise fails by ademption if its subject matter has ceased to exist as part of the testator's property at his death.[22] To take by way of example the specific legacy of "my 200 shares in Marks & Spencer plc" to A and the specific devise of "my farm Blackacre" to L; if during his lifetime the testator sells his Marks & Spencer shares and gives away his farm Blackacre, the specific legacy and the specific devise both fail by ademption. Moreover A is not entitled to receive the proceeds of sale of these shares, even if the testator set the proceeds apart so that they can be traced at his death: the subject matter of the specific legacy was the testator's Marks & Spencer shares, not their proceeds of sale.[23] The principle of ademption is considered more fully in the next chapter.[24]

Neither a general legacy nor a demonstrative legacy fails by ademption in this way. If the testator gives general legacies of "£3,000 to D" and "500 shares in ICI plc to H," it is immaterial whether the testator has £3,000 in money, or 500 shares in ICI, at his death. The subject matter of a general legacy is to be provided by the personal representatives out of the testator's general estate.[25] Thus the personal representatives may need to realise assets in order to raise the £3,000, or the money needed to buy 500 shares in ICI. In *Re O'Connor's W.T.*[26] T by his will gave a general legacy to B of 10,000 preference shares in a private company J. & K. Connor Ltd. At his death T held only 9,000 of these shares. The court held that B was entitled to have 1,000 shares (making up the 10,000) purchased for him by T's personal representative within 12 months from T's death: if it was not possible to purchase them in that time, B was entitled to be paid a sum equal to the market value of 1,000 shares as at the end of 12 months from T's death.[27] However a general legacy may fail for uncertainty. Thus, in the case of a general legacy of company shares, if the company is wound up so that it no longer exists at the testator's death, the gift fails for uncertainty because the personal

[21] *Ante*, pp. 269 and 271–272.
[22] *Ashburner* v. *Macguire* (1786) 2 Bro.C.C. 108.
[23] *Harrison* v. *Jackson* (1877) 7 Ch.D. 339.
[24] *Post*, pp. 345 *et seq.*
[25] For the incidence of general legacies see section 2 of this chapter.
[26] [1948] Ch. 628; see also *Robinson* v. *Addison* (1840) 2 Beav. 515.
[27] B may also be entitled to interest, see *post*, pp. 322 *et seq.*

representatives can neither purchase the shares nor ascertain their market value.[28]

A demonstrative legacy is treated as a general legacy so far as it cannot be satisfied out of the specified fund or specified part of the testator's property primarily designated for its payment. Accordingly, in the case of T's demonstrative legacy "of £1,000 to J out of my current account with Lloyds Bank plc," if T's current account with this bank is overdrawn at the date of T's death the demonstrative legacy to J does not fail by ademption, and J is entitled to have £1,000 provided for him by the personal representatives out of T's general estate.[29]

To sum up, a specific legacy and a specific devise are both liable to fail by ademption, whereas a general legacy and a demonstrative legacy are both immune from ademption and in this respect are more advantageous to the beneficiary.

2. Abatement (1) *Order of abatement under the statutory order.* The statutory order of application of assets, set out in Part II of the First Schedule to the Administration of Estates Act 1925 (which was considered in Chapter 10), regulates the burden of the deceased's expenses, debts and liabilities as between the beneficiaries and is applicable on the death of any person after 1925 unless the order is varied by the deceased's will.[30] Under this statutory order property specifically devised or bequeathed falls within paragraph 6. On the other hand, a general legacy falls within paragraph 5, *i.e.* the pecuniary legacy fund, because the expression "pecuniary legacy" in the Administration of Estates Act 1925 is defined in section 55(1)(ix) as including a general legacy. It follows that under the statutory order general legacies must abate in payment of the deceased's expenses, debts and liabilities before any resort is made to specific legacies and specific devises.[31] The expression "pecuniary legacy" in the Act also includes a free of inheritance tax provision by the testator.[32] Thus if by his will T gives to his son S his French villa Greenacre free of any inheritance tax payable in respect of T's death (such tax to be paid out of T's general personal estate), this provision is treated as a pecuniary legacy to S of the amount of inheritance tax payable on Greenacre, and as such it is liable to abate under paragraph 5 of the statutory order, though of course Greenacre itself falls within paragraph 6.

A demonstrative legacy falls within the definition of a "pecuniary legacy" in section 55(1)(ix) so far as it is not discharged out of the speci-

---

[28] *Re Gray* (1887) 36 Ch.D. 205 (the general legacy "fails, not because of any ademption, but because it has become . . . utterly impossible to determine what amount of money should be set apart" for the legatee): *cf. Re Borne* [1944] Ch. 190.

[29] *Mullins* v. *Smith* (1860) 1 Dr. & Sm. 204, 210; *Fowler* v. *Willoughby* (1825) 2 Sim. & Stu. 354; *Vickers* v. *Pound* (1858) 6 H.L.C. 885; *Walford* v. *Walford* [1912] A.C. 658, 662–663; *Re Webster* (1936) 156 L.T. 128.

[30] For the special rules applicable to debts charged on the deceased's property and to the incidence of inheritance tax see *ante,* pp. 274 and 279.

[31] For an example see *ante,* pp. 266–267.

[32] Administration of Estates Act 1925, s.55(1)(ix); Inheritance Tax Act 1984, Sched. 6, para. 1; Finance Act 1986, s.100(1). See also *Re Turnbull* [1905] 1 Ch. 726.

fied fund or specified part of the testator's estate primarily designated for its payment: to this extent a demonstrative legacy falls within paragraph 5. On the other hand, a demonstrative legacy is treated as a specific legacy so far as it can be discharged out of this designated property: to this extent a demonstrative legacy falls within paragraph 6.[33] The justification for this distinction is that the testator is presumed to have intended the demonstrative legacy to be payable in priority to his general legacies so far as the demonstrative legacy can be satisfied out of the designated property.[34]

Summarising the liability to abatement under the statutory order, a general legacy and a demonstrative legacy so far as it is not discharged out of the designated property both fall within paragraph 5. By way of contrast, a specific legacy, a specific devise, and a demonstrative legacy so far as it can be discharged out of the designated property all fall within paragraph 6 and in this respect are more advantageous to the beneficiary. A demonstrative legacy is said to have "the best of both worlds"[35]—being immune from ademption (like a general legacy) and, so far as it can be discharged out of the designated property, being preferred on abatement under the statutory order (like a specific legacy).

(2) *Gifts in the same class abate rateably.* Paragraph 6 of the statutory order provides that property specifically devised or bequeathed is to bear the burden of expenses and debts falling on it "rateably according to value." It follows that any property specifically devised or bequeathed and any demonstrative legacy so far as it can be discharged out of the property primarily designated for its payment must abate rateably.[36] For the purpose of this rateable abatement under paragraph 6, the property affected is valued as at the death of the testator.[37]

Paragraph 5 of the statutory order does not refer to rateable abatement but there is a well-settled general rule that all general legacies abate rateably on the principle of the maxim "equality is equity."[38] Demonstrative legacies so far as they cannot be discharged out of the designated property are treated as, and therefore abate rateably with, the general legacies. This general rule applies whenever the property from which general legacies are payable[39] is insufficient to satisfy them in full. This may occur, for instance, because the testator's estate did not include sufficient of this property to satisfy his general legacies, or because a loss occurred or this property fell in value after the testator's death, or because the burden of the testator's expenses and debts falls on this property. For the purpose of this rateable abatement, a general

[33] See *Re Turner* [1908] 1 Ir. 274 (T's will gave specific legacies and devises, and demonstrative legacies payable out of specified railway stock held by T; T's other assets were insufficient to pay expenses and debts: held specific legacies and devises and demonstrative legacies so far as they could be satisfied from railway stock must all abate rateably).

[34] *Acton* v. *Acton* (1816) 1 Mer. 178; *Creed* v. *Creed* (1844) 11 Cl. & F. 491, 509; *Livesay* v. *Redfern* (1837) 2 Y. & C.Ex. 90; *Robinson* v. *Geldard* (1851) 3 M. & G. 735, 745.

[35] Snell's *Principles of Equity* (28th ed., 1982), p. 358.

[36] *Re Turner, supra.*

[37] *Re John* [1933] Ch. 370; *Re Cohen* [1960] Ch. 179: see *ante*, pp. 271–272.

[38] *Miller* v. *Huddlestone* (1851) 3 Mac. & G. 513, 523. Interest on a legacy is not an additional legacy for the purpose of abatement, *Re Wyles* [1938] Ch. 313.

[39] For the incidence of general legacies see section 2 of this chapter.

legacy of something other than money (*e.g.* company shares—"I give 500 shares in ICI plc to H") is valued as at the end of 12 months from the testator's death and not as at the death of the testator.[40]

(3) *Testator's intention to give priority.* Of course, the testator may by his will vary the statutory order or give priority to a particular legacy or devise. For instance, the testator may direct that a particular general legacy (*e.g.* to his wife) shall have priority over any other legacy or devise whatsoever contained in his will (*i.e.* taking priority even over specific legacies and devises) *or* (alternatively) over any other general legacies given by his will.[41]

In order to give priority to a particular legacy or devise the testator must show by his will a clear intention to do so.[42] Thus a direction by a testator that a legacy to his wife was to be paid to her immediately after his decease out of the first money to be received by his executors did not give her priority over the other general legacies, but merely specified the *time* for payment of her legacy.[43] Again a legacy given to an executor for his trouble did not take priority over other legacies.[44]

3. Income and interest. In general, a specific legacy or specific devise carries with it all the income or profits accruing from its subject matter after the death of the testator, whereas a general or demonstrative legacy carries interest at the rate of 6 per cent. per annum from the time at which it is payable, *i.e.* usually from the end of one year (the executor's year) after the testator's death. The rules as to income and interest are considered later in section 3 of this chapter.

4. Expenses. Unless the testator directs otherwise by his will, any expenses incurred by the personal representatives in the upkeep and preservation of the subject matter of a specific devise or specific legacy during the period between the testator's death and the assent or transfer to the beneficiary must be paid by the beneficiary. In *Re Rooke*[45] T by her will made a specific gift of her freehold house and its contents to B and the executors incurred expenses in the upkeep and preservation of the house and its contents during this period. Maugham J. held

---

[40] *Blackshaw* v. *Rogers,* cited in *Simmons* v. *Vallance* (1793) 4 Bro.C.C. 345; *Auther* v. *Auther* (1843) 13 Sim. 422, 440: see also *Re Hollins* [1918] 1 Ch. 503.

[41] *Cf. Marsh* v. *Evans* (1720) 1 P.Wms. 668. See also *Re Compton* [1914] 2 Ch. 119 (legacies by T of certain company stock "all now standing in my name as general and not as specific legacies": held T intended these specific legacies to be treated as general legacies and they must abate as such).

[42] *Miller* v. *Huddlestone, supra.* For the case law see Williams, Mortimer and Sunnucks, *Executors Administrators and Probate* (16th ed., 1982), pp. 898 *et seq.*

[43] *Blower* v. *Morret* (1752) 2 Ves.Sen. 420; *Re Schweder's Estate* [1891] 3 Ch. 44 (general legacy to be paid to wife within three months after death: no priority); *Cazenove* v. *Cazenove* (1890) 61 L.T. 115.

[44] *Duncan* v. *Watts* (1852) 16 Beav. 204. For the effect of a charging clause see *ante,* p. 246.

[45] [1933] Ch. 970: see also *Re Pearce* [1909] 1 Ch. 819 (expenses of upkeep, care and preservation of furniture, horses and carriages, and yacht: held payable by specific legatee); *Re Wilson* [1967] Ch. 53, 65. But if T by his will gives to B such articles of furniture and personal effects as B shall select, the expenses of preservation incurred prior to B's selection are not payable by B, *Re Collins' W.T.* [1971] 1 W.L.R. 37. If a contingent specific gift does not carry intermediate income, it does not bear these expenses prior to the occurrence of the contingency, *Re Eyre* [1917] 1 Ch. 351, 356.

that these expenses were not payable out of T's estate as part of the administration expenses but must be paid by B. As Maugham J. pointed out, it is difficult to explain on what principle the income or profits accruing after T's death ought to be paid to B if B is not also to be made liable for the upkeep and preservation of the subject matter of the specific gift from T's death.[46]

On the other hand, any expenses incurred by the personal representatives in preserving the other assets are payable out of the testator's estate as part of the administration expenses and are not payable by the general or demonstrative legatees.

C. ANNUITIES

Classification of annuities. An annuity given by will is a legacy of money payable by instalments or, more accurately, viewing each instalment of the annuity as a separate legacy, "a series of legacies payable at intervals."[47]

Annuities given by will may be classified under the same three heads as other legacies:

(i) *a specific annuity, i.e.* a gift of an existing annuity belonging to the testator at his death[48] (*e.g.* "I give to A the perpetual annuity to which I am entitled under my father's will"), or a gift of an annuity or rentcharge out of specified property of the testator belonging to him at his death[49] (*e.g.* "I give to B during her life an annuity or equitable rentcharge of £100 to be charged upon and payable exclusively out of my farm Blackacre"):

(ii) *a general annuity, i.e.* a gift of an annuity to be provided out of the testator's general estate (*e.g.* "I give to C during her life an annuity of £200 to begin from my death and to be payable by equal quarterly payments, the first payment thereof to be made at the expiration of three months from my death"): and

(iii) *a demonstrative annuity, i.e.* a gift of an annuity which is in its nature a general annuity, but which is directed to be satisfied primarily out of a specified fund or specified part of the testator's property.[50]

Under each of these three heads, whether an annuity is payable out of the corpus or only out of the income of the relevant property depends on the proper construction of the particular will.[51] To take the simple situation where "there is in a will a bequest of an annuity,"[52] the residuary legatees or the other persons becoming entitled to the testator's resi-

---

[46] [1933] Ch. 970, 974.

[47] *Re Earl of Berkeley* [1968] Ch. 154, 165.

[48] *Smith* v. *Pybus* (1804) 9 Ves. 566.

[49] *Creed* v. *Creed* (1844) 11 Cl. & F. 491; *Long* v. *Short* (1717) 1 P.Wms. 403: *cf. Re Trenchard* [1905] 1 Ch. 82: see Rentcharges Act 1977, s.2(3).

[50] *Mann* v. *Copland* (1817) 2 Madd. 223; *Livesay* v. *Redfern* (1836) 2 Y. & C.Ex. 90; *Paget* v. *Huish* (1863) 1 H. & M. 663, esp. at pp. 667–671; *Re Briggs* (1881) 45 L.T. 249.

[51] See generally *Theobald on Wills* (14th ed., 1982), pp. 521 *et seq.*

[52] *i.e.* a general annuity given directly to the annuitant in general terms, without any trust to pay it.

duary estate can only take that estate on the terms of paying or providing for the payment of the annuity in full. The annuity is a charge upon the whole income and corpus of the residuary estate just as much as if it were an ordinary pecuniary legacy."[53]

Again, the duration of an annuity created by a will depends on the proper construction of the will.[54] For instance, if a testator gives an annuity to A, an individual, prima facie the annuity is only for the life of A.

> "An annuity may be perpetual, or for life, or for any period of years: but, in the ordinary acceptation of the term used, if it should be said that a testator had left another an annuity of £100 *per annum*, no doubt would occur of the gift being an annuity for the life of the donee. It is the gift of an annual sum of £100; that is, of as many sums of £100 as the donee shall live years."[55]

On the other hand, if a testator gives an annuity to a corporation or an unincorporated body capable of existing for an indefinite period of time, the annuity is prima facie perpetual.[56]

The differences in the effects of specific, general, and demonstrative annuities relate to ademption and abatement. In addition it is necessary to consider what provision personal representatives should make for the payment of general annuities, from what date annuities are payable, and whether arrears of an annuity carry interest. Abatement is considered last.

Ademption of a specific annuity. Like any other specific legacy, a specific annuity fails by ademption if its subject matter, or the specified property out of which it is payable, has ceased to exist as part of the testator's property at his death.[57]

But, of course, neither a general annuity nor a demonstrative annuity fails by ademption. A demonstrative annuity is treated as a general annuity so far as it cannot be satisfied out of the specified fund or specified part of the testator's property primarily designated for its payment.[58]

Providing for payment of general annuities. (1) *Appropriation of assets.* In the ordinary case, where a general annuity is charged upon the whole income, or the whole income and corpus, of the residuary estate, the annuitant is entitled to have sufficient assets appropriated to

---

[53] *Re Coller's Deed Trusts* [1939] Ch. 277, 280. For the incidence of general legacies (including general annuities) see section 2 of this chapter.

[54] See generally Hawkins and Ryder on the *Construction of Wills* (1965), pp. 206 *et seq.*

[55] *Blewitt* v. *Roberts* (1841) Cr. & Ph. 274, 280: see also *Nichols* v. *Hawkes* (1853) 10 Hare 342 (Wills Act 1837, s.28 does not apply to annuity created *de novo* by T's will); *Blight* v. *Hartnoll* (1881) 19 Ch.D. 294: *cf. Townsend* v. *Ascroft* [1917] 2 Ch. 14.

[56] *Re Jones* [1950] 2 All E.R. 239.

[57] *Cowper* v. *Mantell (No. 1)* (1856) 22 Beav. 223 (T made will, giving a specific annuity to A out of T's leasehold property Blackacre; later T assigned Blackacre to trustees on certain trusts: held annuity was adeemed).

[58] *Mann* v. *Copland* (1817) 2 Madd. 223 (the annuity "may stand, though the Fund out of which it is directed to be paid does not exist"); *Attwater* v. *Attwater* (1853) 18 Beav. 330 (T gave X an annuity "from my funded property"; it was insufficient to pay it: held deficiency must be made good from his residuary estate).

answer the annuity as will make it practically certain that the annuity will be fully paid: subject to this being done, the practice of the court is to direct that the remainder of the residuary estate shall be distributed to the residuary beneficiaries.[59] If the appropriated assets prove insufficient, the annuitant is nevertheless entitled to follow the assets so distributed into the hands of those entitled to them, because they are still subject to the annuity.[60] In order to facilitate distribution and to stop the annuitant from following the distributed assets in this way, a testator may by his will confer power on his executors to satisfy the annuity by appropriating sufficient assets to answer it, and direct that after appropriation the annuitant shall have no right to resort to any part of the estate except the appropriated fund.

(2) *Direction to purchase annuity.* An annuitant for life is generally not entitled to require the capitalised value of his annuity to be paid to him.[61] The will gives him an annuity, not a legacy of a lump sum. But if by his will T directs that an annuity be purchased for A for life, A is entitled to take the purchase-money instead of the annuity: "it would be an idle form [for the court] to direct an annuity to be purchased, which annuitants might sell immediately afterwards."[62] Moreover A is entitled to take the purchase-money even though T by his will shows an intention that the annuity is to be held by his trustees as a personal provision for A.[63] Again, a declaration by T in his will that A shall not be allowed to accept the value of the annuity,[64] or to alienate it,[65] is ineffective in the absence of a valid gift over.[66] If A does take the purchase-money instead of the annuity, he is probably entitled to interest on the purchase-money from T's death because the annuity would have commenced from T's death.[67]

If A survives T, but dies before T's personal representatives purchase an annuity for him, A's personal representatives are entitled to take the

---

[59] *Harbin* v. *Masterman* [1896] 1 Ch. 351 (annuity payable solely out of income: fund set aside to answer annuity by its income, and remainder of residuary estate ordered to be distributed to residuary beneficiaries); *Re Parry* (1889) 42 Ch.D. 570; *Re Coller's Deed Trusts* [1939] Ch. 277, 284 ("in practice, and as a matter of administration, the distribution of the corpus or the income subjected to the annuity is not held up altogether in cases where the annuitant cannot be prejudiced by a partial distribution").

[60] *Re Evans and Bettell's Contract* [1910] 2 Ch. 438. For the effect of an appropriation under Administration of Estates Act 1925, s.41 see *post*, p. 366, n. 64.

[61] *Wright* v. *Callender* (1852) 2 De G.M. & G. 652.

[62] *Stokes* v. *Cheek* (1860) 28 Beav. 620, 621.

[63] *Re Browne's Will* (1859) 27 Beav. 324 (power for trustees to apply annuity for A's benefit if ill or incapacitated).

[64] *Stokes* v. *Cheek, supra.*

[65] *Woodmeston* v. *Walker* (1831) 2 Russ. & M. 197.

[66] See *Hunt-Foulston* v. *Furber* (1876) 3 Ch.D. 285; *Re Mabbett* [1891] 1 Ch. 707; *Hatton* v. *May* (1876) 3 Ch.D. 148.

[67] *Re Robbins* [1907] 2 Ch. 8 (amount of purchase-money is sum required to purchase annuity as from T's death); *Re Brunning* [1909] 1 Ch. 276: but, in the case of a gift of a definite sum of money on trust to apply it in the purchase of an annuity for A, interest has been held to run from one year after T's death, *Re Friend* (1898) 78 L.T. 222 (gift of £1,000 to executors to be laid out in purchase of annuity for A; A took £1,000, instead of annuity: held interest ran from one year after T's death); *Gibson* v. *Bott* (1802) 7 Ves. 89, 96; *Palmer* v. *Craufurd* (1819) 3 Sw. 482. The rate of interest is 6 per cent. per annum, see *post*, p. 323.

purchase-money because the right to take it vested in A at T's death.[68] This is so even though A did not elect to take the purchase-money before his death[69] and had already received an instalment of the annuity before his death,[70] and even though the annuity is directed to be purchased after the death of a tenant for life, who survives A.[71] The same principle applies whether T directs that a definite sum of money (*e.g.* £6,000) be applied in the purchase of the annuity, or that a sum sufficient to purchase a definite annuity (*e.g.* of £500 per annum for A for life) be applied for this purpose.[72]

If, instead of directing the purchase of an annuity for A, T confers a power on the trustees of his will to purchase an annuity for A, the trustees have power to pay the purchase-money to A instead of purchasing an annuity.[73]

Date from which annuities are payable. An annuity given by will begins to run from the testator's death unless the testator shows a contrary intention in his will.[74] Thus the first payment is to be made (in arrear) at the end of one year from the death, unless the annuity is directed to be paid (say) monthly, in which case the first payment is to be made at the end of one month from the death.[75]

Interest on arrears of an annuity. The long-standing general rule is that no interest is payable on arrears of an annuity.[76] Interest is only allowed by the court in exceptional circumstances—for instance, "where the non-payment of the annuity has been the fault of the person out of whose income it would be payable."[77] This general rule is anomalous. "An annuity given by will is a series of legacies payable at intervals": interest is payable on an unpaid general or demonstrative legacy and "it is hard to see why it should not also be payable on the arrears of an annuity."[78] If a testator gives a legacy of £1,000 to his nephew and an annuity of £150 per annum to his niece for her life, and due to difficul-

---

[68] *Re Robbins, supra,* (A died 16 days after T: held A's personal representatives entitled to purchase-money).

[69] *Re Robbins, supra.*

[70] *Re Brunning* [1909] 1 Ch. 276 (T died on September 21, 1907; T's executors made quarterly payment of annuity to A up to December 20, 1907; A died before purchase of annuity: held A's executors entitled to purchase-money required to purchase annuity on December 20, 1907, plus interest from that date).

[71] *Bayley* v. *Bishop* (1803) 9 Ves. 6.

[72] *Re Robbins, supra,* at p. 12; *Dawson* v. *Hearn* (1830) 1 Russ. & My. 606: see also *Wakeham* v. *Merrick* (1868) 37 L.J.Ch. 45.

[73] *Messeena* v. *Carr* (1870) L.R. 9 Eq. 260; *Re Mabbett* [1891] 1 Ch. 707.

[74] *Gibson* v. *Bott* (1802) 7 Ves. 89, 96; *Re Robbins* [1907] 2 Ch. 8; *Pettinger* v. *Ambler* (1866) 35 Beav. 321 (T by will gave annuity to A to be raised out of a reversionary interest of T: held annuity was payable from T's death).

[75] *Houghton* v. *Franklin* (1822) 1 Sim. & St. 390. But see *post,* p. 358.

[76] *Torre* v. *Browne* (1855) 5 H.L.Cas. 555, esp. 577–580; *Re Berkeley* [1968] Ch. 744, esp. at pp. 760–762.

[77] *Re Berkeley* [1968] Ch. 154, 165. Another instance of exceptional circumstances is "where the annuitant has held some legal security which, but for the interference of the court, he might have made available for the obtaining of interest," *Torre* v. *Browne, supra,* at p. 578.

[78] Per Cross J. in *Re Berkeley* [1968] Ch. 154, 165 (he added, "the rule is one that I at least would be glad to see swept away by the Law Commission in some tidying-up operation"): see also *Re Hiscoe* (1902) 71 L.J.Ch. 347.

ties in realising his assets no payments are made to either of them for four years after his death, the legacy carries interest from the end of the executor's year but no interest is payable to the niece. Without legislation[79] this rule can only be altered by the House of Lords,[80] but a testator is of course free to override this anomalous rule by a direction in his will that interest is to be paid on arrears of an annuity.

Abatement. (1) *Order of abatement under the statutory order.* Under the statutory order of application of assets the pecuniary legacy fund falls within paragraph 5, and the expression "pecuniary legacy" in the Administration of Estates Act 1925 is defined as including "an annuity, a general legacy, a demonstrative legacy so far as it is not discharged out of the designated property, and any other general direction by a testator for the payment of money . . . "[81] In all probability "an annuity" in this context means a *general* annuity. If so, a general annuity, and a demonstrative annuity so far as it is not discharged out of the designated property, fall within paragraph 5, whereas a specific annuity, and a demonstrative annuity so far as it can be discharged out of the designated property, fall within paragraph 6. A demonstrative annuity is payable in priority to general legacies and annuities so far as the demonstrative annuity can be satisfied out of the designated property.[82]

(2) *Annuities in the same class abate rateably.* Property falling within paragraph 6 of the statutory order abates "rateably according to value." This includes a specific annuity and a demonstrative annuity so far as it can be discharged out of the designated property.

To turn to the abatement of general annuities[83] under paragraph 5; this requires detailed consideration.

(a) ABATEMENT OF ACTUARIAL VALUE. If the property from which (say) two general annuities (or a general legacy and a general annuity) are payable is insufficient to satisfy them in full, the general rule applies that they must abate rateably unless the testator T has shown by his will a clear intention to give priority to a particular legacy or annuity.[84] In order to achieve a rateable abatement, the rule of practice is to make an actuarial valuation of each annuity (so that the value can be treated as a legacy of a lump sum) and then abate this value (and also any general legacy) rateably, and pay this abated value to the annuitant.[85] Thus, where this rule of practice applies, each annuitant is entitled to be paid

---

[79] The Law Commission has advised that no action be taken on the proposal to abolish this rule; the Commission ascertained that there was a strong body of informed opinion in favour of retaining the rule because to abolish it would create "a disproportionate amount of work and expense": Law Commission, 5th Annual Report (1969–70) Law Com. No. 36, para. 63.

[80] *Re Berkeley* [1968] Ch. 744, 761.

[81] s.55(1)(ix).

[82] *Livesay* v. *Redfern* (1836) 2 Y. & C.Ex. 90: see also *Creed* v. *Creed* (1844) 11 Cl. & F. 491 (specific annuity payable in priority to general legacies charged in aid on same property).

[83] See generally *Theobald on Wills* (14th ed., 1982), pp. 526 *et seq.*

[84] *Miller* v. *Huddlestone* (1851) 3 Mac. & G. 513.

[85] *Wright* v. *Callendar* (1852) 2 De G.M. & G. 652: *Wroughton* v. *Colquhoun* (1847) 1 De G. & Sm. 357; *Re Cox* [1938] Ch. 556.

a lump sum, by way of exception to the general rule against this.[86] The reason for this rule of practice when T has given two general annuities is clear from the hypothetical example put by Simonds J. in *Re Cox*[87]:

"Suppose an annuity of £100 is bequeathed to one annuitant, A, who is ninety years of age, and a similar annuity to another, B, who is nineteen years of age, and suppose that the whole estate available for satisfaction of the annuities is only £1,000. If both the income and the capital of that sum are applied year by year until it is exhausted in payment of the two annuities, A will probably get his annuity paid in full for the whole of his life, but B will not do so. There is thus an inequality in this treatment which the testator is presumed not to have intended. The only fair way of dealing with annuities as between annuitants of different ages is to make an actuarial valuation of the annuities, and to pay the [abated] value of each so ascertained to the annuitants . . . "

The reason for this rule of practice when T has given a general legacy and a general annuity is that a rateable abatement is best achieved by treating the actuarial value of the annuity as a legacy of a lump sum.

In making an actuarial valuation of each annuity the health of each annuitant is disregarded.[88] However, if an annuitant survives the testator but dies before the date for valuation,[89] the sum due to his estate is based on the amount of his annuity which was payable before his death, and not on its actuarial value.[90]

(b) ESTATE "ACTUARIALLY SOLVENT." This rule of practice has been applied in some cases where the estate is "actuarially solvent" when the rule of practice is applied, so that no abatement is needed, *i.e.* the available assets are sufficient to pay the actuarial value of each annuity (and also any general legacy) in full, but are nevertheless insufficient to enable a sum to be set aside and invested to answer the annuities by its income (and also to pay any general legacy in full).[91] The justification for applying the rule of practice in these circumstances is that the testator's intentions as expressed cannot be carried out, and the court has to do the best it can to give effect to those intentions as nearly as may be.[92]

(c) LIMITS TO THE RULE OF PRACTICE. There are limits to the application of this rule of practice:

(i) The rule never applies if there is a single annuity and no other leg-

---

[86] For the other exception to this general rule, see *ante*, p. 303.
[87] [1938] Ch. 556, 563.
[88] *Re Bradberry* [1943] Ch. 35, 40–41 (the risks attendant to the annuitant's occupation are also disregarded).
[89] Usually the court directs an annuity to be valued as at the date of the court's order directing a valuation, *Re Bradberry, supra,* at pp. 45–47 (reviewing the case law): see D. R. Boult (1944) 60 L.Q.R. 383. For the consequences of adopting this date see Theobold, *op. cit.* pp. 529 *et seq.*
[90] *Re Bradberry, supra,* ("where facts are available, they are to be preferred to prophecies").
[91] *Re Cottrell* [1910] 1 Ch. 402 (legacies and an annuity); *Re Cox* [1938] Ch. 556 (annuities).
[92] *Re Bradberry, supra,* at p. 40.

acy or annuity is payable *pari passu* with it[93]—for the rule to apply, at least two annuities (or at least one annuity and one legacy) must be payable *pari passu*.

(ii) The rule is excluded if the testator shows a contrary intention in his will, as by giving directions to meet the contingency of his estate being insufficient.[94]

(iii) The rule is a rule of convenience, not a rule of law, and it is not applicable in a case where the estate is actuarially solvent "if there is no commercial risk of insufficiency."[95] This was the test used by the Court of Appeal in *Re Hill*,[96] where T by his will gave annuities for life to A, B, C and D whose ages ranged from 59 to 64 years; the annuities were charged on capital as well as income. The estate was actuarially solvent but was nevertheless insufficient to answer all the annuities by its income. If the annuities were paid out of income and, so far as need be, out of capital, the estate would last for 54 years if (contrary to human expectation of life) all the annuitants lived so long. As soon as one of the annuities ceased to be payable, the income of the estate would be sufficient to meet the remaining annuities. The Court of Appeal decided that the rule of practice was not applicable because there was no commercial risk that the annuities would not be paid in full if they were paid (as T directed) out of income and, so far as need be, out of capital, as and when they fell due for payment.

(iv) Finally the rule is not applied if the "settled legacy" method of abatement (now to be described) is more appropriate in the circumstances. Say T by his will gives an annuity to A for life, and directs that a fund be set aside to answer the annuity by its income (with power to resort to capital if need be), and after A's death gives the fund (or what is left of it) to B. If T also gives another general legacy or annuity, and his estate is insufficient to enable a sum to be set aside to answer A's annuity by its income and to pay the other legacy or annuity in full, there must be an abatement but the decided cases differ as to which method of abatement is to be used. In some cases[97] the court has adopted the "settled legacy" method. Where this method is used it is necessary to calculate the amount of the fund needed to answer A's annuity by its income (so that this amount can be treated as a settled legacy), then abate this amount (and also the other legacy or the actuarial value of the other annuity) rateably, and pay A's annuity out of the income and (so far as need be) the capital of this abated amount.[98]

[93] *Wright* v. *Callendar* (1852) 2 De G.M. & G. 652.
[94] *Re de Chassiron* [1939] Ch. 934 (trustees to draw on capital to pay annuities in full: held T intended older annuitants to be paid in full, even though nothing might be left for younger annuitants, and so rule was excluded by T's contrary intention).
[95] [1944] Ch. 270, 277.
[96] [1944] Ch. 270: this test was not applied in *Re Cottrell, supra*, and on its facts this decision is now open to doubt.
[97] *Re Nicholson* [1938] 3 All E.R. 270 (the headnote is wrong); *Re Thomas* [1946] Ch. 36: see also *Re Carew* [1939] Ch. 794 (where the will was construed as giving a settled legacy for A for life and subject thereto for B: "settled legacy" abatement ordered).
[98] This method postpones B to A, but B keeps his interest in remainder in the capital of the abated amount, except in so far as it has to be used to pay A's annuity. This is all in accordance with T's intentions.

But in other cases[99] the court has adopted the rule of practice already considered, so that the actuarial value of A's annuity (abated if necessary) is paid to him, and if there is any surplus after payment of the other legacy or the actuarial value of the other annuity, this surplus is payable to B and not to the residuary beneficiary.[1] Probably the "settled legacy" method gives effect to the testator's intentions more nearly than this rule of practice, and the settled legacy method seems likely to be adopted in the future in similar circumstances.

However if, instead of giving the fund (or what is left of it) to B, T directs that after A's death it is to fall into residue, the rule of practice is applicable and the "settled legacy" method is not appropriate.[2]

2. INCIDENCE OF GENERAL LEGACIES

The rules which govern the incidence of general legacies (including general annuities) cannot be stated with any certainty.[3] Obviously rules are needed in order to determine (a) which assets are applicable for the payment of general legacies, and (b) the order in which such assets are to be applied for this purpose. The rules in force on the death of a testator before 1926 were at any rate clear and well settled, though perhaps in need of reform. Unfortunately it is not certain to what extent the Administration of Estates Act 1925 has altered these rules where the testator dies after 1925. The primary responsibility for the present uncertainty rests with the draftsman of the Act but the judicial decisions since 1925 are themselves in a state of confusion and require consideration by the House of Lords.[4] In the meantime any draftsman of a will needs to consider the insertion in the will of an express provision as to the incidence of general legacies.

A. THE RULES BEFORE 1926

Before 1926 general legacies were payable only out of the testator's general personal estate, *i.e.* out of personal estate which was not the subject of an effective specific legacy.[5] This rule applied unless any contrary intention was shown by the testator in his will.

---

[99] *Re Farmer* [1939] Ch. 573; [1939] 1 All E.R. 319, 322; *Re Wilson* [1940] Ch. 966.

[1] This method suffers from disadvantages, *e.g.* it destroys the gift to B outright if there is no surplus, and postpones B to the other legatee or annuitant, as well as (rightly) to A: see *Re Thomas, supra,* at p. 39 for these and other disadvantages.

[2] *Re Cottrell* [1910] 1 Ch. 402: see also *Re Richardson* [1915] 1 Ch. 353 and *Re Ellis* [1935] Ch. 193, where a life tenant in a legacy of money was treated as an annuitant, and the rule of practice applied, because the legacy was directed to fall into residue after his death.

[3] See generally E. C. Ryder [1956] C.L.J. 80; *Theobald on Wills* (14th ed., 1982), pp. 791 *et seq.*

[4] Ryder, *loc. cit.* p. 100; Theobald, *op. cit.* p. 793; *Re Taylor's Estate* [1969] 2 Ch. 245, 253 ("it is not unlikely that in some future [case] the riddle will go before some higher court to which the problem of interpreting the Act and reconciling the authorities may seem simpler than it appears to me. Failing that it may conceivably be considered for a measure of aggiornamento at the hands of the Law Commission and the Legislature").

[5] *Robertson* v. *Broadbent* (1883) 8 App.Cas 812. But see *post*, pp. 429–430.

General personal estate alone applicable. Thus, before 1926, personal estate which was the subject of an effective specific legacy was exempt from the payment of general legacies. So, too, was the whole of the testator's realty. No doubt the exemption of specific legacies gave effect (and would today still give effect) to the likely intention of most testators.[6] However, it appears improbable that by 1925 the exemption of the whole of a testator's realty gave effect to the likely intention of most testators[7]: in this respect the old rules probably needed reform, so as to make the testator's general real estate (which was not the subject of an effective specific devise) liable for the payment of general legacies.

General personal estate liable pari passu. Before 1926 every part of the testator's general personal estate was liable *pari passu* for the payment of general legacies, whether or not it was effectively disposed of by will or went as on intestacy. If T by his will gave his residuary personal estate to X and Y as tenants in common in equal shares, and X predeceased T so that his share lapsed and went on intestacy to T's next-of-kin, the burden of T's general legacies fell *pari passu* on Y's share and the next-of-kin's share of T's residuary personal estate.

Contrary intention shown by will. The testator was free to direct by his will that his general legacies should be paid out of any property he chose to specify. Thus the rule that general legacies were payable only out of the testator's general personal estate was subject to any contrary intention shown by the testator in his will.[8] In this connection two well-known rules of construction became established:

(1) *The rule in Greville v. Brown.* Under the rule in *Greville v. Brown*,[9] if a testator by his will gave general legacies and gave the residue of his real and personal property as one mass, this charged the realty with the legacies in aid of the personalty: accordingly the legacies were payable primarily out of the personalty, but were payable out of the realty so far as the personalty proved to be insufficient. The justification for the rule was that, by giving the residue of his real and personal property as one mass, the testator showed that he intended the legacies to be treated as a deduction from the entire mass.[10] It was immaterial how the residuary gift was worded if there was in substance a single gift, comprising both residuary realty and residuary personalty, to the same person or persons, whether they took beneficially or as trustees.[11] Again the rule applied whether the general legacies appeared in the will before or after

---

[6] *Ibid.* at p. 815.

[7] For a discussion of the reasons why realty was exempt see Theobald, *op. cit.* p. 792.

[8] For the case law on contrary intention see Hawkins and Ryder on the *Construction of Wills* (1965), pp. 367 *et seq.*

[9] (1859) 7 H.L.C. 689: see also *Elliott v. Dearsley* (1881) 16 Ch.D. 322; *Re Boards* [1895] 1 Ch. 499.

[10] *Ibid*, at p. 697.

[11] *Greville v. Brown, supra,* ("all the rest, residue and remainder of any property I may die possessed of, or entitled to, of what nature soever"); *Re Bawden* [1894] 1 Ch. 693 ("all the real and personal estate to which at my death I shall be beneficially entitled . . . and not otherwise disposed of": rule applicable—the testator need not use the word "residue").

the residuary gift.[12] However, the rule did not apply if the gift was of "all my real estate and the residue of my personal estate" because the realty was regarded as given separately from the residuary personalty, so that the residue of his real and personal property was not given as one mass.[13]

(2) *The rule in Roberts* v. *Walker.* Under the rule in *Roberts* v. *Walker*,[14] if a testator by his will *directed* payment of legacies out of a mixed fund of realty and personalty, the legacies were payable rateably out of the realty and personalty in proportion to their respective values. This rule applied in the common case of a gift by a testator of his residuary real and personal estate[15] to trustees upon trust for sale and conversion, and upon trust to pay the legacies given by his will out of the moneys arising from the sale and conversion of his residuary real and personal estate: accordingly in this case the legacies were payable rateably out of the residuary realty and residuary personalty.[16] Of course, if the testator gave general legacies and gave his residuary real and personal estate to trustees upon trust for sale and conversion, but did *not direct* payment of the legacies out of the mixed fund, the rule in *Roberts* v. *Walker* was not applicable—but, under the rule in *Greville* v. *Brown*, the realty was charged with the legacies in aid of the personalty.[17]

B. THE RULES AFTER 1925

The vital question now arises—to what extent has the Administration of Estates Act 1925 altered these pre-1926 rules where the testator dies after 1925? The only provisions of the Act which need to be considered are section 33, in relation to the administration of assets on a partial intestacy, and section 34(3) which refers to the statutory order of application of assets set out in Part II of the First Schedule. Accordingly the effect on the incidence of general legacies of 1. Section 33, and 2. Section 34(3) and the statutory order, is examined in turn.

1. Effect of section 33. The effect on the incidence of general legacies of section 33 of the Act is only material if the testator dies partially intestate. Section 33(1) provides that "on the death of a person intestate as to any real or personal estate" such estate (if not already money) shall be held by his personal representatives upon trust for sale and conversion into money. Section 33(2) must be quoted in full:

---

[12] *Elliott* v. *Dearsley, supra; Re Balls* [1909] 1 Ch. 791: see also *Re Hall* (1884) 51 L.T. 795 (rule applied to additional legacy by codicil to legatee under will).
[13] *Wells* v. *Row* (1879) 48 L.J.Ch. 476; *Re Salt* [1895] 2 Ch. 203.
[14] (1830) 1 R. & My. 752; see also *Allan* v. *Gott* (1872) L.R. 7 Ch.App. 439; *Re Spencer Cooper* [1908] 1 Ch. 130.
[15] Or of all his real and personal estate, *Stocker* v. *Harbin* (1841) 3 Beav. 479; *Salt* v. *Chattaway* (1841) 3 Beav. 576.
[16] *Re Spencer Cooper, supra.* The rule was also applicable where a power to sell realty and personalty was conferred on trustees provided the testator showed an intention to create a mixed fund for the payment of legacies, *Allan* v. *Gott, supra:* cf. *Boughton* v. *Boughton* (1848) 1 H.L.C. 406 and *Tench* v. *Cheese* (1855) 6 De G.M. & G. 453.
[17] *Elliott* v. *Dearsley* (1881) 16 Ch.D. 322.

"Out of the net money to arise from the sale and conversion of such real and personal estate (after payment of costs), and out of the ready money of the deceased (so far as not disposed of by his will, if any), the personal representative shall pay all such funeral, testamentary and administration expenses, debts and other liabilities as are properly payable thereout having regard to the rules of administration contained in this Part of this Act, and out of the residue of the said money the personal representative shall set aside a fund sufficient to provide for any pecuniary legacies bequeathed by the will (if any) of the deceased."

The special rule applicable to debts charged on the deceased's property under section 35 of the Act is, of course, not affected by section 33(2). Finally, section 33(7) enacts that section 33 has effect subject to the provisions contained in the testator's will.

(1) *Section 33(2) makes undisposed-of property primarily liable.* If a testator dies after 1925 partially intestate, and section 33(2) applies in respect of the property undisposed of by his will, then under section 33(2) the net money arising from the sale and conversion of that property and the testator's ready money (if undisposed of by his will) are first to be applied in payment of the testator's expenses, debts and liabilities, and next a pecuniary legacy fund is to be set aside out of the residue of that money. Thus section 33(2), where it applies, has altered the old rules as to the incidence of general legacies by throwing their burden primarily on the undisposed-of property, whether it is realty or personalty or both.

In *Re Worthington*[18] T by her will gave general legacies and gave all the residue of her estate both real and personal to A and B in equal shares. A predeceased T, and A's share consequently lapsed and went as on T's intestacy. If the pre-1926 rules still applied unaltered on a death after 1925, the incidence of the legacies was governed by the rule in *Greville* v. *Brown*, and they were payable primarily out of the residuary personalty (whether or not it went as on intestacy), with residuary realty only liable in aid. Instead the Court of Appeal held that the legacies were payable primarily out of the lapsed share of residue which went as on intestacy. It follows that, where section 33(2) is applicable, the old rules have clearly been altered so as to make the undisposed-of property primarily liable for legacies after the payment of expenses, debts and liabilities.

If the undisposed-of property within section 33(2) includes both property in and property outside the United Kingdom, under section 33(2) the legacies are payable rateably out of the property in and the property outside the United Kingdom.[19] This is important as regards the incidence of inheritance tax. As has already been noted, so far as a legacy is payable out of property outside the United Kingdom, the legatee

---

[18] [1933] Ch. 771; followed in *Re Berrey's W.T.* [1959] 1 W.L.R. 30.
[19] *Cf.* the rule in *Roberts* v. *Walker* (1830) 1 R. & My. 752: see Hawkins and Ryder, *op. cit.* p. 373.

must bear his own inheritance tax in the absence of any free of inheritance tax provision in the will.[20]

(2) *When is section 33(2) applicable?* If section 33(2) is applicable, its effect on the incidence of general legacies is clear. Unfortunately there is a little uncertainty as to when section 33(2) is applicable. First to consider two situations where section 33(2) is applicable:

(i) T dies wholly intestate as to one or more assets of his estate: each such asset (if not already money) is held upon the statutory trust for sale and conversion imposed by section 33(1),[21] and section 33(2) applies to the net money arising from the sale and to any undisposed-of ready money of T.[22]

(ii) T dies wholly intestate as to a share in his residuary estate (*e.g.* A's share of T's residuary estate which lapsed and went as on T's intestacy in *Re Worthington*): such share is held upon the statutory trust for sale and conversion imposed by section 33(1), and again section 33(2) applies to the net money arising from the sale.[23]

But a different situation arises where T creates an effective trust for sale by his will and some beneficial interest thereunder (*e.g.* a life interest or a share of capital) fails. T by his will makes certain gifts, including general legacies, and gives his residuary real and personal estate to trustees upon trust for sale and conversion, and to hold the money arising from such sale and conversion upon trust for his nieces X and Y as tenants in common in equal shares. T dies after 1925. X predeceases T, and X's share consequently lapses and goes as on T's intestacy. The express trust for sale in T's will is nevertheless effective, and this express trust for sale excludes the statutory trust for sale imposed by section 33(1) because there cannot be two subsisting trusts for sale at the same time, and section 33 is expressly made subject to the provisions contained in T's will.[24] But does section 33(2) nevertheless apply to X's share which goes as on T's intestacy? In all probability section 33(2) does not apply to X's share because section 33(2) appears only to apply to the net money arising from the statutory trust for sale and to any undisposed-of ready money of T at his death.[25]

However, if the express trust for sale in T's will fails owing to the *complete* failure of its objects (*e.g.* because, in the above example, both X and Y predeceased T and both their shares lapsed), then the statutory

---

[20] *Ante,* p. 281.

[21] *Cf. Re McKee* [1931] 2 Ch. 145, 159, 160 and 165–166; *Re Plowman* [1943] Ch. 269.

[22] *Re Martin* [1955] Ch. 698 (intestacy as to realty so that s.33(1) and (2) applicable: but legacies held payable out of realty under para. 1): see *post,* p. 317.

[23] *Re Berrey's W.T.* [1959] 1 W.L.R. 30 (gift of residue by T to A, B, C and D equally; B predeceased T, causing B's share to lapse and go as on T's intestacy: held s.33(1) and (2) applied to B's share, and general legacies were payable primarily out of B's share).

[24] *Re McKee, supra,* esp. at pp. 159 and 165–166; *Re Taylor's Estate* [1969] 2 Ch. 245.

[25] *Re McKee, supra,* at pp. 165–166 (on the meaning of "real and personal estate" in s.33); *Re Taylor's Estate, supra; Re Beaumont's W.T.* [1950] Ch. 462 as explained in *Re Berrey's W.T., supra,* at p. 40. But *cf.* Albery (1969) 85 L.Q.R. 464, 467 who suggests that "ready money" in s.33(2) includes the proceeds of sale arising under an express trust for sale in T's will; *sed quaere.*

trust for sale imposed by section 33(1) is applicable, and section 33(2) applies to the net money arising from the sale.

2. Effect of section 34(3) and the statutory order. The effect on the incidence of general legacies of section 34(3) and the statutory order of application of assets needs to be considered in several different situations:

   (i) if the testator dies partially intestate and section 33(2) is applicable, but the legacies cannot be paid in full out of the pecuniary legacy fund set aside out of the undisposed-of property falling within section 33(2)—this undisposed-of property is first applicable in payment of the testator's expenses, debts and liabilities;

  (ii) if the testator dies partially intestate but section 33(2) is not applicable; and

 (iii) if the testator dies fully testate—in that case section 33 is never applicable.

Section 34(3) of the Administration of Estates Act 1925 provides that the testator's real and personal estate shall, subject to any provisions contained in his will, be applicable towards the discharge of "the funeral, testamentary and administration expenses, debts and liabilities payable thereout" in the statutory order mentioned in Part II of the First Schedule. Under the statutory order the testator's undisposed-of property "subject to the retention thereout of a fund sufficient to meet any pecuniary legacies" is primarily liable under paragraph 1, and the testator's property included in a residuary gift "subject to the retention out of such property of a fund sufficient to meet any pecuniary legacies, so far as not provided for as aforesaid" is next liable under paragraph 2. As has been noted already, no distinction is made between realty and personalty in the statutory order, and all the realty and personalty falling within any particular paragraph is liable rateably for the testator's expenses, debts and liabilities.[26]

Under paragraphs 1 and 2 the order of resort is different to that specified in section 33(2)—under both paragraphs 1 and 2 the pecuniary legacy fund is set aside *first*, and the *balance* of the undisposed-of property, or property included in a residuary gift, is liable for expenses, debts and liabilities.[27] Probably the different order of resort specified in section 33(2) is due to a drafting error. Unfortunately different orders of resort may well produce different practical results—for instance, as regards the incidence of inheritance tax on the legatees if the undisposed-of property is not sufficient to pay all the expenses, debts and liabilities and legacies in full, and resort has to be made to property of a different nature included in a residuary gift.

The effect on the incidence of general legacies of section 34(3) and the statutory order depends on their proper construction, as to which there appear to be two main views.

  (1) *First construction—the old rules still apply.* One view is that section 34(3) and the statutory order have not altered the old rules as to the inci-

[26] *Ante*, p. 266.
[27] *Re Anstead* [1943] Ch. 161 (the headnote is wrong); *Re Wilson* [1967] Ch. 53, 70.

dence of general legacies. If this view is correct, a pecuniary legacy fund is to be retained out of the testator's undisposed-of property under paragraph 1 only if and so far as this property is answerable for legacies under the old rules. Similarly, a pecuniary legacy fund is to be retained out of the testator's property included in a residuary gift under paragraph 2 only if and so far as this property is answerable for legacies under the old rules. In effect this view construes paragraphs 1 and 2 as if they read, "subject to the retention . . . " *if and so far as appropriate under the rules as to the incidence of legacies* "of a fund sufficient to meet any pecuniary legacies."[28] This view is supported by at least two first instance decisions on the construction of paragraph 2, namely *Re Thompson* and *Re Anstead,* and by two more first instance decisions on the construction of paragraph 1, namely *Re Beaumont's Will Trusts* and *Re Taylor's Estate.*

In *Re Thompson*[29] T by his will gave general legacies and gave all his real and personal estate not otherwise disposed of to certain charities. If the old rules still applied on a death after 1925, the incidence of his general legacies was governed by the rule in *Greville* v. *Brown.* In order to determine the incidence of death duties, it was necessary to decide whether the general legacies were payable (i) rateably out of residuary realty and residuary personalty, or (ii) primarily out of the residuary personalty, the residuary realty only being liable in aid under the rule in *Greville* v. *Brown.* Clauson J. decided in favour of the latter alternative on the ground that section 34(3) and paragraph 2 of the statutory order had not altered the old rules as to the incidence of general legacies. In his judgment he said[30]:

> "It is suggested that the effect of that provision is to alter the law, and to provide that the fund which is to be retained out of residuary realty and personalty in order to meet pecuniary legacies is to be retained in the following way: that a proportionate part is to be retained out of realty and personalty pro rata of the amount of the realty and personalty respectively. The provision does not say so, and the provision is not concerned with any such matter. The provision is concerned with the way in which funeral testamentary and administration expenses, debts and liabilities are to be met. There is no indication there that there is any intention of altering the law . . . " (as to the incidence of general legacies).

The absence of any reference to legacies in section 34(3) must be regarded, at the least, as a strong indication that the statutory order only deals with the incidence of the testator's expenses, debts and liabilities. Whether or not the statutory order was meant to alter the rules as to the incidence of legacies, the references to the pecuniary legacy fund in paragraphs 1, 2 and 5 of the statutory order were unavoidable: the statu-

---

[28] *Re Taylor's Estate, supra,* at pp. 251–253.

[29] [1936] Ch. 676. See also *Re Rowe* [1941] Ch. 343 where Farwell J. (perhaps *obiter*) agreed with *Re Thompson*: in *Re Rowe* T's will read, "I devise all my real estate and bequeath all the residue of my personal estate" to X and Y equally: held a specific devise and realty was not liable for legacies. But "I devise all my real estate" may be a general devise, *Re Wilson* [1967] Ch. 53: see *ante*, p. 269.

[30] [1936] Ch. 676, 682.

tory order had to indicate at what point the pecuniary legacy fund became liable for the testator's expenses, debts and liabilities.[31] Moreover, the words in paragraphs 1 and 2, "subject to the retention . . . ," are "a curious formula" to have used if the legislature intended to impose an obligation to retain a pecuniary legacy fund regardless of the old rules.[32]

In *Re Anstead*[33] it was again necessary to decide which assets were applicable for the payment of general legacies in order to determine the incidence of death duties. T by his will gave general legacies and gave the residue of his real and personal estate upon certain trusts. The will contained no direction as to the incidence of general legacies, and if the old rules still applied on a death after 1925 their incidence was governed by the rule in *Greville* v. *Brown*. Uthwatt J. decided that under paragraph 2 of the statutory order the first thing to be done was to set aside a pecuniary legacy fund out of residue—this was to be set aside primarily out of the residuary personalty, the residuary realty only being liable in aid if the residuary personalty proved insufficient (for which Uthwatt J. cited *Re Thompson*). The testator's expenses, debts and liabilities were then payable out of the balance of the residuary estate under paragraph 2, and the pecuniary legacy fund only became liable for expenses, debts and liabilities under paragraph 5. Thus Uthwatt J. decided that the pecuniary legacy fund was to be retained out of residue under paragraph 2 in accordance with the old rules, and not rateably out of the residuary realty and residuary personalty.

The other two decisions which support this view were on the construction of paragraph 1, which of course refers to the retention of a pecuniary legacy fund in similar language to paragraph 2. In *Re Beaumont's Will Trusts*[34] T by her will gave pecuniary legacies free of duty, and gave all her real estate and all her personal estate not otherwise disposed of to trustees upon trust for sale and conversion, and, after payment of her expenses and debts, to stand possessed of the residue for A, B, C, and D equally. C predeceased T, and C's share consequently lapsed and went as on T's intestacy and fell within paragraph 1 of the statutory order. In his judgment Danckwerts J. said that section 34(3) of the Act "has in effect made no provision with regard to such things as legacies . . . the position of the legacies depends on the old law"[35] (and he cited *Re Thompson*). Accordingly he decided that the legacies (and the duty on them, which had the effect of an additional legacy) were payable out of the whole estate before division into four equal parts,[36] and not primarily out of C's lapsed share under paragraph 1 of the statutory order.

---

[31] Ryder, *loc. cit.* pp. 84–85 and 98.

[32] *Re Taylor's Estate* [1969] 2 Ch. 245, 252.

[33] [1943] Ch. 161 (the headnote is wrong): in *Re Anstead* T directed his trustees to provide for an annuity given by his will out of his residuary personal estate: no question arose as to this. See also *Re Wilson* [1967] Ch. 53, 71.

[34] [1950] Ch. 462: see also *Re Berrey's W.T.* [1959] 1 W.L.R. 30.

[35] *Ibid.*, at p. 466.

[36] Under the rule in *Greville* v. *Brown* the burden fell primarily on T's personalty, with realty liable in aid.

The same situation arose in *Re Taylor's Estate*[37] (a case decided in the Durham Chancery Court) and again the court held that the legacies were payable out of the residuary estate as a whole in accordance with the old law, and not primarily out of the lapsed share under paragraph 1 of the statutory order.

(2) *Second construction—paragraphs 1 and 2 of the statutory order determine incidence.* The other view is that section 34(3) and the statutory order have altered the old rules as to the incidence of general legacies. According to this view a pecuniary legacy fund must be retained out of the testator's undisposed-of property under paragraph 1, irrespective of whether it would have been answerable for legacies under the old rules. Logically this view also requires that a pecuniary legacy fund (so far as not provided for out of any undisposed-of property) should be retained out of the testator's property included in a residuary gift under paragraph 2, irrespective of whether it would have been answerable for legacies under the old rules. All the decisions supporting this view have turned on the wording of paragraph 1, and not paragraph 2, but it appears highly unlikely that the reference to the retention of a pecuniary legacy fund in paragraph 2 is to be construed in any different way from the similar reference in paragraph 1.[38] Assuming that this view is correct, if the undisposed-of property within paragraph 1 (or the property included in a residuary gift within paragraph 2) includes both realty and personalty, it is not clear whether the legacies are payable primarily out of the personalty within that paragraph, the realty within that paragraph being only liable in aid, or whether the legacies (like the expenses and debts) are payable rateably out of the realty and the personalty within that paragraph.[39] The latter alternative seems more likely to be adopted.

Now for the cases which support this view. The clearest decision is that in *Re Midgley*.[40] T by her will gave pecuniary legacies and gave her residuary real and personal estate to trustees upon trust for sale and, after payment of her expenses and debts, to hold the residue upon trust for six named persons equally. By a codicil T revoked the gift to one of these persons, and consequently that person's one-sixth share went as on T's intestacy and fell within paragraph 1 of the statutory order. Harman J. held that paragraph 1 required the legacies to be paid out of this one-sixth share. He asked,[41] "What, then, is to be done with the fund which has been retained thereout?" (*i.e.* out of the undisposed-of property under paragraph 1). "The answer, it seems to me, is that it must be used to meet the pecuniary legacies, because it has been retained for that purpose. It is, if I may say so, a tortuous way of legislating . . . " Of course no one challenges the proposition that a fund retained to meet pecuniary legacies should be used to pay them (unless the fund

---

[37] [1969] 2 Ch. 245 (the Chancellor considered the construction of the statutory provisions at pp. 250–253).

[38] See *Re Wilson* [1967] Ch. 53, 70.

[39] *Re Martin* [1955] Ch. 698, 704–705; Ryder, *loc. cit.* pp. 99–100 suggests that under para. 2 the personalty is primarily liable.

[40] [1955] Ch. 576.

[41] *Ibid.* at p. 583.

becomes liable for expenses and debts under paragraph 5). The crucial difference between the two views is over the *retention* of a fund. According to the first view, a fund is to be retained out of the undisposed-of property only if and so far as this property is answerable for legacies under the old rules. On the other hand, according to this decision of Harman J. in *Re Midgley*, a fund must be retained out of the undisposed-of property irrespective of whether it would have been answerable for legacies under the old rules.

Of the other cases which support this view, *Re Gillett's Will Trusts*[42] is a weaker authority because counsel for the next-of-kin entitled on intestacy conceded that under paragraph 1 the legacies must be paid out of the testator's undisposed-of property unless the will showed a contrary intention. The other case to be mentioned, *Re Martin*,[43] is another decision of Danckwerts J. By his will T gave pecuniary legacies, gave all his real estate to X, and gave his residuary personal estate to trustees upon certain trusts which did not fail. By a codicil T revoked the gift of his real estate to X, and consequently the realty went as on T's intestacy and section 33(1) and (2) applied to it. The legacies were therefore payable out of the realty pursuant to section 33(2).[44] Danckwerts J. decided that the legacies were payable out of the realty, but he based his decision on paragraph 1 of the statutory order, construing paragraph 1 as if it required a pecuniary legacy fund to be retained out of the undisposed-of realty, regardless of the old rules under which the legacies were payable out of the general personal estate. The earlier decision of Danckwerts J. in *Re Beaumont's Will Trusts*[45] ("the position of the legacies depends on the old law") appears to be incompatible with his reasoning in *Re Martin*.

The lamentable conclusion to be drawn from this review of these statutory provisions and of more than half a century's case law on their construction is that the effect of the Administration of Estates Act 1925 has been to produce lasting uncertainty as to what rules govern the incidence of general legacies. It is most unfortunate that since 1925 no appellate court has ever had to decide between these two constructions of section 34(3) and the statutory order.

Express provision in will as to incidence of legacies. There is however one comfort to be drawn from a study of these statutory provisions—they all take effect subject to the provisions contained in the will of the testator.[46] Accordingly the draftsman of a will may (and often should) insert in the will an express provision as to the incidence of

[42] [1950] Ch. 102: see *Re Berrey's W.T.* [1959] 1 W.L.R. 30, 35.
[43] [1955] Ch. 698. See also *Re Lamb* [1929] 1 Ch. 723 (assumed, without argument, para. 1 applied) and *Re Worthington* [1933] Ch. 771 (para. 1 cited as well as s.33(2))—both were cases where s.33(2) applied.
[44] See *Re Berrey's W.T.*, *supra* and *ante*, p. 312, n. 23, where Danckwerts J. regarded the C.A. decision in *Re Worthington* as binding authority.
[45] *Ante*, p. 315.
[46] ss.33(7) and 34(3); Sched. 1, Pt. II, para. 8(*a*): see *Re Wilson* [1967] Ch. 53 (gift of specific and general legacies; gift of "all my real estate and the residue of my personal estate" to X: held will showed intention that legacies were to be paid exclusively from personal estate—real estate not liable for general legacies but liable for expenses and debts under para. 2); *Re Taylor's Estate* [1969] 2 Ch. 245, 250; *Re Feis* [1964] Ch. 106, 116–117.

general legacies and thereby exclude whatever rules would otherwise be applicable. Often by his will a testator gives his residuary real and personal estate to trustees upon trust for sale and conversion, and out of the proceeds of such sale and conversion and his ready money to pay his funeral, testamentary and administration expenses and debts, and the general legacies given by his will or any codicil thereto. Such a direction ensures that, if some beneficial interest in his residuary estate fails, the general legacies are payable out of the whole residuary estate.[47]

A direction in a will as to the incidence of general legacies can remove the uncertainty which the Administration of Estates Act 1925 has produced. A free of inheritance tax provision in a will can avoid the trap set for testators by the rule that property outside the United Kingdom bears its own inheritance tax.[48]

3. INCOME AND INTEREST

In this section the rules governing the income or interest carried by gifts by will are considered. By his will the testator may make a gift of property (i) to a person beneficially or (ii) to trustees upon trust for persons in succession (*e.g.* upon trust for A for life and subject thereto for B absolutely). In each case the question arises what income or interest does the gift by will carry? But in the case of the trust for persons in succession, a second question also arises—what constitutes income to be paid to the life tenant and what constitutes capital of the trust? The answer to this second question forms part of the law of trusts and is not discussed in this book.[49]

A. Specific Legacies and Devises

1. Immediate specific gifts. A specific legacy or specific devise which takes effect immediately carries with it all the income or profits accruing from its subject matter after the testator's death. For instance, under a specific legacy of company shares the legatee is entitled to the dividends after the testator's death.[50] Similarly, under a specific devise of

---

[47] *Cf.* Form 8 of the Statutory Will Forms 1925 (prescribed under Law of Property Act 1925, s.179 and which may be incorporated in a will); Form 8 makes the legacies payable primarily out of personalty.

[48] See *ante*, p. 281.

[49] The rule in *Allhusen* v. *Whittell* which relates to administration is considered at the end of this section. For the duty to convert under the rule in *Howe* v. *Earl of Dartmouth* (1802) 7 Ves. 137 (applicable to unauthorised investments comprised in a residuary bequest of personalty to be enjoyed by persons in succession), and the duty to apportion under this rule (or the rule in *Gibson* v. *Bott* (1802) 7 Ves. 89), the rule in *Re Earl of Chesterfield's Trusts* (1883) 24 Ch.D. 643, and the rule in *Bouch* v. *Sproule* (1887) 12 App.Cas. 385, see Snell's *Principles of Equity* (28th ed., 1982), pp. 225–230 and 371–376, or Pettit, *Equity and the Law of Trusts* (5th ed., 1984), pp. 355–368.

[50] *Re West* [1909] 2 Ch. 180 (specific legacy of company shares carried dividends from death of testatrix); *Re Marten* [1901] 1 Ch. 370: see also *Chester* v. *Urwick* (1856) 23 Beav. 420 (specific legacy of one or other stocks at discretion of executors: held legatee entitled to dividends from testator's death) and *cf. Re Collins' W.T.* [1971] 1 W.L.R. 37, 42–43.

Blackacre which is subject to a tenancy at the testator's death, the devisee is entitled to the rent after the testator's death.

(1) *Apportionment of income.* In order to ascertain the amount of income accruing after the testator's death it may be necessary to apportion income under section 2 of the Apportionment Act 1870. This section provides that "All rents, annuities, dividends, and other periodical payments in the nature of income . . . shall, like interest on money lent, be considered as accruing from day to day, and shall be apportionable in respect of time accordingly."

(a) EFFECT OF APPORTIONMENT ACT 1870. To consider the specific devise of Blackacre to X by the testator T. If at his death T has a cause of action against the tenant of Blackacre for rent already due, this cause of action is an asset of T's estate at his death and (like rent actually paid to T before his death) falls into T's residuary estate.[51] On the other hand, if rent falls due for payment after T's death, under section 2 of the Act it is apportionable in respect of the period for which it is paid: if this period overlaps T's death, X is entitled to so much of the rent as is apportioned to the time after T's death but any rent apportioned to the time before T's death falls into T's residuary estate.[52]

The Apportionment Act applies to the dividends[53] of all companies registered under the Companies Acts, whether public or private in the company law sense,[54] provided the dividend is declared in respect of some definite, though not necessarily regularly recurring, period, so that the dividend can be apportioned in respect of that period.[55] To consider the specific legacy of company shares to X by T, if a dividend on these shares is declared in T's lifetime, the dividend falls into T's residuary estate, even though it is not payable until after T's death.[56] On the other hand, if the dividend is declared after T's death, under section 2 of the Act it is apportionable in respect of the period for which it is declared: if this period overlaps T's death, X is entitled to so much of the dividend as is apportioned to the time after T's death but any dividend apportioned to the time before T's death falls into T's residuary estate.[57]

A testator may exclude the operation of the Apportionment Act by

---

[51] *Ellis* v. *Rowbotham* [1900] 1 Q.B. 740; *Re Aspinall* [1961] Ch. 526 (T died at 8.30 a.m. on Xmas day: held at his death T had no cause of action for rent payable on Xmas day because cause of action accrued later at midnight).

[52] *Re Aspinall, supra.*

[53] Defined in s.5 of the Act to include "all payments made by the name of dividend, bonus, or otherwise out of the revenue of trading or other public companies . . ." but not "payments in the nature of a return or reimbursement of capital": see also *Re Griffith* (1879) 12 Ch.D. 655 (bonus on company shares out of surplus profits distributable every five years apportionable under the Act).

[54] *Re Lysaght* [1898] 1 Ch. 115; *Re White* [1913] 1 Ch. 231. See also *Re Griffith, supra* (Act applies to unincorporated life assurance society with power to sue or be sued under special Act of Parliament).

[55] *Re Jowitt* [1922] 2 Ch. 442.

[56] *Lock* v. *Venables* (1860) 27 Beav. 598; *De Gendre* v. *Kent* (1867) 4 Eq. 282.

[57] *Re Beavan* (1885) 53 L.T. 245; *Re Edwards* [1918] 1 Ch. 142. As to dividends on cumulative preference shares see *Re Wakley* [1920] 2 Ch. 205 (specific legacy of cumulative preference shares to X by T who died in 1905; in 1907 company declared dividends in respect of that year in order to satisfy "arrears" of dividends since before T's death: held X entitled to whole dividend).

words expressly so stating or requiring that conclusion by necessary implication,[58] but not by any general inference from his will.[59] A suitable precedent of an exclusion clause provides that "all interest dividends and other payments in the nature of income arising from property of mine in respect of any period partly before and partly after my death shall be treated as accruing wholly after my death and shall not be apportioned."[60]

(b) APPORTIONMENT ACT NOT APPLICABLE. Occasionally the Apportionment Act 1870 is not applicable—for instance, it does not apply to the profits accruing from the testator's own business of which he was the proprietor,[61] or from a share in a private partnership.[62] In these cases the profits are treated as having accrued entirely on the final day of the period for which they are declared. To consider a specific legacy by T of his partnership share to X, if after T's death profits are declared for a period which overlaps T's death, X is entitled to the whole of the profits and no apportionment is made.[63]

(2) *Liabilities*. A legatee or devisee taking under an immediate specific legacy or devise must bear the liabilities incident to the subject matter of the gift after the testator's death.[64] To consider again the specific devise of Blackacre to X by the testator T, if at T's death Blackacre is let to a tenant under a lease containing a covenant by the landlord to keep the exterior of the demised premises in repair, X must bear the expense of repairing in accordance with this covenant after T's death.[65] There are, however, two limits to the burden which X must bear:

(i) If in his lifetime T entered into a binding contract to have certain building work done on Blackacre, X as devisee is entitled to have this work carried out for his benefit after T's death at the expense of T's estate. In *Re Rushbrook's W.T.*[66] T by his will gave his house Whiteacre to Y. Before T's death the house was damaged by fire and T contracted with a builder to effect repairs for the sum of

---

[58] Apportionment Act 1870, s.7: see *Re Lysaght* [1898] 1 Ch. 115 (specific legacy of company shares, with declaration that "every share . . . shall carry the dividend accruing thereon at my death": held Act excluded and legacy carried whole dividend for year in which testator died without apportionment); *Re Meredith* (1898) 78 L.T. 492: *cf. Re Edwards* [1918] 1 Ch. 142. See for possible reform Law Reform Committee, 23rd Report, *The powers and duties of trustees*, Cmnd. 8733 (1982), pp. 25 and 64 (recommending Act should not apply, subject to any contrary intention in the will).

[59] *Re Joel's W.T.* [1967] Ch. 14, 23–24.

[60] *Hallett's Conveyancing Precedents* (1965), p. 1028.

[61] *Re Cox's Trusts* (1878) 9 Ch.D. 159.

[62] *Jones* v. *Ogle* (1872) 8 Ch.App. 192; *Re Lynch-White* [1937] 3 All E.R. 551.

[63] *Ibbotson* v. *Elam* (1866) L.R. 1 Eq. 188; *Browne* v. *Collins* (1871) 12 Eq. 586; *Re Robbins* [1941] Ch. 434.

[64] The outgoings must be apportioned if income is apportioned, *Re Joel's W.T.* [1967] Ch. 14, 30–31. As to expenses incurred by the personal representatives in the upkeep and preservation of the subject matter of a specific devise or specific legacy, see *ante*, p. 300.

[65] *Re Day's W.T.* [1962] 1 W.L.R. 1419 (X liable on covenants "of a kind incident to the relationship of landlord and tenant"); *Mansel* v. *Norton* (1883) 22 Ch.D. 769. As to the liabilities to be borne by a specific legatee of a leasehold see *Theobald on Wills* (14th ed., 1982), p. 804.

[66] [1948] Ch. 421: *cf. Re Day's W.T., supra,* (no binding contract to carry out any particular work).

£550. After T's death his executors purported to disclaim responsibility for the repairs. The court held that Y was entitled to have a sum not exceeding £550 expended in repairs out of T's estate.

(ii) If the covenant in the lease relates to something which was to be done by T preparatory to the complete establishment of the relation of landlord and tenant, then the burden of the covenant falls on T's estate and not on X. An instance is a covenant to repair where the object of the covenant was to ensure that the premises were put initially into a condition fit for the occupation of the tenant.[67]

Of course, if Blackacre is subject to a mortgage debt at T's death, section 35 of the Administration of Estates Act 1925 applies and Blackacre is primarily liable for the payment of the mortgage debt, unless T has shown a contrary intention.[68]

2. Contingent or deferred specific gifts. A specific legacy or specific devise may be contingent (e.g. "to X if he attains the age of 30 years"), or deferred to a future date which must come sooner or later (e.g. a gift "to X after the death of my wife A"), or both contingent and deferred.

Section 175 of the Law of Property Act 1925 applies to contingent or deferred specific gifts in a will coming into operation after 1925. It provides as follows:

"(1) A contingent or future specific devise or bequest of property, whether real or personal, and a contingent residuary devise of freehold land, and a specific or residuary devise of freehold land to trustees upon trust for persons whose interests are contingent or executory shall, subject to the statutory provisions relating to accumulations, carry the intermediate income of that property from the death of the testator, except so far as such income, or any part thereof, may be otherwise expressly disposed of.

(2) This section applies only to wills coming into operation after the commencement of this Act."

Section 175 mentions a contingent or deferred specific devise or bequest ("future" in the section means deferred[69]), and a specific devise to trustees upon trust for persons whose interests are contingent or deferred (again "executory" in the section appears to mean deferred[70]), but the section does not mention a specific bequest to trustees upon trust for persons whose interests are contingent or executory. The omission is puzzling but such a specific bequest to trustees probably falls within the earlier reference to "a contingent or future specific . . . bequest."[71]

Where it applies, section 175 makes a contingent or deferred specific

---

[67] Re Day's W.T., supra: see also Eccles v. Mills [1898] A.C. 360 (covenant by landlord to finish laying down land in grass: held burden fell on his estate and not on specific devisee); Re Hughes [1913] 2 Ch. 491; Re Smyth [1965] I.R. 595.

[68] Ante, pp. 274 et seq.

[69] Re McGeorge [1963] Ch. 544, 550–552.

[70] Ibid.

[71] See P. V. Baker (1963) 79 L.Q.R. 184, 186. For the rules applicable to wills coming into operation before 1926 see Hawkins and Ryder on the Construction of Wills (1965), p. 78.

gift of property carry the intermediate income of that property, but subject to the rule that the income can only be accumulated and added to the capital for as long as the statutory rule against accumulations permits.[72] Of course, section 175 does not apply where the intermediate income is otherwise expressly disposed of by the testator.[73] However, if the will contains a contingent or deferred specific devise or bequest, and also a residuary gift, the residuary gift is not construed as an express disposition of the intermediate income, so as to prevent section 175 from applying.[74]

Section 175 probably accords with the likely intentions of a testator who makes a contingent specific gift, but the same cannot be said of a deferred specific gift. If a testator makes a specific gift "to X after the death of my wife A," it seems reasonable to assume that he does not wish X to have any income which accrues before A's death. Unfortunately section 175 applies to a deferred, as well as a contingent, specific gift.

Where there is a beneficiary living who is contingently entitled, section 31 of the Trustee Act 1925 often governs the destination of the intermediate income carried by the specific gift. Under this section the personal representatives have power during the infancy of the beneficiary to apply the whole or part of the income for his maintenance, education or benefit (accumulating any surplus income), and after the beneficiary has attained full age the personal representatives must pay the whole income to him until he either attains a vested interest, or dies, or his interest fails.[75] Section 31 applies so far as a contrary intention is not expressed in the will.[76] The section is not applicable to intermediate income carried by a deferred specific gift, and such income must be accumulated and added to the capital for as long as the statutory rule against accumulations permits.[77]

B. GENERAL LEGACIES

The rules now to be considered governing the interest carried by general legacies also apply to demonstrative legacies but (as has already been explained) do not apply to general annuities.

---

[72] *Re McGeorge, supra,* (deferred specific devise, which was vested subject to being divested, held to carry intermediate income under s.175 for permitted accumulation period): for the rule against accumulations see Law of Property Act 1925, ss.164–166, as amended by Perpetuities and Accumulations Act 1964, s.13.

[73] *Re Hatfield* [1958] Ch. 469 (specific devise by T to A for life, remainder to his sons successively in tail male, remainder to B for life, remainder to his sons successively in tail male, remainder to C in fee simple; T died, A died without issue, and B disclaimed his life interest; B had no son: held until the birth of a son to B the income was payable to C, and was expressly disposed of, and s.175(1) did not apply).

[74] *Re McGeorge, supra.*

[75] Trustee Act 1925, ss.31(1) and (2) and 68(17), as amended by Family Law Reform Act 1969, s.1(3) and (4), Sched. 1, Pt. I and Sched. 3, para. 5(1). See generally Snell's *Principles of Equity* (28th ed., 1982), pp. 272 *et seq.*

[76] s.69(2); *Re Turner's W.T.* [1937] Ch. 15.

[77] *Re McGeorge, supra.*

Interest runs from time for payment. The basic principle is that a general legacy carries interest from the time at which it is payable. Unless the testator directs otherwise, the appropriate rate of interest is 6 per cent. per annum,[78] and it is simple interest (*i.e.* interest is computed only upon the principal), and not compound interest, which is payable. The justification for this rule is that the interest payable compensates the legatee for any delay in paying him his legacy and prevents the residuary beneficiary from benefiting unduly from this delay. The interest payable is not to be regarded as an additional legacy given by the testator but rather as a sum payable in the course of the due administration of the estate.[79]

The rule is not confined to a general legacy of a sum of money but applies, for instance, to a general legacy of company shares. In *Re Hall*[80] T by his will gave several general legacies of shares in a particular company. At his death T held sufficient shares to satisfy these legacies, and more than three years later his executor transferred the shares to the legatees. The court held that each legatee was entitled to interest in respect of the period from the date at which his legacy was due to be satisfied (*i.e.* from the end of one year after T's death) until the date of satisfaction of his legacy, and that the legatee was not entitled to the dividends accruing from the shares during this period. The legatee only became entitled to the dividends accruing from the shares after the transfer or appropriation of the shares to him.

Time for payment. The time for payment of a legacy (1) may be fixed by the testator in his will and, if not, (2) has to be fixed by rules of law.

(1) *Time fixed by the testator.* If by his will a testator directs a legacy to be paid "immediately after my death," the legacy carries interest from the date of the testator's death because the testator has fixed this date as the time for payment.[81] Similarly, a legacy directed to be paid to X at the age of 21 years bears interest from X's 21st birthday, whether the legacy is vested or contingent.[82] Again, a legacy directed to be paid on the death of a tenant for life carries interest from the death of the tenant for life.

---

[78] R.S.C., Ord. 44, r. 10. The rate was increased from 5 per cent. by R.S.C. (Amendment No. 2) 1983 (S.I. 1983 No. 1181), which came into operation on October 1, 1983.

[79] *Re Wyles* [1938] Ch. 313, 315–316. A partial payment made to a legatee on account of the principal and interest of a legacy is treated (unless the will provides otherwise) as made first in respect of arrears of interest and then in respect of principal, *Re Morley's Estate* [1937] Ch. 491 (T's will gave 922 legacies).

[80] [1951] 1 All E.R. 1073.

[81] *Re Riddell* [1936] W.N. 252; *Re Pollock* [1943] Ch. 338: *cf. Webster* v. *Hale* (1803) 8 Ves. 410 (legacy to be paid "as soon as possible": held no date fixed for payment, and interest payable from one year after testator's death). For the effect of Administration of Estates Act 1925, s.44, see *post*, p. 358.

[82] *Heath* v. *Perry* (1744) 3 Atk. 101; *Crickett* v. *Dolby* (1795) 3 Ves. 10; *Tyrrell* v. *Tyrrell* (1798) 4 Ves. 1; *Lord* v. *Lord* (1867) L.R. 2 Ch. 782 (legacies to be paid when certain litigation ended: held interest ran from end of litigation 18 years after death of testatrix); *Holmes* v. *Crispe* (1849) 18 L.J.Ch. 439 (legacies to be paid when testator's estate sufficient: held interest ran from then). But if X attains 21 years before T's death the legacy is payable one year after T's death, *Re Palfreeman* [1914] 1 Ch. 877.

(2) *Time fixed by rules of law.* If no time for payment is mentioned in the will, the time for payment of a general legacy is fixed by rules of law:

(a) IMMEDIATE GENERAL LEGACY. The normal rule is that an immediate legacy is payable one year after the testator's death, *i.e.* at the end of the executor's year. This rule has been adopted for the sake of convenience: it may well be impracticable for the personal representatives to pay the legacy at the end of the executor's year but it is treated as payable at that time, so that the legacy carries interest from that time until the legacy is actually paid.[83] The rule is applicable though the testator's estate does not produce any income[84]—for instance, because it consists mainly of a reversionary interest which cannot be sold to advantage.[85]

The same rule applies to a general legacy upon trust for A for life and subject thereto for B absolutely. Thus the legacy carries interest from the end of the executor's year and A is not entitled to any interest in respect of the executor's year.[86] As Lord Eldon pointed out,[87] "If an annuity is given, the first payment is paid at the end of the year from the death: but if a legacy is given for life, with remainder over, no interest is due till the end of two years. It is only interest of the legacy; and till the legacy is payable, there is no fund to produce interest."

A legacy which is vested but is liable to be divested in a certain event (*e.g.* given to a child X, with a gift over to Y in the event of X dying under the age of 21) also carries interest from the end of the executor's year.[88]

(b) CONTINGENT OR DEFERRED GENERAL LEGACY. A general legacy which is contingent or deferred (or both) carries interest from the time at which it becomes payable. Such a general legacy is not mentioned in section 175 of the Law of Property Act 1925 and accordingly does not carry intermediate income under that section,[89] as does a contingent or deferred specific gift.

It follows that a general legacy to an unborn child only carries interest from the birth of the child,[90] and a general legacy to X if he attains the age of 18 years only carries interest from X's 18th birthday.[91] Again, a general legacy given to a person appointed executor and conditional on his accepting the office only carries interest from the time he accepts the office.[92]

---

[83] *Wood* v. *Penoyre* (1807) 13 Ves. 325a, 333–334.
[84] *Pearson* v. *Pearson* (1802) 1 Sch. & Lef. 10.
[85] *Re Blachford* (1884) 27 Ch.D. 676 (T died in 1869; her main asset was a reversionary interest which fell into possession in 1881: held legatee was entitled to interest on his legacy from one year after T's death); *Walford* v. *Walford* [1912] A.C. 658.
[86] *Re Whittaker* (1882) 21 Ch.D. 657.
[87] *Gibson* v. *Bott* (1802) 7 Ves. 89, 96.
[88] *Taylor* v. *Johnson* (1728) 2 P.Wms. 504.
[89] *Re Raine* [1929] 1 Ch. 716.
[90] *Rawlins* v. *Rawlins* (1796) 2 Cox. 425.
[91] *Re George* (1877) 5 Ch.D. 837; *Re Dickson* (1885) 29 Ch.D. 331; *Re Inman* [1893] 3 Ch. 518.
[92] *Angermann* v. *Ford* (1861) 29 Beav. 349; *Re Gardner* (1893) 67 L.T. 552 (legacy given to infant as executor: held interest ran from time he accepted office after attaining full age). As to accepting office see *Lewis* v. *Matthews* (1869) L.R. 8 Eq. 277.

(c) LEGACY DIRECTED TO BE SEVERED. A legacy which the testator directs to be severed from his general estate may carry interest for a beneficiary from the end of the executor's year, though his beneficial interest in the legacy is contingent or deferred. Whether it does so depends on the purpose for which severance is directed. Thus a general legacy given to trustees upon trust to invest and hold the legacy, and the investments representing it, upon trust for X if he attains the age of 18 years is treated under the general rule as payable by the executor to the trustees at the end of the executor's year, and the legacy carries interest from the end of the executor's year. The same result follows if T by his will directs that the legacy be severed (or set apart) by his executor from his general estate and held for the benefit of X if he attains the age of 18 years: in that case the legacy is treated as severable by the executor at the end of the executor's year and it carries interest from the end of the executor's year.[93] But if by his will T directs that the legacy be set apart merely for convenience of administration (*e.g.* so as to enable the rest of his estate to be distributed) and not for some purpose connected with the legacy, or if without any such direction the executor in fact sets the legacy apart, the legacy only carries interest for X from his 18th birthday, and meanwhile the interest accruing from the fund which has been set apart falls into T's residuary estate.[94]

Interest runs from death under four exceptional rules. There are four exceptional rules under which a general legacy carries interest from the date of the testator's death.

(1) *Satisfaction of a debt.* A legacy to a creditor of the testator, which operates as a satisfaction of his debt, carries interest from the date of the testator's death and not from the end of the executor's year.[95] But this rule is not applicable if by his will the testator fixed a time later than the testator's death for payment of the legacy.[96]

(2) *Legacy charged only on realty.* A legacy which is charged only on realty carries interest from the date of the testator's death if the legacy is vested.[97] Again this rule is not applicable if by his will the testator fixed a later time for payment of the legacy. The normal rule that an immediate legacy is payable at the end of the executor's year was taken by the Court of Chancery from the practice of the ecclesiastical courts but it was not applied to a legacy charged only on realty.[98] However, this exceptional rule has a narrow area of operation. It does not apply to a legacy directed to be paid out of the proceeds of sale of realty devised

---

[93] *Re Medlock* (1886) 55 L.J.Ch. 738; *Johnston* v. *O'Neill* (1879) 3 L.R.Ir. 476 ("the rule that the interest follows the capital prevails and the legatee gets his legacy with its interim accretions"); *Re Couturier* [1907] 1 Ch. 470; *Re Pollock* [1943] Ch. 338.

[94] *Festing* v. *Allen* (1844) 5 Hare 573; *Re Judkin's Trusts* (1884) 25 Ch.D. 743; *Re Inman* [1893] 3 Ch. 518.

[95] *Clark* v. *Sewell* (1744) 3 Atk. 96, 98–99; *Re Rattenberry* [1906] 1 Ch. 667: for satisfaction of a debt by a legacy see *post*, pp. 446–448.

[96] *Adams* v. *Lavander* (1824) M'Cl. & Y. 41.

[97] *Maxwell* v. *Wettenhall* (1722) 2 P.Wms. 26; *Shirt* v. *Westby* (1808) 16 Ves. 393: the rule does not apply if a legacy is charged on realty in aid of the personalty, *Freeman* v. *Simpson* (1833) 6 Sim. 75.

[98] *Pearson* v. *Pearson* (1802) 1 Sch. & Lef. 10, 11.

upon trust for sale—in that case the legacy has been held to carry interest from one year after the testator's death, when the sale might reasonably have been effected.[99]

(3) *Testator's infant child.* If a testator gives a legacy to his infant child, or to an infant to whom he stands *in loco parentis,* the legacy carries interest from the date of the testator's death so as to provide maintenance for the child.[1] This rule is very old and it originated from the court presuming that the legacy was intended by the testator to carry interest in order to provide for the child's maintenance if the will made no other provision for maintenance.[2] The rule is not applicable if the testator has by his will made some other provision for the child's maintenance. Thus the rule is excluded if the testator makes express provision for the child's maintenance out of his residuary estate.[3] Moreover, the rule only applies where the legacy is given directly to the child, and it is not applicable if the legacy is given to trustees upon trust for the child.[4]

The rule applies even though the legacy to the child is not payable until the child attains full age, or is contingent upon his attaining full age or previously marrying.[5] But the rule does not apply if the specified contingency has no reference to the child's infancy. In *Re Abrahams*[6] T by his will gave a legacy to each son of his who should attain the age of 25 years and a further legacy to each son who should attain the age of 30 years. The court held that the rule did not apply because these specified events had no reference to the son's infancy: each legacy therefore carried interest from the time at which it became payable, and not from the date of T's death.

The effect of this rule (where it applies) is to make the legacy carry interest from the date of the testator's death, instead of from the time for payment fixed by the testator in his will or by the rules of law which have already been considered. The rate of interest carried is 5 per cent. per annum if the income available is sufficient.[7] The interest may be applied for the child's maintenance, either under the statutory power of

---

[99] *Turner* v. *Buck* (1874) L.R. 18 Eq. 301; *cf. Re Waters* (1889) 42 Ch.D. 517.

[1] *Re Bowlby* [1904] 2 Ch. 685 (infant child); *Wilson* v. *Maddison* (1843) 2 Y. & C.C.C. 372 (testator *in loco parentis* to child). If the child is *en ventre sa mère* at the testator's death, the legacy carries interest only from the child's birth, *Rawlins* v. *Rawlins* (1796) 2 Cox. 425.

[2] *Harvey* v. *Harvey* (1722) 2 P.Wms. 21 (father gave legacies to his children payable at 21: "it should be presumed that the father who gave these legacies, intended they should carry interest . . . for everyone must suppose it to have been the intention of the father, that his children should not want bread during their infancy"); *Heath* v. *Perry* (1744) 3 Atk. 101, 102; *Wynch* v. *Wynch* (1788) 1 Cox 433.

[3] *Hearle* v. *Greenbank* (1749) 3 Atk. 695, 716; *Donovan* v. *Needham* (1846) 9 Beav. 164; *Re George* (1877) 5 Ch.D. 837. If a share of residue is also given to the child contingently on attaining 21, the statutory power of maintenance (now in Trustee Act 1925, s.31) out of the income of this share of residue does not exclude this exceptional rule, *Re Moody* [1895] 1 Ch. 101: *sed quaere* and *cf. Re Abrahams* [1911] 1 Ch. 108, 114.

[4] *Re Pollock* [1943] Ch. 338 (legacy by T to trustees upon trust for T's son if he attains 25: held legacy was severed and carried interest from end of executor's year).

[5] *Re Bowlby* [1904] 2 Ch. 685.

[6] [1911] 1 Ch. 108: see also *Re Jones* [1932] 1 Ch. 642 and the exceptional rule considered in (4) below.

[7] Trustee Act 1925, s.31(3) (5 per cent. "subject to any rules of court to the contrary"): *cf.* R.S.C., Ord. 44, r. 10 (6 per cent.).

maintenance[8] or pursuant to an order of the court. Any surplus interest not applied for the child's maintenance is accumulated and added to the capital of the legacy.[9]

(4) *Intention to provide for maintenance of infant.* If a testator gives a legacy to an infant and shows in his will an intention to provide for the infant's maintenance,[10] the legacy carries interest from the date of the testator's death,[11] unless the testator has by his will made some other provision for the infant's maintenance.[12] Under this rule the legatee need not be the child or quasi-child of the testator, but the legatee must be an infant.[13]

This rule, unlike the previous one, applies to a legacy which is contingent upon an event having no reference to the legatee's infancy. Thus in *Re Jones*[14] legacies by T to each of his infant daughters, contingent upon attaining the age of 25 years, were held to carry interest from the date of T's death until each daughter attained that age, because T showed in his will his intention to provide for their maintenance and made no other provision for this.

To sum up the effect of these technical rules in the case of a contingent legacy given by T to an infant who is not T's child—*e.g.* given by T "to my nephew James if he attains the age of 18 years." Such a legacy carries interest from the time at which the contingency is satisfied so that the legacy is payable,[15] except in the following cases:

(i) it carries interest from the end of the executor's year if T by his will directs the legacy to be severed from his general estate for some purpose connected with the legacy; and

(ii) it carries interest from the date of T's death, unless T by his will makes some other provision for the legatee's maintenance, if T stands *in loco parentis* to the legatee (and the other requirements of exception (3) are satisfied) or if T shows in his will his intention to provide for the infant's maintenance (so that exception (4) applies).

It may well be preferable for the draftsman of a will to insert an express direction as to the date from which a general legacy to an infant is to carry interest, rather than leave these technical rules applicable.

---

[8] Trustee Act 1925, ss.31 and 68(1)(17), as amended by Family Law Reform Act 1969, s.1(3) and (4), Sched. 1, Pt. I and Sched. 3, para. 5(1).

[9] *Ibid.*: see *Re Bowlby, supra.*

[10] Or education, *Re Selby-Walker* [1949] 2 All E.R. 178.

[11] *Re Churchill* [1909] 2 Ch. 431 (legacy by T to infant grand-nephew, to vest at 21; power for trustees to apply legacy for his benefit whilst under 21: held legacy carried interest from T's death as T intended to provide for maintenance): see also *Re Stokes* [1928] Ch. 716 (statutory power to maintain applicable and treated as showing intention to provide for infant's maintenance).

[12] *Re West* [1913] 2 Ch. 345.

[13] *Raven v. Waite* (1818) 1 Sw. 553.

[14] [1932] 1 Ch. 642 (the headnote is wrong).

[15] *Re Raine* [1929] 1 Ch. 716 (legacy to godchild S if he should attain 21; held legacy carried interest only from date S attained 21).

C. RESIDUARY GIFTS

1. Immediate residuary gifts. A residuary bequest of personalty or a residuary devise of realty[16] which takes effect immediately carries with it all the income or profits accruing from its subject matter after the testator's death.

In examining the effects of contingent or deferred residuary gifts, it is necessary to consider residuary bequests and residuary devises separately because section 175 of the Law of Property Act 1925 does not apply to residuary bequests.

2. Contingent or deferred residuary bequests. (1) *Contingent residuary bequests.* A residuary bequest of personalty which is contingent (but not otherwise deferred) carries with it the intermediate income of residuary personalty, so far as the income is not otherwise disposed of by the will.[17] Thus, whilst the contingent event on which vesting depends remains undecided, any intermediate income not otherwise disposed of is *either* (i) to be dealt with in accordance with section 31 of the Trustee Act 1925 if there is a beneficiary living who is contingently entitled,[18] *or* (ii) to be accumulated and added to the capital for as long as the statutory rule against accumulations permits, but at the end of the permitted accumulation period any income subsequently accruing whilst the event remains undecided goes as on the testator's intestacy.[19] This old rule that a contingent residuary bequest carries intermediate income has been justified by Cross J. in *Re Geering*[20] as follows:

> "The reason behind the rule . . . is that the testator has made, as it were, an immediate appropriation of the property in question for the benefit of the person, born or unborn, to whom he gives it contingently, and that it is in accordance with his probable intention that the income which accrues before the contingency happens or becomes impossible should be accumulated so far as the law allows to abide the event if the testator has not directed it to be applied in some other way."

(2) *Deferred residuary bequests.* On the other hand, a residuary bequest of personalty which is deferred to a future date which must come sooner or later does not carry with it intermediate income arising between the testator's death and that date: if this intermediate income is not disposed of by the will, it goes as on the testator's intestacy. The rule applies to any deferred residuary bequest, whether it is vested[21]

---

[16] Rents accruing before death form part of the testator's personal estate, *Constable* v. *Constable* (1879) 11 Ch.D. 681 (rent apportioned to period prior to death under Apportionment Act 1870 passed as personalty, not realty).

[17] *Green* v. *Ekins* (1742) 2 Atk. 473; *Trevanion* v. *Vivian* (1752) 2 Ves.Sen. 430 (gift of residuary personalty to A if he attains 21: held gift carried intermediate income which must be accumulated); *Bective* v. *Hodgson* (1864) 10 H.L.C. 656.

[18] *Ante*, p. 322.

[19] *Re Taylor* [1901] 2 Ch. 134. For the statutory rule against accumulations see Law of Property Act 1925, ss.164–166, as amended by Perpetuities and Accumulations Act 1964, s.13.

[20] [1964] Ch. 136, 144.

[21] *Berry* v. *Geen* [1938] A.C. 575; *Re Oliver* [1947] 2 All E.R. 162, 166.

(*e.g.* a gift "to X after the death of A"), vested subject to being divested[22] (*e.g.* a gift "to X after the death of A, but if X dies before A to X's children equally"), or contingent[23] (*e.g.* "to X after the death of A if X attains 30 years of age"). As Cross J. put it in *Re Geering*,[24] "The very fact that a testator defers a gift of residue to a future date is itself prima facie an indication that he does not intend the legatee to have the income of residue accruing before that date."

3. Contingent or deferred residuary devises. Section 175 of the Law of Property Act 1925 (which applies to wills coming into operation after 1925[25]) provides that "a contingent residuary devise of freehold land, and a . . . residuary devise of freehold land to trustees upon trust for persons whose interests are contingent or executory shall, subject to the statutory provisions relating to accumulations, carry the intermediate income of that property from the death of the testator, except so far as such income, or any part thereof, may be otherwise expressly disposed of."

(1) *Contingent residuary devises.* A residuary devise of realty which is contingent (but not otherwise deferred) falls within section 175, whether made directly to the devisee or to trustees upon trust for a beneficiary whose interest is contingent. Thus a contingent residuary devise, like a contingent residuary bequest, carries intermediate income unless the income is otherwise expressly disposed of by the will. This intermediate income is *either* (i) to be dealt with in accordance with section 31 of the Trustee Act 1925 if there is a beneficiary living who is contingently entitled,[26] *or* (ii) to be accumulated and added to the capital for as long as the statutory rule against accumulations permits.[27]

(2) *Deferred residuary devises.* Section 175 does not mention a deferred residuary devise but it does apply to a residuary devise to trustees upon trust for persons whose interests are "executory," and "executory" appears to mean deferred.[28] The omission of a deferred residuary devise from section 175 is hard to explain[29] but it may be of little practical significance since a deferred gift of realty now inevitably takes effect through the medium of a trust.[30] Where it applies, section 175 makes a deferred residuary devise carry intermediate income for as long as the

---

[22] *Re Gillett's W.T.* [1950] Ch. 102: *cf. Re Nash's W.T.* [1965] 1 W.L.R. 221.

[23] *Re Geering* [1964] Ch. 136, not following *Re Drakeley's Estate* (1854) 19 Beav. 395 and *Re Lindo* (1888) 59 L.T. 462.

[24] *Ibid.* at p. 145.

[25] For the rules applicable to wills coming into operation before 1926 see Hawkins and Ryder on the *Construction of Wills* (1965), p. 78.

[26] *Ante*, p. 322.

[27] See *ante* n. 19.

[28] *Re McGeorge* [1963] Ch. 544, 550–552.

[29] Hawkins and Ryder, *op. cit.* p. 79, relying on the reference in s.175 to a contingent residuary devise, suggests that a deferred contingent residuary devise may be, but that a deferred vested residuary devise is not, within s.175. See also Cross J. in *Re McGeorge, supra*, at p. 552.

[30] P. V. Baker (1963) 79 L.Q.R. 184, 186.

statutory rule against accumulations permits, unless the income is otherwise expressly disposed of by the will.[31]

To sum up, section 175 of the Law of Property Act 1925 has produced some useful, and some most unfortunate, effects:

(i) A residuary bequest which is contingent (but not otherwise deferred) has always carried intermediate income. Section 175 makes a specific legacy, a specific devise, and a residuary devise if each is contingent (but not otherwise deferred) carry intermediate income if the will came into operation after 1925. This reform probably accords with the likely intentions of a testator, and moreover each type of contingent gift now has the same effect.

(ii) A residuary bequest which is deferred does not carry intermediate income. Unfortunately section 175 makes a specific legacy, a specific devise, and some (if not all) types of residuary devise carry intermediate income though they are deferred. This reform frustrates the likely intentions of a testator, and moreover the different types of deferred gift do not all have the same effect.

There is a strong case for amending section 175 to make it accord with the likely intentions of a testator. It would also be helpful if the section codified the rules, stating in clear language which types of gift do, and which do not, carry intermediate income.[32]

D. The Rule in Allhusen v. Whittell

The object of the rule. If by his will T settles his residuary estate for persons in succession—*e.g.* upon trust for A for life and subject thereto for B absolutely—it is presumed that T intends each of these persons successively to enjoy the same property, *i.e.* his net residuary estate after payment of his funeral and testamentary expenses, debts and liabilities, and legacies. It follows that A is not entitled to receive the income accruing from the portion of T's estate needed for the payment of these outgoings. Under the rule in *Allhusen* v. *Whittell* [33] these outgoings are treated as having been paid partly out of capital and partly out of the income accruing from that portion of the capital during the period between T's death and the payment of these outgoings by the personal representatives. To consider an example, T has given general legacies amounting to £11,000 and T's personal representatives pay these legacies one year after T's death. If T's estate has yielded income during that year at the rate of 10 per cent. after deduction of income tax, these legacies are treated as having been paid out of £10,000 capital and £1,000 income. The tenant for life A is not entitled to the £1,000 income accruing from the £10,000 capital needed for the payment of these lega-

---

[31] s.31 of the Trustee Act 1925 does not apply to a deferred residuary devise, *Re McGeorge, supra,* (a decision on a deferred specific devise).

[32] P. V. Baker, *loc. cit.* pp. 186–187.

[33] (1867) L.R. 4 Eq. 295: the rule applies to residuary realty. *Marshall* v. *Crowther* (1874) 2 Ch.D. 199. The rule has been held not to apply to an absolute gift to A which is liable to be divested by a gift over to B on a certain event, *Re Hanbury* (1909) 101 L.T. 32.

cies, and T's net residuary estate is ascertained by deducting £10,000 (not £11,000) from the capital of T's gross residuary estate.

The rule in *Allhusen* v. *Whittell* "was founded on the broad equitable principle that where residue was limited to persons in succession, their successive enjoyment should be an enjoyment of the same fund."[34] The rule is to be applied in a common-sense manner so as to give effect to this equitable principle. "The actual accountancy will not be difficult so long as the true object is borne in mind."[35]

Outgoings within the rule. If a debt or liability itself carries interest (as does unpaid inheritance tax), the outgoing consists of the total amount paid by the personal representatives, whether in respect of the debt or liability or the interest carried by it. This total amount ought to be paid partly out of capital and partly out of the income accruing from that portion of the capital in accordance with the rule.[36]

A contingent debt or liability of T falls within the rule—such as an annuity for life payable by T under a covenant made by T during his lifetime. Accordingly, when T's personal representatives pay such an annuity, each instalment is to be paid partly out of capital and partly out of the income accruing from that portion of the capital during the period between T's death and the payment of that instalment.[37] Each successive instalment therefore includes more accruing income and less capital than the previous instalment. A payment made by the personal representatives to X in consideration of X accepting an assignment of T's onerous leaseholds also falls within the rule.[38] On the other hand (and rather illogically), a contingent legacy given by T in his will has been held to fall outside the rule, on the ground that the fund to pay the legacy remains part of residue yielding income for the tenant for life until the contingency occurs, and if a contingent legacy fell within the rule the destination of the income accruing from the fund might remain uncertain for a long period whilst the contingent event remained undecided.[39]

Period for calculation of income. If the outgoings are paid at about the end of the executor's year, the outgoings are treated as having been paid partly out of capital and partly out of the income accruing from that portion of the capital during the executor's year. But if any substantial

---

[34] *Per* Sargant J. in *Re McEuen* [1913] 2 Ch. 704, 713.

[35] *Ibid.* at p. 717. *Cf.* Law Reform Committee, 23rd Report, *The powers and duties of trustees,* Cmnd. 8733 (1982), p. 22 (witnesses described the rule "as complex, fiddlesome and resulting in a disproportionate amount of work and expense"); for possible reform see *ibid.,* pp. 24–25 and 64.

[36] *Re Wills* [1915] 1 Ch. 769, 779 (but "in the case of small estates or estates of moderate size it might very often be a good rough and ready rule to allow the interest on the estate duty to be paid out of income, and the capital to be paid out of capital"); *Re McEuen* [1913] 2 Ch. 704, 717.

[37] *Re Perkins* [1907] 2 Ch. 596; *Re Poyser* [1910] 2 Ch. 444; *Re Berkeley* [1968] Ch. 744; *cf. Re Darby* [1939] Ch. 905 (rule not applicable if T took property on which annuity charged, but T not under any personal liability to pay annuity).

[38] *Re Shee* [1934] Ch. 345.

[39] *Allhusen* v. *Whittell* (1867) L.R. 4 Eq. 295, 303–304; *Re Fenwick's W.T.* [1936] Ch. 720.

outgoing is paid some time before,[40] or some time after,[41] the end of the executor's year, the period for calculation of the accruing income is the period from T's death until such outgoing is paid or satisfied. Income is calculated at the average rate of interest yielded by the residuary estate as a whole after deduction of income tax.[42]

The rule does not require "extremely elaborate and minute calculations" to be made in every case[43]—for instance, if a number of small outgoings are paid on different days over a period, the personal representatives are not required to calculate the accruing income separately in respect of each outgoing. Again "if, for instance, a particular asset of a testator, such as . . . an amount on deposit with a bank, were applied with the intermediate interest on it in the discharge of the whole or the bulk or some one large item of the liabilities of the estate at any time at . . . say, three months or six months after the death, the executors might well . . . leave the matter there,"[44] without making any other adjustment by reference to the exact rate of interest yielded by the residuary estate as a whole.

Excluded by contrary intent in the will. The rule in *Allhusen* v. *Whittell* may be, and often is, excluded by the testator showing a contrary intent in his will[45]—*e.g.* "I direct that the rule known as the rule in *Allhusen* v. *Whittell* shall not apply in the administration of my estate and the execution of the trusts of this Will and any codicil hereto."[46]

---

[40] *Re McEuen* [1913] 2 Ch. 704.
[41] *Re Wills* [1915] 1 Ch. 769.
[42] *Re Wills, supra,* (average rate of interest in each year of the calculation); *Re Oldham* [1927] W.N. 113 (deduction of income tax).
[43] *Re McEuen* [1913] 2 Ch. 704, 716.
[44] *Ibid.* at p. 717.
[45] See the Statutory Will Forms 1925, Form 8(7)(c) (which authorises trustees to adjust as they think fit the incidence, as between capital and income, of payments made in due course of administration).
[46] The common form clause excluding apportionment of income under the rule in *Howe* v. *Earl of Dartmouth* (1802) 7 Ves. 137 does not exclude the rule in *Allhusen* v. *Whittell, Re Ullswater* [1952] Ch. 105.

CHAPTER 12

FAILURE OF GIFT BY WILL OR
INTEREST ON INTESTACY

A gift by will may fail for any one or more of the following reasons, which are considered in turn in this chapter:

A. The beneficiary or his spouse is an attesting witness.
B. The beneficiary predeceases the testator, causing the gift to lapse.
C. The dissolution or annulment of the deceased's marriage to the beneficiary causes the gift to fail.
D. The gift fails by ademption.
E. The gift fails for uncertainty.
F. The beneficiary is guilty of the murder or manslaughter of the deceased.
G. The beneficiary disclaims.

This list is not exhaustive. Abatement has already been considered in Chapter 11. A gift by will may also fail because it infringes some rule of law, such as the rule against inalienability,[1] or is made for a purpose contrary to public policy.[2] Again, a contingent gift by will may fail because the contingency is never satisfied.[3]

As will be explained, heads F and G are also applicable to a beneficiary on an intestacy. Head B is not applicable on an intestacy but, of course, a person who predeceases an intestate cannot take on intestacy because the intestacy rules require the intestate's spouse or next-of-kin to survive the intestate in order to be eligible to take.[4] Similarly, head C is not applicable on an intestacy but a former spouse, whose marriage to the intestate has been dissolved or annulled, cannot take on intestacy. Again, a contingent interest under the statutory trusts applicable on intestacy may fail because the contingency of attaining the age of 18 years or marrying is not satisfied.

The effect of the failure of a particular gift is considered at the end of this chapter. So, too, is the effect on an intestacy of failure under heads F and G.

---

[1] Sometimes called the rule against perpetual trusts: for this rule, see Megarry and Wade, *The Law of Real Property* (5th ed., 1984), pp. 296 *et. seq.*

[2] See, *e.g. Re Caborne* [1943] Ch. 224 (provision void as tended to encourage break-up of existing marriage); *Re Johnson's W.T.* [1967] Ch. 387.

[3] Sometimes this is referred to as failure by lapse; see, *e.g. Re Parker* [1913] 1 Ch. 162 and *Re Fox's Estate* [1937] 4 All E.R. 664.

[4] See Chap. 4: a child *en ventre sa mère* at the intestate's death is treated as then living, *ante*, p. 90, n. 61.

A. ATTESTING WITNESS AND HIS OR HER SPOUSE

Section 15 of the Wills Act 1837 deprives an attesting witness[5] and his or her spouse of any benefit under the will which the witness attests: the attestation is valid but any beneficial gift in the will to the witness or his or her spouse is "utterly null and void." "Every time . . . that a beneficiary [or the spouse of a beneficiary] is an attesting witness, section 15 of the Wills Act 1837, deprives him of his benefit and defeats the testator's intention. This is considered necessary to ensure reliable, unbiased, witness of due execution."[6] Not surprisingly, critics have questioned whether this drastic rule is really justified.[7]

There are, however, several limits to the operation of this general rule:

1. Privileged will. The rule does not apply to a will intended to be an informal will and made by a privileged testator, because such a will does not require any attesting witnesses. Thus if a soldier, whilst in actual military service, makes a will intended by him to be an informal will, a gift in it to one of the attesting witnesses is valid.[8]

2. Superfluous attesting witness to formal will. If the testator dies after May 29, 1968, the Wills Act 1968 provides that the attestation of his will by any beneficiaries (or their spouses) is to be disregarded if without them the will is duly executed.[9] It follows that if a will is attested by three witnesses, only one of whom is a beneficiary (or the spouse of a beneficiary), the general rule is excluded and the beneficiary may take his benefit under the will. On the other hand, if more than one of three witnesses is a beneficiary (or the spouse of a beneficiary), the general rule is applicable and none of the witnesses (or their spouses) may take any benefit under the will.

3. Beneficiary signed but not as a witness. The general rule does not apply if the beneficiary (or his or her spouse) signed the will otherwise than as an attesting witness—for example, with the intention of recording his agreement with the gifts made by the testator in the will.[10] However, there is a rebuttable presumption that any person (except the

---

[5] Presumably s.15 applies to a witness who acknowledges his signature under the amended s.9 of the Wills Act 1837, though such a witness is not required to attest: see *ante*, p. 36.

[6] *Per* Russell L.J. in *In the Estate of Bravda* [1968] 1 W.L.R. 479, 492.

[7] See Law Reform Committee, 22nd Report (*The Making and Revocation of Wills*), (1980) Cmnd. 7902, pp. 6–7 (recommending no change); (1981) 125 S.J. 283; Davey [1980] Conv. 64, 75; Yale (1984) 100 L.Q.R. 453.

[8] *Re Limond* [1915] 2 Ch. 240.

[9] s.1. For the formalities required for due execution, see Chap. 2. If the testator died before May 30, 1968, the general rule applies even though there were two other attesting witnesses, so that the beneficiary's attestation was superfluous: *In the Estate of Bravda*, *supra*.

[10] *In the Goods of Sharman* (1869) L.R. 1 P. & D. 661 (beneficiary's signature omitted from grant as she did not intend to attest testator's signature); *In the Goods of Smith* (1889) 15 P.D. 2 (wife, a beneficiary, signed will to verify its contents: her signature omitted from probate); *Kitcat* v. *King* [1930] P. 266: but see *In the Estate of Bravda*, *supra*, at pp. 488, 491 and 493.

testator) whose signature appears at the end of a will signed as an attesting witness. Accordingly, the general rule applies unless this presumption is rebutted.[11]

4. Beneficiary not spouse of witness when will executed. A beneficiary who marries an attesting witness after the execution of the will may take a benefit under the will: section 15 only disqualifies a beneficiary who is the spouse of an attesting witness when the will is executed.[12]

5. Gifts on trust. The general rule only applies to beneficial gifts and not to gifts to an attesting witness (or his or her spouse) as trustee. If T by her will gives £200 to X and "£200 to Brompton Church, to be disposed of as [X] wishes," and X's wife is one of the two attesting witnesses, the first gift is void but the second gift is valid because X is a trustee for the purpose of directing the disposition of the legacy.[13]

6. Gift made or confirmed by another will or codicil. The general rule does not apply:

(i) if the gift to the beneficiary B is contained in a will or a codicil which was not attested by B or B's spouse, even though some other document was so attested[14]; *or*

(ii) if the gift to B is contained in a document which was attested by B or B's spouse, but this document was confirmed by a will or codicil not so attested.[15]

To consider situation (i) again. B is the residuary beneficiary under T's will, which was not attested by B or B's spouse. By a codicil T revokes certain legacies given by his will, thereby swelling his residuary estate. It is immaterial that B or B's spouse attested this codicil—the general rule is not applicable because B takes the swollen residuary estate under T's will and not under the codicil.[16]

But the general rule is applicable if the will or codicil which contains the gift to B, and each document which confirmed this will or codicil, was attested by B or B's spouse. In that case B cannot take because he cannot point to a document under which he claims which neither B nor B's spouse attested.[17]

---

[11] *In the Estate of Bravda, supra.*

[12] *Thorpe* v. *Bestwick* (1881) 6 Q.B.D. 311: see *Re Royce's W.T.* [1959] Ch. 626.

[13] *Cresswell* v. *Cresswell* (1868) L.R. 6 Eq. 69: see also *Re Ray's W.T.* [1936] Ch. 520 (gift by T's will to the person who should be Abbess at T's death; an attesting witness later became Abbess: held gift was valid as she took in trust for the purposes of the convent—it was immaterial that she might, as a member of the convent, get some benefit in some shape or form out of the administration of the fund).

[14] *Re Marcus* (1887) 57 L.T. 399 (gifts to B and C by T's will; B attested codicils but not the will and C attested both the will and the codicils: held B could take but C could not); *Gurney* v. *Gurney* (1855) 3 Drew. 208.

[15] *Anderson* v. *Anderson* (1872) L.R. 13 Eq. 381; *Re Trotter* [1899] 1 Ch. 764 (B, a solicitor, attested will and second codicil: held B could take benefit of a charging clause in will under first codicil which confirmed will): cf. *Burton* v. *Newbery* (1875) 1 Ch.D. 234 (republication of will by second codicil does not validate gift to attesting witness in first codicil not republished). For confirmation (or republication), see *ante*, pp. 80 *et seq.*

[16] *Gurney* v. *Gurney, supra.*

[17] *Re Marcus, supra,* at p. 400.

7. Witness or spouse takes under secret trust. If T by his will gives property to X, and X takes this property upon a secret trust for Y, the general rule is not applicable though Y or Y's spouse attested T's will.[18] The reason is that Y does not take his beneficial interest under T's will, but by virtue of the secret trust imposed upon X who takes under the will.[19]

B. LAPSE

Doctrine of lapse.[20] Under this doctrine a gift by will lapses and fails if the beneficiary dies before the testator.[21] Similarly a gift by will to a corporate body lapses if it is dissolved before the death of the testator.[22] The doctrine of lapse is said to be a consequence of the ambulatory character of a will, which has no effect until the death of the testator and therefore confers no benefit on persons who previously die.[23]

(1) *Declaration against lapse ineffective but substitutional gift effective.* A testator cannot exclude the doctrine of lapse by declaring in his will that it is not to apply to his will.[24] On the other hand, a testator may give the subject matter of a gift to some other beneficiary in the event of the original beneficiary predeceasing the testator.[25] The testator may give it to the personal representatives of the original beneficiary to be held as part of his estate[26]—for instance, by a gift to A "but if he shall die in my lifetime to his legal personal representatives," or with a direction that if A dies in the testator's lifetime, the gift shall operate as if A had survived the testator and had taken the gift but had died immediately afterwards (which of course achieves the same result).[27] Again (and this is much more common), the testator may make a gift to A, but if he shall die in the testator's lifetime to such of A's children living at the

---

[18] *Re Young* [1951] Ch. 344; *O'Brien* v. *Condon* [1905] 1 I.R. 51. For secret trusts see Snell's *Principles of Equity* (28th ed., 1982), pp. 109 *et seq.*
[19] *Ibid.* at p. 350.
[20] See generally H. A. J. Ford (1962) 78 L.Q.R. 88.
[21] *Elliott* v. *Davenport* (1705) 1 P.Wms. 83; *Maybank* v. *Brooks* (1780) 1 Bro.C.C. 84 (legacy given to M, his executors, administrators, or assigns; M predeceased testator: held legacy lapsed).
[22] *Re Servers of the Blind League* [1960] 1 W.L.R. 564; *Re Stemson's W.T.* [1970] Ch. 16; *Re Finger's W.T.* [1972] 1 Ch. 286. A gift by T's will to a corporation with charitable objects does not fail by lapse owing to its dissolution in T's lifetime if (i) it is really a gift for charitable purposes (unless the gift shows the corporation's continued existence is essential), or (ii) T shows a general charitable intention; see generally Snell's *Principles of Equity* (28th ed., 1982), pp. 166 *et seq.*
[23] *Jarman on Wills* (8th ed., 1951), p. 438.
[24] *Re Ladd* [1932] 2 Ch. 219 (T had a general testamentary power of appointment and by her will appointed to her husband "to the intent that this my will shall take effect whether I survive or predecease my husband"; the husband predeceased T: held the appointment to him failed by lapse and his executors did not take); *Browne* v. *Hope* (1872) L.R. 14 Eq. 343 (declaration that gift to vest on execution of will does not prevent lapse).
[25] *Sibley* v. *Cook* (1747) 3 Atk. 572; *Re Greenwood* [1912] 1 Ch. 393, 396.
[26] For the consequences see *Re Cousen's W.T.* [1937] Ch. 381: see also (1962) 78 L.Q.R. 88, 90 *et seq.*
[27] *Re Greenwood, supra.*

testator's death as attain the age of (say) 21 years or marry in equal shares.[28]

(2) *Gift to joint tenants.* The nature of the gift made by the testator may exclude the doctrine of lapse. Thus if T by his will makes a gift to two or more persons as *joint tenants* (*e.g.* to A, B and C jointly), no lapse can occur unless all the beneficiaries die before the testator. If A and B both die before T, C takes the whole gift if he survives T,[29] but if C also dies before T the gift lapses. However, the doctrine of lapse is fully applicable if there are words of severance in T's will, so that the beneficiaries take as *tenants in common* (*e.g.* to X, Y and Z *equally*): in that case if X dies before T, the gift of a third share to X lapses.[30]

(3) *Class gift.* The doctrine of lapse does not apply to a class gift to persons who are to be ascertained from some general description either at the testator's death or subsequently, whether they take as joint tenants or tenants in common. An instance is a gift by T's will "to all my children as tenants in common in equal shares": all the persons coming within this description at the testator's death take the subject matter of the gift equally. It follows that if one of T's children predeceases T, there is no lapse because that child never becomes a member of the class as he is not living at T's death.[31] A gift may be to a class, though some individual members of the class are named: thus a gift "to my children including [or excluding] X" is a class gift.[32] But a gift "to Y and the children of Z" is prima facie not a class gift because Y falls outside the general description[33]: however, T's will may, on its proper construction, show that T intended this gift to take effect as a class gift, so that if Y predeceases T there is no lapse.[34]

On the other hand, if T by his will makes a gift "to my three brothers as tenants in common in equal shares," this is a gift to individuals and not a class gift: each brother takes a distinct third share which is quantified from the beginning and which does not vary in size according to the number of the recipients. If one of the three brothers predeceases T, the gift to him of a third share lapses.[35] But if the gift is "to such of my three brothers as shall be living at my death as tenants in common in equal shares," there is no lapse if one of them predeceases T, because T

[28] Alternatively the substitutional gift may be in favour of A's children and remoter issue *per stirpes* in equal shares, so as to include descendants of a deceased child of A.
[29] *Morley* v. *Bird* (1798) 3 Ves. 629.
[30] *Page* v. *Page* (1728) 2 P.Wms. 489; *Peat* v. *Chapman* (1750) 1 Ves.Sen. 542; *Re Wood's Will* (1861) 29 Beav. 236. Of course T by his will may make a substitutional gift of X's share to Y and Z.
[31] *Doe d. Stewart* v. *Sheffield* (1811) 13 East. 526; *Shuttleworth* v. *Greaves* (1838) 4 M. & Cr. 35. For the effect of the original, and the amended, s.33 of the Wills Act 1837 see *post,* p. 343.
[32] *Shaw* v. *M'Mahon* (1843) 4 D. & War. 431: see *Re Jackson* (1883) 25 Ch.D. 162. There may be a *composite* class gift—"to the children of A and the children of B."
[33] *Re Chaplin's Trusts* (1863) 33 L.J. Ch. 183; *Re Allen* (1881) 44 L.T. 240.
[34] *Kingsbury* v. *Walter* [1901] A.C. 187 (a "special" class gift).
[35] *Re Smith's Trusts* (1878) 9 Ch.D. 117.

has made provision for this event: the other two brothers living at T's death take the subject matter of the gift equally.[36]

(4) *Effect of republication of will.* If T makes his will containing a gift to X, and after X's death T makes a codicil which republishes his will, this does not prevent the gift to X from lapsing or make it take effect as a gift to X's personal representatives.[37] The will is read as if it had been executed at the time of its republication[38] but this makes no difference—there is still a gift to X which fails by lapse.

Occasionally republication may alter the construction of a will as to the identity of the beneficiary and thereby save a gift which otherwise would have lapsed. In *Re Hardyman*[39] the testatrix by her will gave a legacy "in trust for my cousin his children and his wife." This referred to the cousin's wife living at the date of the will. This wife died and the testatrix, knowing of her death, made a codicil which referred to and thereby republished her will. After the death of the testatrix the cousin married again. Romer J. held that, as a result of its republication, the will referred to any lady whom the cousin might marry and not to the dead first wife. As a result of its republication the will, said Romer J., "is a will which the testatrix tells me expressed her wishes as they were at the date of the codicil."[40] The cousin's second wife was therefore entitled to an interest in the legacy. If the will had not been republished the will would have been construed as referring to the first wife and any gift to her would have failed by lapse. Of course, if the will had referred to the first wife by her name "Betty," republication would not have altered the construction of the will as to the identity of the beneficiary, and any gift to the first wife would have failed by lapse.

Presumption where uncertainty as to which survived. Owing to the doctrine of lapse, the order of deaths of T, a testator, and B, a beneficiary under T's will, is crucial. If B survived T for however short a time, B may take under T's will. But if B predeceased T, the doctrine of lapse applies and B cannot take under T's will unless one of the exceptions to the doctrine of lapse (which have still to be considered) is applicable. The order of deaths may also be crucial (i) on an intestacy, (ii) on the death of joint tenants, in order to ascertain which of them benefits by the right of survivorship, and (iii) under the terms of a gift in a will—for instance, a gift by T "to X if my wife shall die in my lifetime," and T and his wife are both swept off a ship by the same wave and never seen again.[41]

Before 1926 there was no legal presumption as to the order of deaths if the evidence left this uncertain. If any person sought to establish a claim which depended upon B having survived T, the onus of proof lay on the claimant to establish that fact by affirmative evidence: if he did not do

---

[36] See *Re Woods* [1931] 2 Ch. 138; *Re Peacock* [1957] Ch. 310 (a gift to a group, having for purposes of lapse the characteristics of a class gift).
[37] *Hutcheson* v. *Hammond* (1790) 3 Bro.C.C. 127; *Re Wood's Will* (1861) 29 Beav. 236.
[38] See *ante,* p. 80.
[39] [1925] Ch. 287.
[40] *Ibid.* at p. 293.
[41] *Underwood* v. *Wing* (1855) 4 De G.M. & G. 633; *Wing* v. *Angrave* (1860) 8 H.L.C. 183: see also *Re Rowland* [1963] Ch. 1.

so, his claim failed.[42] Thus if a husband and wife perished in a ship-wreck and the evidence left it uncertain which of them survived the other, a claim by the personal representatives of either of them to bene-fit under the will or intestacy of the other necessarily failed.[43]

(1) *Death presumed in order of seniority.* Section 184 of the Law of Prop-erty Act 1925 now raises a presumption as to the order of deaths by pro-viding as follows:

"In all cases where, after the commencement of this Act, two or more persons have died in circumstances rendering it uncertain which of them survived the other or others, such deaths shall (subject to any order of the court), for all purposes affecting the title to property, be presumed to have occurred in order of seniority, and accordingly the younger shall be deemed to have survived the elder."

Accordingly where section 184 applies there is a statutory presumption that the parties died in order of seniority, the elder first and the younger last. The words in brackets, "(subject to any order of the court)," are probably meaningless in this context.[44] Certainly these words do not give the court any discretion to disregard the statutory presumption on the ground that it would be unfair or unjust to act upon it.[45]

(2) *Uncertainty as to which survived.* Section 184 applies where it is uncertain which of them survived the other, whether the deaths occurred in a common disaster (the case of *commorientes*, such as a bomb explosion[46] or the sinking of a ship[47]), or whether the deaths occurred separately (the husband's ship may disappear at sea on an unknown date and the wife may die at home after the ship has sailed[48]). In *Hickman* v. *Peacey*[49] five persons were killed in the same house by the explosion of a German bomb dropped during an air raid in 1940; two of them had made wills in favour of some of the others. The House of Lords (by a majority) held that section 184 was applicable in all cases where it could not be proved that one person had in fact survived the other, and it was immaterial whether the deaths appeared to be simul-taneous or consecutive. As Lord Macmillan put it,[50]

"Can you say for certain which of these two dead persons died first?

[42] *Underwood* v. *Wing, supra; Wing* v. *Angrave, supra; Re Phené's Trusts* (1870) 5 Ch.App. 139 ("the true proposition is, that those who found a right upon a person having survived a particular period must establish that fact affirmatively by evidence").
[43] *Underwood* v. *Wing, supra; Wing* v. *Angrave, supra.*
[44] *Per* Lord Simonds in *Hickman* v. *Peacey* [1945] A.C. 304, 346–347, "I have tried in vain to give any reasonable meaning and effect" to the words. For other explanations see *Re Lindop* [1942] Ch. 377, 382 (words make it clear presumption is rebuttable by evidence); *Re Grosvenor* [1944] Ch. 138, 143 and see 148–149 (words may refer to subsequent orders of the court in the event of fresh evidence becoming available); *Hickman* v. *Peacey, supra* at p. 316 (words provide for case where insufficient evidence as to respective ages of deceased persons).
[45] *Re Lindop, supra.*
[46] *Hickman* v. *Peacey* [1945] A.C. 304 (bomb in German air raid). See also *Re Bate* (1947) 116 L.J.R. 1409 (gas poisoning from gas oven in kitchen).
[47] *Re Rowland* [1963] Ch. 1.
[48] *Hickman* v. *Peacey, supra,* at pp. 314–315.
[49] *Supra.*
[50] *Ibid.* at pp. 323–324.

If you cannot say for certain, then you must presume the older to have died first. It is immaterial that the reason for your inability to say for certain which died first is either because you think they both died simultaneously or because you think they died consecutively but you do not know in what sequence."

(3) *Exclusion of the statutory presumption.* By way of exception the statutory presumption does not apply as between spouses if the older spouse dies intestate. Thus if an intestate and his or her younger spouse die in circumstances rendering it uncertain which of them survived the other, the statutory presumption that the younger survived the older does not apply on intestacy and instead the younger spouse is presumed not to have survived the older intestate.[51] Again, the statutory presumption is not applicable for the purposes of inheritance tax payable on death and instead each of the deceased persons is assumed to have died at the same instant.[52] If T and his only child B are both killed in the same road accident in circumstances rendering it uncertain which of them survived the other, under the statutory presumption B (as the younger) is presumed to have survived T and may therefore take T's estate under T's will or intestacy, but nevertheless inheritance tax on T's estate is only payable in respect of T's death and not again in respect of B's death.[53]

Where it is applicable, the statutory presumption has the merit of providing a definite (albeit arbitrary) solution if the order of deaths is uncertain but there is sufficient evidence as to the respective ages of the deceased persons. However, this solution may sometimes defeat the wishes which a testator would have expressed if he had put his mind to the problem. For instance, if T by his will gives his entire estate to his spouse W (who is younger than T), and T and W die in circumstances rendering it uncertain which of them survived the other, under the statutory presumption W is presumed to have survived T and therefore takes T's estate, which then passes to the beneficiaries entitled under W's will[54] or to W's next-of-kin entitled on her intestacy. It may well be a better solution for T to provide by his will that W shall only take if she survives T for (say) a period of one month: such a *commorientes* clause prevents W from taking under the statutory presumption and also guards against the possibility that W may only survive T for a very short time.

Exceptions to the doctrine of lapse. There are three exceptions to the doctrine of lapse, the first two being statutory exceptions under the Wills Act 1837 and the third being based on case law.

[51] Administration of Estates Act 1925, s.46(3) as amended by Intestates' Estates Act 1952, s.1(4): see *ante*, pp. 83–84.
[52] Inheritance Tax Act 1984, s.4(2).
[53] Under Inheritance Tax Act 1984, s.4(1) inheritance tax is charged in respect of B's death on the value of B's estate *immediately before B's death*: at that moment T was still alive and B had not inherited T's estate, s.4(2).
[54] See *Re Rowland* [1963] 1 Ch. 1.

(1) *Entail.* By section 32 of the Wills Act 1837[55] there is no lapse if T by his will gives property to A in tail, and A predeceases T, but A leaves issue living at T's death capable of inheriting under the entail. The exception applies subject to any contrary intention appearing in T's will.

(2) *Gift to the testator's child or remoter descendant.* Section 33(1) of the Wills Act 1837 provides that—

"where—
    (a) a will contains a devise or bequest to a child or remoter descendant of the testator; and
    (b) the intended beneficiary dies before the testator, leaving issue; and
    (c) issue of the intended beneficiary are living at the testator's death,
then, unless a contrary intention appears by the will, the devise or bequest shall take effect as a devise or bequest to the issue living at the testator's death."

This provision which is quoted as amended by section 19 of the Administration of Justice Act 1982, applies if the testator dies after December 31, 1982.[56] Section 33 in its original form applies if the testator dies before January 1, 1983.[57] As will be explained, there are significant differences between the amended, and the original, section 33.

(a) THE REQUIREMENTS OF SECTION 33(1). For the amended section 33(1) to apply, T's will must contain a devise or bequest to B, who is T's child or remoter descendant. The original section 33 also required the devise or bequest to be for an interest not determinable at or before B's death, and therefore did not apply to a gift to B of a life interest, or an interest in joint tenancy,[58] or an interest contingent on B attaining 25 years of age if B died under that age.[59] The amended section 33(1) does not impose this additional requirement. Neither the amended nor the original section applies to an appointment by will under a special power,[60] but each of them applies to an appointment by will under a general power.[61]

Both the amended and the original section require issue of B to be "living" at T's death. For the purposes of the amended section, any issue of B who is conceived before T's death and is born alive after T's

[55] s.32 is applicable to entails of personalty, Law of Property Act 1925, s.130(1).
[56] Administration of Justice Act 1982, ss.73(6) and 76(11).
[57] s.33 in its original form reads, "where any person being a child or other issue of the testator to whom any real or personal estate shall be devised or bequeathed for any estate or interest not determinable at or before the death of such person shall die in the lifetime of the testator leaving issue, and any such issue of such person shall be living at the time of the death of the testator, such devise or bequest shall not lapse, but shall take effect as if the death of such person had happened immediately after the death of the testator, unless a contrary intention shall appear by the will."
[58] *Re Butler* [1918] 1 I.R. 394.
[59] *Re Wolson* [1939] Ch. 780: *cf. Re Wilson* (1920) 89 L.J. Ch. 216.
[60] *Holyland* v. *Lewin* (1883) 26 Ch.D. 266.
[61] *Eccles* v. *Cheyne* (1856) 2 K. & J. 676: see Wills Act 1837, s.27 and *post*, pp. 428 *et seq.*

death is treated as living at T's death.[62] In all probability this was not so under the original section.[63]

Neither the amended nor the original section requires the *same* issue left by B at his death to be living at T's death. Thus the section applies where T by her will gives all her property to her daughter B, who predeceases T leaving an only child C, who also predeceases T after bearing a child D who survives T.[64] Again, the section applies though B is already dead at the date of T's will.[65]

For the purposes of the amended section, the illegitimacy of any person is to be disregarded.[66] This was so under the original section if T died after 1969, whenever he made his will.[67]

(b) THE OPERATION OF SECTION 33(1). If the requirements of the original section 33 were satisfied, then, unless a contrary intention appeared by T's will,[68] T's gift to B did not lapse but took effect as if B had died immediately after T. The gift therefore fell into B's estate and had to be administered by B's personal representatives as an asset of B's estate. If B's estate was insolvent, the original section 33 swelled B's assets and benefited B's creditors.[69] If B's estate was solvent, the subject matter of T's gift passed to those persons beneficially entitled under B's will[70] or intestacy[71] at B's real date of death.[72] Thus, though B's issue living at T's death saved the gift to B from lapse, B's issue only benefited if they were beneficially entitled under B's will or intestacy. Under the original section 33, B's issue living at T's death did not stand in B's shoes and take the gift in place of B—they merely enabled the gift to B to take effect.

The amended section 33(1) operates in a different way. If the requirements of the amended section 33(1) are satisfied, then, unless a contrary intention appears by T's will, the devise or bequest to B takes effect as a devise or bequest to B's issue living at T's death and B's issue take *per*

---

[62] Amended s.33(4)(*a*).

[63] *Elliot* v. *Joicey* [1935] A.C. 209., esp. at pp. 229–233, disapproving *Re Griffiths' Settlement* [1911] 1 Ch. 246.

[64] *In the Goods of Parker* (1860) 1 Sw. & Tr. 523: see *Jarman on Wills* (8th ed., 1951), pp. 463–464.

[65] *Mower* v. *Orr* (1849) 7 Hare 473; *Wisden* v. *Wisden* (1854) 2 Sm. & G. 396.

[66] Amended s.33(4)(*b*).

[67] Family Law Reform Act 1969, s.16(1). Before this Act, s.33 applied if B was legitimated, *Re Brodie* [1967] Ch. 818, and this is still so, Legitimacy Act 1976, ss.1–3 and 5(1) and (3), Sched. I, paras. 1(1) and 2(1): for the status conferred by adoption see Adoption Act 1976, s.39, and *post*, p. 442.

[68] *Re Meredith* [1924] 2 Ch. 552.

[69] *Re Pearson* [1920] 1 Ch. 247 (T by his will made gift to his son B, who predeceased T but left issue living at T's death; B died an undischarged bankrupt: held the gift passed to B's trustee in bankruptcy).

[70] *Johnson* v. *Johnson* (1843) 3 Hare 157; *Re Hayter* [1937] 2 All E.R. 110 (B by his will gave "everything I die possessed of" to X: held a general residuary gift which included property which passed to B under s.33 on the later death of T).

[71] *Eager* v. *Furnivall* (1881) 17 Ch.D. 115: see Ryder (1971) 24 C.L.P. 157, 174–177.

[72] *Re Basioli* [1953] Ch. 367 (reviewing the cases); *Re Hurd* [1941] Ch. 196: see *Re Hone's Trusts* (1883) 22 Ch.D. 663. If T was the person beneficially entitled under B's will (or intestacy), this produced a "circle" which had to be broken at some point: see *Re Hensler* (1881) 19 Ch.D. 612 (T devised Blackacre to son B, who predeceased T but left issue living at T's death; B's will gave his estate to T: held Blackacre did not pass back to T under B's will); *Re Basioli, ibid.* at p. 376; Ryder, *loc. cit.* pp. 175–176.

stirpes, if more than one in equal shares.[73] In short, under the amended section 33(1) B's issue stand in B's shoes and take the gift in place of B. To consider an example, T's will contains a gift to his child B, who dies before T leaving issue, *i.e.* B's two children C and D. Next D's two children, E and F are born and D dies. At T's death B's issue C, E and F are living. Under section 33(1) the gift to B takes effect as a gift to C (a one-half share), and E and F (a one-quarter share each). The amended section 33(1) has the considerable merit of operating in the same way as express substitutional gifts in a will commonly operate—benefiting B's issue and not B's estate.[74]

(c) CLASS GIFT TO TESTATOR'S CHILDREN OR REMOTER DESCENDANTS. The original section 33 did not apply to a class gift because (as was explained earlier) the doctrine of lapse does not apply to a class gift to persons who are to be ascertained at T's death or subsequently.[75] To consider once more the example of a class gift by T's will "to all my children as tenants in common in equal shares." If B, one of T's children, predeceased T but left issue living at T's death, the original section 33 did not apply and B's personal representatives did not take under the gift.[76] The result was the same even if B was T's only child.[77]

If the testator dies after December 31, 1982, the amended section 33(2) applies to a class gift to T's children or remoter descendants. The requirements are that (*a*) T's will contains a devise or bequest to a class of persons consisting of children or remoter descendants of T; (*b*) a presumptive member of the class[78] dies before T, leaving issue; and (*c*) issue of that member are living at T's death. If these requirements are satisfied, then, unless a contrary intention appears by T's will, the devise or bequest takes effect as if the class included the issue of its deceased member living at T's death, and the issue take the deceased member's share *per stirpes*, if more than one in equal shares.[79]

The amended section 33(2) does not create an exception to the doctrine of lapse, which is not applicable to a class gift. Where this provision applies, it adds the issue of a deceased presumptive member to the class eligible to take in order to give effect to the testator's likely intention, which he did not express in his will.

(3) *Gift to discharge a moral obligation.* If T by his will makes a gift to C in discharge of a moral obligation recognised by T in his will, and

---

[73] Amended s.33(3), which provides that B's issue take through all degrees according to their stock, in equal shares if more than one, any gift or share which their parent would have taken and so that no issue take whose parent is living at T's death and so capable of taking. If the gift to B was contingent, *quaere* whether B's issue take subject to the same contingency.

[74] *Ante*, p. 336.

[75] *Ante*, p. 337.

[76] *Olney* v. *Bates* (1855) 3 Drew. 319; *Browne* v. *Hammond* (1858) Johns. 210. The original s.33 of course applied to a gift to individuals, *Re Stansfield* (1880) 15 Ch.D. 84 (T's will gave "to my nine children as tenants in common in equal shares": held not a class gift and s.33 applied).

[77] *Re Harvey's Estate* [1893] 1 Ch. 567.

[78] Amended s.33(2)(*b*) refers to "a member of the class": in the context this means a *presumptive* member.

[79] Amended s.33(3); see *ante*, n. 68.

which still exists at T's death, the gift does not lapse, though C predeceases T, because the court infers that T intended the gift to pass to C's
estate. As Farwell J. put it in *Stevens* v. *King*,[80]

> "I think that the cases . . . have established the rule that, if the
> Court finds, upon the construction of the will, that the testator clearly
> intended not to give a mere bounty to the legatee, but to discharge
> what he regarded as a moral obligation, whether it were legally bind-
> ing or not, and if that obligation still exists at the testator's death,
> there is no necessary failure of the testator's object merely because the
> legatee dies in his lifetime; and therefore death in such a case does
> not cause a lapse."

This exception to the doctrine of lapse is based on case law and its
ambit remains somewhat uncertain. The exception has been held applicable where T makes a gift in discharge of a debt of his which is barred
by limitation,[81] or by the law of bankruptcy,[82] or in discharge of a debt
of T's deceased son.[83] It may be that the exception is confined to the recognition by T in his will of a moral obligation to pay one or more debts,
and does not extend to the recognition of any other forms of moral obligation.

C. Dissolution of Testator's Marriage to Beneficiary

Section 18A(1) of the Wills Act 1837[84] provides that if T's marriage to S
is dissolved or annulled or declared void by a court after T has made a
will, any devise or bequest to S shall lapse.[85] The will also takes effect as
if any appointment of S as an executor and trustee of the will were omitted. Section 18A(1) has these effects except in so far as a contrary intention appears by the will.

If by the will T made a gift to S for life, remainder to R absolutely, and
S's life interest lapses by virtue of section 18A(1), R's interest in remainder is treated as if it had not been subject to S's life interest.[86] Apart
from this, section 18A does not make provision for the effect of the failure of S's interest on the other dispositions in T's will. In *Re Sinclair*[87] T
by his will gave his whole estate to his wife S or, if S predeceased him or

---

[80] [1904] 2 Ch. 30, 33.
[81] *Williamson* v. *Naylor* (1838) 3 Y. & C. 208.
[82] *Philips* v. *Philips* (1844) 3 Hare 281; *Re Sowerby's Trust* (1856) 2 K. & J. 630; *Turner* v.
Martin (1857) De G.M. & G. 429.
[83] *Re Leach's W.T.* [1948] Ch. 232.
[84] s.18A was added by the Administration of Justice Act 1982, s.18(2). See Law Reform
Committee, 22nd Report (*The Making and Revocation of Wills*), (1980) Cmnd. 7902,
pp. 19–22, which by a majority recommended the change made by s.18(2).
[85] This is without prejudice to any right of S to apply for financial provision under the
Inheritance (Provision for Family and Dependants) Act 1975 (*ante*, p. 118), Wills Act 1837,
s.18A(2).
[86] *Ibid.* s.18A(3). If R's interest in remainder "was contingent upon the termination of
S's life interest," it is treated as if it had not been so contingent, *ibid.* S is mortal; S's death
is not a contingent event which may or may not happen. Perhaps this provision applies
where R's remainder was subject to a contingency to be satisfied at S's death, *e.g.* remainder to R absolutely if he survives S.
[87] [1985] Ch. 446.

failed to survive him for one month, to the Imperial Cancer Research Fund. Later T's marriage to S was dissolved and under section 18A(1) T's gift to S lapsed. T died and S survived T for one month. The Court of Appeal held that the contingent gift to the Research Fund failed because S did not predecease T or fail to survive him for one month. T therefore died intestate. The word "lapse" in section 18A(1) meant "fail" and could not be read as indicating that the other provisions of T's will should take effect as if S had predeceased T. It is most unfortunate that section 18A did not provide that for all the purposes of T's will S should be deemed to have predeceased T. Nothing more would have been needed and section 18A would then have "fitted together" with most wills, just as a codicil needs to fit together with a will.

Section 18A applies if T dies after December 31, 1982.[88] Prior to 1983 divorce or nullity had no effect on a will. Judicial separation still has no effect on a will, though it has on an intestacy.[89]

D. ADEMPTION

Ademption of specific gifts. A specific legacy or a specific devise fails by ademption if its subject matter has ceased to exist as part of the testator's property at his death. As was explained in Chapter 11, neither a general legacy nor a demonstrative legacy fails by ademption in this way.

To consider some examples of ademption:

(i) a specific legacy by T of "my 200 shares in Tilley & Co. Ltd." to A; if T sells or gives away his shares in Tilley & Co. Ltd. during his lifetime, the specific legacy fails by ademption.[90] If T sells his shares, A is not entitled to receive the traceable proceeds of sale, because the subject matter of the gift was the shares themselves and not their proceeds of sale.[91] If T sells or gives away some of his shares, the legacy fails to that extent.[92]

(ii) a specific legacy by T of a chattel, *e.g.* "the gold watch which my father gave me"; if T loses the chattel,[93] or destroys it, or sells it, or gives it away, in each case the legacy fails by ademption.

(iii) a specific legacy by T of a debt, *e.g.* "I give to F the money now due to me from G"; if G pays the debt to T during his lifetime, whether voluntarily or under compulsion, again the legacy fails by ademption.[94] If G pays part of the debt to T, the legacy fails to that extent.[95]

---

[88] Administration of Justice Act 1982, ss.73(6) and 76(11).
[89] *Ante*, p. 84.
[90] *Ashburner* v. *Macguire* (1786) 2 Bro.C.C. 108.
[91] *Harrison* v. *Jackson* (1877) 7 Ch.D. 339.
[92] *Humphreys* v. *Humphreys* (1789) 2 Cox. 184.
[93] *Durrant* v. *Friend* (1851) 5 De G. & S. 343 (specific legacy of chattels; T and the chattels perished together at sea: held adeemed and insurance money for chattels fell into residue).
[94] *Ashburner* v. *Macguire, supra; Re Bridle* (1879) 4 C.P.D. 336 (specific legacy of mortgage debt which was paid off in T's lifetime: held adeemed and immaterial T kept sum paid by mortgagor separate); *Gardner* v. *Hatton* (1833) 6 Sim. 93: *Re Robe* (1889) 61 L.T. 497; *Sidney* v. *Sidney* (1873) L.R. 17 Eq. 65. *Cf. Re Heilbronner* [1953] 1 W.L.R. 1254.
[95] *Aston* v. *Wood* (1874) 43 L.J.Ch. 715.

(iv) a specific devise by T of "my farm Blackacre" to L; if T sells and conveys, or gives away, his farm Blackacre during his lifetime, the specific devise fails by ademption. Again, if T sells and conveys Blackacre, L is not entitled to receive the traceable proceeds of sale.[96]

Failure of specific gifts speaking from death. However a specific gift which speaks from the death of the testator[97] is not subject to the doctrine of ademption in its strict sense. Examples include a specific gift of "the cars which I own at the date of my death," or "all shares in Tilley & Co. Ltd. of or to which I may be possessed or entitled at my death." Such a specific gift does, of course, fail if at his death the testator has no assets which answer to the description in the will.[98] But such a specific gift cannot fail under the doctrine of ademption in its strict sense, which is only applicable where the subject matter of the gift is to be ascertained at some time prior to death (*e.g.* "the cars which I own at the date of my will" or "my 200 shares in Tilley & Co. Ltd."[99]), and has ceased to exist as part of the testator's property at his death.

Change in name or form, but not in substance, does not adeem. A change in substance in the subject matter of a specific gift causes ademption but a mere change in name or form does not do so.[1] This principle has been applied in cases where T gives a specific legacy of particular company shares owned by him at the date of the will, and the shares are subsequently altered in some way in the course of an amalgamation or reconstruction before his death. In *Re Clifford*[2] T by his will gave "twenty-three of the shares belonging to me" in the L Co. Ltd.: at the date of his will T held 104 £80 shares in the company and this gift was a specific legacy of 23 of these £80 shares. Before T's death the company changed its name and sub-divided each £80 share into four new £20 shares, and at his death T held 416 new £20 shares in lieu of his 104 original £80 shares. Swinfen Eady J. held that this change had not adeemed the specific legacy because the subject matter remained in substance, though changed in name and form: the legatee therefore took 92 of the new £20 shares, which were "identical in all but name and form" with 23 original £80 shares. The same principle was applied in *Re Leeming*[3] where T gave a specific legacy of "my ten shares" in K Co. Ltd.: at the date of his will T held 10 £4 shares in this company. After the date of the will the company went into voluntary liquidation for the purpose of reconstruction as a new company with the same name, and at his death T held 20 £5 ordinary and 20 £5 preference shares in the new company in place of his 10 original £4 shares in the old company. The

[96] *Re Bagot's Settlement* (1862) 31 L.J.Ch. 772, 774.
[97] For specific gifts which speak from the death of the testator under the Wills Act 1837, s.24; see *post*, p. 424.
[98] *Re Slater* [1907] 1 Ch. 665.
[99] *Re Gibson* (1866) L.R. 2 Eq. 669.
[1] *Re Slater, supra,* at pp. 671–672.
[2] [1912] 1 Ch. 29: see also *Re O'Brien* (1946) 115 L.J.Ch. 340.
[3] [1912] 1 Ch. 828: *cf. Re Kuypers* [1925] Ch. 244 (original shares given still existed though with rights curtailed: new shares issued in compensation for loss of rights did not pass).

court held that the specific legacy had not been adeemed: the legatee took all T's shares in the new company because they were really in substance the same as the shares in the old company.

On the other hand, a change in substance causes ademption. Thus a gift by T's will of his present stock in the Lambeth Waterworks Company is adeemed by the subsequent acquisition of this company (and other metropolitan waterworks companies) by the Metropolitan Water Board: the Metropolitan Water Board stock issued to T before his death as compensation differs in substance from his Lambeth Waterworks Company stock, being different stock in a different concern operating over a much larger area.[4]

Ademption by contract. If T by his will makes a specific gift of his farm Blackacre to L, and later T enters into a binding contract to sell Blackacre to P but T dies before completion, this adeems the specific gift to L and L is not entitled to the purchase price payable by P.[5] But L is entitled (to the same extent as T would have been) to enjoy Blackacre or its rents and profits from T's death until the time for completion of the sale to P.[6] This result follows from the doctrine of conversion. Under this doctrine T, by contracting to sell Blackacre, disposes of his beneficial interest in Blackacre except in so far as T remains entitled to enjoy Blackacre until the time for completion.

If, on the other hand, T first enters into a binding contract to sell Blackacre to P, and afterwards T by his will makes a specific gift of Blackacre to L, the gift is generally construed as passing all T's interest, whatever it may be, to L, so that L is entitled to the purchase price payable by P.[7] The same result follows if the will is made before the contract, but is confirmed by a codicil which is made after, or substantially contemporaneously with, the contract.[8]

Ademption by exercise after death of option to purchase. Under the anomalous, but unfortunately well settled, rule in *Lawes* v. *Bennett*,[9] if T by his will makes a specific gift of Whiteacre to L, and later T grants to Q an option to purchase Whiteacre, the exercise by Q of the option after T's death adeems the specific gift to L. Thus L is not entitled to the purchase price payable by Q,[10] but L is entitled to enjoy Whiteacre or its rents and profits from T's death until Q exercises his option.[11] In short, an option to purchase which is exercised after T's death adeems a specific gift in the same way as a binding contract for sale made by T before his death. In the case of an option to purchase (unlike a binding contract

---

[4] *Re Slater* [1907] 1 Ch. 665, 671–673 and 674–675. Statutes often provide that specific bequests of, *e.g.* government stock, shall not be adeemed by a conversion offer.

[5] *Farrar* v. *Earl of Winterton* (1842) 5 Beav. 1; *Watts* v. *Watts* (1873) L.R. 17 Eq. 217; *Re Galway's W.T.* [1950] Ch. 1; *Re Edwards* [1958] Ch. 168; *Re Sweeting* [1988] 1 All E.R. 1016 (conditional contract): *cf. Re Thomas* (1886) 34 Ch.D. 166 (contract not binding as T's title defective). See generally P. H. Pettit (1960) 24 Conv.(N.S.) 47.

[6] *Watts* v. *Watts, supra.*

[7] *Re Calow* [1928] Ch. 710, esp. at p. 714.

[8] See *Re Pyle* [1895] 1 Ch. 724: for republication see *ante*, p. 80.

[9] (1785) 1 Cox 167. See generally Snell's *Principles of Equity* (28th ed., 1982), pp. 484 *et seq.*

[10] *Weeding* v. *Weeding* (1860) 1 J. & H. 424.

[11] *Townley* v. *Bedwell* (1808) 14 Ves. 591.

for sale) T at his death is still entitled to his beneficial interest in Whiteacre, subject to Q's interest which is contingent upon Q's exercise of the option. After his death T's beneficial interest passes to L under the specific gift, and Q's subsequent exercise of the option ought not to, but does, adeem this specific gift retrospectively.

The decision in *Re Carrington*[12] is a classic instance of the application of this anomalous rule. T by his will made specific gifts of 420 shares held by him in C Ltd. Later T granted to Q an option (exercisable within one month of T's death) to purchase all his shares in C Ltd. T died and Q duly exercised the option. The Court of Appeal reluctantly held that the specific gifts of the 420 shares had been adeemed by Q's exercise of his option after T's death and the purchase price payable by Q fell into T's residuary estate.

If, on the other hand, T first grants to Q an option to purchase Whiteacre, and afterwards T by his will makes a specific gift of Whiteacre to L, then again the gift is generally construed as passing all T's interest (whatever it may be) to L, so that L is entitled to the purchase price payable by Q.[13] The same result follows if the will is made before the grant of the option, but is confirmed by a codicil made after,[14] or substantially contemporaneously with,[15] the grant of the option.

Effect of republication of will. If a specific gift in a will has been adeemed, and the testator later makes a codicil which republishes his will, in general this does not save the specific gift from ademption.[16] For instance, if T by his will makes a specific gift of Blackacre to L, and T sells and conveys Blackacre to P, and later T makes a codicil which confirms his will, this does not make the specific gift to L take effect as a gift of the traceable proceeds of sale of Blackacre.

Nevertheless, republication may alter the construction of a will as to the subject of a specific gift, and thereby save a gift which otherwise would have failed by ademption. One instance has just been mentioned in relation to a contract of sale or an option to purchase.[17] Another instance is the decision in *Re Reeves*.[18] A testator by his will made in 1921 gave to his daughter "all my interest in my present lease" of Blackacre. At the date of his will the testator held a lease granted in 1917 and due to expire in 1924. Later the testator took a new lease for a term of 12 years and by a codicil made in 1926 confirmed his will. The court held

---

[12] [1932] 1 Ch. 1: see also *Re Rose* [1949] Ch. 78.

[13] *Drant* v. *Vause* (1842) 1 Y. & C.C.C. 580: see generally Hawkins and Ryder on the *Construction of Wills* (1965), pp. 60 *et seq.*

[14] *Emuss* v. *Smith* (1848) 2 De G. & Sm. 722: for republication see *ante*, p. 80.

[15] *Re Pyle* [1895] 1 Ch. 724 (T by will made specific devise of Whiteacre; T by codicil confirmed will and on same day granted lease to Q containing option to purchase Whiteacre; Q exercised option after T's death: held specific devisees took purchase price).

[16] *Drinkwater* v. *Falconer* (1755) 2 Ves.Sen. 623, 626; *Powys* v. *Mansfield* (1837) 3 My. & Cr. 359, 375–376; *Cowper* v. *Mantell (No. 1)* (1856) 22 Beav. 223; *Sidney* v. *Sidney* (1873) L.R. 17 Eq. 65; *Macdonald* v. *Irvine* (1878) 8 Ch.D. 101, esp. at p. 108; *Re Galway's W.T.* [1950] Ch. 1.

[17] *Ante*, p. 347.

[18] [1928] Ch. 351; see *Re Champion* [1893] 1 Ch. 101. For another instance see *Re Harvey* [1947] Ch. 285, following *Re Warren* [1932] 1 Ch. 42: cf. *Re Newman* [1930] 2 Ch. 409 and *Re Galway's W.T., supra*. See also J. D. B. Mitchell (1954) 70 L.Q.R. 353, 364 *et seq.*

that the daughter was entitled to the new lease. The testator had republished his will by confirming it, and the will, speaking as if it had been executed at the date of the codicil,[19] referred to the new and not to the expired old lease. But republication does not make a gift pass property which does not answer the description in the will: if by his will the testator had given "my lease of Blackacre dated September 25, 1917," republication would not have made the will refer to the new lease.[20]

No intention to adeem needed. Ademption occurs whether or not the testator intended ademption to occur.[21] Indeed, the doctrine of ademption may often defeat the intention which a testator would have expressed if he had appreciated how the doctrine operates.[22] A testator may, however, insert a provision against ademption in his will—e.g. by a gift of "my 200 shares in Tilley & Co. Ltd. *or the investments representing the same at my death if they shall have been converted into other holdings.*"[23] However, such a provision may give rise to difficulties of identification, especially if many years elapse between the will and the death.

The ademption of legacies by portions under the principle that equity leans against double portions is considered in Chapter 15.[24]

E. Uncertainty

A gift by will is void for uncertainty if, after considering any admissible evidence[25] and applying any relevant rules of construction, it is impossible to identify the subject matter or the object of the gift. Of course, the court tries to put a meaning on the words of a gift rather than "repose on the easy pillow of saying that the whole is void for uncertainty."[26]

Uncertainty of subject matter. For instance, gifts by a testator's will of "some of my best linen"[27] and of "a handsome gratuity to be given to each of the executors"[28] have been held void for uncertainty as to their subject matter. In another case T owned four houses in Sudeley Place; by his will T made separate gifts to each of his four sons of "all that

---

[19] For the date from which a will speaks see *post*, pp. 424 *et seq.*
[20] *Re Reeves* [1928] Ch. 351, 357–358.
[21] *Ashburner* v. *Macguire* (1786) 2 Bro.C.C. 108; *Stanley* v. *Potter* (1789) 2 Cox 180.
[22] *Harrison* v. *Jackson* (1877) 7 Ch.D. 339, 341.
[23] *Re Lewis's W.T.* [1937] Ch. 118.
[24] *Post*, pp. 449 *et seq.*
[25] *Post*, pp. 418 *et seq.*
[26] *Per* Jessel M.R. in *Re Roberts* (1881) 19 Ch.D. 520, 529.
[27] *Peck* v. *Halsey* (1726) 2. P.Wms. 387 (if it were "so much of my bed linen, as they [the legatees] should chuse, or as my executors should chuse for them, this would be good, and by the choice of the legatees or executors is reducible to a certainty").
[28] *Jubber* v. *Jubber* (1839) 9 Sim. 503.

newly built house, being No.   , Sudeley Place" (using similar terms
for each gift). The court held that the four gifts failed for uncertainty
because the will showed that T intended to give a particular house to
each of his sons (so the sons were not intended to select in turn), but the
will did not indicate which house each was intended to take.[29]

By way of contrast, a direction by will to executors to let X enjoy a flat
during her lifetime and "to receive a reasonable income from my other
properties" was held valid on the ground that this required an objective
assessment of reasonable income, which the court could undertake if
need be.[30] In another case T's will read, "I give devise and bequeath
unto my brother Mr. Harry Pateman [address] Also sister Mrs. Jane
Slade [address] Also sister Mrs. Ethel James [address]." The court
inferred that the will was intended to deal with the whole of T's property and held that T's whole estate passed under this gift, though T had
omitted any mention of the subject matter of the gift.[31]

Uncertainty of object. The decision in Re Stephenson[32] is an example
of a gift failing for uncertainty of objects. T by his will gave his residuary estate "unto the children of the deceased son (named Bamber) of my
father's sister share and share alike." This sister (as T was aware) had
three deceased sons, each with the surname Bamber, and each had left
children. The Court of Appeal held that the gift was void for uncertainty
as it was impossible to ascertain which son's children were intended to
take.

But, by way of exception to the general rule, "a charitable bequest
never fails for uncertainty."[33] This means that if the testator has shown
a general charitable intention, a gift does not fail for uncertainty of
objects merely because the testator has not indicated which particular
charity he wishes to benefit. For instance a gift by will on trust for "the
following charitable societies, viz.   to be divided in equal shares
among them" (the objects not being named) is valid and the court
directs a scheme in order to give effect to the gift.[34] However, this
exception to the general rule is not applicable if the gift is not exclusively charitable.[35] Thus in Chichester Diocesan Fund and Board of Finance

[29] Asten v. Asten [1894] 3 Ch. 261: cf. Tapley v. Eagleton (1879) 12 Ch.D. 683 (T owned
three houses in King Street; gift by T's will of "two houses in King Street" to X for life:
held X was entitled to select); Boyce v. Boyce (1849) 16 Sim. 476 (selector dead); Re Knapton
[1941] Ch. 428 (T by will gave "one house to each of my nephews and nieces:" held if they
disagreed they must choose in turn, the order of choice to be determined by lot).
[30] Re Golay [1965] 1 W.L.R. 969: but see R. E. M. (1965) 81 L.Q.R. 481: see also Talbot v.
Talbot [1968] Ch. 1 (option by will to purchase farm at "a reasonable valuation": option
held valid).
[31] Re Stevens [1952] Ch. 323.
[32] [1897] 1 Ch. 75.
[33] Re White [1893] 2 Ch. 41, 53.
[34] Re White, supra, where the gift was "to the following religious societies . . . "; this
was treated as prima facie confined to charities. For application in accordance with the
directions of the Crown under the Royal Prerogative where the gift is direct, and not by
way of a trust, see Re Bennett [1960] Ch. 18.
[35] For qualifications to the "exclusively charitable" requirement, including the Charitable Trusts (Validation) Act 1954, see Snell's Principles of Equity (28th ed., 1982), pp. 157 et
seq.

v. *Simpson*[36] a testator by his will directed his executors to apply his residuary estate for such "charitable or benevolent" objects in England as they might in their absolute discretion select. The House of Lords held that the gift was void for uncertainty because it was not confined to charitable objects, but extended to objects which were benevolent but not charitable.

In the law lords' judgments in this case reference was made to the principle that a testator may not delegate his testamentary power. To quote, for instance, from the judgment of Lord Simonds,[37]

"It is a cardinal rule, common to English and to Scots law, that a man may not delegate his testamentary power. To him the law gives the right to dispose of his estate in favour of ascertained or ascertainable persons. He does not exercise the right if in effect he empowers his executors to say what persons or objects are to be his beneficiaries. To this salutary rule there is a single exception. A testator may validly leave it to his executors to determine what charitable objects shall benefit, so long as charitable and no other objects may benefit."

Nevertheless, despite this principle, a testator may by his will confer on another person,[38] or on the trustees of the testator's will,[39] a power of appointment and thereby delegate his testamentary power.[40] In *Re Park*[41] T by his will gave his residuary estate to his trustee in trust to pay the income to such person (other than his sister Jane) or charitable institution as his sister Jane should from time to time during her life-time direct in writing. Clauson J. held that this "intermediate" power (*i.e.* intermediate between a general and a special power) was valid, and he referred in his judgment to "the well settled principle" that a testator by his will may confer on any person a general or a special power. The decision in *Re Park* would have been the same if Jane had been a trustee of the testator's will.[42]

Thus the principle that a testator may not delegate his testamentary power appears to have quite a narrow ambit. Perhaps the principle is best regarded as a general justification for certain provisions in wills being held void for uncertainty.[43] In practice the court is likely to decide whether a particular provision in a will is void for uncertainty by refer-ence to decided cases, rather than by reference to this principle.

[36] [1944] A.C. 341. For the sequel see *Re Diplock* [1948] Ch. 465, C.A.; and *Ministry of Health* v. *Simpson* [1951] A.C. 251, H.L.; *post*, p. 404.

[37] *Ibid.* at p. 371 (and see Viscount Simon L.C., at p. 348, Lord Macmillan, at p. 349, Lord Porter, at p. 364): see also *Houston* v. *Burns* [1918] A.C. 337, 342 and *Att.-Gen.* v. *National Provincial and Union Bank of England* [1924] A.C. 262, 264 and 268.

[38] *Re Park* [1932] 1 Ch. 580: see also *Re Hughes* [1921] 2 Ch. 208, 212 and *Re Jones* [1945] Ch. 105. *Cf. Re Carville* [1937] 4 All E.R. 464 ("to each of my executors £100 . . . The residue to be disposed of as the executors shall think fit": held by Clauson J. residue went as on intestacy).

[39] *Re Abrahams' W.T.* [1969] 1 Ch. 463, 474–476.

[40] See generally D. M. Gordon (1953) 69 L.Q.R. 334.

[41] [1932] 1 Ch. 580.

[42] *Re Abrahams' W.T., supra*, at p. 475.

[43] *e.g. Houston* v. *Burns* [1918] A.C. 337 (residue to be applied by trustees "for such pub-lic, benevolent, or charitable purposes" in connection with named parish as trustees should think proper: held void for uncertainty); *Att.-Gen.* v. *National Provincial and Union Bank of England* [1924] A.C. 262 (patriotic or charitable purposes void for uncertainty).

F. Murder or Manslaughter of the Testator or Intestate

A sane person who commits murder[44] or manslaughter[45] is generally debarred by public policy from taking any benefit under the will or intestacy of his victim.[46] Moreover this forfeiture rule applies where the killer is convicted of manslaughter by reason of diminished responsibility,[47] but it does not apply if the killer was insane—an insane killer may take a benefit under the will or intestacy of his victim.[48]

However, unless the killer stands convicted of murder, the court has power under the Forfeiture Act 1982 to modify the effect of this forfeiture rule if the court is satisfied that the justice of the case so requires, having regard to the conduct of the offender and of the deceased and any other material circumstances.[49] Under this power to modify the court can grant complete or partial relief from the effect of the forfeiture rule.[50]

Again, unless the killer stands convicted of murder, the killer may apply for provision to be made under the Inheritance (Provision for Family and Dependants) Act 1975,[51] but the application must inevitably fail if the deceased's will or intestacy would have made reasonable provision for the applicant if the forfeiture rule had not applied.[52]

G. Disclaimer

Beneficiary is free to disclaim. A beneficiary under a will may disclaim the gift to him. "The law certainly is not so absurd as to force a man to take an estate against his will."[53] Similarly a beneficiary entitled

---

[44] *In the Estate of Crippen* [1911] P. 108 (intestacy); *Re Sigsworth* [1935] Ch. 89 (will or intestacy): as to burden of proof see *Re Dellow's W.T.* [1964] 1 W.L.R. 451.

[45] *In the Estate of Hall* [1914] P. 1 (will): probably the forfeiture rule does not apply to every type of manslaughter: see *Gray* v. *Barr* [1971] 2 Q.B. 554, 569 and 581 (manslaughter varies infinitely in its seriousness); *R.* v. *Chief National Insurance Commissioner, Ex. p. Connor* [1981] Q.B. 758, 765; *Re K* [1985] Ch. 85, 95–98. See generally Youdan (1973) 89 L.Q.R. 235.

[46] Or statutory nomination or *donatio mortis causa* of his victim. As to joint tenants see *Re K* [1985] Ch. 85, 100 (forfeiture severs a beneficial joint tenancy); see also *Schobelt* v. *Barber* (1966) 60 D.L.R. (2d) 519; *Re Pechar* [1969] N.Z.L.R. 574, 584–588.

[47] *Re Giles* [1972] Ch. 544 (will or intestacy).

[48] *Re Houghton* [1915] 2 Ch. 173 (insane killer may take on his victim's intestacy); *Re Pitts* [1931] 1 Ch. 546. There is a presumption of sanity, *Re Pollock* [1941] Ch. 219.

[49] Forfeiture Act 1982, ss.1–2, 5 and 7. If the killer stands convicted, proceedings for modification cannot be brought more than three months after conviction, s.2(3); *Re Royse* [1985] Ch. 22. Property acquired before October 13, 1982 by a person other than the killer in consequence of the forfeiture rule is protected, s.2(7); *Re K* [1985] Ch. 85, 98–99, [1986] Ch. 180 (only property actually transferred to other person, not property held by personal representative pending administration).

[50] *Ibid.* s.2(1) and (5); see *Re K* [1985] Ch. 85, [1986] Ch. 180 (probation for H's manslaughter: W granted complete relief from forfeiture of her interests under H's will and in matrimonial home as surviving joint tenant).

[51] *Ibid.* ss.3 and 5.

[52] *Re Royse* [1985] Ch. 22: see *ante*, p. 108.

[53] Per Abbot C.J. in *Townson* v. *Tickell* (1819) 3 B. & Ald. 31.

under the intestacy rules may disclaim his interest on intestacy.[54] The beneficiary may disclaim by a deed of disclaimer[55] or by conduct.

If a beneficiary does disclaim a benefit under a will, he may subsequently retract his disclaimer provided that no one has altered his position in reliance on the disclaimer.[56]

Limits on freedom to disclaim. There are, however, certain limits on a beneficiary's freedom to disclaim:

(i) If the beneficiary has already unequivocally accepted the gift, the beneficiary cannot disclaim it.[57]

(ii) In general the beneficiary is free to disclaim an onerous gift[58] in a will and accept another beneficial gift in the same will,[59] but occasionally the will requires him to take both or neither of the gifts.[60]

(iii) If a single gift includes two or more different assets, the beneficiary must take all the assets or none of them. For instance, a gift to B by T's will of his leasehold house Blackacre together with its contents constitutes a single gift, and not two separate gifts, and therefore B is not free to disclaim the gift of Blackacre and accept the gift of its contents.[61]

(iv) One of two or more joint beneficiaries cannot disclaim, though he can release his interest to the other joint tenants[62]—"the only disclaimer which can be made by joint tenants is a disclaimer which is made by them all."[63]

EFFECT OF FAILURE

A legacy or specific devise which fails falls into residue or goes on intestacy. In general, the subject matter of any legacy or specific devise which fails passes under the residuary gift (if any) contained in the testator's will or, if not effectively disposed of by the will, goes on intestacy.[64]

---

[54] *Re Scott* [1975] 1 W.L.R. 1260; *cf.* Goodhart (1976) 40 Conv.(N.S.) 292; Oughton (1977) 41 Conv.(N.S.) 260.

[55] *Townson* v. *Tickell, supra.*

[56] *Re Cranstoun* [1949] Ch. 523: see also *Re Paradise Motor Co.* [1968] 1 W.L.R. 1125, 1143.

[57] *Re Hodge* [1940] Ch. 260; *cf. Re Wimperis* [1914] 1 Ch. 502.

[58] *e.g.* a gift of a lease with an unduly heavy rent, or a gift subject to a condition imposing an onerous personal obligation, as in *Re Hodge, supra* ,(devise of Blackacre to H subject to personal obligation to pay £2 per week to S for life, and if H disposed of Blackacre to invest £2,000 on trust for S for life and after her death for S's children).

[59] *Warren* v. *Rudall* (1861) 1 J. & H. 1.

[60] *Talbot* v. *Earl of Radnor* (1834) 3 M. & K. 252; *Fairtlough* v. *Johnstone* (1865) 16 Ir.Ch. 442.

[61] *Re Joel* [1943] Ch. 311; *Guthrie* v. *Walrond* (1882) 22 Ch.D. 573 ("all my estate and effects in the Island of Mauritius": held a single gift which could only be disclaimed as a whole).

[62] *Re Schär* [1951] Ch. 280.

[63] *Ibid.* at p. 285.

[64] See generally Hawkins and Ryder on the *Construction of Wills* (1965), pp. 64 *et seq.*

(1) *Residuary bequest*. Prima facie a residuary bequest includes the subject matter of any legacy which fails for any reason.[65] As Grant M.R. put it in *Leake* v. *Robinson*,[66] "I have always understood that, with regard to personal estate, everything which is ill given by the will does fall into the residue. . . . It is immaterial how it happens that any part of the property is undisposed of. . . . " If T by his will gives "my 200 shares in Tilley & Co. Ltd." to A and "all the residue of my personal estate" to B, the word "residue" is *not* contrued as referring to all T's personal estate except the 200 shares: instead, if the gift to A fails, the "residue" includes the 200 shares because the gift to B is a residuary bequest. The same result follows if T gives "all the rest of," or "all the remainder of," or "all other," his personal estate to B.[67] However, this common law rule that a residuary bequest includes the subject matter of any legacy which fails is not applicable if the will shows a contrary intention. Accordingly, the rule is not applicable if the testator shows an intention to exclude the subject matter of a legacy from his residuary bequest in any event, irrespective of whether the legacy fails: in that event, if the legacy fails, the subject matter goes on intestacy.[68]

(2) *Residuary devise*. Under section 25 of the Wills Act 1837, unless a will shows a contrary intention, a residuary devise[69] includes the subject matter of any specific devise which fails for any reason. Thus, as a result of section 25, a residuary devise operates in the same way as a residuary bequest.[70]

A residuary gift which fails goes on intestacy. If a residuary gift in a will fails completely, the residuary estate goes on intestacy. Again, if a gift of a share in the residuary estate fails, prima facie that share goes on intestacy. Accordingly, if T by his will gives his residuary real and personal estate to X and Y absolutely as tenants in common in equal shares, and the gift to X fails for any reason, prima facie X's share goes on T's intestacy and does not pass to Y. A residuary gift sweeps up property not effectively disposed of by any other form of gift, but it does not sweep up property not effectively disposed of by the residuary gift itself.[71] However, this rule is not applicable if the will shows a contrary intention. For instance, T may direct that if the disposition of a share of

---

[65] *Cambridge* v. *Rous* (1802) 8 Ves. 12 (lapsed legacies); *Blight* v. *Hartnoll* (1883) 23 Ch.D. 218 (legacy void for remoteness); *Re Backhouse* [1931] W.N. 168 (disclaimed legacy).

[66] (1817) 2 Mer. 363, 393.

[67] *Re Mason* [1901] 1 Ch. 619, 624–625; *Re Barnes' W.T.* [1972] 1 W.L.R. 587.

[68] *Re Fraser* [1904] 1 Ch. 726; *Wainman* v. *Field* (1854) Kay. 507, but see *Blight* v. *Hartnoll*, *supra*, at p. 223. Also the subject matter may, on the construction of the will, fall into a particular residue of that description of property, and not into general residue, *De Trafford* v. *Tempest* (1856) 21 Beav. 564 and see Hawkins and Ryder, *op. cit.* pp. 66–68.

[69] s.25 only applies to general residuary devises, *Springett* v. *Jenings* (1871) L.R. 6 Ch.App. 333; *cf. Re Davies* [1928] Ch. 24.

[70] *Re Mason* [1901] 1 Ch. 619, C.A., [1903] A.C. 1, H.L. (specific devise to attesting witness fell into devise of "all other my freehold messuages and tenements at Wimbledon aforesaid and elsewhere," which was held to be residuary).

[71] *Skrymsher* v. *Northcote* (1818) 1 Sw. 566, 570.

his residue fails, that share is to accrue to the other share, and under such a direction X's share does pass to Y.[72]

Gifts which do not fail. The principles so far considered are not, of course, applicable if the gift (whether a legacy, specific devise or residuary gift) does not fail, though one or more of the beneficiaries cannot take. This occurs (i) in the case of a gift to A, B and C as joint tenants if A and B both die before the testator, but C survives him and takes the whole by survivorship[73]; and (ii) in the case of a class gift to persons who are to be ascertained at the testator's death or subsequently. If a presumptive member of the class dies in the testator's lifetime,[74] or is incapable of taking by reason of his being an attesting witness,[75] or is guilty of the manslaughter of the testator,[76] this does not cause the gift to fail if at least one other member of the class takes. Again, if any property is given by will to X subject to a charge in favour of Y (*e.g.* charged with a legacy of £1,000 for Y), and the gift to Y fails, this causes the charge to fail and X takes the entire property free from the charge.[77] Finally, if any property is given by will to X absolutely and trusts are engrafted on X's absolute interest which fail, under the rule in *Lassence* v. *Tierney* the absolute gift to X takes effect so far as the trusts have failed. This rule is considered later.[78]

Acceleration of subsequent interest. The doctrine of acceleration may be applicable if T by his will gives any real or personal property to X for life and this gift to X fails. It may fail because X or his spouse was an attesting witness, or X predeceased T, or T's marriage to X was dissolved or annulled, or X was guilty of the murder or manslaughter of T, or X disclaimed the gift.

(1) *Gift in remainder vested.* If after X's life interest there is a vested gift in remainder (*e.g.* a gift in remainder to Y absolutely), the remainder is accelerated and takes effect in possession immediately.[79] "An interest is

---

[72] For examples of contrary intention see *Evans* v. *Field* (1839) 8 L.J.Ch. 264; *Re Palmer* [1893] 3 Ch. 369 and *Re Allan* [1903] 1 Ch. 276. For the effect of Wills Act 1837, s.15 see *Re Doland's W.T.* [1970] Ch. 267 (trust of 2 per cent. share of residue for X, whose wife was an attesting witness; proviso that if "any of the trusts . . . shall fail" gift to Y and Z equally: held under Wills Act 1837, s.15 the will must be treated as though it contained no trust in favour of X which could fail—X's share went on intestacy and not under proviso).
[73] *Morley* v. *Bird* (1798) 3 Ves. 629.
[74] *Doe* d. *Stewart* v. *Sheffield* (1811) 13 East. 526; *Shuttleworth* v. *Greaves* (1838) 4 M. & Cr. 35: see also *Re Woods* [1931] 2 Ch. 138 and *cf. Re Midgley* [1955] Ch. 576.
[75] *Fell* v. *Biddolph* (1875) L.R. 10 C.P. 701 (the headnote is wrong); *Re Coleman and Jarrom* (1876) 4 Ch.D. 165 ("the true rule is that those members of the class who are at the testator's death capable of taking take, and that those who become incapable of taking—whether by dying in the testator's lifetime, or by attesting the will, or by some other operation of law—do not take").
[76] *Re Peacock* [1957] Ch. 310.
[77] *Tucker* v. *Kayess* (1858) 4 K. & J. 339: *secus* if the testator intended to sever the gift to Y from the property given to X for all purposes, irrespective of whether the gift to Y failed.
[78] See *post*, pp. 434–435.
[79] *Lainson* v. *Lainson* (1854) 5 De G.M. & G. 754 (X's life interest revoked by codicil: vested remainder accelerated); *Jull* v. *Jacobs* (1876) 3 Ch.D. 703 (X an attesting witness: vested remainder accelerated); *Re Flower's Settlement Trusts* [1957] 1 W.L.R. 401, 405. If X's life interest lapsed by virtue of divorce or annulment, Y's interest is treated as if it had not been subject to X's life interest, Wills Act 1837, s.18A(3); see *ante*, p. 344.

postponed that a prior interest may be enjoyed. If that prior interest is determined, whether by the death of a prior beneficiary or for any other cause, the reason for postponement disappears and there is no reason why there should not be acceleration."[80] If the gift to Y is expressed to take effect "after the death" of X, this does not prevent acceleration—the gift to Y is construed as a gift taking effect on the death of X *or on any earlier failure or determination of X's interest.*[81] In short, "after his death for Y absolutely" is construed in the same sense as the useful phrase *"subject as aforesaid* for Y absolutely." But T may by his will exclude the doctrine of acceleration by making it plain that the expression "after the death" of X refers to X's death in the literal sense and nothing else.

The doctrine of acceleration applies though the vested gift in remainder is vested in Y subject to being divested[82] (*e.g.* a gift in remainder to Y absolutely, but if Y dies before X and leaves issue, to Y's issue absolutely in equal shares *per stirpes*). In this case under the doctrine of acceleration Y's interest takes effect in possession immediately, but Y's interest nevertheless remains liable to be divested in accordance with the terms of T's will.[83]

(2) *Gift in remainder contingent.* On the other hand, if after X's life interest there is only a contingent gift in remainder (*e.g.* a gift in remainder to the first child of Y absolutely, and at T's death Y has no child), normally the remainder is not accelerated whilst the remainder remains contingent.[84] But if this gift in remainder subsequently becomes vested (*i.e.* in this example, if a child is born to Y), under the doctrine of acceleration the remainder is then accelerated and takes effect in possession.[85]

Failure of interest on intestacy. An interest on intestacy may fail because the beneficiary is guilty of the murder or manslaughter of the intestate,[86] or the beneficiary disclaims his interest.[87] At least three different situations may arise.

---

[80] *Re Hodge* [1943] Ch. 300, 301–302 (X disclaimed: held annuities in remainder accelerated).

[81] *Re Flower's Settlement Trusts, supra.*

[82] *Re Taylor* [1957] 1 W.L.R. 1043 (X disclaimed: held vested remainder accelerated but remained liable to be divested); *Re Conyngham* [1921] 1 Ch. 491.

[83] *Re Taylor, supra; Re Conyngham, supra.*

[84] *Re Townsend's Estate* (1886) 34 Ch.D. 357 (X's wife an attesting witness; gift in remainder to X's child or children; X was childless: held no acceleration possible until X has a child—then "the interest of the children in remainder would be accelerated"); *Re Taylor, supra,* at pp. 1045 and 1049; *Re Scott* [1975] 1 W.L.R. 1260. But *cf. Re Dawson's Settlement* [1966] 1 W.L.R. 1456, esp. at pp. 1465–1467 where Goff J. held that a remainder which is contingent may be accelerated if the person contingently entitled is *in esse* and "the contingency is in no way related to the words of futurity or the determination of the prior interest," *e.g.* attaining 21 or marrying: see Prichard [1973] C.L.J. 246. If Y's interest in remainder was "contingent upon the termination of X's life interest," which lapsed by virtue of divorce or annulment, Y's interest is treated as if it had not been so contingent, Wills Act 1837, s.18A(3): see *ante,* p. 344, n. 86.

[85] *Re Townsend's Estate, supra; Re Taylor, supra.* For the effect of acceleration on class closing see *post,* p. 438.

[86] *Ante,* p. 352.

[87] *Ante,* p. 352.

(1) *Interest of surviving spouse fails.* If the surviving spouse is debarred by her murder or manslaughter of the intestate from taking any benefit on intestacy, the intestate's issue take the whole estate.[88] The same result follows if the surviving spouse disclaims his interest on intestacy.

(2) *Another member of the same class takes.* In *Re Callaway*[89] T by her will gave her whole estate to her daughter D, who murdered T and was therefore debarred from taking under T's will or intestacy. T died a widow and T's issue entitled under the intestacy rules were her adult son S and daughter D. Vaisey J. held that D was disqualified from being counted as a member of the class of issue entitled on intestacy and accordingly S was solely entitled to T's estate. He rejected the Crown's claim to take (as *bona vacantia*) the half share to which D would have been entitled on intestacy but for the murder.[90]

If in this case T had died a natural death but D had disclaimed her interest under both T's will and T's intestacy, the disclaimer would have barred D from being counted as a member of the class of issue entitled on intestacy and again S would have been solely entitled to T's estate.[91]

(3) *The next class takes.* If all the members of the class of next-of-kin entitled under the intestacy rules are either disqualified by murder or manslaughter or barred by disclaimer, that class is disregarded and the next class of next-of-kin (of which there are members in existence capable of taking) are entitled.[92]

---

[88] *Re Giles* [1972] Ch. 544.

[89] [1956] Ch. 559.

[90] But see pp. 563–565 where Vaisey J. stated that, but for case law authority, he would have decided that T's whole estate (or alternatively D's half share on intestacy) was undisposed of and passed to the Crown as *bona vacantia*.

[91] See *Re Scott* [1975] 1 W.L.R. 1260, 1270–1271.

[92] *Re Scott, supra* (brother and sister both disclaimed: next class of next of kin held entitled, not the Crown): see E. C. Ryder (1976) 40 Conv.(N.S.) 85.

CHAPTER 13

DISTRIBUTION OF THE ESTATE

In its narrower sense, the process of administration of the deceased's estate is complete when the personal representatives have got in the estate and paid, or made provision for the payment of, the expenses, debts, and liabilities of the deceased, and any inheritance tax payable in respect of his death. In its wider (and probably more accurate[1]) sense, administration embraces the culmination of this process—the distribution of the estate by the personal representatives to the persons entitled under the deceased's will or intestacy. These persons may be beneficially entitled to the distributed assets or they may hold the distributed assets as trustees.

A. DISTRIBUTION TO THE PERSONS ENTITLED

Time for distribution. Section 44 of the Administration of Estates Act 1925 provides that a personal representative is not bound to distribute the deceased's estate before the expiration of one year from the death.[2] As already explained, a different rule governs the time for payment of the deceased's debts. A personal representative has a duty to pay the deceased's debts with due diligence, and due diligence may require that payment should be made before the expiration of one year from the death.[3]

Accordingly, a personal representative cannot be compelled to pay a legacy before the expiration of one year from the death, even though by his will the testator directed the legacy to be paid within (say) six months after his death.[4] This rule may produce hardship if the legatee (*e.g.* the deceased's widow) is in immediate need of money. The court has power to make an interim order in favour of an applicant under the Inheritance (Provision for Family and Dependants) Act 1975 if the applicant is in immediate need of financial assistance.[5]

Of course, a personal representative is free to pay a legacy, or to distribute the residuary estate, before the expiration of the executor's year if he chooses.[6] And section 43(1) of the Administration of Estates Act

---

[1] See *Harvell* v. *Foster* [1954] 2 Q.B. 367.

[2] s.44 is expressed to be "subject to the foregoing provisions of this Act": this may refer to ss.36(10) and 43(2) of the Act, for which see *post*, pp. 376–377.

[3] *Ante*, pp. 257–258.

[4] See *Pearson* v. *Pearson* (1802) 1 Sch. & Lef. 10, 12; *Brooke* v. *Lewis* (1822) 6 Madd. 358. But the legacy carries interest from the time for payment fixed by the testator in his will, *ante*, p. 323.

[5] See *ante*, pp. 131–132.

[6] *Pearson* v. *Pearson, supra*; *Angerstein* v. *Martin* (1823) 1 Turn. & R. 232, 241; *Re Palmer* [1916] 2 Ch. 391, 398 and 401.

358

1925 empowers a personal representative to permit a person entitled to land to take possession of it (or receive the rents payable by tenants[7]) prior to an assent or conveyance in his favour; this does not prejudice the right of the personal representative to resume possession or to convey the land.

On the other hand, a personal representative is not bound to distribute the deceased's estate at the expiration of one year from the death—it may take longer than this to complete the administration of the estate.

Ascertaining the persons entitled. In general, personal representatives are under a duty to distribute to the persons properly entitled under the deceased's will or intestacy.[8] It is therefore important for personal representatives to ascertain all the persons properly entitled, or at any rate to protect themselves against liability in case they fail to do so. If doubt arises as to the proper construction of the will, the personal representatives may apply to the court for this to be determined.[9] Again, it may be advisable to ask the court to conduct an inquiry to ascertain the beneficiaries.[10] For example, such an inquiry may be needed if the deceased died intestate at an advanced age, and the class of next-of-kin entitled under the intestacy rules are his uncles and aunts of the whole blood on the statutory trusts, so that the class includes the issue of each deceased uncle or aunt, taking *per stirpes*. In such a case the personal representatives may experience great difficulty in ascertaining all the persons entitled.

What other protection is there for personal representatives in case they fail to ascertain all the persons properly entitled?

(1) *Advertising for claims.* Under section 27 of the Trustee Act 1925[11] personal representatives may give notice of their intention to distribute and require any person interested to send in particulars of his claim to the personal representatives within a stated time, not being less than two months. The requirements imposed by this section as to advertising this notice and making searches have already been considered in relation to ascertaining the debts and liabilities of the deceased.[12] If the personal representatives satisfy these requirements, they may distribute to the persons entitled having regard only to the claims (whether formal or not) of which the personal representatives then have notice. In that event, the personal representatives are not, in respect of the distributed assets, "liable to any person of whose claim the . . . personal representatives have not had notice at the time of . . . distribution."[13] In *Re*

---

[7] Administration of Estates Act 1925, s. 55(1)(xii).

[8] *Re Diplock* [1948] Ch. 465, 503: *Re Hayes' W.T.* [1971] 1 W.L.R. 758, 765.

[9] *Post*, p. 400.

[10] See generally Heward's *Guide to Chancery Practice* (4th ed., 1972), pp. 79 *et seq.; post*, p. 400.

[11] As amended by Law of Property (Amendment) Act 1926, ss.7, 8(2) and Sched.

[12] *Ante*, pp. 259 *et seq.*

[13] Trustee Act 1925, s.27(2).

Aldhous[14] T died partially intestate and T's executor gave notice in accordance with the requirements of section 27; the executor received no claims from any person claiming to be entitled as T's next-of-kin and, believing that there were no next-of-kin, the executor paid the assets undisposed of by T's will to the Treasury Solicitor on behalf of the Crown as *bona vacantia*. In fact, unknown to the executor, there were next-of-kin of T who were entitled to these assets under the intestacy rules. Danckwerts J. said he thought it was plain that, if proceedings were brought by the next-of-kin against the executor in respect of this payment to the Treasury Solicitor, the executor would be protected by section 27—this protection is "effective not only in respect of claims of creditors but in respect of the claims of next-of-kin of a deceased person or, I suppose, of persons entitled under the will of a deceased person to share in the estate of that person."[15] There seems little reason to doubt that section 27 protects personal representatives against the claims of unknown beneficiaries entitled under the deceased's will or intestacy, as well as against the claims of unknown creditors.[16]

Section 27 does not prejudice the remedy of an unpaid beneficiary against a recipient of the deceased's assets. This is considered later.[17]

(2) *Leave of the court to distribute.* The court may make a "Benjamin Order" giving the personal representatives leave to distribute on a particular footing set out in the order, *e.g.* on the footing that a missing beneficiary under the testator's will was unmarried and predeceased the testator,[18] or that a son who died in the lifetime of the testatrix left no child who survived her.[19] The particular footing set out in the order is, of course, based on probable inferences from the proved facts, but the order does not constitute a positive declaration of rights[20] and, accordingly, it does not prevent any missing beneficiary (if he subsequently appears) from pursuing his remedy against a recipient of the deceased's assets.[21] Sometimes a Benjamin Order is made after an inquiry by the court has proved inconclusive,[22] but such an order may be made without any prior inquiry by the court if suitable advertise-

---

[14] [1955] 1 W.L.R. 459: see also *Newton* v. *Sherry* (1876) 1 C.P.D. 246 (personal representative protected against claim of unknown next of kin by Law of Property Amendment Act 1859, s.29, now replaced by Trustee Act 1925, s.27, which is worded differently); *Re Letherbrow* [1935] W.N. 34 and 48 (advertisements for next of kin); *Re Ward* [1971] 1 W.L.R. 1376.

[15] *Ibid.* at p. 462.

[16] See Law Reform Committee, 19th Report (*Interpretation of Wills*), Cmnd. 5301 (1973), paras. 51 and 65(8), which recommended s.27 should be amended to put this "beyond argument."

[17] *Post*, pp. 403 *et seq.*

[18] *Re Benjamin* [1902] 1 Ch. 723 (P disappeared in September 1892; P's father died in June 1893 and by his will gave P a share of residue; despite inquiries and advertisements nothing heard of P: order that trustees be at liberty to distribute upon the footing P did not survive his father): see also *Re Taylor's Estate* [1969] 2 Ch. 245; *Re Lowe's W.T.* [1973] 1 W.L.R. 882, 887; *Re Green's W.T.* [1985] 3 All E.R. 455.

[19] *Re Beattie*, unreported, see Mosse (1936) 81 L.J.News. 163.

[20] *Hansell* v. *Spink* [1943] Ch. 396, 399; *Re Green's W.T., supra* at p. 462 ("The true view is that a *Re Benjamin* order does not vary or destroy beneficial interests. It merely enables trust property to be distributed in accordance with the practical probabilities . . .").

[21] *Post*, pp. 403 *et seq.*

[22] As in *Re Benjamin, supra*, (Master unable to certify whether P alive or dead, or, if dead, when he died); *Re Lowe's W.T., supra.*

ments for a missing beneficiary produce no claims,[23] or even without any advertisements if the inference from the proved facts is irresistable.[24]

A Benjamin Order protects personal representatives, who distribute on the footing set out in the order, from liability. Moreover, unlike section 27 of the Trustee Act 1925, the protection is not conditional on the personal representatives having complied with statutory requirements as to advertising and making searches.[25] Before making a Benjamin Order the court itself decides what further advertisements (if any) ought to be made. Such an order is also advantageous to the known beneficiaries as the share of the missing beneficiary becomes distributable amongst them, though subject to the (usually remote) possibility of the missing beneficiary appearing and recovering his share from them.

(3) *Adoption.* The duty of personal representatives to distribute to the persons properly entitled is modified by statute in cases where an adoption could affect entitlement. A personal representative is not under a duty to enquire whether any adoption has been effected or revoked before he distributes any property, though that fact could affect entitlement to the property.[26] The personal representative is not liable if he distributes the property without regard to that fact if he has not received notice of it before the distribution; however this protection of the personal representatives does not prejudice the remedy of the true beneficiary against a recipient of the deceased's assets.[27]

Beneficiary owes money to the estate. The situation to be considered is this:

(1) B as a beneficiary under T's will or intestacy is entitled to money from T's estate; and

(2) B owes money to T's estate.

In this situation B is not permitted to take any money out of T's estate until he has made good the money which he owes to T's estate.[28]

---

[23] As in *Re Beattie, supra,* (advertisements to ascertain if deceased son left any child); *Re Taylor's Estate, supra.*

[24] As in *Re Green's W.T., supra* (by her will T, who died in 1976, gave her estate to her son B; B was gunner in a bomber which went missing in a raid on Berlin in 1943; nothing ever heard of the bomber or its crew: irresistible inference crew perished, though T believed B somewhere somehow was still alive).

[25] *Ante,* p. 259.

[26] Adoption Act 1976, s.45(1): see also Legitimacy Act 1976, s.7(1)—no duty to enquire whether any person is illegitimate or has been adopted by one of his natural parents, and could be legitimated (or if deceased be treated as legitimated). Family Law Reform Act 1969, s.17 conferred similar protection on personal representatives as regards illegitimacy but has been repealed by Family Law Reform Act 1987, ss.20 and 33(4) and Sched. 4.

[27] Adoption Act 1976, s.45(2) and (3); Legitimacy Act 1976, s.7(2) and (3). For the remedy against a recipient see *post,* pp. 403 *et seq.*

[28] *Re Rhodesia Goldfields Ltd.* [1909] 1 Ch. 239, 247 ("the rule is of general application that . . . where a fund is being distributed, a party cannot take anything out of the fund until he has made good what he owes to the fund"). See generally B. S. Ker (1954) 18 Conv.(N.S.) 176.

Accordingly, T's personal representatives have the right to apply any money due to B as a beneficiary in satisfaction of any money due from B to T's estate. To take the situation where T by his will gave his residuary estate to A and B equally, and T's personal representatives have £500 in hand ready to distribute, but B owes another £500 to T's estate. The personal representatives are entitled to say to B, "The real residue is £1,000, for you must pay the £500 you owe. Half £1,000 is £500. Therefore we can give the other beneficiary [A] £500 in our hands, and we need give you [B] nothing, because you have to pay us £500, which we should then have to hand back to you."[29] In effect, B is told that his share of residue must be treated as having been paid out of the £500 owing to T's estate which he has in his pocket.[30] The result would have been the same if A and B had been entitled to T's residuary estate under the intestacy rules.[31] Again, the same rule applies if B is entitled to a legacy of £750 under T's will, but B owes £500 to T's estate—T's personal representatives need only pay B £250.

(1) *Money payable to B.* This right of "retainer" can only be exercised by T's personal representatives if B is entitled to a sum of money from T's estate. It cannot be exercised if B is entitled to a specific legacy of something other than money, such as government stock, even though the stock can easily be sold.[32]

(2) *Money payable by B.* The other requirement is that B owes money[33] to T's estate. If the debt owed by B is payable by instalments, the personal representatives may retain any instalments already due, but they are not entitled to retain future instalments not yet due out of a legacy presently payable, because this would make B pay his debt before it becomes due.[34] Again, this requirement is not satisfied if the debt due to T's estate is owed by B and another person jointly.[35]

The right of retainer is exercisable against the beneficiary B in respect of money which B owes to T's estate, but not in respect of money which anyone else owes to T's estate. It follows that if T by his will makes a gift to his children living at his death, and provides that the children of any deceased child shall take "such share as their parent would have taken if living," T's personal representatives cannot retain a debt due to T's

---

[29] *Per* Scrutton L.J. in *Re Melton* [1918] 1 Ch. 37, 59.

[30] *Turner* v. *Turner* [1911] 1 Ch. 716, 719.

[31] *Re Cordwell's Estate* (1875) L.R. 20 Eq. 644.

[32] *Re Savage* [1918] 2 Ch. 146 (specific legacy of colonial stock: rule not applicable—"you must have money payable against money payable"); *Re Taylor* [1894] 1 Ch. 671 (specific legacy of profits of business to B: held executors had right to retain profits as against debt due from B to T's estate): *cf. Re Eiser's W.T.* [1937] 1 All E.R. 244 (executors need not retain income payable under discretionary trust).

[33] It suffices if B is liable in damages to T's estate, *Re Jewell's Settlement* [1919] 2 Ch. 161, 173–177 (damages equal to surrender value of lapsed insurance policy).

[34] *Re Abrahams* [1908] 2 Ch. 69.

[35] *Turner* v. *Turner* [1911] 1 Ch. 716 (debt due to T's estate from two partners jointly: held executors not entitled to retain legacy given to one partner); *Re Pennington and Owen Ltd.* [1925] Ch. 825.

estate from a deceased child out of the share payable to that child's children because the children do not owe the debt.[36]

(3) *Effect of limitation or bankruptcy.* If T's personal representatives could have recovered from B all the money due from him to T's estate, this right of retainer merely saves them the bother of obtaining and enforcing judgment against B. But the right of retainer is exercisable by T's personal representatives in circumstances where they could not have recovered from B all the money due. For instance, it is exercisable:

(i) where the debt due from B was statute-barred at T's death[37]; or
(ii) where B goes bankrupt after he has become entitled as a beneficiary under T's will or intestacy to money from T's estate.[38] However, if T's personal representatives subsequently prove in B's bankruptcy for the money due from B, they cannot then exercise the right of retainer[39]; accordingly, the personal representatives need to consider whether it is more advantageous to T's estate for them to exercise the right of retainer or to prove in B's bankruptcy. Again, if B subsequently obtains his discharge from bankruptcy, T's personal representatives cannot then exercise the right of retainer because the debt has gone.[40] The position is different if B was an undischarged bankrupt when he became entitled as a beneficiary. In that case T's personal representatives may prove in B's bankruptcy and receive a dividend *pari passu* with the other creditors, but the personal representatives cannot exercise the right of retainer because there was never a time when there were cross-obligations to pay in full.[41]

Beneficiary an infant. As a general rule, an infant (*i.e.* a person who is under 18 years of age[42]) cannot give a valid receipt for money or securities to which he is entitled as a beneficiary under a will[43] or intestacy, and neither can his parents,[44] guardian,[45] or adult spouse on his behalf.

(1) *Receipt by married infant for income.* The first exception to this general rule is statutory. Under section 21 of the Law of Property Act

---

[36] *Re Binns* [1929] 1 Ch. 677, *secus* in the case of an advancement to T's deceased child because an advancement is a payment on account of that child's share, at pp. 682–685; *Re Bruce* [1908] 2 Ch. 682.

[37] *Courtenay* v. *Williams* (1844) 3 Hare 539, affirmed (1846) 15 L.J.Ch. 204 (debt still exists though remedy by action barred); *Re Akerman* [1891] 3 Ch. 212.

[38] *Re Watson* [1896] 1 Ch. 925; *Re Melton* [1918] 1 Ch. 37; *Re Lennard* [1934] Ch. 235.

[39] *Stammers* v. *Elliott* (1868) 3 Ch.App. 195.

[40] *Re Watson, supra,* at p. 933; *Re Sewell* [1909] 1 Ch. 806 (composition in bankruptcy).

[41] *Cherry* v. *Boultbee* (1839) 4 My. & Cr. 442 ("there never was a time at which the same person was entitled to receive the legacy and liable to pay the entire debt"); *Re Hodgson* (1878) 9 Ch.D. 673.

[42] Family Law Reform Act 1969, s.1(1) and (2). See *Re Hellmann's Will* (1866) L.R. 2 Eq. 363 (legacy may be paid when infant comes of age according to English law or law of domicil, whichever first happens) and *Re Schnapper* [1928] Ch. 420; and see Dicey and Morris, *The Conflict of Laws* (11th ed., 1987), p. 1011.

[43] *Harvell* v. *Foster* [1954] 2 Q.B. 367, 377 and 383.

[44] *Dagley* v. *Tolferry* (1715) 1 P.Wms. 285 (£100 legacy to B, an infant, paid to B's father: executor held liable to pay legacy again to B's trustee in bankruptcy); *Rotheram* v. *Fanshaw* (1748) 3 Atk. 628, 629.

[45] *Re Cresswell* (1881) 45 L.T. 468.

1925 a married infant has power to give valid receipts for all income (but not capital) to which the infant is entitled, including statutory accumulations of income made during the minority.[46]

(2) *Provision in will.* The testator may by his will authorise payment of a legacy or share of residue to an infant beneficiary at a fixed age (*e.g.* at 17 years of age) or on marriage, or (alternatively) direct that the receipt of an infant beneficiary who has attained a fixed age or married shall be a good discharge. If personal representatives make a payment pursuant to such a provision in the will, they get a good discharge notwithstanding the infancy of the beneficiary.[47] Under such a provision personal representatives have a discretion (which they may surrender to the court) to decide whether in all the circumstances payment would be for the infant's benefit.[48]

(3) *Appointment of trustees.* Instead of making a gift by will direct to an infant, a testator may (and often does) make the gift to one or more trustees upon trust for the infant; in that case the receipt of the trustees is a good discharge to the personal representatives because the trustees are the persons entitled to the gift under the will.[49]

If, under the will (if any) of the deceased, the gift is not made to trustees for the infant, the personal representatives have power under section 42(1) of the Administration of Estates Act 1925 to appoint a trust corporation or two or more individuals not exceeding four (whether or not including one or more of the personal representatives) to be the trustee or trustees of the property for the infant. Section 42(1) applies whenever the deceased died. However, this power is only exercisable where the infant is *absolutely* entitled under the will or on intestacy to a devise, or legacy, or to the residue of the estate or any share therein. Thus the power cannot be exercised where the infant is only contingently entitled under the will or the intestacy rules. It follows that, if the deceased died intestate, the power can only be exercised (i) if the infant is absolutely entitled as the deceased's surviving spouse, or (ii) if there is no preceding life interest and the infant has married, so as to become absolutely entitled under the statutory trusts.[50] If, pursuant to section 42(1), personal representatives duly appoint trustees and vest the infant's property in them, the personal representatives, as such, are discharged from all further liability in respect of that property.[51] Henceforth each of the personal representatives is only liable, as a trustee, if he was appointed one of the trustees of the infant's property. If personal representatives have power to appoint trustees under section 42(1) (the

[46] See Trustee Act 1925, s.31(2)(i).
[47] *Re Somech* [1957] Ch. 165.
[48] *Ibid.*
[49] *Cooper* v. *Thornton* (1790) 3 Bro.C.C. 96 (legacy of £100 given to X to be divided between himself and his family: held X took the legacy as trustee and payment to X discharged the executor).
[50] *Re Yerburgh* [1928] W.N. 208; *Re Wilks* [1935] Ch. 645, 650: see also *Re Kehr* [1952] Ch. 26 (s.42 applies where infant absolutely entitled under intestacy rules of deceased's German domicil). For the statutory trusts see *ante*, p. 90.
[51] Administration of Estates Act 1925, s.42(1); see *Harvell* v. *Foster* [1954] 2 Q.B. 367, 384 (this case is discussed *ante*, p. 198).

infant being absolutely entitled), but the personal representatives do not do so, they remain liable to the infant in their capacity of personal representatives.[52]

(4) *Payment into court.* Personal representatives may pay money or securities to which an infant is entitled into court; the receipt or certificate of the proper officer is a sufficient discharge to the personal representatives.[53] However, since 1925 payment into court is seldom necessary because (as is explained below) personal representatives now have a wide power of appropriation under section 41 of the Administration of Estates Act 1925.

(5) *Maintenance and advancement.* Finally, personal representatives may make payments of income or capital for the benefit of an infant pursuant to any express power contained in the testator's will, the statutory powers of maintenance and advancement,[54] or any order made by the court.[55]

B. Appropriation

Prior to 1926 a personal representative had no adequate power to appropriate assets so as to be entitled (for instance) to make an appropriation to satisfy a vested pecuniary legacy given to an infant. Such an appropriation was not binding on the infant because he was not competent to consent to it.[56] Since 1925 a personal representative has a wide power of appropriation under section 41 of the Administration of Estates Act 1925. The section applies whenever the deceased died.[57] If a personal representative exercises this power, two main consequences follow:

(i) henceforth the beneficiary's interest is in the appropriated assets—if they increase in value he gets the benefit, but if they diminish in value he bears the loss[58]; and

(ii) the appropriation clears the other assets for distribution to the other beneficiaries. For instance, if the personal representative duly appropriates assets so as to satisfy a pecuniary legacy given to an infant, and distributes the residuary estate, the residuary beneficiaries are discharged from any liability to the infant.

---

[52] *Harvell* v. *Foster, supra.*

[53] Trustee Act 1925, ss.63 and 68(1)(17): see R.S.C., Ord. 92, r. 2.

[54] Trustee Act 1925, ss.31, 32, and 68(1)(17) (s.31 as amended by Family Law Reform Act 1969, s.1(3) and (4), Sched. 1, Pt. 1 and Sched. 3 para. 5(1)); Administration of Estates Act 1925, s.47(1)(ii).

[55] See generally Snell's *Principles of Equity* (28th ed., 1982), pp. 272 *et seq.*

[56] *Re Salomons* [1920] 1 Ch. 290 (before 1926 advisable to pay infant's legacy into court or obtain order of court approving appropriation in an administration action). Land Transfer Act 1897, s.4 gave a power of appropriation, but s.4 was never put into effective operation as the power to prescribe provisions for valuation was never implemented.

[57] s.41(9).

[58] *Ballard* v. *Marsden* (1880) 14 Ch.D. 374, 376; *Re Richardson* [1896] 1 Ch. 512; *Re Marquis of Abergavenny's Estate Act Trusts* [1981] 1 W.L.R. 843, 846.

Statutory power of appropriation. Section 41 applies whether the deceased died testate or intestate.[59] Under the section the personal representative may appropriate any part of the deceased's real or personal estate,[60] in its actual condition at the time of appropriation, in or towards satisfaction of any legacy or any other interest or share in the deceased's property, whether settled or not. However, an appropriation must not affect prejudicially any specific devise or bequest[61]; accordingly, the subject matter of an effective specific devise or bequest must not be appropriated in satisfaction of a general legacy or a share of residue. Apart from this, the power of appropriation is exercisable in such manner as to the personal representative may seem just and reasonable, according to the respective rights of the persons interested in the deceased's property.

(1) *When consent required.* Whether the personal representative needs the consent of any person to the appropriation depends on which of the following three alternatives is applicable.

(a) BENEFICIARY ABSOLUTELY ENTITLED. If the appropriation is made for the benefit of a person absolutely and beneficially entitled in possession, the consent of that person is required.[62] Thus, a beneficiary who is absolutely entitled to an immediate legacy of £1,000 may insist on payment in cash, and refuse to take company shares comprised in the deceased's estate in satisfaction of his legacy. If the beneficiary is an infant, the consent may be given on his behalf by his parents, guardian, or, if there is no guardian, by the court.[63]

(b) SETTLED INTEREST. An appropriation may be made in or towards satisfaction of a settled legacy, share or interest; *i.e.* any legacy, share or interest to which a person is not absolutely entitled in possession at the date of appropriation.[64] This includes, for example, a contingent or deferred legacy.

If the appropriation is made in respect of any settled legacy, share or interest, the consent of either the trustee thereof, if any (not being the personal representative), or the person who may for the time being be

[59] s.41(9).

[60] Including property over which a testator exercises a general power of appointment, including the statutory power to dispose of entailed interests, s.41(9).

[61] s.41(1), proviso (i).

[62] s.41(1), proviso (ii). At common law executors may appropriate to one of themselves, *Re Richardson* [1896] 1 Ch. 512, and an administrator may appropriate to himself, *Barclay v. Owen* (1889) 60 L.T. 220.

[63] ss.41(1), proviso (ii) and (1A) and 55(1)(iv), as amended by County Courts Act 1984, s.148(1) and Sched. 2, para. 13; if the beneficiary is mentally incapable see s.41(1), provisos (ii) and (iv) as amended by Mental Health Act 1959, s.149(1) and Sched. 7, Pt. I and Mental Health Act 1983, s.148(1) and Sched. 4, para. 7. An infant surviving spouse may require, or consent to, the appropriation of the matrimonial home comprised in an intestate's residuary estate, see Intestates' Estates Act 1952, Sched. 2, para. 6(2); if the surviving spouse is mentally incapable see para. 6(1).

[64] s.41(8). This includes an annuity; s.41(9) authorises the setting apart of a fund to answer an annuity by means of the income of that fund or otherwise—presumably an appropriation under s.41 with the annuitant's consent clears the other assets for distribution to the other beneficiaries: *cf.* the effect of an appropriation not made under s.41, *ante*, p. 303.

entitled to the income is required.[65] Again, the consent of an infant may be given on his behalf.[66] Apart from the consent of the trustee, no consent is required on behalf of any person not yet born, or who cannot be found or ascertained at the time of appropriation.[67]

(c) NO CONSENT REQUIRED. No consent to the appropriation is required if, independently of the personal representative, there is no trustee of a settled legacy, share or interest, and no person of full age and capacity entitled to the income thereof. However, in this case the appropriation must be of an investment authorised by law or by the deceased's will,[68] whereas under heads (a) and (b) above this is not necessary.[69]

(2) *Protection of non-consenting persons.* In making the appropriation, the personal representative must have regard to the rights of any person not yet born, or who cannot be found or ascertained, and of any other person whose consent is not required (*e.g.* a person entitled in remainder to a settled legacy).[70] An appropriation duly made binds all the persons interested in the deceased's property whose consent is not required.[71]

(3) *Valuation.* An appropriation is made at the value of the appropriated assets as at the date of the appropriation, and not as at the deceased's death.[72] For example, if company shares comprised in the deceased's estate are appropriated by the personal representative with the legatee's consent towards satisfaction of a general legacy of £1,000, the value of the company shares must be ascertained as at the date of the appropriation; if at that date their value is £800, the appropriation satisfies the legacy to the extent of £800—the appropriation has the same effect as a payment of £800 in cash to the legatee.[73]

For the purpose of appropriation the personal representative may ascertain and fix the value of the respective parts of the deceased's estate (and of the deceased's liabilities) as he may think fit, and for this purpose the personal representative must employ a duly qualified valuer where this is necessary.[74] The personal representative may also make any conveyance which may be requisite for giving effect to the appropriation,[75] For instance, in the above example, the personal representative may execute a transfer of the company shares to the legatee so that he may be registered as owner.

[65] s.41(1), proviso (ii).
[66] See *supra*, n. 63.
[67] s.41(1), proviso (iii).
[68] s.41(1), proviso (v).
[69] s.41(1), proviso (ii) and s.41(2); but if the beneficiary is mentally incapable see s.41(1), proviso (iv).
[70] s.41(5).
[71] s.41(4). For the protection of a purchaser of land from a person to whom it has been appropriated see ss.41(7) and (8) and 55(1)(xix).
[72] *Re Charteris* [1917] 2 Ch. 379, 386; *Re Collins* [1975] 1 W.L.R. 309 ("a rule of administration too well established to require further discussion").
[73] The same result follows from an appropriation towards satisfaction of a share of residue, *Re Gollin's Declaration of Trust* [1969] 1 W.L.R. 1858.
[74] s.41(3): *cf. Re Bythway* (1911) 104 L.T. 411 (executrix not entitled to appropriate to herself unquoted company shares at her own valuation).
[75] ss.41(3) and 55(1)(iii).

Express power in will. Section 41 does not prejudice any other power of appropriation conferred by law[76] or by the deceased's will. A testator by his will often confers on his personal representatives an express power to appropriate without the necessity of obtaining the consent of any person, or (alternatively) provides that the statutory power of appropriation shall be exercisable without any of the consents made requisite by section 41.[77] If the consents are dispensed with in this way, no *ad valorem* stamp duty is payable in respect of the appropriation.[78]

C. ASSENTS

Right of beneficiary during administration. What is the true status of a beneficiary under a will or intestacy during the administration of the deceased's estate?

(1) *No equitable interest in unadministered assets.* As a general rule, a beneficiary under a will or intestacy has no legal or equitable proprietary interest in the unadministered assets of the deceased's estate.[79] The entire ownership of the unadministered assets is in the deceased's personal representative. Whatever property comes to a personal representative by virtue of his office comes to him "in full ownership without distinction between legal and equitable interests. The whole property [is] his."[80] The personal representative holds this property for the purpose of carrying out the administration of the deceased's estate. Of course, equity imposes on him fiduciary duties (sometimes called "trusts"), *e.g.* to get in the estate, to preserve the assets, to deal properly with them, and to apply them in due course of administration for the benefit of creditors and beneficiaries.[81] But equity does not treat the unadministered assets as if they constituted a trust fund held upon trust for the beneficiaries. For equity to have done so—

> "would have been in plain conflict with the basic conception of equity that to impose the fetters of a trust upon property, with the resulting creation of equitable interests in that property, there had to be specific subjects identifiable as the trust fund. An unadministered estate was incapable of satisfying this requirement . . . until administration was complete no one was in a position to say what items of

[76] See Law of Property Act 1925, s.28(3) and (4) (power to partition land held in undivided shares) and Administration of Estates Act 1925, s.39(1); Trustee Act 1925, s.15(*b*) (power to sever and apportion blended trust funds or property): as to the common law power of appropriation see *Re Lepine* [1892] 1 Ch. 210; *Re Beverley* [1901] 1 Ch. 681.

[77] See the Statutory Will Forms 1925, Form 6.

[78] *Jopling* v. *I.R.C.* [1940] 2 K.B. 282 (stocks and shares appropriated to satisfy legacy of £5,000: held *ad valorem* stamp duty payable on transfers): but no stamp duty is claimed in respect of an appropriation in satisfaction of a share of a testator's residue.

[79] *Commissioner of Stamp Duties (Queensland)* v. *Livingston* [1965] A.C. 694 (gift of share of all real and residuary personal estate: the judgment of the P.C. analyses the case law); *Lord Sudeley* v. *Att.-Gen.* [1897] A.C. 11 (gift of share of residuary real and personal estate); *Dr. Barnardo's Homes National Incorporated Association* v. *Commissioners for Special Purposes of the Income Tax Acts* [1921] 2 A.C. 1 (gift of residuary estate); *Eastbourne Mutual B.S.* v. *Hastings Corporation* [1965] 1 W.L.R. 861 (interest as sole next-of-kin on intestacy).

[80] *Commissioner of Stamp Duties (Queensland)* v. *Livingston, supra,* at p. 707.

[81] *Ibid.* at p. 707: see also *Re Hayes' W.T.* [1971] 1 W.L.R. 758, 764–765.

property would need to be realised for the purposes of that administration or of what the residue, when ascertained, would consist or
what its value would be."[82]

(2) *Beneficiary has a chose in action to ensure due administration.* The
true status of a beneficiary under a will or intestacy is that he has a
chose in action to have the deceased's estate properly administered.[83]
He may, for instance, bring an action to have the estate administered by
the court, or for some other less sweeping remedy.[84] His remedies are
considered in Chapter 14.

This chose in action is transmissible by the beneficiary. In *Re Leigh's
Will Trusts*[85] T by her will made a specific gift to B of "all shares which I
hold and any other interest . . . which I may have" in S Ltd. T never had
any shares or other interest in S Ltd., but, both at the date of her will
and her death, she was the sole administratrix and sole beneficiary of
the unadministered estate of her husband, who had died intestate. His
estate included some shares in, and a debt due from, S Ltd. Buckley J.
held that the specific gift to B was effective. T could not tie the hands of
the new administrator of her husband's estate, but she could transmit to
her executors her chose in action to ensure due administration. As sole
beneficiary, T also had a right to require the new administrator to
administer the husband's estate in any manner T (or her executors)
might require, consistent with the rights of anyone else against the
estate. T, by making this specific gift by her will, had imposed a duty on
her executors to exercise this right, so as to ensure so far as possible that
the shares and the debt became available to satisfy the specific gift.

(3) *Specific gift by will.* There may be a single exception to the general
rule that the entire ownership of the unadministered assets is in the
deceased's personal representative. It has been said that a beneficiary
entitled under a specific bequest or devise takes an equitable interest in
the subject matter of the gift at the death of the testator,[86] though the
legal estate vests in the personal representative, who may, of course,
resort to the property for payment of the deceased's expenses, debts and
liabilities. However, this exception appears to be of doubtful validity as
it is not consistent with the principle that "whatever property came to
the executor *virtute officii* came to him in full ownership, without distinction between legal and equitable interests. The whole property was
his."[87] It may well be that, until a personal representative assents to a
specific gift, the specific legatee or devisee (like any other beneficiary)

[82] *Ibid.* at p. 708.
[83] *Ibid.* at p. 717.
[84] A pecuniary or residuary legatee (or a creditor) may follow and recover assets
improperly abstracted from the estate, but he does so on behalf of the estate, so that the
assets are restored to the estate for use in due course of administration; the remedy
"asserts the estate's right of property, not the property right of creditor or legatee," *ibid.* at
pp. 713–714. For this remedy see *post*, p. 408.
[85] [1970] Ch. 277: see P.V.B. (1970) 86 L.Q.R. 20.
[86] I.R.C. v. *Hawley* [1928] 1 K.B. 578, 583, *Re Neeld* [1962] Ch. 643, 687–688 and 691: see
also *Williams* v. *Holland* [1965] 1 W.L.R. 739, 743–744; *Re K* [1986] Ch. 180, 188.
[87] *Commissioner of Stamp Duties (Queensland)* v. *Livingston* [1965] A.C. 694, 707 and see
p. 712: see *Kavanagh* v. *Best* [1971] N.I. 89, 93–94.

has, during the period of administration, only a chose in action to have the deceased's estate properly administered.[88]

Assent in respect of pure personalty. At common law, an assent by a personal representative merely indicates that he does not require certain property of the testator for purposes of administration and that the property may pass under the testator's will.

(1) *Subject matter of assent.* Originally the common law power to assent applied to bequests of leaseholds, as well as of pure personalty, and it was extended to devises of realty by the Land Transfer Act 1897.[89] However, section 36 of the Administration of Estates Act 1925 introduced different provisions which are applicable to an assent to the vesting of an estate or interest in land, whether freehold or leasehold. Assents in respect of land are considered later. The Administration of Estates Act 1925 did not affect the common law power to assent in respect of pure personalty and this is considered first.

At common law an executor[90] (and probably an administrator[91]) may assent in respect of any gift of pure personalty by will, whether the gift is specific, general, or residuary. It is said that an administrator cannot assent in respect of pure personalty which passes on intestacy, though there appears to be no case law authority for this.[92]

(2) *Form of assent.* At common law an assent is not required to be (and in practice seldom is) made in writing. It may be made expressly (*e.g.* by a few informal words spoken by the executor[93]), or it may be implied from the conduct of the executor. Whether there has been an assent is generally a question of fact.[94] A useful instance of the implication of an assent is the case of *Attenborough* v. *Solomon*,[95] which has already been considered.[96] In that case T by his will appointed X and Y to be executors and trustees and gave his residuary estate to X and Y upon trust for sale and distribution as directed by the will. Within one year of T's death X and Y paid all his debts and expenses and legacies. Fourteen years after T's death X pledged certain silver plate comprised in the residuary estate. The House of Lords held that long before the date of the pledge X and Y had assented to the dispositions of the will taking effect, so that at the date of the pledge X and Y held the residuary estate

[88] *Re Hayes' W.T.* [1971] 1 W.L.R. 758, 764 (*per* Ungoed-Thomas J., "no legatee, devisee or next-of-kin has any beneficial interests in the assets being administered").
[89] s.3 (not applicable to copyholds, s.1(4)).
[90] An assent by one executor binds the other executors, even where the bequest is to himself, *Townson* v. *Tickell* (1819) 3 B. & Ald. 31, 40; see *ante*, pp. 232 *et seq.*
[91] *i.e.* an administrator with the will annexed: see Williams, *Law Relating to Assents* (1947), p. 96 citing *Gundry* v. *Brown* (1678) Rep. *temp.* Finch 370.
[92] See Williams, *op. cit.* pp. 4 and 122–123; *cf.* Garner (1964) 28 Conv.(N.S.) 298, 300–301.
[93] *Doe* d. *Sturges* v. *Tatchell* (1832) 3 B. & Ad. 675; *Barnard* v. *Pumfrett* (1841) 5 My. & Cr. 63, 70.
[94] *I.R.C.* v. *Smith* [1930] 1 K.B. 713 (an outstanding mortgage does not necessarily prevent inference of an assent to a residuary gift): an assent to a gift of a life interest operates as an assent to the gift in remainder (and vice versa), *Stevenson* v. *Mayor of Liverpool* (1874) L.R. 10 Q.B. 81. See generally Williams, *op. cit.* pp. 102 *et seq.*
[95] [1913] A.C. 76: see also *Wise* v. *Whitburn* [1924] 1 Ch. 460.
[96] *Ante*, p. 234.

(including the plate) as trustees, and not as executors, and therefore X had no power to make a valid pledge because trustees must always act jointly. As Lord Haldane put it, as soon as an executor "has assented, and this he may do informally and the assent may be inferred from his conduct, the dispositions of the will become operative."[97] He inferred from the facts (including the form of the estate accounts) that, within one year of T's death, X and Y considered that they had done all that was required of them as executors and were content that the dispositions of the will should take effect. This inference was strengthened by the lapse of time since then, during which X and Y had done nothing as executors.

(3) *Effect of assent.* An assent indicates that the executor does not require certain property for administration purposes and that the property may pass under the testator's will. The assent in effect activates the gift of the property by the testator's will. "The will becomes operative so far as its dispositions of personalty are concerned only if and when the executor assents to those dispositions."[98] If the property is given by the will to the executor himself, either beneficially or as trustee, after he has assented to the gift the property is vested in him as beneficiary or trustee (as the case may be), and not as personal representative.

Moreover, in the case of a specific legacy, but not a general legacy or a residuary bequest, three other consequences follow from an assent:

(i) After the executor has assented to a specific legacy, the legatee may bring an action at common law to recover possession of the subject matter of the legacy from the executor[99] or a third party.[1] A beneficiary cannot enforce his claim to a general legacy,[2] or a share of residue, or his rights on intestacy,[3] by an action at common law. However, even in the case of a specific legacy, the *legal* title to the subject matter may not be capable of assignment by an assent. For instance, company shares are only transferable in the manner provided by the articles of the company,[4] *i.e.* by entering the name of the transferee in the register of members of the company.[5] After an executor has assented to a specific legacy of company shares, he holds the shares as trustee for the legatee until the legal title is duly transferred to the legatee.[6]

(ii) An assent to a specific legacy relates back to the death of the testator and the legatee becomes entitled to the income or profits accruing from its subject matter since the testator's death. In *Re*

---

[97] [1913] A.C. 76, 83.
[98] *Ibid.* at p. 82.
[99] *Doe d. Lord Saye and Sele* v. *Guy* (1802) 3 East. 120; *Re Culverhouse* [1896] 2 Ch. 251; *Re West* [1909] 2 Ch. 180, 185.
[1] *Stevenson* v. *Mayor of Liverpool* (1874) L.R. 10 Q.B. 81; *Re West* [1909] 2 Ch. 180.
[2] *Deeks* v. *Strutt* (1794) 5 T.R. 690.
[3] *Jones* v. *Tanner* (1827) 7 B. & C. 542.
[4] Companies Act 1985, s.182(1).
[5] See, *ibid.* s.183(1) and (3).
[6] *Re Grosvenor* [1916] 2 Ch. 375, 378.

West[7] T by a codicil gave a specific legacy of certain company shares to A and T's executors transferred these shares to A. Some years after T's death a later codicil was found; by this later codicil T revoked the previous codicil and gave a specific legacy of these shares to B. Swinfen Eady J. held that, when the executors assented to this legacy, B became entitled to these shares as from T's death and also to the dividends accruing from them since T's death. B could therefore recover the shares and these dividends from A.

(iii) After an executor has assented to a specific legacy, the costs of transferring its subject matter to the legatee must be borne by the legatee.[8] Thus, a specific legatee of jewellery and china must bear the costs incurred in packing and delivering these articles to her,[9] and a specific legatee of company shares must bear the costs of transferring the shares to him.[10] A testator may, of course, exclude this rule by a direction in his will that the costs of transferring the subject matter of a specific legacy shall be paid out of his residuary estate.[11]

Assent in respect of land. Section 36(1) of the Administration of Estates Act 1925 confers power on a personal representative to "assent to the vesting, in any person who (whether by devise, bequest, devolution, appropriation or otherwise) may be entitled thereto, either beneficially or as a trustee or personal representative, of any estate or interest" in land, whether freehold or leasehold.[12] Section 36 applies to any assent (or conveyance) made after 1925, whenever the testator or intestate died.[13]

This statutory power to assent in respect of land may be exercised by any personal representative,[14] whether the deceased died testate or intestate. The reference in section 36(1) to an assent in favour of a person entitled by "devolution" covers the case of a beneficiary entitled under the intestacy rules. Again, an assent may be made in favour of a personal representative of a beneficiary who is entitled under the deceased's will or intestacy but who dies before distribution, or (alternatively) who predeceased the deceased but nevertheless takes

---

[7] [1909] 2 Ch. 180: see also *I.R.C.* v. *Hawley* [1928] 1 K.B. 578 and *cf. Dr. Barnado's Homes National Incorporated Association* v. *Commissioners for Special Purposes of the Income Tax Acts* [1921] 2 A.C. 1, 8 and 11 (an assent to a residuary bequest does not relate back to death).

[8] *Re Grosvenor* [1916] 2 Ch. 375 (assent to specific legacies of company shares: held costs of transfer to be borne by legatees); *Re Sivewright* [1922] W.N. 338: *Re Leech* [1923] 1 Ch. 161. As to specific gifts of foreign assets see *Re Fitzpatrick* [1952] Ch. 86 and authorities cited.

[9] *Re Sivewright, supra; Re Leach, supra.*

[10] *Re Grosvenor, supra.*

[11] Such a direction may extend to expenses incurred by the personal representative in the upkeep and preservation of the subject matter of a specific legacy, see *ante*, p. 300.

[12] Administration of Estates Act 1925, s.55(1)(xix).

[13] *Ibid.* s.36(12).

[14] *Ibid.* s.55(1)(xi) provides that "personal representative" means the executor, original or by representation, or administrator for the time being of the deceased. All the personal representatives (still living) to whom a grant has been made in respect of the land must concur in an assent, ss.2(2) and 24, and see *ante*, p. 233.

under the deceased's will under an exception to the doctrine of lapse.[15] The reference to a person "otherwise" entitled apparently authorises an assent in favour of a purchaser, at any rate if the assent carries out a contract for sale made by the deceased in his lifetime, though *ad valorem* stamp duty is payable on such an assent.[16] It remains uncertain whether section 36(1) authorises an assent in favour of a purchaser from a beneficiary.[17]

(1) *Subject matter of assent.* The statutory power to assent applies to any estate or interest in freehold or leasehold land "to which the testator or intestate was entitled . . . and which devolved upon the personal representative."[18] The question what land devolves upon a personal representative on a death after 1925 has already been considered; the land devolving includes land appointed by the deceased in his will under a general power of appointment, and an entailed interest in land, provided it has been barred by and passes under a gift contained in the deceased's will.[19]

It follows that the statutory power to assent is not applicable to land which is conveyed to the personal representative after the death of the deceased, because the land did not devolve upon the personal representative.[20] In this case the personal representative should convey the land to the person entitled by a deed under seal.

(2) *Form of assent.* An assent to the vesting of an equitable interest in land is not required to be made in writing. A personal representative may assent orally, or impliedly by his conduct, to the vesting of an equitable interest in land.[21] However, the rule is different for an assent to the vesting of a legal estate in land, with respect to which section 36(4) provides as follows:

> "An assent to the vesting of a legal estate shall be in writing, signed by the personal representative, and shall name the person in whose favour it is given and shall operate to vest in that person the legal estate to which it relates; and an assent not in writing or not in favour of a named person shall not be effectual to pass a legal estate."

Apart from this provision, no particular form of assent is prescribed except in the case of registered land.[22]

Plainly an assent by a personal representative to the vesting of a legal estate in land in *another person* (whether beneficially, or as a trustee, or as a personal representative of another deceased person) must be made

---

[15] *Ante,* pp. 340 *et seq.*
[16] *G.H.R. Co. Ltd.* v. *I.R.C.* [1943] K.B. 303.
[17] See Williams, *op. cit.* pp. 13 *et seq.*
[18] Administration of Estates Act 1925, s.36(1).
[19] *Ibid.* ss.1(1), 3, 36(1) and 55(1)(xix): see *ante,* pp. 209 *et seq.*
[20] *Re Stirrup's Contract* [1961] 1 W.L.R. 449 (assent under seal took effect as conveyance): but see Elphinstone (1961) 25 Conv.(N.S.) 490.
[21] *Re Edwards' W.T.* [1982] Ch. 30, 40 (W owned Blackacre and died intestate, leaving H solely entitled; H obtained letters of administration and occupied Blackacre for 20 years until H died; no assent in writing by H in his own favour: held H had assented by his conduct to vesting of equitable interest in himself, so that it passed to H's executors).
[22] See Land Registration Act 1925, s.41(4); Land Registration Rules 1925, r. 170 and Sched., Forms 56 and 57.

in signed writing, and the person in whose favour the assent is given must be named in the assent. If an assent does not comply with this rule, it is not effectual to pass the legal estate.

Does the same rule apply to an assent by a personal representative to the vesting of a legal estate in land in *himself* (whether beneficially, or as a trustee, or as a personal representative of another deceased)? In *Re King's Will Trusts*[23] Pennycuick J. held that the same rule applies. In that case T by her will appointed A and B to be executors and trustees and made a specific devise of Blackacre to them upon trust. A and B obtained probate, A died, and B appointed X to be a trustee of the will. B then died, and B's executor C became executor by representation of T. X appointed Y to be a trustee of the will, and X then died. None of them, A, B or C, ever made any written assent to the vesting of the legal estate in Blackacre.[24] Pennycuick J. held that the legal estate in Blackacre was still vested in C as executor by representation of T, and he rejected the argument that, prior to the appointment of X, the legal estate had become vested in B in his capacity as trustee. Pennycuick J. pointed out that a written assent by a personal representative in favour of himself in some other capacity is an everyday occurrence in conveyancing practice, and, referring to section 36(4), he continued:

"The first sentence of subsection (4) [up to the semi-colon], accordingly contemplates that for this purpose a person may by assent vest in himself in another capacity, and such vesting, of course, necessarily implies he is divesting himself of the estate in his original capacity. It seems to me impossible to regard the same operation as lying outside the negative provision contained in the second sentence of the subsection. To do so involves making a distinction between the operation of divesting and vesting a legal estate and that of passing the legal estate. I do not think that this highly artificial distinction is legitimate. On the contrary, the second sentence appears to me to be intended as an exact counterpart to the first."

This construction of section 36(4) has been criticised on the ground that a legal estate does not "pass" if a personal representative merely assents in his own favour, so as to alter the capacity in which he holds the legal estate; accordingly it is argued that such an assent need not be in writing, but can be made orally or impliedly by conduct.[25] However, the construction adopted by Pennycuick J. seems to accord both with the wording and the object of section 36(4). The first sentence of section 36(4) lays down a rule applicable to any assent to the vesting of a legal estate, including an assent by a personal representative in his own favour; the second sentence of section 36(4) sets out the consequences if this rule is disregarded and does not create an exception to this rule.[26]

---

[23] [1964] Ch. 542: see *Re Edward's W.T., supra,* at pp. 33 and 40; *Beebe* v. *Mason* (1980) 254 E.G. 987.

[24] Pennycuick J. held that the deed of appointment by which B appointed X to be a trustee did not constitute a written assent satisfying s.36(4), *ibid.* at pp. 548–549.

[25] For criticisms see Barnsley, *Conveyancing Law and Practice* (2nd ed., 1982), pp. 332–334; Garner (1964) 28 Conv.(N.S.) 298; R. R. A. Walker (1964) 80 L.Q.R. 328. See also Farrand, *Contract and Conveyance* (2nd ed., 1973), pp. 111 *et seq.* (analysing the previous meagre case law).

[26] Ryder (1976) 29 C.L.P. 60, 63.

Moreover, even if the criticism is justified and the decision in *Re King's Will Trusts* is overruled at some future date, a signed written assent by a personal representative in his own favour (whether beneficially, or as a trustee, or as a personal representative of another deceased) will still remain highly desirable, so as to provide documentary evidence of the title to the legal estate.

The person in whose favour an assent (or conveyance) of a legal estate is made by a personal representative may (and should for his own protection) require that notice of it be written on, or endorsed on, or permanently annexed to, the probate or letters of administration at the cost of the deceased's estate; he may also require that the probate or letters of administration be produced to prove that this has been done.[27] This provision protects him against the possibility that the personal representative may execute another assent or conveyance in respect of the same property.[28]

The question whether a personal representative can cease to hold property in that capacity and start to hold it in the capacity of trustee *without any assent or conveyance in his own favour* is considered later in this chapter.[29]

(3) *Effect of assent.* An assent in respect of land is a form of conveyance.[30] Section 36(4) provides that an assent to the vesting of a legal estate in land shall operate to vest the legal estate in the person named in whose favour it is given.[31] On the other hand, an assent in respect of pure personalty activates the gift of the property by the testator's will, so that the property passes under the will and not under the assent.

Section 36 regulates the effect of an assent in respect of land as follows:

  (i) An assent relates back to the death of the deceased unless a contrary intention appears.[32] As has been noted already, at common law only an assent to a specific legacy relates back to the death of the testator.

  (ii) Section 36(7) provides that an assent or conveyance by a personal representative in respect of a legal estate is, in favour of a purchaser for money or money's worth,[33] "sufficient evidence that the person in whose favour the assent or conveyance is given or made is the person entitled to have the legal estate conveyed to him and upon the proper trusts, if any." The purchaser is protected in this way unless notice of a previous assent or conveyance affecting that legal estate has been placed on or annexed to the probate or administration. It follows that if T's personal representatives assent to the vesting of a legal estate in Blackacre

[27] Administration of Estates Act 1925, s.36(5).
[28] *Ibid.* s.36(6) and (7): see *ante,* pp. 222–224.
[29] *Post,* pp. 382–383.
[30] See Law of Property Act 1925, s.52. The statutory covenants for title may be implied in an assent, Administration of Estates Act 1925, s.36(3) and Law of Property Act 1925, s.76(1)(F) and Sched. 2, Pt. VI.
[31] See also s.36(2), which also applies to an assent to the vesting of an equitable interest.
[32] *Ibid.*
[33] *Ibid.* s.36(11): see *ante,* p. 221, n. 4.

in V, and V subsequently sells to P, the assent is sufficient evidence that V was entitled to the legal estate, and P is not concerned (or entitled) to investigate whether V really was entitled to the legal estate under T's will or intestacy. But an assent is only "sufficient," and not conclusive, evidence. In *Re Duce and Boots Cash Chemists (Southern) Ltd.'s Contract*[34] the assent to X by T's executor contained a recital which showed that Blackacre was settled land under T's will, and ought to have been vested in the tenant for life and not in X. Bennett J. said that the effect of section 36(7) is that "a purchaser when investigating title may safely accept [an assent] as evidence that the person in whose favour it has been made was the person entitled to have the legal estate conveyed to him unless and until, upon a proper investigation by a purchaser of his vendor's title, facts come to the purchaser's knowledge which indicate the contrary. When that happens, in my judgment, the . . . assent cannot be and ought not to be accepted as sufficient evidence of something which the purchaser has reason to believe is contrary to the fact, still less so when, as in the present case, he knows it to be contrary to the fact."[35] Accordingly Bennett J. decided that the purchaser was entitled to object to the title.

(iii) Normally, an assent made in signed writing requires no stamp duty,[36] and an assent made under seal no longer requires a 50p deed stamp.[37] If any assent or conveyance is made for value it must be stamped *ad valorem*.[38]

As already explained, after an executor has assented to a specific legacy of pure personalty the costs of transferring its subject matter to the legatee must be borne by the legatee. Probably the costs of an assent to the vesting of freehold or leasehold land in a specific devisee or legatee are payable as a testamentary expense, and do not have to be borne by the devisee or legatee,[39] though the costs of a vesting assent by personal representatives under the Settled Land Act 1925 fall on the settled property.[40]

(4) *Protection of personal representative.* A personal representative has power to give an assent subject to any legal estate or charge by way of legal mortgage,[41] *e.g.* an assent in respect of the deceased's house subject to a mortgage or charge securing the deceased's debt to a building society.[42] As a condition of giving an assent or making a conveyance, a personal representative may require security for the discharge of any

---

[34] [1937] Ch. 642.
[35] *Ibid.* at p. 650.
[36] Administration of Estates Act 1925, s.36(11); *Kemp* v. *I.R.C.* [1905] 1 K.B. 581: see also Settled Land Act 1925, s.14(2).
[37] Finance Act 1985, s.85(1) and Sched. 24.
[38] *G.H.R. Co. Ltd.* v. *I.R.C.* [1943] K.B. 303; *Jopling* v. *I.R.C.* [1940] 2 K.B. 282.
[39] Williams, *op. cit.* p. 44.
[40] Settled Land Act 1925, s.8(2).
[41] Administration of Estates Act 1925, s.36(10): *Williams* v. *Holland* [1965] 1 W.L.R. 739, 743–744.
[42] See *ibid.* s.35 which is discussed *ante*, pp. 274 *et seq.*

duties, debt, or liability to which the property is subject.[43] An instance is unpaid inheritance tax, payable in respect of the testator's death, to which his freehold house is subject under a direction in the will.[44] In order to protect himself the personal representative needs to insist on proper security being given for the discharge of this tax before he assents to the vesting of the house in the person entitled. If the personal representative fails to do so, he runs the risk of having to pay this tax without necessarily having an effective remedy to indemnify himself.[45] However, an assent or conveyance by the personal representative does not, except in favour of a purchaser of a legal estate for money or money's worth, prejudice the right of the personal representative to be indemnified out of the property against any such duties, debt or liability.[46]

(5) *Compelling the personal representative to assent.* The personal representative is not entitled to postpone the giving of an assent merely by reason of the subsistence of any such duties, debt or liability if reasonable arrangements have been made for discharging them.[47] Thus the devisee of the testator's freehold house may call for an assent to be made in his favour, though inheritance tax in respect of the house still has to be paid, if reasonable arrangements have been made for discharging it. If the personal representative refuses to assent, the devisee may apply to the court for directions under section 43(2) of the Administration of Estates Act 1925.

Under section 43(2) any person who, as against the personal representative, claims possession of land which devolved on the personal representative, or an assent or conveyance in respect of it, or to be registered as proprietor of it under the Land Registration Act 1925, may apply to the court for directions, and the court may make such vesting or other order as may be deemed proper. But such a person is not entitled to require the personal representative to execute an assent in his favour before the end of the executor's year.[48] Moreover, even after the executor's year has ended, the personal representative may still be justified in refusing to execute an assent, *e.g.* he may need to sell the property in order to apply the proceeds of sale in payment of the deceased's expenses, debts and liabilities,[49] or there may be doubt as to the construction of the gift of the property by the deceased's will.[50]

[43] *Ibid.* s. 36(10). See also Settled Land Act 1925, s.8(3) and (6).
[44] *Ante,* p. 282.
[45] *Cf. Re Rosenthal* [1972] 1 W.L.R. 1273 (specific devise of house to S; house transferred to S without any security for discharge of unpaid estate duty on it; S sold the house, went to live abroad, and failed to pay duty: held trustees not entitled to recoup duty falling on house out of residue, but must bear it themselves).
[46] Or, except in favour of a purchaser of a legal estate for money or money's worth, the right of the personal representative to recover the property, *ibid.* s.36(9) and (11): for the right to follow the property see s.38 and *post,* p. 408. For the definition of purchaser see s.55(1)(xviii): see also *Re Lander* [1951] Ch. 546, 551–552.
[47] *Ibid.* s.36(10).
[48] *Re Neeld* [1962] Ch. 643, 688; *cf.* Administration of Estates Act 1925, s.44 which is expressed to be "subject to the foregoing provisions of this Act."
[49] See *Williams* v. *Holland* [1965] 1 W.L.R. 739.
[50] *Re Neeld, supra,* at pp. 688–689.

D. Personal Representative or Trustee?

Personal representative holds office for life. After a grant of representation has been made to him, a person holds the office of personal representative for the whole of his life,[51] unless the grant was of limited duration,[52] or he is subsequently removed from office.[53] Though a personal representative has fully administered the deceased's estate, he retains the capacity to represent the estate in any future legal proceedings,[54] or to recover any assets which fall into the deceased's estate on the subsequent death of a testator, whose gift by will to the deceased takes effect under an exception to the doctrine of lapse.[55]

A personal representative continues to hold office as such, though he no longer holds any property in that capacity. To consider the situation where T by his will appoints X and Y to be the executors and trustees of his will, and gives all his property to X and Y upon trust for sale and, subject to the payment of his expenses, debts and liabilities, to hold the net proceeds of sale and any of his property for the time being unsold, and all the investments respectively representing the same, in trust for his widow W for life, and after her death for his son S absolutely. At T's death the entire ownership of T's property vests in X and Y in their capacity as executors,[56] and during the administration of T's estate W and S are entitled to a chose in action to have T's estate properly administered.[57] X and Y become the trustees of T's will at T's death,[58] but during the administration of T's estate X and Y hold T's property in their capacity as executors, and not as trustees. After T's death X and Y obtain probate, pay all T's expenses, debts and liabilities, and immediately assent to the vesting of T's property in themselves. As already explained, an assent to the vesting of a legal estate in land must be made in signed writing; an assent in respect of pure personalty or an equitable interest in land is not required to be made in writing.[59] After making this assent X and Y hold T's property in their capacity as trustees, and the beneficiaries W and S are each entitled to equitable interests in the trust property.[60] X and Y still remain the executors of T's estate, though they no longer hold any property in that capacity.

Distinctions between personal representative and trustee. Broadly speaking, the function of a personal representative is to wind up a deceased's estate, whereas the function of a trustee is to hold property on trust. Despite this basic difference in function, in many respects the

---

[51] *Attenborough* v. *Solomon* [1913] A.C. 76, 83; *Harvell* v. *Foster* [1954] 2 Q.B. 367, 383.

[52] *e.g.* a grant of letters of administration (with the will annexed) for the use and benefit of a minor, who was appointed executor: the grant terminates when the minor attains 18 years of age or dies.

[53] *Ante,* pp. 202 *et seq.*

[54] *Harvell* v. *Foster, supra.*

[55] *Ante,* pp. 340 *et seq.*

[56] *Attenborough* v. *Solomon* [1913] A.C. 76, 82–83; Administration of Estates Act 1925, ss.1(1) and 3.

[57] *Ante,* p. 369.

[58] And X and Y may therefore appoint new trustees of T's will before X and Y make any assent, *Re King's Will Trusts* [1964] Ch. 542: see also *Re Hobson* [1929] 1 Ch. 300.

[59] *Ante,* pp. 370 and 372.

[60] *Attenborough* v. *Solomon, supra.* at pp. 82–86.

office of personal representative resembles that of a trustee. Indeed the fiduciary duties of a personal representative are sometimes called "trusts."[61] Again, the provisions of the Trustee Act 1925 apply to a personal representative where the context admits.[62] Moreover, as the Court of Appeal pointed out in *Harvell* v. *Foster*,[63] even

> "the Administration of Estates Act 1925 (the title of which is not without significance), includes in Part III (headed 'Administration of Assets') section 33, which provides that the estate of an intestate is vested in the personal representative 'upon trust' for sale, calling in and conversion, . . . and . . . Part IV of the same Act, being the part devoted to the devolution of the estates of persons dying intestate and headed 'Distribution of Residuary Estate' is expressed throughout in terms of trusts."

In the case of a partial intestacy, section 49 of the Act even provides that the personal representative "shall, subject to his rights and powers for the purposes of administration, be a trustee" for the persons entitled under the intestacy rules.

However, the rules applicable to personal representatives do differ in certain respects from the rules applicable to trustees. These differences may make it essential to decide whether persons, who were both personal representatives and trustees, were at the relevant time holding the property in question in their capacity of personal representatives or in their capacity of trustees. The following are instances where the rules differ:

(1) *Several authority of executors.* Joint executors, and perhaps joint administrators, have joint *and several* authority (subject to important exceptions), whereas trustees must always act jointly. This difference (which was crucial in the case of *Attenborough* v. *Solomon*) has already been considered.[64]

(2) *Receipt of sole personal representative.* A sole personal representative, acting as such, may give a valid receipt for, or direct the application of, the proceeds of sale of land.[65] A sole trustee may not do so, unless the sole trustee is a trust corporation.[66]

(3) *Personal representative's duty is to the estate.* A trustee "has a duty to hold the balance evenly between the beneficiaries to whom the property belongs and for whom the trustee holds it."[67] On the other hand, a personal representative's duty during the administration of the deceased's estate is to consider the interest of the estate as a whole. Even when a personal representative is carrying out his duty to

---

[61] *Commissioner of Stamp Duties (Queensland)* v. *Livingston* [1965] A.C. 694, 707: see *ante*, p. 368.
[62] Trustee Act 1925, s.68(1)(17); see also s.69(1).
[63] [1954] 2 Q.B. 367, 380.
[64] *Ante*, pp. 234 and 370.
[65] Law of Property Act 1925, s.27(2) as amended by Law of Property (Amendment) Act 1926, Sched.
[66] *Ibid.*; Settled Land Act 1925, s.18(1); Trustee Act 1925, s.14.
[67] *Re Hayes' W.T.* [1971] 1 W.L.R. 758, 764.

distribute the net assets to the persons entitled, he is not concerned with the conflicting interests of beneficiaries under any trust declared in the will, but only with the trustee of that trust, who is the person entitled under the will; and this is so even if the personal representative is himself the trustee of that trust.[68]

In *Re Hayes' Will Trusts*[69] T by his will appointed P, Q, R and S to be the executors and trustees of his will, devised Blackacre to them upon certain trusts, and conferred on them power to sell Blackacre to S at its estate duty valuation. During the administration of T's estate the executors agreed the estate duty valuation with the district valuer, and then contracted to sell Blackacre to S at this agreed valuation. Ungoed-Thomas J. said that their power to agree a valuation was a "purely personal representative administration power."[70] In agreeing the estate duty valuation, the executors were not under a duty to hold the balance evenly between S (who benefited from a low valuation) and the other beneficiaries (who benefited from a high valuation); their duty as executors was to consider the interest of the estate as a whole.

(4) *Death of sole representative.* If a sole (or last surviving) personal representative dies without having fully administered the deceased's estate, and there is no chain of representation through proving executors, a grant of administration *de bonis non* is made in respect of the deceased's unadministered estate, so as to enable the administration of the estate to be completed.[71] But if at his death the deceased held property as a sole (or last surviving) trustee, the property devolves on the trustees's personal representatives.[72] This makes it essential to decide whether at his death the deceased held the relevant property in his capacity as a personal representative or as a trustee.

(5) *Surety's guarantee.* A surety's guarantee covers a breach by an administrator of his duties as administrator, but not of his duties as a trustee. This difference (and the decision in *Harvell* v. *Foster*) has already been explained.[73]

(6) *Limitation period applicable.* In general, the period of limitation in respect of any claim to the personal estate of a deceased,[74] or in respect of an action to recover any land of a deceased,[75] whether under a will or intestacy, is 12 years, whereas the period of limitation for an action by a beneficiary to recover trust property, or in respect of any breach of trust, is six years.[76]

---

[68] *Ibid.* at p. 765.
[69] *Supra:* see also *Re Charteris* [1917] 2 Ch. 379.
[70] *Supra,* at p. 764.
[71] *Ante,* p. 180.
[72] *Ante,* pp. 209 *et seq.*
[73] *Ante,* p. 198.
[74] Limitation Act 1980, s.22 (but the period of limitation for an action to recover arrears of interest on a legacy is six years): no limit applies in case of fraud or property retained or converted to his own use by the personal representative, s.21(1) and (2). For limitation see *post,* pp. 392 *et seq.*
[75] *Ibid.* s.15(1) and (6) and Sched. 1, para. 2.
[76] *Ibid.* s.21(3): again no limit applies in case of fraud or property retained or converted to his own use by the trustee, s.21(1) and (2).

Transition from personal representative to trustee. Three different situations need consideration.

(1) *Personal representative not a trustee under the will.* In general, a personal representative does not become a trustee of property which T by a gift in his will (whether specific, general or residuary) gives to B absolutely, without creating any trust for B by his will. In that case it is the duty of the personal representative (acting as such) to distribute the property to B.[77] Thus, if T by his will gave his residuary estate by a direct gift to B absolutely (without creating any trust for B), and the personal representative has paid the deceased's expenses, debts and legacies (or, as it is sometimes put, has cleared the estate), the personal representative still remains liable for the residue in his capacity as personal representative, and does not become a trustee in the proper sense.[78]

If B, to whom T makes a direct gift by his will, is an infant, so that immediate distribution is impossible, it is the duty of the personal representative (acting as such) to retain the property in trust for B and to transfer it to B after he attains full age. In *Harvell* v. *Foster*[79] T by his will gave all his estate to his daughter absolutely and appointed her sole executrix. At T's death she was an infant, and letters of administration with the will annexed were granted to her husband for her use and benefit until she should attain full age. After T's debts and expenses had been paid the husband disappeared with most of the assets. The Court of Appeal, in giving judgment, said that—

"the duty of an administrator, as such, must at least extend to paying the funeral and testamentary expenses and debts and legacies (if any) and where, as here, immediate distribution is impossible owing to the infancy of the person beneficially entitled, retaining the net residue in trust for the infant. At least until the administrator can show that he has done this, it cannot, in our judgment, be said of him that he has duly administered the estate according to law."[80]

Moreover the Court of Appeal said that the administrator remains liable for the net residue in his capacity of personal representative until he transfers it to the infant after she has attained full age.[81] The administrator retains the net residue "in trust" for the infant in his capacity as personal representative, and he does not thereby become a trustee in the proper sense.[82]

Again, in general, a personal representative does not become a

---

[77] See *Re Richardson* [1920] 1 Ch. 423 (gift of residuary estate to B); *Re Mackay* [1906] 1 Ch. 25; *Re Barker* [1892] 2 Ch. 491 (postponed legacy): and *cf. Re Oliver* [1927] 2 Ch. 323. But an executor who has assented to a specific legacy of company shares holds the shares as trustee for the legatee until the legal title is duly transferred to the legatee, *Re Grosvenor* [1916] 2 Ch. 375 and see *ante*, p. 371.

[78] *Re Mackay, supra,* at pp. 30–31; *Harvell* v. *Foster* [1954] 2 Q.B. 367.

[79] *Supra* (this case is also discussed *ante*, p. 198): see also *Re Davis* [1891] 3 Ch. 119; *Re Mackay, supra.*

[80] *Ibid.* at p. 383.

[81] *Ibid.* at p. 384. Alternatively the personal representative may appoint trustees for the infant under s.42(1) of the Administration of Estates Act 1925, see *ante*, p. 364.

[82] *Re Davis, supra,* at p. 124 (*per* Lindley L.J.—"an executor was always in a loose sense a trustee for creditors and legatees").

trustee of property which T by a gift in his will gives to other persons X and Y upon trust. In that case it is the duty of the personal representative (acting as such) to distribute the property to X and Y. The claim of the beneficiaries under the trust is against X and Y if they fail to recover from the personal representative the property which is properly distributable to X and Y under T's will.[83]

(2) *Personal representative a trustee under the will.* A personal representative becomes a trustee of property under T's will because:

   (i) a trust of that property is created by the will (often the trust is for beneficiaries taking successive interests in the property under the will[84]); and

   (ii) the personal representative is appointed to be a trustee of the property by the will or (alternatively) no effective appointment of any other trustee of the property is made by the will.[85]

When a personal representative assents in his own favour as trustee, he changes his capacity from personal representative to trustee. The decision of the House of Lords in *Attenborough* v. *Solomon*[86] is a classic instance of this occurring in a case where T by his will appointed X and Y to be executors and trustees, and gave his residuary estate to X and Y upon trust for sale and distribution as directed by the will. The same principle applies where T by his will makes a specific gift of property on trust,[87] or a gift of a general legacy on trust. In *Phillipo* v. *Munnings*[88] T by his will appointed X his executor and gave a general legacy of £400 to X upon trust to invest and apply the income for the maintenance of Y until he attained 24 years of age and then upon other trusts. X paid T's expenses and debts, and set apart and invested the sum of £400 out of T's estate. The court held that, when X appropriated this sum, he ceased to hold it as executor and thereafter held it as trustee. The appropriation had the same effect as if T by his will had given the legacy to a different person as trustee, and X had paid the legacy to that person.

The question arises whether a personal representative may cease to hold property in that capacity, and start to hold it in the capacity of trustee of the will, without any assent or conveyance in his own favour.[89] There is some case law authority for the principle that, as soon as a personal representative has cleared the estate by discharging all the

---

[83] *Re Oliver* [1927] 2 Ch. 323, 330–331. For the effect of an assent to a specific legacy of company shares see *ante*, n. 77.

[84] *Phillipo* v. *Munnings* (1837) 2 My. & Cr. 309 (£400 legacy held on trust); *Re Swain* [1891] 3 Ch. 233 (residue held on trust); *Re Timmis* [1902] 1 Ch. 176; *Re Oliver* [1927] 2 Ch. 323 (£2,000 legacy held on trust). See also *Re Claremont* [1923] 2 K.B. 718 (trust to sell residuary personalty and apply proceeds for benefit of T's two nieces): Law of Property Act 1925, s.34(3) (gift of land to tenants in common operates as gift to trustees of will for purposes of Settled Land Act 1925, or to personal representatives, upon the statutory trusts).

[85] *Re Cockburn's W.T.* [1957] Ch. 438.

[86] [1913] A.C. 76: see *ante*, p. 370.

[87] *Wise* v. *Whitburn* [1924] 1 Ch. 460 ("the effect of the assent was to strip the executors of their title as executors and to clothe them with a title as trustees"); *Dix* v. *Burford* (1854) 19 Beav. 409.

[88] (1837) 2 My. & Cr. 309: see also *Clegg* v. *Rowland* (1866) L.R. 3 Eq. 368, 372–373; *O'Reilly* v. *Walsh* (1872) 6 I.R.Eq. 555, 7 I.R.Eq. 167.

[89] See generally Ryder (1976) 29 C.L.P. 60; Stebbings [1984] Conv. 423.

deceased's expenses, debts and liabilities, and legacies, he automatically begins to hold the residuary estate as a trustee on the trusts declared by the will. In *Re Cockburn's Will Trusts*[90] Danckwerts J. felt "no doubt about the matter at all. Whether persons are executors or administrators, once they have completed the administration in due course, they become trustees holding for the beneficiaries either on an intestacy, or under the terms of the will, and are bound to carry out the duties of trustees. . . . "

However, the principle that a personal representative may change his capacity from personal representative to trustee without any assent or conveyance in his own favour cannot be regarded as settled law. Apart from the cases of *Re Ponder*[91] and *Re Yerburgh*,[92] which are mentioned later because both relate to an intestacy, the other cases usually cited in support of this principle (*i.e. Eaton* v. *Daines*,[93] *Re Pitt*,[94] and *Re Cockburn's Will Trusts*[95]) were all decisions on whether personal representatives had power to appoint new trustees of the will. In each of these cases the personal representatives may already have assented in their own favour by their conduct[96]: indeed, the fact that the personal representatives had cleared the estate was evidence of such an assent and the reports of these cases do not state that there had been no assent. Moreover, there is some authority against this principle. In *Attenborough* v. *Solomon* Lord Haldane said that "the will becomes operative so far as its dispositions of personalty are concerned only if and when the executor assents to those dispositions."[97]

In the present state of the authorities it is not safe to assume that personal representatives, who have cleared the estate, cease to hold land comprised in the testator's residuary estate in their capacity of personal representatives, and start to hold the land in their capacity as trustees, though they have made no written assent or conveyance in their own favour.[98] In order to put their change of capacity beyond doubt, personal representatives should make a written assent in their own favour as trustees.

(3) *Intestacy*. The decision in *Re Ponder*[99] concerned the estate of X, who died intestate in 1919, leaving a widow and two infant sons. His

[90] [1957] Ch. 438, 439.
[91] [1921] 2 Ch. 59.
[92] [1928] W.N. 208.
[93] [1894] W.N. 32.
[94] (1928) 44 T.L.R. 371 (T died in 1917; administratrix cleared the estate and in 1927 appointed trustees of the will in her place: held appointment valid).
[95] [1957] Ch. 438, [1957] 2 All E.R. 522 (T died in 1947; administrators cleared the estate and made partial distribution to a residuary beneficiary: held administrators had power to appoint new trustees of the will).
[96] Assuming (as is probable) that an administrator with the will annexed may assent at common law, see *ante*, p. 370. In *Re Cockburn's W.T.*, *supra*, the property included land as well as pure personalty (as reported in [1957] 2 All E.R. 522), but the administrators may at least have assented in respect of pure personalty.
[97] [1913] A.C. 76, 82–83: see also *Re Trollope's W T* [1927] 1 Ch 596, 605.
[98] In *Re King's W.T.* [1964] Ch. 542 (which was considered *ante*, p. 374) the devise was specific: see Ryder, *loc. cit.* pp. 71–73.
[99] [1921] 2 Ch. 59.

widow obtained letters of administration, paid his expenses and debts, and invested each son's share of X's personalty in her name. Sargant J. held that the widow had ceased to hold these assets as administratrix and instead held them as a trustee; it followed that the court had jurisdiction to appoint the Public Trustee to be a trustee of these assets jointly with the widow. If this decision was good law, it involved the implication that the administratrix had become a trustee, though the pre-1926 intestacy rules applicable to personalty did not declare any trust for the next of kin. However, it seems doubtful whether the case was rightly decided. Probably the widow held these assets as administratrix in trust for the sons.[1] She had a duty as administratrix to distribute each son's share to him when he attained full age, and she was not a trustee of these assets so as to be entitled (for instance) to appoint new trustees in place of herself and retire from the trust.

As has been pointed out already, the provisions of the Administration of Estates Act 1925 applicable on a death intestate after 1925 do refer to personal representatives holding on trust.[2] Two questions therefore arise:

   (i) do personal representatives ever become trustees in the proper sense under these provisions, so as to be entitled (for instance) to appoint new trustees in their place and retire from the trust?[3] and

   (ii) if so, do the personal representatives automatically cease to hold the deceased's estate in that capacity, and start to hold it as trustees, as soon as they have cleared the estate?

The case law is meagre. In *Re Yerburgh*[4] X died intestate in 1926, leaving a widow and two infant children. His administrators cleared the estate and applied to the court for directions. Romer J. is reported as saying—

"that s.33 of the Administration of Estates Act had imposed certain duties on legal personal representatives under which they became trustees when the estate had been fully administered. They ceased to be legal personal representatives and became trustees at a particular date . . . the old law applied and determined the time when [they] ceased to be legal personal representatives and became trustees for sale. At the moment when that event happened they ought to make a vesting assent under s.36, vesting the property in themselves as trustees."

This brief judgment answers "yes" to the first question,[5] but the answer of Romer J. to the second question is not clear. Did Romer J. mean that

---

[1] See *Harvell* v. *Foster* [1954] 2 Q.B. 367, 379–380 and 382–384: *cf. Re Cockburn's W.T.* [1957] Ch. 438, 440. As to realty of an intestate who died before 1926, see *Re Ponder, supra,* and *Toates* v. *Toates* [1926] 2 K.B. 30.

[2] *Ante,* p. 379.

[3] Under Trustee Act 1925, s.36(1).

[4] [1928] W.N. 208: see also *Re Cockburn's W.T., supra,* at p. 439.

[5] But see *Re Trollope's W.T.* [1927] 1 Ch. 596, 603–605 (on the effect of Administration of Estates Act 1925, s.39); *Harvell* v. *Foster* [1954] 2 Q.B. 367, 384 (on the effect of s.42(1) where an infant is absolutely entitled); *Re Wilks* [1935] Ch. 645, 650–651.

an assent was *desirable* to evidence an automatic change in capacity, or (alternatively) was *essential* to effect the change in capacity? Perhaps the only safe conclusion to draw is that more case law is needed on both these questions.

CHAPTER 14

REMEDIES

A. LIABILITY OF PERSONAL REPRESENTATIVE

Devastavit. If a personal representative commits any breach of the duties of his office, causing a loss of assets, he is said to commit a *devastavit*, *i.e.* a wasting of the assets of the deceased's estate. A personal representative is personally liable to the deceased's creditors and beneficiaries for any loss caused by his *devastavit*.

(1) *Nature of a devastavit*. Occasionally the duties of the office of personal representative are termed "trusts"[1] and a breach of those duties is referred to as a "breach of trust."[2] The will of the testator may contain a gift of his residuary estate to his executors "upon trust" to carry out one or more of those duties, *e.g.* to pay the testator's expenses and debts. However, it is sometimes essential to distinguish between a *devastavit* and a breach of any trust created by the testator's will. For instance, a personal representative by virtue of his office has a duty to pay the debts of the deceased with due diligence, having regard to the assets in his hands which are properly applicable for that purpose. This duty may be modified by the testator's will as against the beneficiaries, but not as against the creditors.[3] If the personal representative commits a breach of this duty, he is liable to the creditors for any loss suffered by them as a result of his *devastavit*, irrespective of his liability under any trust or power contained in the testator's will.

The following are instances of a breach by a personal representative of the duties of his office, which, if it causes loss to the deceased's creditors or beneficiaries, renders the personal representative personally liable for a *devastavit*:

(i) any breach by a personal representative of his duty to collect and get in the deceased's estate with reasonable diligence, *e.g.* undue delay in commencing an action against a debtor of the deceased, which enables the debtor to escape payment by pleading limitation[4];

(ii) any breach of his duty to take reasonable care in preserving the deceased's estate[5];

(iii) any breach of his duty to deal properly with the assets of the

---

[1] *Commissioner of Stamp Duties (Queensland)* v. *Livingston* [1965] A.C. 694, 707.
[2] *Re Marsden* (1884) 26 Ch.D. 783.
[3] *Re Tankard* [1942] Ch. 69, 72 and 74: see *ante*, p. 258.
[4] *Hayward* v. *Kinsey* (1701) 12 Mod.Rep. 568, 573: see *ante* p. 214.
[5] *Ante*, pp. 217–218.

deceased's estate, *e.g.* improperly converting the assets to his own use[6];

  (iv) any breach of his duty to pay the debts of the deceased with due diligence, *e.g.* failing to pay a debt, though he has assets in hand properly applicable for that purpose[7];

   (v) any breach of his duty to protect the estate against unenforceable claims, *e.g.* paying a debt which he need not pay[8];

  (vi) any breach of his duty to administer the deceased's estate, if it is insolvent, in accordance with the statutory rules as to the payment of debts, *e.g.* failing to observe the order of priority of debts[9]; and

 (vii) any breach of his duty to distribute the estate to the persons properly entitled under the deceased's will or intestacy.[10]

(2) *Devolution of personal representative's liability for a devastavit.* If a personal representative commits a *devastavit*, and dies, his liability for the *devastavit* devolves on his personal representative to the extent of his available assets.[11]

(3) *Effect of acquiescence in devastavit.* If a creditor or beneficiary acquiesced in a *devastavit*, the personal representative is not, in general, liable to him. The same principle applies if a person acquiesced in a breach of trust.[12] The onus of proving acquiescence in the *devastavit* lies on the personal representative.[13] In order to satisfy this onus, the personal representative must show that the creditor or beneficiary acquiesced in the *devastavit* with full knowledge of all the facts.[14] However, there is no hard and fast rule that he must also have had knowledge of the legal consequences of those facts; the court considers all the circumstances of the acquiescence in order to decide whether it is fair and equitable for him to succeed against the personal representative for his *devastavit*.[15]

Acquiescence by one creditor or beneficiary does not affect the rights of any other person who has not acquiesced. If the personal representative is liable for his *devastavit* to any other person, then, under section 62 of the Trustee Act 1925,[16] the court may, in its discretion, impound all or any part of the interest of a beneficiary who has instigated,

---

[6] *Marsden* v. *Regan* [1954] 1 W.L.R. 423 (executrix gave away the deceased's furniture: held a *devastavit*).

[7] *Ante,* p. 257.

[8] *Re Rownson* (1885) 29 Ch.D. 358, 363–364; *Midgley* v. *Midgley* [1893] 3 Ch. 282, 284, 299 and 304: for payment of statute-barred debts see *ante,* p. 263.

[9] *Ante,* pp. 292–293.

[10] *Hilliard* v. *Fulford* (1876) 4 Ch.D. 389: see *ante,* p. 359.

[11] Administration of Estates Act 1925, s.29: s.29 also applies to an executor *de son tort* who commits a *devastavit*: see *post,* p. 410.

[12] *Fletcher* v. *Collis* [1905] 2 Ch. 24: see generally Snell's *Principles of Equity* (28th ed., 1982), pp. 292 *et seq.*

[13] *Re Marsden* (1884) 26 Ch.D. 783, 790.

[14] *Ibid.*

[15] *Holder* v. *Holder* [1968] Ch. 353, approving *Re Pauling's S.T. (No. 1)* [1962] 1 W.L.R. 86, 108 (affirmed [1964] Ch. 303); *Re Freeston's Charity* [1978] 1 W.L.R. 741, 754–755.

[16] As amended by Married Women (Restraint upon Anticipation) Act 1949, s.1(4) and Sched. 2.

requested,[17] or consented in writing to the breach of duty by the personal representative,[18] by way of indemnity to the personal representative. The court does not impound the interest of a beneficiary under this section unless the beneficiary knew the facts which rendered what he was instigating, requesting, or consenting to in writing, a breach of duty by the personal representative, though the beneficiary need not know that those facts amounted in law to a breach of duty.[19]

Liability to account. As already explained, a personal representative has a statutory duty to exhibit on oath a full inventory of the estate, and render an account of the administration of the estate, when required to do so by the court.[20] He must also keep clear and accurate accounts and permit the interested parties to inspect them free of charge.[21] By this means they may ascertain how the personal representative has carried out the administration.

But in equity the liability of the personal representative to account does not merely provide the interested parties with information as to how the personal representative has carried out the administration. It also provides a means of remedying many breaches of duty by a personal representative in the conduct of the administration. A personal representative may be ordered by the court to account in an administration action or (alternatively) in an action for specific relief.[22] A personal representative generally has to account for (1) his receipts and (2) his payments.

(1) *Accounting for receipts.* Under the form of order to account which is usually made against a personal representative (called an order for "a common account"), the personal representative must bring in an account showing the assets of the deceased's estate which he or his agent actually received. An executor, who owes a debt to the deceased's estate, is treated as having paid the debt to himself as executor, and he must therefore account for the amount of the debt as an asset of the estate which he received.[23] An administrator, who owes a debt to the deceased's estate, must account in the same way.[24]

---

[17] *Griffith* v. *Hughes* [1892] 3 Ch. 105 (the instigation or request may be oral).

[18] Trustee Act 1925, s.62 applies to a breach of the duties incident to the office of a personal representative, as well as to a breach of trust, s.68(1)(17). Apart from s.62, equity has jurisdiction to impound the interest of a beneficiary who instigated a breach of trust, to the extent to which he benefited by the breach, *Raby* v. *Ridehalgh* (1855) 7 De G.M. & G. 104.

[19] *Re Somerset* [1894] 1 Ch. 231, 270 and 274.

[20] Administration of Estates Act 1925, s.25, as amended by Administration of Estates Act 1971, s.9: for applications for an inventory and an account see *ante*, p. 216.

[21] *Freeman* v. *Fairlie* (1812) 3 Mer. 29, 43–44; *Ottley* v. *Gilby* (1845) 8 Beav. 602 (legatee entitled to inspect, but not to a copy of the accounts at the expense of the estate); *Re Bosworth* (1889) 58 L.J.Ch. 432.

[22] *Post*, pp. 396 *et seq.*

[23] *Ingle* v. *Richards (No. 2)* (1860) 28 Beav. 366 (debt which executor owed to T was asset in his hands, for which he must account as asset of T's estate); *Re Bourne* [1906] 1 Ch. 697; *Jenkins* v. *Jenkins* [1928] 2 K.B. 501; *Commissioner of Stamp Duties* v. *Bone* [1977] A.C. 511, 518.

[24] Administration of Estates Act 1925, s.21A (added by Limitation Amendment Act 1980, s.10 and amended by Limitation Act 1980, s.40(2) and Sched. 3): s.21A also applies to an executor by representation.

Sometimes a personal representative is ordered by the court to account upon the footing of wilful default, *i.e.* to account, not only for assets which he or his agent actually received, but also for assets which he would have received but for his own wilful default. In this context wilful default means a breach of duty by the personal representative which caused a loss of assets. The breach of duty may constitute a *devastavit*[25] or a breach of trust.[26] Wilful default does not require conscious wrongdoing by the personal representative.[27]

The personal representative may be ordered to account upon the footing of wilful default in respect of the whole estate or (alternatively) in respect of a particular asset or transaction. In *Re Tebbs*[28] the executors of T's will sold T's land to a company pursuant to an option to purchase conferred on the company by will. The sale was made four years after T's death at probate value of the land, instead of at its (higher) current market value as required by the option. This was a breach of trust by the executors. A residuary beneficiary sought an order against the executors for an account to be taken upon the footing of wilful default in respect of T's whole estate. The court ordered an account upon the footing of wilful default in respect of this land, but ordered a common account in respect of the rest of T's estate. As one act of wilful default (*i.e.* the breach of trust) had been proved, the court had jurisdiction to make an order for an account upon the footing of wilful default in respect of T's whole estate.[29] What test ought the court to apply in exercising its discretion whether to make such an order? Slade J. said that the test to apply was to ask, "is the past conduct of the trustees such as to give rise to a reasonable prima facie inference that other breaches of trust[30] not yet known to the plaintiff or the court have occurred?"[31] The evidence before the court did not give rise to such a prima facie inference, so as to justify a "roving inquiry"[32] by the taking of an account upon the footing of wilful default in respect of T's whole estate.

(2) *Accounting for payments.* The personal representative must discharge himself as regards the assets he received by showing that he dealt with them in due course of administration. For instance, he may show that he applied the assets in paying expenses and debts of the deceased which were properly payable by him, or that he distributed the assets pursuant to an order of the court. He can also discharge him-

---

[25] *Re Stevens* [1898] 1 Ch. 162.

[26] *Re Tebbs* [1976] 1 W.L.R. 924: see also *Re Wrightson* [1908] 1 Ch. 789, 799–800 (active breach of trust: no "roving inquiry" ordered to ascertain other breaches); *Bartlett* v. *Barclays Bank Trust Co. Ltd. (No. 2)* [1980] Ch. 515, 546 (wilful default means a "passive" as distinct from an "active" breach of trust): but surely an "active" breach, as much as a "passive" breach, may give rise to a reasonable prima facie inference that other breaches have occurred.

[27] *Bartlett* v. *Barclays Bank Trust Co. Ltd. (No. 2), supra*: see J. E. Stannard [1979] Conv. 345; *cf.* J. A. Andrews (1981) 1 Legal Studies 303, 310–311 and 322.

[28] *Supra.*

[29] *Sleight* v. *Lawson* (1857) 3 K. & J. 292; *Re Youngs* (1885) 30 Ch.D. 421, 431–432.

[30] Or *devastavits*: the test appears equally applicable whether the breaches of duty constitute breaches of trust or *devastavits*.

[31] *Ibid.* at p. 930. *Cf. Re Wrightson, supra,* and *Bartlett* v. *Barclays Bank Trust Co. Ltd., supra.*

[32] *Ibid.* at p. 929.

self by showing that the assets were lost in some way for which he is not responsible.[33] But if the personal representative has made a wrongful application of the assets, this is disallowed when the court takes the account of his payments.[34] For example, if it is found that the personal representative has paid £1,000 to a person as a creditor, who in fact was not a creditor of the deceased, this payment is disallowed and the personal representative must replace the £1,000 which he misapplied.[35]

Liability for co-representative. Under section 30(1) of the Trustee Act 1925, a personal representative is chargeable only for money and securities actually received by him notwithstanding his signing any receipt for the sake of conformity, and is answerable and accountable only for his own acts, receipts, neglects, or defaults, and not for those of any other personal representative "unless the same happens through his own wilful default."[36] This provision (and the decision in *Re Vickery*[37] on the meaning of wilful default) has already been considered in relation to the liability of a personal representative in case loss occurs following delegation to an agent. In all probability, this provision did not alter the established rules of equity relating to the liability of a personal representative for his co-representative.[38]

Under these rules of equity, an executor X is not vicariously liable for his co-executor Y if Y commits a *devastavit* or a breach of trust.[39] Nevertheless, X is fully liable for his own *devastavit* or breach of trust. To mention some instances of X's liability:

(i) X is liable for his own breach of "the duty of all executors to watch over, and, if necessary, to correct the conduct of each other."[40] Thus, in *Styles* v. *Guy*,[41] X was held liable for a *devastavit* because he failed to compel his co-executor Y to pay a debt which was due from Y to the testator T; six years after T's death Y became bankrupt and the debt was lost. X was not vicariously liable for Y's default, but the court held X was liable for his own *devastavit* and ordered him to pay the amount of Y's debt with interest from T's death.

(ii) X is liable for his own breach of the duty of executors to deal properly, and in the ordinary course of business, with the assets of the deceased's estate. To quote Lord Cottenham in *Terrell* v. *Matthews*,[42] "If money be required for the payment of debts or

---

[33] *Job* v. *Job* (1877) 6 Ch.D. 562; see *ante*, pp. 217–218. As to loss of assets in the hands of an agent see *ante*, pp. 237 *et seq.*

[34] *Re Stevens* [1898] 1 Ch. 162, 169–170 and 172.

[35] *Re Stuart* (1896) 74 L.T. 546, 547.

[36] s.30(1) applies to a personal representative, ss.68(1)(17) and 69(1).

[37] [1931] 1 Ch. 572; see *ante*, pp. 240 *et seq.*

[38] *Re Brier* (1884) 26 Ch.D. 238, 243 (discussed *ante*, pp. 240–241): *cf. Re Munton* [1927] 1 Ch. 262, 274–275. As to the effect of an express indemnity clause see *Mucklow* v. *Fuller* (1821) Jacob 198.

[39] *Hargthorpe* v. *Milforth* (1594) Cro.Eliz. 318; *Styles* v. *Guy* (1849) 1 Mac. & G. 422, 429 (*devastavit*); *Williams* v. *Nixon* (1840) 2 Beav. 472.

[40] *Styles* v. *Guy, supra* at p. 433.

[41] *Supra*; see also *Booth* v. *Booth* (1838) 1 Beav. 125 (liable as stood by, knowing cotrustee was committing a breach of trust); *Williams* v. *Nixon* (1840) 2 Beav. 472; *Candler* v. *Tillett* (1855) 22 Beav. 257.

[42] (1841) 1 Mac. & G. 433n., 434–435.

legacies, one executor is safe in joining in the sale of stock or other property, and permitting another executor to receive the proceeds for that purpose . . . [43]; but if he joins in such sales when the money is not required, and he had not reasonable grounds for believing that it was so required, he is liable for the money so received by his co-executor."[44] It follows that if X, in the ordinary course of business in administering the estate, hands over the sole control of certain assets to his co-executor Y, and X commits no breach of his duty to watch over Y's conduct, X is not liable for loss caused by Y's misappropriation of those assets.[45]

These rules of equity relating to the liability of an executor for his co-executor are also applicable to the liability of an administrator for his co-administrator.[46]

Defence of limitation. When is limitation a defence to a claim made against a personal representative by (1) a creditor of the deceased, and (2) a beneficiary under the deceased's will or intestacy?

(1) *Claim by creditor.* A personal representative may plead the defence of limitation to a claim by any person in respect of a cause of action which accrued during the lifetime of the deceased, in just the same way as the deceased might have done if he was still alive.[47] Time continues to run against the claimant during the interval between the death and the grant of representation to the deceased's estate.[48] Moreover, time still continues to run if the claimant becomes the executor or administrator of his debtor.[49]

(a) CHARGE BY WILL FOR PAYMENT OF DEBT. To consider the situation where T at his death owes a simple contract debt to C, and T by his will charges a particular asset of his estate with the payment of this debt. C's action against T's personal representative, if founded on the simple contract debt, is barred after six years from the date on which his cause of action accrued,[50] but C's action to enforce the charge (whether on real or personal property) is only barred after 12 years from the date when his right to receive the money accrued.[51] Accordingly, it may be important to decide whether T, in providing by his will for the payment of his debts, has merely directed their payment or has created a charge for their payment.

---

[43] *Terrell* v. *Matthews, supra.*
[44] *Chambers* v. *Minchin* (1802) 7 Ves. 186; *Shipbrook* v. *Hinchinbrook* (1810) 16 Ves. 477; *Underwood* v. *Stevens* (1816) 1 Mer. 712.
[45] *Re Gasquoine* [1894] 1 Ch. 470: *cf. Lowe* v. *Shields* [1902] 1 I.R. 320 and *Clough* v. *Bond* (1838) 3 My. & Cr. 490.
[46] *Lees* v. *Sanderson* (1830) 4 Sim. 28; *Clough* v. *Bond, supra,* at pp. 496–498.
[47] In general, a personal representative may, if he thinks fit, pay a statute-barred debt of the deceased, see *ante,* p. 263.
[48] *Rhodes* v. *Smethurst* (1838) 4 M. & W. 42, (1840) 6 M. & W. 351 ("if the statute begins to run it must continue to run"); *Boatwright* v. *Boatwright* (1873) 17 Eq. 71.
[49] *Bowring-Hanbury's Trustee* v. *Bowring-Hanbury* [1943] Ch. 104.
[50] Limitation Act 1980, s.5; *Barnes* v. *Glenton* [1899] 1 Q.B. 885. An action founded on a specialty debt is barred after 12 years, *ibid.* s.8.
[51] *Ibid.* s.20(1).

In *Scott* v. *Jones*[52] T by his will gave all his personal estate to his
executors for the payment of his debts. T died in 1816. The House of
Lords held that this direction did not amount to a trust or charge so as to
give C, who was a simple contract creditor of T, the benefit of any longer
period of limitation; at T's death his executors took T's personalty subject to a liability under the general law to pay T's debts, and this direction added nothing to that liability. Since 1925 no distinction is made
between realty and personalty in relation to liability for T's debts.[53]
Accordingly, since 1925, if T by his will gives all his real and personal
estate to his executors for the payment of his debts, this direction probably does not create any charge so as to give simple contract creditors
the benefit of a 12 year period of limitation.[54] The result may be the
same if T by his will gives all his real and personal estate to his executors upon trust for sale and to pay his debts out of the proceeds of sale.[55]

(b) DEVASTAVIT. If a personal representative commits a *devastavit* by
distributing assets without providing for payment of a debt, the creditor's action against the personal representative personally for the *devastavit* is barred after six years from the date of distribution.[56] The same
period of limitation applies where the creditor claims an account
against the personal representative so as to remedy his *devastavit*.[57]
Thus, a personal representative, who distributed assets more than six
years before the creditor commences an action against him for an
account, cannot be compelled to account for those assets.

(2) *Claim by beneficiary.* To turn to the defence of limitation to a claim
made by a beneficiary under the deceased's will or intestacy.

(a) PURE PERSONALTY. Section 22 of the Limitation Act 1980 provides
that:

  (i) "no action in respect of any claim to the personal estate[58] of a
      deceased person or to any share or interest in any such estate
      (whether under a will or on intestacy) shall be brought after the
      expiration of twelve years from the date on which the right to
      receive the share or interest accrued," and
 (ii) "no action to recover arrears of interest in respect of any legacy,
      or damages in respect of such arrears, shall be brought after the

---

[52] (1838) 4 Cl. & F. 382: see also *Freake* v. *Cranefeldt* (1838) 3 My. & Cr. 499. *Cf.* a pre-1926
direction to pay debts out of realty, which did create a charge, *Re Stephens* (1889) 43 Ch.D.
39; *Re Balls* [1909] 1 Ch. 791; *Re Raggi* [1913] 2 Ch. 206.
[53] *Ante*, p. 266.
[54] See generally Williams, Mortimer and Sunnucks, *Executors, Administrators and Probate* (1982), pp. 809–811.
[55] See *Scott* v. *Jones, supra,* at pp. 397–398: but *cf.* Williams, Mortimer and Sunnucks, *op.
cit.* p. 811, and Preston and Newsom, *Limitation of Actions* (3rd ed., 1953), pp. 180, 191.
[56] Limitation Act 1980, s.2: *Re Gale* (1883) 22 Ch.D. 820 (immaterial creditor receives
interest on his mortgage from beneficiaries after the *devastavit*); *Lacons* v. *Warmoll* [1907] 2
K.B. 350 (contingent debt); *Re Blow* [1914] 1 Ch. 233.
[57] Limitation Act 1980, s.23: see *Re Blow, supra; Re Lewis* [1939] Ch. 232: the defence of
limitation must be raised before the court directs the account to be taken, *Re Williams*
[1916] 2 Ch. 38.
[58] Personal estate excluding the deceased's leaseholds, Limitation Act 1980, s.38(1).

expiration of six years from the date on which the interest became due."

In all probability, the right of a legatee to receive an immediate general legacy accrues at the testator's death, though he cannot recover the legacy until the end of the executor's year; accordingly, the 12 years' limitation period runs from the testator's death,[59] at any rate if there are assets applicable for the payment of the legacy.[60] In the case of a residuary legatee under a will or a beneficiary entitled on intestacy, if an asset falls into the deceased's estate many years after his death, the 12 years' limitation period in respect of that asset runs from the date on which it came into the hands of the personal representative. Thus, a personal representative is always liable to account to such a beneficiary for assets which came into his hands within the last 12 years before the beneficiary brings an action against him.[61]

(b) LAND. An action by a beneficiary to recover any land is barred after the expiration of 12 years from the date on which his right of action accrued.[62] For this purpose land includes any legal estate or equitable interest in land, a rentcharge, and any interest in the proceeds of sale of land held upon trust for sale.[63]

(c) NO LIMITATION PERIOD APPLICABLE. There are two important exceptions to the rules so far considered applicable to a claim by a beneficiary to pure personalty or land. Under section 21(1) of the Limitation Act 1980[64] no period of limitation applies to an action by a beneficiary:

(i) in respect of any fraud,[65] or fraudulent breach of trust, or fraudulent breach of the duties incident to the office of a personal representative, to which the personal representative was a party or privy; or
(ii) to recover from the personal representative property or the proceeds thereof in his possession, or previously received by him and converted to his use.[66]

If either of these exceptions is applicable, so that no period of limitation

---

[59] *Waddell* v. *Harshaw* [1905] 1 Ir.R. 416; *Re Deeney* [1933] N.I. 80: the right to receive a contingent legacy accrues when the contingency is satisfied, *Rudd* v. *Rudd* [1895] 1 Ir.R. 15.
[60] *Re Ludlam* (1890) 63 L.T. 330, 332; *Bright* v. *Larcher* (1859) 27 Beav. 130 (on appeal, 4 De G. & J. 608).
[61] *Re Johnson* (1884) 29 Ch.D. 964 (next-of-kin entitled on intestacy held not barred in respect of reversionary interest which fell into deceased's estate within limitation period before action); *Adams* v. *Barry* (1845) 2 Coll. 285 (residuary legatee).
[62] Limitation Act 1980, s.15(1): see *ibid.* s.15(6) and Sched. 1, para. 2.
[63] *Ibid.* s.38(1); see also s.18(1).
[64] For definition of "trust" and "trustee" see Limitation Act 1980, s.38(1) and Trustee Act 1925, s.68(1)(17).
[65] *Re Sale Hotel and Botanical Gardens Co. Ltd.* (1897) 77 L.T. 681 (moral fraud not required), reversed on another point, (1898) 78 L.T. 368: *cf. Collings* v. *Wade* [1896] 1 Ir.R. 340 (fraud must amount to dishonesty).
[66] *Re Howlett* [1949] Ch. 768 (trustee, chargeable with occupation rent for his own use of trust property, is treated as still having it in his own pocket, and no period of limitation applies). see also *Re Timmis* [1902] 1 Ch. 176. If the personal representative, acting honestly and reasonably, has made a distribution to himself as beneficiary, his liability is limited to the excess over his proper share, Limitation Act 1980, s.21(2).

applies, the equitable doctrine of *laches*[67] may be available as a defence for the personal representative.

(3) *Extension of limitation period.* The disability of the claimant,[68] or fraud, concealment, or mistake[69] may extend or postpone the period of limitation. Again, if a personal representative acknowledges[70] the claim of a creditor to recover any debt or other liquidated money claim, or the claim of a beneficiary to the deceased's personal estate or any share or interest therein, the claimant's right of action is deemed to have accrued on the date of the acknowledgment.[71] In order to be effective, an acknowledgment must be made in signed writing by the personal representative (or his agent) to the claimant (or his agent).[72] Similarly, if a personal representative (or his agent) makes any payment to the claimant (or his agent) in respect of such a claim, the claimant's right of action is deemed to have accrued on the date of the payment.[73] An acknowledgment of, or payment in respect of, any claim to the deceased's personal estate or any share or interest therein by one of several personal representatives is binding on the deceased's estate[74] Any acknowledgment, or payment, makes the relevant period of limitation start to run afresh but cannot revive any right of action already barred by limitation.[75]

Power of court to grant relief from liability. Under section 61 of the Trustee Act 1925,[76] the court has power, in its discretion,[77] to relieve a personal representative either wholly or partly from personal liability for any breach of trust,[78] or any breach of the duties incident to the office of a personal representative, if it appears to the court that the personal representative:

(i) "has acted honestly and reasonably," and
(ii) "ought fairly[79] to be excused for the breach . . . and for omitting

---

[67] Limitation Act 1980, s.36(2); for *laches* see *Lindsay Petroleum Oil Co.* v. *Hurd* (1874) L.R. 5 P.C. 221, 239–240.

[68] Limitation Act 1980, ss.28, 38 (infancy or of unsound mind).

[69] *Ibid.* s.32.

[70] The personal representative must acknowledge an existing liability, *Re Flynn (No. 2)* [1969] 2 Ch. 403; *Bowring-Hanbury's Trustee* v. *Bowring-Hanbury* [1943] Ch. 104. For an acknowledgment in a will see *Howard* v. *Hennessey* [1947] Ir.R. 337.

[71] Limitation Act 1980, ss.29(5) and 38(9). As to an acknowledgment of the title of the person entitled to a right of action to recover land, see *ibid.* ss.29 and 31(1).

[72] *Ibid.* s.30: see *Bowring-Hanbury's Trustee* v. *Bowring-Hanbury, supra.*

[73] *Ibid.* ss.29(5), 30(2) and 38(9): as to payment of part of the interest due, see s.29(6).

[74] *Ibid.* s.31(8). As to an acknowledgment of, or payment in respect of, a debt by one of several personal representatives, see s.31(6), (7) and (9): *Re Macdonald* [1897] 2 Ch. 181 (on effect of Lord Tenterden's Act 1828, s.1, now repealed).

[75] *Ibid.* s.29(7).

[76] For definition of "trust" and "trustee" see Trustee Act 1925, s.68(1) (17): see *Re Kay* [1897] 2 Ch. 518; *Marsden* v. *Regan* [1954] 1 W.L.R. 423.

[77] *Marsden* v. *Regan, supra,* at p. 437 ("this matter of relief is essentially one for the judge in his discretion").

[78] *Re Rosenthal* [1972] 1 W.L.R. 1273 (s.61 does not apply to breach of trust merely contemplated by trustees).

[79] *Marsden* v. *Regan, supra,* at p. 434 ("in fairness to the executor and to other people who may be affected").

to obtain the directions of the court in the matter in which he committed such breach."

The onus of proving that he acted honestly and reasonably rests on the personal representative.[80] If this first requirement is made out, the court considers whether the personal representative ought fairly to be excused, looking at all the circumstances of the particular case.[81] One material circumstance is whether the personal representative is a trust company,[82] or a professional man,[83] undertaking the office in return for remuneration; if so, the court is less likely to grant relief to such a personal representative than to one who acts gratuitously.

Each case depends on its own particular circumstances, but it may be helpful to consider one instance where partial relief was granted. In *Re Kay*[84] T died in June, having by his will given an immediate legacy of £300, and a life interest in the remainder of his estate, to his widow. He left assets of £22,000, and debts believed to amount to not more than £100. His executor X, believing T's estate to be solvent with substantial assets, paid the £300 legacy to the widow, and allowed her to receive the income from the estate for her household expenses. In August, Y made a rather indefinite claim against T's estate for rents collected by T on Y's behalf. In November, X published the usual advertisements for creditors. In December, Y issued a writ claiming an account of these rents. X, being advised (wrongly) that there was a complete defence to this action, continued to allow the widow to receive the income until two years later, when the action came to trial, and ultimately Y obtained judgment against T's estate for more than £26,000. It followed that T's estate was insolvent and that X had committed a *devastavit* by distributing assets to the widow. The court relieved[85] X from his liability to Y for this *devastavit* in respect of the £300 legacy and the income paid to the widow before Y issued the writ. Romer J. said that X had acted reasonably in making these payments to the widow until T's debts could be fully ascertained. Admittedly "a prudent and reasonable executor ought to advertise for creditors as soon as possible after his testator's death,"[86] but X's delay in advertising had not affected Y's claim. However, Romer J. refused to grant relief to X in respect of the income paid to the widow after Y issued the writ, because this disclosed a serious and substantial claim against T's estate. Thereafter X had not acted reasonably—he neither ascertained the extent of Y's claim nor applied to the court for directions.

---

[80] *Re Stuart* [1897] 2 Ch. 583 (onus on trustee to show he acted reasonably).

[81] *National Trustees Company of Australasia Ltd.* v. *General Finance Company of Australasia Ltd.* [1905] A.C. 373, 381.

[82] *Ibid.* (trust company made wrong distribution, on its solicitors' bad advice: P.C. refused relief); *Re Pauling's S.T.* [1964] Ch. 303, esp. at pp. 338–339.

[83] *Re Windsor Steam Coal Co. (1901) Ltd.* [1929] 1 Ch. 151, 164–165.

[84] [1897] 2 Ch. 518. See also *Re Lord de Clifford's Estate* [1900] 2 Ch. 707 (executors paid sums for administration purposes to their solicitors, who became bankrupt); *Re Roberts* (1897) 76 L.T. 479 (executor failed to get in debt due to testator's estate); *Re Grindey* [1898] 2 Ch. 593; *Marsden* v. *Regan* [1954] 1 W.L.R. 423. For a survey of the cases see L. A. Sheridan (1955) 19 Conv (N s.) 420.

[85] Under Judicial Trustees Act 1896, s.3 (the repealed predecessor of Trustee Act 1925, s.61).

[86] *Re Kay, supra*, at p. 522.

B. Administration Proceedings

Administration proceedings include:

(a) Actions for the administration of the deceased's estate by the court. If the court makes an order for administration, the whole or some part of the administration may be carried out under the direction of the court.

(b) Actions for specific relief, such as the determination of a particular question arising in the administration of the deceased's estate.

There is no rigid dividing line between actions for administration and actions for specific relief. As will be explained, in an action for administration the court may order specific relief instead. Again, the plaintiff in an action for specific relief usually applies, in addition, for an order for the administration of the deceased's estate if and so far as this is necessary.

It must be emphasised at the outset that administration proceedings are often non-contentious, in the sense that they are commenced so as to obtain the guidance of the court on difficulties arising in the administration of the estate. A personal representative is always entitled to seek the guidance of the court in matters of difficulty. Indeed, it is in his own interest to do so, as he is protected from liability if he acts in accordance with the directions of the court.

Actions for administration

(1) *Jurisdiction over administration.* In the High Court of Justice an action for the administration of the estate of a deceased person is assigned to the Chancery Division.[87] Such an action may be commenced by writ or by originating summons,[88] though an originating summons is not appropriate to a claim based on an allegation of fraud,[89] or where there is likely to be a substantial dispute of fact.[90]

The following also have jurisdiction over the administration of a deceased's estate:

(i) the county court, if the estate does not exceed £30,000 in amount or value[91];

(ii) the Public Trustee, if the estate is solvent, its gross capital value is less than £1,000, and the persons beneficially entitled are persons of small means[92]; and

---

[87] Supreme Court Act 1981, s.61 and Sched. 1, para. 1.

[88] R.S.C., Ord. 5, r. 1; Ord. 85, r. 4.

[89] *Ibid.* Ord. 5, r. 2(*b*).

[90] *Ibid.* Ord. 5, r. 4(2).

[91] County Courts Act 1984, ss.23 and 147: County Courts Jurisdiction Order 1981 (S.I. 1981 No. 1123): if the estate exceeds £30,000, the parties may confer jurisdiction on a specified county court by a signed memorandum, County Courts Act 1984, s.24.

[92] Public Trustee Act 1906, ss.2(4) and 3(1); *Re Devereux* [1911] 2 Ch. 545 (gross capital value at date of application to Public Trustee). As to transfer from the court to the Public Trustee, see *ibid.* s.3(5). For the powers of the Public Trustee see Public Trustee Rules 1912 (S.R. & O. 1912 No. 348), rr. 14–15.

(iii) the bankruptcy court, if the deceased died insolvent.[93]

Henceforth this consideration of administration proceedings concentrates on proceedings in the Chancery Division.

(2) *Parties to administration action.* An administration action may be commenced by the personal representatives, by a creditor of the deceased[94] (suing either on his own behalf,[95] or on behalf of himself and all other creditors), or by any beneficiary interested in the deceased's estate under his will or intestacy.[96]

No order for the administration of the deceased's estate can be made until a personal representative has obtained a grant of representation to the estate,[97] and the personal representative (or each of them, if more than one) must be made a party to the action.[98] Thus an order for administration cannot be made against an executor *de son tort*,[99] though he may be compelled to account for the assets of which he has taken possession.[1]

If no grant of representation has been made, a creditor[2] or beneficiary[3] may apply to the court for the appointment of a receiver of the deceased's estate (and, if necessary, a manager of his business), so as to preserve the assets until a grant of representation is made. But, if a probate action has already begun, it is usually preferable to apply for the appointment of an administrator pending suit, who has the wider rights and powers of a general administrator, other than the right of distributing the residue of the estate after payment of the deceased's debts and expenses.[4]

(3) *Order for administration.* As already explained, if the court makes an order for general administration, the personal representatives must not exercise their powers without first obtaining the sanction of the court.[5] An order for administration (but not the mere commencement of

[93] *Ante*, p. 286: see *Re Bradley* [1956] Ch. 615. No petition can be presented to the bankruptcy court after proceedings for administration have been commenced in another court, but that court may transfer the proceedings to the bankruptcy court if satisfied that the estate is insolvent, Insolvency Act 1986, s.271 as modified by Administration of Insolvent Estates of Deceased Persons Order 1986 (S.I. 1986 No. 1999).
[94] *Re Hargreaves* (1890) 44 Ch.D. 236 (annuitant, whose annuity is not in arrear, is not entitled to bring administration action). A business creditor of a personal representative, entitled by subrogation to payment out of the deceased's assets, may obtain an administration order, *Re Shorey* (1898) 79 L.T. 349.
[95] *Re James* [1911] 2 Ch. 348.
[96] *Peacock* v. *Colling* (1885) 54 L.J.Ch. 743 (a beneficiary contingently entitled may bring administration action): *cf. Clowes* v. *Hilliard* (1876) 4 Ch.D. 413.
[97] *Rowsell* v. *Morris* (1873) L.R. 17 Eq. 20; *Re Sutcliffe* [1942] Ch. 453. A creditor may obtain an order for administration against an administrator *pendente lite, Re Toleman* [1897] 1 Ch. 866: *cf. Dowdeswell* v. *Dowdeswell* (1878) 9 Ch.D. 294 (order for general administration cannot be made against administrator *ad litem*).
[98] R.S.C., Ord. 85, r. 3(1).
[99] *Rowsell* v. *Morris, supra,* (order for administration cannot be made against personal representative of executor *de son tort*): *cf. Re Lovett* (1876) 3 Ch.D. 198.
[1] *Coote* v. *Whittington* (1873) L.R. 16 Eq. 534: see *post*, p. 410.
[2] *Re Sutcliffe* [1942] Ch. 453 (creditor may have to undertake, if required, to take a grant of representation himself).
[3] *Re Oakes* [1917] 1 Ch. 230.
[4] *Ante*, p. 185.
[5] *Ante*, p. 235.

an administration action) also stops time running under the Limitation Act against the claims of creditors of the deceased.[6] After the court has made an order for administration, a further order may be made for the transfer to the same court of any other pending High Court action brought by, or against, the personal representatives.[7]

The court is not bound to make an order for administration unless, in the opinion of the court, the questions at issue between the parties cannot properly be determined otherwise than under such an order.[8] Thus, if a testator by his will directs his executors to take proceedings to have his estate administered by the court, the court is not bound to make an order for administration.[9] If the court does make an order for administration, and orders the whole administration to be carried out under the direction of the court, the costs incurred are likely to be considerable.[10] For instance, in a beneficiary's action against an executor the usual form of order[11] directs the following accounts and inquiries to be taken and made:

(i) An account of the property not specifically devised or bequeathed by the testator come to the hands of the defendant, the executor of the will of the testator, or to the hands of any other person or persons by the order or for the use of the defendant.[12]

(ii) An account of the testator's debts and funeral and testamentary expenses, *or where deceased died more than six years before judgment*, an inquiry whether there is any debt or funeral or testamentary expense of the testator remaining unpaid.

(iii) An account of legacies and annuities.

(iv) An inquiry what parts if any of the testator's property are outstanding or undisposed of, and whether any part of such property so outstanding or undisposed of is subject to any and what incumbrances.

Ultimately, after the Chancery master has certified the result of the accounts and inquiries ordered, the court makes an order for payment or distribution to the beneficiaries entitled.

Instead of ordering the whole administration to be carried out under the direction of the court, the court may make a limited order. To consider some instances:

(i) The court may order such particular accounts or inquiries as are needed, or otherwise determine the particular questions which

---

[6] *Re Greaves* (1881) 18 Ch.D. 551.

[7] R.S.C., Ord. 4, r. 4.

[8] R.S.C., Ord. 85, r. 5(1): see *Re Blake* (1885) 29 Ch.D. 913.

[9] *Re Stocken* (1888) 38 Ch.D. 319.

[10] See Law Reform Committee, 23rd Report, *The powers and duties of trustees*, Cmnd. 8733 (1982), p. 56 ("an extremely clumsy, costly and time consuming procedure and in practice it is only in wholly exceptional cases that its use can be recommended").

[11] See Chancery Masters' Practice Forms (in *The Supreme Court Practice*, Vol. 2), Form No. 10: the usual form of order in a creditor's action is Form No. 11.

[12] If the will gives a life interest in residue, *add* distinguishing between capital and income. If an account on the footing of wilful default is ordered, *add* or which without the wilful neglect or default of the defendant might have come to his hands.

arise in the administration. Thus the court may order appropriate specific relief in an action for administration.

(ii) If the plaintiff (being a creditor or a beneficiary) alleges that no accounts, or insufficient accounts, have been furnished by the personal representatives, the court may order that proceedings in the action be stayed for a specified period, and that in the meantime the personal representatives shall furnish the plaintiff with proper accounts.[13] In addition, in order (if necessary) to prevent proceedings by other creditors or beneficiaries, the court may make an order for administration and direct accounts and inquiries, but at the same time order that no proceedings are to be taken under the order for administration, or under the accounts and inquiries, without the leave of the judge in person.[14]

Appointment of judicial trustee. On the application of a personal representative or beneficiary, the Chancery Division may, in its discretion, appoint a person to be a judicial trustee to complete the administration of the deceased's estate.[15] A judicial trustee may be appointed to act alone, or jointly with any other person, and, if sufficient cause is shown, in place of the existing personal representatives.[16] The appointment of a judicial trustee provides "a middle course"[17] in cases where the administration of the estate by the personal representatives out of court has broken down, and it is not desired to put the estate to the expense of the whole administration being carried out under the direction of the court. A judicial trustee, as an officer of the court, "acts in close concert with the court and under conditions enabling the court to supervise his transactions,"[18] but, unlike the position of a personal representative after an order for general administration has been made, a judicial trustee may exercise his powers without first obtaining the sanction of the court.[19]

Appointment of substitute for, or removal of, personal representative. The Chancery Division also has power in its discretion

(i) to appoint a substituted personal representative in place of all or any of the existing personal representatives of the deceased, or

(ii) if there are two or more existing personal representatives, to terminate the appointment of one or more (but not all) of them.[20]

---

[13] R.S.C., Ord. 85, r. 5(2).

[14] Ibid.: see Re Viscount Furness [1943] Ch. 415.

[15] Judicial Trustees Act 1896, ss.1 and 2 (as amended by Administration of Justice Act 1982, s.57); Judicial Trustee Rules 1983 (S.I. 1983 No. 370). As to remuneration of a judicial trustee, see ante, p. 249.

[16] Ibid.; Re Ratcliff [1898] 2 Ch. 352, 355–356. A judicial trustee cannot be appointed in respect of only part of the estate vested in executors, Re Wells [1968] 1 W.L.R. 44.

[17] Re Ridsdel [1947] Ch. 597, 605.

[18] Ibid · see Judicial Trustees Act 1896, s. 1(3) and (4).

[19] Ibid.

[20] Administration of Justice Act 1985, s.50(1) and (2): see ante, p. 143. As to remuneration of a substituted personal representative, see ante, p. 248.

The power is exercisable on an application relating to the deceased's estate by a personal representative of the deceased or a beneficiary under the deceased's will or intestacy.[21] This provides an alternative course to the appointment of a judicial trustee[22] in cases where an exercise of the power is appropriate in order to secure the proper administration of the deceased's estate out of court.

Actions for specific relief. Instead of bringing an action for the administration of the deceased's estate by the court, a personal representative, creditor, or beneficiary may bring an action for specific relief, *i.e.* for the determination of any question, or for any relief, which could be determined, or granted, in an administration action.[23] Such an action for specific relief is nearly always begun by originating summons. The personal representative (or each of them, if more than one) must be made a party.[24] Often the personal representative is the plaintiff, seeking the guidance of the court in particular matters of difficulty which arise in the course of the administration of the deceased's estate out of court. In such an action the personal representative has a clear duty to lay before the court all the relevant facts which are within his knowledge.[25]

To list a few typical examples[26] of the specific relief which may be sought in such an action:

(i) The determination of any question arising in the administration of the deceased's estate, *e.g.* the question whether upon the true construction of the testator's will the rule in *Allhusen* v. *Whittell*[27] is applicable.

(ii) The determination of any question as to the composition of any class of beneficiaries, *e.g.* an inquiry as to the deceased's next-of-kin entitled under the intestacy rules.[28]

(iii) The determination of any question as to the rights or interest of a person claiming to be entitled under the deceased's will or intestacy, *e.g.* the question whether a specific gift has been adeemed,[29] or from what date a particular general legacy carries interest.[30]

---

[21] *Ibid.* s.50(1) and (5).

[22] On an application under section 50 the court may appoint a judicial trustee, *ibid.* s.50(4), and on an application for a judicial trustee the court may exercise its power under section 50, Judicial Trustees Act 1896, s.1(7) as amended by section 50(6).

[23] R.S.C., Ord. 85, r. 2. The court's jurisdiction to construe a will, or control the administration of a deceased's estate, cannot be ousted by the terms of the will, *Re Wynn* [1952] Ch. 271.

[24] R.S.C., Ord. 85, r. 3(1).

[25] *Re Herwin* [1953] Ch. 701, 708–709 and 714–715.

[26] For other examples see R.S.C., Ord. 85, r. 2(2) and (3).

[27] (1867) L.R. 4 Eq. 295: see *ante*, p. 330. For power of court to authorise action by personal representatives to be taken in reliance on opinion of counsel of 10 years' standing on question of construction see Administration of Justice Act 1985, s.48.

[28] See Chancery Masters' Practice Forms, Form No. 7. If the inquiry proves inconclusive the court may make a Benjamin Order, see *ante*, p. 360.

[29] *Ante*, p. 345.

[30] *Ante*, pp. 322 *et seq.*

(iv) An order requiring a personal representative to furnish and, if necessary, verify accounts.[31]

(v) An order directing a personal representative to do, or not to do, a particular act, *e.g.* directing whether he should carry on the deceased's business,[32] or whether he should take, or defend, legal proceedings on behalf of the estate.[33] If, without the direction of the court, a personal representative takes, or defends, legal proceedings, he is not allowed his costs out of the estate unless the costs were properly incurred for the benefit of the estate.[34]

Costs in administration proceedings. A personal representative is entitled to the costs of administration proceedings (in so far as they are not recovered from, or paid by, any other person) out of the estate as a matter of course.[35] The court may only order otherwise on the ground that the personal representative has acted unreasonably, or has in substance acted for his own benefit rather than for the benefit of the estate.[36] The costs of all other parties to administration proceedings are in the discretion of the court.[37]

In the case of an action begun by originating summons for specific relief (*e.g.* to determine the proper construction of the testator's will), the costs of all parties[38] are normally allowed out of the estate where there is some difficulty which justifies the application to the court.[39]

C. DEFENCES OF PERSONAL REPRESENTATIVE TO CREDITOR'S ACTION

Instead of commencing administration proceedings, a creditor of the deceased may bring an action against the personal representative to recover a debt due from the deceased.[40] In general the personal representative may plead any defence to the action which would have been open to the deceased, and in addition the personal representative may plead certain special defences:

1. Plene administravit, *i.e.* that the personal representative has fully administered all the assets of the deceased which have come to his

---

[31] A legatee is entitled to inspect the accounts at the expense of the estate, but he must normally pay any expenses incurred in furnishing him with a copy, *Ottley* v. *Gilby* (1845) 8 Beav. 602; *Re Bosworth* (1889) 58 L.J.Ch. 432: *cf. Re Skinner* [1904] 1 Ch. 289 (executors' gross neglect to account).

[32] *Ante,* pp. 224 *et seq.*

[33] For the practice where the proposed legal proceedings are against a beneficiary see *Re Moritz* [1960] Ch. 251; *Re Eaton* [1964] 1 W.L.R. 1269; and where the proposed defence is against an adverse claim to the entire estate, *Re Dallaway* [1982] 1 W.L.R. 756; *Re Evans* [1986] 1 W.L.R. 101.

[34] *Re Beddoe* [1893] 1 Ch. 547; *Stott* v. *Milne* (1884) 25 Ch.D. 710.

[35] R.S.C., Ord. 62, r. 6(2). His costs are taxed on the indemnity basis, *ibid.* r. 14.

[36] *Ibid.*

[37] Supreme Court Act 1981, s.51(1).

[38] The costs of the personal representative on the indemnity basis, and of other parties on the standard basis, R.S.C., Ord. 62, rr. 12 and 14.

[39] *Re Buckton* [1907] 2 Ch. 406: *cf. Re Halston* [1912] 1 Ch. 435 (adverse litigation).

[40] For causes of action against the deceased which survive against his estate, see *ante,* p. 212.

hands. If the plaintiff creditor joins issue on this plea, the burden of proof lies on him to show that the personal representative still has, or ought to have, assets in his hands.[41]

If the personal representative's defence of *plene administravit* succeeds, the plaintiff (assuming that he is otherwise successful in the action) may only obtain judgment against future assets, *i.e.* against assets of the deceased coming to the personal representative's hands after the date of the judgment.[42] So far as the personal representative's defence of *plene administravit* fails, the plaintiff (on the same assumption) may obtain judgment against the personal representative as such for a sum equal to the amount of the unadministered assets proved against him, but as to any balance only against future assets.[43]

2. Plene administravit praeter, *i.e.* that the personal representative has fully administered all the assets of the deceased which have come to his hands, except assets of a stated amount which he admits are still in his hands. If this defence succeeds, the plaintiff (on the same assumption) may obtain judgment against the personal representative as such for a sum equal to the amount of the assets admitted, but as to any balance only against future assets.

3. Existence of debts having priority over the plaintiff's debt[44] and no assets ultra. If this defence succeeds, the plaintiff may only obtain judgment against future assets.

"The law as regards the consequences of a failure to plead *plene administravit* bears very hardly on a personal representative."[45] If a personal representative fails to plead these special defences, and the plaintiff obtains judgment against him, the personal representative thereby conclusively admits that at the date of judgment he had sufficient assets to satisfy the claim.[46] Accordingly, if the plaintiff levies execution but the judgment is not satisfied, a presumption arises that the personal representative has committed a *devastavit* in the interval between judgment and execution.[47] The personal representative is personally liable to the plaintiff for this *devastavit* unless the personal representative is able to rebut this presumption in some way, *e.g.* by proving that during this interval he handed over the assets to a receiver appointed by the court.[48]

[41] *Giles* v. *Dyson* (1815) 1 Stark. 32; *Reeves* v. *Ward* (1835) 2 Bing.N.C. 235.
[42] Called a judgment of assets *quando acciderint* or *in futuro*: for leave to issue execution on such a judgment see R.S.C., Ord. 46, r. 2(1)(c).
[43] *Jackson* v. *Bowley* (1841) Car. & M. 97.
[44] For the order of priority of debts see *ante*, pp. 288 *et seq.*
[45] *Midland Bank Trust Co.* v. *Green (No. 2)* [1979] 1 W.L.R. 460, 469.
[46] *Batchelar* v. *Evans* [1939] Ch. 1007; *Marsden* v. *Regan* [1954] 1 W.L.R. 423 (personal representative does not thereby admit that he had sufficient assets to satisfy judgment for costs to be taxed); *Midland Bank Trust Co.* v. *Green (No. 2), supra*; *I.R.C.* v. *Stannard* [1984] 1 W.L.R. 1039, 1041.
[47] *Leonard* v. *Simpson* (1835) 2 Bing.N.C. 176.
[48] *Batchelar* v. *Evans, supra*: *cf. Marsden* v. *Regan, supra*, (presumption not rebutted, but relief from liability granted under Trustee Act 1925, s.61).

D. Liability of Recipient of Assets

At the outset it is essential to distinguish between two different equitable remedies:

(a) First, there is the equitable right to claim a refund from a person to whom the deceased's assets have been wrongly paid by the personal representative. This remedy is available against the recipient of the assets from the personal representative, and the recipient is not excused from repayment because he has spent the assets wrongly paid to him. However, as in the case of any personal claim, this remedy is only fully effective if the defendant is solvent.

(b) Secondly, there is the equitable right to trace and recover property from the holder of it, whether or not he was the recipient from the personal representative. If the property has become mixed with other property, the appropriate remedy may be a declaration of charge on the mixed fund. The equitable right to trace, being a proprietary claim, remains effective despite the insolvency of the holder of the property. However, the right to trace is lost if the property ceases to be identifiable, and there is no right to trace against a bona fide purchaser of the property for value without notice.

Each of these remedies may be available in a case where the deceased's assets have been wrongly distributed by the personal representative. The first remedy (of claiming a refund) was created by the Court of Chancery in the seventeenth century as it gradually wrested from the ecclesiastical courts jurisdiction over the administration of the estates of deceased persons.[49] This first remedy is certainly applicable in the administration of estates, though it may not be applicable in the execution of trusts,[50] and it must now be more fully considered. The second remedy (of tracing) is a more general remedy, which is not confined to the administration of estates, and only certain rules, which are particularly applicable to tracing as a remedy in the administration of estates, are considered here.[51]

Unfortunately a word of warning is needed on terminology. Though these two remedies are markedly different, each of them is sometimes referred to as the remedy of "following the assets" and on occasion this phrase appears to be used in a sense embracing both these remedies at once.[52]

Right of creditor, legatee or next-of-kin to claim refund. If D's personal representative wrongly pays assets to Y, instead of to X who, as

---

[49] *Per* Lord Simonds in *Ministry of Health* v. *Simpson* [1951] A.C. 251, 266: see also *Re Diplock* [1948] Ch. 465, 489.

[50] *Ibid.* at pp. 265–266: see also *Butler* v. *Broadhead* [1975] Ch. 97.

[51] *Post*, p. 408. For the remedy of tracing generally see Snell's *Principles of Equity* (28th ed., 1982), pp. 295 *et seq.*, or Hanbury and Maudsley's *Modern Equity* (12th ed., 1985), pp. 630 *et seq.*, or Pettit's *Equity and the Law of Trusts* (5th ed., 1984), pp. 446 *et seq.*

[52] The right to "follow" the assets is referred to in Administration of Estates Act 1925, s.38(1); Trustee Act 1925, ss.26(2) and 27(2); Legitimacy Act 1976, s.7(3); and Adoption Act 1976, s.45(3).

creditor, legatee, or next-of-kin of D, is properly entitled to them, X has an equitable right to claim a refund from Y^{53} of such an amount as X cannot recover from the personal representative. This claim against Y does not carry interest.[54]

(1) *Basis of liability.* As Lord Simonds put it in *Ministry of Health* v. *Simpson*,[55] this remedy was developed "by the Court of Chancery in the administration of assets of a deceased person to avoid the evil of allowing one man to retain money legally payable to another." It is immaterial whether the money is legally payable to X as an unpaid or underpaid creditor, legatee or next-of-kin of D. The evil to be avoided, and the remedy applicable, is the same. The defendant Y "has no great reason to complain that he is called upon to replace what he has received against his right."[56]

If X is a creditor of D, X is entitled to payment out of any of D's assets regardless of the rules regulating the burden of D's debts as between the beneficiaries, and therefore X may generally claim a refund from any of the beneficiaries. But, as the creditor's remedy is equitable, the court may order the beneficiaries to refund upon such terms (*e.g.* as to the order of refunding) as the court deems it equitable to impose, so as to regulate the burden of the debt as between them.[57]

The leading authority on this remedy is the decision of the House of Lords in *Ministry of Health* v. *Simpson*. In 1936 the deceased, Caleb Diplock, died intestate as to his residuary estate. He left a will by which he purported to dispose of his residuary estate by directing his executors to apply it for such "charitable or benevolent" objects in England as they might in their absolute discretion select. The executors, acting in good faith, distributed over £200,000 from the residuary estate among 139 charities before the next-of-kin challenged the validity of the residuary gift, which was held to be void for uncertainty by the House of Lords.[58] The next-of-kin exhausted their primary remedy against the executors in respect of the wrongful distribution of the estate,[59] and claimed to recover the balance from the wrongly paid charities. The

[53] Or, if Y has died, from Y's personal representative or legatee, *March* v. *Russell* (1837) 3 My. & Cr. 31.

[54] *Re Diplock* [1948] Ch. 465, 506–507. Interest may be recoverable under the equitable right to trace, *ibid.* at pp. 557–558.

[55] [1951] A.C. 251, 268. As to a creditor's claim, Lord Davey said in *Harrison* v. *Kirk* [1904] A.C. 1, 7, "the Court of Chancery, in order to do justice and to avoid the evil of allowing one man to retain what is really and legally applicable to the payment of another man, devised a remedy by which, where the estate had been distributed either out of court or in court without regard to the rights of a creditor, it has allowed the creditor to recover back what has been paid to the beneficiaries or the next-of-kin who derive title from the deceased testator or intestate."

[56] *David* v. *Frowd* (1833) 1 My. & K. 200, 211.

[57] *National Assurance Co.* v. *Scott* [1909] 1 I.R. 325 (creditor held entitled to refund from residuary legatees and, if need be, from pecuniary legatees). But if D's estate was administered by the court, and the creditor failed to prove for his debt, the creditor may only recover from each beneficiary the sum he was properly liable to bear, *Gillespie* v. *Alexander* (1827) 3 Russ. 130, 138; *Greig* v. *Somerville* (1830) 1 R. & M. 338; *Davies* v. *Nicolson* (1858) 2 De G. & J. 693, 702; *Todd* v. *Studholme* (1857) 3 K. & J. 324, 336–337.

[58] *Chichester Diocesan Fund and Board of Finance* v. *Simpson* [1944] A.C. 341: see *ante*, pp. 350–351.

[59] The executors paid £15,000 under a compromise approved by the court.

claim against the charities was made under two alternative heads, *i.e.* (i) under the equitable right to claim a refund and (ii) under the equitable right to trace. In *Re Diplock*[60] the Court of Appeal held that both these remedies were applicable. An appeal by one charity (a hospital) against its liability under head (i) was unanimously rejected by the House of Lords in *Ministry of Health* v. *Simpson*. The House of Lords held that, as the next-of-kin had exhausted their primary remedy against the executors, the next-of-kin were entitled to claim a refund from this hospital in respect of the money wrongly distributed to it by the executors. The hospital had spent this money on erecting new buildings, so that the next-of-kin had lost their right to trace, but the hospital was nevertheless under a personal liability to refund.[61]

(2) *Two requirements.* The equitable right to claim a refund is applicable if two requirements are satisfied:

(a) WRONG PAYMENT BY PERSONAL REPRESENTATIVE. The first requirement is that the personal representative must have wrongly paid assets of the deceased's estate to Y. This requirement is satisfied if the personal representative distributed assets to Y, who had no title at all and was a stranger to the estate. Of course, in the *Diplock* case each of the charities was a stranger to the estate.[62] This requirement is also satisfied if the personal representative distributed more assets to Y than he was properly entitled to receive, *e.g.* a half-share of residue instead of the third share to which he was properly entitled. In that case Y is liable to refund the excess to which he was not entitled.

In order to determine whether Y received more assets than he was properly entitled to receive, it may be necessary to ascertain the extent of the available assets at the time of the distribution to Y. If by his will D gives a legacy of £500 each to X and Y, and D's executor pays Y's legacy in full at a time when the executor has sufficient assets available to pay X's legacy in full, Y does not receive more assets than he is properly entitled to receive. It follows that X has no right to claim a refund from Y if these other assets are subsequently lost, whether accidentally[63] or owing to a *devastavit* committed by the executor.[64] X has the burden of proving that Y received more assets than he was properly entitled to receive at the time of the distribution to Y.[65]

There is no requirement that the deceased's estate must have been administered by the court.[66] Again, there is no requirement that the personal representative must have paid Y under a mistake of fact. The remedy is equally applicable if the personal representative paid Y under

[60] [1948] Ch. 465 (reviewing the case law).

[61] *Ministry of Health* v. *Simpson* [1951] A.C. 251, 276: *cf.* G. H. Jones (1957) 73 L.Q.R. 48, 61 *et seq.*

[62] *Re Diplock* [1948] Ch. 465, 502: see *Re Lowe's W.T.* [1973] 1 W.L.R. 882, 887 (wrong payment to Crown).

[63] *Fenwick* v. *Clarke* (1862) 4 De G.F. & J. 240 (accidental loss of other assets when bank unexpectedly failed); *Re Winslow* (1890) 45 Ch.D. 249.

[64] *Peterson* v. *Peterson* (1866) L.R. 3 Eq. 111; *Re Lepine* [1892] 1 Ch. 210.

[65] *Peterson* v. *Peterson, supra.*

[66] *Ministry of Health* v. *Simpson* [1951] A.C. 251, 268.

a mistake of law, as occurred in the *Diplock* case,[67] or if the personal representative made the wrong payment to Y deliberately, knowing that Y was not properly entitled.[68] Moreover, Y's liability to refund does not depend upon his knowledge, or assumed knowledge, that he is not properly entitled. In *Ministry of Health* v. *Simpson* the hospital received and spent the money in good faith, believing that it was properly entitled, but was nevertheless held liable to refund the money.[69]

(b) ANY REMEDY AGAINST PERSONAL REPRESENTATIVE EXHAUSTED. The second requirement is that X must exhaust his primary remedy (if any) against the personal representative in respect of his wrong payment to Y. This second requirement certainly has to be satisfied if X claims as D's legatee or next-of-kin[70] and probably the same rule applies if X claims as D's creditor.[71]

X's claim against Y for a refund is limited to the amount which X cannot recover from the personal representative.[72] Sometimes X cannot recover anything from the personal representative and in that event X may claim a refund from Y of the whole amount which was wrongly paid to Y. This situation arises, for instance:

  (i) if the personal representative is liable to X for a *devastavit* but is wholly without assets[73]; *or*
 (ii) if the personal representative is protected from liability to X because the personal representative acted under an order of the court in paying Y, *e.g.* under a Benjamin Order giving the personal representative leave to distribute on the footing that X, a missing beneficiary, predeceased D[74]; *or*
(iii) if the personal representative is protected from liability to X by statute, *e.g.* by section 27 of the Trustee Act 1925 which protects the personal representative against the claims of X, an unknown creditor or beneficiary, if the personal representative satisfies the statutory requirements as to advertising and making searches before he distributes.[75]

(3) *Defences.* X's claim against Y for a refund is liable to be defeated by the defence of limitation. If X claims as a legatee or next-of-kin entitled to D's pure personalty, section 22 of the Limitation Act 1980 is appli-

---

[67] *Ibid.* at pp. 269–270.
[68] *Ibid.* at p. 270.
[69] *Ibid.* at p. 276.
[70] *Orr.* v. *Kaines* (1750) 2 Ves.Sen. 194 (X an underpaid legatee); *Re Diplock* [1948] Ch. 465, 503–505; *Ministry of Health* v. *Simpson* [1951] A.C. 251, 267–268.
[71] *Hodges* v. *Waddington* (1684) 2 Vent. 360; *Hunter* v. *Young* (1879) 4 Ex.D. 256.
[72] *Re Diplock, supra*, at pp. 503–505 (X may issue a writ against Y for a refund before exhausting his remedy against the personal representative).
[73] *Ibid.*
[74] See *ante*, p. 360: see also *Re Gess* [1942] Ch. 37, 39 (leave of court to distribute on footing deceased's debts and liabilities had been ascertained), discussed *ante*, p. 261.
[75] See *ante*, p. 260 (unknown creditor) and p. 359 (unknown beneficiary). For other similar statutory protection of the personal representative, see (i) Trustee Act 1925, s.26 (deceased's leasehold), discussed *ante*, p. 230; (ii) Adoption Act 1976, s.45(3) and Legitimacy Act 1976, s.7 (adoption or legitimation), discussed *ante*, p. 361; (iii) Inheritance (Provision for Family and Dependants) Act 1975, s.20(1), discussed *ante*, pp. 105–106; (iv) Administration of Justice Act 1982, s.20(3) (rectification), see *ante*, p. 56.

cable and the period of limitation is 12 years from the date when X's right to receive his share or interest accrued.[76] Thus the same period of limitation applies to X's claim against Y for a refund as applies to X's claim against the personal representative.[77] If X claims as a creditor of D, X must bring his action within six years from the accrual of his cause of action.[78]

Again, if X acquiesces in the distribution to Y by the personal representative and thereby releases X's claim in respect of the assets paid to Y, X cannot thereafter claim a refund from Y.[79]

Right of personal representative to claim refund. In general, a personal representative cannot exercise the equitable right to claim a refund from Y, a beneficiary to whom he distributed the deceased's assets.[80] Exceptionally, a personal representative is entitled to claim a refund from Y if a debt, of which the personal representative had no notice at the time of the distribution, is afterwards discovered and the personal representative is obliged to pay it.[81] The personal representative is not entitled to a refund from Y if the personal representative had notice of the debt at the time of distribution.[82] However, it is immaterial that at the time of distribution the personal representative had notice of the existence of a contingent liability of the deceased, e.g. for possible calls on unpaid company shares. If this liability arises and the personal representative is obliged to discharge it, he may claim repayment from Y of the capital value of the assets distributed to him, unless at the time of distribution the personal representative knew that the claim had already fallen due for payment.[83]

A personal representative who, by a mistake of law (and not a mistake of fact), has overpaid one beneficiary Y cannot obtain repayment from Y[84]; the personal representative must make good the sum overpaid from his own pocket so that the other beneficiaries are paid in full.[85] But the personal representative is entitled to deduct the sum overpaid from any other sum falling due to Y from the personal rep-

[76] Re Diplock [1948] Ch. 465, 507–516; affirmed Ministry of Health v. Simpson [1951] A.C. 251, 276–277: for s.22, see ante, p. 392.
[77] Re Diplock, supra, at p. 514; Ministry of Health v. Simpson, supra, at p. 277.
[78] Limitation Act 1980, s.5: if X claims a specialty debt, the period is 12 years, ibid. s.8.
[79] Blake v. Gale (1886) 32 Ch.D. 571: see Ridgway v. Newstead (1861) 3 De G.F. & J. 474 (legatee's position altered) and cf. Re Eustace [1912] 1 Ch. 561 (mere delay).
[80] Orr v. Kaines (1750) 2 Ves.Sen. 194; Hodges v. Waddington (1679) 2 Cas. in Ch. 9.
[81] Nelthrop v. Hill (1669) 1 Cas. in Ch. 135, 136; German v. Lady Colston (1678) 2 Rep.Ch. 137: for the effect of advertising for claims, see ante, p. 260. A personal representative may also be entitled to claim a refund from Y if he distributed to Y under a court order: Newman v. Barton (1690) 2 Vern. 205; Noell v. Robinson (1686) 2 Ventr. 358.
[82] Jervis v. Wolferstan (1874) L.R. 18 Eq. 18, 25.
[83] Jervis v. Wolferstan, supra, (repayment of capital but not of intermediate income received by beneficiary); Whittaker v. Kershaw (1890) 45 Ch.D. 320: see ante, pp. 262–263.
[84] Re Diplock [1948] Ch. 465, 479–480 ("as regards common law claims for money had and received the action will not lie where the money has been paid under a mistake of law").
[85] Hilliard v. Fulford (1876) 4 Ch.D. 389, 394 (the personal representatives "who have made the error will have to pay for it"): see Goff and Jones, The Law of Restitution (3rd ed., 1986), pp. 128–129.

resentative,[86] unless in the particular circumstances this would be inequitable.[87] To this extent the personal representative may recoup his overpayment.

Right to trace. Legatees, devisees and next-of-kin are all entitled to exercise the equitable right to trace and recover property from the holder of it, other than a bona fide purchaser for value without notice or any person deriving title under him.[88] An unsatisfied creditor of the deceased is also entitled to exercise the equitable right to trace for the purpose of obtaining payment,[89] except against such a purchaser or any person deriving title under him.[90] The Administration of Estates Act 1925[91] provides that an assent or conveyance by a personal representative in respect of any property does not prejudice the equitable right of any person to trace the property in this way.

X may exercise his equitable right to trace, though he has not exhausted his remedy (if any) against the personal representative in respect of his wrong payment to Y. However, in so far as X has already recovered from the personal representative, X loses his equitable right to trace.[92]

E. EXECUTOR DE SON TORT

The term executor *de son tort* (or executor in his own wrong[93]) is applied to a person who is not an executor or administrator but who nevertheless acts in some way as if he were an executor. Such a person is called an executor (and not an administrator) *de son tort* even though the deceased left no will.

A person appointed executor by the testator in his will can only establish his title by means of a grant of probate.[94] If such a person acts in some way as executor without any grant of probate, he is treated by the court as an executor *de son tort* (and not as an executor) because he cannot establish his title as executor.[95] On the other hand, once probate has been granted, this establishes his title as executor as from the testator's death. Logically he ought then to be regarded as an executor (and not as an executor *de son tort*) as from the testator's death.[96]

---

[86] *Livesey* v. *Livesey* (1827) 3 Russ. 287 (overpayments of annuity deductible from future payments of annuity); *Dibbs* v. *Goren* (1849) 11 Beav. 483; *Re Musgrave* [1916] 2 Ch. 417.

[87] *Re Horne* [1905] 1 Ch. 76: *cf. Re Musgrave, supra,* at p. 425 and *Re Ainsworth* [1915] 2 Ch. 96, 104–106.

[88] *Re Diplock* [1948] Ch. 465.

[89] *Salih* v. *Atchi* [1961] A.C. 778, 793; *Davies* v. *Nicolson* (1858) 2 De G. & J. 693.

[90] *Dilkes* v. *Broadmead* (1860) 2 De G.F. & J. 566 (marriage consideration); *Spackman* v. *Timbrell* (1837) 8 Sim. 253; *Salih* v. *Atchi, supra,* at 793—though the creditor "cannot follow the property against the purchaser, he can follow the purchase price in the hands of the [beneficiary]," or rely on his equitable right to claim a refund from the beneficiary: see also Administration of Estates Act 1925, s.32(2).

[91] *Ibid.* ss.38(1), (3) and 55(1) (xviii): see also *ibid.* s.36(9) and (11).

[92] *Re Diplock* [1948] Ch. 465, 556–557.

[93] Administration of Estates Act 1925, s.28.

[94] *Ante,* pp. 168–169.

[95] *Att.-Gen.* v. *The New York Breweries Co. Ltd.* [1898] 1 Q.B. 205, affirmed [1899] A.C. 62.

[96] *Sykes* v. *Sykes* (1870) L.R. 5 C.P. 113 (the headnote is misleading): *cf. Webster* v. *Webster* (1804) 10 Ves. 93.

Acts creating liability as executor de son tort. Section 28 of the Administration of Estates Act 1925 provides as follows:

"If any person, to the defrauding of creditors or without full valuable consideration, obtains, receives or holds any real or personal estate of a deceased person or effects the release of any debt or liability due to the estate of the deceased, he shall be charged as executor in his own wrong to the extent of the real and personal estate received or coming to his hands, or the debt or liability released, after deducting—

(a) any debt for valuable consideration and without fraud due to him from the deceased person at the time of his death; and

(b) any payment made by him which might properly be made by a personal representative."

Probably the section made no material change in the rules in force before 1926 specifying what acts made a person liable as executor *de son tort*.

(1) *Intermeddling.* If a person intermeddles with any of the deceased's assets in England or Wales[97] as if he were an executor, this makes him liable as executor *de son tort*. The rule applies to intermeddling with the deceased's realty[98] as well as his personalty. Examples include carrying on the deceased's business,[99] selling his goods,[1] and receiving payment of debts due to the deceased.[2] Again the act of transferring title from English personal representatives to foreign personal representatives constitutes an intermeddling with the deceased's English estate. In *New York Breweries Company, Ltd.* v. *Attorney-General*[3] an English limited company transferred a deceased American's shares and debenture in the company into the names of his American executors, who had not obtained probate of the deceased's will in England. The House of Lords held that the company had made itself an executor *de son tort* because it had vested these English assets of the deceased in persons who were not English personal representatives. In *I.R.C.* v. *Stype Investments (Jersey) Ltd.*[4] at C's death a Jersey company held English land on trust for C in fee simple, with the benefit of a contract for the sale of the land to P for £20 million. After C's death the company completed the sale and directed P to pay the price to its Jersey bank account. In an action by the Inland Revenue Commissioners claiming capital transfer tax, the Court of Appeal held that the company was an executor *de son tort* because it had diverted £20 million, part of C's English assets, to Jersey out of the reach of C's personal representatives when constituted in England.[5]

---

[97] *Beavan* v. *Lord Hastings* (1856) 2 K. & J. 724 (intestate's brother obtained representation in Belgium but did not intermeddle with English assets: not executor *de son tort*).
[98] Administration of Estates Act 1925, s.28.
[99] *Padget* v. *Priest* (1787) 2 T.R. 97; *Hooper* v. *Summersett* (1810) Wightw. 16.
[1] *Read's Case* (1604) 5 Co.Rep. 33b; *Nulty* v. *Fagan* (1888) 22 L.R.Ir. 604.
[2] *Sharland* v. *Mildon* (1846) 5 Hare 469.
[3] [1899] A.C. 62.
[4] [1982] Ch. 456.
[5] *Ibid.* at p. 474 ("the act of transferring title from English personal representatives to Jersey personal representatives constituted an intermeddling with the English estate").

(2) *As if he were an executor.* To become liable as executor *de son tort* a person must intermeddle as if he were an executor. If he intermeddles out of humanity or necessity, this does not make him an executor *de son tort*.[6] For instance, he will not become an executor *de son tort* if he receives payment of a debt due to the deceased solely for the purpose of paying the deceased's reasonable funeral expenses.[7] The same is true if he takes possession of an intestate's goods for the purpose of keeping them in safe custody until an administrator is appointed.[8]

Liability of executor de son tort. (1) *Liability to creditors and beneficiaries.* In general an executor *de son tort* is liable to creditors and beneficiaries of the deceased as if he were the lawful executor.[9] But under section 28 of the Administration of Estates Act 1925 he is only liable "to the extent of the real and personal estate received or coming to his hands."[10] Unlike a personal representative, an executor *de son tort* is not under any duty to collect and get in the deceased's assets.[11]

Under section 28, in determining the extent of the liability of an executor *de son tort*, two deductions are to be made from the assets for which he is liable. These two deductions are as follows:

(i) Any debt for valuable consideration and without fraud due to the executor *de son tort* from the deceased at death. Thus an executor *de son tort* may apparently "retain" for his own debt as against another creditor, even though the other creditor is of a higher degree[12] and even though the executor *de son tort* has reason to believe that the deceased's estate is insolvent. In this respect, unfortunately, an executor *de son tort* is treated more favourably than a personal representative.[13]

(ii) Any payment made by the executor *de son tort* which might properly be made by a personal representative. An executor *de son tort* may therefore deduct payments made by him in discharge of the deceased's funeral expenses and debts in due course of administration of the deceased's estate.[14] "In many cases it may be very convenient, and even necessary, that an executor *de son tort*

---

[6] This is not expressed in Administration of Estates Act 1925, s.28 but is probably still the law.

[7] *Camden* v. *Fletcher* (1838) 4 M. & W. 378. *A fortiori* giving directions for the deceased's funeral does not make him an executor *de son tort*, *Harrison* v. *Rowley* (1798) 4 Ves. 212, 216.

[8] *Peters* v. *Leeder* (1878) 47 L.J.Q.B. 573.

[9] Unlike an executor, in the absence of liability by estoppel, an executor *de son tort* is not personally liable to the lessor for breach of covenant in respect of the deceased's leasehold of which he has taken possession, because the lease is not vested in him, *Mayor, Aldermen and Burgesses of Stratford-upon-Avon* v. *Parker* [1914] 2 K.B. 562.

[10] Or, if he effected the release of any debt or liability due to the deceased's estate, to the extent of the debt or liability released.

[11] For duty of a personal representative see Administration of Estates Act 1925, s.25 as amended by Administration of Estates Act 1971, s.9; *ante*, p. 214.

[12] *Ante*, pp. 289 *et seq.*

[13] *Ante*, pp. 292–293. Before 1926 an executor *de son tort* was not permitted to retain for his own debt, *Curtis* v. *Vernon* (1790) 3 T.R. 587.

[14] *Oxenham* v. *Clapp* (1831) 2 B. & Ad. 309.

should dispose of the assets of the deceased in due course of administration."[15]

The liability of an executor *de son tort* to à creditor or beneficiary ceases if, before they bring an action against him, he delivers or accounts for all the assets received by him to the lawful personal representative of the deceased.[16] By this means an executor *de son tort* may purge his wrongdoing in receiving the assets.

An executor *de son tort* may be cited by a creditor or beneficiary to take probate if he has been duly appointed as executor[17] but he cannot be compelled to take a grant of letters of administration.[18]

(2) *Liability for inheritance tax.* An executor *de son tort* is liable for the inheritance tax attributable to the value of any property with which he intermeddles. He is treated as a person in whom such property is vested and in that capacity he is personally liable for inheritance tax chargeable in respect of the death of the deceased,[19] but he is not liable for tax beyond the extent of such property.[20]

(3) *Liability to the personal representatives.* An executor *de son tort* is liable to the lawful personal representatives under the general law (*e.g.* in tort[21] or quasi-contract) for his acts of interference with the deceased's assets.[22] However, the executor *de son tort* may mitigate the damages awarded against him by showing that he has made payments in due course of administration of the deceased's estate: the lawful personal representatives would have been bound to make these payments and to this extent the deceased's estate has suffered no loss.[23]

[15] *Per* Lord Tenterden C.J. in *Oxenham* v. *Clapp, supra,* at p. 313.
[16] Again this is not expressed in Administration of Estates Act 1925, s.28 but is probably still the law; *Anon.* (1702) 1 Salk. 313; *Padget* v. *Priest* (1787) 2 T.R. 97; *Curtis* v. *Vernon* (1790) 3 T.R. 587, 2 H.Bl. 18; *Hill* v. *Curtis* (1865) L.R. 1 Eq. 90.
[17] *Ante,* p. 149.
[18] *Ante,* p. 159.
[19] Inheritance Tax Act 1984, ss.199(4) and 200(1) and (4): see *I.R.C.* v. *Stype Investments (Jersey) Ltd.* [1982] Ch. 456, 466; *I.R.C.* v. *Stannard* [1984] 1 W.L.R. 1039. An executor *de son tort* may also be liable for inheritance tax on a chargeable transfer made by an *inter vivos* disposition of the deceased, s.199(1) and (4) and see s.204(6). If owing to the wide definition of "personal representatives" in s.272 an executor *de son tort* is also liable as a personal representative under s.200(1), then probably under s.204(1) no liability arises for assets which he might have received but for his own neglect or default, because he is under no duty to get in assets.
[20] *Ibid.* s.204(3).
[21] *Whitehall* v. *Squire* (1703) Carth. 103 (conversion of deceased's horse); *Fyson* v. *Chambers* (1842) 9 M. & W. 460 (conversion of deceased's household goods).
[22] See *I.R.C.* v. *Stype Investments (Jersey) Ltd., supra,* at pp. 476–477; *Official Solicitor* v. *Stype Investments (Jersey) Ltd.* [1983] 1 W.L.R. 214.
[23] *Whitehall* v. *Squire, supra; Padget* v. *Priest* (1787) 2 T.R. 97, 100; *Mountford* v. *Gibson* (1804) 4 East. 411, 450 and 454. If an executor *de son tort* pays a creditor of the deceased in due course of administration, the creditor is not liable to the lawful personal representatives if the creditor reasonably believed that the executor *de son tort* was the lawful personal representative, *Thomson* v. *Harding* (1853) 2 E. & B. 630, and *cf. Mountford* v. *Gibson* (1804) 4 East 441.

CHAPTER 15

THE CONSTRUCTION OF WILLS

The construction of wills is a branch of the law which needs a whole book,[1] rather than a chapter. This chapter can only serve as an introduction to the general principles of construction, the rules governing the admissibility of evidence, and a few of the detailed rules of construction.

The proper construction of a testator's will is important at two stages:

(i) before his death, when his will is being drafted so as accurately to express the wishes of the testator[2]; and

(ii) after his death, when the meaning and effect of his will must be ascertained in order that a grant of probate or letters of administration may be made to the persons entitled and his estate may be properly administered.

A. General Principles of Construction

Object to ascertain the testator's expressed intention.[3] In construing a will the object of the court is to ascertain the intention of the testator as expressed in his will when it is read as a whole. Sometimes extrinsic evidence (*i.e.* extrinsic to the will) is admissible to assist in the interpretation of the will,[4] but the language of the will is central to its construction because the object is "to discover the meaning of the words as intended by the testator."[5] As Lord Simon L.C. put it in *Perrin* v. *Morgan*[6]:

"The fundamental rule in construing the language of a will is to put on the words used the meaning which, having regard to the terms of the will, the testator intended. The question is not, of course, what the testator meant to do when he made his will, but what the written words he uses mean in the particular case—what are the 'expressed intentions' of the testator."

---

[1] See *Theobald on Wills* (14th ed., 1982); *Williams on Wills* (6th ed., 1987); *Hawkins and Ryder on the Construction of Wills* (1965); *Jarman on Wills* (8th ed., 1951).

[2] *Per* Knight Bruce L.J. in *Lowe* v. *Thomas* (1854) 5 De G.M. & G. 315, 317, "the numerous class of persons who, in wills and otherwise, speak as if the office of language were to conceal their thoughts, have no right to complain of being taken to mean what their language expresses."

[3] For the general principles of construction see Theobald, *op. cit.* pp. 185 *et seq.*

[4] See *post*, pp. 418 *et seq.*

[5] Phipson (1904) 20 L.Q.R. 245, 254.

[6] [1943] A.C. 399, 406.

(1) *The court cannot rewrite a will.* Apart from its powers under the Inheritance (Provision for Family and Dependants) Act 1975,[7] the court has no power to rewrite a will for a testator after his death in order to achieve a more sensible result. The function of a court of construction is to construe the testator's will, not to make a new will for him.[8] To quote Jenkins L.J. in *Re Bailey*[9]:

" . . . it is not the function of a court of construction to improve upon or perfect testamentary dispositions. The function of the court is to give effect to the dispositions actually made as appearing expressly or by necessary implication from the language of the will applied to the surrounding circumstances of the case."

(2) *The court does not guess.* Moreover the court does not ascertain the intention of the testator by conjecture or guess-work. Lord Wensleydale warned against this in *Abbott v. Middleton*[10]:

"The use of the expression that the intention of the testator is to be the guide, unaccompanied with the constant explanation that it is to be sought in his words, and a rigorous attention to them, is apt to lead the mind insensibly to speculate upon what the testator may be supposed to have intended to do, instead of strictly attending to the true question, which is what that which he has written means."

Presumption words to be given their ordinary meaning. Prima facie the words and phrases used in a will are to be given their ordinary meaning—"the strict, plain, common meaning of the words themselves."[11]

Obviously, this presumption cannot be applied if the word or phrase has more than one ordinary meaning. For instance, the word "money" has several ordinary meanings, ranging from coin (the narrowest meaning) to the whole of a person's real and personal property (the widest meaning, as used in the phrase, "It's her money he's after").[12] If a word or phrase has more than one ordinary meaning, the court determines the meaning intended by the testator by considering all the provisions of the will,[13] construed with the aid of any admissible extrinsic evidence.[14] Needless to say, a skilled draftsman avoids the use of such an ambiguous word as "money."

This presumption that a word or phrase bears its ordinary meaning may be rebutted in two ways:

---

[7] *Ante*, pp. 126 *et seq.*

[8] *Scalé* v. *Rawlins* [1892] A.C. 342; *Re Lewis's W.T.* [1985] 1 W.L.R. 102 (T's devise of farm did not pass T's shares in company which owned farm). For rectification of a will see *ante*, pp. 55–56.

[9] [1951] Ch. 407, 421.

[10] (1858) 7 H.L.C. 68, 114: see *Re Rowland* [1963] Ch. 1, 11–12 and 17–18.

[11] *Shore* v. *Wilson* (1842) 9 Cl. & F. 355, 565: see *Gorringe* v. *Mahlstedt* [1907] A.C. 225, 227 ("the ordinary and usual meaning of the words").

[12] *Perrin* v. *Morgan* [1943] A.C. 399, 406–408 ("When Tennyson's Northern Farmer counselled his son not to marry for money, but to go where money is, he was not excluding the attractiveness of private property in land"); *Re Barnes' W.T.* [1972] 1 W.L.R. 587.

[13] *Perrin* v. *Morgan, supra*; *Re Whitmore* [1902] 2 Ch. 66, 70; *Re Barnes' W.T., supra*.

[14] *Post*, pp. 418 *et seq.*

(1) *The dictionary principle.* If it appears, from an examination of all the provisions of the will construed with the aid of any admissible extrinsic evidence, that the testator used that word or phrase in a different sense from its ordinary meaning, the word or phrase is to be construed in that different sense. This rule is often called the "dictionary principle" because the testator in his will has supplied his own dictionary. A testator is free to use words to mean whatever he wishes if he makes the sense in which he is using them clear in his will—he can make "black" mean "white" if he makes the dictionary sufficiently clear in his will.[15] Thus the dictionary principle applies if a testator includes a definition clause in his will, stating that a particular word in his will is used in some special sense. And the dictionary principle is equally applicable if the will, construed as a whole, states this indirectly; for example, if the testator uses that word in other parts of his will in this special, though unmistakable, sense. In *Re Davidson*[16] T's residuary gift to "my grandchildren" was held to include the children of T's stepson because T's will described him as "my son" and one of his two children as "my granddaughter."

(2) *Secondary meaning makes sense.* If the ordinary meaning does not make sense when the will is read in the light of the surrounding circumstances in which it was made, and the word or phrase has a secondary meaning which does make sense, the word or phrase is to be given that secondary meaning. This rule applies, for instance, to words descriptive of relationship. In *Re Smalley*[17] a testator gave all his property to "my wife Eliza Ann Smalley." He left a lawful wife Mary Ann Smalley and also Eliza Ann Mercer whom he had "married" and who lived with him and who believed herself, and was reputed in the neighbourhood, to be his wife. The Court of Appeal decided that Eliza Ann Mercer was entitled: the surrounding circumstances showed that the testator had used the words "my wife" in his will in their secondary meaning of his *reputed* wife. This rule differs from the dictionary principle in one respect. Under this rule the word or phrase must be capable of bearing the secondary meaning to be put on it; extrinsic evidence alone (unlike the rest of the will) cannot make "black" mean "white."

If the presumption in favour of the ordinary meaning is not rebutted, the ordinary meaning of a word or phrase prevails even though it may produce results which appear capricious.[18] To quote Buckley J. in *Re James's Will Trusts*,[19] "a testator is entitled to be capricious or eccentric in his testamentary dispositions if he chooses."

Presumption technical words to be given their technical meaning. Prima facie technical legal words and expressions used in a will are to

[15] *Per* Harman J. in *Re Cook* [1948] Ch. 212, 216 (a case on the meaning of technical words), *post*, p. 415).

[16] [1949] Ch. 670: see also *Re Lynch* [1943] 1 All E.R. 168.

[17] [1929] 2 Ch. 112: see *Allgood* v. *Blake* (1873) L.R. 8 Exch. 160, 163–164; *Re Jebb* [1966] Ch. 666.

[18] *Gilmour* v. *MacPhillamy* [1930] A.C. 712: *cf. Bathurst* v. *Errington* (1877) 2 App.Cas. 698, 709–711 (two possible meanings: not adopt capricious meaning).

[19] [1962] Ch. 226, 234: see also *Hart* v. *Tulk* (1852) 2 De G.M. & G. 300, 313–314; *Bird* v. *Luckie* (1850) 8 Hare 301, 306.

be given their technical meaning.[20] In *Re Cook*[21] T by her will, made on a printed will form, gave "all my personal estate whatsoever" to her named nephew and nieces. T's estate mainly consisted of realty. Harman J. held that T's realty was not disposed of by her will and devolved as on her intestacy. He said[22]:

"It seems unlikely that she intended to dispose only of the personal estate in the lawyer's sense of that word . . . but this is a case where a layman has chosen to use a term of art. The words 'all my personal estate' are words so well-known to lawyers that it must take a very strong context to make them include real estate. Testators can make black mean white if they make the dictionary sufficiently clear, but the testatrix has not done so. It may well be that she thought 'personal estate' meant 'all my worldly goods'; I do not know. In the absence of something to show that the phrase ought not to be so construed, I must suppose that she used the term 'personal estate' in its ordinary meaning as a term of art."

This presumption that technical legal words and expressions are to be given their technical meaning may be rebutted in the same two ways as the presumption in favour of the ordinary meaning.[23] Thus, under *the dictionary principle*, a testator is free to use technical legal words and expressions to mean whatever he wishes if he makes the sense in which he is using them clear in his will—he can make the expression "personal estate" include real estate if he makes the dictionary sufficiently clear in his will. In *Re Bailey*[24] T by her home-made will gave the house in which she lived to X and several pecuniary legacies to persons named, and concluded, "I leave Y as my residuary legatee." T's estate mainly consisted of realty. Romer J. held that there was sufficient context in the will, read in the light of the surrounding circumstances, to show that the technical words "residuary legatee" (prima facie referring to personalty) were used in the wider sense of "residuary beneficiary," and therefore Y was entitled to T's residuary realty.

The will is to be read as a whole. The testator's intention is to be ascertained from an examination of the whole of his will, construed with the aid of any admissible extrinsic evidence. "The fundamental and overriding duty binding the court is to ascertain the intention of the testator as expressed in his will read as a whole."[25] The testator's

---

[20] *Doe d. Winter* v. *Perratt* (1843) 6 M. & G. 314, 342–343: see also *Re Harcourt* [1921] 2 Ch. 491, 503 ("when a testator has used words which have acquired a definite meaning in conveyancing and have for a long time been used in the drafting of wills and settlements and other like documents with that meaning, it requires a very strong case to justify their interpretation in a different sense"); *Falkiner* v. *Commissioner of Stamp Duties* [1973] A.C. 565, 577–578 (justifying the technical meaning rule).

[21] [1948] Ch. 212: see also *Re Du Cros' S.T.* [1961] 1 W.L.R. 1252, 1256 ("male issue" means male descendants in the exclusively male line) and *cf. Re Drake* [1971] Ch. 179 ("male descendants" not technical expression). For the word "heir" see Theobald, *op. cit.* pp. 408 *et seq.*

[22] *Ibid.* at p. 216.

[23] *Ante*, pp. 413–414. For an example of a secondary meaning making sense see *Re Glassington* [1906] 2 Ch. 305.

[24] [1945] Ch. 191: *cf. Re Gibbs* [1907] 1 Ch. 465.

[25] *Per* Ungoed-Thomas J. in *Re Macandrew's W.T.* [1964] Ch. 704, 719.

"general" intention, when ascertained with reasonable certainty in this way, "is competent not only to *fix* the sense of *ambiguous* words, but to *control* the sense even of *clear* words, and to *supply* the place of *express* words, in cases of difficulty or ambiguity."[26]

(1) *Resolving ambiguity.* If the court is faced with a choice between two (or more) possible meanings of an ambiguous word or phrase (*e.g.* the word "money"[27]), the court determines the meaning intended by the testator by considering all the provisions of the will, construed with the aid of any admissible extrinsic evidence.

(2) *Rebutting presumption in favour of ordinary or technical meaning.* As already explained, under the dictionary principle the ordinary or technical meaning of a word or phrase may be discarded if it is inconsistent with the testator's general intention, as expressed in his will read as a whole.[28]

(3) *Supplying, omitting or changing words.* This general intention may even supply by implication words omitted from the will (by, perhaps, the proverbial "blundering attorney's clerk"[29]). But the court exercises great caution over reading words into a will and only does so if it is clear from the will itself, "from the four corners of the document,"[30] (i) that something has been omitted from the will and (ii) what the omission was. Of course, it is not necessary that the precise words omitted should be clear from the will but the substance of the omission must be clear.[31] In *Re Whitrick*[32] T by her will left her entire estate to her husband and provided that "in the event of my husband . . . and myself both dying at the same time" her estate should be held upon trust for X, Y and Z equally. T's husband predeceased her and consequently, according to the literal meaning of the words used, the gift to X, Y and Z failed and T's entire estate passed as on her intestacy. The Court of Appeal held that it was clear from the will as a whole that T intended, by means of the gift to X, Y and Z, to provide for the contingency of her husband not surviving her. The will was therefore read as if it had directed that X, Y and Z were to take in the event of the husband predeceasing T, as well as in the event of them both dying at the same time.

In the same way, the will is read as if certain words were omitted or changed if it is clear from the will itself (i) that an error has been made in the wording and (ii) what the substance of the intended wording

[26] *Re Haygarth* [1913] 2 Ch. 9, 15, quoting from *Hawkins on Wills* (2nd ed., 1912), p. 6.
[27] *Ante*, p. 413.
[28] *Ante*, pp. 413–414 and 415.
[29] *Re Redfern* (1877) 6 Ch.D. 133, 138: perhaps the attorney's blundering clerk was meant.
[30] *Re Whitrick* [1957] 1 W.L.R. 884, 887.
[31] *Ibid.* at pp. 892–893: *cf. Re Follett* [1955] 1 W.L.R. 429 (substance of omission not clear).
[32] *Supra*: the court approved the principle stated in *Jarman on Wills* (7th ed., 1930), Vol. I, p. 556, "Where it is clear on the face of a will that the testator has not accurately or completely expressed his meaning by the words he has used, and it is also clear what are the words which he has omitted, these words may be supplied in order to effectuate the intention as collected from the context." See also *Re Smith* [1948] Ch. 49 (implication of gift of residue to husband absolutely); *Re Riley's W.T.* [1962] 1 W.L.R. 344; *Re Doland's W.T.* [1970] Ch. 267.

was.[33] Thus it may be clear from the will itself which of two provisions in the will, which are irreconcilable with each other,[34] ought to be changed, and in what way. Failing this, the court applies the well-established "rule of despair"[35] that the later of the two irreconcilable provisions must prevail because it is the last expression of the testator's wishes.[36]

It must be emphasised that this power of the court to supply, omit or change words, as part of the process of construing a will, is very limited in its scope. The requirement that the substance of the intended wording must be clear from the will itself is particularly demanding. It may be obvious from the will that an error has been made in its wording, but a court of construction cannot supply, omit or change words if the will leaves the substance of the intended wording in doubt. This can, however, be remedied by the rectification of the will if this remedy is available.[37]

Intention to revoke as clear as original gift. It is a "very clear and strong rule"[38] that if a will or codicil contains a gift in clear terms, a later codicil is not construed as revoking the gift unless the intention to revoke is as clear as the original intention to give.[39] In *Re Freeman*[40] T by his will appointed A to be one of his executors and gave him a legacy of £1,000 if he should prove the will, and also gave him a share of residue. By a codicil T revoked the appointment of A as executor and the legacy of £1,000, appointed B to be an executor in place of A, and declared that his will should be construed as if the name of B were inserted throughout instead of the name of A. The Court of Appeal held that this declaration did not impliedly revoke the gift to A of the share of residue. As Buckley L.J. put it[41]:

"The . . . principle is that a clear gift in a will is not to be cut down by anything subsequent which does not with reasonable certainty indicate the intention of the testator to cut it down. If there be a plain gift in a will the Court will not say it is defeated by something ambiguous in a codicil which does not plainly cut down the previous gift."

---

[33] *Hart* v. *Tulk* (1852) 2 De G.M. & G. 300 ("fourth" schedule read as fifth schedule in accordance with general intention); *Key* v. *Key* (1853) 4 De G.M. & G. 73; *Re Bacharach's W.T.* [1959] Ch. 245 (words of will rearranged in accordance with general intention).

[34] Two gifts of residue, one after the other, are reconcilable by construing the second gift as meant to sweep up any shares of the first residue which fail, and possibly lapsed legacies, *Re Isaac* [1905] 1 Ch. 427; *Re Gare* [1952] Ch. 80. See also *Re Alexander's W.T.* [1948] 2 All E.R. 111 (bequest of same bracelet to A and later in will to B: held each entitled to half bracelet).

[35] *Re Potter's W.T.* [1944] Ch. 70, 77.

[36] *Re Hammond* (1938) 54 T.L.R. 903 (I give to X "the sum of one hundred pounds (£500)": held £500).

[37] *Ante,* pp. 55–56.

[38] *Follett* v. *Pettman* (1883) 23 Ch.D. 337, 342; *Re Resch's W.T.* [1969] 1 A.C. 514, 547–548.

[39] *Doe d. Hearle* v. *Hicks* (1832) 1 Cl. & F. 20, 24; *Re Stoodley* [1915] 2 Ch. 295 ("a clear unambiguous gift in a will can only be revoked by codicil by words at least equally clear and unambiguous as those of the original gift").

[40] [1910] 1 Ch. 681: see also *Re Percival* (1888) 59 L.T. 21; *Re Wray* [1951] Ch. 425; *cf. Re Crawshay* [1948] Ch. 123.

[41] *Ibid.* at p. 691.

B. ADMISSIBILITY OF EVIDENCE

Probate conclusive as to the words of the will. A grant of probate (or letters of administration with the will annexed) is conclusive as to what the words of the will are. A court of construction must not look at the original will for the purpose of correcting any error alleged to exist in the wording of the probate copy of the will.[42] Extrinsic evidence is not admissible in a court of construction to fill up total blanks in the will.[43]

However, a court of construction may look at the original will for the purpose of considering the manner in which it is set out. Thus the presence (or absence) of marks of punctuation,[44] the use of capital letters, the arrangement of the words,[45] and the presence of blanks[46] or erasures[47] in the original will may be taken into consideration in construing the will, whether or not they appear in the probate copy.[48] Again, if two testamentary documents have been admitted to probate, a court of construction may decide that the earlier document has no operative effect, all its provisions having been revoked or repeated in the later document.[49]

Evidence to prove existence of object or subject-matter of gift. Obviously extrinsic evidence is admissible to prove the existence of any person or property described in the will. "You must always, of course, have evidence who are the persons mentioned, and you must also have evidence of what are the things bequeathed."[50] For instance, if by his will T gives to "my nephew John Turner the car which I own at the date of my death" (*or* "at the date of my will"), evidence is admissible to prove the existence of a person who, and of a chattel which, falls within the description used in the will. Such evidence is essential "in order to establish contact between the language in the will and the outside world."[51]

Distinction between direct and circumstantial extrinsic evidence. The question now arises—what extrinsic evidence is admissible as an

---

[42] *Oppenheim* v. *Henry* (1853) 9 Hare 802, note (*b*); *Gann* v. *Gregory* (1854) 3 De G.M. & G. 777; *Re Cliff's Trusts* [1892] 2 Ch. 229. Such an error can only be corrected by an amendment made by the Family Division to the grant.

[43] *Baylis* v. *Att.-Gen.* (1741) 2 Atk. 239 (to Mr.   ); *Hunt* v. *Hort* (1791) 3 B.C.C. 311 (bequest to Lady   : court could not supply a total blank by parol evidence): see *post*, p. 423. *Cf.* a partial blank, *In the Estate of Hubbuck* [1905] P. 129 (*post*, p. 419).

[44] *Houston* v. *Burns* [1918] A.C. 337 (commas); *Gauntlett* v. *Carter* (1853) 17 Beav. 586 (commas); *Re Steel* [1979] Ch. 218 (absence of commas); *Child* v. *Elsworth* (1852) 2 De G.M. & G. 679, 683 (full stop); *Morrall* v. *Sutton* (1845) 1 Ph. 533, 538 (brackets); *Compton* v. *Bloxham* (1845) 2 Coll. 201 (colon).

[45] *Re Steel, supra,* (indentation or the lack of it).

[46] *Re Harrison* (1885) 30 Ch.D. 390 ("I know of no rule that for the purpose of construing a will you may not look at the original will itself").

[47] *Re Battie-Wrightson* [1920] 2 Ch. 330 (name of bank erased; later in will legacy to X of balance "at the said bank": held court may look at original will to ascertain name of bank); *Manning* v. *Purcell* (1855) 24 L.J.Ch. 522.

[48] Normally a photostat copy of the will is annexed to the grant, so that reference to the original will is seldom necessary.

[49] *Re Hawksley's Settlement* [1934] Ch. 384.

[50] Per James L.J. in *Sherratt* v. *Mountford* (1873) 8 Ch.App. 928, 929: see *Sunford* v. *Raikes* (1816) 1 Mer. 646.

[51] Albery (1963) 26 M.L.R. 353, 359.

aid in the construction of a will so as to ascertain the testator's expressed intention? At the outset it is essential to distinguish between *direct* and *circumstantial* extrinsic evidence of the testator's testamentary intention. If by his will T gives a legacy of £100 "to Mrs. G," the fact that T was acquainted with a lady named Mrs. Gregg, whom he habitually referred to as "Mrs. G," is *circumstantial evidence* of T's intended meaning.[52] On the other hand, the fact that T told a friend that he intended to give a legacy of £100 to "Mrs. Gregg" is *direct evidence* of T's intended meaning. Evidence of any instructions the testator gave for his will and of any declarations made by him as to what he intended to do, or had done, by his will constitutes direct evidence of his intended meaning.

If the testator dies before January 1, 1983, the admissibility of extrinsic evidence to assist in the interpretation of his will is governed by case law. If the testator dies after December 31, 1982, section 21 of the Administration of Justice Act 1982 is applicable.[53]

Admission of direct extrinsic evidence on death before 1983. If the testator dies before 1983, direct extrinsic evidence of his intended meaning is not admissible[54] except in cases of equivocation. Such evidence is also admissible to rebut equitable presumptions but these are not rules of construction.

(1) *Equivocation.*[55] There is an equivocation if a description of an object or subject in a will is applicable to two or more persons or things. To consider some examples:

(i) There is an equivocation as to the *object* of a gift if T by his will makes a gift to "my son John," and T has two sons called John[56]; or to "my granddaughter   ," and there are three of them[57]; or to "my nephew Arthur Murphy," and there is more than one nephew who satisfies the description[58]; or to "The Clergy Society," and there are several societies popularly so called.[59]

(ii) There is an equivocation as to the *subject* of a gift if T by his will makes a gift of his manor of Dale, and T has two manors of that name, South Dale and North Dale.[60]

If the will, construed as a whole with the aid of any extrinsic evidence admissible under the armchair principle,[61] shows to which of the

---

[52] See *Abbot* v. *Massie* (1796) 3 Ves. 148 (the nature of the evidence is not reported).

[53] Administration of Justice Act 1982, ss.73(6) and 76(11).

[54] *Doe* d. *Hiscocks* v. *Hiscocks* (1839) 5 M. & W. 363; *Charter* v. *Charter* (1874) L.R. 7 H.L. 364 (see *post*, p. 421); *Re Atkinson's W.T.* [1978] 1 W.L.R. 586, 590: see Phipson (1904) 20 L.Q.R. 245, 252–253 and 268–271. However, T's instructions may be admissible as *circumstantial* evidence of T's intended meaning, *Re Ofner* [1909] 1 Ch. 60 (T gave legacy to grandnephew "Robert": evidence admissible that T wrote "Robert," referring to grandnephew Richard, in instructions to solicitor).

[55] See generally *Theobald, op. cit.* pp. 214 *et seq.*

[56] *Lord Cheyney's Case* (1590) 5 Co. 68a, 68b (T supposed elder son John to be dead).

[57] *In the Estate of Hubbuck* [1905] P. 129: see *Price* v. *Page* (1799) 4 Ves. 680 ("   Price the son of   Price").

[58] *Re Jackson* [1933] Ch. 237: see *Doe* d. *Morgan* v. *Morgan* (1832) 1 C. & M. 235.

[59] *Re Clergy Society* (1856) 2 K. & J. 615.

[60] *Miller* v. *Travers* (1832) 8 Bing. 244, 248: see *Re Battie-Wrightson* [1920] 2 Ch. 330.

[61] *Post*, pp. 421–422.

persons or things the testator was referring, there is no equivocation.[62] But, if it does not, direct extrinsic evidence is admissible of declarations of intention by the testator showing to which he was referring.[63] If the equivocation cannot be resolved, the gift fails for uncertainty.[64]

If part of the description does not apply to any possible person (or thing), it may be rejected, leaving the remainder of the description equivocal. Thus there is an equivocation if by his will T makes a gift to "my nephew Arthur Charles Brown," and at the date of his will T has two or more nephews named Arthur Brown and no nephew named Charles Brown.[65] The remainder of the description must, however, be sufficient to describe with legal certainty one of the competing persons (or things), if the other of them did not exist.[66] On the other hand, if T's gift is to "my nephew Arthur Charles Brown," and at the date of his will T has one nephew named Arthur Brown and another nephew named Charles Brown, there is no equivocation because part of the description ("Arthur") applies to one person and another part ("Charles") applies to the other person.[67]

Sometimes the term "latent ambiguity" is used instead of equivocation. The latter term seems preferable because a description which is equally applicable to two or more persons or things constitutes an equivocation, even though their existence is mentioned elsewhere in the will.[68]

(2) *Equitable presumptions.* Direct extrinsic evidence is admissible of the testator's declarations of intention in order to rebut certain equitable presumptions which are explained later in this chapter,[69] *i.e.* to rebut:

   (i) the presumption of the satisfaction of a debt by a legacy[70];
   (ii) the presumption of the satisfaction of a legacy by another legacy[71]; and
   (iii) the presumption of the satisfaction of a portion-debt by a legacy.[72]

If extrinsic evidence is admitted to rebut an equitable presumption, contrary evidence supporting the equitable presumption is also admissible.[73] But if no equitable presumption is applicable, the general

---

[62] *Doe* d. *Westlake* v. *Westlake* (1820) 4 B. & Ald. 57.

[63] *Lord Cheyney's Case, supra; In the Estate of Hubbuck, supra,* (T's instructions for her will); *Price* v. *Page, supra.*

[64] *Asten* v. *Asten* [1894] 3 Ch. 261 (*ante,* pp. 349–350).

[65] *Re Ray* [1916] 1 Ch. 461; *Bennett* v. *Marshall* (1856) 2 K. & J. 740.

[66] *Re Ray, supra:* cf. *Miller* v. *Travers* (1832) 8 Bing. 244.

[67] *Doe* d. *Hiscocks* v. *Hiscocks* (1839) 5 M. & W. 363; *Charter* v. *Charter* (1874) L.R. 7 H.L. 364. It is not clear why this rule became law, see *Charter* v. *Charter, ibid.* at p. 383.

[68] *Doe* d. *Gord* v. *Needs* (1836) 2 M. & W. 129 ("George Gord the son of Gord"; George, son of George Gord, and George, son of John Gord, both mentioned elsewhere in will: evidence of T's declarations of intention admissible).

[69] *Post,* pp. 446 *et seq.*

[70] *Wallace* v. *Pomfret* (1805) 11 Ves. 542.

[71] *Hurst* v. *Beach* (1821) 5 Madd. 351, 360; *Hall* v. *Hill* (1841) 1 Dr. & War. 94, 124–128.

[72] *Re Tussaud's Estate* (1878) 9 Ch.D. 363 ("if in any way a presumption arises, you admit evidence to rebut that presumption").

[73] *Kirk* v. *Eddowes* (1844) 3 Hare 509, 517 (a decision on ademption of a legacy by a portion).

rule applies and extrinsic evidence of the testator's declarations of intention is not admissible.[74]

Circumstantial extrinsic evidence admissible under armchair principle on death before 1983. Circumstantial extrinsic evidence of the testator's intended meaning is admissible as an aid in construction in cases of uncertainty or ambiguity. This rule is often referred to as the "armchair principle." "You may place yourself, so to speak, in [the testator's] armchair, and consider the circumstances by which he was surrounded when he made his will to assist you in arriving at his intention."[75]

(1) *Identity of object of gift.* The decided cases usually concern the identity of either the object or the subject matter of a gift. Reverting to T's gift of a legacy of £100 to "Mrs. G," uncertainty arises from the incomplete description of the object of the gift and evidence that T was acquainted with a lady named Mrs. Gregg, whom he habitually referred to as "Mrs. G," is therefore admissible as circumstantial evidence of T's intended meaning.[76] The case of *Charter* v. *Charter*[77] is an instance of uncertainty arising from a misdescription of the object of the gift. T, a farmer, by his will appointed "my son, Forster Charter" as his executor and gave him his residuary estate. T had had a son named Forster Charter, who had died some years before, and at the date of the will T had two sons named William Forster Charter and Charles Charter. Probate in common form was granted to William. Charles applied for revocation of this grant on the ground that he was the person appointed executor. At the trial Lord Penzance admitted evidence of the surrounding circumstances when T made his will, *i.e.* that Charles was living at home with his parents and working on T's farm, that William had lived away from home for some years and seldom visited T, and that T did not call him "Forster" but always "William" or "Willie." Lord Penzance decided in favour of Charles, and William failed in an appeal to the House of Lords which was evenly divided. The House of Lords held that declarations by T of his intention to benefit Charles had been improperly admitted in evidence because there was no equivocation. Lord Cairns and Lord Selborne nevertheless upheld the decision of Lord Penzance. They pointed to a provision in the will under which the executor was directed to pay an annuity and allow maintenance to T's widow "so long as they reside together in the same house": this provision was only appropriate when applied to persons who were living together at the date of the will. The evidence of surrounding circumstances established that Charles, but not William, was living at home with his parents at that time.

---

[74] *Hurst* v. *Beach, supra; Hall* v. *Hill, supra; Re Shields* [1912] 1 Ch. 591.

[75] *Per* James L.J. in *Boyes* v. *Cook* (1880) 14 Ch.D. 53, 56.

[76] See *Abbott* v. *Massie* (1796) 3 Ves. 148; *Price* v. *Page* (1799) 4 Ves. 680 (gift of legacy to " Price the son of Price"); *Re Ofner* [1909] 1 Ch. 60 (single instance of T's use of wrong name admissible); *Re Tetsall* [1961] 1 W.L.R. 938.

[77] (1874) L.R. 7 H.L. 364: see also *Doe* d. *Hiscocks* v. *Hiscocks* (1839) 5 M. & W. 363; *Bernasconi* v. *Atkinson* (1853) 10 Hare 345.

(2) *Identity of subject matter of gift.* To turn to cases where there was uncertainty as to the identity of the subject matter of the gift. In *Ricketts* v. *Turquand*[78] T by his will devised "all my estate in Shropshire, called Ashford Hall," and the House of Lords held that evidence was admissible to show the extent of the land in Shropshire which T during his lifetime habitually called his Ashford Hall estate. Again, in *Kell* v. *Charmer*[79] T, a jeweller, by his will gave "to my son William the sum of i.x.x. To my son Robert Charles the sum of o.x.x." The court held that evidence was admissible that in carrying on his business T used private symbols to denote his prices and that, according to this system, the letters "i.x.x." and "o.x.x." represented £100 and £200 respectively.

(3) *Limits on effect of evidence.* Circumstantial evidence of the testator's intended meaning is admitted in cases of uncertainty or ambiguity so as to ascertain the testator's expressed intention in his will. However, such evidence cannot make words in a will bear a meaning which on the face of the will they are incapable of bearing.[80] Extrinsic evidence alone cannot make "black" mean "white."

As regards the object of a gift, a "very strong presumption"[81] arises that the person who completely satisfies the description in the will was meant and this presumption cannot be overcome by circumstantial extrinsic evidence except in "exceptional circumstances."[82] In *National Society for the Prevention of Cruelty to Children* v. *Scottish National Society for the Prevention of Cruelty to Children*[83] T gave a legacy "to the National Society for the Prevention of Cruelty to Children," which was the exact name of an English society. T had lived all his life in Scotland and the legacy appeared in his will amid a series of legacies to Scottish charities. The legacy was claimed by the Scottish National Society for the Prevention of Cruelty to Children, which evidence showed had been brought to T's notice shortly before T made his will: there was no evidence that T had taken any interest in the English society. The House of Lords decided that the English society was entitled to the legacy. Lord Loreburn said that "what a man has said ought to be acted upon unless it is clearly proved that he meant something different from what he said. . . . I do not think that in this case any ambiguity has been established."[84]

Probably, on the analogy of this case, the same rule applies as regards the subject of a gift.[85]

---

[78] (1848) 1 H.L.Cas. 472: see also *Webb* v. *Byng* (1855) 1 K. & J. 580 ("all my Quendon Hall estates in Essex"); *Castle* v. *Fox* (1871) 11 Eq. 542 ("my mansion and estate called Cleeve Court"); *Re Glassington* [1906] 2 Ch. 305 (my "real estate" passed T's interest under a trust for sale of realty as T had no realty at date of will) and *cf. Re Sykes* [1940] 4 All E.R. 10; *Re Lewis's W.T.* [1985] 1 W.L.R. 102.

[79] (1856) 23 Beav. 195.

[80] *Higgins* v. *Dawson* [1902] A.C. 1; *Re Mulder* [1943] 2 All E.R. 150, 151; *Re Lewis's W.T., supra.*

[81] *National Society for the Prevention of Cruelty to Children* v. *Scottish National Society for the Prevention of Cruelty to Children* [1915] A.C. 207, 212 and 216.

[82] *Ibid.* ("in some abnormal case of a special character").

[83] [1915] A.C. 207: see also *Re Satterthwaite's W.T.* [1966] 1 W.L.R. 277; *Re Carlisle* [1950] N.I. 105.

[84] *Ibid.* at pp. 212–213.

[85] But see *Re Seal* [1894] 1 Ch. 316, 322–323.

Admission of extrinsic evidence on death after 1982. If the testator dies after December 31, 1982, section 21 of the Administration of Justice Act 1982 makes both direct and circumstantial extrinsic evidence of the testator's intention admissible to assist in interpretation in three situations:

(1) *In so far as any part of a will is meaningless.* Thus if T employs in his will a word or symbol which has no meaning to anyone else, both direct and circumstantial extrinsic evidence of his intention is admissible to assist in the interpretation of the word or symbol. For example, such evidence is admissible if T gives to his son "the sum of o.x.x.,"[86] or gives Blackacre "to K. then to L."[87] If T died before 1983, only circumstantial extrinsic evidence is admissible.

However extrinsic evidence is probably not admissible to fill up a total blank in the will[88] ("I give £100 to   "), because there is nothing which the evidence can assist in interpreting. Again, if T's will reads, "I give nothing to my son," extrinsic evidence is not admissible that T intended "nothing" to denote £20,000, because this part of the will is not meaningless.

(2) *In so far as the language[89] used in any part of a will is ambiguous on the face of it.* A classic instance is a gift by T's will of "my money" or "my effects."[90] If T died before 1983, only circumstantial extrinsic evidence is admissible: if T dies after 1982, both direct and circumstantial extrinsic evidence of his intention is admissible.

(3) *In so far as evidence, other than evidence of the testator's intention, shows that the language used in any part of a will is ambiguous in the light of surrounding circumstances.* This obviously applies where there is an equivocation. But it also applies where there is no equivocation—for instance, where T makes a gift to "my nephew Arthur Charles Brown," and at the date of his will T has one nephew named Arthur Brown and another nephew named Charles Brown.[91] The extrinsic evidence of T's intention is admissible, not to show that the language is ambiguous, but to assist in the interpretation of language which is shown to be ambiguous in the light of surrounding circumstances.

If the testator died before 1983, direct extrinsic evidence of his intention is only admissible in cases of equivocation. If the testator dies after 1982, section 21 of the Administration of Justice Act 1982 makes such evidence much more generally admissible. However, the function of the

[86] See *Kell* v. *Charmer* (1856) 23 Beav. 195 (before 1983, circumstantial evidence of T's use of private symbols in his jeweller's business admissible, see *ante*, p. 422).
[87] See *Clayton* v. *Lord Nugent* (1844) 13 M. & W. 200 (before 1983, key written on separate card not admissible as direct evidence): but circumstantial evidence was admissible, *Abbot* v. *Massie* (1796) 3 Ves. 148 (*ante*, p. 421).
[88] *Ante*, p. 418.
[89] See *Re Williams* [1985] 1 W.L.R. 905, 912–913 (language includes numerals as much as words or letters, but *quaere* whether it includes a division of legatees in a will into three groups).
[90] *Re Williams, supra*, at p. 911 (obvious examples): for gifts of "money" see *ante*, p. 413.
[91] *Ante*, p. 420: for another instance see *Re Smalley* [1929] 2 Ch. 112 (before 1983, circumstantial evidence admissible, see *ante*, p. 414).

direct and circumstantial extrinsic evidence, admissible in all these three situations under section 21, is "to assist in . . . interpretation," not to make a new will for the testator. Accordingly, such evidence cannot make "black" mean "white." To quote Nicholls J. in *Re Williams*[92]:

> "The evidence may assist by showing which of two or more possible meanings a testator was attaching to a particular word or phrase. . . . That meaning may be one which, without recourse to the extrinsic evidence, would not really have been apparent at all. So long as that meaning is one which the word or phrase read in its context is capable of bearing, then the court may conclude that, assisted by the extrinsic evidence, that is its correct construction. But if, however liberal may be the approach of the court, the meaning is one which the word or phrase cannot bear, I do not see how in carrying out a process of . . . interpretation . . . the court can declare that meaning to be the meaning of the word or phrase. Such a conclusion, varying or contradicting the language used, would amount to rewriting part of the will. . . . "

C. Date from Which a Will Speaks

A will speaks from death as to property. Section 24 of the Wills Act 1837 provides that "every will shall be construed, with reference to the real estate and personal estate comprised in it,[93] to speak and take effect as if it had been executed immediately before the death of the testator, unless a contrary intention shall appear by the will." Thus, the description of the subject matter of a gift is prima facie to be construed as comprising all the property which satisfies the terms of the description at the death of the testator, including property acquired by him since he made his will.[94] For example, a devise by a testator of "all my freehold land" prima facie comprises all the freehold land to which the testator is entitled at his death, including any acquired by him since the date of his will.[95]

(1) *Specific gift.* Section 24 applies to specific gifts, as well as to general and residuary gifts. A specific legacy by T of "all my shares in Marks & Spencer plc" speaks from T's death and is construed as a gift of all the shares in Marks & Spencer to which T is entitled at his death, unless a contrary intention appears in the will.[96] Similarly, a specific devise by T of "all my lands in the county of Kent" is construed as a gift of all T's

---

[92] [1985] 1 W.L.R. 905, 912.

[93] *Langdale (Lady)* v. *Briggs* (1856) L.J.Ch. 27, 49 ("with reference to the real estate and personal estate comprised in it" means "so far as the will comprises dispositions of real and personal estate").

[94] Before the Wills Act 1837 it was a rule of law that realty acquired after the date of a will could not be devised; s.3 of the Act made it lawful for a testator to devise his after-acquired realty.

[95] *Langdale (Lady)* v. *Briggs* (1856) 8 De G.M. & G. 391: see *Re Kempthorne* [1930] 1 Ch. 268.

[96] *Goodlad* v. *Burnett* (1855) 1 K. & J. 341 (gift of "my New Three-and-a-quarter per Cent. Annuities": held gift passed all Annuities of which T died possessed): see also *Trinder* v. *Trinder* (1866) L.R. 1 Eq. 695; *Re Bancroft* [1928] Ch. 577.

lands in the county of Kent at the date of his death, unless a contrary intention appears in the will.[97] In each of these examples the subject matter of the gift is generic, the subject matter being so described as to be capable of increase or decrease between the date of the will and the date of T's death.

On the other hand, if the subject matter is described with such particularity as to show that an object in existence at the date of the will was intended, a contrary intention appears in the will and section 24 does not apply. For instance, a specific legacy by T of "my 200 shares in Marks & Spencer plc" refers to the 200 shares owned by T at the date of the will and accordingly, if T sells these shares before his death, the legacy fails by ademption, even though T later buys other shares in the same company.[98] In the same way, a specific legacy of "my piano" has been held to refer to the piano which T possessed at the date of her will; T later sold this piano and bought another one, and the court held that the legacy failed by ademption.[99] Again, a specific devise by T of his "house and effects known as Cross Villa situated in Templeton" has been held to refer to the premises known as Cross Villa at the date of T's will. At that date the premises comprised half an acre of land with a house upon it. T later divided part of the land from the rest by a hedge and erected two more houses upon this part of the land. The court held that the devise passed the whole premises known as Cross Villa at the date of T's will, including the part of the land with the two new houses later erected upon it.[1]

(2) *Reference in will to the present time.* If T by his will devises "all the freehold land of which I am possessed *at the date of this my will*," obviously section 24 is excluded and the devise does not pass any freehold land acquired by T after the date of his will. But a reference in T's will to property *"now"* or *"at present"* possessed by him may refer to (i) the date of his will, or (ii) the date of his death. Such a reference to the present time makes it necessary to consider the particular language of T's will in order to ascertain whether a contrary intention appears excluding section 24.[2] For instance, if such a reference to the present time is an essential part of the description of the subject matter of a specific gift, a contrary intention appears excluding section 24 and the reference is construed as referring to the date of T's will.[3] On the other

[97] *Re Evans* [1909] 1 Ch. 784, 786; *Re Davies* [1925] Ch. 642; *Castle* v. *Fox* (1871) L.R. 11 Eq. 542 (my "mansion and estate called Cleeve Court"): *cf. Webb* v. *Byng* (1855) 1 K. & J. 580. Where s.24 applies, a gift only passes after-acquired property which falls within the description of the subject-matter of the gift, *Re Portal and Lamb* (1885) 30 Ch.D. 50 (devise of "my cottage and all my land at S": T later bought large house adjoining his small cottage: held s.24 applied but house did not satisfy description).

[98] *Re Gibson* (1866) L.R. 2 Eq. 669 (gift of "my one thousand North British Railway preference shares"; T later sold this holding and bought other shares in the same company: held s.24 was excluded by T's contrary intention and the specific legacy failed by ademption).

[99] *Re Sikes* [1927] 1 Ch. 364; see also *Re Gibson, supra,* at p. 672 ("my Holy Family picture"); *Castle* v. *Fox* (1871) L.R. 11 Eq. 542, 551–552 and 555; *Theobald, op. cit.* p. 221.

[1] *Re Evans* [1909] 1 Ch. 784.

[2] *Re Whitby* [1944] Ch. 210; *Cole* v. *Scott* (1849) 1 Mac. & G. 518, *Hutchinson* v. *Burrow* (1861) 6 H. & N. 583.

[3] *Re Whitby, supra,* (construction of exclusion clause).

hand, if such a reference to the present time is not an essential part of the description of the subject matter of the gift, but merely an additional description, the reference does not exclude the operation of section 24: accordingly, in the absence of any controlling context, the will speaks from T's death and the reference is construed as referring to the date of T's death. This construction was adopted in *Re Willis*[4] where T devised "all that my freehold house and premises situate at Oakleigh Park, Whetstone . . . and known as 'Ankerwyke,' and in which I now reside." Eve J. held that the phrase "in which I now reside" was merely an additional description of the subject matter of the gift and, speaking from T's death under section 24, the phrase referred to the date of T's death. The devise therefore passed the house and premises known as "Ankerwyke" at the date of T's death, including two adjoining plots of land purchased by T after the date of his will and occupied by T as part of "Ankerwyke."

(3) *Testator's later acquisition of different interest.* If T by his will makes a gift of "my leasehold house, 54 Narcissus Road," of which T is the lessee at the date of his will, and T later acquires the freehold reversion, it was held in *Re Fleming's Will Trusts*[5] that the gift passes T's entire interest in the property at his death. To quote from Templeman J.'s judgment in this case,[6] "a gift of property discloses an intention to give the estate and interest of the testator in that property at his death; a mere reference in the will to the estate and interest held by the testator at the date of his will is not sufficient to disclose a contrary intention." On occasion the same result has been reached in reliance (at least in part) on section 24,[7] but this result is probably best explained as based on the testator's intention to pass the property for whatever interest he has at his death.

Similarly, if T by his will makes a gift of his share in a partnership business, in which he has a third share at the date of his will, and T later acquires his two partners' shares and carries on the business as sole owner until his death, the gift passes T's entire interest in the business at his death.[8]

However, if T by his will shows an intention to give the leasehold interest in Blackacre which he holds at the date of his will, *and nothing else*, his intention must prevail. If at his death T no longer holds this leasehold interest, the gift fails by ademption; such a gift does not pass

[4] [1911] 2 Ch. 563: see also *Re Champion* [1893] 1 Ch. 101 (where North J. adopted this construction and the C.A. relied on republication by codicil); *Re Horton* [1920] 2 Ch. 1.

[5] [1974] 1 W.L.R. 1552 (no merger occurred, but T's freehold estate and leasehold interest both passed under the gift): see also *Struthers* v. *Struthers* (1857) 5 W.R. 809; *Miles* v. *Miles* (1866) L.R. 1 Eq. 462; *Cox* v. *Bennett* (1868) L.R. 6 Eq. 422; *Saxton* v. *Saxton* (1879) 13 Ch.D. 359 (gift of "all my term and interest in the leasehold . . . premises . . . No. 1, Berkeley Gardens . . . subject to the payment of the ground rent and performance of the covenants affecting the same": held subsequently acquired freehold passed). As to renewal of a lease see *Wedgwood* v. *Denton* (1871) L.R. 12 Eq. 290.

[6] *Ibid.* at p. 1555.

[7] *Miles* v. *Miles, supra; Saxton* v. *Saxton, supra*: s.23 of the Wills Act 1837 was relied on (at least in part) in *Struthers* v. *Struthers, supra, Cox* v. *Bennett, supra,* and *Saxton* v. *Saxton, supra: sed quaere* whether s.23 is relevant.

[8] *Re Russell* (1882) 19 Ch.D. 432 (s.23 relied on).

any other leasehold interest in Blackacre granted to T after the date of his will.[9]

A will speaks from its date as to the object of a gift. Section 24 applies with regard to the subject matter of a gift but it does not in any way affect the construction of a will with regard to the object of a gift.[10] In general, a will speaks from its date as to the object of a gift, unless a contrary intention appears in the will. Accordingly, words in a will indicating an existing person prima facie refer to a person in existence at the date of the will. Thus, where T by his will gave to "Lord Sherborne and his heirs my Oliver Cromwell cup . . . for an heirloom," and the person who was Lord Sherborne at the date of the will died before T, the Court of Appeal held that the gift lapsed and did not take effect in favour of the person who was Lord Sherborne at T's death.[11] Similarly, a gift by T to "the eldest son of my sister Frances" is a gift in favour of the person who answers the description at the date of the will, and the gift lapses if that person dies before T.[12]

The general rule that a will speaks from its date as to the object of a gift is, of course, excluded if a contrary intention appears in the will. For instance, a gift by T of a legacy to "the Lord Mayor of London for the time being" takes effect in favour of the person who holds this office at T's death.[13] As is explained later, this general rule does not apply to a class gift or to an individual gift to each member of a class.[14]

Effect of republication.[15] (1) *Subject of a gift.* If a will speaks from its date as to the subject matter of a gift (section 24 not being applicable because a contrary intention appears by the will), and later the will is republished by a codicil, the effect is to make the will speak *from the date of the codicil* as to the subject matter of the gift, unless a contrary intention appears. In *Re Reeves*[16] a testator by his will made in 1921 gave to his daughter "all my interest in my present lease" of Blackacre. At the date of his will the testator held a lease granted in 1917 and due to expire in 1924. Later the testator took a new lease for a term of 12 years and by a codicil made in 1926 confirmed his will. The court held that the daughter was entitled to the new lease. The testator had republished his will by confirming it, and the will, speaking as if it had been executed at the date of the codicil, referred to the new and not to the expired old lease. But republication does not make a gift pass property which does

[9] *Cox* v. *Bennett, supra,* at p. 426; *Re Reeves* [1928] Ch. 351.
[10] *Bullock* v. *Bennett* (1855) 7 De G.M. & G. 283.
[11] *Re Whorwood* (1887) 34 Ch.D. 446.
[12] *Amyot* v. *Dwarris* [1904] A.C. 268: see also *Foster* v. *Cook* (1791) 3 Bro.C.C. 347 (gift by T's will to the child, wherewith his wife was pregnant; this child was stillborn: held gift did not take effect in favour of another child of which wife was pregnant at T's death); *Re Coley* [1903] 2 Ch. 102 (the wife of my son).
[13] *Re Daniels* (1918) 118 L.T. 435: the general rule may not apply to a gift to the holder of an office, *In the Estate of Jones* (1927) 43 T.L.R. 324.
[14] *Post,* pp. 435 *et seq.*
[15] For the requirements of republication see *ante,* p. 80.
[16] [1928] Ch. 351: see also *Re Champion* [1893] 1 Ch. 101 (land "now in my occupation" included land acquired by I between making and republishing his will); *Re Fraser* [1904] 1 Ch. 726; *Grealey* v. *Sampson* [1917] 1 Ir.R. 286; *Goonewardene* v. *Goonewardene* [1931] A.C. 647.

not answer the description in the will: if by his will the testator had given "my lease of Blackacre dated September 25, 1917," republication would not have made the will refer to the new lease.[17] Again, republication does not make the will speak from the date of the codicil if a contrary intention appears.[18]

(2) *Object of a gift.* Similarly, if a will speaks from its date as to the object of a gift, and later the will is republished by a codicil, the effect is to make the will speak *from the date of the codicil* as to the object of the gift, unless a contrary intention appears. The decision in *Re Hardyman*,[19] which has already been considered,[20] is an instance.

D. EXERCISE OF POWERS

General powers of appointment to which section 27 applies. Section 27 of the Wills Act 1837 makes a general gift by T's will of real or personal estate operate to exercise a power conferred on T to appoint such property "in any manner he may think proper," unless a contrary intention appears by T's will. If section 27 is applicable, T need not expressly show an intention in his will to exercise the general power. "It has been often said, and is now a platitude, that the object of the section was to abolish the distinction between property and a general power over property, because an ordinary man considers in the latter case that the property is his own."[21]

(1) *Powers within section 27.* Section 27 applies to any power of appointment[22] which satisfies each of the following three requirements:

(i) At T's death the power must be capable of being exercised by T by his will[23]; section 27 does not apply to a power exercisable by T by deed but not by will.[24] It is immaterial whether the power exercisable by T by his will had already been created at the date of T's will. Under section 24 of the Wills Act 1837 a will speaks from death as to property and accordingly section 27 applies to a power which is vested in T at his death, though the power was created after the date of T's will.[25]

(ii) The terms of the power must not impose any condition incompatible with the operation of section 27, *e.g.* a condition that T

---

[17] *Re Reeves, supra,* at pp. 357–358.
[18] *Grealey* v. *Sampson, supra,* at p. 305.
[19] [1925] Ch. 287.
[20] *Ante,* p. 338.
[21] *Re Jacob* [1907] 1 Ch. 445, 449.
[22] But not to a power of revocation and new appointment, *Re Brace* [1891] 2 Ch. 671: see also *Re Salvin* [1906] 2 Ch. 459.
[23] *Re Powell's Trusts* (1869) 39 L.J.Ch. 188 (power to appoint to any persons by will only is within s.27); *Hawthorn* v. *Shedden* (1856) 3 Sm. & G. 293.
[24] *Phillipps* v. *Cayley* (1890) 43 Ch.D. 222, 232 and 234.
[25] *Boyes* v. *Cook* (1880) 14 Ch.D. 53; *Airey* v. *Bower* (1887) 12 App.Cas. 263. But s.27 does not apply to a power created after T's death, *Re Young* [1920] 2 Ch. 427.

may only exercise the power by a will "expressly referring to this power."[26]

(iii) T must be entitled to appoint "in any manner he may think proper," *i.e.* to any objects he may think proper. Obviously section 27 does not apply to a special power of appointment among a limited class of objects, *e.g.* T's children.[27] Again, section 27 does not apply to a "hybrid" power to appoint in favour of anyone except one or more excepted persons, *e.g.* except "her present husband, or any friend or relative of his."[28] But a hybrid power to appoint in favour of anyone except X becomes a general power free from exception after the death of X.[29] It follows that if X dies before T, at T's death T has power to appoint to any objects he may think proper and section 27 applies to the power.[30]

(2) *General gifts within section 27.* Section 27 applies to "a general devise of the real estate of the testator, or of the real estate of the testator in any place or in the occupation of any person mentioned in his will, or otherwise described in a general manner," and to "a bequest of the personal estate of the testator, or any bequest of personal property described in a general manner." The section applies both to residuary gifts of property[31] and to specific gifts of property described in a general manner. For instance, a specific devise by T of "all my realty in the County of Kent" carries realty in that county over which T had a general power of appointment at his death. Similarly, a bequest by T of "all my stocks and shares,"[32] or a bequest of "all my shares in Marks & Spencer plc,"[33] in each case passes property of that description over which T had a general power.

Moreover, section 27 applies to a gift by T of general pecuniary legacies because this constitutes a "bequest of personal property described in a general manner." If and so far as T's own assets are insufficient for their payment,[34] the legacies are payable out of personal property over which T had a general power.[35] As Stuart V.-C. explained the rule in *Hawthorn v. Shedden*[36]:

---

[26] *Phillips* v. *Cayley, supra; Re Tarrant's Trust* (1889) 58 L.J.Ch. 780: see also *Re Davies* [1892] 3 Ch. 63. But a condition imposing special formalities as to execution and attestation need not be observed in a formal will when a power is exercised, Wills Act 1837, s.10: see *ante*, pp. 7–8.

[27] *Cloves* v. *Awdry* (1850) 12 Beav. 604.

[28] *Re Byron's Settlement* [1891] 3 Ch. 474.

[29] *Re Harvey* [1950] 1 All E.R. 491: *Re Byron's Settlement, supra,* at p. 480.

[30] *Re Harvey, supra,* at p. 494.

[31] *Re Spooner's Trust* (1851) 2 Sim.(N.S.) 129 ("constituting my son . . . my residuary legatee": held s.27 applied).

[32] *Re Jacob* [1907] 1 Ch. 445; *Turner* v. *Turner* (1852) 21 L.J.Ch. 843: *cf. Re Brown's Trusts* (1855) 1 K. & J. 522.

[33] *Re Doherty-Waterhouse* [1918] 2 Ch. 269 ("all my shares in the Halifax Corporation New Market consolidated stock": held s.27 applied).

[34] For the rules governing the incidence of general legacies see *ante*, pp. 308 *et seq.*

[35] *Hawthorn* v. *Shedden* (1856) 3 Sm. & G. 293; *Re Wilkinson* (1869) L.R. 4 Ch.App. 587; *Re Seabrook* [1911] 1 Ch. 151. An express direction in T's will for the payment of his debts has the same effect, *Laing* v. *Cowan* (1858) 24 Beav. 112; *Re Davies' Trusts* (1871) L.R. 13 Eq. 163, 166.

[36] *Supra,* at p. 303.

"General pecuniary legacies with no particular fund indicated for their payment are bequests of personal property described in a general manner, and therefore, where the proper assets of the testator are inadequate without resort to personal estate over which the testator had a general power of appointment, general pecuniary legacies are within the operation of the 27th section, and the will must be held to include and extend to the personal estate subject to the power of appointment, so far as necessary to satisfy general pecuniary legacies."

(3) *Contrary intention.* The operation of section 27 is excluded if "a contrary intention shall appear by the will," *i.e.* if it appears from the will that T, having the power in mind, did not intend to exercise it.[37] The onus of establishing such a contrary intention from the will lies on those who assert it.[38] In practice such a contrary intention very seldom appears from T's will.

The mere fact that T describes the subject matter of his gift as *"my* realty in the county of Kent" or *"my* stocks and shares" is not any indication of a contrary intention[39]—if it were, this would frustrate the object of section 27, which would hardly apply at all. Again, if T by his will makes an express appointment to X under his general power and gives his residuary estate to Y, and the appointment to X fails for any reason (*e.g.* by lapse), the property subject to the power passes under the residuary gift to Y pursuant to section 27. T's attempted express appointment to X does not indicate that T intends to exclude the property subject to the power from the operation of the residuary gift, if the appointment to X fails.[40]

Powers of appointment to which section 27 does not apply. As already explained, section 27 does not apply to a special power of appointment, or to a hybrid power to appoint in favour of anyone except one or more excepted persons. In order to exercise such a power of appointment by will, there must be a sufficient indication in the will of an intention to exercise the power.[41] In general, a reference either to the power or to the property subject to the power constitutes a sufficient

[37] *Scriven* v. *Sandom* (1862) 2 J. & H. 743 (there must be something in T's will inconsistent with the view that the general gift was meant to exercise the power); *Re Thirlwell* [1958] Ch. 146.

[38] *Re Jarrett* [1919] 1 Ch. 366, 370; *Re Thirlwell, supra.*

[39] *Re Jacob* [1907] 1 Ch. 445 ("all stocks, shares and securities which I possess or to which I am entitled": held s.27 applied); *Re Doherty-Waterhouse* [1918] 2 Ch. 269; *Re Spooner's Trust* (1851) 2 Sim.(N.S.) 129.

[40] *Re Spooner's Trust, supra,* (express appointment by T's will to six children equally; one child predeceased T: held his share passed under T's residuary gift pursuant to s.27); *Re Elen* (1893) 68 L.T. 816 (express appointment to X on contingency which failed); *Re Jarrett* [1919] 1 Ch. 366 (express appointment in will revoked by codicil). See also *Re Stokes* [1922] 2 Ch. 406 and *Re Box's Settlement* [1945] 1 All E.R. 547.

[41] *Re Ackerley* [1913] 1 Ch. 510 (special power); *Re Lawrence's W.T.* [1972] Ch. 418, esp. pp. 428–432 (hybrid power). If the instrument creating the power lays down any special requirement for its exercise, this must also be complied with, *Re Lawrence's W.T., supra,* at p. 430. But a condition imposing special formalities as to execution and attestation need not be observed in a formal will when a power is exercised, Wills Act 1837, s.10, and see *ante,* pp. 7–8.

indication for this purpose.[42] The testator's intention is, of course, to be gathered from an examination of the whole of his will, with the aid of any admissible extrinsic evidence. The decided cases, which are not easily reconcilable, turn on particular wording in particular wills and do not lay down any general principles.[43] "Matters of construction must in the end . . . depend upon the impression made upon the reader's mind by the words that have been used. Such, indeed, is the purpose of language."[44]

Power to bar entail by will. Under section 176 of the Law of Property Act 1925 a tenant in tail[45] has power to bar his entail in any real or personal property by will, and thus dispose of the fee simple in realty, or absolute interest in personalty, or any lesser interest[46] in such property. A testator may exercise this power to bar his entail if the following requirements are satisfied:

(i) the testator is of full age and holds the entail in possession[47] (and not in remainder) at his death;

(ii) his will is either executed after 1925 or republished by a codicil executed after 1925; and

(iii) his will refers specifically *either* to the property (*e.g.* "Blackacre"), *or* to the instrument under which it was acquired (*e.g.* "the property I acquired under my father's will"), *or* to entailed property generally (*e.g.* "all entailed property").[48]

E. Whether Gift is Absolute or for Life

Presumption that devise passes fee simple. Section 28 of the Wills Act 1837 enacts that a devise of real estate to any person without any words of limitation shall be construed to pass the fee simple, or other the whole interest of which the testator has power to dispose, unless a contrary intention appears by his will.[49] The section applies to any will made or republished after 1837.[50] Thus, T's devise of Blackacre "to X" passes T's fee simple estate in Blackacre to X, unless a contrary intention is shown by T's will. The rule applies to a devise by T of any *existing* interest, *e.g.* a devise by T "to X" of a rentcharge (which is vested in T in fee simple at his death) passes the rentcharge to X in fee simple, unless a

---

[42] *Re Ackerley, supra,* at pp. 514–515: see also *Re Holford's Settlement* [1945] Ch. 21 (reviewing some of the case law: "the principle . . . is clear. The difficulty lies in the application of it").

[43] *Re Knight* [1957] Ch. 441, 449–450 and 453.

[44] *Ibid.* at p. 453.

[45] Including an owner of a base fee in possession who has power to enlarge it into a fee simple without the consent of any other person, Law of Property Act 1925, s.176(3): but not a tenant in tail restrained by statute from barring his entail, or a tenant in tail after possibility of issue extinct, *ibid.* s.176(2).

[46] If he merely disposes of a lesser interest such as a life interest, then, subject to the life interest, the entail devolves in the normal way, *ibid.* ss.130(4) and 176(1).

[47] See *ibid.* s.205(1)(xix).

[48] *Acheson* v. *Russell* [1951] Ch. 67 ("the object of the section . . . must surely be to avoid any risk of a disentail being effected by inadvertence or involuntarily").

[49] *Gravenor* v. *Watkins* (1871) L.R. 6 C.P. 500.

[50] Wills Act 1837, s.34.

contrary intention is shown. However, the rule is not applicable to a devise by T of a *new* interest created by his will, *e.g.* a devise by T "to X" of a new rentcharge, issuing out of T's land Blackacre, passes a rent-charge to X *for life*, unless a contrary intention is shown.[51]

Since 1925 a testator who wishes to create an entail in any real or personal property by his will must employ the formal expressions which were effective to create an entail in a deed before 1926, *i.e.* the word "heirs" followed by words of procreation or the words "in tail."[52]

Presumption that bequest is absolute. A bequest by T of personal estate "to X" gives X an absolute interest, unless a contrary intention is shown by T's will. But, if T's will also contains a direction that on X's death the same property is to go to Y, this shows T's intention to give X only a life interest.[53]

Gift over of what remains. Home-made wills sometimes contain a gift of property "to X," followed by a direction that on X's death *what remains* of the property (or words to that effect) is to go to Y. The decided cases indicate that at least three different constructions are possible:

   (i) One construction is that X takes absolutely, and the gift over to Y is void, either because it is repugnant to X's absolute interest[54] or because, construed as a trust, it fails for uncertainty of subject-matter.[55]

  (ii) Another construction is that X takes a life interest, coupled with a power to dispose of capital (perhaps only *inter vivos*, or only by will), and subject thereto Y takes absolutely.[56]

 (iii) A third construction is that X takes a life interest and subject thereto Y takes absolutely.[57] This construction treats the gift over

---

[51] *Nichols* v. *Hawkes* (1853) 10 Hare 342.

[52] Law of Property Act 1925, s.130(1): see also s.130(3) and *Re Jones* [1934] Ch. 315. For the effect since 1925 of informal expressions, which would have created an entail in a will before 1926 (*e.g.* "to X and his issue," "to X and his descendants," or "to X and his children"), see *ibid.* s.130(2); *Hawkins and Ryder on the Construction of Wills* (1965), pp. 256 *et seq.* For the effect of a gift to X, but if he die without issue, to Y, see Wills Act 1837, s.29, and Law of Property Act 1925, s.134, as amended by Family Law Reform Act 1969, s.1(3) and Sched. 1, Pt. I; *Hawkins and Ryder, op. cit.* pp. 265 *et seq.*

[53] *Re Russell* (1885) 52 L.T. 559; *Re Houghton* (1884) 53 L.J.Ch. 1018; *Sherratt* v. *Bentley* (1833) 2 My. & K. 149.

[54] *Perry* v. *Merritt* (1874) L.R. 18 Eq. 152 (gift of residuary personalty to X "for her own absolute use and benefit": gift over to Y after X's death held void for repugnancy); *Henderson* v. *Cross* (1861) 29 Beav. 216 (gift to X to spend both principal and interest during his lifetime: gift over to Y should X not spend it held void for repugnancy); *Re Jones* [1898] 1 Ch. 438 (gift to X "for her absolute use and benefit so that during her lifetime for the purpose of her maintenance and support she shall have the fullest power to sell and dispose of my said estate absolutely").

[55] *Pushman* v. *Filliter* (1795) 3 Ves. 7; *Bull* v. *Kingston* (1816) 1 Mer. 314.

[56] *Re Stringer's Estate* (1877) 6 Ch.D. 1; *Re Pounder* (1886) 56 L.J.Ch. 113 (X took for life, with power to dispose of capital *inter vivos* but not by will); *Re Sanford* [1901] 1 Ch. 939 (X took for life, with general power of appointment): *cf. Re Jones, supra.*

[57] *Constable* v. *Bull* (1849) 3 De G. & Sm. 411; *Bibbens* v. *Potter* (1879) 10 Ch.D. 733 (gift over to Y was by codicil); *Re Sheldon and Kemble* (1885) 53 L.T. 527 (at the decease of X what might remain of my property to go to Y); *In the Estate of Last* [1958] P. 137 (at X's death "anything that is left" to go to Y).

to Y of *what remains* of the property as if it were a gift over to Y of *all* the property.

Obviously each of the decided cases turned on the particular wording in a particular will.[58] The same question arises in each case—what intention did the testator express in his will read as a whole with the aid of any admissible extrinsic evidence?

Presumption as to effect of gift to spouse. If a testator dies after December 31, 1982,[59] section 22 of the Administration of Justice Act 1982 provides that a gift by the testator's will to his spouse shall be presumed to be absolute if two requirements are satisfied:

(i) The gift is made to the spouse "in terms which in themselves would give an absolute interest to the spouse,"—for instance, T gives "my house Blackacre to my wife Jane" *or* "all my property to my husband John." On the other hand this requirement is not satisfied if T's gift is "to my wife Jane (*or* husband John) *for life.*"

(ii) The testator purports by the same instrument to give his issue an interest in the same property—for instance, "after her (*or* his) death I give Blackacre (*or* all my property *or* what remains of all my property) to my children equally." On the other hand this requirement is not satisfied if the gift over is to "my nephew George" *or* "the Oldcastle Dogs' Home."

If these two requirements are satisfied, under section 22 Jane takes Blackacre (*or* John takes all T's property) absolutely and T's children take nothing. However, section 22 is excluded where a contrary intention is shown—for instance, where T adds, "I direct that my wife Jane shall take only a life interest in Blackacre and after her death I give Blackacre to my children equally."

The purpose of section 22 is to prevent the creation of an "unintended" life interest for the spouse by a home-made will.[60] A testator who makes his own will often assumes (wrongly) that it is possible to give successive absolute interests in property, so that his spouse may first enjoy the full rights of an absolute owner and at her death these rights may pass to another person. Such a testator may well have no conception of the nature of a life interest, but he may nevertheless make his will in language which read as a whole (under the law applicable prior to 1983) expressed an intention to give a life interest, rather than an absolute interest, to his spouse. If the testator dies after 1982, section 22 applies but (rather oddly) only where the purported gift over is to the testator's issue.

---

[58] *Re Minchell's W.T.* [1964] 2 All E.R. 47, 49 (the will provided "an outstanding example of the toast of the Chancery Bar, 'Here's to the man who makes his own will.' He plainly did not . . . brood on the rules of construction in his leisure time. . . . 'One testator's nonsense is no guide to another testator's nonsense' ").

[59] Administration of Justice Act 1982, ss.73(6) and 76(11).

[60] See Law Reform Committee, 19th Report, *Interpretation of Wills,* Cmnd. 5301 (1973), paras. 60–62 and 65.

The rule in Lassence v. Tierney. Under the rule in *Lassence* v. *Tierney*[61] (more accurately called the rule in *Hancock* v. *Watson*[62]), "it is settled law that if you find an absolute gift to a legatee in the first instance, and trusts are engrafted or imposed on that absolute interest which fail, either from lapse, or invalidity, or any other reason, then the absolute gift takes effect so far as the trusts have failed to the exclusion of the residuary legatee or next-of-kin as the case may be."[63] The rule applies to an absolute gift of realty as well as of personalty.[64] The rule reconciles two inconsistent provisions in T's will, *e.g.* (i) an initial gift of property to B absolutely, and (ii) a subsequent provision that the property given to B shall be held upon trust for B for life and after his death for B's children absolutely as tenants in common in equal shares. If B dies childless, so that the trust for B's children fails, under the rule the absolute gift to B takes effect; the property therefore passes under B's will or intestacy and does not pass under T's residuary gift or as on T's intestacy. The rule imputes to T an intention to modify the absolute gift to B only so far as is necessary to give effect to the trusts.[65]

(1) *Initial absolute gift.* The real difficulty usually lies in determining whether there is an initial absolute gift to B and this is a question of construction. If there is, the first requirement of the rule in *Lassence* v. *Tierney* is satisfied. The rule applies whether the initial gift is made directly to B or to trustees on trust for B.[66] To consider an instance of an initial absolute gift, in *Hancock* v. *Watson*[67] T by his will gave his residuary personal estate to trustees upon trust for his wife for life and after her death to be divided into five portions, two of which he "gave" to B; his will continued, "But it is my will and mind that the two fifth portions allotted to [B] shall remain in trust, and that she be entitled to take only the interest . . . of the shares so bequeathed to her during her natural life" and after her death be held upon other trusts, which failed. The House of Lords held that there was an initial absolute gift of two fifth shares to B, because T used the words "I give" and referred to these shares as "allotted" to B. Accordingly, after B's death these two fifth shares formed part of B's estate.

On the other hand, this first requirement is not satisfied if the words of gift to B run straight on into a whole series of limitations, so as to form one system of trusts under which B takes only a limited interest.[68]

(2) *Engrafted trusts fail.* The other requirement of the rule in *Lassence* v. *Tierney* is that the trusts engrafted on B's absolute interest in the property do not (in the events which happen) exhaust the whole bene-

---

[61] (1849) 1 Mac. & G. 551.

[62] [1902] A.C. 14.

[63] *Per* Lord Davey in *Hancock* v. *Watson, supra,* at p. 22.

[64] *Moryoseph* v. *Moryoseph* [1920] 2 Ch. 33.

[65] *Fyffe* v. *Irwin* [1939] 2 All E.R. 271, 282.

[66] *Re Harrison* [1918] 2 Ch. 59 (rule applies to legacy bequeathed to trustees on trust for B).

[67] *Supra.* For the extensive case law see *Theobald on Wills* (14th ed., 1982), pp. 505 *et seq.*

[68] *Re Payne* [1927] 2 Ch. 1; *Lassence* v. *Tierney, supra:* see also *Re Cohen's W.T.* [1936] 1 All E.R. 103 (estate to be equally distributed amongst T's seven named children "subject to the provisions and directions hereinafter contained": held no initial absolute gift to a child).

ficial interest in the property. These trusts may be declared later in T's will or in a codicil,[69] and the cause of their failure is immaterial.[70] Under the rule the absolute gift to B takes effect so far as the trusts do not exhaust the whole beneficial interest in the property.[71]

F. Rules for Ascertaining Classes

Wills often contain gifts to a class of beneficiaries. To mention some examples, T by his will may give:

(i) £100 to each of the children of A (an individual gift to each member of a class);

(ii) £10,000 to the children of B in equal shares absolutely (a class gift in the strict sense, because the size of a child's share depends on the number of children who fall within the class[72]); and

(iii) £10,000 to the children of C who attain the age of 21 years in equal shares absolutely (again a class gift in the strict sense).

In each of these examples the question may arise whether children who come into existence after T's death are eligible to take. Of course, T might have expressed his intention clearly in his will, *e.g.* by giving £100 to each of the children of A "who shall be living at my death." But, if T has not done so, the question must be answered by applying certain rules of construction known as the class-closing rules.[73] Which rule is applicable depends upon whether the gift is:

(1) an individual gift to each member of a class (as in example (i) above); *or*

(2) a class gift where each member of the class takes a share at birth (as in example (ii) above); *or*

(3) a class gift where a contingency is imposed on each member of the class (as in example (iii) above).

In the explanation which follows of the class-closing rules reference will be made to persons who are "living" at a particular time or who "come into existence" before a particular time. In applying these rules it is necessary to remember that a child who is *en ventre sa mère* at that time (and who is subsequently born alive) is by a legal fiction treated as already "living," or as having already "come into existence," at that

---

[69] *Norman* v. *Kynaston* (1861) 3 De G.F. & J. 29.

[70] *Watkins* v. *Weston* (1863) 3 De G.J. & S. 434 (B died childless); *Re Coleman* [1936] Ch. 528 (trusts in part void for perpetuity).

[71] *Re Coleman, supra,* (engrafted trusts after B's death were (i) discretionary trusts during life of B's widow and (ii) after her death trust for B's children: discretionary trust void for remoteness, and under rule income during widow's life formed part of B's estate).

[72] *Pearks* v. *Moseley* (1880) 5 App.Cas. 714, 723. For the nature of a class gift see *ante,* p. 337.

[73] See generally *Hawkins and Ryder on the Construction of Wills* (1965), Chap. 8; J. H. C. Morris (1954) 70 L.Q.R. 61; S. J. Bailey [1958] C.L.J. 39.

time if the child may thereby become entitled to benefit as a member of the class.[74]

1. Individual gift to each member of a class. In the case of an individual gift to each member of a class, the class closes at the testator's death. If T by his will gives a legacy of £100 to each of the children of A, only children of A living at T's death take under the gift[75]; if no child of A is living at T's death the gift fails.[76] The same rule applies if the gift imposes a contingency on each member of the class, *e.g.* if T gives a legacy of £100 to each of the children of A who attain the age of 21 years or marry. In that case only children of A living at T's death are eligible to take under the gift, though it is immaterial whether each of them satisfies the contingency before or after T's death; if no child of A is living at T's death the gift fails.[77]

The object of this drastic class-closing rule is to enable the personal representatives to distribute T's residuary estate. The rule is a rule of convenience which fixes the maximum number of members of the class at T's death, so that the personal representatives may know the total sum required to meet their legacies and may safely distribute the remainder of T's estate. If the class did not close at T's death, the personal representatives could not safely distribute T's residuary estate until it had become impossible for further children of A to be born.

The rule is modified if the will postpones payment of the legacies and distribution of the residue until the death of a life tenant, *e.g.* if T gives his estate upon trust for X for life, and after X's death to pay £100 to each of the children of A and hold the remainder on trust for Y absolutely. In that case the class remains open until the death of the life tenant and therefore embraces children of A who are living at T's death or who come into existence before X's death.[78]

The rule is altogether excluded, so that any children of A coming into existence after T's death may take, if the inconvenience prevented by the rule either does not exist or is expressly contemplated by the testator.[79] An instance of the first exception is where the testator directs a fund of specified amount to be set aside out of which alone the legacies are made payable.[80] The second exception was held to be applicable in a case where the testator showed a clear intention that the class should include any children coming into existence after his death and directed a sufficient fund to be set aside for this purpose.[81]

---

[74] *Trower* v. *Butts* (1823) 1 S. & S. 181 (such a child is "within the reason and motive of the Gift"); *Storrs* v. *Benbow* (1853) 3 De G.M. & G. 390; *Re Salaman* [1908] 1 Ch. 4 (such a child is treated as born if he thereby takes a direct benefit); *Elliot* v. *Joicey* [1935] A.C. 209: *cf. Re Corlass* (1875) 1 Ch.D. 460 (child *en ventre* illegitimate, though legitimated before birth). But see *Re Gardiner's Estate* (1875) 20 Eq. 647 (which appears wrongly decided).

[75] *Ringrose* v. *Bramham* (1794) 2 Cox 384.

[76] *Re Belville* [1941] Ch. 414 (T by his will gave £10,000 each to any daughters of X born after the date of his will: held daughter conceived after T's death could not take).

[77] *Rogers* v. *Mutch* (1878) 10 Ch.D. 25.

[78] *Att.-Gen.* v. *Crispin* (1784) 1 Bro.C.C. 386.

[79] *Re Belville, supra,* at pp. 418–419.

[80] *Evans* v. *Harris* (1842) 5 Beav. 45.

[81] *Defflis* v. *Goldschmidt* (1816) Mer. 417 (court directed master to inquire what would be a sufficient sum to set aside to answer legacies of £2,000 payable to each child of A who might thereafter be born, having regard to A's age): *cf. Butler* v. *Lowe* (1839) 10 Sim. 317.

2. Class gift where each member takes a share at birth. Under a class gift in the strict sense the members of the class share the same subject-matter of the gift, whether equally or in specified proportions. If the class has not yet closed, the personal representatives cannot safely distribute a share to a person who is already a member of the class, because the minimum size of that share is not yet fixed. However, the personal representatives can safely distribute the remainder of the testator's estate. As already explained, in the case of an individual gift to each member of a class, the object of the class-closing rule is to enable the personal representatives to distribute the testator's residuary estate. But, in the case of class gifts in the strict sense, the relevant class-closing rules serve a different purpose—to enable the personal representatives to distribute a share of the subject matter of the gift to a person who is already a member of the class.

A class gift where each member takes a share at birth may be (1) immediate or (2) postponed.

(1) *Immediate gift.* In the case of an immediate class gift where each member takes a share at birth, the class closes at the testator's death if any member of the class is then in existence[82]; if no member of the class is then in existence, no class-closing rule applies and the class remains open indefinitely.[83] To consider the gift by T's will of £10,000 to the children of B in equal shares absolutely. If one or more children of B are living at T's death, then the class closes immediately and they alone take under the gift. On the other hand, if no child of B is living at T's death, then the class remains open indefinitely and all the children of B born thereafter take under the gift. This rule that the class closes at the testator's death if any member of the class is then in existence applies to an immediate class gift which is vested, even though payment is directed to be postponed until the youngest member of the class attains full age,[84] or even though a member's share is liable to be divested in a certain event (*e.g.* on his death under 21 years of age[85]).

(2) *Postponed gift.* A class gift may be postponed by a preceding life or other interest,[86] *e.g.* a gift by T's will of £10,000 upon trust for X for life

---

[82] *Viner* v. *Francis* (1789) 2 Cox 190 (£2,000 to the children of my late sister B); *Re Chartres* [1927] 1 Ch. 466, 471; *Re Manners* [1955] 1 W.L.R. 1096.

[83] *Shepherd* v. *Ingram* (1764) Amb. 448; *Weld* v. *Bradbury* (1715) 2 Vern. 705; *Harris* v. *Lloyd* (1823) 1 T. & R. 310; *Re Chartres, supra*; *Re Bleckly* [1951] Ch. 740, 749.

[84] *Re Manners, supra*, (gift by T's will to my grandchildren (the children of my son X) "to be administered towards their maintenance and education until the youngest is 21 . . . and then distributed equally among them": held grandchildren alive at T's death alone took): see also *Scott* v. *Harwood* (1821) 5 Madd. 332.

[85] *Davidson* v. *Dallas* (1808) 14 Ves. 576; *Scott* v. *Harwood, supra*.

[86] *e.g.* a life interest which is determinable or subject to a condition subsequent, *Re Aylwin's Trusts* (1873) L.R. 16 Eq. 585 (life interest determinable on bankruptcy or insolvency): or an absolute interest subject to a gift over, *Ellison* v. *Airey* (1748) 1 Ves.Sen. 111 (to X absolutely, but if X dies under 21 unmarried, to the children of B). See also *Oppenheim* v. *Henry* (1853) 10 Hare 441 (gift to all my grandchildren, to be divided among them at the end of 20 years after my death, income to be accumulated meanwhile: held class closed at end of 20 years).

and after X's death for the children of B in equal shares absolutely. In this case the class closes at the time when the postponement ends,[87] but if at that time there is as yet no member of the class, no class-closing rule applies and the class remains open indefinitely.[88] To consider this last example of a postponed class gift. If one or more children of B are living at T's death or come into existence before X's death, the class closes at X's death and only embraces children of B who are living at T's death or who come into existence before X's death. If any such child dies after T's death but before distribution of the £10,000, the child's share passes as an asset of his estate to his personal representatives.[89] On the other hand, if no child of B is living at T's death or comes into existence before X's death, then the class remains open indefinitely and all the children of B born thereafter take under the gift. This rule that the class closes at the time when the postponement ends applies to a class gift which is vested, even though payment is directed to be postponed until the youngest member of the class attains full age,[90] or even though a member's share is liable to be divested in a certain event.

Thus the same class-closing rule applies to any class gift where each member takes a share at birth, whether the gift is immediate or postponed, except that the crucial "class-closing time" is the testator's death in the case of an immediate gift, and the end of the period of postponement in the case of a postponed gift. This rule differs in one vital respect from the more drastic rule applicable in the case of an individual gift to each member of a class—under this rule, if at the class-closing time there is as yet no member of the class, the class remains open indefinitely.

This class-closing rule, in common with the other rules, is sometimes called a rule of convenience (though it may appear inconvenient to B's children who come into existence after the class has closed). In truth, it is a rule of construction and it is based upon the supposition that T would not wish B's children who are in existence at T's death (or, in the case of a postponed gift, who come into existence before the time when the postponement ends) to have to wait for distribution of the capital until it is no longer possible for further children of B to be born.[91]

(3) *Acceleration of class gift by failure of preceding interest.* To return to the gift by T's will of £10,000 upon trust for X for life and after X's death for the children of B in equal shares absolutely. If X's life interest fails because (for instance) he predeceases T, the class gift to the children of B

---

[87] *Ellison* v. *Airey, supra; Devisme* v. *Mello* (1782) 1 Bro.C.C. 537; *Ayton* v. *Ayton* (1787) 1 Cox 327; *Middleton* v. *Messenger* (1799) 5 Ves. 136; *Walker* v. *Shore* (1808) 15 Ves. 122; *Holland* v. *Wood* (1871) L.R. 11 Eq. 91.

[88] *Chapman* v. *Blissett* (1735) Cas.t.Talb. 145; *Hutcheson* v. *Jones* (1817) 2 Madd. 124; *Re Chartres* [1927] 1 Ch. 466, 471–472; *Re Bleckly* [1951] Ch. 740, 749 and 755.

[89] *Devisme* v. *Mello, supra*: but if the child held as a joint tenant the right of survivorship operates.

[90] *Smith* v. *Jackson* (1823) 1 L.J.(o.s.)Ch. 231 (gift to children of T's granddaughters to be paid when youngest attained 21 years).

[91] *Re Ward* [1965] Ch. 856, 865. See generally for the basis of the rules S. J. Bailey [1958] C.L.J. 39, 45–48.

is accelerated and becomes an immediate (and not a postponed) gift, so that the crucial class-closing time is the testator's death.[92]

If X survives T, but X disclaims his life interest and thereby accelerates the class gift to the children of B, does this have the same effect on class-closing as if X had predeceased T? Probably the answer is no—the crucial class-closing time is still X's death. In *Re Davies*[93] X (who had three children) disclaimed her life interest under T's will, and Vaisey J. held that the vested class gift in remainder to the issue of X was accelerated, and that X's three children took to the exclusion of any other issue of X who might come into existence prior to X's death. If X had not disclaimed, any issue of X who came into existence prior to X's death would have been eligible to take, but Vaisey J. rejected the argument that (despite the acceleration) the shares of X's three children remained liable to be diminished by other issue coming into existence prior to X's death. However, in *Re Harker's Will Trusts*[94] Goff J. accepted this argument and refused to follow the decision in *Re Davies*. He decided that, despite the acceleration of the class gift in remainder, the class of beneficiaries must remain open until X's death. The class-closing rules were not applicable in *Re Harker's Will Trusts* because the trust was for X for life and after his death for X's children, and it was impossible for further children of X to come into existence after X's death.[95] It appears likely that the decision in *Re Harker's Will Trusts* will be followed and will also be applied in a case where the class-closing rules are applicable. X, by disclaiming his life interest after T's death, cannot change the composition of the class of beneficiaries entitled under the class gift in remainder. The class-closing rules are rules of construction and the proper construction of T's will cannot be altered after T's death by X's disclaimer.

3. Class gift where contingency is imposed on each member. To turn to the other type of class gift where a contingency is imposed on each member of the class, *e.g.* a gift by T's will of £10,000 to the children of C who attain the age of 21 years in equal shares absolutely. In this case the relevant class-closing rule is known as the rule in *Andrews v. Partington*.[96]

(1) *Immediate gift.* In the case of an immediate class gift where a contingency is imposed on each member, the class closes at the testator's death if any member of the class who has satisfied the contingency is then in existence[97]; if not, the class closes as soon as one member satis-

---

[92] *Sprackling* v. *Ranier* (1761) Dick. 344: as to T's revocation of X's life interest by a codicil see *Eavestaff* v. *Austin* (1854) 19 Beav. 591; *Re Johnson* (1893) 68 L.T. 20. For acceleration see *ante*, pp. 355–356.

[93] [1957] 1 W.L.R. 922: see also *Re Taylor* [1957] 1 W.L.R. 1043, 1047–1048 and *Re Chartres* [1927] 1 Ch. 466.

[94] [1969] 1 W.L.R. 1124 (X for life, on his death to X's children equally on attaining 21; X surrendered his life interest; later one child of X attained 21: held the remainder was accelerated but the class remained open until X's death): see also *Re Kebty-Fletcher's W.T.* [1969] 1 Ch. 339.

[95] *Re Harker's W.T.* [1969] 1 W.L.R. 1124, 1128: see also *Re Kebty-Fletcher's W.T., supra; post*, p. 441.

[96] (1791) 3 Bro.C.C. 401.

[97] *Picken* v. *Matthews* (1878) 10 Ch.D. 264; *Balm* v. *Balm* (1830) 3 Sim. 492.

fies the contingency.[98] Thus, taking this last example, the class closes at
T's death if any child of C who has attained the age of 21 years is then in
existence; if not, the class closes as soon as a child of C attains the age of
21 years. Once the class closes, any child already in existence may take
under the gift if the child subsequently satisfies the contingency, but
any child not already in existence is excluded from taking.

(2) *Postponed gift.* Again the class gift may be postponed by a preceding life or other interest,[99] *e.g.* a gift by T's will of £10,000 upon trust for
Y for life and after Y's death for the children of C who attain the age of
21 years in equal shares absolutely. In this case the class closes at the
time when the postponement ends if any member of the class who was
in existence after T's death has satisfied the contingency[1]; if not, the
class closes as soon as one member satisfies the contingency.[2] Applying
this rule to this example, the class closes at Y's death if any child of C,
who was in existence after T's death, has attained the age of 21 years; if
not, the class closes as soon as a child of C attains the age of 21 years.

In short, the same class-closing rule applies to any class gift where a
contingency is imposed on each member, whether the gift is immediate
or postponed, except that the crucial class-closing time is the testator's
death in the case of an immediate gift, and the end of the period of postponement in the case of a postponed gift. The rule differs in one vital
respect from both the rules so far considered—under this rule, if at the
class-closing time there is as yet no member who has satisfied the contingency, the class does remain open but only until one member satisfies the contingency.

This rule, like the other rules, is a rule of construction[3] and is based
upon the supposition that T would not wish a child of C who has satisfied the contingency to have to wait for distribution of the capital until
it is no longer possible for further children of C to be born.[4]

4. Gift of income to a class. The rules so far considered do not apply
to a gift of income to members of a class, *e.g.* a gift by T's will of property upon trust to pay the income thereof to the children of D in equal
shares during some defined period. In this case the class does not close
and each instalment of income is payable to the children of D for the

---

[98] *Andrews* v. *Partington, supra; Re Mervin* [1891] 3 Ch. 197. It is immaterial that no member of the class is in existence at the testator's death, *Re Bleckly* [1951] Ch. 740, 749–750.

[99] *e.g.* a life interest which is determinable or subject to a condition subsequent, *Re
Smith* (1862) 2 J. & H. 594 (life interest determinable on bankruptcy or insolvency); *Re
Bleckly* [1951] Ch. 740 (whilst wife or widow of X): or an absolute interest subject to a gift
over, *Gillman* v. *Daunt* (1856) 3 K. & J. 48. As to postponement by a direction to accumulate
see *Watson* v. *Young* (1885) 28 Ch.D. 436; *Re Stephens* [1904] 1 Ch. 322; *Re Watt's W.T.* [1936]
2 All E.R. 1555.

[1] *Re Smith, supra; Re Canney's Trusts* (1910) 101 L.T. 905; *Gillman* v. *Daunt, supra.* See also
Re Faux (1915) 113 L.T. 81 (one-half of income to A for life and other half to B for life: held
postponement did not end at A's death, B still being alive); *Re Paul's S.T.* [1920] 1 Ch. 99.

[2] *Clarke* v. *Clarke* (1836) 8 Sim. 59; *Re Smith, supra; Locke* v. *Lamb* (1867) L.R. 4 Eq. 372; *Re
Emmet's Estate* (1879) 13 Ch.D. 484. It is immaterial that no member of the class comes into
existence until after the time when the postponement ends, *Re Bleckly, supra.*

[3] *Re Bleckly, supra,* at pp. 747 and 750.

[4] *Re Ward* [1965] Ch. 856, 865.

time being living.[5] For example, if D has three children at T's death, the first instalment of income is payable in third shares to D's three children; if another child of D is then born, the next instalment is payable in quarter shares to D's four children. This rule that the class does not close applies whether the members of the class take a share of income at birth[6] (as in the last example), or on satisfying a contingency[7] (*e.g.* a gift of income to the children of D who attain the age of 21 years in equal shares). Of course, the suppositions on which the class-closing rules applicable to class gifts of capital are based have no validity in the case of a gift of income to a class.[8]

5. Class gifts to which class-closing rules apply. The class-closing rules do not, of course, apply to a gift to particular persons individually; for instance, a gift of property by T's will "to be divided equally between the children of A, namely B, C and D" is not a class gift.[9] Again, the class-closing rules do not apply in the case of a gift on trust for X for life and after X's death for X's children, because it is impossible for further children of X to come into existence after X's death: accordingly T cannot be taken to have intended a distribution before all X's children come into existence.[10]

The class-closing rules have been applied to a class gift made by T's will to a *limited* class of relatives, *i.e.* to a class which is not capable of infinite expansion, being limited to one or more particular generations. Instances include class gifts made by T's will to the children of X,[11] T's grandchildren,[12] T's brothers and sisters,[13] the nephews and nieces of X,[14] T's great-nephews and nieces,[15] and T's cousins.[16] On the other hand, the class-closing rules have been held not to apply to a gift by T's will to an *unlimited* class of relatives, such as the issue (or the descendants) of X who attain the age of 21 years. T cannot have intended all X's issue, born in any generation at any time in the future, to take and the question of construction inevitably arises—what class of issue did T intend should take? This question is to be answered without regard to the class-closing rules.[17] If the gift is to all of a limited class of relatives,

---

[5] *Re Ward* [1965] Ch. 856 (not following *Re Powell* [1898] 1 Ch. 227).

[6] *Re Ward, supra.*

[7] *Re Wenmoth's Estate* (1887) 37 Ch.D. 266.

[8] *Re Ward, supra*, at p. 865.

[9] *Bain* v. *Lescher* (1840) 11 Sim. 397 (B predeceased T and his share lapsed): see also *Havergal* v. *Harrison* (1843) 7 Beav. 49 ("my brothers and sister"): see *ante*, p. 337.

[10] *Re Harker's W.T.* [1969] 1 W.L.R. 1124, 1128; *Re Kebty-Fletcher's W.T.* [1969] 1 Ch. 339.

[11] *Viner* v. *Francis* (1789) 2 Cox 190 (the children of my late sister X); *Re Bleckly* [1951] Ch. 740 (children of my son X who attain 21).

[12] *Oppenheim* v. *Henry* (1853) 10 Hare 441 (my grandchildren); *Gimblett* v. *Purton* (1871) L.R. 12 Eq. 427 (such of my grandchildren as attain 21); *Re Manners* [1955] 1 W.L.R. 1096.

[13] *Re Gardiner's Estate* (1875) L.R. 20 Eq. 647.

[14] *Dimond* v. *Bostock* (1875) L.R. 10 Ch.App. 358 (nephews and nieces of my late husband X, who were living at his death, excepting P and Q).

[15] *Balm* v. *Balm* (1830) 3 Sim. 492.

[16] *Baldwin* v. *Rogers* (1853) 3 De G.M. & G. 649 (my first cousins by my mother's side).

[17] *Re Cockle's W.T.* [1967] Ch. 690 (gift by T's will upon trust for X for life and after X's death for the issue of X who attain 21 years or being female marry in equal shares absolutely; X had no issue at T's death: held only issue in existence at X's death were intended to take); *Re Deeley's Settlement* [1974] Ch. 454 (again a postponed gift); *Re Drummond* [1986] 1 W.L.R. 1096.

it only raises the question as to when the gift should be closed as a matter of convenience, and the class-closing rules provide the answer.

6. Rules excluded by contrary intention. The class-closing rules, being rules of construction, are not applicable if the testator has clearly shown a contrary intention by his will. A gift by will to "all or any" the children of C who attain the age of 21 years is not sufficient by itself to indicate a contrary intention.[18] Again, a gift to all the children of C "whether now born or hereafter to be born" does not indicate a contrary intention because the words of futurity are capable of referring only to the period before the application of the relevant class-closing rule would close the class.[19] But the emphatic phrase children of C "whenever born" is a particular reference to the future expressly unlimited in time, and therefore excludes the application of the class-closing rules[20]: it is equivalent to the phrase "at whatever time they may be born," which has the same effect.[21]

G. ADOPTED, LEGITIMATED AND ILLEGITIMATE CHILDREN

The position of adopted, legitimated and illegitimate children for the purposes of intestacy has already been considered.[22] Now it is necessary to turn to gifts by will.

Adopted child. Under the Adoption Act 1976 an adopted child is treated as the legitimate child of the married couple who adopted him (or, in any other case, as the legitimate child of his adopter),[23] and not as the child of his natural parents.[24] This principle applies to the construction of the will of a testator who dies after December 31, 1975, subject to

[18] Re Bleckly [1951] Ch. 740, 751: see also Prescott v. Long (1795) 2 Ves. 690 ("all and every the child and children of his son"); Re Canney's Trusts (1910) 101 L.T. 905; Re Emmet's Estate (1880) 13 Ch.D. 484 ("all and every the children" of X).
[19] i.e. in the case of an immediate gift, the period until T's death, Sprackling v. Ranier (1761) 1 Dick. 344; Dias v. De Livera (1879) 5 App.Cas. 123 (children which may hereafter be procreated): in the case of a postponed gift, the period until the end of the period of postponement, Scott v. Earl of Scarborough (1838) 1 Beav. 154, 168: see also Re Chapman's S.T. [1977] 1 W.L.R. 1163.
[20] Re Edmondson's W.T. [1972] 1 W.L.R. 183 (an appointment by deed).
[21] Re Edmondson's W.T., supra, at p. 188. See also Scott v. Earl of Scarborough, supra, (children of A, B and C "now born or who shall hereafter be born, during the lifetime of their respective parents": class-closing rule excluded); Re Ransome [1957] Ch. 348 (such of the children of C as shall be living at time youngest child of C attains 21 years: class-closing rule excluded); Re Tom's Settlement [1987] 1 W.L.R. 1021 ("closing date" in deed); cf. Re Clifford's S.T. [1981] Ch. 63 (compound class). As to the exclusion of the rules by a power of advancement applicable to vested presumptive shares, see Re Henderson's Trusts [1969] 1 W.L.R. 651.
[22] Ante, pp. 94–96.
[23] Adoption Act 1976, s.39(1), (2) and (4): this rule applies to an adoption order made by a court in any part of the U.K., the Isle of Man or the Channel Islands, and to certain foreign adoptions, ibid. s.38. For the protection of personal representatives see ante, p. 361.
[24] Ibid. s.39(2); as to the effect of adoption by one of the child's natural parents see ibid. s.39(3) and Legitimacy Act 1976, s.4 as amended by Adoption Act 1976, s.73(3) and Sched. 3. The adopted child retains any interest vested in possession in him before the adoption, ibid. s.42(4).

any contrary indication,[25] and it is immaterial whether the adoption order is made before or after the testator's death.[26] Thus, if T dies in 1976, having by his will given property upon trust for his son X for life and after X's death for X's children in equal shares absolutely, any child adopted by X (whether before or after T's death) will be entitled to take, unless there is a contrary indication in T's will. If X is T's daughter, the same result follows, subject to a curious exception which may be applicable in the case of a child adopted by a woman after she has attained 55 years of age.[27]

The Adoption Act 1976 sets out two rules of construction (complete with statutory examples) which are applicable to the will of a testator who dies after 1975, subject to any contrary indication. The rules relate to a disposition[28] by will which depends on the date of birth of a child or children. The disposition is to be construed as if:

(i) the adopted child had been born on the date of adoption,[29] and
(ii) two or more children adopted on the same date had been born on that date in the order of their actual births,

but these rules do not affect any reference to the age of a child.[30] To take the statutory example of a gift by T's will to the children[31] of A "living at my death or born afterwards." T dies in 1976 and after T's death A adopts a child, who was born in 1974. This child is entitled to take under the gift as a child of A born (applying rule (i)) after T's death, though the child does not answer to the description of a child of A living at T's death. The second statutory example is another gift by T's will to the children[32] of A "living at my death or born afterwards before any one of such children for the time being in existence attains a vested interest and who attain the age of 21 years." A's adopted child is entitled to take under this gift if he is adopted before any other child

---

[25] *Ibid.* ss.42(1), 46(3) and 72(1). In the case of a testator who died before January 1, 1976, the Adoption Act 1958, ss.16, 17 and provisions containing references to those sections continue to apply, *ibid.* s.73(1) and Sched. 2, para. 6.

[26] *Ibid.* s.39(6). If the testator T died before January 1, 1976, the adoption order must have been made before T's death (Adoption Act 1958, s.16(2) and 17(2)): but if T's will or codicil was executed before April 1, 1959, (i) the adoption order must have been made before its execution, unless it was confirmed by codicil executed after March 31, 1959 (*ibid.* Sched. 5, para. 4(3), (4)), and (ii) the adopted child cannot take if T's will or codicil was executed before January 1, 1950 (*ibid.* Sched. 5, para. 4(1), (2)) unless, exceptionally, the child is entitled to take at common law, *Re Fletcher* [1949] Ch. 473; *Re Gilpin* [1954] Ch. 1; *Re Jebb* [1966] Ch. 666, but see J. H. C. Morris (1966) 82 L.Q.R. 196.

[27] *Ibid.* s.42(5) provides that "where it is necessary to determine for the purposes of a disposition of property effected by an instrument [*i.e.* T's will] whether a woman can have a child, it shall be presumed that once a woman has attained the age of 55 years she will not adopt a child after execution of the instrument [this may mean after T's death, s.46(3)], and, . . . if she does so that child shall not be treated as her child or as the child of her spouse (if any) for the purposes of the instrument." If T's daughter X disclaims or releases her life interest, it may be necessary to determine whether X can have a child: *quaere* in what other circumstances it is "necessary".

[28] See *ibid.* s.46.

[29] As to the effect of adoption by one of the child's natural parents, see *ibid.* s.43 (which sets out a statutory example).

[30] *Ibid.* s.42(2).

[31] Or grandchildren. Another statutory example is to A for life "until he has a child," and then to his child or children.

[32] Or grandchildren.

attains a vested interest and if he attains the age of 21 years, which is measured from his true date of birth and not from the date of his adoption. Finally, to consider a gift by T's will to the eldest son of B. At T's death in 1976 B has a natural son (born in 1974) and an adopted son (born in 1973 and adopted in 1975). If "eldest" is a reference to the age of a child, the adopted son takes; but probably it is not and, if so (applying rule (i)), the natural son takes.

By way of exception, an adoption does not affect the devolution of any property limited (expressly or not) to devolve along with any peerage or dignity or title of honour, unless a contrary intention is expressed in the will.[33]

Legitimated child. Under the Legitimacy Act 1976 a legitimated person (and any other person) is entitled to take any interest under the will of a testator who dies after December 31, 1975 as if the legitimated person had been born legitimate, subject to any contrary indication.[34] As in the case of adoption, it is immaterial whether the legitimation occurs before or after the testator's death.[35] Again, in the case of legitimation, similar rules of construction are applicable to a disposition by will which depends on the date of birth of a child or children as apply (as explained above) in the case of adoption.[36] For instance, if T dies in 1976 having by his will (which was made before 1970) made a gift to the children of C "living at my death or born afterwards," a child of C who is legitimated after T's death by his parents' marriage is entitled to take under the gift as a legitimate child of C born (under the rule of construction) on the date of his legitimation.[37]

Illegitimate child. At common law a gift by will to children, or other relations, was prima facie construed as referring only to legitimate children, or persons tracing their relationship exclusively through legitimate links.[38] This rule of construction was reversed by section 15 of the Family Law Reform Act 1969, which applies to a disposition of property by a will or codicil made after December 31, 1969 and before April 4,

---

[33] *Ibid.* s.44; adoption does not affect the descent of any peerage or dignity or title of honour.

[34] Legitimacy Act 1976, s.5(1), (3) and (6) and s.10. In the case of a testator who died before January 1, 1976, the Legitimacy Act 1926, ss.3 and 5 continue to apply, Legitimacy Act 1976, Sched. I, para. 2. For the protection of personal representatives see *ante*, p. 361.

[35] If the testator T died before January 1, 1976, the legitimation must have occurred before T's death, Legitimacy Act 1926, s.3(1).

[36] Legitimacy Act 1976, s.5(4), (5): as to the effect of posthumous legitimation see *ibid.* s.5(6), and as to devolution of property limited to devolve along with any dignity or title of honour see *ibid.* Sched. 1, para. 4.

[37] Legitimacy Act 1976, s.5(4). If T's will had been made after 1969 an *illegitimate* child of C would have been entitled to take: *ibid.* s.5(5) gives statutory examples but in each example legitimation appears to have no practical effect if T's will was made after 1969, because the illegitimate child, or a person related through him, would have been entitled to take anyway, unless a contrary intention appeared in the will, Family Law Reform Act 1969, s.15; Legitimacy Act 1976, s.6(1), (3).

[38] For this rule, and the exceptions to it, see generally *Hawkins and Ryder on the Construction of Wills* (1965), pp. 131 *et seq.*; *Theobald on Wills* (14th ed., 1982), pp. 351 *et seq.*

1988. If the will or codicil was executed before 1970, it is not treated as made after December 31, 1969 although it was confirmed by a codicil executed after that date.[39]

(1) *Rules of construction under the Family Law Reform Act 1969.* Section 15(1) of the Act lays down two rules of construction:

(i) Any reference (express or implied) to the child or children of any person D is to be construed as, or as including, a reference to any illegitimate child of D. If T's will (made after 1969) gives property upon trust for D for life and after D's death for D's children in equal shares absolutely, any illegitimate child of D (whether born before or after T's death[40]) is entitled to take.

(ii) Any reference (express or implied) to a person or persons related in some other manner to any person D is to be construed as, or as including, a reference to anyone who would be so related if he, or some other person through whom the relationship is deduced, had been born legitimate. A gift by T's will (made after 1969) to D's grandchildren therefore includes both the illegitimate child of a legitimate child of D and the legitimate child of an illegitimate child of D.[41]

(2) *Exceptions.* These rules of construction only apply to references to a child or other relation where the reference is to a person who is to benefit or be capable of benefiting under the disposition, or for the purpose of designating such a person, to someone else to or through whom that person is related.[42] Accordingly, these rules do not apply to a gift to E absolutely "if he dies without leaving children"; the word "children" therefore means legitimate children and, if E dies leaving one illegitimate child but no legitimate children, the condition is satisfied and E takes absolutely.[43] Again, these rules of construction do not affect the construction of the word "heir" or "heirs" or of any expression which is used to create an entail,[44] or the devolution of any property which would (apart from these rules) devolve along with a dignity or title of honour.[45] Finally, these rules of construction apply "unless the contrary intention appears." A testator is free to exclude the operation of these rules by his will, *e.g.* by making a gift to D's *legitimate* children.[46]

(3) *Rules of construction under the Family Law Reform Act 1987.* Section 19 of the Family Law Reform Act 1987 changes these rules of construc-

---

[39] Family Law Reform Act 1969, s.15(8): see also *ibid.* s.1(7). For the general rule that a republished will or codicil operates as if it had been made at the time of its republication see *ante*, pp. 80–81.

[40] *Ibid.* s.15(7) abolishes any rule of law that a gift to illegitimate children born after T's death is void as contrary to public policy.

[41] *Quaere* whether it also includes the illegitimate child of an illegitimate child of D, see E. C. Ryder (1971) 24 C.L.P., 163–164; Law Commission Report on Illegitimacy, Law Com. No. 118, p. 104. See also Prichard [1981] Conv. 343 ("as on intestacy" in will).

[42] Family Law Reform Act 1969, s.15(2).

[43] See E. C. Ryder, *loc. cit.* pp. 164–166.

[44] Family Law Reform Act 1969, s.15(2).

[45] *Ibid.* s.15(5).

[46] See E. C. Ryder, *loc. cit.* pp. 166–167.

tion and abolishes most of these exceptions.[47] It applies to dispositions[48] by will or codicil made after April 3, 1988.[49] Under section 19 references (whether express or implied) to any relationship between two persons are to be construed without regard to whether the father and mother of either of them, or the father and mother of any person through whom the relationship is deduced, were married to each other at any time. This new rule of construction applies whether or not the reference is to a person who is to benefit or be capable of benefiting under the disposition. Again it applies to the construction of the word "heir" or "heirs" and to any expression which is used to create an entailed interest,[50] but not to the devolution of any property which would otherwise devolve along with a dignity or title of honour.[51] Finally, the new rule of construction applies "unless the contrary intention appears."

H. Age of Majority

In a will the expressions "full age," "infant," "infancy," "minor," "minority" and similar expressions are to be construed by reference to the provision that a person attains full age on attaining the age of 18.[52] This construction applies, in the absence of a definition or of any indication of a contrary intention, if the will was made after December 31, 1969. A will or codicil executed before 1970 is not treated as made after 1969 although it was confirmed by a codicil executed after 1969.[53]

The construction of any expression specifying a particular age (for example, "twenty-one") is not altered by the Family Law Reform Act 1969.[54]

I. Satisfaction

Satisfaction of a debt by a legacy. If T owes a debt to C, and later T makes a will or codicil giving to C a pecuniary legacy of an amount equal to, or greater than, the debt, an equitable presumption arises that the legacy is intended to satisfy the debt. If at T's death C accepts the legacy, he cannot also claim payment of the debt.[55] And if later during T's lifetime T pays off the debt, the legacy is adeemed.[56]

(1) *Requirements.* This equitable presumption only arises if three requirements are fulfilled:

[47] See Law Commission Second Report on Illegitimacy, Law Com. No. 157.
[48] Including an oral disposition, *ibid.* s.19(6), *e.g.* a privileged will made orally.
[49] Family Law Reform Act 1987 (Commencement No. 1) Order 1988 (S.I. 1988 No. 425). A will or codicil executed before, but confirmed by codicil executed on or after, April 4, 1988 is not treated as made on or after that date, *ibid.* s.19(7).
[50] *Ibid.* s.19(2).
[51] *Ibid.* s.19(4).
[52] Family Law Reform Act 1969, s.1.
[53] *Ibid.* s.1(7): for republication see *ante,* pp. 80–81.
[54] See E. C. Ryder, *loc. cit.* pp. 158–160; Cretney (1970) 120 N.L.J. 144, 145.
[55] *Talbot* v. *Duke of Shrewsbury* (1722) Prec.Ch. 394.
[56] *Re Fletcher* (1888) 38 Ch.D. 373 (legacy of same amount as debt).

(i) T must already owe the debt to C before T makes the will or codicil giving the pecuniary legacy to C. No presumption of satisfaction arises if T incurs the debt to C afterwards, because when he made the will or codicil T cannot have intended the legacy to satisfy a non-existent debt.[57]

(ii) T must give to C a pecuniary legacy of an amount equal to, or greater than, the debt.[58] A legacy of an amount less than the debt raises no presumption of satisfaction, even *pro tanto*.[59] Again, a devise of land,[60] or a gift of residue or a share of residue,[61] raises no presumption of satisfaction.

(iii) The pecuniary legacy must be as beneficial to C as the debt. The presumption is not applicable if the debt is secured but the legacy is not,[62] or if the debt is immediately due at T's death but the legacy is payable at a future time under an express term to this effect in the will.[63] But the presumption is probably applicable if T gives an immediate legacy to C but does not fix any time for payment by his will; such a legacy is only payable one year after T's death but it carries interest from T's death[64] and is therefore treated as being as beneficial to C as the debt.[65]

(2) *Rebutting the presumption.* This "artificial"[66] presumption may be rebutted by extrinsic evidence that T did not intend the legacy to satisfy the debt, but intended to give the legacy regardless of his liability to pay the debt; as already explained, direct extrinsic evidence of T's declarations of intention is admissible for this purpose.[67] The presumption may also be excluded by T's expression of a contrary intention in a will or codicil made by T after he incurred the debt to C.[68] In *Chancey's Case*[69] it was held that a direction in T's will that his debts and legacies should be paid expressed a contrary intention and therefore C was entitled to the payment of both the debt and the legacy. Moreover, it is now settled that a direction in T's will that his debts should be paid

[57] *Cranmer's Case* (1702) 2 Salk. 508: see also *Horlock* v. *Wiggins* (1889) 39 Ch.D. 142 (separation deed, containing covenant to pay £100, and will, giving £100 legacy, were contemporaneous: held no presumption of satisfaction).

[58] *Re Manners* [1949] Ch. 613 (covenant by T to pay annuity; T gave annuity by will: held presumption of satisfaction applicable but rebutted).

[59] *Eastwood* v. *Vinke* (1731) 2 P.Wms. 613, 616. But *cf. Fitzgerald* v. *National Bank Ltd.* [1929] 1 K.B. 394 (T owed C £100 carrying 5 per cent. interest; T gave C £100 legacy: held presumption of satisfaction applied, though unpaid interest was due to C at T's death).

[60] *Eastwood* v. *Vinke, supra; Richardson* v. *Elphinstone* (1794) 2 Ves. 463.

[61] *Barret* v. *Beckford* (1750) 1 Ves.Sen. 519; *Devese* v. *Pontet* (1785) 1 Cox C.C. 188.

[62] *Re Stibbe* (1946) 175 L.T. 198: *cf. Re Haves* [1951] 2 All E.R. 928.

[63] *Clark* v. *Sewell* (1744) 3 Atk. 96 (legacy payable one month after T's death); *Adams* v. *Lavender* (1824) M'Cle. & Yo. 41 (legacy payable within six months after T's death): see also *Re Van Den Bergh's W.T.* [1948] 1 All E.R. 935 (annuity given by will determinable on attempted alienation).

[64] For this exceptional rule see *ante*, p. 325.

[65] *Re Rattenberry* [1906] 1 Ch. 667: but *cf. Re Horlock* [1895] 1 Ch. 516.

[66] *Horlock* v. *Wiggins* (1888) 39 Ch.D. 142, 147: *Re Horlock* [1895] 1 Ch. 516, 518 ("no sooner was [the rule] established than learned Judges of great eminence expressed their disapproval of it, and invented ways to get out of it").

[67] *Wallace* v. *Pomfret* (1805) 11 Ves. 542: see *ante*, p. 420.

[68] *Gaynon* v. *Wood* (1717) 1 P.Wms. 409n.

[69] (1725) 1 P.Wms. 408.

expresses a contrary intention.[70] Most wills contain such a direction and accordingly this artificial presumption is usually excluded.

Satisfaction of a legacy by another legacy. If a testator T gives two general legacies of the same amount to the same legatee B, the question arises whether the legacies are cumulative (so that B takes both of them) or substitutional (so that B takes only one of them). T may have expressed his intention to make the legacies cumulative or (alternatively) substitutional in his will read as a whole. If not, the following rules apply:

(1) *Legacies in the same instrument.* If by the same will (or the same codicil) T gives two general legacies of the same amount[71] to B, an equitable presumption arises that the legacies are *substitutional* and that B is intended to take only one of them.[72] Minor differences in the way in which the two legacies are given do not rebut this presumption.[73]

(2) *Legacies in different instruments.* But if T gives two legacies of the same amount to B by different instruments (*e.g.* one legacy by a will and the other by a codicil), prima facie the legacies are *cumulative* and B takes both of them.[74] This is a rule of construction and not an equitable presumption. It "rests upon the perfectly sound basis, which is not to be weakened, that a testator intends each and every disposition which he makes to take effect where these are not mutually inconsistent."[75]

(3) *Legacies in different instruments given from same motive.* If T gives two legacies of the same amount to B by different instruments, and T expresses the same motive in each instrument for giving each legacy, an equitable presumption arises that the legacies are *substitutional* and that B is intended to take only one of them.[76] The court only raises this presumption where there is the double coincidence of the same amount and the same motive in each instrument, *e.g.* each instrument contains a legacy of £100 to B "for his trouble as executor." If the instruments merely describe B as "my servant," this is not construed as an expression of T's motive for giving each legacy and the legacies are prima facie cumulative.[77]

---

[70] *Re Manners* [1949] Ch. 613; *Re Huish* (1890) 43 Ch.D. 260: *cf. Re Hall* [1918] 1 Ch. 562.

[71] If the two legacies are of different amounts, they are prima facie cumulative, *Curry* v. *Pile* (1787) 2 Bro.C.C. 225.

[72] *Garth* v. *Meyrick* (1779) 1 Bro.C.C. 30 (two legacies of £1,000 old South Sea annuities); *Holford* v. *Wood* (1798) 4 Ves. 76 (two annuities of £30 for life); *Manning* v. *Thesiger* (1835) 3 My. & K. 29.

[73] *Holford* v. *Wood, supra,* ("to B I give an annuity of £30 for his life payable quarterly. . . . I give to B the butler £30 a year for his life": held B took only one annuity).

[74] *Hooley* v. *Hatton* (1773) 1 Bro.C.C. 390; *Hurst* v. *Beach* (1821) 5 Madd. 351, 358; *Roch* v. *Callen* (1848) 6 Hare 531; *Re Davies* [1957] 1 W.L.R. 922.

[75] *Re Resch's W.T.* [1969] 1 A.C. 514, 548: see also *Wilson* v. *O'Leary* (1872) L.R. 7 Ch.App. 448, 454 (this rule "is not to be frittered away by a mere balance of probabilities"). For a summary of the case law as to what constitutes a clear indication of an intention to make the legacies substitutional see *Theobald on Wills* (14th ed., 1982), pp. 237 *et seq.*

[76] *Benyon* v. *Benyon* (1810) 17 Ves. 34 (£100 by will, and £100 by codicil, to B, in each case for his trouble as executor: held substitutional); *Hurst* v. *Beach, supra,* at pp. 358–359; *Re Royce's W.T.* [1959] Ch. 626. *Cf. Wilson* v. *O'Leary, supra,* at pp. 454–455.

[77] *Roch* v. *Callen* (1848) 6 Hare 531.

The equitable presumptions in (1) and (3) above that the legacies are substitutional may be rebutted by extrinsic evidence that T intended the legacies to be cumulative, and direct extrinsic evidence of T's declarations of intention is admissible for this purpose.[78] But direct extrinsic evidence is not admissible on T's death before 1983 to rebut the rule of construction in (2) above that the legacies are cumulative[79]: on T's death after 1982 section 21 of the Administration of Justice Act 1982 is applicable.[80]

Equity leans against double portions. Two applications of the principle that equity leans against double portions need consideration, i.e. (i) the presumption of the satisfaction of a portion-debt by a legacy and (ii) the presumption of the ademption of a legacy by a portion.[81] This principle imputes to a father an intention to achieve equality amongst his children. In Re Vaux[82] Lord Greene M.R. explained the presumption of the ademption of a legacy by a portion as follows,

"The rule against double portions rests upon two hypotheses: first of all, that under the will the testator has provided a portion and, secondly, that by the gift *inter vivos* which is said to operate in ademption of that portion either wholly or *pro tanto*, he has again conferred a portion. The conception is that the testator having in his will given to his children that portion of the estate which he decides to give to them, when after making his will he confers upon a child a gift of such a nature as to amount to a portion, then he is not to be presumed to have intended that that child should have both, the gift *inter vivos* being taken as being on account of the portion given by the will."

(1) *Testator must be father or in loco parentis.* These two equitable presumptions only apply to portions provided for a child by his father or by some other person who stands *in loco parentis* to the child.[83] The presumptions have been held not to apply to a provision made by the child's mother unless she stood *in loco parentis* to the child.[84] A person stands *in loco parentis* to a child if that person intends to undertake the parental duty of making financial provision for the child.[85] Whether a person intends to undertake this duty is decided from evidence of his general conduct towards the child and particularly from evidence of any financial provision made by him for the child. For instance, an uncle who intends to undertake this duty may put himself *in loco parentis* to

---

[78] Hurst v. Beach, supra, at pp. 360–361; Hall v. Hill (1841) 1 Dr. & War. 94, 124–128: see ante, p. 420.

[79] Hurst v. Beach, supra; Hall v. Hill, supra.

[80] Ante, pp. 423–424.

[81] The third application of the principle is the satisfaction of a portion-debt by a portion: see generally Snell's Principles of Equity (28th ed., 1982), pp. 512 et seq.

[82] [1939] Ch. 465, 481.

[83] Fowkes v. Pascoe (1875) 10 Ch.App. 343, 350.

[84] Re Ashton [1897] 2 Ch. 574 (reversed on other grounds [1898] 1 Ch. 142).

[85] Powys v. Mansfield (1837) 3 My. & Cr. 359, 367.

his nieces, though they continue to live with their father,[86] and so may a grandfather to his grandchildren.[87]

(2) *Nature of a portion.* Not every gift made by a father or person *in loco parentis* to a child is treated as a portion. A gift constitutes a portion if it is made for the purpose of establishing a child in life or of making a permanent provision for him.[88] Most gifts by will are treated as portions,[89] though a legacy to a daughter of a diamond necklace is not a portion.[90] Similarly, a provision for a child made by a marriage settlement constitutes a portion.[91] Again, payments of money or transfers of property made for establishing a child in a profession or in business constitute portions,[92] but not payments of money made for the child's education or maintenance, or by way of temporary assistance to a child.[93] If there is no evidence as to the purpose for which a payment was made, a gift to a child of a sum sufficiently substantial in itself to be in the nature of a permanent provision is prima facie a portion.[94] However, the court does not add up a series of small gifts (such as birthday and Christmas presents) so as to make a portion.[95]

(3) *Satisfaction of a portion-debt by a legacy.* If T (a father or person standing *in loco parentis*) incurs a legal obligation to provide a portion for a child C, and later T makes a will or codicil giving a legacy or share of residue (constituting a portion) to C, an equitable presumption arises that the legacy or share of residue is intended to be a complete or partial satisfaction of the portion-debt.[96] Unless this presumption is rebutted, C cannot take both, but C is entitled to elect whether to take the por-

---

[86] *Ibid.*

[87] *Pym* v. *Lockyer* (1841) 5 My. & Cr. 29; *Rogers* v. *Soutten* (1839) 2 Keen 598 (grandfather to illegitimate grandchild): see also *Booker* v. *Allen* (1831) 2 Russ. & My. 270 (near relation to child whose father had died).

[88] *Taylor* v. *Taylor* (1875) L.R. 20 Eq. 155, 157. This was a decision on the Statute of Distribution 1670 which required an advancement "by portion" to be brought into account by a child on a distribution on intestacy; see also the hotchpot rule in Administration of Estates Act 1925, s.47(1)(iii), for which see *ante*, pp. 91–93.

[89] *e.g. Re Furness* [1901] 2 Ch. 346, 348 (£20,000 legacy to daughter a portion); *Thynne* v. *Earl of Glengall* (1848) 2 H.L.Cas. 131 (gift of half his residuary personal estate a portion).

[90] *Re Tussaud's Estate* (1878) 9 Ch.D. 363, 367.

[91] *Taylor* v. *Taylor* (1875) L.R. 20 Eq. 155, 157.

[92] *Taylor* v. *Taylor, supra,* (payment of admission fee to Inn of Court for intending barrister and for purchase of mining plant for son's business); *Re George's W.T.* [1949] Ch. 154 (gift *inter vivos* of live and dead farming stock to son to set him up in farming business held a portion); *Hardy* v. *Shaw* [1976] Ch. 82.

[93] *Taylor* v. *Taylor, supra,* (payment of fee to special pleader for intending barrister to read in chambers, payments made to curate to assist him in his living expenses, and payment of army officer's debts); *Re Scott* [1903] 1 Ch. 1 (paying off part of son's mortgage debt was by way of temporary assistance and not a portion).

[94] *Re Hayward* [1957] Ch. 528 (nominations amounting to £507 in favour of a son aged 43: held not prima facie an advancement for purposes of hotchpot on intestacy—if son had been 20 years younger the result might have been different); *Hardy* v. *Shaw, supra,* at p. 88.

[95] *Schofield* v. *Heap* (1858) 27 Beav. 93; *Watson* v. *Watson* (1864) 33 Beav. 574.

[96] *Weall* v. *Rice* (1831) 2 Russ. & M. 251; *Warren* v. *Warren* (1783) 1 Bro.C.C. 305 (partial satisfaction).

tion-debt or (alternatively) the legacy or share of residue.[97] For instance, if on C's marriage T covenants to pay £10,000 to the trustees of C's marriage settlement, and later T makes a will giving a legacy of £10,000 (or more) to these trustees, an equitable presumption arises that the legacy is intended to be a complete satisfaction of T's obligation under his covenant[98]: if, instead, T gives a legacy of £6,000, the presumption is that the legacy is intended to be a partial satisfaction. The beneficiaries under the settlement are entitled to elect whether to take under T's covenant or under T's will.

Of course, if T is not the father of (or a person standing *in loco parentis* to) the creditor, or if the debt is an ordinary debt and not a portion-debt, the position is governed by the ordinary rules relating to the satisfaction of a debt by a legacy.[99]

(4) *Ademption of a legacy by a portion.* If T (a father or person standing *in loco parentis*) makes a will or codicil giving a legacy or share of residue[1] (constituting a portion) to a child C, and later T provides (or incurs a legal obligation to provide) a portion for C, an equitable presumption arises that the later portion adeems the legacy or share of residue, either wholly[2] or partially.[3] For instance, if T makes a will giving a legacy of £10,000 to C, and later T provides a portion of £10,000 (or more) for C, an equitable presumption arises that the legacy is wholly adeemed: if, instead, T provides a portion of £6,000, the presumption is that the legacy is adeemed to the extent of £6,000.

If T is not the father of (or a person standing *in loco parentis* to) the legatee under his will, there is generally no presumption that a later *inter vivos* gift by T to that legatee adeems the legacy.[4] The legatee remains entitled to the legacy, despite the later gift, unless (exceptionally) a presumption of ademption arises because both the legacy and the later gift were expressly given for a particular purpose (*e.g.* given for the purchase of a house by the legatee),[5] or pursuant to a specific moral obligation (*e.g.* given "according to the wish of my late beloved husband").[6]

---

[97] *Thynne* v. *Earl of Glengall* (1848) 2 H.L.C. 131; *Lord Chichester* v. *Coventry* (1867) L.R. 2 H.L. 71, 87 and 90–94. But if T *provides* the portion for C before making his will, no presumption of satisfaction arises and C takes both provisions, *Taylor* v. *Cartwright* (1872) L.R. 14 Eq. 167, 176.

[98] If T by his will had given the legacy to C, this would have satisfied C's beneficial life interest in the £10,000 under the settlement, but not the beneficial interests of C's spouse and issue, *Re Blundell* [1906] 2 Ch. 222.

[99] See *ante*, pp. 446–448.

[1] *Montefiore* v. *Guedalla* (1859) 1 De G.F. & J. 93 (share of residue). As to a devise of realty see *Davys* v. *Boucher* (1839) 3 Y. & C. 397, 411 (of doubtful authority, as revocation of all wills is now governed by Wills Act 1837, s.20).

[2] *Re Pollock* (1885) 28 Ch.D. 552, 555–556; *Re Vaux* [1939] Ch. 465, 481–482. For the effect of inheritance tax see *Re Turner's W.T.* [1968] 1 W.L.R. 227.

[3] *Pym* v. *Lockyer* (1841) 5 My. & Cr. 29 (ademption may be *pro tanto*).

[4] *Ex p. Pye* (1811) 18 Ves. 140 (father not *in loco parentis* to his illegitimate child).

[5] *Re Corbett* [1903] 2 Ch. 326 (legacy to hospital's endowment fund adeemed by later *inter vivos* gift for same purpose); *Re Jupp* [1922] 2 Ch. 359: cf. *Pankhurst* v. *Howell* (1870) 6 Ch.App. 136.

[6] *Re Pollock* (1885) 28 Ch.D. 552 (legacy by T's will of £500 to X "according to the wish of my late beloved husband": T later gave £300 to X as "legacy" from T's husband: held legacy adeemed to extent of £300): cf. *Re Aynsley* [1915] 1 Ch. 172.

(5) *A stranger cannot benefit.* Equity leans against double portions so as to achieve equality amongst children, but not so as to benefit a stranger, *i.e.* a person who is neither a child of T nor a person to whom T stood *in loco parentis*. The presumptions of satisfaction and ademption which arise under this principle must not be applied so as to benefit a stranger.[7] To consider some examples:

(i) T makes a will giving a legacy of £10,000 to his child C and his residuary estate to C and S (a stranger) absolutely in equal shares. Later T provides a portion of £10,000 for C. C's legacy and share of residue are not adeemed because ademption would merely benefit S.[8]

(ii) T makes a will giving his residuary estate to his children B and C and a stranger S absolutely in equal shares. Later T provides a portion of £10,000 for C and this partially adeems C's share of residue. T's net estate available for distribution amounts to £60,000. S takes £20,000 (*i.e.* one third of £60,000), B takes £25,000, and C takes £15,000 (which, together with his previous portion of £10,000, amounts to £25,000 in all).[9]

(iii) T makes a will giving a legacy of £10,000 to his child C but T does not dispose of his residuary estate. Later T provides a portion of £10,000 for C. If T's residuary estate passes as on intestacy to T's widow S, probably C's legacy is not adeemed because ademption would merely benefit S.[10] The result would be the same if T by his will had given his residuary estate to S.

(6) *Rebutting the presumptions.* The equitable presumptions of satisfaction and ademption may be rebutted (i) by intrinsic evidence from the different nature of the two provisions, or (ii) by extrinsic evidence of T's actual intention.[11] Evidence of T's declarations of intention is admissible as direct extrinsic evidence.[12]

It is easier to rebut the presumption of the satisfaction of a portion-debt by a legacy than the presumption of the ademption of a legacy by a portion.

"When the will precedes the settlement [which provides the portion] it is only necessary to read the settlement as if the person making the provision had said, 'I mean this to be in lieu of what I have given by my will.' But if the settlement [which creates the portion-debt] precedes the will, the testator must be understood as saying, 'I give this in lieu of what I am already bound to give, if those to whom I am so

---

[7] *Meinertzagen* v. *Walters* (1872) L.R. 7 Ch.App. 670; *Re Heather* [1906] 2 Ch. 230; *Re Vaux* [1938] Ch. 581 (not considered on appeal [1939] Ch. 465).

[8] Example (i) is based on *Re Heather, supra.*

[9] Example (ii) is based on *Meinertzagen* v. *Walters, supra,* and *Re Vaux, supra,* at p. 590.

[10] Example (iii) is based on *Re Vaux, supra,* but in that case children as well as the widow took on intestacy: *cf. Meinertzagen* v. *Walters* (1872) L.R. 7 Ch.App. 670, 673 and 674.

[11] *Weall* v. *Rice* (1831) 2 Russ. & My. 251, 267–268.

[12] *Re Tussaud's Estate* (1878) 9 Ch.D. 363 (satisfaction); *Kirk* v. *Eddowes* (1844) 3 Hare 509 (ademption): see *ante,* p. 420.

bound will accept it.' It requires much less to rebut the latter than the former presumption."[13]

It follows that factors which rebut the presumption of satisfaction will not necessarily rebut the presumption of ademption.

The presumption of satisfaction, at any rate, is rebutted by intrinsic evidence if there are substantial differences between the limitations contained in the two provisions; this indicates T's intention to provide a double portion.[14] Moreover each of the presumptions is rebutted if the provisions are not *ejusdem generis*.[15] Thus, a legacy of a sum of money is not adeemed by a later gift *inter vivos* of stock-in-trade,[16] unless T puts a money value on the stock-in-trade at the time when he gives it so that it can be regarded as a gift of money.[17]

---

[13] *Per* Lord Cranworth in *Lord Chichester* v. *Coventry* (1867) L.R. 2 H.L. 71, 87.

[14] *Weall* v. *Rice, supra,* ("it is not possible to define what are to be considered as slight differences between two provisions"): *cf. Thynne* v. *Earl of Glengall* (1848) 2 H.L.Cas. 131 (slight differences: presumption of satisfaction applied) and *Lord Chichester* v. *Coventry, supra,* (substantial differences: presumption of satisfaction rebutted).

[15] *Re Jacques* [1903] 1 Ch. 267.

[16] *Holmes* v. *Holmes* (1783) 1 Bro.C.C. 555.

[17] *Re George's W.T.* [1949] Ch. 154; *Bengough* v. *Walker* (1808) 15 Ves. 507.

DRAFTING A WILL

The draftsman of a will needs a sound knowledge of the law of succession. The precedents of clauses which follow are intended to illustrate the link between drafting and substantive law.

Commencement of will and revocation of prior dispositions

I JOHN ROBSON of 10 The Grove Oldcastle in the County of Northumberland Headmaster HEREBY REVOKE all former wills codicils and testamentary dispositions made by me and DECLARE this to be my last will

The commencement identifies the nature of the document[1] and the testator. The revocation clause does not revoke a statutory nomination made by the testator.[2] If the testator has foreign property which is disposed of by a foreign will, this general revocation clause is not appropriate.[3]

Declaration will (or disposition) intended not to be revoked by particular Marriage

I DECLARE that at the time I make this Will I am expecting to be married to John Brown of 3 Percy Way Oldcastle and that I intend that this Will shall not be revoked by my marriage to the said John Brown

This clause complies with section 18(3) of the Wills Act 1837.[4] If the testatrix marries John Brown, her will is not revoked. In drafting a clause so as to satisfy statutory requirements, it is good practice to follow the statutory wording closely.

I DECLARE that at the time I make this Will I am expecting to be married to John Brown of 3 Percy Way Oldcastle and that I intend that the disposition contained in clause 3 of this Will shall not be revoked by my marriage to the said John Brown and that the dispositions contained in clauses 4 and 5 of this Will shall be revoked by my marriage to the said John Brown

This clause complies with section 18(4) of the Wills Act 1837.[5] If the testatrix had not declared her intention that clauses 4 and 5 should be revoked by her marriage to John Brown, her marriage to John Brown would not have revoked clauses 4 and 5. But in that case it would have been better for the testatrix to use the preceding clause complying with section 18(3).

---

[1] *Ante*, p. 1.
[2] *Ante*, p. 17.
[3] See *Re Wayland* [1951] 2 All E.R. 1041 (*ante*, p. 67).
[4] *Ante*, p. 61.
[5] *Ante*, p. 61.

The body of the deceased

I WISH my body to be cremated and my ashes scattered beside Innominate Tarn on Haystacks in Cumbria

This wish has no legal but only moral force.[6] Some draftsmen are reluctant to insert wishes as to the disposal of the testator's body in his will in case no one reads the will until after his funeral.[7]

Appointment of executors and trustees

I APPOINT my wife Dorothy Jones to be sole executrix of this Will

If the will only contains immediate absolute gifts, there is no need to appoint trustees of the will.

I APPOINT my brother CHARLES ROBSON of 25 Princes Street Oldcastle Chemist and PERCY GRAINGER of 6 Grey Street Oldcastle Solicitor to be the executors and trustees of this Will [and the trustees thereof for the purposes of the Settled Land Act 1925] and I declare that the expression "my Trustees" in this Will shall (where the context permits) include the trustees or trustee for the time being hereof whether original or substituted

(i) This clause (and the preceding clause) each contains an absolute appointment. As already explained, an appointment of an executor may be qualified in one or more respects and a substituted executor may be appointed.[8] If a bank is to be appointed, the bank will readily supply its current recommended form of appointment (authorising remuneration for the bank) for use by the draftsman.[9]

(ii) The definition of "my Trustees" is inserted so as to ensure that any powers conferred by the will on "my Trustees" are not construed as personal to the original trustees.[10]

(iii) The appointment of trustees for the purposes of the Settled Land Act 1925 is appropriate where the testator's will creates a settlement for the purposes of the Act.[11]

(iv) If the testator holds settled land, which was settled previously to his death and not by his will and which remains settled after his death, the testator *may* appoint the persons, if any, who are at his death the trustees of the settlement to be his special executors in regard to the settled land. However, such an express appointment serves no useful purpose because, in default of express appointment, the testator is *deemed* to have made such an appointment[12]: the testator cannot choose other persons to be his special executors.

[6] *Ante*, p. 6. For this wish see A. Wainwright, *Fellwanderer* ("if you, dear reader, should get a bit of grit in your boots as you are crossing Haystacks in the years to come, please treat it with respect. It might be me").

[7] *Ante*, pp. 6–7.

[8] *Ante*, pp. 140–141. For a clause appointing the partners in a firm of solicitors see *ante*, p. 140, n. 3.

[9] A typical clause reads, "I appoint Bards Bank plc (hereafter called "the Bank") to be the executor and trustee of this will and I declare that the Bank's terms and conditions for acting as executor and trustee (including the scale of remuneration) last published before the date of my death shall apply with power to charge remuneration in accordance with any later published terms of the Bank for the time being in force."

[10] *Ante*, pp. 234–235.

[11] See Settled Land Act 1925, s.30.

[12] Administration of Estates Act 1925, s.22(1): see *ante*, pp. 142 and 177.

Appointment of guardians[13]

In the event of my husband dying in my lifetime I APPOINT my brother DAVID BEAN of 16 Green Street Oldcastle Grocer to be the guardian of my infant children

This includes children born after the date of the will.

I APPOINT my brother THOMAS JONES Tax Inspector and my sister MARY JONES Schoolteacher both of 3 Cheviot View Oldcastle to be the guardians of my infant children [including my infant adopted children] to act jointly with my wife during her life and after her death with any guardian or guardians appointed by her and if none then alone

The adopter of a child under an adoption order may appoint one or more guardians of the child.[14]

Specific legacies

I GIVE to my daughter MARY SMITH of 206 Matilda Road Melbourne Australia absolutely free of tax my Wedgwood dinner set And I direct that the cost of packing insuring and delivering the same to the said Mary Smith shall be borne by my residuary estate

The costs of transferring the subject-matter of a specific legacy to the beneficiary must be borne by the beneficiary unless there is (as here) a direction to the contrary.[15] If the dinner set is in the United Kingdom at the death of the testatrix, inheritance tax is a testamentary expense.[16] However, it is useful to insert an express direction as to whether each gift is to be free from, or subject to, tax.

I GIVE to my daughter PAMELA ROBSON of 10 The Grove Oldcastle absolutely free of tax all my personal chattels as defined by section 55(1)(x) of the Administration of Estates Act 1925 [and not by this Will or any codicil hereto otherwise effectually disposed of] and my motor car whether or not used by me for business purposes

The motor car is given in this way because, if used for business purposes, it falls outside the statutory definition of personal chattels.[17]

I GIVE to my son WILLIAM ROBSON of Reivers Way Oldcastle absolutely free of tax all my shares stock and debentures in Firth Tractors Ltd. And I direct (i) that any charge or lien thereon shall in exoneration of property comprised in this gift be paid and satisfied out of my residuary estate (ii) the cost of transferring the same to the said William Robson shall be borne by my residuary estate and (iii) all dividends interest and other payments in the nature of income arising therefrom in respect of any period partly before and partly after my death shall be treated as accruing wholly after my death and shall not be apportioned

(i) This specific legacy speaks from death under section 24 of the Wills Act 1837.[18] It therefore passes bonus shares issued to the testator after the date of the will.

[13] *Ante*, p. 7. Most of the precedents which follow are based on *Hallett's Conveyancing Precedents* (1975) with the kind permission of the author.
[14] *Ante*, p. 7.
[15] *Ante*, p. 372.
[16] *Ante*, p. 279.
[17] *Ante*, p. 84.
[18] *Ante*, p. 424.

(ii) If at the testator's death he has no assets which answer the description in the will, the bequest fails.[19]

(iii) If, for instance, the company's articles impose a charge on the testator's shares for money owed to the company by the testator, under section 35 of the Administration of Estates Act 1925 the shares are primarily liable for the payment of the charge unless the testator shows a contrary intention.[20] Direction (i) shows a contrary intention.

(iv) A specific legatee must bear the cost of transferring the shares, stock and debentures to him unless there is (as here) a direction to the contrary.[21]

(v) Direction (iii) excludes apportionment under the Apportionment Act 1870.[22] This direction does not pass to the legatee dividends declared in respect of a period wholly before the death.

I GIVE to my son WILLIAM ROBSON of Reivers Way Oldcastle absolutely free of tax my 1,200 ordinary £1 shares in Thomas Smith Ltd. together with any bonus shares issued in respect of any of the said shares And I direct that if any of the said shares hereinbefore given to the said William Robson shall by any means otherwise than by a sale by me (such sale not being effected in pursuance of an offer to shareholders conditional on the acquisition of a controlling interest in Thomas Smith Ltd.) be converted into money or into some other form of investment or security then the gift hereof shall not be adeemed but shall extend to the money or other investment or security which shall at the time of my death have been substituted therefor or shall in any other way represent the same

(i) This specific legacy does not speak from the death of the testator because the subject-matter is described with such particularity as to show that the testator was referring to the 1,200 shares owned by him at the date of the will.[23] Such a legacy does not pass bonus shares issued after the date of the will[24]: hence the express reference to bonus shares so that they pass.

(ii) The direction is inserted to prevent ademption in case the testator parts with these shares as the result, for instance, of a take-over bid before his death. However, such a direction may give rise to difficulties in identifying which assets represent the original 1,200 shares at the testator's death. Such a direction is not appropriate if the specific legacy speaks from death. Instead of inserting such a direction a testator may prefer to give a general pecuniary legacy in place of a specific legacy which is adeemed.

(iii) Directions (i), (ii), and (iii), which follow the previous specific legacy which speaks from death, are also appropriate where the specific legacy (as here) does not speak from the death of the testator.

General pecuniary legacies

I GIVE to my sister PAMELA SMITH of 15 The Rise Durham absolutely free of tax the sum of Five thousand pounds (£5,000) to be paid to her immediately after my death [AND I DIRECT that such sum free of tax shall

---

[19] *Ante*, p. 346.
[20] *Ante*, pp. 274 *et seq.*
[21] *Ante*, p. 372.
[22] *Ante*, pp. 319–320.
[23] *Ante*, p. 425.
[24] *Re Kuypers* [1925] Ch. 244; *Re O'Brien* (1946) 62 T.L.R. 594.

have absolute priority over all dispositions (general or specific) made hereby or by any codicil hereto]

(i) A "free of tax" provision is inserted so that the legacy does not bear any inheritance tax.[25]

(ii) The direction that the legacy is to be paid immediately after the testator's death makes the legacy carry interest from the testator's death. If this direction is omitted, the legacy carries interest from one year after the testator's death.[26]

(iii) If inserted, the final direction ensures that this legacy is the last gift to abate. Under the statutory order of application of assets specific gifts abate after general pecuniary legacies, unless a contrary intention is shown.[27] This final direction varies the statutory order.

I GIVE to my Trustees free of tax the sum of Twenty thousand pounds (£20,000) with interest thereon at the rate of 7 per cent. per annum from my death until investment or appropriation upon trust to invest the same in or upon any of the investments hereby authorised for the investment of trust moneys with power to vary any such investments and I direct that my Trustees shall hold the said sum of Twenty thousand pounds (and any interest thereon) and the investments for the time being representing the same (hereinafter called "my Trust Legacy") and the income thereof as from investment or appropriation In Trust contingently for my son DEREK ROBSON if and when he attains the age of 18 years or marries under that age And I DIRECT that the statutory powers of maintenance accumulation and advancement conferred by sections 31 and 32 of the Trustee Act 1925 shall apply to the foregoing trust [with the following modifications namely that the power of maintenance shall be exercisable free from any obligation to apply a proportionate part only of income where other income is applicable for maintenance purposes and the power of advancement shall authorise the application of the whole or any part (instead of being limited to one-half) of my Trust Legacy]. But if the said DEREK ROBSON shall die unmarried under the age of 18 years then I declare that subject to any and every exercise of the said statutory powers my Trust Legacy and the income thereof and all statutory accumulations of the income shall sink into and form part of my residuary estate

(i) This clause is suitable if the legatee is under 18 years of age and the legacy is to carry intermediate income so that it is available for maintenance.

(ii) This clause makes the legacy carry interest from the testator's death at 7 per cent. per annum (instead of from one year after the testator's death at the normal 6 per cent.)[28]

(iii) It may be useful to modify in this way the statutory powers conferred by sections 31 and 32 of the Trustee Act 1925.

I GIVE to the ROYAL NATIONAL LIFEBOAT INSTITUTION the sum of Five hundred pounds (£500) to be applicable for the general purposes thereof and I declare that the receipt of the person who professes to be the Treasurer or other proper officer for the time being thereof shall be a sufficient discharge for the same

[25] Ante, pp. 281 et seq.
[26] Ante, pp. 323–324.
[27] Ante, pp. 298 et seq.
[28] Ante, pp. 322 et seq.

(i) Unfortunately, it is quite common for a charity to be misdescribed in a will.[29] A draftsman needs to verify the name of the charity.

(ii) A receipt clause is desirable.

Gifts of residue

Subject to the payment of my funeral and testamentary expenses and debts and the legacies given by this Will or any codicil hereto and the tax on all gifts in this Will or any codicil hereto given free of tax I GIVE all my property both real and personal of whatever nature and wherever situated not hereby or by any codicil hereto otherwise disposed of to my husband James Smith absolutely [contingently on his surviving me by one month But if the said James Smith shall not so survive me then I direct that he shall be treated as having died in my lifetime and the intermediate income thereof shall not belong to him and I GIVE the same property (including the said intermediate income) to my daughter MARGARET PARK of 19 Hill Road Durham absolutely]

This form of residuary gift is suitable where residue is given absolutely.

1. (a) I GIVE all my property both movable and immovable of whatever nature and wherever situated not hereby or by any codicil hereto otherwise disposed of to my Trustees Upon trust to sell call in collect and convert into money such property (so far as not already consisting of money) at such time or times and in such manner as my Trustees shall think fit

(b) My Trustees shall have the fullest power at their absolute discretion (without being responsible for loss) to postpone the sale or conversion of the whole or any part or parts of my said property (even though of a terminable hazardous or wasting nature) during such time as my Trustees shall think fit and to retain any property of mine of whatever nature as an authorised investment

(c) Out of the whole or such part or respective parts as my Trustees shall in their absolute discretion think fit of the proceeds of sale and conversion of my said property and any ready money forming part of such property my Trustees shall (in exoneration of any property which would otherwise be liable for payment of the same) pay discharge or provide for my funeral and testamentary expenses and debts and any general legacies and annuities given by this Will or any codicil hereto and any tax from which any gifts by this Will or any codicil hereto are expressed to be free

(d) My Trustees shall at their discretion invest the residue of the said proceeds of sale and conversion and ready money in or upon any of the investments hereby authorised with power to vary or transpose such investments for or into others of a nature hereby authorised and shall stand possessed of such residue and of such part of my said property hereinbefore given to my Trustees as shall for the time being remain unsold and of all investments from time to time respectively representing the same (hereinafter together referred to as "my Trust Fund") and the income thereof Upon the trusts and with and subject to the powers and provisions hereinafter declared and contained concerning the same

---

[29] See *Re Songest* [1956] 1 W.L.R. 897, 1311; *Re Satterthwaite's W.T.* [1966] 1 W.L.R. 277 (consequences of using the yellow pages to find animal charities).

(e) In the administration of my estate and the execution of the trusts of this Will and any codicil hereto

(i) The income of any property of mine for the time being unsold shall (as well during the first year after my death as afterwards) be applied as if it were income arising from authorised investments of the proceeds of sale thereof comprised in my Trust Fund

(ii) No reversionary property of mine not actually producing income shall be treated as producing income

(iii) The rule known as the rule in *Allhusen* v. *Whittell* shall not apply and any actual income of property later sold for or applied in payment or discharge of or provision for expenses debts legacies annuities tax or other matters directed in paragraph (c) of this clause to be paid discharged or provided for by my Trustees shall be applied as if it were income arising from my Trust Fund

(iv) All interest dividends and other payments in the nature of income arising from property of mine in respect of any period partly before and partly after my death shall be treated as accruing wholly after my death and shall not be apportioned

(v) All interest dividends and other payments in the nature of income arising from my Trust Fund in respect of any period partly before and partly after the time when a person entitled to the income thereof ceases to be so entitled shall be treated as accruing wholly after such time and shall not be apportioned.

2. My Trustees shall stand possessed of my Trust Fund (a) upon trust to pay the income thereof to my sister Jane Swinburne of 3 Coquet View Oldcastle during her life and subject as aforesaid (b) upon trust (as to the entirety of my Trust Fund and the income thereof) for all or any the children or child of the said Jane Swinburne living at the death of the survivor of myself and the said Jane Swinburne and the issue then living of any then deceased child of hers who (whether children or remoter issue of hers) attain the age of 21 years or marry if more than one in equal shares but so that the issue of any deceased child of hers shall take in equal shares *per stirpes* only the share which such deceased child of hers would have taken had he or she survived such survivor as aforesaid and attained a vested interest

(i) This form of residuary gift is suitable where residue is given on trust.

(ii) It does not bar entails belonging to the testator,[30] but it does exercise a general power of appointment conferred on the testator, unless a contrary intention appears by the will.[31]

(iii) Clause 1(e), (i) to (v) excludes certain apportionment rules as follows:
  (i) excludes apportionment under *Howe* v. *Earl of Dartmouth*[32];
  (ii) excludes the rule in *Re Earl of Chesterfield's Trusts*[33];
  (iii) excludes the rule in *Allhusen* v. *Whittell*[34];
  (iv) excludes apportionment under the Apportionment Act 1870[35] on the death of the testator; and

---

[30] *Ante*, p. 431.
[31] *Ante*, pp. 428 *et seq.*
[32] (1802) 7 Ves. 137: see Snell's *Principles of Equity* (28th ed., 1982), pp. 226–229.
[33] (1883) 24 Ch.D. 643: see Snell, *op. cit.* pp. 229–230.
[34] (1867) L.R. 4 Eq. 295: see *ante*, pp. 330 *et seq.*
[35] *Ante*, pp. 319–320.

(v) does the same on the death of the life tenant Jane Swinburne.

(iv) Clause 2(b) is a gift to a composite class, consisting of Jane Swinburne's children and remoter issue, who are living at the death of the survivor of the testator and Jane Swinburne, and who attain the age of 21 years or marry. The children and remoter issue take *per stirpes*.

Statutory power of appropriation extended

The statutory power of appropriation conferred by section 41 of the Administration of Estates Act 1925 shall be exercisable by my Trustees without any of the consents made requisite by that section and shall include power to appropriate in favour of any of my Trustees entitled to a share or interest in my estate

If the consents are dispensed with in this way, no *ad valorem* stamp duty is payable in respect of an appropriation to a legatee.[36]

Investment clause

Money liable to be invested under this my Will may be invested or applied in the purchase of or at interest upon the security of such stocks funds shares securities or other investments or property of whatsoever nature and wheresoever situate (including the purchase of any land or dwelling-house of whatever tenure and whether situate in the United Kingdom or elsewhere for use as a residence) and whether involving liabilities or not or upon such personal credit with or without security as my Trustees shall in their absolute discretion think fit and to the intent that my Trustees shall have the same powers in all respects as if they were absolute owners beneficially entitled

This is a very wide investment clause. The express reference to the purchase of a dwelling-house to be used as a residence is advisable.[37]

Trustee charging clause

Any of my Executors or my Trustees who shall be an individual engaged in any profession or business may be employed by my Executors or my Trustees and shall be entitled to charge and be paid all professional or other reasonable and proper charges for any business done or services rendered or time spent by him or his firm in connection with the administration of my estate or the trusts powers or provisions of this Will or any codicil hereto whether or not within the usual scope of his profession or business and although not of a nature requiring the employment of a professional or business person

This is a usual form of charging clause.[38]

Testimonium and attestation clause

IN WITNESS whereof I the said JOHN ROBSON have to this my last Will [contained in this and the three preceding sheets of paper] set my hand this *First* day of *March* 1983

---

[36] *Ante*, p. 368.
[37] See *Re Power's W.T.* [1947] Ch. 572.
[38] *Ante*, pp. 245 *et seq.*

SIGNED by the above named Testator
JOHN ROBSON as his last Will in the
presence of us both present at the
same time who in his presence and
in the presence of each other have
hereunto subscribed our names as
witnesses

John Robson

Arthur Brown
6, Grey Street
Oldcastle

Legal Executive

6 P. Wood,
4, The Mount,
Oldcastle,
Secretary.

(i) It is not necessary for the testator to sign *each* page of his will or codicil but many practitioners consider this to be good practice.

(ii) The will should be dated so that, if the testator executes two or more wills, their order of execution can readily be ascertained.[39] It does not matter whether the date appears at the head of the will or in the testimonium: the latter is more common, perhaps because the space for the date in the testimonium serves as a reminder when the will is executed.

(iii) This attestation clause[40] does not refer to an acknowledgment by a witness of his previous signature because, though this is permissible if the testator dies after 1982,[41] it is likely to be a rare occurrence.

Codicil

This is a codicil of me JOHN ROBSON of 10 The Grove Oldcastle in the County of Northumberland Headmaster to my last Will dated the First day of March 1983
1. I REVOKE the appointment of my brother CHARLES ROBSON as an executor and trustee of my said Will [and as trustee thereof for the purposes of the Settled Land Act 1925]
2. I HEREBY APPOINT my son WILLIAM ROBSON of Reivers Way Oldcastle to be an executor and trustee of my said Will [and a trustee thereof for the purposes of the Settled Land Act 1925] in the place of the said CHARLES ROBSON and I declare that my said Will shall be construed and take effect in all respects as if the said WILLIAM ROBSON had been originally appointed as an executor and trustee thereof [and as trustee thereof for the purposes of the Settled Land Act 1925]

---

[39] See *Re Howard* [1944] P. 39 (*ante*, p. 68).
[40] *Ante*, p. 37. If the testator is blind or illiterate, or the will is signed by an amanuensis for the testator, see *ante*, p. 50, nn. 76 and 77.
[41] *Ante*, p. 36.

3. In all other respects I confirm my said Will

IN WITNESS whereof I the said JOHN ROBSON have hereunto set my hand this   day of   19

SIGNED by the above named Testator
JOHN ROBSON as a Codicil to his
last Will in the presence of us
both present at the same time who
in his presence and in the presence
of each other have hereunto
subscribed our names as witnesses

(i) A codicil should only be used to effect a simple purpose, such as substituting one executor and trustee for another, or adding, or revoking, or altering the amount of a legacy.

(ii) The draftsman of a codicil should insist upon having the testator's last will before him.[42] A will and its codicils should fit together.

(iii) Clause 3 republishes the will.[43]

THE NON-CONTENTIOUS PROBATE RULES 1987

S.I. 1987 No. 2024 (L.10)

ARRANGEMENT OF RULES

1. Citation and commencement
2. Interpretation
3. Application of other rules
4. Applications for grants through solicitors
5. Personal applications
6. Duty of registrar on receiving application for grant
7. Grants by district probate registrars
8. Oath in support of grant
9. Grant in additional name
10. Marking of wills
11. Engrossments for purposes of record
12. Evidence as to due execution of will
13. Evidence of will of blind or illiterate testator
14. Evidence as to terms, condition and date of execution of will
15. Attempted revocation of will
16. Affidavit as to due execution, terms, etc., of will
17. Wills proved otherwise than under section 9 of the Wills Act 1837
18. Wills of persons on military service and seamen
19. Evidence of foreign law
20. Order of priority for grant where deceased left a will

---

[42] *Ante*, pp. 78–79.
[43] *Ante*, p. 80.

SCHEDULES

First Schedule—Forms
Second Schedule—Revocations

Citation and commencement

1. These Rules may be cited as the Non-Contentious Probate Rules 1987 and shall come into force on 1st January 1988.

Interpretation

2.—(1) In these Rules, unless the context otherwise requires—

"the Act" means the Supreme Court Act 1981;
"authorised officer" means any officer of a registry who is for the time being authorised by the President to administer any oath or to take any affidavit required for any purpose connected with his duties;
"the Crown" includes the Crown in right of the Duchy of Lancaster and the Duke of Cornwall for the time being;
"grant" means a grant of probate or administration and includes, where the context so admits, the resealing of such a grant under the Colonial Probates Acts 1892 and 1927[1];
"gross value" in relation to any estate means the value of the estate without deduction for debts, incumbrances, funeral expenses or inheritance tax (or other capital tax payable out of the estate);
"oath" means the oath required by rule 8 to be sworn by every applicant for a grant;
"personal applicant" means a person other than a trust corporation who seeks to obtain a grant without employing a solicitor, and "personal application" has a corresponding meaning;
"registrar" means a registrar of the Principal Registry and includes—
   (a) in relation to an application for a grant made or proposed to be made at a district probate registry, and
   (b) in rules 26, 41 and 61(2) in relation to a grant issued from a district probate registry, and
   (c) in relation to rules 46, 47 and 48,
the registrar of that district probate registry;
"registry" means the Principal Registry or a district probate registry;
"the Senior Registrar" means the Senior Registrar of the Family Division or, in his absence, the senior of the registrars in attendance at the Principal Registry;
"statutory guardian" means a surviving parent of a minor who is the guardian of the minor by virtue of section 3 of the Guardianship of Minors Act 1971[2];
"testamentary guardian" means a person appointed by deed or will

[1] 1892 c. 6, 1927 c. 43.
[2] 1971 c. 3.

to be guardian of a minor under the power conferred by section 4 of
the Guardianship of Minors Act 1971[2];
"the Treasury Solicitor" means the solicitor for the affairs of Her Majesty's Treasury and includes the solicitor for the affairs of the Duchy
of Lancaster and the solicitor of the Duchy of Cornwall;
"trust corporation" means a corporation within the meaning of section 128 of the Act as extended by section 3 of the Law of Property
(Amendment) Act 1926.[3]

(2) A form referred to by number means the form so numbered in the
First Schedule; and such forms shall be used wherever applicable, with
such variation as a registrar may in any particular case direct or
approve.

Application of other rules

3. Subject to the provisions of these Rules and to any enactment, the
Rules of the Supreme Court 1965[4] shall apply, with the necessary modifications, to non-contentious probate matters, save that nothing in
Order 3 shall prevent time from running in the Long Vacation.

Application for grants through solicitors

4.—(1) A person applying for a grant through a solicitor may apply at
any registry or sub-registry.
(2) Every solicitor through whom an application for a grant is made
shall give the address of his place of business within England and
Wales.

Personal applications

5.—(1) A personal applicant may apply for a grant at any registry or
sub-registry.
(2) Save as provided for by rule 39 a personal applicant may not apply
through an agent, whether paid or unpaid, and may not be attended by
any person acting or appearing to act as his adviser.
(3) No personal application shall be proceeded with if—
   (a) it becomes necessary to bring the matter before the court by
       action or summons;
   (b) an application has already been made by a solicitor on behalf
       of the applicant and has not been withdrawn; or
   (c) the registrar so directs.
(4) After a will has been deposited in a registry by a personal applicant, it may not be delivered to the applicant or to any other person
unless in special circumstances the registrar so directs.
(5) A personal applicant shall produce a certificate of the death of the

[3] 1926 c. 11.
[4] S.I. 1965/1776.

deceased or such other evidence of the death as the registrar may approve.

(6) A personal applicant shall supply all information necessary to enable the papers leading to the grant to be prepared in the registry.

(7) Unless the registrar otherwise directs, every oath or affidavit required on a personal application shall be sworn or executed by all the deponents before an authorised officer.

(8) No legal advice shall be given to a personal applicant by an officer of a registry and every such officer shall be responsible only for embodying in proper form the applicant's instructions for the grant.

Duty of registrar on receiving application for grant

6.—(1) A registrar shall not allow any grant to issue until all inquiries which he may see fit to make have been answered to his satisfaction.

(2) Except with the leave of a registrar, no grant of probate or of administration with the will annexed shall issue within seven days of the death of the deceased and no grant of administration shall issue within fourteen days thereof.

Grants by district probate registrars

7.—(1) No grant shall be made by a district probate registrar—
  (a) in any case in which there is contention, until the contention is disposed of; or
  (b) in any case in which it appears to him that a grant ought not to be made without the directions of a judge or a registrar of the Principal registry.

(2) In any case in which paragraph (1)(b) applies, the district probate registrar shall send a statement of the matter in question to the Principal Registry for directions.

(3) A registrar of the Principal Registry may either confirm that the matter be referred to a judge and give directions accordingly or may direct the district probate registrar to proceed with the matter in accordance with such instructions as are deemed necessary, which may include a direction to take no further action in relation to the matter.

Oath in support of grant

8.—(1) Every application for a grant other than one to which rule 39 applies shall be supported by an oath by the applicant in the form applicable to the circumstances of the case, and by such other papers as the registrar may require.

(2) Unless otherwise directed by a registrar, the oath shall state where the deceased died domiciled.

(3) Where the deceased died on or after 1st January 1926, the oath shall state whether or not, to the best of the applicant's knowledge, information and belief, there was land vested in the deceased which

was settled previously to his death and not by his will and which remained settled land notwithstanding his death.

(4) On an application for a grant of administration the oath shall state in what manner all persons having a prior right to a grant have been cleared off and whether any minority or life interest arises under the will or intestacy.

Grant in additional name

9. Where it is sought to describe the deceased in a grant by some name in addition to his true name, the applicant shall depose to the true name of the deceased and shall specify some part of the estate which was held in the other name, or give any other reason for the inclusion of the other name in the grant.

Marking of wills

10.—(1) Subject to paragraph (2) below, every will in respect of which an application for a grant is made—
    (a) shall be marked by the signatures of the applicant and the person before whom the oath is sworn; and
    (b) shall be exhibited to any affidavit which may be required under these Rules as to the validity, terms, condition or date of execution of the will.
(2) The registrar may allow a facsimile copy of a will to be marked or exhibited in lieu of the original document.

Engrossments for purposes of record

11.—(1) Where the registrar considers that in any particular case a facsimile copy of the original will would not be satisfactory for purposes of record, he may require an engrossment suitable for facsimile reproduction to be lodged.
(2) Where a will—
    (a) contains alterations which are not to be admitted to proof; or
    (b) has been ordered to be rectified by virtue of section 20(1) of the Administration of Justice Act 1982,[5]
there shall be lodged an engrossment of the will in the form in which it is to be proved.
(3) Any engrossment lodged under this rule shall reproduce the punctuation, spacing and division into paragraphs of the will and shall follow continuously from page to page on both sides of the paper.

Evidence as to due execution of will

12.—(1) Subject to paragraphs (2) and (3) below, where a will contains no attestation clause or the attestation clause is insufficient, or where it

---

[5] 1982 c. 53.

appears to the registrar that there is doubt about the due execution of the will, he shall before admitting it to proof require an affidavit as to due execution from one or more of the attesting witnesses or, if no attesting witness is conveniently available, from any other person who was present when the will was executed; and if the registrar, after considering the evidence, is satisfied that the will was not duly executed, he shall refuse probate and mark the will accordingly.

(2) If no affidavit can be obtained in accordance with paragraph (1) above, the registrar may accept evidence on affidavit from any person he may think fit to show that the signature on the will is in the handwriting of the deceased, or of any other matter which may raise a presumption in favour of due execution of the will, and may if he thinks fit require that notice of the application be given to any person who may be prejudiced by the will.

(3) A registrar may accept a will for proof without evidence as aforesaid if he is satisfied that the distribution of the estate is not thereby affected.

Execution of will of blind or illiterate testator

13. Before admitting to proof a will which appears to have been signed by a blind or illiterate testator or by another person by direction of the testator, or which for any other reason raises doubt as to the testator having had knowledge of the contents of the will at the time of its execution, the registrar shall satisfy himself that the testator had such knowledge.

Evidence as to terms, condition and date of execution of will

14.—(1) Subject to paragraph (2) below, where there appears in a will any obliteration, interlineation, or other alteration which is not authenticated in the manner prescribed by section 21 of the Wills Act 1837,[6] or by the re-execution of the will or by the execution of a codicil, the registrar shall require evidence to show whether the alteration was present at the time the will was executed and shall give directions as to the form in which the will is to be proved.

(2) The provisions of paragraph (1) above shall not apply to any alteration which appears to the registrar to be of no practical importance.

(3) If a will contains any reference to another document in such terms as to suggest that it ought to be incorporated in the will, the registrar shall require the document to be produced and may call for such evidence in regard to the incorporation of the document as he may think fit.

(4) Where there is a doubt as to the date on which a will was executed, the registrar may require such evidence as he thinks necessary to establish the date.

[6] 1837 c. 26.

Attempted revocation of will

15. Any appearance of attempted revocation of a will by burning, tearing or otherwise destroying and every other circumstance leading to a presumption of revocation by the testator, shall be accounted for to the registrar's satisfaction.

Affidavit as to due execution, terms, etc., of will

16. A registrar may require an affidavit from any person he may think fit for the purpose of satisfying himself as to any of the matters referred to in rules 13, 14 and 15, and in any such affidavit sworn by an attesting witness or other person present at the time of the execution of a will the deponent shall depose to the manner in which the will was executed.

Wills proved otherwise than under section 9 of the Wills Act 1837

17.—(1) Rules 12 to 15 shall apply only to a will that is to be established by reference to section 9 of the Wills Act 1837 (signing and attestation of wills).

(2) A will that is to be established otherwise than as described in paragraph (1) of this rule may be so established upon the registrar being satisfied as to its terms and validity, and includes (without prejudice to the generality of the foregoing)—

    (a) any will to which rule 18 applies; and

    (b) any will which, by virtue of the Wills Act 1963,[7] is to be treated as properly executed if executed according to the internal law of the territory or state referred to in section 1 of that Act.

Wills of persons on military service and seamen

18. Where the deceased died domiciled in England and Wales and it appears to the registrar that there is prima facie evidence that a will is one to which section 11 of the Wills Act 1837 applies, the will may be admitted to proof if the registrar is satisfied that it was signed by the testator or, if unsigned, that it is in the testator's handwriting.

Evidence of foreign law

19. Where evidence as to the law of any country or territory outside England and Wales is required on any application for a grant, the registrar may accept—

    (a) an affidavit from any person whom, having regard to the particulars of his knowledge or experience given in the affidavit, he regards as suitably qualified to give expert evidence of the law in question; or

[7] 1963 c. 44.

(b) a certificate by, or an act before, a notary practising in the country or territory concerned.

Order of priority for grant where deceased left a will

20. Where the deceased died on or after 1 January 1926 the person or persons entitled to a grant in respect of a will shall be determined in accordance with the following order of priority, namely—
   (a) an executor (but subject to rule 36(4)(d) below);
   (b) any residuary legatee or devisee holding in trust for any other person;
   (c) any other residuary legatee or devisee (including one for life) or where the residue is not wholly disposed of by the will, any person entitled to share in the undisposed of residue (including the Treasury Solicitor when claiming bona vacantia on behalf of the Crown), provided that—
      (i) unless a registrar otherwise directs, a residuary legatee or devisee whose legacy or devise is vested in interest shall be preferred to one entitled on the happening of a contingency, and
      (ii) where the residue is not in terms wholly disposed of, the registrar may, if he is satisfied that the testator has nevertheless disposed of the whole or substantially the whole of the known estate, allow a grant to be made to any legatee or devisee entitled to, or to a share in, the estate so disposed of, without regard to the persons entitled to share in any residue not disposed of by the will;
   (d) the personal representative of any residuary legatee or devisee (but not one for life, or one holding in trust for any other person), or of any person entitled to share in any residue not disposed of by the will;
   (e) any other legatee or devisee (including one for life or one holding in trust for any other person) or any creditor of the deceased, provided that, unless a registrar otherwise directs, a legatee or devisee whose legacy or devise is vested in interest shall be preferred to one entitled on the happening of a contingency;
   (f) the personal representative of any other legatee or devisee (but not one for life or one holding in trust for any other person) or of any creditor of the deceased.

Grants to attesting witnesses, etc.

21. Where a gift to any person fails by reason of section 15 of the Wills Act 1837,[8] such person shall not have any right to a grant as a beneficiary named in the will, without prejudice to his right to a grant in any other capacity.

---

[8] 1837 c. 26.

Order of priority for grant in case of intestacy

22.—(1) Where the deceased died on or after 1 January 1926, wholly intestate, the person or persons having a beneficial interest in the estate shall be entitled to a grant of administration in the following classes in order of priority, namely—

(a) the surviving husband or wife;

(b) the children of the deceased and the issue of any deceased child who died before the deceased;

(c) the father and mother of the deceased;

(d) brothers and sisters of the whole blood and the issue of any deceased brother or sister of the whole blood who died before the deceased;

(e) brothers and sisters of the half blood and the issue of any deceased brother or sister of the half blood who died before the deceased;

(f) grandparents;

(g) uncles and aunts of the whole blood and the issue of any deceased uncle or aunt of the whole blood who died before the deceased;

(h) uncles and aunts of the half blood and the issue of any deceased uncle or aunt of the half blood who died before the deceased.

(2) In default of any person having a beneficial interest in the estate, the Treasury Solicitor shall be entitled to a grant if he claims bona vacantia on behalf of the Crown.

(3) If all persons entitled to a grant under the foregoing provisions of this rule have been cleared off, a grant may be made to a creditor of the deceased or to any person who, notwithstanding that he has no immediate beneficial interest in the estate, may have a beneficial interest in the event of an accretion thereto.

(4) Subject to paragraph (5) of rule 27, the personal representative of a person in any of the classes mentioned in paragraph (1) of this rule or the personal representative of a creditor of the deceased shall have the same right to a grant as the person whom he represents provided that the persons mentioned in sub-paragraphs (b) to (h) of paragraph (1) above shall be preferred to the personal representative of a spouse who has died without taking a beneficial interest in the whole estate of the deceased as ascertained at the time of the application for the grant.

Order of priority for grant in pre-1926 cases

23. Where the deceased died before 1st January 1926, the person or persons entitled to a grant shall, subject to the provisions of any enactment, be determined in accordance with the principles and rules under which the court would have acted at the date of death.

Right of assignee to a grant

24.—(1) Where all the persons entitled to the estate of the deceased (whether under a will or on intestacy) have assigned their whole interest in the estate to one or more persons, the assignee or assignees shall replace, in the order of priority for a grant of administration, the assignor or, if there are two or more assignors, the assignor with the highest priority.

(2) Where there are two or more assignees, administration may be granted with the consent of the others to any one or more (not exceeding four) of them.

(3) In any case where administration is applied for by an assignee the original instrument of assignment shall be produced and a copy of the same lodged in the registry.

Joinder of administrator

25.—(1) A person entitled in priority to a grant of administration may, without leave, apply for a grant with a person entitled in a lower degree, provided that there is no other person entitled in a higher degree to the person to be joined, unless every other such person has renounced.

(2) Subject to paragraph (3) below, an application for leave to join with a person entitled in priority to a grant of administration a person having no right or no immediate right thereto shall be made to a registrar, and shall be supported by an affidavit by the person entitled in priority, the consent of the person proposed to be joined as administrator and such other evidence as the registrar may direct.

(3) Unless a registrar otherwise directs, there may without any such application be joined with a person entitled in priority to administration—

    (a) any person who is nominated under paragraph (3) of rule 32 or paragraph (3) of rule 35;

    (b) a trust corporation.

Additional personal representatives

26.—(1) An application under section 114(4) of the Act to add a personal representative shall be made to a registrar and shall be supported by an affidavit by the applicant, the consent of the person proposed to be added as personal representative and such other evidence as the registrar may require.

(2) On any such application the registrar may direct that a note shall be made on the original grant of the addition of a further personal representative, or he may impound or revoke the grant or make such other order as the circumstances of the case may require.

Grants where two or more persons entitled in same degree

27.—(1) Subject to paragraphs (2) and (3) below, where, on an application for probate, power to apply for a like grant is to be reserved to such other of the executors as have not renounced probate, the oath shall state that notice of the application has been given to the executor or executors to whom power is to be reserved.

(2) Where power is to be reserved to partners of a firm, notice for the purposes of paragraph (1) above may be given to the partners by sending it to the firm at its principal or last known place of business.

(3) A registrar may dispense with the giving of notice under paragraph (1) above if he is satisfied that the giving of such a notice is impracticable or would result in unreasonable delay or expense.

(4) A grant of administration may be made to any person entitled thereto without notice to other persons entitled in the same degree.

(5) Unless a registrar otherwise directs, administration shall be granted to a person of full age entitled thereto in preference to a guardian of a minor, and to a living person entitled thereto in preference to the personal representative of a deceased person.

(6) A dispute between persons entitled to a grant in the same degree shall be brought by summons before a registrar.

(7) The issue of a summons under this rule in a district probate registry shall be notified forthwith to the registry in which the index of pending grant applications is maintained.

(8) If the issue of a summons under this rule is known to the registrar, he shall not allow any grant to be sealed until such summons is finally disposed of.

Exceptions to rules as to priority

28.—(1) Any person to whom a grant may or is required to be made under any enactment shall not be prevented from obtaining such a grant notwithstanding the operation of rules 20, 22, 25 or 27.

(2) Where the deceased died domiciled outside England and Wales rules 20, 22, 25 or 27 shall not apply except in a case to which paragraph (3) of rule 30 applies.

Grants in respect of settled land

29.—(1) In this rule "settled land" means land vested in the deceased which was settled previously to his death and not by his will and which remained settled land notwithstanding his death.

(2) The special executors in regard to settled land constituted by section 22 of the Administration of Estates Act 1925[9] shall have a prior right to a grant of probate limited to settled land.

(3) The person or persons entitled to a grant of administration limited to settled land shall be determined in accordance with the following order of priority, namely—

    (i) the trustees of the settlement at the time of the application for the grant;

    (ii) the personal representatives of the deceased.

(4) Where the persons entitled to a grant in respect of the free estate are also entitled to a grant of the same nature in respect of settled land, a grant expressly including the settled land may issue to them.

---

[9] 1925 c. 23.

(5) Where there is settled land and a grant is made in respect of the free estate only, the grant shall expressly exclude the settled land.

Grants where deceased died domiciled outside England and Wales

30.—(1) Subject to paragraph (3) below, where the deceased died domiciled outside England and Wales, a registrar may order that a grant do issue to any of the following persons—

(a) to the person entrusted with the administration of the estate by the court having jurisdiction at the place where the deceased died domiciled; or

(b) where there is no person so entrusted, to the person beneficially entitled to the estate by the law of the place where the deceased died domiciled or, if there is more than one person so entitled, to such of them as the registrar may direct; or

(c) if in the opinion of the registrar the circumstances so require, to such person as the registrar may direct.

(2) A grant made under paragraph (1)(a) or (b) above may be issued jointly with such person as the registrar may direct if the grant is required to be made to not less than two administrators.

(3) Without any order made under paragraph (1) above—

(a) probate of any will which is admissible to proof may be granted—

(i) if the will is in the English or Welsh language, to the executor named therein; or

(ii) if the will describes the duties of a named person in terms sufficient to constitute him executor according to the tenor of the will, to that person; and

(b) where the whole or substantially the whole of the estate in England and Wales consists of immovable property, a grant in respect of the whole estate may be made in accordance with the law which would have been applicable if the deceased had died domiciled in England and Wales.

Grants to attorneys

31.—(1) Subject to paragraphs (2) and (3) below, the lawfully constituted attorney of a person entitled to a grant may apply for administration for the use and benefit of the donor, and such grant shall be limited until further representation be granted, or in such other way as the registrar may direct.

(2) Where the donor referred to in paragraph (1) above is an executor, notice of the application shall be given to any other executor unless such notice is dispensed with by the registrar.

(3) Where the donor referred to in paragraph (1) above is mentally incapable and the attorney is acting under an enduring power of attorney, the application shall be made in accordance with rule 35.

Grants on behalf of minors

32.—(1) Where a person to whom a grant would otherwise be made is a minor, administration for his use and benefit, limited until he attains the age of eighteen years, shall, unless otherwise directed, and subject to paragraph (2) of this rule, be granted to the parents of the minor jointly, or to the statutory or testamentary guardian, or to any guardian appointed by a court of competent jurisdiction; provided that where the minor is sole executor and has no interest in the residuary estate of the deceased, administration for the use and benefit of the minor limited as aforesaid, shall, unless a registrar otherwise directs, be granted to the person entitled to the residuary estate.

(2) A registrar may by order assign any person as guardian of the minor, and such assigned guardian may obtain administration for the use and benefit of the minor, limited as aforesaid, in default of, or jointly with, or to the exclusion of, any person mentioned in paragraph (1) of this rule; and the intended guardian shall file an affidavit in support of his application to be assigned.

(3) Where there is only one person competent and willing to take a grant under the foregoing provisions of this rule, such person may, unless a registrar otherwise directs, nominate any fit and proper person to act jointly with him in taking the grant.

Grants where a minor is a co-executor

33.—(1) Where a minor is appointed executor jointly with one or more other executors, probate may be granted to the executor or executors not under disability with power reserved to the minor executor, and the minor executor shall be entitled to apply for probate on attaining the age of eighteen years.

(2) Administration for the use and benefit of a minor executor until he attains the age of eighteen years may be granted under rule 32 if, and only if, the executors who are not under disability renounce or, on being cited to accept or refuse a grant, fail to make an effective application therefor.

Renunciation of the right of a minor to a grant

34.—(1) The right of a minor executor to probate on attaining the age of eighteen years may not be renounced by any person on his behalf.

(2) The right of a minor to administration may be renounced only by a person assigned as guardian under paragraph (2) of rule 32, and authorised by the registrar to renounce on behalf of the minor.

Grants in case of mental incapacity

35.—(1) Unless a registrar otherwise directs, no grant shall be made under this rule unless all persons entitled in the same degree as the incapable person referred to in paragraph (2) below have been cleared off.

(2) Where a registrar is satisfied that a person entitled to a grant is by reason of mental incapacity incapable of managing his affairs, administration for his use and benefit, limited until further representation be granted or in such way as the registrar may direct, may be granted in the following order of priority—

    (a) to the person authorised by the Court of Protection to apply for a grant;

    (b) where there is no person so authorised, to the lawful attorney of the incapable person acting under a registered enduring power of attorney;

    (c) where there is no such attorney entitled to act, or if the attorney shall renounce administration for the use and benefit of the incapable person, to the person entitled to the residuary estate of the deceased.

(3) Where a grant is required to be made to not less than two administrators, and there is only one person competent and willing to take a grant under the foregoing provisions of this rule, administration may, unless a registrar otherwise directs, be granted to such person jointly with any other person nominated by him.

(4) Notwithstanding the foregoing provisions of this rule, administration for the use and benefit of the incapable person may be granted to such two or more other persons as the registrar may by order direct.

(5) Notice of an intended application under this rule shall be given to the Court of Protection.

Grants to trust corporations and other corporate bodies

36.—(1) An application for a grant to a trust corporation shall be made through one of its officers, and such officer shall depose in the oath that the corporation is a trust corporation as defined by these Rules and that it has power to accept a grant.

(2) (a) Where the trust corporation is the holder of an official position, any officer whose name is included on a list filed with the Senior Registrar of persons authorised to make affidavits and sign documents on behalf of the office holder may act as the officer through whom the holder of that official position applies for the grant.

    (b) In all other cases a certified copy of the resolution of the trust corporation authorising the officer to make the application shall be lodged, or it shall be deposed in the oath that such certified copy has been filed with the Senior Registrar, that the officer is therein identified by the position he holds, and that such resolution is still in force.

(3) A trust corporation may apply for administration otherwise than as a beneficiary or the attorney of some person, and on any such application there shall be lodged the consents of all persons entitled to a grant and of all persons interested in the residuary estate of the deceased save that the registrar may dispense with any such consents as aforesaid on such terms, if any, as he may think fit.

(4) (a) Subject to sub-paragraph (d) below, where a corporate body would, if an individual, be entitled to a grant but is not a trust corporation as defined by these Rules, administration for its use and benefit, limited until further representation be granted, may be made to its nominee or to its lawfully constituted attorney.

   (b) A copy of the resolution appointing the nominee or the power of attorney (whichever is appropriate) shall be lodged, and such resolution or power of attorney shall be sealed by the corporate body, or be otherwise authenticated to the registrar's satisfaction.

   (c) The nominee or attorney shall depose in the oath that the corporate body is not a trust corporation as defined by these Rules.

   (d) The provisions of paragraph (4)(a) above shall not apply where a corporate body is appointed executor jointly with an individual unless the right of the individual has been cleared off.

Renunciation of probate and administration

37.—(1) Renunciation of probate by an executor shall not operate as renunciation of any right which he may have to a grant of administration in some other capacity unless he expressly renounces such right.

(2) Unless a registrar otherwise directs, no person who has renounced administration in one capacity may obtain a grant thereof in some other capacity.

(3) A renunciation of probate or administration may be retracted at any time with the leave of a registrar; provided that only in exceptional circumstances may leave be given to an executor to retract a renunciation of probate after a grant has been made to some other person entitled in a lower degree.

(4) A direction or order giving leave under this rule may be made either by the registrar of a district probate registry where the renunciation is filed or by a registrar of the Principal Registry.

Notice to Crown of intended application for grant

38. In any case in which it appears that the Crown is or may be beneficially interested in the estate of a deceased person, notice of intended application for a grant shall be given by the applicant to the Treasury Solicitor, and the registrar may direct that no grant shall issue within 28 days after the notice has been given.

Resealing under Colonial Probates Acts 1892 and 1927

39.—(1) An application under the Colonial Probates Acts 1892 and 1927[10] for the resealing of probate or administration granted by the

---

[10] 1892 c. 6, 1927 c. 43.

court of a country to which those Acts apply may be made by the person to whom the grant was made or by any person authorised in writing to apply on his behalf.

(2) On any such application an Inland Revenue affidavit or account shall be lodged.

(3) Except by leave of a registrar, no grant shall be resealed unless it was made to such a person as is mentioned in sub-paragraph (a) or (b) of paragraph (1) of rule 30 or to a person to whom a grant could be made under sub-paragraph (a) of paragraph (3) of that rule.

(4) No limited or temporary grant shall be resealed except by leave of a registrar.

(5) Every grant lodged for resealing shall include a copy of any will to which the grant relates or shall be accompanied by a copy thereof certified as correct by or under the authority of the court by which the grant was made, and where the copy of the grant required to be deposited under subsection (1) of section 2 of the Colonial Probates Act 1892 does not include a copy of the will, a copy thereof shall be deposited in the registry before the grant is resealed.

(6) The registrar shall send notice of the resealing to the court which made the grant.

(7) Where notice is received in the Principal Registry of the resealing of a grant issued in England and Wales, notice of any amendment or revocation of the grant shall be sent to the court by which it was resealed.

Application for leave to sue on guarantee

40. An application for leave under section 120(3) of the Act or under section 11(5) of the Administration of Estates Act 1971[11] to sue a surety on a guarantee given for the purposes of either of those sections shall, unless the registrar otherwise directs under rule 61, be made by summons to a registrar and notice of the application shall be served on the administrator, the surety and any co-surety.

Amendment and revocation of grant

41.—(1) Subject to paragraph (2) below, if a registrar is satisfied that a grant should be amended or revoked he may make an order accordingly.

(2) Except on the application or with the consent of the person to whom the grant was made, the power conferred in paragraph (1) above shall be exercised only in exceptional circumstances.

Certificate of delivery of Inland Revenue affidavit

42. Where the deceased died before 13th March 1975 the certificate of delivery of an Inland Revenue affidavit required by section 30 of the

[11] 1971 c. 25.

Customs and Inland Revenue Act 1881[12] to be borne by every grant shall be in Form 1.

Standing searches

43.—(1) Any person who wishes to be notified of the issue of a grant may enter a standing search for the grant by lodging with the Senior Registrar, or sending to him by post, a notice in Form 2.

(2) A person who has entered a standing search will be sent an office copy of any grant which corresponds with the particulars given on the completed Form 2 and which—

    (a) issued not more than twelve months before the entry of the standing search; or

    (b) issues within a period of six months after the entry of the standing search.

(3) (a) Where an applicant wishes to extend the said period of six months, he or his solicitor may lodge at, or send by post to, the Principal Registry written application for extension.

    (b) An application for extension as aforesaid must be lodged, or received by post, within the last month of the said period of six months, and the standing search shall thereupon be effective for an additional period of six months from the date on which it was due to expire.

    (c) A standing search which has been extended as above may be further extended by the filing of a further application for extension subject to the same conditions as set out in sub-paragraph (b) above.

Caveats

44.—(1) Any person who wishes to show cause against the sealing of a grant may enter a caveat in any registry or sub-registry, and the registrar shall not allow any grant to be sealed (other than a grant ad colligenda bona or a grant under section 117 of the Act) if he has knowledge of an effective caveat; provided that no caveat shall prevent the sealing of a grant on the day on which the caveat is entered.

(2) Any person wishing to enter a caveat (in these Rules called "the caveator"), or a solicitor on his behalf, may effect entry of a caveat—

    (a) by completing Form 3 in the appropriate book at any registry or sub-registry; or

    (b) by sending by post at his own risk a notice in Form 3 to any registry or sub-registry and the proper officer shall provide an acknowledgement of the entry of the caveat.

(3) (a) Except as otherwise provided by this rule or by rules 45 or 46, a caveat shall be effective for a period of six months from the date of entry thereof, and where a caveator wishes to extend the said period of six months, he or his solicitor may lodge at, or send by post to, the registry or sub-registry at

[12] 1881 c. 12.

which the caveat was entered a written application for extension.

(b) An application for extension as aforesaid must be lodged, or received by post, within the last month of the said period of six months, and the caveat shall thereupon (save as otherwise provided by this rule) be effective for an additional period of six months from the date on which it was due to expire.

(c) A caveat which has been extended as above may be further extended by the filing of a further application for extension subject to the same conditions as set out in sub-paragraph (b) above.

(4) An index of caveats entered in any registry or sub-registry shall be maintained at the same registry in which the index of pending grant applications is maintained, and a search of the caveat index shall be made—

(a) on receipt of an application for a grant at that registry; and

(b) on receipt of a notice of an application for a grant made in any other registry,

and the appropriate registrar shall be notified of the entry of a caveat against the sealing of a grant for which application has been made in that other registry.

(5) Any person claiming to have an interest in the estate may cause to be issued from the registry in which the caveat index is maintained a warning in Form 4 against the caveat, and the person warning shall state his interest in the estate of the deceased and shall require the caveator to give particulars of any contrary interest in the estate; and the warning or a copy thereof shall be served on the caveator forthwith.

(6) A caveator who has no interest contrary to that of the person warning, but who wishes to show cause against the sealing of a grant to that person, may within eight days of service of the warning upon him (inclusive of the day of such service), or at any time thereafter if no affidavit has been filed under paragraph (12) below, issue and serve a summons for directions.

(7) On the hearing of any summons for directions under paragraph (6) above the registrar may give a direction for the caveat to cease to have effect.

(8) Any caveat in force when a summons for directions is issued shall remain in force until the summons has been disposed of unless a direction has been given under paragraph (7) above.

(9) The issue of a summons under this rule shall be notified forthwith to the registry in which the caveat index is maintained.

(10) A caveator having an interest contrary to that of the person warning may within eight days of service of the warning upon him (inclusive of the day of such service) or at any time thereafter if no affidavit has been filed under paragraph (12) below, enter an appearance in the registry in which the caveat index is maintained by filing Form 5 and making an entry in the appropriate book; and he shall serve forthwith on the person warning a copy of Form 5 sealed with the seal of the court.

(11) A caveator who has not entered an appearance to a warning may at any time withdraw his caveat by giving notice at the registry or subregistry at which it was entered, and the caveat shall thereupon cease to

have effect; and, where the caveat has been so withdrawn, the caveator shall forthwith give notice of withdrawal to the person warning.

(12) If no appearance has been entered by the caveator or no summons has been issued by him under paragraph (6) of this rule, the person warning may at any time after eight days of service of the warning upon the caveator (inclusive of the day of such service) file an affidavit in the registry in which the caveat index is maintained as to such service and the caveat shall thereupon cease to have effect provided that there is no pending summons under paragraph (6) of this rule.

(13) Unless a registrar of the Principal Registry by order made on summons otherwise directs, any caveat in respect of which an appearance to a warning has been entered shall remain in force until the commencement of a probate action.

(14) Except with the leave of a registrar of the Principal Registry, no further caveat may be entered by or on behalf of any caveator whose caveat is either in force or has ceased to have effect under paragraphs (7) or (12) of this rule or under rule 45(4) or rule 46(3).

Probate actions

45.—(1) Upon being advised by the court concerned of the commencement of a probate action the Senior Registrar shall give notice of the action to every caveator other than the plaintiff in the action in respect of each caveat that is in force.

(2) In respect of any caveat entered subsequent to the commencement of a probate action the Senior Registrar shall give notice to that caveator of the existence of the action.

(3) Unless a registrar of the Principal Registry by order made on summons otherwise directs, the commencement of a probate action shall operate to prevent the sealing of a grant (other than a grant under section 117 of the Act) until application for a grant is made by the person shown to be entitled thereto by the decision of the court in such action.

(4) Upon such application for a grant, any caveat entered by the plaintiff in the action, and any caveat in respect of which notice of the action has been given, shall cease to have effect.

Citations

46.—(1) Any citation may issue from the Principal Registry or a district probate registry and shall be settled by a registrar before being issued.

(2) Every averment in a citation, and such other information as the registrar may require, shall be verified by an affidavit sworn by the person issuing the citation (in these Rules called the "citor"), provided that the registrar may in special circumstances accept an affidavit sworn by the citor's solicitor.

(3) The citor shall enter a caveat before issuing a citation and, unless a registrar of the Principal Registry by order made on summons otherwise directs, any caveat in force at the commencement of the citation

proceedings shall, unless withdrawn pursuant to paragraph (11) of rule 44, remain in force until application for a grant is made by the person shown to be entitled thereto by the decision of the court in such proceedings, and upon such application any caveat entered by a party who had notice of the proceedings shall cease to have effect.

(4) Every citation shall be served personally on the person cited unless the registrar, on cause shown by affidavit, directs some other mode of service, which may include notice by advertisement.

(5) Every will referred to in a citation shall be lodged in a registry before the citation is issued, except where the will is not in the citor's possession and the registrar is satisfied that it is impracticable to require it to be lodged.

(6) A person who has been cited to appear may, within eight days of service of the citation upon him (inclusive of the day of such service), or at any time thereafter if no application has been made by the citor under paragraph (5) of rule 47 or paragraph (2) of rule 48, enter an appearance in the registry from which the citation issued by filing Form 5 and shall forthwith thereafter serve on the citor a copy of Form 5 sealed with the seal of the registry.

Citation to accept or refuse or to take a grant

47.—(1) A citation to accept or refuse a grant may be issued at the instance of any person who would himself be entitled to a grant in the event of the person cited renouncing his right thereto.

(2) Where power to make a grant to an executor has been reserved, a citation calling on him to accept or refuse a grant may be issued at the instance of the executors who have proved the will or the survivor of them or of the executors of the last survivor of deceased executors who have proved.

(3) A citation calling on an executor who has intermeddled in the estate of the deceased to show cause why he should not be ordered to take a grant may be issued at the instance of any person interested in the estate at any time after the expiration of six months from the death of the deceased, provided that no citation to take a grant shall issue while proceedings as to the validity of the will are pending.

(4) A person cited who is willing to accept or take a grant may, after entering an appearance, apply ex parte by affidavit to a registrar for an order for a grant to himself.

(5) If the time limited for appearance has expired and the person cited has not entered an appearance, the citor may—

(a) in the case of a citation under paragraph (1) of this rule, apply to a registrar for an order for a grant to himself;

(b) in the case of a citation under paragraph (2) of this rule, apply to a registrar for an order that a note be made on the grant that the executor in respect of whom power was reserved has been duly cited and has not appeared and that all his rights in respect of the executorship have wholly ceased; or

(c) in the case of a citation under paragraph (3) of this rule, apply to a registrar by summons (which shall be served on the person cited) for an order requiring such person to take a grant within a specified time or for a grant to himself or to some other person specified in the summons.

(6) An application under the last foregoing paragraph shall be supported by an affidavit showing that the citation was duly served.

(7) If the person cited has entered an appearance but has not applied for a grant under paragraph (4) of this rule, or has failed to prosecute his application with reasonable diligence, the citor may—

(a) in the case of a citation under paragraph (1) of this rule, apply by summons to a registrar for an order for a grant to himself;

(b) in the case of a citation under paragraph (2) of this rule, apply by summons to a registrar for an order striking out the appearance and for the endorsement on the grant of such a note as is mentioned in sub-paragraph (b) of paragraph (5) of this rule; or

(c) in the case of a citation under paragraph (3) of this rule, apply by summons to a registrar for an order requiring the person cited to take a grant within a specified time or for a grant to himself or to some other person specified in the summons;

and the summons shall be served on the person cited.

Citation to propound a will

48.—(1) A citation to propound a will shall be directed to the executors named in the will and to all persons interested thereunder, and may be issued at the instance of any citor having an interest contrary to that of the executors or such other persons.

(2) If the time limited for appearance has expired, the citor may—

(a) in the case where no person has entered an appearance, apply to a registrar for an order for a grant as if the will were invalid and such application shall be supported by an affidavit showing that the citation was duly served; or

(b) in the case where no person who has entered an appearance proceeds with reasonable diligence to propound the will, apply to a registrar by summons, which shall be served on every person cited who has entered an appearance, for such an order as is mentioned in paragraph (a) above.

Address for service

49. All caveats, citations, warnings and appearances shall contain an address for service in England and Wales.

Application for order to attend for examination or for subpoena to bring in a will

50.—(1) An application under section 122 of the Act for an order requiring a person to attend for examination may, unless a probate action has been commenced, be made to a registrar by summons which shall be served on every such person as aforesaid.

(2) An application under section 123 of the Act for the issue by a registrar of a subpoena to bring in a will shall be supported by an affidavit setting out the grounds of the application, and if any person served with the subpoena denies that the will is in his possession or control he may file an affidavit to that effect in the registry from which the subpoena issued.

Grants to part of an estate under section 113 of the Act

51. An application for an order for a grant under section 113 of the Act to part of an estate may be made to a registrar, and shall be supported by an affidavit setting out the grounds of the application, and
  (a) stating whether the estate of the deceased is known to be insolvent; and
  (b) showing how any person entitled to a grant in respect of the whole estate in priority to the applicant has been cleared off.

Grants of administration under discretionary powers of court, and grants ad colligenda bona

52. An application for an order for—
  (a) a grant of administration under section 116 of the Act; or
  (b) a grant of administration ad colligenda bona,
may be made to a registrar and shall be supported by an affidavit setting out the grounds of the application.

Applications for leave to swear to death

53. An application for leave to swear to the death of a person in whose estate a grant is sought may be made to a registrar, and shall be supported by an affidavit setting out the grounds of the application and containing particulars of any policies of insurance effected on the life of the presumed deceased together with such further evidence as the registrar may require.

Grants in respect of nuncupative wills and copies of wills

54.—(1) Subject to paragraph (2) below, an application for an order admitting to proof a nuncupative will, or a will contained in a copy or reconstruction thereof where the original is not available, shall be made to a registrar.

(2) In any case where a will is not available owing to its being retained in the custody of a foreign court or official, a duly authenticated copy of the will may be admitted to proof without the order referred to in paragraph (1) above.

(3) An application under paragraph (1) above shall be supported by an affidavit setting out the grounds of the application, and by such evidence on affidavit as the applicant can adduce as to—

    (a) the will's existence after the death of the testator or, where there is no such evidence, the facts on which the applicant relies to rebut the presumption that the will has been revoked by destruction;

    (b) in respect of a nuncupative will, the contents of that will; and

    (c) in respect of a reconstruction of a will, the accuracy of that reconstruction.

(4) The registrar may require additional evidence in the circumstances of a particular case as to due execution of the will or as to the accuracy of the copy will, and may direct that notice be given to persons who would be prejudiced by the application.

Application for rectification of a will

55.—(1) An application for an order that a will be rectified by virtue of section 20(1) of the Administration of Justice Act 1982[13] may be made to a registrar, unless a probate action has been commenced.

(2) The application shall be supported by an affidavit, setting out the grounds of the application, together with such evidence as can be adduced as to the testator's intentions and as to whichever of the following matters as are in issue:—

    (a) in what respects the testator's intentions were not understood; or

    (b) the nature of any alleged clerical error.

(3) Unless otherwise directed, notice of the application shall be given to every person having an interest under the will whose interest might be prejudiced by the rectification applied for and any comments in writing by any such person shall be exhibited to the affidavit in support of the application.

(4) If the registrar is satisfied that, subject to any direction to the contrary, notice has been given to every person mentioned in paragraph (3) above, and that the application is unopposed, he may order that the will be rectified accordingly.

Notice of election by surviving spouse to redeem life interest

56.—(1) Where a surviving spouse who is the sole or sole surviving personal representative of the deceased is entitled to a life interest in part of the residuary estate and elects under section 47A of the Administration of Estates Act 1925[14] to have the life interest redeemed, he may give written notice of the election to the Senior Registrar in pursuance of subsection (7) of that section by filing a notice in Form 6 in the Principal Registry or of the district probate Registry from which the grant issued.

[13] 1982 c. 53.
[14] 1925 c. 23.

(2) Where the grant issued from a district probate registry, the notice shall be filed in duplicate.

(3) A notice filed under this rule shall be noted on the grant and the record and shall be open to inspection.

Index of grant applications

57.—(1) The Senior Registrar shall maintain an index of every pending application for a grant made in any registry.

(2) Notice of every application for a grant shall be sent by the registry in which the application is made to the registry in which the index is maintained and shall be in the form of a document stating the full name of the deceased and the date of his death.

(3) On receipt of the notice referred to in paragraph (2) above, the registry shall search its current index and give a certificate as to the result of that search to the registry which sent the notice.

(4) The requirements of paragraph (2) above shall not apply in any case in which the application for a grant is made in the registry in which the index is maintained.

(5) In this rule "registry" includes a sub-registry.

Inspection of copies of original wills and other documents

58. An original will or other document referred to in section 124 of the Act shall not be open to inspection if, in the opinion of the registrar, such inspection would be undesirable or otherwise inappropriate.

Issue of copies of original wills and other documents

59. Where copies are required of original wills or other documents deposited under section 124 of the Act, such copies may be facsimile copies sealed with the seal of the court and issued either as office copies or certified under the hand of a registrar to be true copies.

Taxation of costs

60. Every bill of costs, other than a bill delivered by a solicitor to his client which falls to be taxed under the Solicitors Act 1974,[15] shall be referred to a registrar of the Principal Registry for taxation and may be taxed by him or such other taxing officer in the Principal Registry as the President may appoint.

Power to require applications to be made by summons

61.—(1) A registrar may require any application to be made by summons to a registrar in chambers or a judge in chambers or open court.

---

[15] 1974 c. 47.

(2) An application for an inventory and account shall be made by summons to a registrar.

(3) A summons for hearing by a registrar shall be issued out of the registry in which it is to be heard.

(4) A summons to be heard by a judge shall be issued out of the Principal Registry.

Transfer of applications

62. A registrar to whom any application is made under these Rules may order the transfer of the application to another registrar having jurisdiction.

Power to make orders for costs

63. On any application dealt with by him on summons, the district probate registrar shall have full power to determine by whom and to what extent the costs are to be paid.

Exercise of powers of judge during Long Vacation

64. All powers exercisable under these Rules by a judge in chambers may be exercised during the Long Vacation by a registrar of the Principal Registry.

Appeals from registrars

65.—(1) An appeal against a decision or requirement of a registrar shall be made by summons to a judge.

(2) If, in the case of an appeal under the last foregoing paragraph, any person besides the appellant appeared or was represented before the registrar from whose decision or requirement the appeal is brought, the summons shall be issued within seven days thereof for hearing on the first available day and shall be served on every such person as aforesaid.

Service of summons

66.—(1) A judge or registrar of the Principal Registry or, where the application is to be made to a district probate registrar, that registrar, may direct that a summons for the service of which no other provision is made by these Rules shall be served on such person or persons as the judge or registrar may direct.

(2) Where by these Rules or by any direction given under the last foregoing paragraph a summons is required to be served on any person, it shall be served not less than two clear days before the day appointed for the hearing, unless the judge or registrar at or before the hearing dispenses with service on such terms, if any, as he may think fit.

Notices, etc.

67. Unless a registrar otherwise directs or these Rules otherwise provide, any notice or other document required to be given to or served on any person may be given or served in the manner prescribed by Order 65 Rule 5 of the Rules of the Supreme Court 1965.[16]

Application to pending proceedings

68. Subject in any particular case to any direction given by a judge or registrar, these Rules shall apply to any proceedings which are pending on the date on which they come into force as well as to any proceedings commenced on or after that date.

Revocation of previous rules

69.—(1) Subject to paragraph (2) below, the rules set out in the Second Schedule are hereby revoked.

(2) The rules set out in the Second Schedule shall continue to apply to such extent as may be necessary for giving effect to a direction under rule 68.

FIRST SCHEDULE   Rule 2(2)

FORMS

FORM 1   Rule 42
CERTIFICATE OF DELIVERY OF INLAND REVENUE AFFIDAVIT

And it is hereby certified that an Inland Revenue affidavit has been delivered wherein it is shown that the gross value of the said estate in the United Kingdom (exclusive of what the said deceased may have been possessed of or entitled to as a trustee and not beneficially) amounts to £.......... and that the net value of the estate amounts to £..........

And it is further certified that it appears by a receipt signed by an Inland Revenue officer on the said affidavit that £.......... on account of estate duty and interest on such duty has been paid.

[16] S.I. 1965/1776.

FORM 2 Rule 43(1)
STANDING SEARCH

In the High Court of Justice

Family Division

The Principal Registry

I/We apply for the entry of a standing search so that there shall be sent to me/us an office copy of every grant of representation in England and Wales in the estate of—

Full name of deceased: ....

Full address: ....

Alternative or alias names: ....

Exact date of death: ....

which either has issued not more than 12 months before the entry of this application or issues within 6 months thereafter.

Signed ....

Name in block letters ....

Full address ....

Reference No. (if any) ....

FORM 3 Rule 44(2)
CAVEAT

In the High Court of Justice

Family Division

The Principal [or .... District Probate] Registry.

Let no grant be sealed in the estate of (*full name and address*) deceased, who died on the .... day of .... 19 ... without notice to (*name of party by whom or on whose behalf the caveat is entered*).

Dated this .... day of .... 19 .... .

(*Signed*) (*to be signed by the caveator's solicitor or by the caveator if acting in person*)

whose address for service is: ....

Solicitor for the said .... (*If the caveator is acting in person, substitute "In person".*)

FORM 4   Rule 44(5)
WARNING TO CAVEATOR

In the High Court of Justice

Family Division

[*The Registry in which the caveat index is maintained*]

To .... of .... a party who has entered a caveat in the estate of
.... deceased.

You have eight days (starting with the day on which this warning was served
on you):
  (i) to enter an appearance either in person or by your solicitor, at the [*name
      and address of the registry in which the caveat index is maintained*] setting
      out what interest you have in the estate of the above-named ....
      .... of ....
      deceased contrary to that of the party at whose instance this warning is
      issued; or
  (ii) if you have no contrary interest but wish to show cause against the seal-
      ing of a grant to such party, to issue and serve a summons for directions
      by a registrar of the Principal Registry or a district probate registry.

If you fail to do either of these, the court may proceed to issue a grant of
probate or administration in the said estate notwithstanding your caveat.

Dated the .... day of .... 19 .... .

Issued at the instance of ....

[*Here set out the name and interest (including
the date of the will, if any, under which the
interest arises) of the party warning, the name
of his solicitor and the address for service. If the
party warning is acting in person, this must be
stated.*]   Registrar

FORM 5   Rules 44(10), 46(6)
APPEARANCE TO WARNING OR CITATION

In the High Court of Justice

Family Division

The Principal [*or* .... District Probate] Registry

Caveat No. .... dated the .... day of .... 19 ......
[Citation dated the .... day of .... 19......]

Full name and address of deceased: ....

Full name and address of person warning [*or* citor]: ....
(*Here set out the interest of the person warning, or citor, as shown in warning or
citation.*)
Full name and address of caveator [*or* person cited].
(*Here set out the interest of the caveator or person cited, stating the date of the will (if
any) under which such interest arises.*)

Enter an appearance for the above-named caveator [or person cited] in this matter.

Dated the .... day of .... 19..... .

(Signed)

whose address for service is:

Solicitor (or 'In person').

FORM 6   Rule 56
NOTICE OF ELECTION TO REDEEM LIFE INTEREST

In the High Court of Justice

Family Division

The Principal [or .... District Probate] Registry

In the estate of .... deceased.

Whereas .... of .... died on the .... day of .... 19 .... wholly/
partially intestate leaving his/her/lawful wife/husband and .... lawful issue of the said deceased;

And whereas Probate/Letters of Administration of the estate of the said ....
.... were granted to me, the .... [and to .... of
...................] at the Probate Registry on the .... day of .... 19 ....;

And whereas [the said .... has ceased to be a personal representative because ....] and I am [now] the sole personal representative:

Now I, the said ....
hereby give notice in accordance with section 47A of the Administration of Estates Act 1925 that I elect to redeem the life interest to which I am entitled in the estate of the late ....
by retaining £ .... its capital value, and £ .... the costs of the transaction.

Dated the .... day of .... 19 ... .

(Signed)

To the Senior Registrar of the Family Division.

INDEX

493